SECRETARIAL PROCEDURES AND ADMINISTRATION

7TH EDITION

J Marshall Hanna, Ed.D.

Professor of Business Education Emeritus
The Ohio State University

Estelle L. Popham, Ph.D.

Professor of Business Education Emeritus
Hunter College of the City University of New York

Rita Sloan Tilton, Ph.D.

Division of Business
Milwaukee Area Technical College

Published by

K73   **SOUTH-WESTERN PUBLISHING CO.**

CINCINNATI   WEST CHICAGO, ILL.   DALLAS   PELHAM MANOR, N.Y.   PALO ALTO, CALIF.

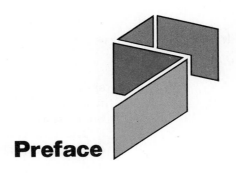

Preface

Today's office is changing at a dizzying speed. New technology enables the office force to achieve higher productivity at lower costs. Scientific managerial techniques dictate the adoption of uniform office systems and procedures. Legislation and enlightened management are opening many business positions from clerk to top executive to persons of both sexes and all ethnic backgrounds. *Secretarial Procedures and Administration*, Seventh Edition, is designed to reflect these changes and to prepare secretaries for job entry as well as advancement.

In today's office environment your decision to become a secretary is a wise one. You will obtain a position to which you can bring marketable skills and know-how in performing the office tasks that contribute to the effectiveness of the executive and the company. You will perform an assistant's function. If you learn how business functions, how to effectively work with business people, and how to continually upgrade your knowledge and skills, your secretarial position can be the beginning step in a successful career path to your ultimate goal.

Secretarial Procedures and Administration, Seventh Edition, prepares you to perform the operational functions of a secretary. You will learn the procedures necessary to function efficiently in today's office with its vast array of new equipment and new organizational patterns. Whether you work as a traditional secretary or as one of the two types of secretaries in a word processing environment (administrative secretary and correspondence secretary), this book prepares you for these operational responsibilities. Basic skills in typewriting and in shorthand are assumed; other skills are presented as if they were new to you. *Secretarial Procedures and Administration* is planned with the experienced secretary in mind, too, for continual updating about the secretarial role is essential.

The top-level secretary makes many decisions, both about how to handle work assignments and about how to deal with colleagues at all levels — supervisees, co-workers, and executives. Throughout the course, therefore, emphasis is placed on development of decision-making competencies so that the secretary can operate with a minimum of supervision and exercise that most-needed skill of all —

skill in human relations. Without good human relations techniques, it is difficult for anyone, no matter how skillful, to be successful in business.

The text consists of 28 chapters organized into 9 parts. Part 1 discusses the changing organizational pattern of secretarial work and the secretary's role in the total office environment. Parts 2, 3, and 4 deal with word processing, the transformation of ideas into typewritten or printed form. These parts cover such topics as typewriting, reprographics, dictation and transcription, composition, incoming and outgoing mail, postal and shipping services, and telephone and telegraph services. Part 5 deals with the management of records and the rules of alphabetic indexing. Parts 6, 7, and 8 encompass such secretarial functions as planning travel and expediting meetings and conferences; collecting, processing, and presenting business data; and handling financial, payroll, and legal responsibilities. Part 9 examines the employment opportunities open to the college-trained secretary, techniques used in applying for a job, the essentials for achieving professional status, and the supervisory-administrative role of the secretary or administrative assistant.

At the end of each chapter is a list of carefully selected suggested readings. You will find many uses for this list — when you are writing a term paper for this or another course, when you are asked to speak on a secretarial subject, or when you want to delve more deeply into a topic during the course.

Case problems at the end of each part are close adaptations of actual office situations and bring realism to the course. As you solve them, try to develop a set of principles that will enable you to cope with similar situations that you may encounter on the job.

The Reference Guide at the end of the book can be of enormous value if you will let it help you become the "word specialist" that a competent secretary must be. It identifies accepted practices for abbreviating and capitalizing words, writing and using numbers, spelling and using plurals and possessives, punctuating, and using words effectively. Following this section are a Communications Guide and a brief Postal Guide. You can see why we say that the book is more than a textbook. You will want to take it to the office with you as a constant on-the-job reference.

The authors hope that through this textbook you will set the highest professional goals for yourself — goals consistent with your abilities. If you *input* your best efforts into the course, you will *output* products that will enable you to achieve your goals, not only in the immediate future but as your ultimate career plans unfold.

J Marshall Hanna   Estelle L. Popham   Rita Sloan Tilton

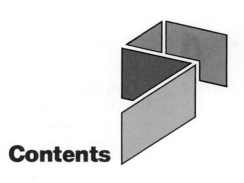

Contents

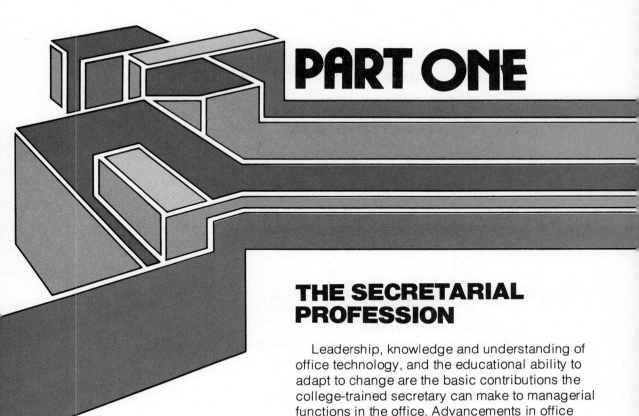

PART ONE

THE SECRETARIAL PROFESSION

Leadership, knowledge and understanding of office technology, and the educational ability to adapt to change are the basic contributions the college-trained secretary can make to managerial functions in the office. Advancements in office technology have provided for the professional secretary new career paths and countless opportunities for decision making in the application of this technology. Part 1 discusses the many dimensions of the secretarial position, its duties and responsibilities, in addition to the administrative and supervisory opportunities available to the secretary.

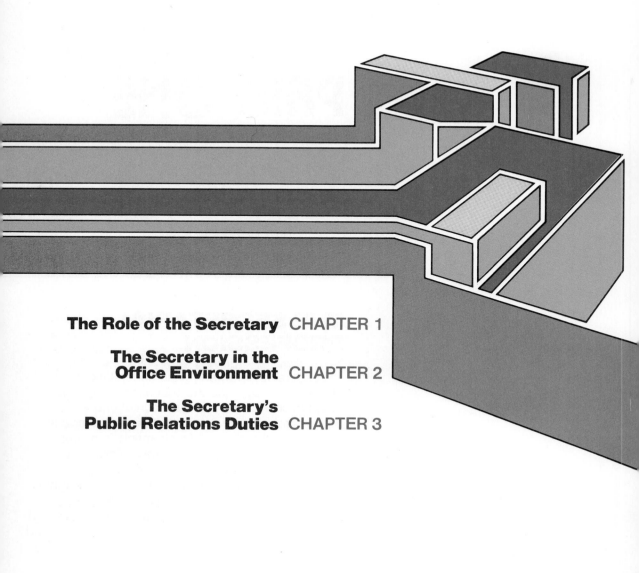

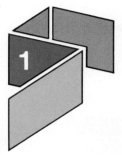

The Role of the Secretary

A secretarial position has always been near the top of the list of opportunities in the office in terms of both salary and prestige. However, in the 70s, legislative acts, technological advancements, and complexities of business organizations have caused drastic changes in secretarial career paths and responsibilities.

Today, there are not only traditional secretaries, who constitute about 85 percent of the secretarial work force, but also two newcomers — the correspondence secretary and the administrative secretary. These two new specialized secretarial roles are part of what is known as the word processing office organization pattern. This book is written with the training needs of all three types of secretaries in mind.

Chapter 1 will define a "secretary" in the traditional mold and describe the secretary's role. Then it will discuss technological advances that are changing the organizational structure of secretarial work and describe the duties of the administrative secretary and the correspondence secretary. After a look at the sociological and psychological factors that are also affecting the secretarial field, the chapter will reevaluate secretarial opportunities in terms of job openings, salaries, and promotional possibilities. After you have read this analysis, you will be better able to make intelligent decisions about your own secretarial future.

DEFINITION OF A SECRETARY

The job classification *secretary* is one of the most misunderstood terms in the office occupations. To attract applicants, a company may advertise for a secretary when the work is purely stenographic or even clerical. Yet in personnel offices concerned with the classification of jobs for salary and promotion purposes, the term must have a specific meaning that indicates both the duties performed and the conditions under which the secretary functions. This job description is helpful:

Secretary — assigned as personal secretary, normally to one individual. Maintains a close and highly responsive relationship with the day-to-day work activities of the supervisor. Works fairly independently, receiving a minimum of detailed supervision and guidance. Performs varied clerical and secretarial duties usually including most of the following:

a. Receives telephone calls, personal callers, and incoming mail; answers routine inquiries, and routes the technical inquiries to the proper persons;

b. Establishes, maintains, and revises the supervisor's files;

c. Maintains the supervisor's calendar and makes appointments as instructed;

d. Relays messages from supervisor to subordinates;

e. Reviews correspondence, memoranda, and reports prepared by others for the supervisor's signature, to assure procedural and typographical accuracy;

f. Performs stenographic and typing work.[1]

From this and similar job descriptions, the National Secretaries Association (International), an organization representing more than 33,000 secretaries, adopted the following definition. A secretary is:

An assistant to an executive, possessing mastery of office skills and ability to assume responsibility without direct supervision, who displays initiative, exercises judgment, and makes decisions within the scope of her authority.

Within this concept a secretary is a highly qualified person who possesses not only "mastery of office skills" but also personality requisites of the highest order. A secretary must know the scope of authority given and must discharge the responsibilities that are within that sphere. The secretary must judge correctly when to follow through alone and when to consult the employer about how to handle a job. Here is a person capable of making many decisions, of composing routine correspondence independently, perhaps of supervising other clerical workers and of keeping their personnel records.

The person who fits the NSA definition is frequently secretary to the chief executive, acting many times as the *alter ego* to a busy employer. Secretaries to the presidents or to the managing officials in large organizations are sometimes given the title and salary of administrative assistant. In other organizations they may perform these functions without being given this title. In the classification system used by the Administrative Management Society (AMS), this employee is called Secretary A with the following job description:

---

[1] U.S. Department of Labor, Bureau of Labor Statistics, *National Survey of Professional, Administrative, Technical and Clerical Pay*, Bulletin 1804 (Washington: U.S. Government Printing Office, 1975).

Performs secretarial duties for a top-level executive or someone responsible for a major functional or geographic operation. Does work of a confidential nature and relieves principal of designated administrative details. Requires initiative, judgment, knowledge of company practices, policy, and organization.

AMS then classifies the secretary who works for an executive responsible for departmental management as Secretary B, with this job description:

Performs secretarial duties for a member of middle management. General requirements are the same as for Secretary A but limited to the area of responsibility of the principal.

It is likely that in a first secretarial position, the beginner will be classified as a Secretary B (or even Stenographer) and with experience and increased knowledge eventually be promoted to Secretary A. In other words, secretarial work can be a position to be promoted *into* as well as *out of*.

The Secretary B must have a thorough knowledge of one branch of the organization but is not expected to demonstrate the broad understanding of the total organization that is demanded of a Secretary A. There is a possibility, too, that an outstanding Secretary B may advance to department head.

TECHNOLOGICAL ADVANCES

Early in the 70s automated word processing equipment became available. This makes possible the mechanization of much of the secretary's production of typed material. This new equipment is very expensive (too expensive to place at every secretary's desk) and must be used to capacity. It is necessary, therefore, to put it in special locations called word processing centers where trained operators specialize in producing typewritten output. In these centers words are processed in much the same way as numbers are processed in data processing centers.

In addition to the availability of new equipment, the cost factor has influenced the rapid growth of automated word processing. The cost of producing a business letter in 1977 was $4.47 according to the Dartnell Institute of Business Research.[2] Other estimates place the cost at more than $5.00. (Included in these estimates are such items as the dictator's time, the transcriber's time, typewriter, paper, light, heat, and office rent.) The expense of operating the office has been taking up a larger part of the overall costs of producing

---

[2]*The Secretary* (May, 1977), p. 46.

goods every year. Naturally, management welcomed the cost-reducing possibilities that could be achieved through automated word processing.

The Emergence of Word Processing

Although words have been processed ever since paper was produced, the term "word processing" has been adopted to describe a new method of improving the efficiency of business communications. It is, according to IBM, "the transition of a written, verbal, or recorded idea to a typewritten form." Word processing adopts the systems approach. One group of employees specializes in performing one function and, with the help of automated equipment, achieves greater productivity. Another group performs the other secretarial tasks required by executives.

The traditional secretary's job is split into two jobs: that of *word processor* or *correspondence secretary* in a word processing center, and that of the *administrative secretary* (sometimes called *administrative-support secretary* because it is not an administrative position) in an administrative support center.[3]

The equipment that gave rise to the word processing concept was the Magnetic Tape Selectric Typewriter (MT/ST). Equally influential was electronic voice-writing equipment, on which the originator of a document records oral dictation which is then transmitted to a center by telephone (see page 185 for an explanation).

Today there are several dozen automatic typewriter manufacturers producing machines that sell for $2,000 to more than $20,000. It is customary for a word processing center to advertise for an operator by the name of the equipment to be used, for instance, Vydec, Lexitron, Xerox, or Redactron.

The capabilities of the equipment are amazing. It is possible to show both copy being typed and stored copy on the screen in front of the operator. Then the operator can correct it and can verify the corrected copy as it appears on the screen. It is possible to merge materials from several sources to produce one document. For instance, one source produces the address, another produces computerized numerical data, and another produces selected paragraphs from a mag (magnetic) card or a series of mag cards. The result might be a letter using paragraph 7 and paragraph 234 of sample form letters to delinquent customers and a summary of the customer's overdue bill covering two invoices. Sending material from

---

[3]The term *administrative secretary* will be used in this book because it is the more commonly used term.

This correspondence secretary is keyboarding individualized material into a portion of a letter that has been stored on magnetic cards.

International Business Machines Corporation

This administrative secretary is taking notes concerning travel arrangements for one of the executives with whom she works.

the word processing center to a distant company location over telephone lines is also possible. This saves time in delivery and the expense of preparing a hard-copy printout.

The Impact of Word Processing Equipment on the Traditional Secretary

Many secretaries work in small organizations where the volume of work may never justify the purchase of word processing typewriters. For them word processing may be merely an interesting development. In larger companies, though, even the secretary who works with one executive will be able to enjoy the advantages of automated processing of many documents. He or she will become a modified administrative secretary, freed from routine duties for more challenging ones. Material can be dictated to a center by either the executive or the secretary. Or perhaps part of the dictation and transcription can be retained in the executive's office and part sent to the center. In some cases the secretary who formerly had an assistant, or even more than one, will be able to handle all of the executive's work alone. In other cases a secretary who formerly worked for one executive may be assigned to two or even more principals, as the following paragraphs indicate.

Reorganization Patterns Under a Word Processing System

Word processing is such a new concept that organization patterns and job titles have not yet been standardized. The centers are organized according to the company's needs — one large center serving all departments, a center for each heavy-volume department, a center for several related departments, and so on. Usually the equipment manufacturer surveys the buyer's organization and recommends the most efficient pattern. The flowchart on page 9 illustrates one possible setup. It shows the interrelation between the word processing center and the administrative support center.

In this plan the administrative secretary gets materials ready for dictation and the principal dictates (or perhaps the administrative secretary dictates if the material is routine). In this word processing unit there are four components:

The receiving station, which logs in the received dictation.

The word processing manager, who decides the order in which work is to be done and assigns the work to individual operators.

The correspondence secretary or word processor, who operates the power equipment.

The center coordinator, who proofreads the transcripts.

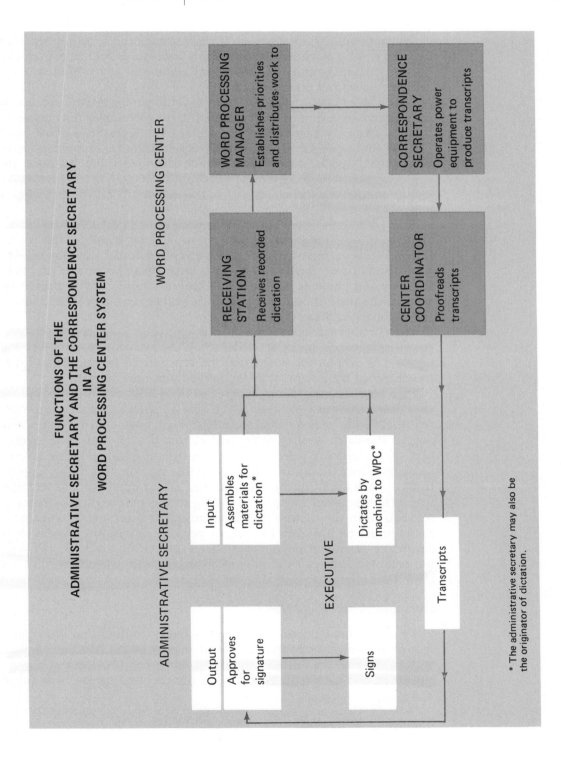

FUNCTIONS OF THE
ADMINISTRATIVE SECRETARY AND THE CORRESPONDENCE SECRETARY
IN A
WORD PROCESSING CENTER SYSTEM

WORD PROCESSING CENTER

WORD PROCESSING MANAGER

Establishes priorities and distributes work to

CORRESPONDENCE SECRETARY

Operates power equipment to produce transcripts

RECEIVING STATION

Receives recorded dictation

CENTER COORDINATOR

Proofreads transcripts

ADMINISTRATIVE SECRETARY

Input

Assembles materials for dictation*

EXECUTIVE

Dictates by machine to WPC*

Output

Approves for signature

Signs

Transcripts

* The administrative secretary may also be the originator of dictation.

The approved transcripts are then sent back to the administrative secretary, who attaches the necessary enclosures and approves the document for signing. The principal signs and the administrative secretary distributes the output.

Group needs determine the number of administrative secretaries in a center; for example, six administrative secretaries may serve as many as twenty principals. Administrative secretaries may have general functions for all other-than-typewriting tasks, or they may be assigned special functions in which they excel. For instance, an administrative secretary may handle all records management or travel arrangements or library research for all of the principals served by a unit.

The correspondence secretary keyboards (types) dictation from voice-writing equipment. Typing as rapidly as possible, the secretary corrects errors by using the typewriter's automatic erasing features. Sometimes the dictator wants only a rough draft so that corrections and changes can be made before a final copy is prepared. Most of the time, though, a final, usable document is produced from the keyboarded material.

The correspondence secretary is responsible, too, for playing out stored mag cards, tapes, or disks when the same material is needed again. The whole document may be reproduced or portions of different stored transcripts may be merged into new output.

English skills are the most important qualification of the correspondence secretary, who must be able to spell and punctuate correctly. The correspondence secretary must have to an exceptional degree the same first qualification required of a traditional secretary: to understand words and their correct use in business communication. Since dictation is from a remote station, there is no opportunity to ask about terms. But the transcriber cannot make sensible transcripts without an understanding of the nature of the business referred to in the dictation. This means that a top-notch word processor must be a highly intelligent person who knows a great deal about the organization's operations. Typewriting speed is not very important; accuracy is. Finally, a correspondence secretary must be interested in mechanical equipment and understand its capabilities.

Management's Reactions

A management consulting company has estimated that word processing techniques can usually result in a decrease of 15 to 30 percent in clerical payroll and overhead for every 100 work stations placed under the program.[4] (This is another indication that word

---

[4]Walter A. Kleinschrod, *Management's Guide to Word Processing* (Chicago: Dartnell Corporation, 1975), p. 15.

processing systems are feasible only in large companies.) One company says that production has doubled with word processing — from 250–300 lines a day previously produced by typists at individual work stations to 500–800 lines a day by correspondence secretaries. In another company 10 employees now handle the work previously done by 42. Naturally, management is sold on the concept for its cost-cutting features.

Management likes word processing too because secretarial output can be measured. Under the traditional system the only supervisor of output was the executive for whom the secretary worked. Such a person was neither trained in nor especially interested in work measurement. Now management is trying to staff the administrative support center and the word processing center with supervisors who know how to apply standards of both quality and quantity.

Some executives, who regard their secretaries as status symbols, resist the reorganization of the secretarial function. They dislike dictating to a machine, and they feel that the whole concept of word processing is dehumanizing.

No more than 20 percent of today's offices are organized for word processing. Many will never be. Yet rapid progress is being made toward automating the offices of large organizations.

SOCIOLOGICAL AND PSYCHOLOGICAL CHANGES AFFECTING THE SECRETARIAL FIELD

The women's movement has created a negative attitude toward secretarial work. In the past, over 95 percent of secretarial jobs have been held by women. Thus it has become popular to deride the field as "women's work" in which women are subservient to men, who have traditionally held practically all of the executive positions. Secretaries are depicted by the propagandists as "go-fers" whose main responsibilities are bringing in coffee, running errands on the lunch hour, and acting as office maids.

The result is described in a *Business Week* article in which executives deplore the scarcity of secretarial applicants even though the positions offer challenges. "These jobs are not low-paying," says John M. Coulter, research director for the Chicago Association of Commerce and Industry. Coulter blames the women's movement for placing a stigma on secretarial work and discouraging young women from taking such jobs.[5]

On the other hand, women's rights efforts have undoubtedly improved the lot of working women at every level, secretaries included. In their drive for equal opportunities, women have been a

[5]*Business Week* (March 19, 1976).

major factor in securing affirmative action legislation which prohibits discrimination in hiring and promoting. Some of the largest corporations in the country have been ordered to pay women employees millions of dollars in back pay for discriminatory promotion practices. Women have opened the doors, although on an admittedly limited basis, into new professions, new management training programs, and new attitudes. In fact, all jobs are acquiring a unisex complexion. "Men's fields" are opening to women, and "women's fields" are opening to men.

PERSONAL SECRETARIAL REQUISITES

A good secretary is a staff assistant and the executive's office memory. As a public relations expert, the secretary must represent the company and the employer effectively to the public. Of equal importance is the ability to work cooperatively with all employees inside the organization: with the executives on a higher level, with co-workers on the same level, and with those to be supervised. Strangely enough, research tells us that human relations problems arise infrequently with those at higher and lower levels and that most personality problems occur in contacts with employees at the same level, in this case with other secretaries.

Because secretaries are close to management, they should look and act like management. Most college students try to conform to the standards of dress and hair styling that will win the acceptance of their peers. When they move into a new environment, that of the office, they must try equally hard to meet new standards, those of business.

Some employees do not realize that good grooming and appropriate business dress are even more important to their business success than are their skills. They "express their individuality" by ignoring business standards for personal appearance — a self-defeating attitude if there ever was one. Companies sometimes react by imposing dress standards such as forbidding pants suits for women or long hair for men. A career-minded employee, though, should require no outside standards. A person's good judgment should compel attention to conservative dress and behavior.

Equally important are good posture and good health habits. The secretary to an executive must be in top physical condition. As pressures on the executive increase, so do they upon the secretary. To meet capably all the demands of the day, the secretary must begin the day well rested and well nourished.

College students usually take a speech course — but not very seriously! Yet the personnel officer in charge of work assignments for 20 college students who were on an internship program between junior and senior years reported that the one universal complaint of the executives with whom the students worked was, of all things, *speech*. The student should analyze speech patterns and, with faculty help, embark on a speech improvement campaign.

IS SHORTHAND OBSOLETE?

A news release from the International Word Processing Association recently stated that "Shorthand skill is becoming an archaic job requirement." Is this statement true? Want ads for stenographers and secretaries in the daily press and job listings in employment offices refute this statement. The 80 percent of offices without word processing systems refute it too. So do over 1,400 members of the National Secretaries Association (International) who have just participated in a survey. They state that more than 50 percent of their companies require entry-level shorthand speeds of 90 words a minute or more; 70 percent require typing speeds of 60 words a minute or more. Three fourths of the secretaries reported that they transcribe from symbol shorthand regularly.

Administrative secretaries need shorthand too, even if they do not transcribe their notes into usable business documents. If they can take shorthand, they can save time and be more productive. Secretaries who dictate to word processing centers can organize their ideas for the dictation into logical sequence by making shorthand notes. This is especially true for the dictation that requires great care. Carefully-thought-through letters come back in usable form rather than in rough draft.

The administrative secretary can save time, too, by using shorthand notes in researching material for reports, in writing rough drafts, or in abstracting material. During interviews with other company personnel, the secretary can use shorthand to provide exact records for future reference. Material for preparing reports on a conference or a committee meeting can be quickly organized from shorthand notes taken during the conference or meeting. And, obviously, shorthand is indispensable for recording telephone conversations, whether the secretary is monitoring a conversation between a principal and an outside caller or is simply taking a message. A final argument for learning shorthand is the advantage it gives the administrative secretary who decides to change jobs. It is often the ace up the sleeve that makes the difference.

As Anderson says: "The business establishment that considers shorthand to be an archaic job requirement has not been studying

THE PERFECT SECRETARY

Yes | No

1. Do you know the full range of your responsibilities and activities in your organization?
2. Do you know your employer's personal goals and ambitions and how they fit into corporate objectives?
3. Are you a well-organized person? Can you help the executive organize time by coordinating schedules and appointments and meeting deadlines — all without nagging?
4. Can you initiate, handle, and follow through on projects within the scope of your authority without running to your employer?
5. Are you courteous, helpful, respectful, and solicitous toward your business associates, visitors, clients, and customers? Do they speak favorably of you?
6. Are you imaginative and creative? Do you suggest original ideas, systems, and procedures for the improvement of your employer's work? Do you adopt such ideas in your own work?
7. Can you move paper efficiently, prying loose papers and projects that have stayed on the executive's or an associate's desk too long?
8. Are your basic secretarial skills (such as filing, stenography, and telephoning) beyond reproach?
9. Are you calm in a crisis? Gracious when tension mounts?
10. Do you give your employer and company absolute loyalty?
11. Can you be trusted with confidential information, both personal and business?
12. Do you read widely, calling pertinent information to your employer's attention?
13. Are you engaged in a self-improvement program, attending classes, lectures, and programs that are management-oriented? Do you try consistently to learn more about your company, your customers, and your industry?
14. Are you articulate? Can you express yourself well, both verbally and in writing, in summarizing information for your employer? Do you give clear instructions?
15. Are you a good manager? Can you assign work to others when necessary, supervising its completion, and taking responsibility for its quality?
16. Can you do basic research for your employer? Can you gather information for a report, for example, and write a rough first draft?

This form evaluates the ability of the secretary to manage people as well as paper and pushbuttons. Few secretaries will rate at the top on all counts.

Adapted from Ruth Gallinot, "How Good Is Your Personal Secretary?" *Time Trap*, edited by R. Alec Mackenzie (New York: American Management Association, 1972), pp. 155–156.

the productivity of its administrative secretaries. And isn't that productivity what word processing is all about?"[6]

REEVALUATION OF SECRETARIAL OPPORTUNITIES

Most of you who read this chapter are already involved in secretarial preparation, and wisely so. But the following material can be used to confirm your vocational choice and to refute such downgrading attitudes as those described earlier in the chapter.

Secretarial work is for many people a satisfying life occupation. In this text, the traditional secretary will be referred to as the *multifunctional secretary* because of general rather than specialized duties, such as those found in the word processing type of organization. The multifunctional secretary is part of the management team. A top-level secretary associates with executives at the exciting core of the company's activities. The secretary is one of the key figures through which executive ideas are implemented.

Job Openings

Secretaryship, unlike some of the supposedly more glamorous fields, offers almost certain employment opportunities in any geographic location. Many an adventurous person has used secretarial work as a means of traveling extensively, both at home and overseas. The secretarial field also provides an "open sesame" to the older person who wants to enter or return to the business world.

Even when there is a high rate of unemployment, especially among the young and inexperienced, jobs are available for secretaries. A look at the help-wanted columns of almost any daily newspaper will confirm this statement. Even more reliable is the work of the U.S. Labor Department's Bureau of Labor Statistics in studying where jobs will be found in the next ten years. Between 1975 and 1985, the secretarial profession is expected to grow by a million and a half new workers.[7]

Secretarial Salaries

The average weekly salaries of secretaries compare favorably with those of other office workers throughout the United States

---

[6]Ruth I. Anderson, "The Need for Shorthand in the Automated Office," *Business Education World* (January–February, 1976), p. 19.

[7]"Where the Jobs Will Open Up Over the Next Decade," *U.S. News & World Report*, Vol. 54, No. 26 (Dec. 27, 1976/Jan. 3, 1977), pp. 82–83.

according to an Annual Survey of Office Employees by the Administrative Management Society. The 1977–78 statistics yield the information shown below.

It is significant that, with the exception of Computer Operator A (technician), Programmer (technician), and Systems Analyst (professional), Secretary A leads the salaries of the office force. Also, Secretary B is eighth among the group. The International Word Processing Association surveys indicate that at the present time salaries of both administrative secretaries and correspondence secretaries are lower than those of multifunctional secretaries.

AVERAGE WEEKLY OFFICE SALARIES IN THE U.S.

1977–78 Administrative Management Society's Annual Survey

Job Category	Average Weekly Salary
Correspondence secretary	$160
Systems analyst	319
Programmer	275
Computer operator A	222
Computer operator B	191
Tabulating machine operator	181
Keypunch operator A	165
Keypunch operator B	149
Secretary A	208
Secretary B	180
Stenographer	164
Typist — Clerk	147
Telephone switchboard operator	158
Offset duplicating machine operator	176
Bookkeeping machine operator	148
Accounting clerk A	193
Accounting clerk B	159
General clerk A	169
General clerk B	139
Mail clerk — File clerk	125

Secretarial salaries have risen rapidly in the last few years. According to IBM, secretarial salaries have increased 68 percent since 1965. This is so not only because of inflation but also because of shortages of competent applicants due to forces discussed earlier.

A final comment about salaries refers to a 1975 survey of members of the National Secretaries Association (International).

The salaries reported by these professionals, who had been employed as secretaries for at least five years, indicated that more than half of them make more than $9,000 a year and that a few make over $15,000. Only 15 percent of the respondents worked at companies which had word processing centers, and only 2 percent were actually part of a word processing system.

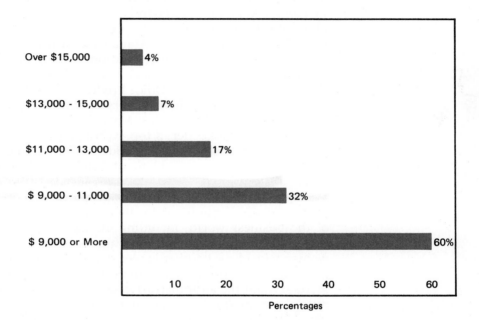

Salaries of 1,420
Members of the
National Secretaries
Association
(1975 Survey)

Promotion Possibilities

For some people, secretarial work is a stepping stone to another career. Probably secretaries have benefited from affirmative action programs as much as — and even more than — any other group. Undoubtedly many an executive, faced with the possibility of court action for violations, has looked around for possible candidates for promotion, focused on the person whose quality of performance was already known, and promoted a secretary. However, chances are that, unless a promotion entails a management job at the former employer's level (and that is highly unlikely), the information dealt with in a new job will be of a lower level and more removed from top management's thinking.

A sampling of former secretaries who were promoted attests to the possibilities for advancement. Elinore Stieha of Rapid City, South Dakota, was appointed Assistant to the President of Black

Hills Power and Light Company. Phyllis Spencer was made Manager, Personnel Administration, of the Oakland, California, plant of Sherwin-Williams Company, paint manufacturer. Carmen Martinez became Purchasing Assistant for the Raytown, Texas, chemical plant of Exxon Corporation. Mary Holstad was appointed to the Iowa Commerce Commission. Betty Raymond became Budget and Cost Control Analyst for American Airlines Field Marketing Services in Tulsa, Oklahoma. Ida Podbilski became Assistant to the President of Stanford Research Institute, Menlo Park, California. Shirley Trottier was promoted to Sales Manager of a firm in Baltimore, Maryland, which specializes in regulation uniforms for military and industrial wear. Bertha Stronach was promoted to Word Processing Training Manager for the Office Products Division of IBM.[8]

Others who began their careers behind the secretary's desk and reached top management are: Marion Stephenson, vice-president of NBC; Josephine Shaeffer, a top executive in a large real estate company; Virginia Rehme, vice-president of a St. Louis bank; and Isabelle Kirchner, vice-president of Prudential Life Insurance Company. The diversity of job titles represented here attests to the variety of promotional opportunities available to secretaries.

Women are being hired for more and more jobs in all categories of the business world, including management. A woman secretary today will find new competition, not only with men but with other women who chose another career path into management.

What about promotional opportunities for the correspondence secretary and the administrative secretary? The correspondence secretary was probably attracted to word processing because of the ability to produce larger volumes of higher quality documents than the multifunctional secretary in a given period. Therefore, one of the numerous advertisements in urban newspapers for a mag card, a Vydec, or a Xerox operator would appeal to such a person. If competent operators are not available, the company must then train its own. The correspondence secretary who has demonstrated competency in English mechanics and in decision making related to equipment capabilities will probably advance through the job titles within the word processing center: from correspondence secretary or word processor, to proofreader, to proofreader trainer, to coordinator-scheduler, to supervisor, to manager of the center, to — who knows?

Administrative secretaries realize that they may have to adjust to the whims of several superiors rather than just one. Still, they see their opportunities for promotion increasing in direct proportion to the number of principals served.

---

[8]Source: Publications of the National Secretaries Association's Certified Professional Secretary program.

SUMMARY

This chapter has indicated some of the changes that are occurring in the secretarial field. These changes logically lead to the following conclusions.

Although many offices are reorganizing for word processing, there are still many that are not and never will. The multifuctional secretary in offices large enough to organize word processing centers need not feel threatened. Rather the multifunctional secretary should welcome the equipment as a way of obtaining freedom from much of the routine typing, so that more challenging work can be accomplished. The secretary of tomorrow must be flexible. Anyone now in secretarial work or preparing for it must accept change and adjust to it. In fact, the areas in which change is occurring may be the areas of greatest opportunity.

Secretarial work provides a satisfying life career. It also offers demonstrated possibilities for promotion into management. Labor shortages continue in this field even in a time of high unemployment. Salaries of secretaries compare favorably with those of other office employees.

Various parts of the text may be of interest to the multifunctional secretary, to the administrative secretary, or to the correspondence secretary. However, all sections of the book should be studied carefully for the development of a strong foundation in secretarial knowledge and skill.

SUGGESTED READINGS

Benét, M. K. *Secretary: A New Look at a Female Ghetto.* New York: McGraw-Hill Book Co., 1973.

Blackburn, Norma Davis. *Secretaryship.* Pacific Palisades: Goodyear Publishing Co., 1974.

Brunson, Evelyn V. *Professional Secretary.* Englewood Cliffs: Prentice-Hall, 1974.

Dallas, Richard J., and James M. Thompson. *Clerical and Secretarial Systems for the Office.* Englewood Cliffs: Prentice-Hall, 1975.

Ettinger, Blanche, and Estelle L. Popham. *Opportunities in Office Occupations*, 4th ed. Louisville: Vocational Guidance Manuals, c/o Data Courier, 1976.

Kleinschrod, Walter A. *Management's Guide to Word Processing.* Chicago: Dartnell Corp., 1975.

McCabe, Helen, and Estelle L. Popham. *Word Processing: A Systems Approach to the Office.* New York: Harcourt Brace Jovanovich, 1977.

"The Office of the Future." *Business Week* (June 30, 1975), pp. 48–50+.

Winter, Elmer L. *Successful Manager-Secretary Team*. West Nyack: Parker Publishing Co., 1974.

PERIODICALS AND SUBSCRIPTION SERVICES

Administrative Management. A monthly magazine available by subscription from Geyer-McAllister Publications, Inc., 51 Madison Avenue, New York, NY 10010.

From Nine to Five. Twice monthly pamphlets on specialized topics, available by subscription from Dartnell Corporation, 4660 Ravenswood Avenue, Chicago, IL 60640.

Management World. A monthly magazine published by the Administrative Management Society, AMS Building, Maryland Road, Willow Grove, PA 19090.

Modern Office Procedures. A monthly magazine available from the Industrial Publishing Co., Division of Pittway Corp., 614 Superior Avenue West, Cleveland, OH 44113.

Office Guide for the Working Woman. A twice-monthly bulletin from the Bureau of Business Practice, Inc., Division of Prentice-Hall, Inc., 24 Rope Ferry Road, Waterford, CT 06386.

Personal Report for the Professional Secretary. Twice-monthly high-level report on research of value to the secretary. By subscription from Research Institute, 589 Fifth Avenue, New York, NY 10017.

P. S. — A Professional Service for Private Secretaries. A twice-monthly bulletin on personal relationships, office procedures, and techniques for the secretary. Bureau of Business Practice, Inc., Division of Prentice-Hall, Inc., 24 Rope Ferry Road, Waterford, CT 06386.

The Office. A monthly magazine available by subscription from Office Publications, Inc., 1200 Summer Street, Stamford, CT 06904.

The Secretary. The official monthly publication of the National Secretaries Association (International), 2440 Pershing Road, Crown Center, Suite G-10. Kansas City, MO 64108; containing association news and interesting features.

Today's Secretary. A monthly magazine (except for July and August) containing timely and informative articles for all levels of secretaries. Gregg Publishing Division, McGraw-Hill Book Company, Inc., 1221 Avenue of the Americas, New York, NY 10020.

Viewpoint. Monthly news sheet of the International Word Processing Association, Maryland Road, Willow Grove, PA 19090.

Word Processing Report. A twice-monthly technical/management newsletter published by Geyer-McAllister Publications, Inc., 51 Madison Avenue, New York, NY 10010.

Word Processing World. Bimonthly magazine published by Geyer-McAllister Publications, Inc., 51 Madison Avenue, New York, NY 10010.

Words. Quarterly magazine of the International Word Processing Association, Maryland Road, Willow Grove, PA 19090.

QUESTIONS FOR DISCUSSION

1. In what ways has this chapter changed your concept of the secretary's role?

2. Do you think that the National Secretaries Association's definition of "secretary" is valid? Why or why not?

3. The National Secretaries Association (International) objects to the use of the terms correspondence secretary and administrative secretary by the International Word Processing Institute. Do you think that the objection is justified? Why or why not?

4. What effect do you think the rapid development of word processing will have on future secretarial opportunities?

5. Have affirmative action programs been beneficial or detrimental to the secretary?

6. How can misconceptions about opportunities in secretarial work be reversed?

7. In the light of your own capabilities and interests, which type of secretary would you prefer to become: a multifunctional secretary, a correspondence secretary, an administrative secretary, or a supervisor in a word processing center?

8. Select the correct verb or pronoun from the parentheses in the following sentences so that there is number agreement between related words. Then consult the Reference Guide to correct your work. Compose an example similar to any sentence you missed.
   (a) Your pair of scissors (is, are) being sharpened; my scissors (needs, need) it, too.
   (b) The number of applicants (seems, seem) large; a number (has, have) asked for interviews.
   (c) (This, These) data (constitutes, constitute) a comprehensive collection of all the facts and figures available now.
   (d) Assignments, and not the examination, (determines, determine) your final grade.
   (e) Not only the letter but also the carbons (is, are) messy.
   (f) The professor, together with the students, (plans, plan) to go through the main post office.
   (g) No book or articles (touches, touch) on this subject.

PROBLEMS

1. Visit a word processing center or talk with either an administrative secretary or a correspondence secretary to determine whether the conclusions in this chapter coincide with those of someone working in one of these jobs.

2. One way to develop the secretarial personality that will later enable you to get a high score on the chart on page 14 is to evaluate yourself today and acquire as yet undeveloped desirable traits. The rating scale below will serve as a guide as you evaluate yourself. Then, to determine whether you perceive yourself as others see you, ask a classmate, a friend, or a family member to check your characteristics

on the same scale. Each point may be rated *excellent*, *so-so*, or *needs improvement*. Next, set up a specific program for improvement, pinpointed to your low ratings. Concentrate on one or two traits at a time until the desirable behavior seems to be instinc- tively yours. Then work on two or three more traits until they are habitual. Repeat the process until you have an attractive, pleasant-to-work-with personality that will earn a high score on this chart.

A SELF-CHECK ON YOUR SECRETARIAL PERSONALITY

Performance Components

Accuracy

How good am I at finding and correcting errors?

Good Judgment

Are my decisions usually thoughtful rather than impulsive?

Follow Through

Do I see a job through — doing implied and specific assignments?

Resourcefulness

Do I usually try various possibilities until I solve a problem?

Initiative

Do I often initiate action in my group?

Organization

Can I develop a work plan that, when necessary, can be flexible in its execution?

Efficiency

Am I aware of the importance of time and the economy of motion in the completion of assignments?

Skill Development

Do I make a definite effort to improve my weakest skills?

Human Relations Components

Consideration

Do I often do kind things without being asked?

Tact

Do I avoid ruffling the feelings of others?

Discretion

Do I refrain from divulging business and personal information?

Loyalty

Do I stand by my family and my friends through thick and thin?

Objectivity

Can I — and do I — look at personal situations impersonally?

Respect

Do I recognize the need for lines of authority as part of a team effort?

Forbearance

Can I hold my tongue and refrain from petty remarks to a co-worker who is being "difficult"?

Attitude

Do I accept work assignments cheerfully?

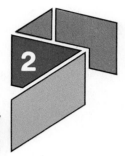

The Secretary in the Office Environment

The first chapter presented an overview of the secretarial profession. You may begin your career as a secretary in a large corporation, a professional office of attorneys or doctors, a small office, a hospital, or a government agency. No matter where you enter employment, you will want to know how you fit into the organizational structure and where you are to complete your duties.

This chapter will introduce you to the office environment. First, the management and division levels of a large business organization will be discussed. Next, the chapter will describe a work station similar to the one you may occupy when you take your first assignment. The three areas of responsibility possible in a secretarial position will then be considered. Finally, you will see how the secretary organizes time and work for top efficiency. Soon you should begin to see yourself in the important position of secretary.

UNDERSTANDING THE ORGANIZATIONAL STRUCTURE

One of the first things you will do as a newly hired secretary is acquaint yourself with the organizational structure of the office. You need to know where your employer fits into the management team. If you join a one-secretary office or a small company, the hierarchy is readily apparent. If you are in a large company, however, the situation is quite different. There you must learn the names of persons to whom your employer reports. You must also know the names of those who report to your employer and of those of equal status with your employer. An organization chart can give you this information. If one is not available, ask questions of your employer and research the files. In general, keep your eyes open! The discussion which follows describes an organization typical of a large firm.

Company Officers

The administration of a company usually consists of a president, an executive vice-president, one or more vice-presidents, a secretary, and a treasurer. Each of these officers will have a staff to provide assistance.

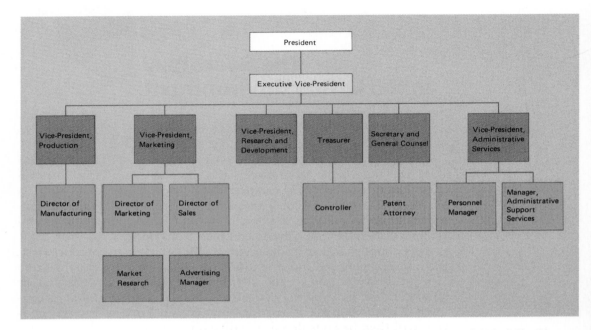

The organization chart for the company described on these pages might look like this. Positions will, of course, vary among companies. This chart clearly identifies the levels of administrative authority in a line structure (one in which authority flows vertically from the top executive to the lowest level employee).

President. In most corporations the president is the chief executive officer who is responsible to the board of directors for the profitable operation of the business. This position is one of liaison between the board of directors, on which the president usually serves, and management personnel. Thus, the president interprets the board's actions to management and management's plans to the board. The office of the president puts board resolutions into effect.

The duties of the person who carries this title are as varied as the activities of the firm. To many people, the president is a company symbol. What this executive does has a bearing on the reputation of the firm and possibly on the community in general. The leadership ability of the holder of this office often determines the type and caliber of management personnel in the organization.

Executive Vice-President, Vice-Presidents, Secretary, and Treasurer. The executive vice-president (or senior vice-president) is second in command in the organization. This officer serves in place of the president and may be selected to succeed a president. Generally, it is the responsibility of the executive vice-president to suggest changes in policy and to coordinate the efforts of the other vice-presidents in carrying out their specific programs and functions. This executive also coordinates the work of various departments.

Often there are two, three, or more vice-presidents. Each is a general officer of the company and, with the president and executive vice-president, is involved in achieving the goals of the firm. Each vice-president is responsible for a special phase of administration, such as production or marketing, and strives to reach the objectives set for that division.

The secretary of the company, often an attorney, is responsible for the legal actions of the business. Typical activities of this office include: scheduling stockholders' meetings, drafting resolutions, recording the proceedings of meetings, executing proxies or powers of attorney, and preparing contracts.

The treasurer, who is the financial officer of the firm, directs all monetary, budget, and accounting activities.

Controller —
Comptroller

Divisions of a Company

A large company is usually organized into departments or divisions. The functions and titles of these divisions vary depending on the type of business in which the company is engaged. For example, a manufacturing firm may have such operational divisions as production, purchasing, marketing, finance, research and development, and administrative services. A retail chain may have the same divisions with the exception of a production department or manufacturing department.

Production. The executive in charge of the production division is the vice-president, production. In some companies this executive's title may be director of manufacturing, director of engineering, or factory manager.

The production division controls and is responsible for all matters pertaining to the manufacture of the company's products. The objective of this division is to manufacture the product in its desired quality, in the proper quantity, and at the lowest possible cost. This division must cooperate closely with other company divisions, such as marketing and finance.

Purchasing. The purchasing division is responsible for procuring materials, machinery, and supplies for the company. The complexity of the division will, of course, depend on the size of the company. In a small company, one person (with perhaps some clerical help) can accomplish all purchasing functions. In a very large corporation, the head of the division may be at the vice-presidential level.

Purchasing functions are specialized according to the needs of the organization. One buyer, for example, may be in charge of purchasing all raw materials for production. Another may be responsible for the packaging requirements for the corporation's various products. Further divisions in the purchasing procedure occur as necessary.

In general, the procedure is this: A department initiates a purchase requisition, providing as many specifications as necessary. The appropriate buyer locates a source of supply; considers quality, quantity, price, and service; and negotiates the purchase.

Marketing. Because a business survives only if it sells its products, there must be an effective marketing/sales organization. The marketing division may be separated into two or more departments, the heads of which report to the vice-president of marketing.

Sales Department. The sales director (or sales manager) usually directs a staff of salespeople. The department may employ the members of the sales staff, give them special training, and assign them to territories. It may supply samples and literature, introduce new products, and perform myriad other activities through the sales staff. In addition to managing the sales department, the sales director may be responsible for developing product policy, approving credit extensions, and preparing a sales budget.

The selling function, of course, is one of the most important activities of the company. How well this function is performed often determines the company's profit.

Advertising Department. The advertising department, also, is concerned with selling. It is responsible for devising a broad advertising plan appropriate to the overall marketing program of the company. This department coordinates its advertising with the selling effort. In some instances it turns over the advertising entirely or partly to an outside advertising agency which, in turn, plans and executes the program. In this event, the advertising department acts as a liaison. It supplies information to the agency about the company's products and marketing goals and approves the agency's proposals.

Market Research Department. The work of a market research department is statistical and interpretive in nature. This department gathers useful data to guide the business in marketing current products or in launching new ones. Its scope is extensive. It continuously reexamines and estimates the market for the company's products. Market research also evaluates new products of other manufacturers and provides management with the information necessary for sound decisions.

Finance Division. The finance division handles the moneys and accounting procedures, recording, analyzing, summarizing, and interpreting the financial affairs of the company. Thus the financial division provides a continuous record of company financial transactions. It is also responsible for devising systems, forms, and procedures to summarize company financial activities. This division is involved in formulating company policy.

Often the financial vice-president is in charge of the finance division. This officer directs the work of the treasurer and the controller. The controller (sometimes spelled *comptroller* but always pronounced *controller*) usually directs all phases of accounting. These phases include the general accounting department; cost accounting department; and the combined tax, internal auditing, and procedures department.

Research and Development Division. Recognizing that their survival depends upon success in developing better products, large companies are increasing their budget allotments for research. Scientists and engineers work to develop new and improved products or production methods. These specialists occupy a position of high status in the company.

Administrative Services Division. Those departments which exist to serve all the others are presented here as administrative services departments. These departments generally report to the vice-president, administrative services.

Personnel Department. The personnel director or manager directs the work of the personnel department. One function of this department is the interviewing and hiring of employees. This responsibility involves exploring labor sources, processing and filing application forms, organizing and conducting interviews, administering tests, and adhering to government standards in fair employment practices. Some personnel departments also maintain training programs for new employees (perhaps excluding sales trainees) and in-service training for present employees. It is the function of the personnel department to provide employee services and fringe benefits; establish health and safety programs; and accomplish the work involved in transferring, promoting, and discharging employees. The department also develops job descriptions and job analyses.

Administrative Support Services. Some companies centralize certain office functions, such as records management, reprographic services, mailing, and word processing, by maintaining a specialized staff to perform these activities. The offices of this staff are located where the services provided are as accessible as individual layouts permit. The company with specialized services relieves the individual office force of some routine office jobs. For example, a company using word processing centers can group all secretaries serving one division into a unified location in the division. This type of organization is called the satellite concept.

In a company without centralized office services, each functional division or department operates as a complete, self-sufficient unit. It handles all of the office duties which would otherwise be turned over to a centralized department.

THE SECRETARY'S WORK STATION

The word "change" aptly describes the office surroundings of today's secretary. Because of the increase in all office activity, the avalanche of paperwork, and the need for more communication at every level of the office hierarchy, there is a tremendous strain on office budgets. As a result, businesses are attempting to decrease costs by mechanizing and systematizing the work of the secretary. In order to economize further, changes in the work environment itself are in process. Saving energy and money in terms of heat and light consumption is the byword in today's and tomorrow's office design. Thus, the conventional office floor plan which provides the secretary with a private office or with a desk placed outside the executive's office is being scrutinized by cost-conscious management.

In the "changed office," employees are placed according to the work flow or work system. Thus each employee's niche is called a work station. This work station is completely self-sufficient, movable, and economic. Each station is adaptable to the needs of the employee and is furnished with the tools and equipment necessary to increase office productivity.

The Conventional Office Design

In a conventional office layout, the secretary's desk may be in any one of three areas. It may be immediately inside the employer's office, outside the employer's office along with secretaries to other principals, or in a nearby location with several other secretaries. If a secretary is assigned to more than one principal, the desk is located so that it is convenient to each of them. Regardless of the arrangement, the boss-secretary team must at least be able to see, if not hear, each other.

The Landscape Office Design

Today's approach to office design is popularly referred to as the landscape or open space concept. This approach utilizes movable

Westinghouse ASD Group

The landscape office design allows office modules, or work stations, to be positioned to best fulfill present needs, yet allows flexibility as those needs change.

partitions and acoustical screens instead of walls in order to provide open spaces rather than doors and hallways. Colorful, modular furniture, paintings, thick carpets, live or artificial plants, and plenty of sunlight and windows typify the new office.

Besides visible changes in the office, the landscape design facilitates work flow and communications. Employees are positioned according to the flow of work and are readily visible to their supervisor. This office planning system emphasizes the fact that employees are a part of the total process and thus an integral part of the company team. Advocates of this approach say that it increases productivity and job satisfaction. In addition, the colorful surroundings have a positive effect on the company's customers.

Ergonomics, the science of work and work place design, is the technical term used to describe this total office planning system. Ergonomics integrates both the physiological and psychological factors involved in creating an effective work area. Thus, it is concerned with the tools and equipment, furniture, acoustics, color, spatial layout, methods of work, and organization of work within an office.

One problem with the office landscape model is the loss of visual and audio privacy. Scientific aids are effective in reducing the noise level and congestion produced by many workers and visitors in a given area. The fact remains, however, that in the open landscape office the square footage available per worker is reduced considerably. Thus distractions are greatly increased. A secretary placed in this situation must develop the ability to concentrate and must show consideration toward co-workers at all times. To meet the demand for privacy, newer installations of the landscape design provide for 20 to 30 percent of the work station area to be enclosed.

Another disadvantage of the landscape office is the need for increased personal and equipment security. The greater accessibility of open space may force an office to maintain a staff of security personnel 24 hours a day.

In the open space design the executive's office generally has two sections: a large area for individual work and a meeting room for group interactions. In the future it is likely that this conference area may become an information center complete with data input and output devices, visual display boards, and other audio-visual aids in communication. Secretaries will ordinarily work with input, output, and retrieval equipment. They will also be responsible for projecting the data visually. Even more than now, the secretary will be the facilitator of communications between the employer and other staff members.

AREAS OF SECRETARIAL RESPONSIBILITY

Secretarial work can be divided into three general areas: (1) routine duties, (2) assigned tasks, and (3) original work. All of these areas apply to the multifunctional secretary, the administrative secretary, and the correspondence secretary.

Routine Duties

All secretarial jobs involve some routine tasks, although automation has substantially reduced the amount of routine work required. The multifunctional secretary and the administrative secretary perform such routine duties as opening the mail, filing, replenishing supplies, answering the telephone, and locking up confidential materials at the end of the day. The correspondence secretary locates already-transcribed materials and reproduces additional copies.

Assigned Tasks

Assigned tasks are those which are given to the secretary by the employer. The task can be simple, complex, or a mixture of both. In any event, it is work that must be done, usually in a limited amount of time. Tasks assigned to either the multifunctional secretary or the administrative secretary may include making travel reservations, drafting and sending a Telex, making a bank deposit, or getting technical material from the library. In completing these assignments the secretary may have to make adjustments in the work schedule to accommodate emergencies. The correspondence secretary performs such assigned tasks as transcribing a letter or report, inserting changes in a report, or merging addresses and content so that identical letters can be sent to several correspondents.

Original Work

Originial work is defined here as that area of responsibility in which the secretary displays initiative in assisting the employer. Work which demonstrates thinking ahead or following through on the part of the secretary is typical of this category.

The secretary's contribution in the area of original work is especially appreciated by the employer. At the same time, it is most gratifying to the secretary. The more efficiently the secretary handles the work in the assigned and routine areas, the more time remains for service of an original nature. Such service earns the attention that may lead to promotion for the secretary.

The opportunities for creative work on the part of the secretary depend largely on the executive's willingness to delegate responsibility. Such action is an indication of progressive leadership. The secretary can, however, increase the scope of responsibility by demonstrating competence in initiating supportive activities. For example, a multifunctional or administrative secretary who wants to perform work of an original nature will anticipate a request for data supporting a business report and supply it before the employer requests it. Or perhaps the secretary will initiate an instant reference system to increase the employer's effectiveness. In addition, the creative secretary may notice an important article in a magazine and call it to the employer's attention.

Although the multifunctional secretary and the administrative secretary may have more opportunities to be creative, it is possible for the correspondence secretary to show originality and creativity as well. For instance, since margins, headings, or spacing can be changed without difficulty, a correspondence secretary may experiment with various formats to improve the appearance of a document. Or perhaps the correspondence secretary may redesign the arrangement of the work station to make materials more accessible. Although these suggestions apply more to improving methods of handling assigned duties, they do demonstrate that the job of the correspondence secretary is not so limiting as to exclude opportunities for creativity.

ORGANIZATION OF TIME AND WORK

An effective secretary makes every minute count. This means actively working during working hours and relaxing during leisure time hours. Punctuality is expected in reporting for work, in completing material for the employer, in submitting periodic reports, in relaying messages, and so on. A lackadaisical attitude about time can be a source of irritation to the employer. It can also directly affect other office workers in their attitude toward time. As in other office-behavior situations, the secretary sets the standard.

The Working Day

Secretaries generally do not punch a time clock, nor do they watch the clock! They may have peculiar time schedules in order to fit their working time to that of their employers. This may mean working during the lunch hour, after closing hours, or even on weekends. Naturally, they are paid for overtime work in terms of either salary or compensatory time off.

The person holding a secretarial position may also have a time schedule different from that of other workers in the same office. The secretary's working time, scheduled to suit the employer's convenience, must at the same time cover a full work week in terms of hours. Any comments of other workers should be ignored, because the secretary is accountable only to the employer. Vacations, too, may be more irregular for the secretary than for other office employees. The secretary must defer to the employer's schedule by remaining on the job when the work load is the heaviest.

Time is the scarcest resource and unless it is managed nothing else can be managed.

Peter Drucker

The Secretary's Work Plan

Planning each work day is a necessity for any secretary. Work does not come in an even flow. There are periods when the employer, and accordingly the secretary, must turn out important work in a limited time. The secretary's own analysis of the time and motion spent on routine tasks may free additional time in anticipation of high-priority work. A thorough analysis of all the activities performed by the secretary may provide clues to where time can be conserved. If the secretary anticipates periodic jams and distributes part of the rush-period work to slack days, it may be possible to reduce, but still not eliminate, the pressures of peak loads.

Work Analysis. Work measurement is common in offices today. The more repetitive clerical tasks performed by the secretary, such as filing, typing, transcribing, and stuffing and sealing envelopes, have received considerable attention from work analysts. Time standards developed for these clerical tasks can serve as guidelines to the secretary. Often these are available from the office administrator.

Every secretary should strive to perform repetitive tasks as efficiently as possible by working with a minimum of motion, effort, time, and fatigue. As an interested secretary, you may wish to analyze the factors involved in completing each task so as to reduce motion, effort, time, fatigue, or any combination of these.

For a complete, organized analysis, you may consider all duties over a period of several weeks on a form or chart similar to the one below. At predetermined time intervals, you record the current activity. This provides a daily account of the tasks performed and the proportion of time given to each activity. A careful study of the chart shows where time is not being used to best advantage. For

WORK ANALYSIS SHEET

Date _October 15_   Position _Secretary to V-P_

TIME		TASK	CLASSIFICATION					TOTAL TIME	Evaluation
Start	Complete		Outside Contact	Intraco. Contact	Subordinates	Adm. Matters	Routine		
8:00	8:10	Housekeeping duties					✓	10	Total time necessary to maintain standards
8:10	8:15	Telephone confirmation of meeting	✓					5	
8:15	9:05	Open, sort, distribute mail		✓	✓		✓	50	Train Susan to distribute
9:05	9:52	Dictation		✓		✓		47	Suggest holding of telephone calls
9:53	11:30	Transcription of memos, letters					✓	97	
12:30	1:00	Explanation of monthly report preparation			✓			30	No need to replicate

A work analysis which incorporates time involved and classification of each task. The amount of time and the type of work involved can suggest to the secretary what work can be delegated to others in the office.

instance, you may spend too much time on something that someone else could do, such as searching in the files, typing a mailing list, and so forth. Be mindful, too, of subtle time wasters, such as filing papers that could be thrown away, duplicating information on several company forms, or recording information that is no longer valid or necessary. Concentrate your energy and your time on those activities which lead to increased efficiency and work productivity. Such activities are most valuable to your employer and to yourself.

Certainly, the secretary alone can implement some time-saving practices. Certain changes, though, require the cooperation and approval of the employer or even the purchase of new equipment.

Daily Schedule. At the end of the day, the secretary takes care of several routine items, such as planning for the next day and straightening the office desk. Thinking ahead, you will prepare an activity plan for the following day. A chart similar to the one on page 35 could be used to list the jobs in order of priority. If you work for more than one principal, it may be difficult to decide which job to do first, second, and so forth. Personalities may enter into the decision. Still, there are certain guidelines which can be used in determining work priority. The old adage, "Rank has its privileges," applies to the business office. For instance, if one employer holds a higher position than the other, generally the higher-ranked employer's work takes precedence. However, if some other item is of an especially urgent nature, it may take priority. Ultimately, you may have to rely on your own judgment to make these determinations.

On rare occasions, your plan may not dovetail with that of your employer. In that event, the principal's plan is followed. One of the many traits of a successful secretary is flexibility.

Before leaving for the day, you should clear and straighten the desk work surface. A cluttered desk is unsightly and does not speak well of the efficient secretary. For security and other reasons, you should lock up all areas where confidential material or expensive equipment is kept.

Periodic Peak Loads. A study of a month's flow of work over the secretary's desk may indicate patterns of fluctuation. For instance, Mondays traditionally bring heavier mail and subsequently heavier dictation. Thus, other Monday plans should be light. A secretary who must issue first-of-the-month statements of account could spread their preparation throughout the month in some organized pattern. Slack periods are ideal for transferring files, typing new record cards, bringing address files up to date, and duplicating sets of frequently requested materials. At all times, then, the secretary should be on the lookout for ways to simplify work.

DAILY WORK PLAN

Date _October 16_

Goals: 1. _Complete research for report_

2. _Select meeting time/place_

3. _Compose notification letters_

4. _____

Priority Code

1 — Urgent
2 — Do today
3 — Do when convenient
4 — Do when all other duties
    are accomplished

Time	Task	Priority	Evaluation
8:00	Open, sort, distribute mail	2	Delegate to Susan
8:30	Library research	1	
9:00	" "	1	
9:30	Compiling data	1	

A daily work plan incorporating a listing of objectives for the day, a time analysis, and the priority of work.

To help meet the demands of periodic peak loads, the secretary makes preliminary preparations, such as addressing envelopes, partially completing forms, preparing enclosures, and purchasing or requisitioning all necessary supplies. In this way, the office will run smoothly even during the busiest times.

Real Emergencies. Even with the best planning, unavoidable emergencies will occur. An unexpected illness or tragedy may upset the normal functioning of the office force. All at once you may be faced with a difficult job and insufficient time in which to perform it.

With experience you will know which jobs are critical and how and when each is to be accomplished. If subordinates are available, some of the work may be delegated to them. Through it all, work calmly and steadily. When an overload situation does occur, try to approach each item as made up of individual tasks. Then, check off each task as it is completed. In this way, you will make steady progress. If, however, the work load is far more than the present office force can handle, you may want to suggest employing temporary help.

Office Memory Devices

A good memory is basic to office efficiency. The secretary needs a good memory to plan the work for the day, to carry out assignments which are pending, and to keep track of assignments which have specific due dates. There are several types of memory aids for the secretary.

Secretarial Desk Manual. Every secretary should compile and keep up to date a loose-leaf desk manual. It should cover each duty, responsibility, and procedure of that desk. It may also provide a useful place in which to keep often-needed company information. Part 9 of this book explains the contents and organization of such a manual.

The Tickler. This efficient office aid, the tickler, derives its name from the accounting term *tick*, meaning to *check off*. A tickler is an accumulating record, by days, of items of work to be done on future days. The items are then ticked off when completed.

The daily calendar can be used as a tickler for recording items to be done on specific dates. Calendar page space is limited, however, so a separate tickler is usually set up and maintained. The most flexible tickler is a file box with 5- by 3-inch colored guide cards.

The secretary enters a tickler item concerning an express shipment due before the end of the week. Notice the abbreviated form of writing memorandums.

There are cards for each month, one to three sets of date guides numbered from 1 to 31, and one card labeled "Future Years." The guide for the current month is placed in the front of the file. A set of day guides is placed behind the guide for the current month. Additional guides may be placed behind the next one or two months. An item of future concern is written on an individual card, and the card is filed behind the guide for the proper month and date. If the item is to be followed up several months later, it is dropped behind the month guide. It will be filed according to date when that month comes to the front.

Since an item is often forwarded and reforwarded, the follow-up date is written in pencil so that it can be erased and changed when necessary. In fact, since this is a memorandum type of record, the entire item is usually written in pencil. Annual items, such as due dates of taxes, insurance premiums, and wedding anniversaries, are refiled for next year's reminders as soon as they are ticked off.

Maintaining a tickler is one of the routine duties of secretarial work. However, the tickler is an important tool. It is the secretary's responsibility to remind the employer of tickler items. The oversight of an item can be very embarrassing and costly to the firm. You will, therefore, want to use the tickler device as a memory aid in these ways:

1. To remind yourself of work to be done.
2. To tick off items accomplished.
3. To record work for a future date.

To be of dependable help to your employer, you must consistently check a tickler for pending activities.

> Sooner or later a busy person learns to write things down. It's the best way to capture things we are apt to forget. *"The strongest memory,"* says an old proverb, *"is weaker than the palest ink."*
>
> Bits and Pieces
> June, 1976

Pending File. The pending file is also a memory aid. It is a file folder in which the secretary temporarily holds mail concerning matters that are pending. It is kept in the secretary's desk, in the employer's desk, or in some other place near at hand. If the secretary's desk has a deep file drawer, the pending file can be kept conveniently there. It is not too satisfactory to keep the folder in a flat position because then the folder and its contents often become dog-eared. The secretary must be careful not to isolate letters in the pending file that should be available in the regular files. This can be avoided by making extra copies of incoming and outgoing letters and filing the originals in their respective files. If a letter is not involved, type a special note about the item and place it in the pending file. Check through the pending file regularly to determine what matters need to be called to your employer's attention. Any letters which have been answered should be released to the regular files and any extra copies should be discarded.

Desk Reference Files. The secretary can organize the office work more efficiently by keeping desk reference files. Such files would include the names of important clients, telephone numbers frequently called, addresses of regular correspondents, items that must be followed through before they are placed in the central files, stock identifications and descriptions, and work in process. These desk reference files save much time that would otherwise be lost in hunting for frequently needed facts. The organization of each secretarial desk differs according to the employer's position and the type of business. The desk reference files you set up will be those you need most. They can be planned only after you are on the job.

The Chronological File. Some secretaries make an extra copy of everything they type in order to maintain a complete chronological file. Many a day has been saved by this ready-reference file. If the secretary is also in charge of the employer's files, it is a good practice to note the location of the file copy on the "chron" copy.

How long you keep the chron copies is a matter of preference. For example, some secretaries keep their chron copies for the past three months in the desk drawer. In addition, chron copies of older correspondence are kept in a file drawer. (Also see pages 320–321 for additional information.)

Outside Assistance

It is good judgment for the secretary to request assistance if the situation warrants such action. When there is not sufficient time to complete a sizable office job, the secretary should ask for additional workers. If a word processing center is not available, this assistance can be secured through the office manager. Also, secretaries will often help each other in rush situations. If those avenues fail, you may obtain the employer's permission to contact an agency that supplies experienced temporary help. Among such agencies are Manpower, Kelly Services, Inc., Olsten Temporary Services, and others.

Sometimes the work requires professional skills or abilities beyond those of the secretary. Or perhaps the job is of such size that it can be done more quickly and less expensively outside. In such cases, with the employer's permission, the multifunctional secretary often turns to a special-service agency. Outside agencies can perform the following services: prepare multiple copies of original letters and mail them; obtain hotel and travel reservations; take full recordings of meetings and prepare transcripts; handle any or all of the operations of reprographics; furnish and maintain mailing lists;

or provide competent help for other jobs of a specialized or technical nature.

Upon completion of the work, the secretary writes a note in the desk manual identifying the agency or the individuals employed. Also, a record of the total cost and a brief evaluation of the service should be kept for future guidance.

Supervision of Subordinates

The secretary may be assigned one or more full-time assistants or temporary helpers. With relatively inexperienced assistants, the supervisor assumes the role of *teacher*. In this capacity, the secretary provides the assistant with opportunities for the development of efficient work habits. In addition, the secretary teaches the proper use of equipment and physical facilities.

When assigning work, the secretary gives thorough directions to subordinates. There should be no doubt as to what is to be done. If the work is complicated, written instructions should supplement the oral directions. Periodically, the secretary checks on the progress of the work, so that any misunderstandings can be avoided. It is also a good idea to give assignments of varying difficulty to subordinates. In this way, they have an opportunity to display exactly what they can do.

In addition to being a teacher, the secretary is also a *student* — a student of human behavior. The secretary studies the abilities of the office assistants. Also, it may be useful to read literature concerning supervision. It is the secretary's responsibility to motivate subordinates so that they work to their full potential and take pride in their work. The supervisor gives credit and praise when due. If criticism becomes necessary, however, the supervisor discusses the *work* and not the *worker*.

At specified intervals, the secretary formally evaluates the subordinate's performance, perhaps by using an evaluation instrument similar to that given on page 40. Note that such an instrument lets the evaluator comment on each factor being rated. This is an advantage both to the evaluator and to the employee. Remember that the responsibility for objective evaluation is implied.

A supplementary evaluation form, such as that shown on page 41, is being used along with the standard evaluation form in more and more offices. The supplementary form attempts to encourage understanding and receptiveness by identifying future action needed by the employee. The completed form provides a basis for discussion during the supervisor-employee conference.

An additional discussion on the elements of supervision appears in Chapter 28.

EMPLOYEE EVALUATION

Name of Employee _Joe A. Morgan_   Department _Word Processing_

Directions: Read over each section carefully. Appraise employee performance by placing
a check mark in the box below the phrase that applies to the employee.
Check only one box in each section. Appraisers are encouraged to use the
"Remarks" sections for additional comments pertinent to the employee's
evaluation.

KNOWLEDGE OF THE JOB Technical job information and practical know-how	Proficient on job; makes the most of experiences--a "self-starter" ☑	Rarely needs assistance but asks for it to save time ☐	Knows job fairly well; regularly requires supervision and instruction ☐	Job knowledge limited; shows little desire or ability to improve ☐

Remarks: _has thorough understanding of machines_

QUALITY OF WORK	Doesn't care; work is inferior in many respects ☐	Work is usually passable; regularly requires reminder to do a better job ☐	Usually does a good job; seldom makes errors ☑	Consistently does an excellent job; errors very rare ☐

Remarks: _____

QUANTITY OF WORK	Slow; output below minimum requirements ☐	Turns out the required amount of work--seldom more ☐	Fast; usually does more than is expected ☑	Exceptionally fast; efficiency unusually high ☐

Remarks: _line count is above average_

ADAPTABILITY Mental alertness; ability to meet changed conditions	Learns new duties easily; meets changed conditions quickly ☑	Grasps new ideas if given a little time; adjusts to new conditions ☐	Routine worker; requires detailed instructions on new duties and procedures ☐	Slow to learn; requires repeated instructions; unable to adjust to changes ☐

Remarks: _____

RELIABILITY Confidence in employee to carry out all instructions conscientiously and completely	Requires frequent follow-up, even on routine duties; apt to put things off ☐	Generally follows directions, but needs occasional follow-up ☐	Conscientious; follows instructions with little need for follow-up ☑	Dependable; on time, does what you want, when you want it ☐

Remarks: _capable of formatting documents without instructions_

Summary Statement: _Mr. Morgan is highly productive and extremely creative in his work._

Signature and Position of Evaluator _P. B. Schultz_

SUPPLEMENTARY EVALUATION FORM

EMPLOYEE *Wilson   Jane   E.*

(last)   (first)   (initial)

This form is not intended to be used for scoring past performance. It is "supplementary to" standard evaluation forms, and should be used to identify characteristics where changes in employee behavior are needed.

	CONTINUE AS NORMAL	TAKE NEW DIRECTION
QUANTITY		
EFFICIENCY: proper use of resources, no wasted time or effort; energy used versus product produced.	☑	☐
SPEED: length of time required to complete tasks. *needs to put tasks in order of priority*	☐	☑
QUALITY		
ACCURACY: amount of mistakes in work performance.	☑	☐
DECISION-MAKING ABILITY: conclusions and actions are timely and accurate; reaching the right answer after proper analysis.	☑	☐
WORK HABITS		
ACCEPTANCE OF RESPONSIBILITY: willing to be the person in charge of a task's success or failure.	☑	☐
CREATIVE ABILITY: finding new ideas and new and better ways of doing things.	☑	☐
DEPENDABILITY: can be counted on to do what is needed when it is needed.	☑	☐
OBSERVATION OF WORKING HOURS: works within the proper time frames.	☑	☐
OPENMINDEDNESS: ability to examine and consider new thoughts and ideas; consider things without a preconceived notion.	☑	☐
PERSONAL RELATIONS		
APPEARANCE: personal impression, clothing, cleanliness, etc.	☑	☐
COOPERATIVENESS: willingness and ability to work with others. *always willing to assist colleagues*	☑	☐
ADAPTABILITY		
ALERTNESS: the ability to grasp instructions; able to meet changing conditions, and to "catch on" quickly.	☑	☐
FLEXIBILITY: ability to meet changing or new situations.	☑	☐
INNOVATIVENESS: coming up with something new; making needed changes. *learns new applications quickly*	☑	☐
SUPERVISION *not applicable*		
DELEGATION OF PROPER RESPONSIBILITY: allows employees to have the opportunity to succeed or fail on their own and use the power that gets things done.	☐	☐
FAIRNESS: applies the rules in a consistent manner toward all employees equally.	☐	☐
GENERAL		
AMBITION: desire to reach a goal or objective; projecting one's self into a new role. *attends company seminars*	☑	☐
ENTHUSIASM: active desire and interest in the work.	☑	☐
HONESTY: truthfulness; not given to fraud or deception.	☑	☐
LOYALTY: maintains allegiance to the work group; does not ell others all the bad stories of the work group.	☑	☐

Source: Walter H. Smith, Jr., "An Evaluation Form that Improves Employee Relations," *Management World*, Vol. 4, No. 11 (November, 1975), p. 27.

When you ask a
subordinate to do
something, take time
to explain why. It's an
excellent habit with a
lot of good side
effects.

Bits and Pieces
June, 1976

SUGGESTED READINGS

Blackburn, Norma Davis. *Secretaryship*. Pacific Palisades: Goodyear Publishing Co., 1974, pp. 87–93 (office environment).

Dallas, Richard J., and James M. Thompson. *Clerical and Secretarial Systems for the Office*. Englewood Cliffs: Prentice-Hall, 1975, pp. 379–390 (supervising).

Keeling, B. Lewis, Norman F. Kallaus, and John J. W. Neuner. *Administrative Office Management*, 7th ed. Cincinnati: South-Western Publishing Co., 1978, Chapter 23 (work analysis), Chapter 24 (employee evaluation forms).

Mackenzie, R. Alec (ed.). *Time Trap*. New York: American Management Association, 1972.

Plan Your Work — A Handbook on How to Work Smarter, Not Harder. Arlington: National Association of Educational Secretaries (1801 N. Moore Street, Arlington, VA 22209).

Simpson, Marian G. *Tested Secretarial Techniques for Getting Things Done*. Englewood Cliffs: Prentice-Hall, 1973, pp. 18–19 (ordering priorities), pp. 26–34 (daily work schedule), pp. 129–150 (working for more than one principal).

QUESTIONS FOR DISCUSSION

1. Considering your interests, abilities, and aptitudes, in which department of a business organization (purchasing, personnel, research, sales, advertising, accounting) would you prefer to work? Give reasons for your choice.

2. You work in an office with a landscape design. What is your responsibility concerning the workers in your immediate area? concerning the security of equipment and confidential files?

3. Determine whether each of the office duties given below is a routine, an assigned, or an original task. Describe the working situation in each case (working with an employer, other company employees, things, or outsiders).
   (a) Filing a piece of correspondence
   (b) Answering the telephone
   (c) Looking up a word in the dictionary
   (d) Answering employer's buzz
   (e) Typing a letter from dictation
   (f) Setting up your own chronological file
   (g) Proofreading a document with another person

4. Many successful secretaries have this to say about completing the daily work plan: "Once you begin a task, complete it before going on to another activity." What do you think is the reasoning behind this statement?

5. The organization chart on page 24 illustrates the line structure of authority. Where would an administrative assistant to the executive vice-president appear on this chart? What would be the relationship between this position and the officers of the company?

6. Your employer frequently calls you for rush dictation late in the afternoon. This calls for much overtime work on your part. What steps would you follow in suggesting the reorganization of your employer's work, so that efficiency could be increased and overtime reduced?

7. In what ways can you reduce the pressures of periodic peak loads? of real emergencies?

8. What is the weakness of using a pending file? How can this danger be averted?

9. What would you do first if all the following happened at the same time: you were typing an urgent Telex; your employer, who was talking on a long-distance call, buzzed you to enter the office; the secretary to the company president walked by your desk into your employer's office; and your subordinate was at your desk wanting to borrow a file from your desk drawer? Explain your reasoning.

10. Suppose your employer needs to convert securities into cash to pay the quarterly income taxes. What kind of item would you put in the tickler? under what dates?

11. In your opinion, what factors should be considered in the employee evaluation process of an organization? Which person in the organization should be responsible for an employee's evaluation?

12. Capitalize the appropriate words in the following sentences. Then refer to the Reference Guide to correct your answers.

(a) He said, "you were a superior student in mathematics 201."
(b) The question is, what went wrong?
(c) How is your typing? Your shorthand? Your Spelling?

13. Show how you would type the number *twenty* in the blanks in the following sentences. Then refer to the Reference Guide to correct your answers.
(a) Send the letter to our new address at 267 _____ Avenue.
(b) The wine is over _____ years old.
(c) _____ copies will supply our needs.
(d) We are living in the _____ century.

PROBLEMS

1. The following items are on your desk on March 2 to be marked for the tickler file. Before filing these items in the regular files, you type a card for each one for the tickler file. Indicate on each card the date under which the card would be filed. Note on the card where the original material is filed.
   (a) Notes for an article to be written for the September *Journal of Accountancy*. The deadline for the article is April 1.
   (b) A note about setting up a conference with a bank official about a short-term loan to meet the April 1 payroll.
   (c) A letter accepting an invitation to speak at a meeting of the School of Business seniors on May 8.
   (d) The program of the annual convention of the International Controllers Institute to be held on April 6 in Brussels. Your employer plans to attend.
   (e) A notice of a meeting on March 8 of the Administrative Committee. Your employer is a member.

2. It is 11:30 a.m. and you are busy completing the last-minute details for a 2:00 conference your employer has called. Everything is going according to your schedule until your employer calls you into the office to tell you the following:
   (a) An additional 10 people will attend the meeting. It will be necessary to change the meeting room and to obtain more copies of the brochures and other papers to be discussed at the meeting.
   (b) Set up a short meeting with the Chief Accountant at 1:30.
   (c) Arrange for an overhead projector and screen for the meeting.
   (d) Bring the Smith contract file into the office immediately.
   (e) Call Henry Carter and request a postponement of the appointment scheduled for 1:30 today.
   On a sheet of paper, type the order in which you would handle these matters. Explain the rationale behind your decisions.

3. It is late Friday afternoon and you are 15 minutes away from your two-week vacation. Your employer is out of town until Monday. You have a number of pending matters on your desk. Decide which of the following items you should handle yourself in the time remaining, which to leave locked in your employer's desk, and which to leave for your replacement

to handle. On a sheet of paper, type your decisions and give the rationale behind them.

(a) Payment of your employer's insurance premium due the following Wednesday. You are authorized to make payment.

(b) Notification of meeting scheduled for Thursday of the following week.

(c) Shorthand notes of a letter dictated by one of the staff members.

(d) Confidential promotion papers concerning a staff member.

(e) Interoffice memorandum requesting technical data to be provided by your employer.

(f) A letter from your employer's daughter at college.

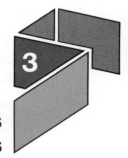

The Secretary's
Public Relations Duties

One of the most interesting and at times challenging duties of the multifunctional or administrative secretary is handling the public relations aspect of the position. Meeting, talking, and working with people outside the office are examples of public relations activities.

The secretary who greets office visitors is acting as the public relations representative of the office. Creating and maintaining a favorable company image requires courtesy, patience, persistence, sensitivity, tact, and the ability to get along well with others. Believe it or not, the Golden Rule applies in the business world just as much as it does in our personal lives.

In addition to the other aspects of public relations, the secretary must consider the personal preference of the employer in receiving callers. In the case of the administrative secretary who may report to several principals, the personal preference of each employer must be known and must be followed.

Skill in dealing with people *inside* and *outside* of the company can be worth uncountable dollars in goodwill. Some of that skill is innate to certain individuals, but for most people it comes with on-the-job experience.

This chapter discusses the public relations functions of the secretarial position. Appropriate behavior in the many situations which arise in meeting the public is described. Also, the efficient handling of appointments is presented.

THE EMPLOYER'S PREFERENCES

As a new secretary, you may learn of your employer's preferences by asking your predecessor. If this is not possible, you may ask your employer general questions. If you develop sensitivity to the reactions of others, you will begin to discern these preferences through experience.

Here are some questions about employer preferences and some suggested answers:

Does the employer want to see everyone who calls? (Many persons pride themselves on their "open door" policy.)

Does the employer prefer to see callers in a certain category (such as salespeople) at specified times only?

You can get direct answers to these two questions; however, the answers must in some situations be modified.

Which personal friends and relatives are likely to call? Which of these should be sent in without announcement?

Who else should be admitted without appointments?

Do not ask these questions directly. You will soon sense the answer. Certain persons can always enter the employer's office without first obtaining your permission: top executives to whom your employer is responsible; their secretaries; co-executives and their secretaries; and the employer's immediate staff. Special-privilege callers come in with confidence. They know they will be welcome, and usually they will introduce themselves to the new secretary.

How should callers be announced to your employer?

When should you try to terminate visits?

Are there callers that your employer prefers to avoid?

Watch your employer's reactions to your ways of handling these problems.

Welcoming the Visitor

When a visitor comes to your desk, courtesy requires that you give that individual your immediate and undivided attention. To finish typing a line, to file another three letters, or to continue chatting with another employee would violate proper business behavior.

Your greeting should be friendly and cheerful. A simple "Good morning" or "Good afternoon" said in a pleasant tone of voice sets the stage for effective communication.

The secretary will especially watch for a person with a *scheduled appointment*. Greeting the caller by name adds a personal touch to the welcome. After the usual pleasantries, the secretary escorts the visitor to the executive's office and makes any necessary introductions in a courteous manner.

After a cheerful, courteous greeting, the secretary listens attentively to the caller to determine the purpose of the visit. Perhaps the visitor may need to be referred to another office. If not, the secretary must choose between interrupting the employer and asking the visitor to wait.

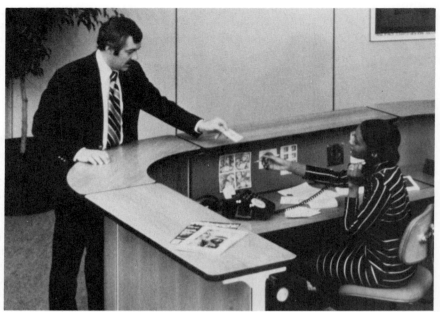

Herman Miller Inc.

If an *unscheduled caller* asks to see your employer, you must learn the caller's name, the company which the caller represents, and the purpose of the visit. The following greetings are appropriate:

Good morning, May I help you?
May I have your name please?
Who shall I say is calling?

The caller's business card provides some of this information and may give a clue to the reason for the visit. However, actually questioning the caller about the purpose of the visit may be necessary. In this case, tact and patience often come into play. An experienced secretary handles the situation gracefully and obtains the information for the employer.

A caller's business may involve a matter *outside the scope of your employer's duties.* You will save everyone's time by determining the nature of the visit first and, if necessary, referring the caller to the proper person. The transfer should be made immediately by telephoning the proper office and explaining the situation. If an appointment is made at once, the secretary directs the caller to the correct office. If an appointment must be made for another day, the secretary confers with the visitor and then sets a mutually convenient time. In most cases the secretary's helpfulness in arranging this appointment will more than offset any inconvenience which the visitor may experience.

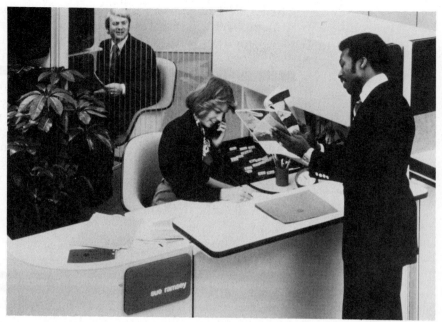

Herman Miller Inc.

If the visitor's business falls under the responsibility of another executive, the considerate secretary will try to arrange a meeting with the right person.

Once you know the visitor's name and reason for calling and are satisfied that the visitor's business is *within your employer's province*, you may write the name and the purpose of the visit on a slip of paper and take it in to your employer. The employer then decides whether to see the caller. If the caller is admitted, the written memorandum will help your employer remember the caller's name in their subsequent conversation.

Deciding Whom to Admit

Experienced secretaries are sometimes inclined to become too protective of the executive's time. Often they turn away too many visitors. The problem is treated humorously in a cartoon which shows a president's door overhung with cobwebs while the secretary explains, "Oh, nobody ever sees the president." This sort of attitude antagonizes almost everybody. A good rule to follow is: *When in doubt, ask whether your employer wants to see the visitor*.

If your desk is placed inside the executive's office, callers will be inclined to bypass you and go directly to your principal. But if your desk is just outside the office, you will probably be fully responsible for determining who may enter. Although certain co-workers, friends, and family may enter the executive's office without your permission, they usually ask courteously if it is convenient to go in.

Clients and customers are always given cordial and gracious treatment by the secretary. Marketing representatives from businesses which supply materials and services related to the employer's work are treated with courtesy and attentiveness.

Never judge a visitor's importance by appearance. Some outstanding people in the artistic, professional, and industrial world are far from prepossessing in appearance. On one occasion the secretary to a college president decided that an early-morning, very ordinary-looking caller was quite unimportant. Because the office was quite busy at the time, the secretary did not inform the president that a visitor was waiting. Finally the caller grew impatient and left. Later the secretary learned that the visitor was a very wealthy alumnus who had intended to give the school a tremendous sum of money. Naturally, the caller never returned.

Remembering Names and Faces

One extremely valuable secretarial technique is remembering names and faces so that you may greet callers in a sincere and natural manner. Unless the caller gives you a business card, write the person's name and the reason for the call on your daily calendar during the conversation. To remember names requires:

1. *Attention to the name as it is spoken.* Listen carefully when the name is pronounced. If in doubt, ask the person how to pronounce it or spell it. Writing the name phonetically in shorthand or in longhand will prevent mispronunciation. Being called by name is pleasant; but having one's name mispronounced is very annoying.

2. *A forceful effort to remember the name.* You can train yourself to remember a person's name by: repeating it when you first hear it; using it when addressing the person; recording it, perhaps in a reference notebook or card file; and associating the person's name and face with the business represented.

The ability to remember faces is another attribute of the superior secretary. Several devices similar to those used in remembering names may be used to develop this skill. The secretary may keep a card file of frequent callers, or may file a business card and associate the name on the card with the face of the caller. To recognize the employer's colleagues, the secretary should watch carefully for their pictures in company publications, newspapers, or magazines. While recording a committee meeting, the secretary might draw a seating chart and list some outstanding features about any unfamiliar faces. This will assist in learning their names later.

Several companies whose success depends upon effective public relations have developed techniques for improving internal

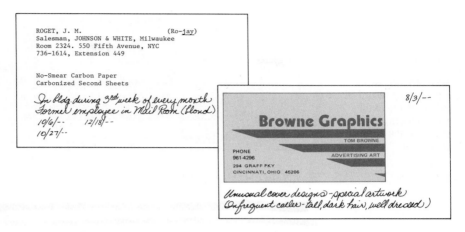

These cards are examples of efficient memory aids. Prepare a card for each caller, recording the name, affiliation, purpose and date of visit, subsequent visits, etc. Or make notations directly on the caller's business card. Shown at the right is a business card affixed to a 5- by 3-inch card.

relations. To help personnel recognize other members of the organization, one advertising agency publishes in its company induction manual an organization chart with the picture, title, and name of each executive.

Keeping a Record of Visitors

A record of visitors which includes names, dates of calls, business affiliations, purposes for calls, and other pertinent information is helpful. Often the secretary uses this record to locate needed facts.

To keep a record of visitors some offices use a printed registration form which the caller is asked to complete. In some cases the secretary may secure the information from the caller and add it to the register at a later time.

Professional offices, such as those of lawyers, doctors, engineers, and public accountants, use daily registers. These are helpful in preparing periodic time reports used in computing costs of services rendered to clients. The register serves as a checklist for each period so that the time spent with each client, as recorded, is also correctly entered and charged for on the proper time report.

Some offices keep an alphabetic card file of visitors, recording all visits as they occur. A card is filed by the caller's name and is cross-referenced to show the business affiliation. Doctors use the card system as a basis for billing patients and as a record of each patient's medical data. Purchasing agents can more easily remember the correct names of products and sales representatives by using such a file.

If the flow of visitors is small, the efficient secretary can keep a simple record of visitors conveniently and permanently on the desk calendar.

REGISTER OF OFFICE VISITORS						
Date	Time	Name and Affiliation	Person Asked For	Person Seen	Purpose of Call	
6/8/7–	9:30	H. Horton, Cove Lighting Fix.	S.G.	✓	Sales rep	
"	10:30	L. Alton, Standard Printing	R.B.	✓	"	
"	11:45	R. Krause, luncheon appt.	R.B.	✓	Merrill cont.	
"	1:40	J. Keller, Flexwood Consultant	S.G.	✓	" "	
"	3:50	Flexwood delivery driver	–	–	Brought samp.	

With this ruled register of visitors, the secretary can easily keep a daily record of helpful information about callers, including the purpose of the call.

THE SECRETARY'S CONTRIBUTIONS

When a visitor approaches the secretary's desk, the secretary must follow the rules of proper business etiquette. This involves making the visitor comfortable, making introductions if necessary, and using good judgment in interrupting the visitor's conference with the employer.

Pleasant Waiting

The secretary, acting in the role of public relations representative, provides the means for a comfortable and pleasant waiting period for the visitor. In order to accomplish this, the secretary may attend to the visitor's hat and coat, offer a cup of coffee or an ashtray, or provide current magazines.

Admitting the Visitor

After an unduly long wait, the secretary may remind the executive that the caller is still waiting. If the executive indicates that it will be only a few more minutes, the secretary may report this to the caller.

Sometimes the executive walks out to greet the caller. Should there be two callers waiting, the secretary should indicate who is first.

If this is the visitor's first call, the secretary will usually lead the way to the employer's office. Before leaving the desk, however, it is always a good idea for the secretary to cover the work on the desk or slip it into a folder unobtrusively. If the executive's door is closed, the secretary knocks, and after a slight pause, enters the office with the visitor. When the proper introductions have been made, the secretary leaves, closing the door quietly.

In some instances the secretary cannot leave the desk to escort the visitor to the executive's office. In this case, a simple suggestion will indicate that the visitor may go in now.

Introductions

When the secretary is responsible for making introductions, the general rule to follow is: **The person given the greater courtesy is named first. In business introductions, this means that the name of the person of higher position is given first.** Titles such as Doctor, Captain, or Sergeant are included if known.

When the executive introduces the secretary to a client, business position takes precedence. Therefore, the client is addressed first. The secretary responds to introductions in a natural way. A "hello" is sufficient.

As office receptionist, the secretary needs to be aware of the following situations where sex, age, and sometimes rank, rather than strict business position, might apply:

Introduction	*Factor in Presentation*	*First Named*
1. Woman and man	Sex	Woman
2. Dignitary (head of state, church dignitary, politician) and employer	Rank	Person with higher position
3. Young person and mature person	Age	Mature person
4. Member of armed forces or college faculty	Rank	Person with higher rank
5. Distinguished visitor and employer	Rank	Visitor
6. Individual to a group	Convenience	The individual, then each person in the group

Handshaking

The practice of shaking hands reduces barriers between people. It is said that the way a person shakes hands, like other forms of body language, reveals a great deal about that person. An enthusiastic handshake, for example, is interpreted as pleasant since it signifies that the person is sincere in offering the greeting.

Handshaking is customary and almost automatic between men. However, when a man and a woman shake hands, usually the woman must make the first move by offering her hand. In an office situation, the business position of the other person involved may preclude the secretary from offering a hand first. A good rule to remember is always to accept an extended hand. To do otherwise would slight the other person and cause embarrassment.

The Difficult Visitor

Being courteous to certain visitors may require considerable discipline and restraint. Some callers are gruff; some are condescending; some are self-important or aggressive; some, even rude. To be gracious to these persons requires strong willpower.

A nuisance visitor can resort to all sorts of dodges to get past the secretary's desk. In such cases, the secretary needs to exercise tact and firmness. Be wary of a person who, without giving a name, says, "I'm a personal friend" or "I have a personal matter to discuss with Miss Jones." The caller with important business has everything to gain by providing a name and stating the purpose of the visit. You may explain to the caller that you are not permitted to admit visitors unannounced. If the caller still refuses to give you this information, offer a piece of paper and request that a short note be written to the executive. Then enclose this note in an envelope and take it to the executive, who can then decide whether to admit the caller.

Some callers try to obtain information from the secretary either about the executive or about the company. Be wary of such inquisitive questions. Do not answer them, except in generalities. A remark such as "I really don't know" will ordinarily stop such questions.

Interrupting a Conference

Sometimes it is necessary to give a message to the employer during a conference. If this occurs, type the message on a slip of paper and take it into the office, usually without knocking if this is less likely to disturb the conference proceedings.

When there is a telephone call for the visitor, ask if you can take the message. If so, type it along with the caller's name, the date, and the time of the call. Then the message can be given to the visitor after the conference. If the one calling insists on speaking to the visitor, go into the conference room and say something like this: "Mr. Lawrence, Ms. Rowett is on the telephone and wants to speak with you. Would you like to take the call here (*indicating which telephone he is to use*) or would you prefer using the telephone on my desk?" If the latter is chosen, the secretary takes care of other business away from the desk to afford the visitor privacy.

Some inconsiderate visitors do not know when to leave. Usually the executive rises as an indication that the conference is over; but occasionally a caller will not take the hint. The secretary may help in this situation by taking a note in to the executive. This provides an opportunity for the executive to announce apologetically that it is time for another meeting. The secretary might even telephone from another person's desk to ask the executive if some kind of interruption is required. Often the mere answering of the telephone by

Mrs. Ahmad

Your secretary just called and asked that
you call back within 20 minutes for a very
important message. There is a telephone
which you can use just outside the conference room. (Dial 9 for an outside line.)

                                         A. A.

Mr. Montenegro

The secretary of Dr. Joseph Chou is on the
line at my desk and asks that you come to
the telephone for an important message from
the doctor. I'll wait outside my office while
you talk. Will you please let me know when
you are ready to leave my office?

                                         A. A.

Shown here are two acceptable ways in which to handle typical interruptions of business conferences. Before acting, the secretary decides what procedure will make the interruption as unobtrusive as possible.

the executive affords a sufficient break in the conversation to make the caller realize that the visit is over. Finally, the secretary can reduce overlong visits by informing the visitor upon entering of another scheduled appointment for the executive in ten minutes.

THE EXECUTIVE'S APPOINTMENT RECORDS

A busy executive may see a number of visitors in the course of each day. Therefore, in order to keep the work of the office running smoothly, the secretary must keep a record of the daily appointments of the executive. It is also a good practice to keep the appointment records from year to year as a general reference source. The effective secretary follows the employer's personal preferences in scheduling appointments, keeps a close watch on the employer's time, and uses good judgment in maintaining the appointment schedule.

Scheduling Appointments

Appointments are scheduled in different ways. For example:

1. The secretary schedules appointments for all recurring meetings at which the executive's presence is necessary (i.e., regularly scheduled conferences of boards or corporation committees) on the calendar at the beginning of the year. Additional recurring appointments are scheduled as new commitments are made.

2. The executive or the secretary may schedule an appointment over the telephone.

3. The executive or the secretary may schedule an appointment by mail.

4. The executive may ask the secretary to schedule an additional conference with someone who is in the office at that time.

5. The secretary may schedule a definite appointment with a caller who happened to come in when the executive was out.

6. The secretary may arrange for an appointment for the executive with outside individuals or businesses.

The secretary uses an appointment book to record the executive's appointments. In maintaining this book, the secretary follows the four "W's" of scheduling appointments. The following information should be recorded on the specific date page of the appointment book:

WHO the person is — the name, business affiliation, and telephone number.

WHAT the person wants — an interview for a position, an opportunity to sell a product, or a business discussion. Indicate any materials that will be needed for the appointment.

WHEN the person wants an appointment and how much time it will take.

WHERE an appointment is to be held, if other than in the executive's office. Be sure to include the address and room number.

If the individual making the appointment is in the office at the time of scheduling, the secretary furnishes a written reminder to that person.

In addition to the official appointment book, the executive generally keeps a pocket diary or calendar as a convenient reference when attending meetings or visiting outside offices. If this is the situation, the secretary would be wise to check with the executive daily for possible conflicting dates and times.

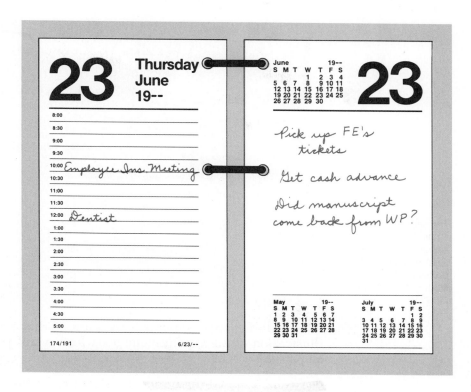

23 Thursday
June
19--

8:00
8:30
9:00
9:30
10:00 *Employee Ins. Meeting*
10:30
11:00
11:30
12:00 *Dentist*
1:00
1:30
2:00
2:30
3:00
3:30
4:00
4:30
5:00

174/191   6/23/--

June   19--
S M T W T F S
            1 2 3 4
5 6 7 8 9 10 11
12 13 14 15 16 17 18
19 20 21 22 23 24 25
26 27 28 29 30

23

Pick up FE's tickets

Get cash advance

Did manuscript come back from WP?

May   19--
S M T W T F S
1 2 3 4 5 6 7
8 9 10 11 12 13 14
15 16 17 18 19 20 21
22 23 24 25 26 27 28
29 30 31

July   19--
S M T W T F S
            1 2
3 4 5 6 7 8 9
10 11 12 13 14 15 16
17 18 19 20 21 22 23
24 25 26 27 28 29 30
31

The Secretary's Desk Calendar

Usually secretaries also keep a desk calendar to remind them of pending matters or appointments which involve the secretaries themselves. A sample page from such a calendar is illustrated on this page.

The secretary's first duty each morning is to remind the executive of the appointment commitments for the day. Pertinent information and files are placed on the executive's desk. Some employers prefer a typed list of the day's appointments along with other matters that must receive attention. This list may be on 8½- by 11-inch paper or even on a 5- by 3-inch card. An illustration of the typed appointment list appears on page 58. Some executives prefer a separate list of matters to be handled that day. The appropriate files are then attached to this list. Any matters not completed that day will be carried over to the next day's list.

Another successful practice is to include in the list any questions the secretary may have. The executive can write the answers directly on the sheet and then leave the paper on the desk. In this way the secretary can get the answers without disturbing the executive.

The administrative secretary who works for several executives maintains a separate appointment listing for each. The procedure

```
                    APPOINTMENTS AND REMINDERS FOR

                        Monday, April 7, 19--

        10:00    Staff Meeting

        11:00    James F. Syzek, Chamber of Commerce, 829-2300,
                 Ext. 509, concerning the center development

        11:30    Sally Bennington, Mutual Life, 829-4502,
                 renewal of policy

        12:00    Luncheon Meeting with Frank Snyder, University Club

         2:00    Budget Meeting


        Today's Reminders:

                 Call Frances Prouloz, 425-0034
                 Follow up on Emerson contract
                 License No. 533-429-3001 expires end of month
                 Review Inundo's proposal
```

The secretary types the employer's appointments in appropriate format and places the list on the employer's desk each morning.

for scheduling appointments is the same as that described above. An illustration of an appointment book for several principals is given on page 59.

Date and Time Preferences. In selecting the date and time for an appointment, consider the personal preferences of the executive. Some guidelines to be considered are:

1. Schedule few, if any, appointments on Monday mornings, because the weekend accumulation of mail requires attention.

2. On any day, allow ample time in the appointment schedule to take care of the mail.

3. Avoid late-afternoon appointments so that the employer can complete the work of the day.

4. Avoid appointments just before a trip because of the last-minute rush of work.

5. Avoid appointments on the first day after the executive's absence of several days, because of the accumulation of work.

6. Suggest two alternate times for the appointment, rather than asking the caller when it would be convenient for an appointment.

Unless told to the contrary, the secretary must seek the approval of the executive in granting appointments. The appointment is tentatively recorded in the appointment book to be later explained to and approved by the executive.

| JANUARY 14 | | | | |
Altman	Cross	McNutt	Haynes	Froehlich
8:00		In Miami 305 989-1011			
8:30					
9:00	R. Binder 821-4211		L. Timmons 356-8254	C. Basil 789-9339	Courthouse 9-5
9:30					
10:00			V. Stein 215-6129	Mrs. Rodder 981-7991	
10:30	L. Samuels 203 420-1481				
11:00				T. Benjamin 201-621-0219	
11:30					
12:00	T. Bandino Lunch 873-1891		Lunch	Lunch	
12:30				R. Braun 239-7969	
1:00			F. Perez 888-6239	S. Solomon 914-6199	
1:30					
2:00	D. Amos 739-4989		J. Silver 219-4569	Leave for Chicago 3 p.m. flight	
2:30					
3:00			J. Taylor 819-1699		
3:30					
4:00	Out from here		B. Matthews 819-8393		
4:30					
5:00			L. Nelsen 766-7916		
5:30					
6:00					
6:30					

Appointment Book for
Five Principals of an
Administrative
Secretary

Avoiding Unkept Appointments. Nothing destroys good relations faster than an appointment not kept. Preventing conflicting appointments is one of the secretary's most difficult problems. Sometimes the executive forgets to tell the secretary about appointments made outside the office. Three suggestions from experienced secretaries may prove helpful:

1. Each morning, try setting aside some time to review the day's appointment schedule with the executive. This may bring to mind an unrecorded appointment.

APPOINTMENTS
FRIDAY, APRIL 9, 19--

Time	Engagements	Memorandums
9:00	Mr. Smith	HR – Call DC Mohr re contract
9:30		
10:00	Meeting with Sales Personnel	See Jane Kuman for annual sales graph
10:30		
11:00		
11:30	Mrs. Alice Carter	
12:00	Dr. Pardi	

Appointment Book
Illustrating
Memorandum Column

2. Provide the executive with a pocket diary to carry at all times. You may ask to see this book until the executive becomes accustomed to giving it to you for checking.

3. At the end of the day, remind the executive of any unusual appointments. These may include a very early morning appointment or a night meeting.

Sometimes an executive may be unavoidably detained in returning to the office for an appointment. In this case, the secretary should, if possible, notify the next visitor by telephone and suggest a later meeting time. Occasionally the executive may forget an appointment. A secretary can be very helpful in quickly locating the executive if this occurs. Also, the executive may, at some point, face an emergency situation which causes an appointment to be canceled or a substitution made prior to the appointment. If this is the case, the secretary should explain the situation to the visitor and apologize for the substitution.

Saying No Tactfully. Obviously appointments should be refused as tactfully as possible. Refusals should be prefaced by a sincere "I'm very sorry, but . . . ." A logical reason for the refusal should always be given. Remember to use your employer's name rather than the impersonal pronoun when explaining the situation to the caller. Other tactful ways to refuse appointments would be to explain that the executive is in conference, must attend a meeting on that day, has a heavy schedule for the next two weeks, or is preparing to leave town. If a caller seems very disappointed over a refusal, you might offer to talk with the caller yourself. From this conversation you could relay a message to the executive or take some other appropriate, helpful action.

The Actual Appointment

From the appointment book, the secretary knows when to expect a person coming for an appointment. If an individual within the company is late for an appointment, it is entirely proper for the secretary to telephone that person's office to see if there has been some delay.

Often, more than one person is involved in an appointment or meeting. If possible, the secretary arranges the executive's office before the meeting and sees that there are enough chairs, pencils, note pads, and ashtrays. When the first conferee arrives, a problem is posed: Shall the secretary tell the executive of the arrival or wait until the entire group has assembled? There is no hard and fast rule. The decision depends on the visitor's status, the executive's activity at the time, and the executive's preference. If the first visitor is very important, the secretary may not only inform the employer of the arrival but may also notify the other conferees to come now. Otherwise, it is appropriate to wait until the whole group is assembled before informing the executive.

Before a meeting, the secretary should give the executive any correspondence or material that will be helpful during the conference. Also, the secretary should remain near the executive's office during the conference in the event that additional information is needed.

When the executive is going to another office for a meeting, the secretary anticipates the papers that will be required and places them in the executive's briefcase.

Scheduling Appointments by Letter

Appointments with persons out of the city are frequently made by letter. A request for an appointment should be answered promptly and completely. A typical letter granting an appointment follows:

```
Dear Mr. Graham

Mrs. Andrews will be pleased to interview you
on Friday, April 3, at 11 a.m.  If you can't
be here at that time, please let me know.  I
shall be glad to reschedule the appointment.

                    Sincerely yours
```

When refusing a request for an appointment, include a tactfully phrased explanation. Note the following example:

> Mrs. Andrews is preparing to leave the city on a speaking tour and has no free time until her return on May 15. She asked me to express her regrets that she cannot meet with you on May 8 as you requested.

Canceling Appointments

If an appointment must be canceled, the secretary usually writes the out-of-town visitors concerned and telephones the local visitors. In the latter case, the executive often asks the secretary to write a letter confirming the cancellation to prevent embarrassment in case the telephone message was not received. If possible, the secretary schedules a new appointment immediately to take the place of the canceled one. The following is a typical letter of cancellation:

> Because Mrs. Andrews has been called out of town unexpectedly, she is disappointed that she cannot keep her appointment with you at 3 p.m. on July 19. When she returns, I shall let you know so that we can arrange a new appointment at a mutually convenient time.

SUGGESTED READINGS

Blackburn, Norma Davis. *Secretaryship*. Pacific Palisades: Goodyear Publishing Co., 1974, pp. 317–324.

Dallas Richard J., and James M. Thompson. *Clerical and Secretarial Systems for the Office*. Englewood Cliffs: Prentice-Hall, 1975, pp. 43–71, 193–203.

Simpson, Marian G. *Tested Secretarial Techniques for Getting Things Done*. Englewood Cliffs: Prentice-Hall, 1973, pp. 181–184, 193–194.

QUESTIONS FOR DISCUSSION

1. Why is the secretary often considered a public relations representative of a company?

2. Describe the uses of a card file for frequent callers, the register of visitors, and the appointment book. Which of these three office tools would you regard as most important, and why? Do most

offices need all three of these kinds of records? Explain your answer fully.

3. Contrast the problems of the administrative secretary with those of the multifunctional secretary in handling visitors.

4. Suppose your employer makes appointments without telling you. If these appointments conflict with those that you have scheduled, what should you do?

5. In the following situations you are asked to introduce the two persons specified. Which person would you afford the greater courtesy by naming first?
    (a) Your employer's 14-year-old daughter and a secretary in the office.
    (b) A well-known politician and your employer, president of the company.
    (c) Your elderly mother and your employer, Carl Samson.
    (d) Ms. Alvarez, a business product sales representative, and your employer, Ralph Hazelton.
    (e) Rabbi Harold Silverman and your employer, Mr. Fishburg.
    (f) Professor James Ford and Alfred Bostick, Dean, College of Business, both visitors in your office.

6. As a new secretary, what steps would you take if you realized your predecessor scheduled the executive's appointments too closely?

7. In what ways do you think that reception work would differ in the offices of each of the following types of business executives?
    (a) A professional person, such as a doctor or lawyer
    (b) A bank executive
    (c) The president of a company which manufactures and sells heavy machinery
    (d) An elected government official

8. Insert the proper word in the blanks. Then refer to the Reference Guide to correct your answers.
    (a) We will be pleased with a response from _____ of the executives. (anyone or any one)
    (b) _____ can leave the meeting. (anyone or any one)
    (c) Will _____ please respond. (someone or some one)
    (d) Will _____ from the committee please reply. (someone or some one)

PROBLEMS

1. Analyze the following situations. How would you handle each of them? If the solution requires a conversation or note, indicate exactly what you would say. On a piece of paper, type your answer to each situation.
    (a) A visitor, while waiting for a scheduled appointment, makes the following statement: "I understand your employer was in New York last week."
    (b) Your employer's daughter has called the office three times within the last hour. Your employer is in a meeting with other officers of the company.

(c) Your employer has called an important meeting in the office for 10:30 a.m. The company's most important customer arrives fifteen minutes early.

(d) A visitor whose appointment you forgot to cancel arrives as scheduled. Your employer is working under pressure to complete an important contract.

(e) An unscheduled visitor comes into the office to talk with your employer.

(f) Two important visitors are in the office with your employer. It is time for your coffee break.

(g) A caller who failed to keep the last two appointments telephones for a third one.

2. As secretary to Sara Prince of Office Interiors, one of your responsibilities is to maintain her appointment book. The following appointments and activities have been scheduled for July 23. Type an appointment listing in attractive style for Mrs. Prince. Note any reminders at the bottom of the page.

(a) Mrs. Prince made a luncheon appointment at the Erie Hotel with L. W. Rasmussen for 12:30.

(b) A letter from S. T. White, of San Francisco, requested a 10 a.m. appointment which was granted by return mail.

(c) S. P. must appoint a committee by the 25th to handle an outing for the Advertisers' Club.

(d) You made a doctor's appointment for 11 a.m. for S. P.

(e) An office conference, which Mrs. Prince must attend, is scheduled for 3:15 p.m.

(f) T. K. Krause telephoned for an appointment and accepted your suggestion to come in for a 20-minute appointment at 2 p.m.

(g) Mr. White wrote that he is unable to keep the scheduled appointment for 10 a.m.

(h) Mr. Thornton, sales manager, requested that S. P. come to his office at 9 a.m. for a conference.

(i) Mrs. Prince asked you to verify a 2 p.m. appointment made with Barbara Hale. Inasmuch as you have scheduled another appointment at 2 p.m., you called Miss Hale and arranged for her to come at 10 a.m.

(j) Mrs. Prince asked you to cancel any afternoon appointments that are scheduled to take place before 2:30 p.m. You called Mr. Krause and arranged for him to come in at 10:30 a.m.

Part 1 CASE PROBLEMS

Case 1-1
CONFORMITY TO COMPANY POLICY

The executive vice-president of Cooper Corporation fired the office manager for incompetence, especially in enforcing company policy. A new manager, Norma Heinz, was hired and told that she must tighten up office discipline. One of her first acts was to send a directive stating that employees must adhere to company hours. They were warned against coming to work late or leaving early and that "any extension of time for lunch or for coffee breaks is to be stopped immediately, for it is just as dishonest to cheat the company of time as it is to cheat the company of money. Any infringement of rules regarding hours of employment will be considered grounds for dismissal."

Helen Loehman, secretary to the sales manager, usually did not lunch with the clerical staff. However, some of her acquaintances in this group invited her to lunch with them on a day when her employer was out of town. Helen accepted the invitation, but it was the wrong day! Her friends were livid with rage at the directive. They decided to resist by returning from this lunch twenty minutes late.

Should Helen avoid criticism by the group by staying with them, or should she go back to work on time? Should she reprimand the group for failure to conform to company policy? As a member of the management team, should she discuss the directive with Norma? with her employer? with the executive vice-president?

Case 1-2
COPING WITH ENVY

After graduation from Hill College as an office administration major, Mary Alton applied for a secretarial position in the company headquarters of Ashton Brothers in St. Louis. She was told that she would have two weeks of orientation in the training department in the mornings and would work in the stenographic pool in the afternoons. She could then expect to be assigned to a secretarial position, possibly in the personnel office. She was delighted with this arrangement, for she was primarily interested in personnel work and hoped to work into a position of interviewer of applicants for office positions.

Everything went well during the first week. The training department requirements were within her competency; and Mary felt that she was getting excellent exposure to company procedures, realizing that her college background, while helpful, was no substitute for actual experience. She thought that she had made friends with other trainees and hoped to form a close friendship with one girl whom she liked especially well.

One morning in the women's lounge, she recognized this colleague's voice saying, "How many letters did you get approved this morning?" Another trainee answered, "Four. I was furious because You-Know-Who had seven accepted. Doesn't she just make you sick? She thinks she is so wonderful just because she is a college graduate." The would-be friend replied, "Yes, she *is* mighty superior. Did you hear her say that she wants to be placed as secretary and maybe work into management later? My sister says that all the secretaries are promoted from inside the company and that seniority is what counts. I suppose she wants to be president of the company some day."

Although by now Mary realized that *she* was "You-Know-Who," she decided that revealing her presence at this point would embarrass the girls and antagonize them further. The second speaker continued, "I think that she plays up to the training director, don't you? I guess that's how people get ahead in business. That's what I've always heard."

When they had left, Mary wondered what action she should take. Should she speak to them about their unfair attitude? Should she discuss the situation with the training director? Should she resign? How can she achieve the relationship toward which she aimed?

**Case 1-3
WHO'S THE BOSS?**

Sarah Gelazny was an administrative secretary assigned to four principals in the executive offices of NJL Company. She reported to Amos Carullo, the manager of the administrative-support unit. One of Sarah's principals was Jo Peretta, who had been in her present position for 15 years and had had her own secretary until the introduction of a word processing center 10 months ago.

Sarah soon found that of all of her principals, Ms. Peretta was her favorite. She seemed more appreciative of the work Sarah did for her, brought her little gifts occasionally, and, as she said, "treated her like a lady." She realized that Ms. Peretta sought her out for doing work. Because Sarah sensed that Ms. Peretta disliked the new structure, she felt sorry for her and whenever possible gave her time for the extras that were formerly handled by Ms. Peretta's secretary. One morning Ms. Peretta asked Sarah to type a confidential memorandum, saying, "I don't want to dictate to that infernal telephone, and anyway just anybody could get hold of the information if it gets out of my office."

As Sarah was typing the memorandum on the only typewriter allowed in the unit, she was interrupted by Amos, who said, "Sarah, you must be working for Ms. Peretta again. You know that your responsibilities do not include taking dictation. You know, too, that your work is to be assigned by me and that you are responsible only to me. You've got to learn who is in charge around here."

What should Sarah do in regard to both Amos and Ms. Peretta? Is the new organization pattern dehumanizing the office? What argument can be made that might cause Ms. Peretta to accept the change? How can Sarah retain good relations with her favorite principal?

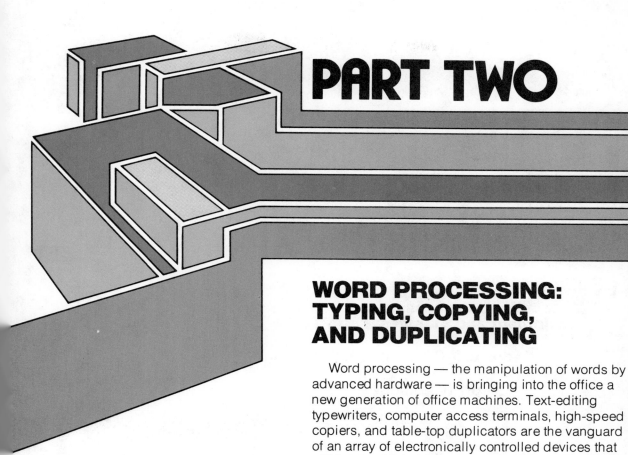

PART TWO

WORD PROCESSING: TYPING, COPYING, AND DUPLICATING

Word processing — the manipulation of words by advanced hardware — is bringing into the office a new generation of office machines. Text-editing typewriters, computer access terminals, high-speed copiers, and table-top duplicators are the vanguard of an array of electronically controlled devices that will bring a high degree of automation to the office. The secretary — the major word processor in the office — is at the center of the change. To cope with these technological advancements, the secretary must be amenable to change and knowledgeable about new equipment and procedures that are not only changing the way office work is done but are restructuring the organizational pattern of the office.

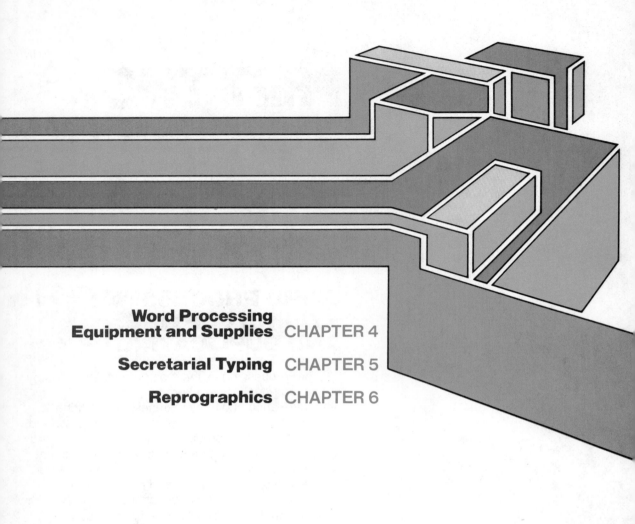

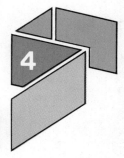

Word Processing Equipment and Supplies

Technological advancements in equipment are responsible for the reorganization (some say revolution) that is taking place in the office. The computer, because of its fantastic operational speed and unquestionable accuracy, has dramatically changed the way numbers are processed in the business world. Likewise, the automatic typewriter, with its editing capability and its capacity to produce error-free typing at high rates of speed, is changing the way words are processed in today's office. Word processing and data processing, however, are more than the application of highly sophisticated machines to office production activities. They are also a concept and a way of organizing the office so as to apply the benefits of technology and of worker specialization to achieve increased office productivity.

The use of automated equipment in the processing of words has reached a high level of acceptance. Large businesses are mechanizing many elements of their word processing. This trend is forecasted to grow at an annual rate of 21 percent. Furthermore, the steady decrease in the cost of word processing equipment is bringing these machines closer to the price range of the middle-sized and even of the small office. The predictions are that in the near future the multifunctional secretary in the small office will have access to some form of automatic editing-typing equipment.

WORD PROCESSING EQUIPMENT

Automatic typewriters are manufactured by several companies, each producing models with different capabilities. This equipment may be classified under three headings: repetitive typewriters, stand-alone text editors, and communicating typewriters.

Repetitive Typewriters

Automatic repetitive (non-editing) typewriters have been in use for many years in the production of form letters which require little or no text manipulation. They are driven by a perforated paper or

Mylar tape or roll that is prepared on a separate machine. This machine, called a perforator, has a standard typewriter keyboard. When the perforated tape or roll is inserted into the repetitive typewriter console, the machine is activated. The tape may be programmed to stop the typewriter at designated places to permit the operator to make manual keyboard insertions, such as inside addresses, amounts, numbers, dates, and so forth. Usually one operator will be assigned to supervise two or more repetitive typewriters. Businesses and letter shops use these machines to produce quantities of identical or nearly identical letters that give the appearance of having been personally typed.

These machines are called non-editing typewriters because it is difficult and impractical to make changes in the copy once the tape or roll has been perforated. For this reason, the automatic repetitive typewriter is rapidly being replaced by machines that do have text-editing features.

Stand-Alone Text Editors

Since stand-alone text editors operate independently and do not need to be connected to other machines, they are described as "stand-alone" or "all-in-one" machines. "Text editor" refers to the capability the machine provides for making type corrections and editorial changes during and after copy is keyboarded.

The stand-alone text editor is the most commonly used word processor for correspondence and short documents requiring limited revisions and for limited quantities of personalized form letters. It consists of a high-speed typewriter equipped with some form of magnetic-medium recording-playback attachment. As the operator types each character or space on the keyboard, a hard copy is produced by the typewriter while the recording unit records the character or space on the mag (magnetic) medium. When a typing mistake is made, the operator simply backspaces and strikes over the incorrect letter, word, or phrase. The process of backspacing and retyping automatically erases the error on the mag medium and replaces it with the corrected copy. This feature permits the operator to type at a rough-draft rate. Some units are equipped with lift-off or cover-up ribbons (see page 81) so the mistake can be corrected on the hard copy as well as on the mag medium. After the text has been recorded on the mag medium, additional copy can be inserted or unwanted copy can be deleted.

When the rough-draft typing has been completed and the copy has been edited, the operator inserts a letterhead or a regular sheet of paper and any desired carbons into the typewriter. Then the machine is changed to the playback mode by pressing a button on the

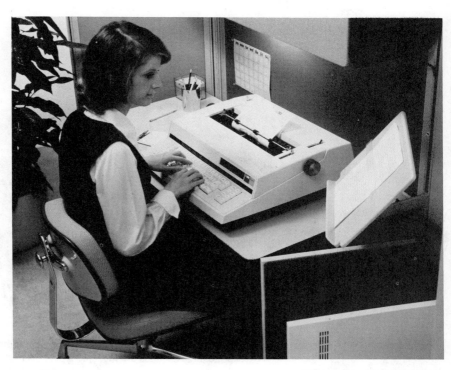

Photo courtesy of A. B. Dick Company

The A. B. Dick Magna I electronic typewriter uses a print wheel mechanism that permits playback from a mag card at the rate of 500 words per minute. It can type out a full page letter in 45 seconds. The operator can select either 10 or 12 pitch type, program the machine to justify the right margin, and provide for automatic underscoring. The Magna I has 95 percent fewer moving parts than a standard electric typewriter.

typewriter console. The machine retypes automatically, completely error free, at the rate of 150 to 500 words per minute. While retyping, the machine may be programmed to make a number of logical production decisions. These include automatically respacing and repositioning words and sentences, controlling the end-of-line hyphens, determining line and page endings, providing numeric column alignment, making high-speed forward and reverse underlining, and stopping for the manual keyboarding of varying information in a form letter.

The mag medium used depends upon the make and model of the machine. The most commonly used media are mag tape, card, and diskette (floppy disk). The tape may be packaged as a roll, cassette, or cartridge. Each medium offers advantages and disadvantages in its ease of handling, storage capacity, and access time. Access time refers to the length of time required to locate a specific point on the

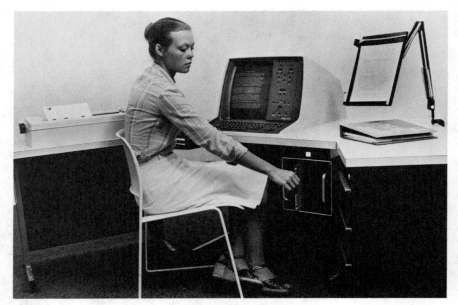

Vydec, Inc.

In the illustrated word processing system, copy is displayed on the cathode ray tube as the secretary types. Editorial changes are made by typing over errors and removing, moving, and inserting copy by use of a cursor. The edited copy is then transferred to a diskette which the secretary is shown inserting into the recorder unit. Finished copy is played back from the diskette by the printer (shown on the left) at the rate of 540 words per minute. While the copy is being printed out from the diskette, the secretary can be entering additional copy on the keyboard.

medium for editing or replay. The diskette provides the fastest access time, and for that reason it is becoming increasingly popular as a mag medium.

The stand-alone editor may be a single- or a dual-medium machine. The single-medium machine facilitates minor editing, such as corrections of typing errors, making short insertions or deletions, and other small changes in copy. Wholesale modifications of copy that may be required in preparing reports, news releases, and manuscripts, however, are difficult to accomplish. To facilitate such extensive editorial changes, some manufacturers produce dual-medium machines. These machines are equipped with two recording-playback units. This feature permits the operator to transfer "good" copy from the original keyboarded rough-draft medium onto the second mag tape, card, or disk. New material is keyboarded in and unwanted material is bypassed as the "good" copy is transferred to the second medium. This dual-medium process is known as transfer-updating.

Memory Capability Machines. Some machines have the added feature of being able to hold keyboarded text in "flux" (also called "float") before it is committed to the mag medium. This permits corrections, deletions, additions, and restructuring of copy to be completed before the copy goes on the medium. Thus, the text is recorded on the medium only once, not twice as is necessary on the dual-medium machine. For example, on the IBM Mag Card II, keyboarded copy is stored temporarily on an internally located, continuous, magnetic tape loop. After editing, the operator may type out directly from the memory loop, or commit the copy to a mag card for storage and later play-out. The transfer from the memory tape to the mag card takes place at the rate of 200 characters per second. Thus, the operator is able to type into memory, read copy in memory, revise copy in memory, play out copy in memory, and create final copy in memory — all with no handling of the mag card.

Display Editors. Some machines use a cathode ray tube (CRT) or gas plasma display (GASPS) to provide a partial- or full-page display of keyboarded copy before the copy is committed to the mag medium. As the operator keyboards, the copy appears on a video screen rather than on a sheet of paper. Typos are corrected by typing directly over the error. Words, lines, and paragraphs may be added at any point in the copy by moving the cursor (a movable pointer) to the desired point on the screen and then keyboarding changes. Also copy can be deleted or moved by using the cursor. Once the copy is fully edited, it can be recorded on the mag card for printout, storage, or both.

The operator is using a cursor (pointer) to remove data from a tabulation on the display screen of an IBM Information Display System. The cursor also may be used to move data from one line or place to another line or place in the copy.

International Business Machines Corporation

Some makes and models of display editors provide for the print-out process to be performed on a separate high-speed printer (see the next section for details). This frees the keyboard console and display screen for use in producing new input, while the copy committed to the mag medium is being played out on the printer.

The display editor is growing in popularity because it makes text editing easier. The operator can see at all times precisely what is being typed and edited and exactly how the copy will look on the typed page.

High-Speed Printer Units. The Selectric typewriter has been used by most manufacturers of text-editing machines for keyboarding in and correcting copy on the mag medium. Usually the same Selectric machine was also used to type out the edited or final copy. The Selectric with its "golf ball" printing element has a maximum operational speed of approximately 175 words per minute. To obtain a higher printout speed, some manufacturers now use separate printer units that can attain much higher rates of speed than the Selectric. One type of printer unit now in use is the "daisy" wheel typing mechanism. This mechanism operates at speeds up to 500 words per minute. It also has the advantage of being a less complicated mechanism since it has only six moving parts versus 500 for the Selectric. Multiple type fonts are available for the "daisy" mechanism. The newest and fastest of the printout methods is the "jet ink" process developed by IBM. This process can print out at computer output speeds.

This typing wheel developed by the Xerox Corporation is the key element in the high-speed capabilities of the company's new electronic typing system. The system operates at a speed of up to 350 words a minute.

Xerox Corporation

This word processing unit has three distinctive features: a full-page screen to show exactly what will be printed out, a dual-tape-drive printer that operates from two cassettes, and a "daisy wheel" printing mechanism that prints out at the rate of 450 words per minute.

Lexitron Corporation

Communicating Typewriters, Shared Logic Systems, and Time-Shared Services

Some models of stand-alone text editors are designed to enable them to communicate via telephone lines with compatible equipment in near and remote locations. Thus, the word processing equipment serves as a communication terminal. When this equipment is used to send processed text from one location to another, the material is first typed, edited, and then transmitted using the mag medium for playback transmission. Western Union permits direct transmission of letters by text editors to Mailgram outlets. Thus, hundreds of personalized form letters can be sent over TWX or Telex lines (see pages 293–294) to Mailgram outlets in different locations nationwide for delivery the next morning. This could be the beginning of a completely new electronic mail system.

Linking the text editor to the in-house computer (referred to as a shared logic system) or to a high-powered, multifunctional, large computer (through a time-shared service) takes communication one step further. When this is done, the text editor becomes primarily a computer input terminal and text manipulator station. The computer records the input from the text editor, performs the text manipulation as directed from the terminal, and furnishes the full output through the computer's high-speed printer. Several text editors may interact simultaneously with one computer. The advantage of the system is that the computer can perform operations that the stand-alone text editor is unable to do. Examples of such operations include mathematical calculations and high-speed printout of repetitive personalized letters against a stored name and address list. Furthermore, the linkup with the computer permits the text editor operator to tap a vast amount of computer-stored information and have it automatically incorporated as part of the printout without the operator keyboarding the copy. The computer-stored information would include such items as standard legal paragraphs for typing legal papers, plot descriptions for typing contracts and deeds, and medical case histories for updating cases.

Noise Factor

A disadvantage of the automatic typewriter and printout units is the noise generated when the machinery is operating. The higher the speed of operation, the higher the noise volume. Specially designed noise abatement covers and acoustically treated work stations tend only, at best, to moderate the noise level. Some people find it very uncomfortable to work in the area of these machines.

Noise-absorbing partitions can help eliminate the problems caused by the sound of some word processing equipment.

Westinghouse Electric Corporation

The secretary needs to be aware that the typewriter/printout unit is a disturbing element in the office. If you use this equipment, be considerate of others. Place the noise-suppressing cover over the machine when operating and run the unit at maximum speed only when such speed is needed.

TYPEWRITERS

The establishment of a word processing center does not take away the administrative secretary's typewriter. In a recent American Management Society study of businesses with word processing centers, over 84 percent of the respondents reported that all administrative secretaries in their companies have typewriters. The remaining 16 percent reported that their administrative secretaries have access to typewriters. For certain typing applications (especially the production of short documents which are rarely revised), the use of a high-quality electric typewriter may be preferable and, in fact, cheaper than the use of automatic typing equipment.

Obviously, the typewriter at the secretary's desk continues to be a major instrument for communication. Thus, all secretaries must be capable of producing quality output. Typing quality, however, is influenced not only by the skill and knowledge of the operator but also by the machine, the ribbon, the paper, and the other supplies used. The remainder of this chapter will be devoted to a discussion of the secretary's typewriter and supplies.

The secretary has three basic types of electric typewriters from which to select: standard type-bar, single-element, and proportional-spacing typewriters.

Standard Type-Bar Electric Typewriters

The standard type-bar electric typewriter is marketed by a number of manufacturers, but it is gradually being replaced in the office by the single-element machine (80 percent of office sales are reportedly for single-element machines). Although designed primarily for correspondence and general office work, the type-bar electric can be equipped for such special purposes as billing, preparing material for the bulletin board, typing name tags for conventions, typing statistical tables, and preparing oversized letters for TV and movie prompting materials.

Single-Element Typewriters

The single-element typewriter eliminates the type-bars and movable carriage, and replaces them with a spherical element of the size

The typist can change the pitch on the IBM Selectric II from 10 to 12 characters per inch merely by moving a lever. The error lift-off ribbon permits the operator to correct typos from the keyboard.

of a golf ball that moves on its own carrier from left to right across the paper. Alphabetic and special symbols are embossed on the surface of the sphere. Striking a key positions the element to type that letter or symbol. There is no problem with jamming the keys, and there is less vibration when the single-element typewriter is used.

The first single-element typewriter to receive wide acceptance was the IBM Selectric. Adler, Cimatron, Facit, Olympia, Royal, and Sperry Remington have single-element machines either on the market or reportedly ready to market soon.

A distinctive feature of the single-element machine, which the type-bar machine cannot match, is that it permits the use of a wide variety of type styles and special symbols. Over 30 interchangeable elements are available, each with a different type style or with different symbols. To change the type style, the operator removes the element and, in a few seconds, inserts one with the desired type style. Furthermore, some single-element machines enable the typist to switch from pica type (ten characters per inch) to elite type (twelve characters per inch) simply by releasing a lever and changing the element.

Proportional-Spacing Typewriters

The ordinary typewriter spaces uniformly for each letter of the alphabet. Printing, however, uses proportional spacing in which

Compare the difference in space consumption between standard typewriter spacing and proportional typewriter spacing, illustrated at the right. Shown also are the styles of expanded spacing that are possible with the proportional-spacing typewriter.

Proportional
Spacing
Type
Style
· iiiii
· ooooo
· wwwww
· mmmmm

E X P A N D E D with one standard space between letters

Standard
Spacing
Type
Style
· iiiii
· ooooo
· wwwww
· mmmmm

E X P A N D E D with a proportional space two units wide between letters

E X P A N D E D with a proportional space three units wide between letters

IBM Corporation

some letters are wider and use much more space than others. This is shown in the illustration above. The proportional-spacing typewriter can produce copy that closely resembles material which has been printed.

Typewriter Variables

Typewriters are available in a wide variety of type styles, line spacings, ribbon mechanisms, cylinder lengths, keyboards, and other special features.

Imperial
Precision built

Script
Your letters are

Small Gothic (Condensed)
clear-cut legibility and

Letter Gothic
jobs, especially

Courier 72
highly legible.

Various Executive Typefaces

Type Sizes and Styles. In addition to the standard type sizes (10 and 12 characters to an inch), type may also be obtained in sizes of 6, 8, 9, 11, 14, and 16 characters to an inch.[1] For specialized work, type sizes and styles are available in wide variety. For example, one typeface is designed for filling in insurance policies and another for billing work. There are also typefaces that optical scanning equipment can read.

Several type styles referred to as executive typefaces provide a distinctive and formal appearance. Styles also vary from a schoolbook face resembling printer's type to an informal script that gives correspondence a personal touch. Lightface, boldface, and italics are other choices. A face consisting of all capital letters is also available.

Line Spacing. Although most typewriters provide the standard six lines to the vertical inch, the line spacing can vary from one line per inch (video type) to eight or more, depending upon the type size and style and the purpose of the typed materials. These limits include type styles that use 3, 3.6, 4, 4.5, 5.8, 6, or 8 lines to the vertical inch.

---

[1]The number of characters per inch is frequently referred to as type "pitch," such as 10 typing pitch or 12 typing pitch.

Although single, double, and triple spacing are standard on most typewriters, machines with line-space settings of 1, 1½, 2, 2½, and 3 lines allow flexibility in adjusting to the line spacing on printed forms.

Special Keyboards. Special-purpose keyboards can be obtained. These keyboards include symbols and characters common to a type of work. For example, there are keyboards for each of the following uses: billing, legal, chemical, engineering, mathematical, library, and each of several foreign languages. When ordering a typewriter, you may specify the keyboard desired.

Special foreign language keyboards are available for special needs. The trilingual keyboard illustrated here is used for typing in English, Spanish, and French. The "dead keys" for the accents, the dieresis, and the circumflex do not advance the carriage (carrier) when struck.

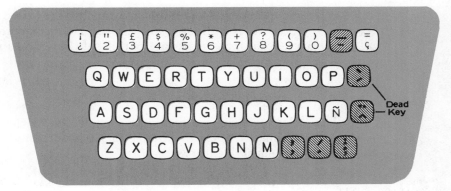

IBM Corporation

Special-Character Keys. The special characters and symbols available on the typewriter can be supplemented by the use of interchangeable type head devices. A wide selection of special characters and symbols for practically any language, profession, or business can be obtained.

Decimal Tabulator. A typewriter used extensively for typing financial and statistical reports can be equipped with decimal tabulation by adding a fifth row of keys. These keys (tabulator keys) permit the operator to move to the exact place in a column of figures in order to align numbers.

Half-Space Key. The half-space key or bar moves the carriage only one half of a space. It is used for central placement of extra-letter corrections; for example, a four-letter word can be typed exactly centered in the space used by a three-letter word. The half-space key is also used for expanded headings and for even distribution of space in justified lines.

Cylinder (Platen) Length. Cylinder lengths vary from 11 to 29 inches. The 13-inch cylinder is most commonly used. Some machines have interchangeable carriages whereby the standard carriage can be removed and an extra-long unit set in its place. This unit might be used for a special project such as a chart, graph, table, or special display.

Cylinder Resiliency. Rubber cylinders range from very soft to extra hard. A soft cylinder can be used for ordinary work involving four or five carbons. When more carbons are needed, the cylinder must be harder. Many typewriters have interchangeable cylinders that can be removed easily and rapidly.

Fabric- and Film-Ribbon Mechanisms. A typewriter can have a fabric- or a film-ribbon mechanism. However, a feature available on some models is that both types of ribbons are carried on the machine, and the typist can switch from one to the other simply by changing the keyboard ribbon control. This is an economy feature. Fabric ribbons are reusable, but film ribbon is designed to run through the machine only once. The fabric ribbon may be used for routine typing and internal communications. The film ribbon can then be reserved for letters, reports, and so forth.

Some typewriters now being marketed are equipped with mechanisms that simplify the ribbon-changing process. Smith-Corona (SCM) typewriters use a pistol-shaped ribbon cartridge which the operator merely plugs into the side of the typewriter. An automatic film threader is used in Hermes 705 typewriters. The threader automatically threads the new ribbon through the ribbon-carrying mechanism. In both systems the hands of the typist do not come in contact with the ribbon.

Self Correcting. So-called self-correcting features are available on many typewriters. These permit the typist to correct typos from the keyboard. The feature consists of a separate correction ribbon attached to the typewriter or provided in a separate ribbon cartridge. Two processes can be used: lift-off and cover-up. In the lift-off process, the correction tape contains a substance that removes the error chemically when a correctable film ribbon is used originally. In the cover-up process, the ribbon deposits a "white-out" material on top of the error. When an error is made, the typist shifts the ribbon control to the correction mode, backspaces, and strikes over the error. The operator again backspaces and types the correct copy. On SCM machines the operator ejects the ribbon cartridge, inserts the correction cartridge, covers over the error, removes the correction cartridge, reinserts the ribbon cartridge, corrects the error and then resumes typing.

Repeat Keys and Reverse Underscoring. Repeat keys (such as the letter "x," underscore, and period) and repeat functions (such as spacing, backspacing, advancing) that continue until the key or bar has been released are common features of most machines.

Special Attachments. A number of special attachments can adapt the machine for special uses. Palm tabulators, cardholders, label holders, multiple-form holders and aligners, an attachment for continuous forms, additional repeat controls, and automatic paper injectors are a few of them.

Double Margin Stops and Tab Systems. Typewriters equipped with double left-hand margin stops are available. This facilitates typing subheads and typing notes in the margin. Some machines (the Facit 1850, for example) have two tabulator systems, and the operator can switch from one to the other by merely flipping a lever. This permits the machine to be set for typing letters on one tabulator system and set for typing invoices or filling in a repeated form on the other system. The operator can go from one to the other without having to reset the tab stops.

Selection of Typewriter Ribbons

Typewriter ribbons are of three types: one-time film, multi-use film, and fabric. Each type has certain properties to recommend it for the specific kind or quality of work desired.

Thinness. The sharpness of typewritten work will depend upon the thinness of the ribbon used: the thinner the ribbon, the sharper the imprint; also, the thinner the ribbon, the more yardage on a spool. This means less-frequent ribbon changes. Ribbons range from cotton (the thickest) to nylon, to coated Mylar, to polyethylene film (the thinnest).

One-Use Film Ribbon. The one-use film ribbon is a continuous, narrow strip of Mylar or polyethylene film (called polyfilm) coated with an ink-releasing agent on one side. It advances at the rate of one strike per space on the ribbon. After the ribbon has passed from one spool to the other, it is discarded.

Multi-Use Film Ribbon. The ink-releasing agent on the multi-use ribbon is formulated to release ink gradually so that the same spot may be struck up to six (some say nine) times. The ink is so uniformly released that there is no variation in print density. The ribbon is designed to travel very slowly from spool to spool. It does not reverse but is discarded when it comes to the end.

In addition to its longer life, the multi-use film ribbon has the advantage of providing security of information. With the one-use ribbon, typed material can be read from the imprinted ribbon on the spent ribbon spool. This is not possible with either the multi-use or fabric ribbons.

Because they print very sharply, do not fill the letters, are the cleanest to handle, and erase easily, film-base ribbons are generally preferred by secretaries for high-quality work.

Fabric Ribbons. Of the fabric ribbons, nylon is the longest wearing and the thinnest. Silk ribbons are very expensive and for that reason are not commonly available. Since the fabric ribbon is more economical and is appropriate for use in preparing most in-house communications and documents, some electric typewriters provide a dual ribbon-carrying mechanism, one for a film ribbon and one for a fabric ribbon. The operator can shift from one ribbon to the other by a regulator on the keyboard. Fabric ribbons are available in several colors and in various concentrations of ink.

Special-Purpose Ribbons. Ribbons designed for special types of work include offset ribbon for typing offset masters, photostat ribbons for preparing copy for photostating, and opaque ribbons for photocopy work. Also available are correction ribbons with the top half inked and the bottom half white-chalked for speedy corrections and a number of combinations of bichrome (two-color) ribbons.

TYPEWRITER RIBBON CHART

FILM — **MYLAR OR** **POLYETHYLENE**	Highest quality ribbon available. Produces sharp, print-like image. Used for prestige correspondence. Excellent for preparing offset masters. Thinnest and strongest of all film ribbons. Breakfree. Lintfree. Both one-time use and multi-use film ribbons are available.
FABRIC — **SILK OR** **NYLON**	Finest quality fabric ribbon. Produces a clear, sharp image that compares well with the film ribbon. Lintfree. Extra long life. Obtainable in light, medium, and heavy inking.
FABRIC — **COTTON**	Available in a variety of grades. Less expensive and has shorter life than silk or nylon. Used primarily for routine correspondence, production typing, and filling in forms. Deposits lint on keys. Obtainable in light, medium, medium-heavy, and heavy inking.

STATIONERY AND SUPPLIES

Most supplies with which a secretary works are available in a wide range of quality. Many factors, particularly the use and quality, must be considered in the selection of supplies.

Bond Paper

Bond paper is so called because originally it was used for printing bonds, which had to have long-lasting qualities. It can be made from all-cotton fiber (sometimes called *rag*), from all-sulfite (a wood pulp), or from any proportion of the two. High-cotton-fiber bond suggests quality and prestige, and it ages without deterioration or chemical breakdown. It has a good, crisp crackle. It is hard to the pencil touch and is difficult to tear. High-sulfite bond is limper, softer to the pencil touch, and easier to tear.

There are excellent all-sulfite papers in crepelike, ripple, or pebble finishes that many companies use exclusively. Letterhead paper is usually made of 25 percent, or more, cotton-fiber bond. Forms for business records usually are made of all-sulfite or high-sulfite bond.

Watermarks. Hold a piece of letterhead paper up to the light. See the design or words? That is the *watermark*. It can be the name or trademark of the company using the paper or the brand name of the paper. Since only better bond paper is watermarked, the mark is a hallmark of quality.

There is a right side and a top edge to the plain watermarked sheets. Always have the watermark read across the sheet in the same direction as the typing. Put watermarked sheets in your stationery drawer in such a manner that they will be in the right position automatically when they are inserted into the typewriter.

Substance. The weight of paper is described by a substance number. The number is based on the weight of a ream consisting of 500 sheets of 17- by 22-inch paper. If the ream weighs 20 pounds, the paper is said to be of substance 20, or 20-pound weight. Two thousand sheets of 8½- by 11-inch paper can be cut from one ream. Paper is produced in a wide range of weights. Regular letterhead paper and envelopes are usually of substance 16, 20, or 24. Airmail stationery, now used primarily for overseas correspondence, is usually of substance 9 or 11.

Erasability. You can erase typing from some bond papers very easily. This feature is usually indicated in the brand name of the paper, such as *Ezerase* or *Corrasable*. Ribbon ink or carbon rests lightly on the surface of the paper at first, until it is gradually absorbed into the paper. Thus, you can quickly and neatly remove fresh typing with a pencil eraser. But you can also easily smear or smudge the surrounding typing.

The most difficult papers on which to make neat erasures and corrections are the inexpensive all-sulfite ones like those you probably used in your typing course. A neat erasure can be made without too much difficulty on a 16-pound high-cotton-fiber bond.

Second Sheets

The thin sheets used for file copies of letters and for multicopy typing are described as *onionskin, manifold*, or simply *second sheets*. They are of lightweight paper of substances 7 to 13, in smooth, glazed, or cockle (rippled) finish. A stack of these sheets can be difficult to control because they tend to slither and slide — mostly onto the floor. To avoid frustration, select a finish that has low "slipperiness." Sheets with cockle finish slip less than others and give the appearance of being of better quality, but they create more bulk in the files than do smooth-finish ones.

Copy sheets are used in many offices. They are second sheets with the word COPY printed on them and are used for copies of matter that should be so identified. When necessary, identify a plain sheet as a copy by typing the word COPY conspicuously in all capital letters, letterspaced, and centered from 7 to 9 line spaces from the top of the sheet.

Letterheads

Letterheads vary widely and depend upon individual taste and the nature of the company's business. Most large companies have a standard company letterhead designed for use by lower-level and middle-level management personnel. These letterheads are produced by offset and are standardized to include the company's name, address, telephone number (including area code), and the name and title of the individual. The letterhead sometimes contains information about the company's products or displays the company's trademark. All letterheads may be ordered with matching envelopes and blank sheets for the two-page letter.

Top executives usually have "prestige" letterheads that differ from the standard company letterhead in style, printing process, weight of paper, and cotton-fiber content. The cotton-fiber content usually ranges from 50 to 100 percent. Some executives use what is called "101 percent rag," meaning 100 percent cotton fiber of unusually fine quality.

LETTERHEADS AND ENVELOPES

Letterheads	Matching Envelopes
Standard Company Use:	
Business size 8½- by 11-inch	No. 10 (4⅛- by 9½-inch)
Usually of 16 or 20# bond, 25% cotton fiber (rag)	Same weight and fiber content as letterhead
Top-Executive Use:	
Standard and Monarch size (Monarch size: 7¼- by 10-inch)	No. 10 and No. 7 (3⅞- by 7½-inch)
Usually 24# bond, 100% cotton-fiber content	Same weight and fiber content as letterhead

Color

Usually white; however, tinted pastel shades are increasing in popularity.

Plain Sheets to Match Letterheads

Same weight, cotton-fiber content, and size as letterhead (*Never use a letterhead for the second or subsequent pages of a letter.*)

Letterheads and Envelopes for Overseas Correspondence

Letterheads: lightweight, 9 to 11# maximum
Envelopes: Bordered for AIRMAIL, weight to match letterheads

Interoffice Letterheads

Business size or half size (8½- by 5½-inch); usually of 16 or 18# sulphite

Interoffice Envelopes

Oversize, strong, perforated, reusable envelopes with many ruled lines for the names of successive addressees

Oversize Envelopes

Strong white or manila envelopes that allow letters and reports to be mailed unfolded; 9- by 12-inch, 10- by 13-inch; gummed flaps with or without metal clasps.

OTHER PAPER SUPPLIES

Carbon Copy Paper

Thin sheets, usually 8# by 13#, in various sizes, colors, and finishes; called second sheets, onionskin, or manifold paper.

Carbon Paper

For description and use, see pages 88–90.

Duplicator Paper

Business[1] and legal[2] sizes, white and colors, various substances; often called by the process the paper is made for, such as mimeograph paper, offset paper. *Duplicating* paper usually refers to paper designed for use with the direct-process duplicator.

Forms

Usually in pads to prevent waste. Multicopy forms may be continuous, accordion-folded, and perforated. After the "chain" is inserted in the typewriter to type the first set, the rest feed through automatically. Accordion-folded forms often have spot-carbon coating on the back of each copy exactly where the typing is to appear on the copy underneath. This eliminates handling interleaved carbon.

Labels, Return Address

Small slips of paper showing company's return address; are usually gummed on the back.

Legal Paper

Top-quality legal size bond; plain or with ruled margins

Manila Sheets

Thin sheets for typing rough drafts or carbons; legal size or business size

Plain Sheets

Paper 8½- by 11-inch, usually 13# to 16#, most often used for reports and for general typing; may or may not be of easy-to-erase bond.

Writing Pads

Ruled Paper: Legal size or business size, usually yellow
Scratch: Assorted sizes; usually sold by the pound

---

[1]*Business size:* 8½- by 11-inch
[2]*Legal size:* 8½- by 13- or 14-inch

The letterhead of a top executive usually shows only the company name, address (no phone number), and the executive's name and title. In addition, the executive may have a personal letterhead which is used mainly for outside work with foundations or charity organizations. Personal letterheads may show only the executive's name and address, or the name only. In general, as an individual's position becomes more elevated in the company, the letterhead becomes more simplified, presenting an appearance of dignity befitting the position. The trend in all letterheads is toward simplicity.

Carbon Paper

Conventional typewriter carbon paper is thin, dark-colored tissue, coated on one side with carbon. It is available in a great variety of sizes, colors, weights, finishes, and qualities. It can be obtained in special-purpose packs as well as in single sheets.

Topcoated Carbon Paper. Most carbon paper now is coated on the uncarboned, or top side, with a metallic, plastic, or varnish finish

---

GUIDE TO SELECTION OF CARBON PAPER FINISH AND WEIGHT

Finish

Soft	USE IF — typewriter has a soft cylinder. USE IF — copies are grayer than desired when using other finishes. DO NOT USE IF — typewriter has elite or smaller typeface.
Hard	USE IF — typewriter has a hard cylinder. USE IF — typewriter has elite or smaller typeface. USE IF — gray copy is acceptable.
Medium	USE — for all typing situations not covered above.

Weight
FOR MAKING ORIGINAL PLUS:

Light	9 or more copies
Medium	5 to 8 copies*
Medium Standard	2 to 7 copies
Standard	1 to 4 copies

*Consider weight of copy paper used and adjust weight of carbon.

that makes the sheet curlfree or curl resistant. The topcoating also reduces wrinkling which can "tree" or "vein" the copy. High-quality topcoated carbon paper is smudgefree, produces a neater copy, and permits more extensive use than does low-quality carbon.

Plastic-Base Copying Film. Although sometimes identified as carbon paper because of a similarity in appearance, plastic-base copying film is described more accurately as *copying film*. It employs ink, not carbon, and is made of film, not paper. A sheet of Mylar or polyethylene film is surfaced with a microscopically thin coating of tiny interconnecting cells, each containing liquid ink. Pressure from the typewriter key or element forces the cells to release the ink on the typing paper. After the key is struck, the ink flows back into the unused area, thus re-inking the sheet. The sheet may then be used repeatedly. Since the ink dries immediately, the copy is smudgefree. Copying film is curlfree, easily handled, and difficult to tear. It never trees. It comes in two weights, standard and light. It has a 50- to 60-time usage. Increasingly, plastic-base copying film is being used by secretaries for top-quality work.

Conventional Carbon Paper. Carbon paper comes in a number of grades, weights, and coatings. Better grades are treated with a wax, varnish, or metallic coating on the uncarboned side to reduce curling and treeing and to extend the wear. This coating also prevents the carbon from going through the tissue and offsetting to the back of the preceding sheet. Special coatings also make the carbon more smudge resistant, cleaner to handle, and capable of producing sharper copies.

Different finishes or coatings are available, ranging from *soft*, which writes like a soft black pencil, to *hard* which writes like a hard gray pencil. The finish to be used depends upon the typewriter (manual or electric), size of typeface, hardness of cylinder, number of copies to be made, and "blackness" of copy desired.

Weights of carbon paper range from light (4#) to heavy (10 to 20#). A lightweight carbon paper with a hard finish produces the sharpest impressions.

Special-Feature Carbon Paper. Carbon paper may be obtained with special features that contribute to efficiency and convenience. Such features include:

1. Extended Edges. An extended uncoated side or bottom edge is provided to permit handling of the carbon sheet without smudging the fingers. A cut corner may also be provided to allow the secretary to remove the carbon paper from the copy sheets more easily.

2. Micrometric Edge. A numbered guide is printed on a clean, extended right edge of the carbon sheet. The guide shows the unused

lines remaining on the page for ease in obtaining uniform top and bottom margins.

3. Carbon Sets. A carbon (copy) set is a preassembled sheet of one-time carbon paper affixed to a sheet of copy paper. Two or more sets combine to make a carbon pack. Carbon sets are convenient to use and no time is lost jog-aligning carbons, copy paper, and letterhead. A major disadvantage, however, is that one-time carbon retains a readable stenciled image of what was written. This produces a "talking wastebasket" — a serious security leak in offices where information must be kept confidential.

The accessibility and convenience of the copying machine has tended to obscure the fact that multiple copies can be made (especially on the automatic typewriter play-out) at less cost than securing the added copies via the copying machine.

OFFICE FORMS

American business *runs* on paper forms. In fact, every business function involves some type of business form at some point in its operation. A function is either initiated by a form, authorized by one, recorded on one, or summarized on one. Thus, everyone in a business organization is involved with "paper work," and the secretary is no exception. A significant portion of the secretary's time is spent in completing forms, copying information on forms, reading forms, interpreting forms, routing forms, filing forms, using forms for reference, and handling and transmitting forms. Furthermore, the secretary is not only a user of forms but may be a designer of them.

Types of Forms

Modern technology and business ingenuity have provided multiple-copy business forms in different configurations that encompass many timesaving features.

Unit-Set and Snap-Out Forms. Unit- or multiple-set forms are preassembled packets with interleaved one-time carbons. Each unit is self-contained, not part of a larger pad. The set is usually bound with a perforated stub at the top or side. This stub permits easy removal of the carbons. Because they are preassembled, unit-set forms are timesaving. They are also convenient since they allow one-motion removal of the carbons.

Carbonless Forms. Unit sets are also assembled using carbonless paper (NCR — No Carbon Required) that permits impressions from copy to copy without the use of carbon tissue. An image-forming dye is built into the paper. The dye is released under pressure and reacts with a mating chemical that is built into the paper or coated onto the back of the sheet above. A blue-purple image on the copy results from the pressure of typewriter keys or handwriting. Using NCR forms saves the time required to manipulate the carbon tissues. It also avoids the smearing and smudging of copies, hands, and clothing that are associated with carbon paper. Eliminating the carbon tissue decreases the bulk of the pack, allowing more copies with one writing.

Continuous Forms. With continuous forms, one set of forms is joined to another in a series of accordion-pleated folds. Continuous forms are used to process, at one time, a large quantity of a specific form such as invoices, statements, purchase orders, payroll checks, and the like. This saves the time required to feed forms into the typewriter repeatedly.

Spot-Carbon-Coated Forms. With spot-carbon-coated forms, no-smudge carbon is applied at designated spots on the back of each form in a pack from which reproduction is desired. Thus, typing on the original copy can reproduce on some copies and can leave blank areas on others. This permits the production of a number of different forms in one writing; for example, a packing slip, a shipping order, an address label, an inventory withdrawal slip, and an invoice — each form containing only the appropriate data.

Forms Control and Design

As a business expands, the number of forms that it needs seems to multiply at an astonishing rate. Consequently, most large business and government organizations have established systems for forms control. Such systems provide for a periodic review and the discontinuance of any forms that have become useless or obsolete. Provision is also made for the establishment of definite procedures for the preparation and approval of new forms.

The secretary may be expected to exercise a similar control over the forms originating in the executive's office. This would include a systematic review of all forms for their possible improvement, the elimination of unneeded forms, and the designing of new forms that will expedite the work of the office. In designing new forms, consider the following factors:

Necessity. Is a separate form really needed? Could it be combined with an existing form? In what ways will a new form save time?

Wording. Does the title clearly indicate the purpose of the form? Does it contain a code number for filing reference? Does the form contain all necessary information? Does it provide *only* necessary information? (Example: The company name is not needed on intra-company forms.) Does the form mechanize the writing of repetitive data? Are code numbers and check boxes used to eliminate unnecessary typing?

Disposition. Does each copy of the form clearly indicate its disposition? Is color coding or some other appropriate means used to facilitate distribution?

Arrangement. Is the form compatible with the equipment on which it is to be used? (Example: If it is to be filled in on a typewriter, do the type lines conform to typewriter vertical line spacing and require a minimum of tabulator stops?) Does the sequence in which the data are to be inserted on the form follow the sequence of the information on the data source? Is there the right amount of fill-in space? Will the arrangement of the form speed operations?

Retention. If the form is to be retained, how and where? Does the form size fit the filing system?

BEFORE DESIGNING A FORM — Answer these questions:

What is the purpose of the form?

How does it affect other procedures? other forms?

Can it be combined with another form?

Where does the information originate? Where does it go?

Where do parts go?

How is the form filed?

Will additional copies ever be needed?

What types of data will appear on the form? Words? Figures? Checkmark responses?

Can the form be sequenced to follow the order of the data source?

OBTAINING OFFICE SUPPLIES

The executive usually delegates to the secretary the responsibility of procuring the proper office supplies. Unless the executive has a special need or high-cost factors are involved, the secretary uses personal judgment in making selections. The procedures for obtaining office supplies differ for the secretary in a large office and the secretary in a small office. However, both must "know" supplies in order to choose those that best fill particular executive and secretarial needs.

The secretary in the small office is a direct buyer. In the large office, however, the secretary may request forms and supplies from a central stock or requisition them from the purchasing department. The secretary who has supervisory responsibilities may select and purchase for a department or company. In this case the sources of product information must be used to learn the comparative factors and to find dependable sources. Businesslike purchasing procedures, of course, must be followed.

Quality of Supplies

Some businesses feel it is important to use only the highest quality stationery, forms, and office supplies; others find medium quality adequate to their situation. Every office uses a pride factor and an economic factor to determine the level of quality it follows. You will not find this quality level precisely stated or written out for you. Nor is it a question you can tactfully ask. You can deduce it, though, by observation of the present supplies and cost records.

Local Sources of Supply

Local office-supply stores cannot carry all varieties of all brands of all office supplies. Each store carries one or two brands of an item (perhaps not your favorite) in the varieties most commonly sold, none of which may exactly fill your needs. Therefore, your selection is limited and often you cannot buy as discriminatingly as you would like.

Salespeople. Representatives of office-supply agencies may call on you with samples or price catalogs. They, too, limit themselves in brands and varieties, so choice is again restricted. The secretary orders over the telephone from the salesperson or from the sales office. Since you cannot possibly know everything about all supplies, it is helpful to have a dependable salesperson of whom you can ask advice. When you are in the market for an item, explain your exact needs. Salespeople are trained to help you make a wise selection.

Brand-Name Supplies. Sometimes you want a *specific variety of a specific brand*. If the variety is not sold locally, you can order it from

A SUGGESTION: To reinforce paper to go into a loose-leaf notebook, attach a strip of tape along the back edge of the paper where the holes will be. Punch holes through both tape and paper.

the manufacturer or ask your local office-supply store to order it for you.

Some pieces of equipment, you may decide, produce better results if you use the supplies that are sold by the manufacturer. These might include using A. B. Dick ink for the mimeograph, or Gestetner correction fluid for Gestetner stencils. If no local source is listed in the telephone book, you can order such supplies directly from the manufacturer.

Collecting Information

Collect specific information about each kind of office supply you use. Suppliers furnish helpful literature. Descriptive, informative folders are often furnished by a salesperson, or are given away at exhibits of office equipment and supplies. Collect and file such information by subject. It will help you to be a better buyer.

Choosing Supplies

Choose supplies that are in the quality range of your office. There is no economy in cheap supplies. Unknown brands may contain inferior materials or may be off-sized. Consequently, they may be more expensive in the long run than the better grades. *Usually you get just about what you pay for.* A carbon paper of good quality gives many more writings. Low-priced duplicating inks with poor-quality oils and pigments make fewer copies than high-grade inks. Also, the ingredients in cheap inks often separate when the machine stands idle, and the oil seeps through the mechanism.

There is no reason for shifting from one brand of supply to another as long as the one in use is satisfactory and fair in price. On the other hand, supplies are constantly being changed. A product may now be made of entirely different materials and hence may be greatly improved since the last time you examined or tested it.

When contemplating a change in brand, get samples of competing products and test them all under the same circumstances. Compare net prices and quality. Analyze the extra service or added efficiency claimed. If the price is higher, you should decide whether the difference is justified.

Overbuying

Some office supplies deteriorate when they are held in stock too long. For example, carbon paper dries and hardens, typewriter ribbons dry out, some paper becomes yellow, liquids evaporate, and erasers harden. New products that come out may be preferable to those you have stocked. It is better, then, to err on the side of under-buying than of overbuying. Repeat orders can always be placed shortly before supplies are needed.

You may tend to overbuy because of quantity prices. An item that costs 50 cents a unit in small quantities usually costs appreciably less when bought in larger quantities. Consequently, it may seem to be economical to order in large amounts. The monetary saving is not always the prime consideration, however.

Some suppliers of paper have arrangements whereby a year's supply may be purchased at one time. Thus you obtain the price advantage of a bulk purchase. The paper is delivered in specific lots at designated intervals through the year. Such a plan provides a price advantage without the problem of storing the paper before it is needed.

Requisitions and Invoices

In a large company, most of the supplies are kept in stock and are obtained by submitting a supply requisition. Items not carried in stock must be requested by submitting a purchase requisition to the purchasing department. This form should provide as detailed a description of the needed item as the secretary can provide.

A secretary or supervisor who has the authority to purchase supplies has added responsibilities. These include making a careful record of each item purchased or ordered, checking out the delivery of the items, and verifying the accuracy of the items and extensions of the invoice or bill that accompanies or follows delivery.

When an item is invoiced (included and charged on an invoice) but is omitted, substituted, or defective, the secretary annotates that fact on the invoice and requests an adjustment.

Storage of Supplies

If you wish to determine how neat and orderly a secretary really is, examine the supply storage cabinet. Certainly a storage cabinet that presents an array of boxes, packages, and articles in complete disorder is no recommendation for efficiency.

The well-arranged storage cabinet has several characteristics. Similar materials are placed together. Materials used most frequently are placed to the front at the most convenient level for reaching. Small items are placed at eye level; bulk supplies and reserve stock are placed on the lower shelves. Shelf depths should be adjustable to fit the items and thus to conserve space.

All packages are identified by oversize lettering made with a marking pen, or by a sample of the contents affixed to the front.

Unpadded stationery items are kept in flip-up, open-end boxes. (There are no carelessly torn-open, paper-wrapped packages.) Loose supplies such as paper clips, are kept separately in marked open boxes. A list of all supplies by shelves is often posted on the inside of the door.

SUGGESTED READINGS

Check the following periodicals for recent articles on automated typewriters, typewriters, text-editing typewriters, typewriter ribbons, and office supplies.

Administrative Management. The Systems Magazine for Administrative Executives, (Monthly). New York: Geyer-McAllister Publications, Inc.

The Office. (Monthly). Stamford, Conn.: Office Publications, Inc.

Word Processing. (Bimonthly). Franklin Lakes, N.J.: International Business Machines Corp.

QUESTIONS FOR DISCUSSION

1. The statement is made in the chapter that: "The automatic typewriter is changing the way words are processed in today's office." In what other ways is the automatic typewriter changing the office scene?

2. Surveys show that stenographers and typists average less than *15 words a minute* when transcribing from shorthand notes or dictation belts. An average of 38 percent of their typing work is retyping. Manufacturers of text-editing typewriters claim that using their equipment increases the typist's productivity over 100 percent. In your judgment, is this claim exaggerated? Explain your answer.

3. The establishment of a word processing center usually permits the pattern of one secretary to one executive to be changed to one administrative secretary to two or more executives. What arguments can you present to convince a reluctant executive that the new pattern will be advantageous?

4. Originally, IBM was the only company manufacturing the single-element typewriter. Several companies have now entered the market, and the single-element typewriter is rapidly replacing the type-bar typewriter in the office. What is your explanation as to why this change is taking place?

5. The proportional-spacing typewriter facilitates justifying (making even) the right margin. Some people feel that a letter with a justified right margin looks too symmetrical and gives the initial impression of being a form letter. Express your opinion. For what special type of work would you recommend the use of a proportional-spacing typewriter?

6. You note that a carbon copy produced by your assistant lacks sharpness and is gray in appearance. Upon further checking you

find that the carbon you examined was the fifth copy. What are some of the factors you would consider in your effort to improve the quality of the copies produced? What procedure would you recommend in your effort to help your assistant improve the quality of the carbon copies?

7. You are aware that your assistant has the habit of taking paper, stamps, and other office supplies for personal correspondence and use. (a) What is your responsibility and how would you handle the situation? (b) Would your responsibility be the same if the person guilty of this infraction were another secretary over whom you have no jurisdiction?

8. You are employed as secretary to the manager of the R & D (Research and Development) Division. This is a highly sensitive area and thus under strict control for security leaks. A major security leak was traced to your wastebasket and to the snap-out forms you have been using. (a) Explain how this could happen. (b) Is there any solution other than discontinuing the use of these forms?

9. Revise the following sentences by eliminating redundant terms. Then refer to the Reference Guide to correct your answers.
   (a) The new administration plans to continue on with the same policies.
   (b) You will receive our check sometime during the month of July.
   (c) You are so much both alike that you could pass as two-twin brothers.
   If the executive frequently dictated these redundant terms, would you point out their redundancy? If so, how?

PROBLEMS

1. A number of companies manufacture typewriters with text-editing capabilities. Each model has certain advantages as well as limitations. Assume that you have the responsibility of submitting specifications for a text-editing typewriter to be installed in a newly organized word processing center for your office. Initially the center will be a one-person operation. The correspondence of the four executives in the office will be processed by one correspondence secretary.
   (a) Set up the criteria you would use for selecting the text-editing typewriter. Gather data on two different makes and select the one you would recommend for purchase. Support your selection with reasons for the decision.
   (b) What qualifications would you suggest for the correspondence secretary who will staff the newly formed word processing center?

2. Many companies and most government agencies require that detailed specifications accompany a request for the purchase of equipment. In the case of a typewriter, for example, the specifications would cover such items as: carriage length, cylinder hardness, line spacing, keyboard, special keys, typeface, and any special features and attachments.

Assume that you are to be secretary to one of the following departments in your college: mathematics, chemistry, library, engineering. (Select the one with which you are most familiar.) You are asked to submit an order, with accompanying specifications, for a typewriter. Compile the specifications.

3. A secretary needs to be informed about office supplies. Select one of the following items and make yourself a semi-authority on it — cost, qualities available, and advantages and disadvantages of each brand or type.
   (a) Carbon paper, copying film, and carbonless paper
   (b) Paper for letterheads and second sheets
   (c) Type cleaners
   (d) Typing error correction products
   (e) Typewriter ribbons

   Prepare a written report on the item. Also be prepared to explain and demonstrate to the class the factors to be considered in item selection and how to use the item.

4. You are employed as the secretary to an architect whose office is located in a small community. Because of the location, all office supplies are ordered via letter from the Mid-West Office Supply, 23 East Town Street, St. Louis, Missouri 63130. Prepare a letter ordering the following supplies. Design the letterhead (create the name and location), and use the current date.

   2,000 letterheads. These are for general use and should be of good quality, but not the very highest grade.
   2,000 envelopes to match the letterheads ordered above.
   1 dozen typewriter ribbons for your IBM Executive typewriter.
   2 boxes of carbon paper.

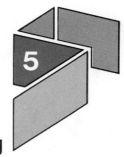

Secretarial Typing

The ability to produce an error-free, correctly styled, and visually attractive letter is an assumed qualification for secretarial work. This is true whether you see yourself as a correspondence secretary operating in a word processing center, an administrative secretary on the support staff of a group of executives, or a multifunctional secretary working on a one-to-one basis with your employer. The quantity of typing varies among the secretarial roles, but the quality cannot vary. Thus, typing competency is not only essential for employment but may be an important factor in determining the satisfaction you get from your work. It can also determine whether you make the "eligible for promotion" list.

Secretarial typing competency is more than speed with accuracy. It is attitude and pride in workmanship; it is economy in the use of time and supplies; it is knowing how to organize for work; it is the search for ways to increase output and efficiency; it is the ability to guide those whom you supervise in their typing assignments.

These qualities come only with time and experience, provided one seeks them out. This chapter is a good place to start. It presents some of the know-how that practicing secretaries and supervisors use in their continual efforts to produce high-quality work as efficiently as possible. Practice any techniques which are new to you and add them to the skills you bring to your work.

Although the techniques described in this chapter are primarily for use with the standard electric typewriter, they have equal application (with the exception of the error-correction procedures) for use with the text-editing typewriter.

YOU AND YOUR TYPEWRITER

You will quickly become at ease with "your" typewriter if you will, first, *explore and learn its capabilities*; and, second, *give it the care it requires*. Remember the adage: The poor workman quarrels with his tools.

Instruction Booklets

Every typewriter has a helpful, reassuring booklet of instructions on its use. The booklet accompanies the machine on delivery but often disappears before the machine does. If your predecessor has not left the instruction booklet for you, request one from the manufacturer. It will save you time and give you confident know-how. There is nothing worse than fighting a strange, militant typewriter that has hidden resources.

Learn the capacities of your typewriter. It may have features of which you are not aware, such as aids to accurate realignment of typing, scales to determine center positions, fractional spacing devices, and tabulation time-savers. The special features of your typewriter are illustrated and explained in the instruction booklet.

Learning to operate the text-editing typewriter, however, usually takes more than following the instruction booklet. A training period may be required. Unless there are other provisions for assistance, contact the manufacturer of the machine and ask for a training session. This training may take place either in the manufacturer's office or under the supervision of a manufacturer's representative in your office. This is a service which manufacturers are eager to provide. The length of the training period required is frequently a factor in determining which machine to purchase.

TIME-SAVERS. Keep a tab stop permanently set for the center of your stationery. You can then center by the backspace method.
When typing columns of figures with varying digits, set two tab stops for each column: one for 100,000 and one for 100.
Keep a desk copy of frequently typed reports. Indicate on each the tab-stop numbers and centering positions for all significant lines.

Typewriter Care

Even though a typewriter is sturdy and almost self-sufficient, it does require a modicum of attention from you. Read the machine-care section of your instruction booklet. Follow it faithfully or follow the recommendations on page 102. No amount of skill is going to produce good copy if the typewriter is not kept in excellent working condition.

CARBON COPIES

The typing techniques concerning carbon copies which are given here may seem commonplace; but the procedures are those used by master typists. They will allow you to produce quality typing and to save motion, time, and material.

Carbon Sheets — Copying Film

You will find the following practices in using carbon-film sheets to be paper-savers and time-savers:

1. Keep your desk supply of carbon-film sheets flat with the carbon-ink side down to prevent curling. Keep the sheets away from heat or dampness, and inside a folder or box.

2. Reverse carbon-film sheets end-for-end each time you use them, because the carbon quickly wears off on spots where the dateline and other letter-part positions fall.

3. Discard a sheet at once if it becomes wrinkled or treed. It will never be usable.

4. Do not discard a sheet just because it looks worn or because the shine is off the carbon side. Instead check the clarity of the last copy typed. Discard the carbon-film sheet only when the copy is faint.

5. Use extended bottom-edge carbon paper with cutoff corners for the most efficient removal and reuse. If the carbon-film sheets are square-cornered, lay them carbon-ink side down and cut off one-inch triangles from the top-left and bottom-right corners. This space provides room to hold the set of typed sheets and to remove the set of carbons intact in one quick, clean pull. See the illustration on page 104.

6. Use carbon-film sheets with cutoff corners as a visual check for the proper insertion of carbons into the carbon pack. With the carbon pack in typing position, the cutoff should be visible in the top-left corner. If the cutoff shows at the right, you have inserted the carbon-ink side up (which happens occasionally to the most careful of secretaries).

The number of carbon copies being prepared in the office has been decreasing because of the accessibility of the copying machine. Making corrections on multiple carbons is a slow, costly, and boring process. Consequently, secretaries have a love affair with the copying machine, and in all too many cases the copier is overused to produce a very costly substitute for the carbon copy. The high cost of operating and maintaining the copying machine and the cost of time lost going to and from the copier results in a very high per-copy cost. Consequently, management consultants are emphasizing that the carbon copy is the least expensive method of producing the necessary copies of outgoing correspondence and short reports. The savings are especially evident when the automatic text-editing typewriter is used. The major additional cost factor in the carbon copy method is the time required to make corrections. Therefore, when playing back edited (error-free) copy on the automatic typewriter, it is far less expensive to produce the additional copies needed via carbon copies than to reproduce the copies via the copying machine. The former method is also less work for the secretary.

TIME-SAVER. To bring an address book up to date, type the new address on a gummed label and paste the label over the old address.

FOR A LONGER LASTING, MORE RESPONSIVE TYPEWRITER

1. **Prevent dust from accumulating.** Dust and eraser grit cripple and prematurely age a typewriter.
   - NEVER erase over the type basket. Move the carriage to one side, then erase. (On the single-element electric, move the typing element to the right or left.)
   - ALWAYS cover the typewriter when you leave for the day. Clean the cover with a damp cloth occasionally.

2. **Dust the typewriter daily.**
   - Use a long-handled brush to dust the hard-to-reach parts.
   - Brush toward you, away from the mechanism.
   - Dust under the machine.

3. **Clean the keys frequently** — *before* the keys fill up. Clean the keys gently; avoid pushing them out of alignment. Do not use a pin; use one of these methods:
   - Roll a type-cleaning sheet (paper with a chemically treated fiber surface that picks up dirt from typeface) into typing position. Set the ribbon for stencil and the pressure control to maximum; then strike each key several times. (This is the cleanest method.)
   - Use a plastic type-cleaner. Repeatedly press the plastic firmly against the type until the keys are clean. Knead and fold the plastic as you work.
   - With a stiff, dry, short-bristled brush, use a tapping — not a gouging — motion. Clean the brush as you work by rubbing it on paper.
   - Use a fluid or spray cleaner — sparingly, as excess fluid can carry dirt particles into the mechanism. Some spray cleaners contain dirt-repellent silicone.
   - For the single-element electric, remove the element; clean with soap, water, and the special brush that comes with the machine.

4. **Protect the cylinder (platen).** Keep the cylinder clean. Ink and dust on the platen cause it to become shiny and to lose its grip.
   - Clean the cylinder with a soft cloth.
   - If the cylinder is removable, lift it out and dust the trough.
   - NEVER lift a typewriter by the cylinder knobs.

5. **Lubricate sparingly.** Too much oil is harmful. Lubricate only the carriage rail — and oil that only lightly. Keep oil away from rubber parts.

6. **Arrange for periodic servicing.** Check the service guarantee. Arrange with a local agency to check and service your typewriter periodically. Investigate the economy of a service contract.

Obviously, then, the copying machine is not a replacement for the carbon copy in all situations. There is a continuing need for the secretary to be skilled in handling carbon paper and in producing carbon copies. The secretary also needs to be able to make the decision when to use carbons and when to use the copier.

Making Up a Carbon Pack

Two methods of making up and inserting a carbon pack are the *desk method* and the *machine method*.

Desk Method. Using the following procedure, assemble the carbon pack and insert it directly into the typewriter.

1. Place a sheet of paper on the desk; on top of that sheet, place a sheet of carbon-film paper, *glossy side down*. Add one set (a second sheet and a carbon) for each extra copy desired. Place a letterhead or a plain sheet of heavier paper on top of the pack for the original copy.

2. Turn the pack around so the glossy sides of the carbon sheets face you.

3. To keep the sheets straight when feeding, use a *leader* — place the pack in the fold of an envelope or in the fold of a narrow folded piece of paper.

4. Straighten the pack by tapping the sheets on the desk.

5. Insert the leadered pack with a quick turn of the cylinder; roll it up, and remove the leader.

Machine Method. Using the following procedure, build the carbon pack right in the machine.

1. Arrange the required number and kinds of sheets for insertion into the typewriter.

2. Insert the sheets normally, turning the cylinder until they are gripped slightly by the feed rolls; then bring all but the last sheet forward over the cylinder.

3. Place the carbon-film sheets between the sheets of paper, with the carbonized surface (glossy side) toward you. Flip each sheet back as you add each carbon.

4. Roll the pack into typing position.

5. When the typing is completed, roll the pack nearly to the bottom of the sheets. Operate the paper-release lever and remove the copy sheets by pulling them out with one hand. The paper fingers will automatically hold the carbon-film sheets in the machine. Remove these sheets with the other hand.

Correct positioning of the cutoffs at the upper left and lower right corners of the carbon paper permits easy removal of the carbons from the pack.

The master typist folds an envelope or a slip of paper over a carbon pack as a leader for inserting the pack into the typewriter rapidly and evenly.

Adjusting the Impression Regulator

Most electric typewriters are equipped with an impression regulator to adjust the pressure with which the key strikes the paper. This regulator should be adjusted to the thickness of the carbon pack. In general, it should be set at the lowest pressure that will produce the required number of copies. Pressure set too high will emboss the letterhead or front sheet, and the carbon impressions will be heavy and lack sharpness.

Avoiding Bottom-Line Slippage

To control bottom-line slippage, roll the pack back to about mid-page. From the back, drop a sheet of paper between the original and the first carbon. Roll the pack forward. As you type near the bottom, the extra sheet will hold the pack securely in place. Steady the top sheet with one forefinger if necessary.

CARBON-COPY TROUBLESHOOTING

Curling   Curling usually may be traced to changes in temperature or humidity. A curlfree carbon paper or copying film is available. Carbon paper should be stored flat in a box.

Cutting   If the typeface is cutting through the carbon paper, check the sharpness of the typeface, the hardness of the roller, and the quality and weight of carbon paper being used. Also check the impression regulator on the electric. Use copying film, as it is tougher.

Illegible Copies   Illegible copies usually indicate that the carbon paper or copying film is too worn or too lightweight for the task, or that the impression regulator is set too low.

Roller Marks   Roller marks on the carbon copies usually indicate that the paper bail is set too tight. Move the rollers off the edge of the paper, using just the paper bail.

Slippage   If the carbons tend to slip in the machine, the carbon paper may have too slick a back (frequently the case with plastic-base copying film) and/or the second sheets may be too slick (too glossy). Use colored second sheets.

Smudges   Smudges on carbon copies usually indicate either careless handling of the carbon pack or the use of carbon paper with too soft a finish.

Uneven Copies   Dark and light copy on the same page usually indicates that the carbon paper or copying film is too worn or that the typewriter has a faulty impression control.

Wrinkling or Treeing   Wrinkling can be caused by failure to smooth the carbon when assembling and feeding the carbon pack into the machine, or feeding the pack into the machine unevenly, or using a pack too heavy to feed evenly into the impression rollers. When starting a carbon pack into the machine, use the paper release or a leader; or use carbon paper coated to prevent treeing.

CORRECTIONS

Typewriter corrections that defy detection are evidence of the master typist. They are an absolute necessity for quality typing. In fact, if any correction is evident in an otherwise excellent piece of typing, the typescript drops from quality level. The three techniques for making nonevident corrections are: careful removal of the error, perfect positioning, and matched typing.

Careful Erasing

A neat erasure results from the skillful use of erasing tools. The erasing tools are easily obtained, but erasing skill must be acquired by patience and practice.

Erasers. Erasers are available in a variety of textures — art gum, soft, semi-abrasive, abrasive, glass fiber, steel blades — and in many forms and shapes — pencil, wheel, stick. An electric eraser is also available.

For corrections, use two kinds of erasers — a soft eraser to remove surface ink and carbon that might smear, and a more abrasive eraser to remove embedded ink. Try various brands and shapes of erasers until you find those that you can use most effectively. Clean the erasers by rubbing them on an emery board.

Erasing Shields. Erasing shields are basic to neat and complete erasures. A fastidious typist develops the habit of having shields quickly available and of using them automatically whenever erasures are to be made. Erasing shields are of two kinds for two different purposes.

An Erasing-Area Shield. Unless you use an electric eraser, use a flat metal or plastic shield with letter-height open spaces to confine the erasing. Such a shield can be used on papers in or out of the typewriter. It permits erasing to the extreme edge of an error yet protects adjacent letters. Lightened or fuzzy letters around an otherwise imperceptible correction are telltale and therefore unacceptable in high-quality typing. The light areas call attention to the erasures.

A Thick, Pressure-Proof Shield. A shield of metal or card stock is used to protect the carbon copies under the page being erased. The shield is placed immediately under the area to be erased and on *top* of the carbon. A curved metal shield that hugs the cylinder gives best protection and is easiest to find among papers on the desk.

NEVER use a set of paper slips behind the carbons as erasing shields. They are time-wasters!

Cover-Ups. To fade out an erasure, rub a whitening agent into the paper before typing the correction. A piece of chalk, a direct-process master correction pencil, an aspirin, or a commercial cover-up stick can be used.

In place of erasing, a white correction fluid marketed under such trade names as White-Out and Liquid Paper may be painted over the error.[1] If this is done carefully and if the fluid matches the paper in whiteness, acceptable results can be achieved.

Another cover-up method is to put a chalk-coated strip of paper, coated side down, over the error and retype the *error* so that some of the chalk transfers and covers it. Then go back and type the correction. A special type of cover-up paper is available for use on carbon copies and with carbon ribbons.

White, self-adhesive correction tape is available in one-line, two-line, and three-line widths. The required length of tape is torn off and placed over the error. Corrections are then typed on top of the tape. Since the correction is obvious, restrict this method to use on copy where appearance may not be important, such as interoffice communications, dummy layouts, and material that is to be duplicated by photographic or offset process.

Lift-Offs. Some models of typewriters are equipped with dual ribbons. A correctable film ribbon (one that deposits a slow-penetrating ink) is used for the typing. Errors are removed by typing over the error with the second ribbon. This ribbon contains a chemical that interacts with the ink and literally fades or lifts off the error.

Perfect Positioning for Corrections

Tips to the Typist

Proofread before copy is removed from the typewriter. This makes corrections easier.

It is easy to reposition the carriage for an immediate correction, unless the error occurs at the very bottom of the page. In that case, do not try to correct it at once, for the sheets almost always slip out of line during erasing and repositioning. Instead, finish typing the page, remove the pack from the typewriter, and then make the correction on each copy separately.

To save time in repositioning, learn the exact relationship of your typing line to your aligning scale. To acquire speed in realigning, watch intently as you type a line of words and notice the exact distance *at the typing point* between the bottom of the typed line and the aligning scale. It is the barest fraction of an inch, but memorizing it visually helps you to realign more quickly and accurately.

You can find the approximate letter position more quickly by keeping the paper guide set at one spot and using it squarely each time you insert sheets into the typewriter. On a reinserted sheet move the carriage to the first letter of the correction. The typing point will be in almost exact position. A quick position test can be made by shifting the ribbon mode to stencil and striking the correct letter.

---

[1]Send a sample of your office stationery to the manufacturer of the correction fluid, and the manufacturer will prepare fluid that matches your letterhead.

ERASING ON RIBBON AND CARBON COPIES

Some brief but important steps in making a complete and neat erasure are:

1. Erase the original first, then the carbon copies. This could save time in case the original cannot be erased satisfactorily.

2. Hold the margin release down and move the carriage to one side to avoid erasing over the type basket. On the single-element electric, move typing element to right or left.

3. Roll the copy forward so that the erasure can be made completely. If the error is near the bottom of the page, roll the paper backward to prevent the carbon pack from slipping.

4. If a punctuation mark is to be erased from a ribbon copy, rub the back of the sheet with your thumbnail. The mark, embedded in the paper, erases more completely if pressed outward.

5. Clean the surfaces of the erasers on an emery board.

6. For each copy to be erased, insert a *pressure-proof* shield under the error and on top of the carbon sheet underneath.

7. For each copy to be erased, position the *erasing-area* shield over the error so as to protect adjacent typing. It may take several positionings to complete the erasure.

8. First use plastic type cleaner, if available, to remove as much of the surface ink or carbon as possible. Press the plastic cleaner down on the error and lift off. Plastic cleaner is also good for removing a smudge from carbon copies. If plastic type cleaner is not available, use a soft eraser.

9. Then use an abrasive eraser with light strokes in *one* direction only. Use a "digging-lift" stroke in place of a "scrubbing" action.

10. If necessary, smooth down roughened areas with the thumbnail. Also rub the back of the sheet on the spot where the correction was made to smooth the surface and press out any depressions.

11. If ink dye remains in the paper and will not erase, try to fade it out by rubbing with a whitening agent.

Tests for Exact Positioning

To position a reinserted page for a correction, use the paper-release lever to move the page sideways and the variable line spacer to roll it up or down. Test the exactness of position by the following procedure:

1. Cover the page of typing with a transparent second sheet. Roll the two sheets into the typewriter to the correction line.

2. Test for exactness of position by typing over a letter near the erased error. Adjust the sheets and type over another letter until the copy is in exact position.

3. Roll the sheets forward a couple of inches. Fold back the thin covering sheet, crease it all the way across, and tear it off. Roll the page into line position, set the carriage at typing point, and type the correction.

   This method wastes paper but assures exact positioning of corrections and is the cleanest way of correcting reinserted carbon copies. Proofreading the copy before it is removed from the typewriter, however, usually makes repositioning unnecessary.

Fractional-Space Positioning for Corrections

Corrections that require one letter more or one letter fewer than the error are inconspicuous if they are centered carefully in the space available.

Squeezing and Spreading. To insert a word containing one letter more than the error, proceed as follows after the erasure has been made:

1. Move the carriage pointer to the space preceding the position of the first letter in the word.

2. Depress and hold down the half-space bar or key, type the first letter of the correction, and release the bar or key.

3. Repeat the process for each letter of the correction.

This procedure will leave one-half space before and after the corrected word.

To insert a word containing one letter fewer than the error:

1. Move the carriage pointer to the space occupied (before erasure) by the first letter of the error.

2. Depress and hold down the half-space bar or key, strike the first letter of the correction, and release the bar or key.

3. Repeat the process for each letter of the correction.

This procedure will leave one and one-half spaces before and after the corrected word.

On machines not equipped with a half-space bar or key, depress the carriage-release lever, move and firmly hold the carriage manually in the half-space position, and strike the key.

Tips to the Typist

Write DRAFT across the top of every rough draft to avoid mistaking it for final copy.

```
askyou
ask you
stilllife
still-life
```

Inserting a Space or Hyphen. To insert a space or a hyphen between two words, erase the two letters which must be separated. Retype the first letter one-half space to the left of its original position. Retype the second letter by fractional forward spacing. Center a hyphen in the space available by using the backspace key. In this manner, you can make a near-perfect correction.

```
alignment
insertion
letter
```

Inserting a Thin Letter in a Word. In some cases you can insert an *l*, an *i*, or a *t* within a typed word by fractional spacing. Experiment with your typewriter to determine in what instances you can use this method of correcting. Keep in mind that the correction will be discernible.

```
Time must be of the
essence/permit inter-
linear corrections.

Time must be of the
            to
essence/permit inter-
```

Making an Insertion Between Lines. When time is of the essence, you may have to make a neat insertion between lines. Use the underline and diagonal keys to indicate the point of insertion. Find the midpoint between the lines for the line of typing. In single-spaced copy type the correction to the right of the diagonal; in double-spaced copy center it over the upper end of the diagonal.

Correcting a Topbound Typescript

Typed pages that are bound at the top can be corrected without unbinding. Feed a blank sheet of paper into the machine in the usual way until the paper shows about a two-inch top margin. Insert the bottom of the sheet to be corrected between the top edge of the blank paper and the cylinder. Roll the cylinder back to the line to be corrected, position the carriage for the correction, and type it.

Matched Typing

To make a correction in carbon on a reinserted page of carbon-copy typing, staple together several slips of paper and a small piece of carbon paper, carbon side out. A good size is 1 by 2½ inches. After positioning the carriage for the first letter of the correction, put this pad behind the ribbon with the carbon side against the paper. Type in the correction lightly.

Certain strikeovers are likely to be almost imperceptible in the specific type style on your typewriter. Experiment in order to learn those that match and blend into the typing. They may include: *d* over *c; h* over *n; o* over *c; E* over *F;* and, *; :* or *?* over the period.

TYPING SPECIALTIES

Typing specialties that expedite, control, and add visual appeal — in short, those that earn praise — are described here.

Special Characters

A number of special characters can be constructed on the typewriter. The chart shows a partial list.

Brackets	[ ]	*Left Bracket.* Type underline, backspace, strike diagonal, turn platen back one line space, and type underline.
		Right Bracket. Type underline, diagonal, backspace, turn platen back one line space, and type underline.
Degree sign	12°	Turn platen back slightly; strike lowercase o.
Ditto mark	"	Turn platen forward slightly; strike the quotation mark.
Division sign	÷	Type hyphen, backspace, and strike the colon.
Equal sign	=	Type hyphen, backspace, turn platen forward a bit, strike the hyphen.
Paragraph mark	¶	Type capital P, backspace, and strike 1.
Plus sign	+	Type hyphen, backspace, and strike diagonal.
Pound sterling	£	Type f, backspace, strike t.

Multipage Typing

A typing job of many pages, and often of many copies, must be organized in advance and controlled while in process so that it can be carried through to a consistent completion. To accomplish this task, formulate the regulations and set them down on paper. This is important for your own reference and for the guidance of those who assist you.

The Job Guide Sheet. Set up a job guide sheet covering every point of form and typing instruction that may be needed for a long typing job. Try to answer in advance every question that will likely be raised. Include the items below and all others that might apply to the specific job.

1. Kind and size of paper to be used

2. Weight and finish of carbon paper to be used

3. Number of copies to be typed

4. Kind and type style of typewriter to be used

5. Page layout:
   Paper-guide scale number
   Left margin — number on typewriter scale
   Right margin — number on typewriter scale
   Top margin — number on line-guide scale (see discussion)
   Bottom margin — number on line-guide scale (see discussion)
   Single- or double-spaced typing
   Paragraph indention — number of spaces
   Tabulation indention — number of spaces
   Tabulation identification — I, A, (1), (a), etc.
   Tabulation spacing — single-spaced or double-spaced
   Headings — examples and placement
   Subheadings — examples and placement

6. Handling of typed pages awaiting assembly (see discussion)

7. Instructions for proofreading (see discussion)

8. Instructions for collating (see discussion)

9. Instructions for binding

10. Distribution of copies

11. Disposal of original-draft pages

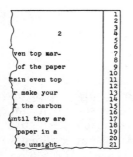

Top and Bottom Margin Guide. Use any of several devices to maintain even top and bottom margins.

Turn the paper into the machine until the top edge just catches under the paper bail. Usually, this will provide a uniform one-inch top margin.

Use carbon paper with the line scale printed on the extended white edge (micro-metric carbon paper).

Make your own numbered line guide by typing line numbers down the extreme right edge of a thin second sheet. Number the lines in ascending order, 1–33, starting at the top to midpage. Starting at midpage, number the lines in descending order, 33–1, to the bottom of the page. Insert this guide at the back of the carbon pack or behind the top sheet with the line numbers showing along the right edge.

Glue a small strip of paper (envelope flap or mailing label) to the side edge of one of the carbon sheets. The strip should protrude from the edge and be approximately two inches from the bottom of the page.

Treatment of Typed Pages. Keep the original and the carbon copies of each page together in the same order in which they were typed until they are ready to be proofread and corrected. Never leave the carbon paper in a set of typed pages, because pressure exerted on the pack will cause unsightly offset marks on each copy. Do not fasten each set of pages together with a paper clip because the clip leaves crimp marks.

Place the bottom copy on top of the set to protect the choice ribbon copy. Since the bottom copy is used for proofreading and marking corrections, it will be ready without further handling of the set of pages. If the bottom set of carbon copies is used for proofreading, any illegibility will be revealed. In this way, an illegible copy will not be passed on inadvertently and proven to be useless. If you are in doubt about any figures especially, consider the set unusable.

Collation. After the sets of pages have been proofread and corrected, they are ready to be collated. Lay out the copies of the last page across the desk so that hand motions in collating are clockwise. Then lay on the copies of the next-to-last page, original on original, first carbon on first carbon, and so on. When all pages are laid out, check and correct each set for proper page sequence before binding.

For a discussion of automatic collating machines, see page 133. If such a machine is available, use it even for small jobs.

Display Typing

Very often a secretary must design a typing layout for reproduction. It may be a notice, an invitation, a program, or the like. The finished piece requires that the units of copy, the decorations, and the white space be in pleasing arrangement and that the headings stand out. To achieve this effect, the secretary types blocks of copy and headings in various line lengths, spacings, and styles, and then experiments with their placement on a dummy layout.

Sample Blocks of Copy. To find the most pleasing size and shape for the blocks of copy, type one paragraph or short unit of copy in different spacings and line lengths. Experiment with this set of samples on the dummy layout. You can vary sizes and shapes by:

1. Single-line spacing or double-line spacing

2. Different line lengths: full width, three-fourths width, etc.

3. Copy typed in columnar arrangement

4. Copy or columns typed with even right margins

Sample Headings. To make sample headings with which to experiment, take the longest heading and type it in different styles by:

Tips to the Typist

When typing a number of duplicate letters, use the letter just typed as the copy for the next letter. Errors will be caught and proofreading time will be saved.

1. Using uppercase and/or lowercase letters

2. Using different spacings between letters; using conventional spacing between letters

3. Varying the styles of underlining: continuous or broken underlining; single or double underlines; use of the underline, the hyphen, or the period key

4. Framing the headings: use of periods, small o's, or asterisks; use of underlines with diagonals; use of hyphens and apostrophes

Justified Typing with Even Right Margins. Even-right-margin or *justified* typing is illustrated below. To justify copy on a typewriter with standard spacing:

1. Set the margins for the exact column width desired. Type each line of copy in double-spaced form the full column width, filling in each unused space at the end with a diagonal.

2. Pencil in a check mark to indicate where you will insert each extra space within the line. Try not to use an extra space after the first word in a line or to isolate a short word with an extra space on each side.

3. Retype the copy, inserting the extra spaces.

```
First, set up the column width;///
then type each line of copy the///
full width of the column filling//
in each unused space at the end///
with a diagonal.
```

```
First, set  up the  column  width;
then type  each line  of copy  the
full width  of the column  filling
in each  unused space  at the  end
with a diagonal.
```

Decorative Typing. Distinctively typed words, designs, and patterns may be used occasionally as "eye-catchers" on the cover page of a notice, the announcement of a meeting, or an item to be posted on the office bulletin board. The illustrations at the left are a few that can be done by straight typing and spacing. Such decorative typing is rarely used in business work. It requires more time than the results justify, and frequently it is out of place on a formal business document.

High-Speed Envelope and Card Routines

You will occasionally have small typing production jobs to do or to supervise. These jobs might include addressing a hundred or so envelopes or making up a 5- by 3-inch card index. Master the following high-speed routines used in specialized typing assignments.

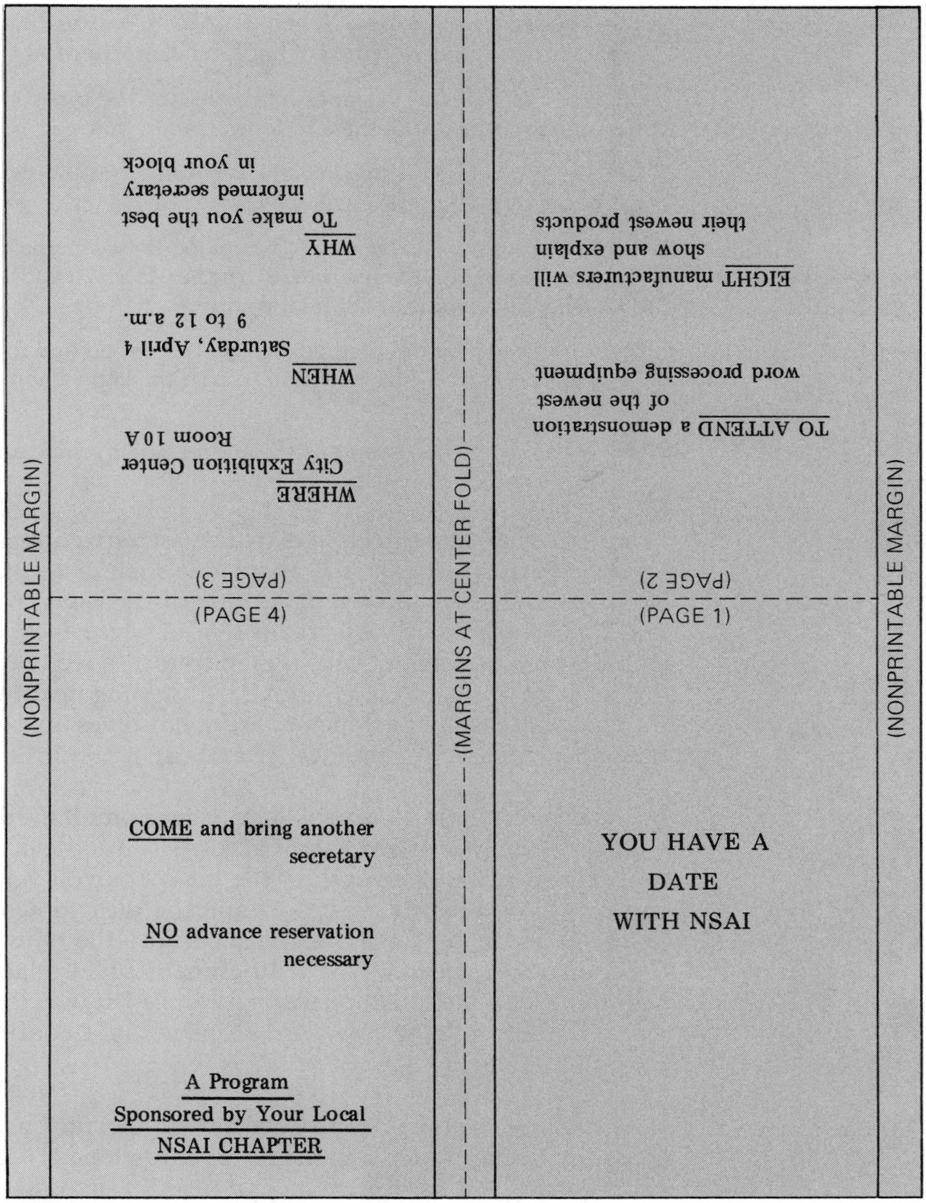

WHY
To make you the best
informed secretary
in your block

WHEN
Saturday, April 4
9 to 12 a.m.

WHERE
City Exhibition Center
Room 10A

EIGHT manufacturers will
show and explain
their newest products

TO ATTEND a demonstration
of the newest
word processing equipment

(PAGE 3)   (PAGE 4)   (PAGE 2)   (PAGE 1)

(NONPRINTABLE MARGIN)   (MARGINS AT CENTER FOLD)   (NONPRINTABLE MARGIN)

COME and bring another
secretary

NO advance reservation
necessary

A Program
Sponsored by Your Local
NSAI CHAPTER

YOU HAVE A

DATE

WITH NSAI

This is a dummy for an invitation to be duplicated on one side of 8½- by 11-inch paper, and then to be French-folded: first across, and then up and down with the final fold at the left. The broken lines show the fold lines; the solid margin lines show the limit of the typing area. The copy in the upper half of the layout must be upside down to be in reading position when the sheet is folded. The typing is done on separate small sheets and pasted on the full-page dummy layout. The stencil or master is then prepared by thermal, facsimile, or photo imaging.

Back-Feeding Envelopes. When you have a number of envelopes to address, you can save time by back-feeding them.

1. Stack the plain envelopes at the left of the typewriter, flap down and bottom edge of the envelopes toward you.

2. Feed the first envelope into the typewriter until only about one half of the bottom of the envelope is free.

3. Place the top of the second envelope between the platen and the bottom of the first envelope. Turn the platen to address position for the first envelope and type the address.

4. With the left hand pick up the next envelope and drop it into feed position as you turn the platen with the right hand to remove the addressed envelope.

5. With the left hand remove the addressed envelope and stack it face down at the left of your machine.

Front-Feeding Envelopes. To front-feed envelopes, roll a just-addressed envelope *back* until about one inch of the top edge is free. Have a stack of envelopes at the side of the typewriter flap up with the flap edge toward you. Drop one of these face up between the cylinder and the top edge of the addressed envelope. Roll the cylinder back until the blank envelope is in typing position, then address it. The addressed envelopes stack themselves in sequence against the paper table on the typewriter and can be removed occasionally.

Front-Feeding Small Cards. To front-feed small cards, make a pleat a half-inch or less deep straight across the middle of a sheet of paper to form a pocket. The depth of the pleat controls how far down you can type on the cards. Paste or tape the pleat down at the sides to hold it in place. Roll the pleated sheet into the typewriter and align the fold of the pleat with the alignment scale. Place the first card into the pleat and position it for typing. Draw a line on the paper along the left edge of the card to serve as a continuing guide for consistent margins.

Government Postal Cards. Government postal cards can be purchased in sheets 4 cards wide and 10 cards long. These sheets can be cut into strips and addressed.

Fill-Ins

The term *fill-in* refers to the insertion of some typed material in a space provided on duplicated or printed letters, bulletins, or business papers. The fill-in may be an address, a salutation, a word, a phrase, or some figures. On interoffice correspondence no attempt is made to disguise fill-ins, but on outgoing mail fill-ins should match the body of the message. The procedure is as follows:

1. Use a ribbon that matches the body of the message in darkness of color.

2. Set the carriage in position to insert the fill-in. Test the position by typing over a period or comma in the text.

3. When the position has been determined, set the paper guide and margins for use in succeeding fill-ins.

4. Salutations and addresses are placed more accurately if the lines are typed from bottom to top, unless a pinpoint placement dot from the master shows where to begin the first line.

Tips to the Typist

When typing on ruled lines, adjust the typing line so the bases of y, g, and p just touch the ruled line.

SUGGESTED READINGS

Anderson, Ruth I., *et al. The Administrative Secretary*. New York: Gregg Division, McGraw Hill Book Co., 1976, pp. 78–121.

Kelly Services Staff. *The Kelly Girl Second Career Guide*. Boston: Little, Brown and Co., 1973, pp. 5–52.

Lojko, Grace R. *Typewriting Techniques for the Technical Secretary*. Englewood Cliffs: Prentice-Hall, 1972.

QUESTIONS FOR DISCUSSION

1. Your textbook states: "Erase the original first, then the carbon copies." What reason is given for this sequence? Can you think of any situation where it would be advisable to erase the carbons before erasing the original?

2. Assume that you have typed six copies of a five-page, double-spaced report on the subject of filing equipment. Before assembling the copies, you discover that you have not capitalized the "f" in *Visu-Flex*, which occurs on each page. What would you do?

3. Suppose the executive has penned in three corrections on the first page of a letter and two on the second — changes made before signing the letter. The time is 4:45 p.m., and the executive plans to leave promptly at 5 p.m. What would you do?

4. If you were assigned the responsibility for typing a long report, what questions would you ask and what items would you decide for yourself before you started the typing?

5. Faulty handling of carbon copies can mar superior workmanship. What precautions should you observe in handling carbon copies?

6. Office costs used to be 20 to 30 percent of the total cost in a company; now they have grown to 40 to 50 percent of all costs. The cost of producing a business letter is 40 percent more than it was ten years ago. List the things a secretary can do to help curb the spiraling cost of a business letter.

7. Fill in the correct word in each of the following sentences. Then refer to the Reference Guide to check your answers.
   (a) The driver feels (bad, badly) about involving you in the accident yesterday.
   (b) The administration is (apt, likely) to change the regulation before it is placed in (affect, effect).
   (c) We will have a full (complement, compliment) of staff by April.
   (d) (Less, fewer) members have paid dues this year.
   (e) They have (already, all ready) prepared their wills.
   (f) The prize is to be divided equally (among, between) the three winners.

PROBLEMS

1. A study shows that it takes the following time to correct one typing error:

	Time Per Error
Original only	8 sec.
Original and 1 carbon	17 sec.
Original and 2 carbons	25 sec.
Original and 3 carbons	35 sec.

   For the following questions assume an average of five correctable errors per letter. Also assume that the total cost for the secretary is $9.00 per hour (this includes hourly rate + fringe benefits + employer payroll taxes + supplies + equipment costs + overhead):
   (a) What is the cost per letter for correcting errors on the original only? original and 1 carbon? original and 2 carbons? original and 3 carbons?
   (b) If an original and 2 carbons are made of each letter, how much would be saved per letter if the policy were to correct errors on originals only and not on the carbons? Do you see any disadvantage to this?
   (c) One business has a policy that no errors are to be erased. Errors are corrected by striking over or "x-ing" out and retyping. Can you present any good arguments against this policy?

2. A secretary must know how to change a typewriter ribbon. As a supervisor, the secretary may need to demonstrate the ribbon-changing process for both film and fabric ribbons to those who are supervised. Practice changing the ribbon on your typewriter and also on typewriters of other makes until you feel qualified to demonstrate the technique.

3. Making undetectable corrections on typewritten material takes practice. This problem will test your skill. Make up a carbon pack of one original and two carbon copies. Type at the top of the page an exact copy of the following sentences:
   (a) How many are coming.
   (b) We received your letter of Augst 3 today.
   (c) There have been fourty replies so far.
   (d) There were both old, and new ones.

   While the pack is still in the typewriter, make any necessary corrections on each of the three copies.

   Continue by typing these sentences exactly as given.
   (e) Our expenses forthe year have greatly increased.
   (f) The following is a summary ofour sales.

(g) Only 154 shares of stock were ssued.

Remove the sheets from the typewriter and slip out the carbons. Then make the necessary corrections on the original and the two carbons.

4. In this chapter you were given detailed instructions on how to perform certain operations on the typewriter. Knowing how these operations are performed, however, is no assurance that you are competent to perform them. Practice each of the following operations until you are prepared to demonstrate it before the class.
   (a) Back-feeding or front-feeding of envelopes
   (b) Front-feeding of small cards
   (c) Assembling and inserting a carbon pack into the typewriter
   (d) Making a correction on multiple carbons in the typewriter

5. There are many techniques that experienced typists use to increase their efficiency, to improve the appearance of the typed copy, or to perform difficult typing assignments. Prepare a short report entitled "A Typewriting Shortcut." In this report describe a typewriting technique or application that you have learned or read and which is not described in this chapter.

6. The office in which you are employed makes an original and three copies of each outgoing letter. The original goes to the addressee, and a copy is provided for the central files, your chronological file, and the executive's file. You are appointed chairperson of a four-member committee assigned to investigate the comparative costs of producing the three copies by the use of carbon paper or by the use of the copy machine. Your committee has finished its investigation and prepared a report.

Type the title page for the report. You wish to make the title page attractive so that it will invite reader attention. Use the names of three of your class members as the other members of your committee.

7. Style manuals differ in their instructions for certain phases of manuscript typewriting. Compare the instructions given in three reference manuals for secretaries, stenographers, and/or typists for:

Method of numbering pages
Typing of headings and subheadings
Margins

Prepare a report indicating points of agreement and points of disagreement in the three manuals.

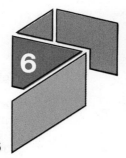

Reprographics

Reprographics is the multiple reproduction of recorded images. Applied to the office, it involves the use of two primary kinds of equipment: copiers and duplicators. *Copiers* use an exposing device and an image-forming process to create copies exactly and directly from existing originals. *Duplicators*, however, make copies from a stencil or master that must be prepared before the duplicated copies can be produced. Technological advancements in copying and duplicating processes have so greatly improved the speed and ease of machine operation, the quality of reproduction, and the per-copy cost factor that some type of copier or duplicator is found in almost every office. In fact, the copying machine has become so commonplace and useful as to cause one enthusiastic secretary to comment: "The copier is the greatest boon to the business world since the telephone and electric lights."

Reprographic equipment is a high-growth market area. The 1975 Xerox Corporation's Annual Report projects that by 1980 there will be more than 11 million reprographic installations and approximately 9.5 trillion copies made annually — a 35 percent increase in five years. The fact that the office equipment industry is geared to meet this demand is evidenced by the multiple types of equipment currently on the market and by the rapidly increasing number of equipment manufacturers. The large investments being made by equipment manufacturers in research and development are certain to result in continued technological improvements in reprographic equipment. This, in turn, will have an impact upon the office.

Technological improvements in the ease and convenience of operating duplicating machines are resulting in more in-office duplicating. The multifunctional and correspondence secretaries need to know how to prepare originals for duplication and, in many cases, need to operate the duplicator as well. The administrative secretary may not prepare the duplicator originals or run off the copies but must know the comparative costs of copying versus duplicating, the quality of work that can be obtained from each copying and duplicating process, and the factors to be considered in determining which process to use. In many cases, the secretary is given carte blanche in determining what reprographic equipment to purchase and how to control its use.

COPYING MACHINES

Copying machines, sometimes called *copiers* and other times called *photocopiers*, are used to quickly reproduce an exact copy of an original. Originals may include typewritten pages, pages from magazines and books, financial reports, photographs, artwork, graphic illustrations, and other legally reproducible materials.

The following are some of the ways in which a copier can save time and increase the efficiency of secretaries.

Copies of an incoming letter can be made and forwarded to several staff members. There is no delay in typing copies or routing the letter from one person to another.

If a sentence or short note can be used to answer a letter, the note can be handwritten or typed on the incoming letter and returned to the sender. The file copy of the original with the answer can be made on the copying machine.

A request for a letter can be accommodated by furnishing a duplicate made on the copying machine. The original letter stays in the files.

Identical extra copies of accounting papers, statements, statistical reports, tables and statistics from magazines, newspaper clippings, drawings, and illustrations can be made quickly for distribution.

Copies of incoming orders and other data can be made immediately and routed to the various branches and departments for their use.

File copies can be made of personal income tax reports and of the receipts and other documents that are used to support tax deductions.

Mailing lists can be updated easily. An original mailing list of up to 42 addresses may be typed once. The copier reproduces each address on special label stock for each mailing. The adhesive-backed labels are peeled off and affixed to the mailing piece. Changes in the mailing list can be made directly on the original.

Duplicator stencils, offset masters, spirit masters, and overhead transparencies can be produced immediately from copy without time-consuming retyping.

Copying Processes

The three basic copier reproduction processes are: (1) electrostatic, (2) thermographic, and (3) diazo.

Electrostatic Process. Most copying machines in general offices use the electrostatic process. There are two types: plain-paper copiers (PPCs), and coated-paper copiers (CPCs).

The IBM Copier II, which is illustrated here, uses the electrostatic copying process.

The plain-paper copier (PPC), such as the Xerox, uses a dry process. A camera throws an image of the document to be copied onto a positively charged selenium-coated drum. When a sheet of plain (untreated) negatively charged paper is passed over the drum, the image adheres to the paper and is permanently affixed by means of heat. A Federal Trade Commission ruling in 1975 required that patents held by the Xerox Corporation on the plain-paper copier process be made available to other manufacturers. Thus, the number of PPCs on the market has greatly increased and costs have been reduced. The plain-paper copier is the fastest growing segment of the copying industry.

The coated-paper copier (CPC), such as the Apeco and the Bell and Howell, is an electrostatic process that reproduces the image directly on coated (chemically treated or sensitized) paper. A toner is used to develop the image on the exposed paper. Some users believe the coated-paper copier produces copies with a higher image contrast than those obtained from the plain-paper copier.

Thermographic Process. The thermographic process is also known as the infrared or heat-transfer process. Material to be copied is placed beneath a heat-sensitive copy sheet. Infrared light is beamed through the sensitized copy onto the original as both sheets feed through the machine. The heat turns the sensitized paper dark in the same places as the original, thus producing the image.

Although copiers using the thermographic process were the first to be marketed for office use, today the process is used primarily to prepare stencils, direct-process masters, and overhead-projector transparencies, and to laminate documents.

Diazo Process. The diazo process is an improved form of blue-printing that has been adapted for use in special kinds of offices, such as engineering, drafting, and advertising. It produces black-on-white copies, but colored paper may be used for special color effects. Special paper that is chemically coated must be used for the reproductions. The original is placed over the coated sheet, and both are exposed to ultraviolet light. Only originals with copy on one side of the sheet can be reproduced by this method.

Color Reproduction

Both Xerox and 3M produce reliable color copiers. Their use, however, is usually limited because of the high per-copy cost to those situations where color is essential. An attachment to the Xerox color copier makes color prints or enlarges color slides on paper. This permits color prints to be made and distributed to an audience after a management presentation using a visual display.

Special Features of Convenience Copiers

The convenience-type electrostatic copier is designed to be simple to operate, to produce a limited number of copies of an original, and to be relatively maintenance free. The number of automated features on these machines is limited.

Automatic Repeat. Many copiers provide a control mechanism that programs the copier to reproduce two or more copies of an original before stopping or proceeding to the next original. The operator sets the multiple-copy control indicating the number of copies of each original to be prepared. As each original feeds into the copier, the desired number of copies are reproduced automatically.

Automatic Document Feeding. On most copiers the operator must feed one original at a time into the machine. When using a machine equipped for automatic feeding, the operator places all the originals to be copied on the feed table and sets the multiple-copy control for the number of copies of each original to be made. The copier automatically feeds each original into the machine as the copies of the preceding original have been completed.

For a description of other automatic features available on high-volume copiers, see pages 130–131.

Speed of Operation

A criterion for judging the relative merits of convenience copiers is the speed of operation. This usually involves two speed figures: the time required for first-copy delivery (it takes longer to produce the first copy than subsequent copies of the same original) and the total number of copies of one original that can be produced per minute. For example, Copier A may have a first-copy delivery of 8 seconds and 20 copies per minute, while Copier B may have a first-copy delivery of 12 seconds and 30 copies per minute. Speed becomes a factor only when the primary use of the copier has been determined. For example, to reproduce one copy of a 40-page report on Copier B will take 2½ minutes longer than on Copier A; yet Copier B will produce 30 copies of the same report in the same time it takes Copier A to produce 20 copies.

COPY QUALITY

If any of the following questions is answered "No," you are not obtaining the highest quality of reproduction from your copying machine.

1. Is the background as white as the original?

2. Is the copy free of specks or spots not on the original?

3. Is the copy free of streaks crossing the paper?

4. Is the intensity of the ink-like impression similar to the original copy?

5. Does the copier compensate for less-than-perfect originals, such as those with dark backgrounds or light images?

6. Does the copier reproduce a pencil original into readable copy?

7. Does the copier adjust to the reproduction of originals on colored paper?

8. Do both black-and-white and colored photographs reproduce with strong images?

9. Can the copier produce good copies from special materials, such as: labels, card stock, transparencies, vellum, and specialty papers?

Copying Abuses

The ease with which copies can be made on the copier has led to the tendency to overcopy — that is, to make more copies than needed. The urge seems to be almost irresistible. In addition to overcopying, there is also the cost of unauthorized personal copying — recipes, materials for clubs and other organizations, bowling scores, and personal letters. While each copy costs only a few pennies, the cumulative total adds many dollars to the monthly copying bill.

To meet the problems of overcopying and unnecessary and unauthorized copying, some companies centralize all copiers in the word processing center and assign full-time operators to the machines. A copy-requisition form must be submitted with each original. Assigning an operator has been known to decrease the volume of unnecessary copying by as much as 20 percent.

Other companies, however, contend that centralizing the copiers increases the time it takes to get copies, takes the secretary away from the work station, and delays work. The cost of the time lost far exceeds the savings gained by eliminating unauthorized copying and overcopying.

Copiers can be equipped with devices, such as an *autotron*, that will insure that only authorized personnel use the machine. Such devices also make it possible to charge copying costs to departments or individuals on a use basis. One such unit consists of six counters installed in the copier. These counters are not able to be reset by the user. The operator must have a key to activate the machine. When any one of the six keys is inserted in the lock, the machine operates and the counter corresponding to that key records the number of copies made.

Another factor in the mounting cost of copying is the temptation, because of convenience, to use the copier rather than the duplicator to produce multiple copies of a page. Multiple copies of a page or several pages can usually be produced on a duplicator at a third or less of the cost of reproducing them on a copier.

The secretary needs to exercise good judgment and restraint to avoid overcommunicating. Don't make two copies when one copy properly routed will do. Don't use the copier for runs that the duplicator can produce at far less cost.

Illegal Copying

Because of the ease of making photocopies and the availability of a copier in the office, there is a temptation to make copies of valuable personal papers and to use or carry the copies in place of the originals. There are rules against, and in some cases penalties for, copying certain papers. These include a driver's license, an automobile registration, a passport, citizenship papers, naturalization papers, immigration papers, postage stamps, copyrighted materials, and securities of the United States government.

DUPLICATING MACHINES

Unlike the copier which reproduces directly from the original, the duplicating machine produces copies from prepared masters and stencils. The three most commonly used types of duplicators for general office use are the fluid, stencil, and offset. The fluid and stencil processes have been widely used because of their simple operation and low initial cost. However, offset duplication has increased in popularity because of the superior quality of the reproduction. In addition, technological improvements have greatly simplified the preparation of the offset master and the operation of the offset equipment.

Fluid (Direct-Process) Duplication

The fluid process, also know as liquid, spirit, direct, and Ditto, is used for relatively short runs and is usually limited to the reproduction of materials to be used for interoffice or company distribution. The term "direct process" comes from the fact that copies are made directly from the master copy as it comes in contact with sheets of paper.

Have you ever dashed to the duplicator to run off a few copies quickly, only to find that first you need to spend ten minutes cleaning up someone else's mess? Suggestion: Initiate a sign-up sheet so that each person must register his or her use of the machine. It's amazing how tidy some people become when they know that the next user will definitely know who left the untidiness.

Copy to be reproduced is transferred in reverse image to the back of a master sheet from a direct-process carbon sheet by one of several methods. The master is then clamped to the cylinder of the duplicating machine carbon side up. The carbon-deposit side of the master comes in contact with the chemically moistened sheets of paper as they pass through the machine. A minute portion of the dye from the master transfers to the paper thus reproducing the copy. Up to 400 copies can be reproduced from one master.

Copies can be produced in purple, black, blue, green, or red. Using various colored carbons in producing the master allows several colors to be reproduced at the same time. Charts, pictures, and ruled forms can be traced onto the master. Also, a computer printout can go directly onto direct-process masters and then multiple copies can be run.

Stencil Duplication (Mimeograph Process)

The stencil process involves a stencil and an inked drum or inked twin cylinders. The stencil is a thin tissue coated with a waxy substance which ink cannot penetrate. The copy to be duplicated is transferred to the stencil by one of several methods. Each method results in pushing aside or removing the wax coating, thus exposing the porous fibers. The stencil is placed around an inked drum or screen, and the ink flows through the exposed fibers to produce the copy as the paper passes through the machine.

The quality of reproduction in stencil duplication is superior to that of the fluid process. Several thousand highly readable copies can be reproduced from one stencil, thus making the process practical for both short runs and also relatively long runs.

Fast-drying emulsion inks make it possible to print on both sides of the paper without slip-sheeting (inserting a blotting paper between sheets). As many as five colors can be reproduced at the same time by using a special multicolor ink pad. One manufacturer produces a model that utilizes snap-in cartridges of printer's ink that are easily interchangeable.

With the stencil process, near-perfect registration (exact positioning on a page, column, and line) can be achieved, making it possible to duplicate fill-ins on printed or duplicated forms. Variable-speed controls permit regulating the speed to lighten or darken the copy. Up to 200 copies per minute can be produced on the single-drum machine and 125 copies per minute can be produced on the twin-drum machine. The machine may be set to shut off automatically upon completion of a preset number of copies.

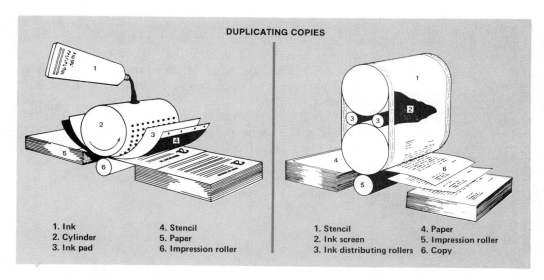

DUPLICATING COPIES

1. Ink	4. Stencil
2. Cylinder	5. Paper
3. Ink pad	6. Impression roller

1. Stencil	4. Paper
2. Ink screen	5. Impression roller
3. Ink distributing rollers	6. Copy

Copies are produced by the stencil process through the meeting of the stencil, the ink, and the paper. The paper is fed, sheet by sheet, between the cylinder and the impression roller. As the paper passes through, the roller lifts, automatically pressing the paper against the stencil. Simultaneously, ink flows through the stencil openings, making a copy on the paper. At the left is a single-drum duplicator; at the right, a twin cylinder.

Offset Duplication

Offset duplication (also known as photo-offset, lithography, photo-offset lithography, and offset lithography) is a process in which the inked impression is first transferred to a rubber roller and then transferred from the roller to the paper. The process is based on the chemical principle that grease and water do not mix and on the lithographic principle of printing from a "flat" surface. The image area (outline) is receptive to ink; the non-image area is receptive to water. Thus this ink and water receptivity defines the image. The copy to be duplicated is reproduced by typing or other methods on the front side of an offset master. The master is placed on a cylinder and is inked as it rotates. The ink on the master deposits the copy in reverse image on a large drum of rubber called a blanket. The image is transferred from the blanket to the copy paper being fed through the machine when the impression roller presses the copy paper against the rubber blanket.

The offset process offers a wide range of possibilities for reproducing printed, handwritten, or typed copy as well as pictures and drawings. Various colors can be used and several colors can be reproduced on the same page, but a separate master and a separate run are required for each color. As there is no offset on the back of the sheets, slip-sheeting is unnecessary. Copies can be run on both sides of a sheet to save both paper cost and bulkiness.

Offset duplicator manufacturers, such as A. B. Dick, Itek, and Addressograph-Multigraph, market table-top, office-size machines designed to produce high-quality work at a low per-copy cost. Their objective is to provide a machine that is competitive for general office duplication. The operation of these machines has been so simplified that they may be operated satisfactorily by most members of the office staff.

As many as 10,000 copies can be reproduced from one offset master and work of the highest quality can be obtained. The wide range of paper and variety of colors that can be used make the process especially appropriate where appearance is of major concern. This is most valuable for materials which are going outside the office to customers and to the general public.

COPIER-DUPLICATORS

The most recent development in office reprographics is the copier-duplicator. This machine uses the copier principle of imaging but, unlike the convenience copier, is designed for high-volume production, such as 100,000 to 500,000 impressions per month per machine. These machines operate at speeds of 4,500 or more copies per

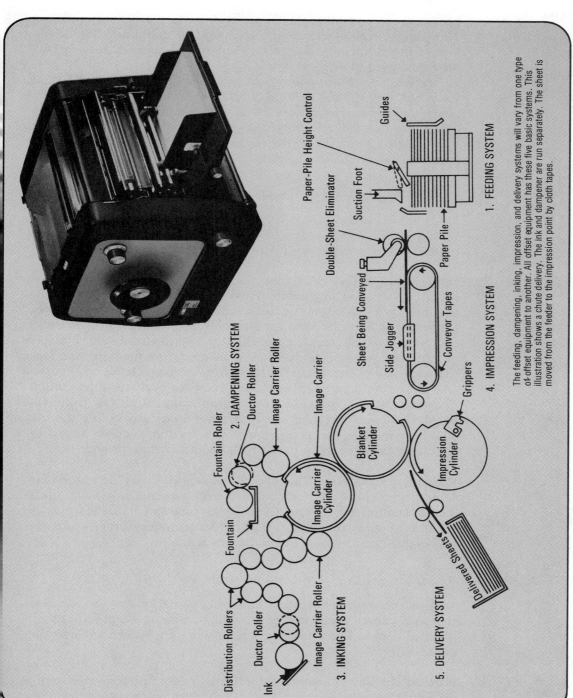

A. B. Dick Company

Distribution Rollers

Fountain Roller

2. DAMPENING SYSTEM

Ductor Roller

Image Carrier Roller

Fountain

Image Carrier

Paper-Pile Height Control

Guides

Double-Sheet Eliminator

Suction Foot

Ductor Roller

Image Carrier Roller

3. INKING SYSTEM

Ink

Image Carrier Cylinder

Blanket Cylinder

Sheet Being Conveyed

Side Jogger

Paper Pile

1. FEEDING SYSTEM

Conveyor Tapes

Impression Cylinder

Grippers

4. IMPRESSION SYSTEM

5. DELIVERY SYSTEM

Delivered Sheets

The feeding, dampening, inking, impression, and delivery systems will vary from one type of offset equipment to another. All offset equipment has these five basic systems. This illustration shows a chute delivery. The ink and dampener are run separately. The sheet is moved from the feeder to the impression point by cloth tapes.

hour and compete favorably in per-copy cost with offset duplicating. They offer the convenience of the copier, the speed and cost advantage of the duplicator, and certain automated features not available on duplicating machines.

Several large office-equipment manufacturers, such as Eastman Kodak, Xerox, IBM, 3M, and Addressograph-Multigraph, provide copier-duplicators which are competing for the market. These machines are expensive to purchase or lease, are generally positioned in word processing or reprographic departments, and are usually operated by trained technicians.

Special Features of Copier-Duplicators

All copier-duplicators will have automatic repeat and document-feeding features (see pages 123–124). In addition, some makes and models have the following features.

Duplexing. The process of reproducing copy on both sides of a sheet of paper is called duplexing. This feature reduces paper cost; for example, a 20-page report can be reproduced on 10 sheets of paper. Duplexing is accomplished mechanically in one of two ways. Under one system all originals are run through and the front side is imaged on the copy paper. The operator then resets the machine and runs the back side of the originals through, producing copies on the back side of the copy paper. This system requires operator intervention. The other system provides in-line duplexing. Both the front and back sides of the original are copied automatically before the machine proceeds to the next original. This system requires no operator intervention and is a major technological breakthrough.

Reduction Capability. The size of the original may be reduced by some copier-duplicators as much as 35 percent. Legal-size documents, computer printouts, and accounting spread sheets may be reduced to letter-size copies. This reduction saves storage space and makes documents easier to handle, yet readable.

Paper-Processing Features

Some copier-duplicators continue automation beyond duplication into paper processing by providing assembled and finished duplicated copies. These machines have what are known as "finishing capabilities."

Sorters. The sorter assembles duplicated pages into sequence to provide multiple sets of a duplicated document, such as a report. The automatic sorter unit is attached in-line to the copier-duplicator, meaning that the copies proceed directly from the copier-duplicator to the sorter without operator intervention. As the multiple copies of the first page of the original come off the copier-duplicator, they are automatically separated into a series of bins, one bin for each copy. The next page of the original is run and the copies are separated into the same bins. This process is repeated until all pages of the original have been copied. Each bin will then contain one complete copied set of the original. Similar sorter attachments for duplicators are also available.

Finishing. In addition to assembling, the Eastman Kodak Ektaprint copier-duplicator carries the process one step further to include in-line finishing. The assembling unit receives the copies, jogs the set, staples one or two corners along one side, and deposits the set in a removable tray. Most copier-duplicators produce the number of desired copies of page one before proceeding to page two. The Kodak Ektaprint system, however, produces one copy of each page of the report, assembles and finishes set one, then proceeds to repeat the process and completes set two. This process is followed until the desired number of sets have been completed. The advantage of the system is that it is not necessary to wait until all the sets have been duplicated before getting the first finished set. The time involved here is called turn-around time — the lapsed time from submission of original to receipt of assembled copies.

This Xerox 9200 copier has a collator which assembles pages into sequence, thus providing multiple sets of the copied material.

Xerox Corporation

AUTOMATED DUPLICATORS

The copier-duplicator offers the convenience of reproducing copy directly from an original without the intermediate step of preparing a master or stencil. To compete, manufacturers of stencil and offset duplicators have produced highly automated machines for high-volume users. Basically the automated duplicator combines three machines into an in-line assembly: (1) an automatic master or stencil making machine, (2) a high-speed duplicating machine, and (3) a sorter to provide assembled copies. The operator produces the master or stencil on the automatic plate or stencil maker and transfers the master or stencil to the duplicator. The duplicated copies feed automatically into a sorter and the operator receives assembled copies. The operation is even further automated by some manufacturers. The master or stencil moves via conveyor belt directly from the plate-stencil maker to the duplicator and attaches itself, and copies are run and assembled without operator intervention. The operator's function is to feed the original into the plate-stencil maker and to set the duplicator for the desired number of copies.

The automatic duplicator is usually placed in a centralized reprographic or word processing department and is run by trained operators only. A. B. Dick, Addressograph-Multigraph, Eastman Kodak, Itek, and Xerox produce high-speed automatic duplicators. The reproductions on these machines are of the highest quality.

AUXILIARY REPROGRAPHIC EQUIPMENT

There are various types of equipment that supplement the work of copiers and duplicators. This equipment is usually located in a reprographic department or word processing center.

Headliners and Composers

Equipment which can use a variety of type sizes and styles to produce copy resembling printing will improve the visual quality of the material to be duplicated or copied.

Headliners. Letter compositor machines are available for in-office use to create display type for headlines, subheads, and similar items for which large type is needed. The operator dials the letters in a heading one at a time. The heading is printed by the compositor on sensitized strips of tape. The tape is pasted on the original. The original is then converted to a master or stencil and duplicated.

Composers. Duplicated material that closely resembles printing, such as that found in magazines, advertising brochures, and important announcements, cannot be obtained from copy prepared on the office typewriter. A VariTyper or IBM Composer would be used to prepare the copy. These machines have a typewriter-like keyboard. They can justify the right margin, permit the easy interchange of type size and style, and provide proportional letter spacing closely resembling the printed page. The VariTyper and IBM Composer are used to produce copy for catalogs, annual reports, company newspapers, and other items where various type styles and sizes are needed.

Finishing Equipment

Collating, stapling, binding, folding, and addressing duplicator output are time-consuming activities. There are machines that will perform these paper-pushing jobs quickly and accurately. They free the office staff for more productive work.

Collators. There are collators that operate independently of the copier or duplicator. The collator contains bins in which piles of papers are placed by the operator. Each bin will contain copies of the same sheet. When activated, the machine will automatically eject the top sheet from each bin and will assemble the sheets in a desired order. Fully automatic collators will stack the completed sets on a stacking bin. If the collator is semi-automatic, the operator is required to gather and stack the assembled sets.

Binders. Binding gives a professional appearance to copied or duplicated materials. Equipment consisting of a puncher and a binder is available for both soft-cover and hard-cover binding. There are both manually and electrically operated punching, binding, and stapling machines.

Folding and Inserting Machines. Machines that fold duplicated sheets, such as letters and advertisements, and insert them into envelopes are significant energy-savers and time-savers to businesses that have large mailings. For example, Insertamate Mailing System distributed by Pitney-Bowes is a fully integrated system that folds, inserts, seals, and meter-stamps mail in one fast, accurate, and simultaneous operation.

Addresser-Printers. The addresser-printer is used to address envelopes to go to names on a mailing list. Each name and address on the mailing list is recorded on some form of plate or card called the data carrier. The data carrier may be a metal or plastic plate or a card with a small stencil or direct-process master insert. A separate data carrier is used for each addressee. As the envelope or addressing tape passes through the addresser-printer, the plate or address card falls in place, one at a time. The address is then duplicated on the envelope or address tape. The addresser-printer may be manually fed or fully automatic. These machines are called addresser-printers because they may be used for other purposes than addressing, such as preparing inventory cards, monthly bills, and routing of multiple forms.

COMMERCIAL DUPLICATION

In every city there are commercial shops that make a specialty of reprographic work. These businesses are usually listed in the *Yellow Pages* under "Letter Shop Service" or "Copying and Duplicating." Such shops will prepare stencils or masters, run the copies, address envelopes, fold and insert the enclosures, and so on. They will do the entire job or any phase of it.

If the office does not have adequate duplicating equipment or if time is short, the secretary may need to turn to an outside shop. Factors that must be investigated and compared include the following: (1) rates charged per copy, (2) quality of prepared copy, (3) cost for collating, (4) cost for binding copies, and (5) time needed for completion. A file of information about the shops available should be maintained by the secretary.

SELECTING THE REPROGRAPHIC PROCESS

The secretary usually makes the decision as to whether copies are to be produced on the copier, copier-duplicator, or duplicator, or by a commercial shop. Several factors enter into this decision: the number of copies required; the urgency; copying and duplicating facilities available in-office, in-company, and at outside agencies; the quality of reproduction desired; and the cost per copy.

If the number of copies required is 10 or less, the use of the copying machine will probably be the least expensive, fastest, and most convenient. If the number required is 100 or more, the duplicator or copier-duplicator will be the fastest, will give the highest quality reproduction, and will result in the lowest per-copy cost. However, when the number of copies required falls between 10 and 100, the choice comes within what is known in the industry as the "gray zone," meaning that the decision is not clearly weighted for copying or for duplicating. The copier-duplicator is economical in this range, but it is a high-volume machine and usually is available only in large companies with a centralized reprographic department. The commercial shop may be the most economical in the 10-to-100-and-above copy range, but the inconvenience and the slow turn-around time of the shop may preclude its use. The convenience and quality of reproduction by duplicator will depend upon: whether equipment for stencil and master imaging is available (see pages 136–138); which duplicator process is used; and what automated features are on the equipment.

The chart on this page provides a convenient summary for comparison of reprographic processes.

COMPARISON OF REPROGRAPHIC PROCESSES

Characteristics	Copiers	Copier-Duplicator	Fluid Process	Stencil Process[1]	Offset Process[1]
Copy quality	Facsimile — as good as original	Same as copiers	Medium quality, multi-color available, purple produces best copy	Good quality with copy separation and good registration	Excellent quality with full-color reproduction
Recommended quantity of copies	1 to 10 copies	11 to unlimited number of copies	10 to 300 copies per master	50 to 3,000 copies per stencil	11 to 10,000 copies per master
Imaging	Direct from original	Direct from original	Typed master or thermal master	Typed stencil, thermal or electronic	Typed master, electrostatic, photographic
Estimated cost of master	No master required	No master required	Master set 10¢ Thermal master 8¢	Stencil 20–25¢ Thermal 40–50¢ Electronic 40–55¢	Typing Master 15–25¢ Electrostatic 50–75¢ Aluminum plate $1–$5
Estimated cost per copy	2½¢ to 10¢	3¢ decreasing to 1¢ for high-volume use plus paper cost	1–3¢ depending on number of copies run	100–1,000, ¾¢ each 1,000 up, ½¢ each	11–100, ¾¢ plus cost of master 100 up, ½¢ plus cost of master

[1]The automated duplicator uses either the stencil or offset process. Quality of copy and estimated per-copy cost are approximately the same as that shown for the process used.

PREPARING MASTERS AND STENCILS

Copy to be duplicated may be transferred to an offset or direct-process master or to a stencil in a number of ways. The traditional and still most widely used method is to image the copy on the master or stencil by typing. Technology, however, has provided new imaging devices that are more convenient, faster, and more versatile than typing. These new devices have been instrumental in keeping the duplicator in a competitive position relative to the copying machine. Imaging equipment is now used extensively in large offices, and the number of small offices purchasing this equipment is growing steadily.

Imaging techniques not only save the time of manually typing and correcting the master and stencil but offer many other advantages. For example, most of the time-consuming process of proofreading the stencil or master is eliminated. If the original is correct, the master or stencil will be correct. In addition, pasting up copy is practical. It provides the flexibility to include a printed graph or map, to prepare a four-page folded program, and to include photographs and other materials that would be impractical if not impossible to attempt to record manually on a stencil or master.

Thermal Imaging

The thermographic (heat-transfer) copier (see pages 122–123) can be used to produce stencils and fluid masters. The original is prepared by typing, writing, or drawing on paper. Erasers, correction tape, or correction fluid may be used to make corrections. Copy can be cut and a paste-up original prepared. The original is then combined with a *thermal stencil* or *master* and passed through the copier. The heat causes a copy of the original to transfer to the stencil or master which may be placed immediately on the duplicator to reproduce copies.

One limitation of the thermal process is that certain colors will not transfer, but a copy of the original can be made on an electrostatic copier that will reproduce most inks and most colors. This copy can then be used in place of the original to produce the thermal stencil or master.

Facsimile Imaging

The facsimile process, sometimes referred to as the *electronic scanning method*, is used for preparing stencils and offset masters. The process is an adaptation of the principle of the photoelectric cell. Material to be reproduced is placed on the left drum of a two-drum machine. An electronic (plastic) stencil or offset plate is

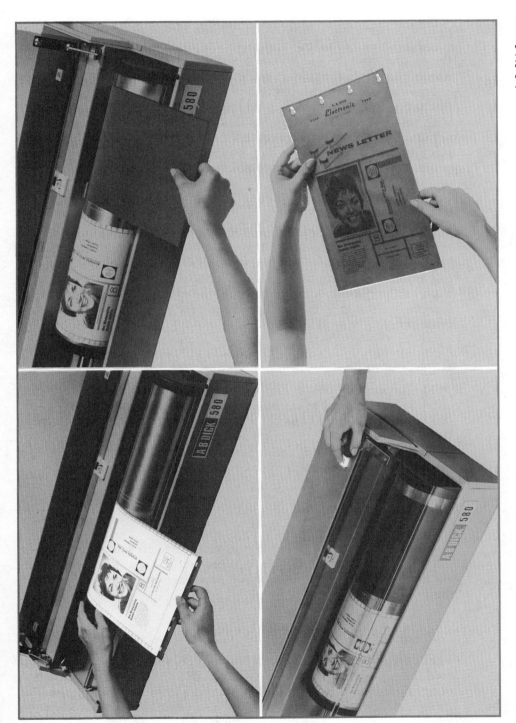

The four steps in preparing a stencil by the facsimile process are (1) the copy to be reproduced is placed on one drum; (2) an electronic stencil is placed on the second drum; (3) the operation switch is activated; and (4) the completed stencil is removed and is ready to be run on the duplicator.

placed on the right drum. As the drums rotate slowly, a photoelectric eye scans each line. This activates a needle that moves across the second drum as the photoelectric eye moves across the first. The needle records the image on the stencil or offset master.

Drawings, forms, printed and typed copy, diagrams, and artwork (including photographs) can be transferred to a stencil or master with relatively high-quality detail. A transparency may be prepared simultaneously with the production of the stencil or master. Thus, reproduced copies can be distributed to a group and the screen-projected transparency can be used for oral presentation.

Photo Imaging

Small desk-top offset platemakers transfer originals to offset masters (plates) within seconds. The original and the chemically sensitized offset master are placed on a flatbed window. When the printing button is pressed, a photographic-type lamp automatically exposes the master. A timer controls the exposure. No film or other intermediate step is required, and the process is almost completely error-proof.

Electrostatic Imaging

The process of producing an offset master on the copying machine is almost as simple and convenient as producing a copy of an original. The original is placed in the copier. A sensitized offset master is substituted for the copy paper. The image is transferred from the original to the offset master which may be immediately used to produce copies on the offset duplicator.

TYPING MASTERS AND STENCILS

Not all offices have imaging equipment and in some situations it may not be possible to use the equipment. The secretary, therefore, should be competent to produce masters and stencils by other methods.

Typing Fluid Masters

Fluid masters are produced for runs of varying length — short, medium, and long — and are packaged in sets with carbon attached and interleaved with tissue that must be removed before use. Although duplicating carbon is highly smudge resistant, it must be handled carefully. A special cleaning cream that removes the dye should be kept available. (Creaming the hands before using the carbon makes stains easier to remove.)

The typing, done on the front of the master, is always visible because the ribbon remains engaged.

If the length of a run exceeds the number of copies possible from the kind of master you have, prepare two masters at the same time. This can be done by placing one master sheet and carbon over another master sheet and carbon and adjusting the touch regulator for the extra copies. In one operation you will have prepared two identical masters.

Until your employer can sign a direct-process master, keep it clean by replacing the tissue (with the signature area cut out) between the carbon and the master.

Drawing on the Master. Artwork and ruled lines can be traced directly on the master by laying the copy on top of the sheet and tracing over the copy. The impression will be transferred to the back of the sheet by the carbon underneath. Halftone effects can be obtained by using a shading plate beneath the carbon copy and rubbing over it. Multicolored drawings can be made by using different colors of carbon paper.

Making Corrections. Corrections can be made by blocking out the error on the back of the master sheet (the front surface is not corrected) with a wax blockout pencil as follows:

1. Separate the master sheet from the carbon. (Some secretaries prefer to insert a master set into the typewriter with the bound edges at the bottom so that it is not necessary to detach the carbon in making corrections.)

2. Lay back the master sheet so that the error rests on the flat part of the typewriter, or put a rigid object as a shield underneath it.

3. Scrape the carbon dye from the error with a razor blade or knife. Remove remaining carbon with a soft typewriter eraser.

4. Cover the error with a wax blockout pencil.

5. Roll the sheet and carbon into approximate position for typing. Slip a small piece of unused carbon paper in back of the error and type the correction. Remove the carbon slip immediately.

A SAFETY HINT! Keep the single-edge razor blade you use for corrections in an empty matchbook, sharp edge inserted where the matches used to be. If you use a double-edge blade, wrap several thicknesses of adhesive tape around the center. Leave the corners free for scraping.

Also, corrections may be made by using a self-adhesive correction tape with the same surface as the master sheet. Cut off the length needed and press it on the back of the master covering the incorrect copy. Do not remove the carbon dye. After the correction tape is in place, slip a small piece of unused carbon paper in back of the correction tape and type the correction. This method is best when more than several letters must be corrected.

A small area on the master can be permanently blocked out by cutting out the area with a razor blade or by covering it on the carbon side with plastic tape. A convenient tool for making neat, precise cutouts is an X-ACTO knife, available at stationery and art supply shops.

Blockouts. Any part of the master may be temporarily blocked out as copies are being run on the duplicator. This makes it possible to produce a number of different forms from the same master. For this reason the direct-process duplicator is widely used in systems work. For example, one master for an order can be drawn up; then by the use of blockout covers, or blockout sections printed on the forms, shipping labels, invoices, work orders, stockroom orders, stock-record cards, back-order sheets, and other forms can be reproduced from the one master. Different forms can be reproduced from the same master by merely inserting a blockout mask that meets the requirements of each form.

Storing and Rerunning Masters. When the production run has been completed, the master can be stored. Place the tissue sheet which originally was a part of the master set against the carbon-deposit side of the master. Place the master and tissue sheet on top of a sheet of paper, and staple all three items together.

Masters can be rerun. A master, however, can reproduce in total only a limited number of copies. Additions, changes, or corrections can be made on a master even after it has been run. For example, it is possible to run a dozen copies from a master, to insert additional information on it, and then to run more copies. Instead of removing the carbon paper from the master copy sheet, fold the carbon sheet under the master and leave it attached when placing the master on the machine for the first run. This method keeps the unit set intact and holds the carbon paper in its original position for making the addition while retaining the original alignment.

Azograph. A disadvantage of the direct process is that the reproducing dye on the master will smudge and rub off unless the master is handled carefully. This problem has been eliminated by the A. B. Dick Company by using the *azograph process*. The azograph master will not smudge or discolor the hands as no dye is formed on the master sheet until it comes in contact with azograph fluid while copies are being duplicated. Both the azograph master and azograph fluid must be used. The two disadvantages of the process are that copies can be produced in blue color only, and the maximum number of copies obtainable from one master is comparatively low, less than 100.

Typing Stencils (Mimeograph Process)

The quality of stencil duplication depends primarily on the quality of the stencil, the care with which it is prepared, and the care given to the cleaning and filing of the stencil for future use.

Kinds of Stencils. Stencils are produced by a number of manufacturers, each of whom makes several different grades and kinds. Some grades are designed for short runs, others for long runs. Some are recommended for typing work, others for handwriting and artwork. Stencils are available, with or without a transparent Pliofilm covering, in a variety of colors. The color, however, has no significance except that some stencil manufacturers use color to identify the type or grade of stencil. Each brand carries full instructions inside or on the cover of the box. For best results, read and follow the instructions carefully.

Stencils come in legal, letter, and note size. Form-topped stencils (stencils with outlines printed on the face of the stencil) may be obtained for handwriting, typing newspaper columns, addressing labels, and setting up four-page folders. Also, continuous stencil sheets are available for use on tabulators and computer-printout equipment.

The tissue or coated sheet cushions the impact of the typewriter keys and broadens the outlines of each letter. The sheet also serves as a depository for the stencil coating.

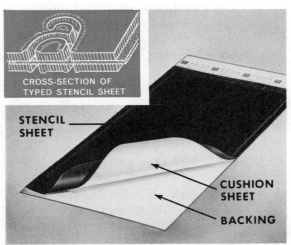

CROSS-SECTION OF
TYPED STENCIL SHEET

STENCIL
SHEET

CUSHION
SHEET

BACKING

A. B. Dick Company

A tissue or coated cushion sheet is usually provided with the stencil. Insert this sheet between the stencil and the backing sheet before the stencil is cut. This sheet cushions the impact of the typewriter keys, serves as a depository for the stencil coating which is removed from the underside of the stencil sheet, and broadens the outlines of each stenciled letter. Some stencils have color-coated cushion sheets to facilitate proofreading.

Preparing the Guide Copy. If you are not experienced in typing stencils, prepare a guide copy to help you. Use a paper sheet the size to be used for running off the copies.

1. Mark on the sheet the limitations or boundary lines shown on the stencil.

2. Indicate the position of all special illustrations or folds so that the typing copy can be adjusted to the right locations; then type the copy to be reproduced on the guide sheet. "Plan before typing" is a basic rule for good stencil reproduction.

3. After preparing the stencil, check the guide copy with the stencil. Many mistakes in duplicating work can be traced to the omission of this step.

Placement of Copy on the Stencil. Several methods may be used to indicate placement of the copy on the stencil. One is to lay the guide copy on the stencil and jot down the line numbers and spaces for each margin and indention according to the scales printed on the stencil. Another method is to lay the guide copy directly under the stencil sheet and mark the places for margins and indentions on the face of the stencil by small dots of correction fluid.

Some duplicating machines permit an adjustment of only about one inch to raise or lower copy on the duplicated sheet; consequently, it is necessary to place the copy carefully for well-proportioned top and bottom margins.

Guide Points for Salutations and Addresses. When typing a stencil for letters that are to have the inside addresses inserted individually on the typewriter, indicate the beginning position of the address by making a tiny dot on the stencil with a pin at the point where the inside address or salutation should start. This is an efficiency aid to the person who will fill in the addresses.

Handwork on Stencils. The drawing of lines, forms, and illustrations; hand lettering; and other artistic work on stencils require the skillful use of styluses, lettering guides, screen plates, and the illuminated drawing board. Best results are obtained when a flexible writing plate is used instead of the cushion sheet under the stencil.

The selection of the correct stylus is important. In general, the wire-loop stylus should be used for solid-line work and signatures; a wheel stylus for charts, graphs, and ruled forms; ball point for fine detail work; and a lettering-guide stylus for lettering. Books and packets are available with headings, cartoons, and the like for stencil tracing.

Typing. For producing good stencils observe the following procedures (as well as any special instructions given with the particular brand of stencil used):

1. *Clean the typewriter type.*
   Unless film-topped stencils are used, it is usually necessary to clean the keys after the typing of each stencil. Letters with less surface, like *i*, *l*, *c*, *e*, *o*, and *w* (as well as the period), should be watched carefully. It may be necessary to clean them during the course of the stencil typing, especially if the typeface is elite. A liquid type cleaner should not be allowed to spatter on the stencil sheets, nor should a stiff brush come into contact with the coating.

2. *Prepare the typewriter.*
   Set the ribbon lever to the "off," "white," or "stencil" position or the letters will not stencilize completely. Release card fingers to avoid their hooking into the stencil. Move the rolls on the paper bail aside so they will not roll on the typed stencil surface.

3. *Follow the instructions.*
   Read the instructions provided by the manufacturer or distributor to determine the correct method of assembling the stencil for insertion into the typewriter. When typing lengthwise on the stencil, do not cut off the bottom of the stencil to accommodate reduced carriage width. Merely cut the *backing sheet* to the required length and fold the stencil around the backing sheet.

4. *Type with care.*
   Experiment to determine the correct pressure. If the pressure is too light, the copy will be uneven; if the pressure is too heavy, the copy will be dense and lack sharpness. To determine the correct pressure, set the indicator at the lowest registration. Move the carriage to the edge of the stencil outside the printing area. While typing a series of periods and commas, gradually raise the pressure to the point where the periods and commas are reproduced clearly and evenly.

5. *Inspect the stencil at the end of each paragraph.*
   See if the typewriter keys are pushing the coating aside properly for clear, evenly stenciled openings. See if any keys need cleaning or if any are making holes in the stencil. Do not roll the stencil backward any more than is absolutely necessary as it may wrinkle or tear. When it is necessary to roll it back, hold one corner of the stencil firmly.

Typing Plate. In place of a cushion sheet, a plastic typing plate called an *equalizer sheet* may be used to produce extra-sharp copies. The equalizer sheet is inserted between the stencil sheet and the backing sheet.

Transparent Cover Sheets. If a stencil has a Pliofilm cover sheet, type right onto it and through it. This film sheet eliminates *type fill* — the accumulation of stencil coating in the keys — and reduces the cutting out of such letters as *o, q, d, b, p*.

Proofreading the Stencil. Every stencil should be checked paragraph by paragraph while it is being typed and also read in its entirety after it is taken from the typewriter. Accuracy is paramount in duplicating work.

Making Corrections. A surprising amount of stencil patching and rearranging is possible. This salvaging work can be done before or after the stencil has been run on the duplicating machine. Experiment with a discarded stencil. The correction or new material to be inserted is typed on an unused section of a spoiled stencil sheet that is still attached to its backing sheet. The piece to be discarded is cut out and the opening neatly trimmed. The new copy is cut with a margin around all sides and placed on the face of the stencil sheet over the opening. Make sure the patch is in proper alignment and the edges do not cover up any other copy on the stencil sheet. The patch is then anchored with patching cement and sealed all around the edges with correction fluid.

Small sections of the stencil can be blocked out by placing a piece of carbon paper over that portion of the stencil. The adhesive action of the ink will hold the blockout paper in place.

To make a good correction:

1. Turn the stencil forward in the typewriter so that the line containing the error is clear of interference. On film-topped stencils, the film must be detached from the stencil heading, as the correction fluid must be applied under the film.

2. When a tissue cushion sheet or equalizer sheet is used, smooth together the edges of the error by rubbing gently with a glass burnisher or the curved end of a paper clip before applying the correction fluid. Lift the stencil away from the cushion or equalizer sheet by inserting a pencil between the stencil and the sheet. This prevents any correction fluid that has leaked through the stencil from adhering to the cushion sheet. Never use the correction fluid over the writing plate of an illuminated drawing board.

3. Using a single vertical stroke of the brush, apply a thin coat of correction fluid to the error. The less fluid the better, as long as the opening is entirely covered.

There are three steps in preparing a stencil for a correction: (1) turn the stencil forward and separate the film from the stencil sheet, (2) burnish, and (3) apply the correction fluid. After the correction fluid has set, type the correction.

4. Let the correction fluid set for about half a minute and remove the pencil. Test with the finger for dryness.

5. Lower the pressure adjustment slightly and type the correction.

When removing the stencil from the typewriter, use the paper release to insure the least damage to the stencil. Then examine the stencil for scratches, unnecessary marks, or holes. All of these should be covered with correction fluid. If other blemishes show up after the stencil is on the machine, paint them out with correction fluid.

Running Off the Copies. A number of models and makes of stencil duplicating machines are in use. A detailed instruction booklet accompanies each machine describing how it should be operated. Study this booklet. If additional help is needed, call on the company servicing the machine.

Cleaning and Filing Stencils. Cleaning may be done by placing the stencil between two sheets of newspaper and rubbing on the surface of the newspaper to remove the ink from the stencil. When water-based, contact-drying inks are used, the stencil can be washed with soap in lukewarm water.

Special stencil wrappers made of absorbent paper stock are available for filing stencils that have been used with oil-base emulsion (or paste) inks. With these wrappers it is not necessary to clean a stencil before filing it; merely place the stencil in the wrapper, close, and rub the wrapper. There are special file cabinets in which to file used stencils. Empty stencil boxes stored on edge can also be used.

Identifying Stencils. A plan should be followed for identifying stencils for future use. When a stencil wrapper is used, one of the duplicated copies may be attached to the wrapper, or the wrapper itself may be run through the duplicator reproducing a copy of the stencil on it.

Preparing Offset Masters

There are three basic types of offset masters — paper masters called mats used for short runs and general production; plastic masters called plates used for medium runs; and metal plates used for long runs and for high-quality reproduction. The paper mat is generally used when the master is prepared on the typewriter.

Typing Offset Masters. Copy to be duplicated is typed (drawn, traced, stamped) directly on the face of the mat. The typing, however, must be done with a carbon-paper or film (Mylar or polyethylene) ribbon or with a special offset fiber ribbon. An alternative to using the carbon ribbon is to use an offset carbon sheet. The carbon sheet is placed face down on the mat, and the typing is done on the back of the carbon sheet.

As in all other duplicating processes, keep the typeface clean and the paper-bail rollers positioned to ride on the master but *outside* the usage area. Type directly on the face of the master, using normal typing pressure. Too heavy a pressure may dent the surface of the master slightly and cause poor reproduction.

For best results, allow an interval of fifteen to thirty minutes between the typing and the running of the master. This time space permits the image to set.

A nonreproducing pencil may be used to help plan the placement of the copy on the master. With this pencil, markings can be made directly on the master as guidelines for typing the copy. The pencil marks will not reproduce.

Writing, lettering, drawing, and ruling may be made directly on the offset mat by using an offset ink, crayon, or pencil that will adhere to the mat and leave a film. Offset carbon paper may be used to trace a form or sketch on the mat.

Making Corrections on Offset Masters. Corrections on offset masters are made by erasing and retyping. A special eraser is produced for this purpose, but any soft (non-gritty) eraser may be used. Only a few light erasing strokes are necessary, as the deposit comes off readily. A faint "ghost" image will remain, but it will not reproduce. Use a normal touch to type in the correction. A second correction cannot be made in the same spot.

To reinsert a typed master into the typewriter, lay a clean sheet of paper over the master to prevent the typewriter rollers from smudging the typing. When proofreading, hold the master along the edges to avoid getting fingerprints on the surface.

Cleaning, Storing, and Rerunning Offset Masters. A properly cleaned and filed master can be rerun any number of times. After a run, moisten a cotton pad with water and gently clean the surface of the master. Remove any ink or solution left along the edges of the master. Cover it with a thin coating of a preservative (gum solution). When it has dried, store the master in a plain, non-oily paper folder in a file drawer.

When rerunning a filed master, take the time to "etch" the master — the process of applying a starting solution that supplies proper amounts of moisture to the surface of the master during the initial wet-out.

PAPER FOR COPIERS AND DUPLICATORS

The secretary may be assigned the responsibility for buying paper for the office copier and duplicator. The purchasing problem is complicated because several of the office copiers use sensitized papers, and each duplicating process requires its own type of paper.

Paper used in duplicating is usually wood sulfite. It comes in a wide variety of colors. The three standard weights for mimeo and duplicating paper are 16, 20, and 24 pounds. Offset paper may carry these same weight identifications or different weights such as 50, 60, or 70 pounds. A 50-pound offset paper weighs slightly less than a 20-pound bond.

Offset paper comes in two general types — coated and uncoated. The coated paper is designed for high-grade work, and offset enamel is the very highest quality. Uncoated paper is used for the majority of in-house work which does not require a high-quality result from the reproduction process.

Paper for stencil duplicating, unlike that for spirit duplicating, is unglazed and absorbent. Since moisture affects the quality of reproduction and the ease with which the paper is handled by the machine, duplicating paper should be kept wrapped in the moisture-proof covers in which it is received. It should be stored in a dry place and stacked flat.

Duplicator paper, like other paper, has a top and a bottom side. The best results are obtained by using the paper top side up. The printed label on the package usually indicates the correct printing side.

An important consideration in buying copier paper is to avoid overstocking. Most copier papers have a "shelf life" which should be checked before buying in quantity. Paper for copiers may be purchased in rolls (which use more storage space) and in a variety of sizes, such as executive, letter, and legal (pre-cut).

SUGGESTED READINGS

Administrative Management, The Systems Magazine for Administrative Executives, (Monthly). New York: Geyer-McAllister Publications. Select recent articles on copiers, duplicators, copier-duplicators, sorters, addresser-printers, copier paper.

Bauer, Dennis E., and John W. Strahl. *Office Reproduction Processes*. San Francisco: Canfield Press, 1975.

Pasewark, William R. *Duplicating Machine Processes*, Stencil, Fluid, Offset and Copier, 2d ed. Cincinnati: South-Western Publishing Co., 1975.

QUESTIONS FOR DISCUSSION

1. What is meant by "overcopying"? Why is it a major problem in the office?

2. What factors and features should be considered in evaluating the quality of reproductions obtained from a specific copier?

3. Which reproduction process would you recommend for each of the following projects, assuming that all types were available to you?
   (a) 5,000 copies of a form letter to be mailed to sales prospects
   (b) 5 copies of an order to be distributed to department heads with the least possible delay
   (c) 300 copies of a notice to be mailed to all salespeople, announcing a new product
   (d) 15 copies of a two-page report to be mailed to department heads
   (e) 750 copies of a four-page house organ that is issued monthly and contains pictures and illustrations
   (f) 45 copies of a one-page announcement showing directions to the recreational area for a company picnic (The notices are to be placed on bulletin boards throughout the plant.)
   (g) 8 copies of the secretary's minutes of the directors' meeting
   (h) 150 copies of a price list duplicated each week (The list covers 144 standard items arranged in alphabetical order. Since the prices fluctuate, a new price list is prepared, duplicated, and distributed weekly to all sales employees.)
   (i) 500 preprinted time cards to be titled each week — one time card for each company employee (The title on the card shows the employee's number, name, address, social security number, and number of income tax exemptions.)

4. List the features you might evaluate in determining the quality of material prepared on a duplicator.

5. By what methods can you personalize a duplicated letter?

6. What auxiliary equipment may be purchased as a supplement to copiers and duplicators?

7. What finishing equipment may be purchased as auxiliaries to copiers and duplicators?

8. What cost elements should be included in arriving at the duplicator or copier cost-per-copy?

9. One of your assistants duplicated a report on a stencil machine. Upon examining the copies, you note the following:
   (a) On some copies, the image at the left is lighter than that at the right.
   (b) The letters are not evenly sharp and are rather broad and heavy.
   (c) The center of some of the circular letters like *o*, *p*, and *d* are all ink.

   What would you suggest that your assistant do to improve the quality of the duplicating work?

10. If necessary, correct the following sentences. Then use the Reference Guide to check your answers.
    (a) The copied materials were placed altogether in the correct folder.
    (b) Everyone of the contestants were eager for the start of the test.
    (c) He is apt to refuse our offer.
    (d) Anyone of the secretaries can open the safe.
    (e) Class attendance was effected by the weather.
    (f) It is allright for you to purchase additional supplies.

PROBLEMS

1. There are many makes, models, and types of duplicators and copiers available. Furthermore, each duplicator and copier process offers certain advantages depending upon the specific reproduction requirements of the office. Careful consideration is required to select the reprographic process and the make and model of machine that will best meet the needs of a specific office. Prepare a list of the factors you would consider in selecting the process and the make and model of machine to be used in an office.

2. Be prepared to demonstrate one of the following:
   (a) Planning the placement of the guide copy on a stencil or offset master
   (b) Typing the stencil or offset master

   (c) Correcting errors on a stencil, direct-process master, and offset master
   (d) Using a copying machine to produce a stencil, offset master, fluid master, or transparency

3. To help the employees you are supervising, prepare an instruction sheet clearly explaining procedures for one of the following activities. Illustrate your explanation, if possible:
   (a) Placing the master copy on a direct-process duplicator and running the copies
   (b) Placing the stencil on a stencil duplicator, running the copies, and removing and preparing the stencil for filing
   (c) Placing the master on the offset duplicator, running the copies,

and removing and preparing the master for filing

(d) Using a copying machine

(e) Using a heat-transfer copier to produce a direct-process master or stencil

(f) Using a copying machine to produce an offset master

(g) Preparing a liquid duplicating master

4. Your company offices occupy six floors in an office building. One high-speed copier-duplicator is installed in a central location on each floor, and each staff person who has copying to do uses that machine. You are aware of several problems: (1) The total cost for copying has been increasing at an alarming rate and you are suspicious that there is much overcopying and copying of personal material being done. (2) You have observed that staff members frequently lose considerable time waiting at the copier for the machine to become available for their use. (3) The copying center has become the quasi-social center for the office personnel. (4) Although the copier-duplicator is centrally located, it is a considerable distance from some of the offices. Secretaries frequently make the round trip to the machine to reproduce only two or three copies. (5) Senior staff members complain that the secretaries are away from the desks too much of the time. Prepare a list of recommendations to improve the situation.

5. You are responsible for duplicating the company's annual report. Select and describe the type of machine you will use for duplicating the report.

6. Follow Steps (a) through (d), below, to prepare a stencil or direct-process or offset master, and run ten copies of the horizontal bar graph shown at the top of page 471. Below the graph, type the five suggestions for preparing bar graphs shown in Chapter 20.

(a) Prepare a guide copy.

(b) When you are satisfied with the accuracy and form of the guide copy, plan your stencil or master placement.

(c) Type the stencil or master and draw lines.

(d) Run ten copies.

Part 2   CASE PROBLEMS

Case 2-1 DEVELOPING POSITIVE ATTITUDES

Foremost Foods has a buddy system under which selected experienced employees are assigned on a one-to-one basis to help new workers adjust to their jobs. This assignment is considered a compliment to the experienced employee.

Blanche Woods, secretary to J. W. Mills, was delighted when Mr. Mills asked her, "Blanche, will you help me out? Ben Falk, who is buddy to Martica Joyer, wants to give up on his assignment. Martica is a 'griper.' She takes a negative attitude toward other employees and toward work assignments. Her supervisor and she are almost at swords' points, and she is becoming a misfit among her colleagues. Yet she does the best work herself that we have had from a beginner in months. She *could* become a real asset and is definitely worth saving. Personally, I like her.

"Ordinarily this situation would be handled by her supervisor, but you know as well as I do how rigid and inflexible Mr. Cruz is. I remember that you told me that you are interested in psychology, so why not give this assignment a fling?"

Blanche decides to accept the challenge but needs help in developing a plan. What recommendations would you make to her?

Case 2-2 EQUIPMENT UTILIZATION

Ray Stamipolous has been secretary to Eileen Eisen, vice-president of marketing, for a number of years. He works on a one-to-one basis in what everybody, including Ms. Eisen, agrees is a pressure job. Ms. Eisen was, however, unenthusiastic about the word processing center that was recently installed on an experimental basis. She often told Ray that she liked to dictate to him rather than to a machine because she had a foreign background and he was so helpful to her with English. In fact, she credited him with "doctoring" her letters until they were exemplary.

When a notice came around stating that the services of the new center would be available to all departments, Ray decided to analyze his duties and plan how, in the face of Ms. Eisen's resistance, he could reorganize his work to utilize the new equipment now available to him.

What principles should guide Ray so far as his relations with his employer are concerned in his decisions? How can he satisfy her and still take advantage of the equipment?

Case 2-3 PURCHASING EQUIPMENT — RESPONSIBILITY WITHOUT AUTHORITY

Myra Lancaster was secretary to William Noble, the purchasing agent. Mr. Noble told her, "Myra, I am so busy with procurement of raw materials for the factory that I wish you would take over the responsibility for learning about new office equipment and supplies. If you find something you think we should have, just call my attention to it."

Myra read all of the office administration magazines, attended business shows, talked to sales representatives about office supplies and equipment, and informed herself in the field so that she became the company authority. She was justifiably proud of improvements made in office efficiency because of her choices.

Before she could buy anything, though, she had to get Mr. Noble's authorization. She felt that she should have been given authority along with responsibility for the purchase of office supplies and equipment if she stayed within the budget and improved operations.

Do you agree that Myra should have this authority? If so, what steps would you suggest that she follow?

Case 2-4 CAUGHT IN THE MIDDLE — EMPLOYER'S REQUEST FOR PREFERENTIAL TREATMENT

Angela Rodino, copywriter for an advertising agency, handed a 24-page market analysis to her secretary, Judy Savitsky, saying, "Take this down to Duplicating and tell them that this is a rush job. We have to have 10 copies, collated and bound by four o'clock tomorrow, even if they have to let some of their other work go until later."

Aware that her employer had a reputation for making everything a rush job, Judy approached Joe Santini, supervisor of duplicating, with the written job order in hand and said cautiously, "Listen, Joe, Ms. Rodino is really in a bind. She has to have 10 copies of this market analysis by four o'clock tomorrow, and she knows that she can depend on you to get her out of this crisis."

Joe was unimpressed. "You tell that boss of yours that she has got to learn that there are other people in this company that need duplicating. She just has to wait her turn. Look at that pile of work orders. Do you think that she has any right to ask to be put ahead of them? I've done my last rush job for Madam Rodino."

Judy considered her alternatives. Should she try again by revealing confidential information that a million-dollar contract was riding on that report? Should she accept Joe's refusal and, if so, what should she say to Ms. Rodino? What else might she suggest to get the report finished by the deadline?

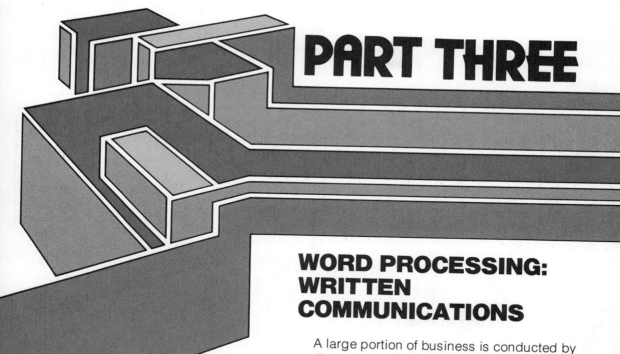

PART THREE

WORD PROCESSING: WRITTEN COMMUNICATIONS

A large portion of business is conducted by mail — not only the communications to and from the outside world but also the many interoffice memorandums that circulate inside the organization and make its operations possible. With the costs of communication increasing, every business document must pay its way. A communication must represent the writer so effectively that its purpose is accomplished and its expense justified.

The secretary contributes significantly to effective handling of the mail — from recording its receipt so that nothing is lost, to organizing it, assembling data required for answering, and finally processing the reply. In most cases the executive dictates the reply to be recorded either in shorthand or by machine. From then on until it is ready for signature, the secretary is responsible, even to the extent of correcting obvious errors and sometimes improving the quality of the dictation. And, with the growth in understanding of the organization's operations that comes with experience, the secretary composes some of the communications. The secretary is the *word specialist*.

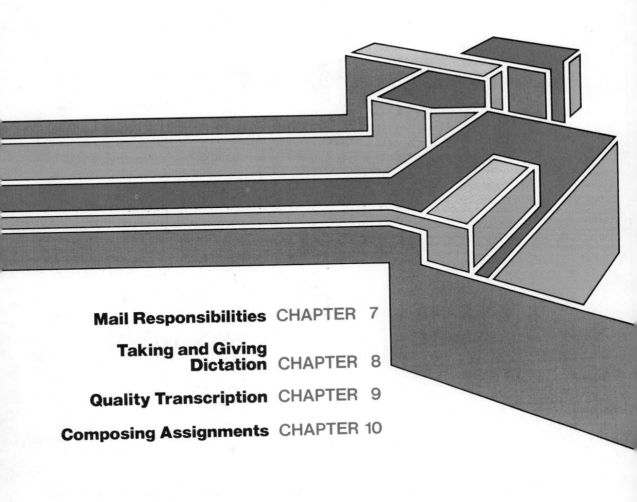

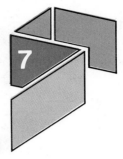

Mail Responsibilities

The secretary expedites the work of the employer. The preparation of the mail for efficient handling is one of the most visible proofs of secretarial competency as an expediter. The first and heaviest mail arrives from the mail room early in the morning, and other deliveries come throughout the rest of the day. Also, special-delivery or hand-delivered mail arrives at irregular intervals and demands immediate attention. Special methods of delivery signal the importance of a piece of mail and indicate that it is to receive priority. In addition, there are the myriad office memorandums that circulate within the organization. The secretary must decide which of these have precedence over mail from outside sources.

Preparing all of the mail for executive action is called *processing* the mail. The decision-making process involved in processing the mail recurs frequently during the day; it is not a once-a-day activity. This chapter indicates how the secretary can develop efficiency in fulfilling the mail-processing role.

MAIL-PROCESSING PERSONNEL

The first step in the processing of mail is opening the envelopes and sorting the contents into groups for expeditious handling. The personnel involved differ according to the way the mail is addressed and, of course, according to the size of the company or firm.

The Mail Room

The mail room personnel receive mail from the post office, from a company mail service, or from a private mail service. It is not unusual for an organization to develop a mail service among its branches and most frequent correspondents. This can speed up delivery by at least a day. The secretary should become familiar with such services and their schedules.

If a letter is addressed to the company and not to an individual in the company, the envelope is opened in the mail room. The mail room is prepared for quantity handling of mail and contains equipment more elaborate than that in the individual offices. The mail clerk follows established procedures for assigning the mail to appropriate departments for action. The clerk also makes a record of the receipt of the mail and the routing assigned to it. It is then usually delivered by messenger to the designated offices. The work of the mail room is becoming more automated. For instance, a mail delivery cart is available that operates without an attendant. It is controlled electronically and programmed as to route, schedule, and time at each stop.

The mail room personnel, too, accumulate outgoing mail, complete its final processing, and dispatch it.

The Secretary

If letters are addressed to specific employees or departments, the mail room delivers the envelopes unopened. The secretary then gives the unopened envelopes to the addressees, with the exception of the employer's mail. That mail is opened, sorted, and processed in other ways that will expedite its handling when it is presented to the employer for action.

In a small office, the secretary opens all mail that is not addressed to a specific employee, assigns it to the appropriate person for answering, and prepares the employer's mail for action.

PROCEDURES FOR PROCESSING MAIL

Steps to follow in opening, reading, and expediting the handling of incoming mail are discussed here. The processing of outgoing mail is described in later chapters.

Opening the Mail

You need special supplies for opening mail. Lay them out before you start to work, arranging them within convenient reach.

You need:	*You may also need:*
An envelope opener	A date or time stamp
A stapler, pins, or clips	A routing stamp or slips
Pencils	An action stamp or slips
The tickler	Cellophane tape for mending

First Sorting. The mail may be sorted three times if it is received in considerable volume. On the first sorting, pull out only the *important business and personal mail for immediate processing*. Lay aside all envelopes that look as if they might contain letters of importance to the executive. How, you ask, can the envelope tell you that the letter is important? Two clues can guide you in sorting: the *source* and the *kind of mail service used*.

1. The sender's name, address, or the postmark tells you the source or gives you a clue to it. You will learn to recognize those business and personal correspondents of high interest to the executive as you become familiar with your employer's business activities and personal associations.

2. A special-delivery letter or a certified letter signals "Important." An airmail package takes precedence over other mailed packages.

After completing the first sorting, stop and process the important mail according to the steps on pages 161–162. Keep in mind that including something unimportant is preferable to missing something important. Unless you are authorized to open personal mail, leave personal letters unopened (even though they are not marked *personal* or *confidential*) and submit them with the processed mail.

Second and Third Sortings. Lay out the mail by kind in a second and a third sorting. (Because of their bulkiness, put aside the publications; later on, open, scan, and perhaps stamp or initial them as your employer's copy.) First, sort the envelope mail into these three groups: business, personal, and advertising.

The bulk of each mail delivery will be *business mail* — that which relates to the purposes of the office. You will quickly learn that business mail has a pattern. Follow this pattern in sorting the group once more into like kinds — envelopes from branch offices, from the home office, from customers or clients, from traveling associates, from suppliers, and so on. Group the first-class window envelopes that usually contain invoices or statements. Put a large *X* on the back of any incorrectly addressed or odd-looking envelope to remind you to attach it to the letter for the executive's attention.

Personal mail also has a pattern. If there is enough volume, sort it again according to the executive's outside activities and financial interests. You may want to maintain special files relating to these activities and interests. (This type of file is discussed in Chapter 14.) Separate the personal financial mail into like kinds — such as the bills, the bank letters, investment-house letters, and stock-ownership letters.

Advertising mail comes in envelopes of all sizes, shapes, and colors — for attention value. You can easily spot it, although the advertisers try hard to fool you. The envelopes rarely, if ever, carry first-class postage. They almost always have open ends with sealed flaps. They have precanceled stamps or printed permit numbers and are not postmarked. Open these when you have time, perhaps after the other mail has been processed and handed to the executive. Organize the contents of advertising mail (it is always full of floating, loose pieces, it seems) and give them to the executive at your convenience sometime during the day. Do not destroy them. The executive likes to keep up on *direct mail* — as it is called in the advertising profession — to know what is being advertised and whether to return the enclosed postcards.

Opening the Envelopes. Keep the sorted groups intact for convenient handling of the letters later. For the easiest removal of contents, open the envelopes along the top edges. The efficient placement of envelopes and the movements involved differ with the kind of opener used. An efficient routine for a right-handed person using a scissors or a letter knife is described as follows:

1. Keep forearm working area free.

2. Place stack of envelopes to the left, flaps up, with top edges to the right.

3. Hold envelope with left hand; slip the knife under the flap and with one quick stroke open the edge or cut off a narrow strip along the flap edge with the scissors.

4. Lay the opened envelope down with the left hand, in the left-side area. Keep the cut edges to the right.

When using a lever-operated letter opener:

1. Stack the envelopes with the top edges parallel to the letter opener.

2. Insert one envelope, press the lever, and lay the envelope to the left side without changing the position of the envelope.

Hand-operated and electric openers are available for desk use. Mail rooms use electric openers that operate at high rates of speed, sometimes processing more than one hundred envelopes a minute.

Removing the Contents. To remove the contents, again keep the forearm working area free. Place the stack of opened envelopes to the left, open edges to the right, flap sides up. Pull out the contents with the right hand. With the left hand, hold the envelope up to the light, glance to see that everything has been removed, and lay it to the far left, keeping the same side up. Use both hands to unfold and flatten the letter and attach enclosures. As you open the letter, scan it to see if it contains the sender's address; if not, retrieve the envelope and attach it to the letter. Scan also to see if the letter mentions enclosures and whether those you found agree with the letter. If not, after checking inside the envelope again, underline the reference notation of the enclosure or the mention of the enclosure in the letter and write *No* nearby. Attach any marked envelope to its enclosed letter to be given to the executive.

This automatic mail opener, suitable for large companies with mail room operations, will quickly open mail of almost any size without presorting.

Pitney-Bowes, Inc.

Mend any torn material. Lay the unfolded letters *face down* in a stack to the right to keep them in the same order as the envelopes in case a letter and its envelope have to be rematched later.

It may be a rule in your office to staple the envelope to the back of each piece of mail received. If not, save all the envelopes for one day, in case you need to identify the sender, to determine the sender's address, to investigate the reasons for delayed receipt, to recheck for missing enclosures, to establish legality of time of mailing, and so on. Specifically, save the envelopes for situations in which:

1. An envelope is incorrectly addressed. In this case, the executive may want to include the correct address in the return letter for the future guidance of the correspondent or as an explanation of why the letter was not answered more promptly.

2. A letter was missent by the post office and had to be forwarded. This information is needed to explain the reason for a delayed answer to the missent letter.

3. A letter does not contain a return address.

4. The return address in the letter differs from that on the envelope. Sometimes an individual uses business, hotel, or club stationery and does not indicate a return address. However, the reply should not be sent to the address given on the letterhead, and so the return address on the envelope is needed.

5. The date of the letter differs too much from the date of its receipt. A comparison of the letter date with the postmark date will reveal whether the fault lies with the sender or with the postal service.

6. Neither a handwritten nor a typewritten signature appears in the letter. The name of the sender may appear as a part of the return address on the envelope.

7. A letter specifies an enclosure that was not attached to the letter nor found in the envelope.

8. A letter contains a bid, an offer, or an acceptance of a contract. The postmark date may be needed as legal evidence.

Registering, Dating, and Time Stamping. It is often desirable for the secretary to keep a *mail register* of important mail for follow-up or tracing purposes. The mail register is used to record special incoming mail (such as registered, certified, special-delivery, or insured mail), expected (separate-cover) mail, and mail that is circulated to the executive's associates. For expected bulk mail it may be necessary to give the mail clerk or receiving clerk a memorandum that a package is coming. Telegrams and cables are also logged in on the mail register.

Secretaries say that the mail register is "worth its weight in gold" as a protective record that verifies the receipt and disposition of mail. Only a few minutes are needed to record the entries since abbreviations are used freely. A ruled form similar to the one illustrated may be used. The blank space in the "SEP. COV. RECEIVED" column, for example, indicates to the secretary that the executive's banquet tickets have not yet arrived. As an aid in tracing lost mail, the secretary usually indicates on the face of the item the number assigned to that item in the mail register.

Another precaution in keeping track of incoming mail is to record the date and time of receipt on the face of each letter between the letterhead and the body. This can be done either with a date-and-time stamp or in longhand.

For several reasons it is important to know the date on which each piece of mail is received:

1. It furnishes a record of the date of receipt.

2. It furnishes an impetus to answer the mail promptly. (Each reply should be regarded as a builder of goodwill, but no reply that is unduly delayed — no matter how courteous or affable it may be — will promote good public relations.)

3. A letter may have arrived too late to take care of the matter to which it refers. The date of receipt authenticates that inability.

M A I L   R E G I S T E R

Name *Arlene Dylan*

Dates this page *3/14 –*

	RECEIVED Date	Time	FROM Name/Address	DATED	ADDRESSED TO Dept	Person	DESCRIPTION Kind of mail/enc/sep cov	SEP COV RECEIVED	REFERRED To	Date	WHERE FILED
1	3/14	9:15 a.m.	F. Gapinsky, New York	3/12	Adv.		Ad pamphlet – layout	—	Adv.	3/14	Adv.
2	3/18	9 a.m.	Steel Equipment Co, Chicago	3/11		MLA	Expected catalogs – file cabinets	3/21	Purch	3/22	Purch.
3	3/20	1 p.m.	G. H. Sims, New York	3/19		MLA	ACA Banquet tickets				
4	3/22	3 p.m.	L. Cox, Lima, Ohio	3/18	Adv.		Book – typefaces	4/10	Adv.	4/11	Adv.
5	3/23	2 p.m.	D. Schmidt, Chicago	3/22		MLA	Special delivery – rush order	—	Sales	3/23	
6	3/24	9 a.m.	I.R.S. – Local	3/23		K. Logan	Quarterly taxes – forms enclosed	—	KL	3/24	
7	3/26	2 p.m.	Jones, Inc. Local	3/26	Acctg		Registered Ch. # 345	—	Cashier	3/26	
8	3/28	9:20 a.m.	R. Fugazzi, Denver	3/26		O. Miller	Insured package	—	Sales	3/28	

4. The letter itself may be undated. The only clue to its date is the date of receipt. (You may find it hard to believe, but undated letters are frequently mailed — even letters typewritten by secretaries.)

Reading, Underlining, and Annotating

After opening the envelopes and dating the contents, you begin the interesting, secretarial part of handling mail. It involves three steps:

1. Read each letter through once, scanning for important facts. Make necessary calendar notations.

2. Underline those words and phrases that tell the story as you read the letter again. Be thrifty with underlining. Call attention only to the necessary words and phrases.

3. Annotate (write in the margin) any necessary or helpful notes to the executive.

Marginal annotations come under two headings:

1. Suggested disposition of routine letters, such as "File," "Ack." (for acknowledge), and "Give to Sales Department." (The secretary anticipates the executive's decision and makes a suggestion for handling, which may or may not be accepted.)

2. Special notes, such as "See our last letter attached" (The secretary will have removed this letter from the files and attached it to the annotated letter); or "When Mr. B. was here, you agreed to give this talk." (Such notes are usually reminders, although some may be of a helpful identifying type — that is, a brief "who's who" of the writer or the company.)

You may be asking, "Shall I, as a new secretary, read, underline, and especially annotate, if my predecessor did not?" The answer is *Yes*. Act as if it is a part of your understanding of a real secretary's service. If the employer questions the routine, abide by the decision. The employer is more likely to praise the practice, however, than to question it; if it is intelligently done, it saves time.

Notations for Filing. Save processing time by adding, at this point, the filing notations on any letters that require no replies. For example, if Clyde Crawford's reply to your letter can be filed without further correspondence, the filing notation should be put on the letter during processing. (Methods of determining where to file letters and when and how to make filing notations are presented in a later chapter.)

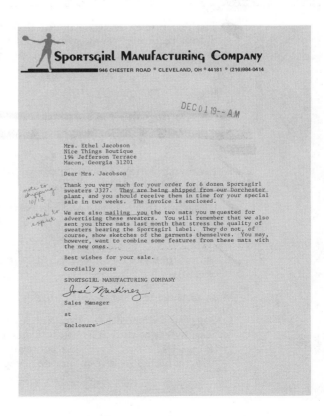

The annotations and the date-time stamp indicate that this letter is ready for presentation to the executive.

Limiting Annotations. Since original letters are sometimes copied on machines and sent outside the organization, an executive may request you to avoid all writing on the face of letters and ask you to add annotations only on the back of them. Some copying processes will not, however, reproduce ink or colored pencil. If you are using a copying process that has this limitation, you need not worry about making notations on the face of the letter. On the other hand, many executives want notations copied to achieve compact yet comprehensive records.

Expediting the Executive's Handling of Mail

You can expedite the executive's handling of specific letters by anticipating and preparing for certain procedural steps that will be taken. You can be of help by adopting the suggestions described below.

Letter Requiring Background Information. In many cases a letter cannot be answered unless additional information is at hand. For instance, suppose you are a secretary to a sales manager who receives a letter canceling an order because the customer is tired of waiting for delivery. You would look up and attach all the pertinent information about the order, its date of receipt, its present whereabouts, and the cause for delay. You may have to judge how much background information you should supply. If the executive will ask you for it anyway, anticipate this request. If it only *might* prove useful, weigh the amount of time required to get it, the amount of time you have to give to it, and the executive's probable attitude concerning the information.

Letter Referring to Previous Correspondence. When there is need to refer to previous correspondence, get it and attach it to the current letter. Write "See attached" in the margin. If the previous correspondence involves a bound file, put the letter on the file, and insert paper markers in the file at the pertinent points.

Letter Requiring Follow-Up. Often a letter may refer to mail that will follow or may contain a request that requires additional action besides the routine answer. Also, sometimes a letter must be answered within a certain time, or other time factors may be involved. In such cases, follow these steps:

1. Select the earliest date when the action should be accomplished.

2. Write that date on the face of the letter with a key (like *T* for *Tickler*, or *FD* for *Follow-Up Date*) so that the executive and you know that a reminder has been recorded.

3. Make a tickler entry under the selected date.

4. If material is expected in a separate mailing, write a note on your calendar page, or send a memo to the mail department describing the mail expected. Indicate such notifications in the margin of the letter. (See also Mail Register, pages 160–161.)

Letter to Be Referred to an Associate. Often an executive passes along to an associate a piece of mail for either action or information. For instance, perhaps the communication is to be acknowledged, answered, or followed up by the associate. It may require the recipient to prepare a report, or it may provide information but not call for immediate action. In preparing this kind of mail for an employer whose action you can anticipate, you might fill out a routing slip or an action slip similar to those illustrated on p. 165, lightly penciling in both the individual's name and the action needed. Give the letter and the slip to your employer. If the suggested action is approved, you may attach the slip to the letter. If there is any possibility that you may need later follow-up, photocopy the letter and indicate on the original the names of the persons to whom you sent the copies, the action to be taken, and your own follow-up date, if any. Photocopying is superseding the routing slip because it speeds up dissemination of information. If you send an original copy out of the office, KEEP A RECORD OF WHERE YOU SENT IT.

Letter Misaddressed to the Executive. When a letter addressed to the executive actually should have been sent to another person, annotate the correct name in the top margin and put the letter with the employer's other mail. Although you will probably be asked to forward the letter to someone else, you should give the addressee the right to see the mail first.

Personal Letter Opened Inadvertently. If you should inadvertently open a personal letter addressed to your employer, stop reading the letter as soon as you discover that it is personal and not business. Refold the letter, replace it in its envelope, and attach a short note bearing your initials to the face of the envelope, "Sorry, opened by mistake."

Enclosed Bill or Invoice. When an envelope contains a bill or an invoice, if possible compare the prices and the terms with those quoted. Always check the mathematical accuracy of the extensions and the total. Then write "OK" on the face of the bill or the invoice if it is correct, or note any discrepancy. Any arithmetic computations in a letter should be checked for accuracy as well.

DATE _____

TO _____

Refer to the attached material and

☐ Please note.
☐ Please note and file.
☐ Please note and return to me.
☐ Please mail to _____
☐ Please note and talk with me
    this a.m. _____ ; p.m. _____

☐ Please answer, sending me a copy.
☐ Please write a reply for my signature.
☐ Please handle.
☐ Please have _____ photocopies made
    for_____
☐ Please sign.
☐ Please let me have your comments.
☐ Please RUSH — immediate action desired.
☐ Please make follow-up for_____

_____

REMARKS:

Signed _____

Please read the attached material and pass
it on to the persons indicated.

Refer to:	Date Received	Date Passed On
Mr. Adams	_____	_____
Mr. Berger	_____	_____
Miss Bessler	_____	_____
Mr. Caldwell	_____	_____
Ms. Carmen	_____	_____
Mr. Davis	_____	_____
Mr. Gephardt	_____	_____
Mrs. Goodman	_____	_____
Ms. Hessler	_____	_____
Mr. Holmes	_____	_____
Miss Kerr	_____	_____
Mr. Perot	_____	_____
Mr. Robinson	_____	_____
Mrs. Rodriguez	_____	_____
Ms. Smith	_____	_____
Ms. Swillinger	_____	_____
Mr. VanDerbeck	_____	_____
Ms. Zimmerman	_____	_____

Return to:

A secretary devised this check-off slip to save the executive's time in distributing information to and requesting action from assistants. There is room for a signature or initials at the bottom because an initialed or signed request is more personal than a printed name.

One of these duplicated slips is attached to mail to be distributed to others. The secretary or executive checks in pencil or ink the names of those who should receive it. Since routing slips must conform with changes in personnel, they are often office-duplicated rather than printed.

Enclosed Check or Money Order. Compare the amount of a check or money order enclosed in an envelope with the amount mentioned in the letter of transmittal or on the copy of the statement or invoice. If it has been mailed alone, check it with the file copy of the bill to verify the correctness of the amount. Handle the remittance according to the procedure of your office. If it is to be turned over immediately to a cashier, indicate the amount in the margin of the letter or invoice, or prepare a memorandum for the executive, reporting the amount and the date of receipt.

Publications Received. Identify each publication permanently with the executive's name or initials. Scan the table of contents and indicate any item that might be of interest to the executive. If an article is of special interest, underline the salient points and paper clip all the preceding pages together so that the publication opens to the indicated material; or attach a note to the front cover calling attention to the article.

Final Arrangement of the Mail

Arrangement of processed and personal mail for presentation to the executive depends on preferences, daily schedule, or even mood. In general, though, the mail is separated into these four groups:

1. For immediate action — Possible order of precedence: telegrams, unopened personal letters, pleasant letters, letters containing remittances, important letters, unpleasant letters

2. To be answered — Routine letters having no great priority

3. To be answered by secretary — Letters that are usually turned over to you for handling (Don't preempt the executive's right to make this decision.)

4. To read for information — Advertisements, publications, routine announcements

One successful secretary recommends the use of a four-pocket organizer for submitting mail, with each pocket clearly identified as to contents. This organizer keeps the mail confidential, even from those who seem able to read letters upside down. In any case, the mail should be covered if the executive is not at the desk when you present the processed mail.

On a day when the employer has only limited time for the mail, you may wish to submit items from Category 1 only. On a day when working with the mail seems to have high priority, send in the first half as soon as it is ready, and take in the rest when it has been processed. If you know that a specific piece of mail is expected, take it in as soon as it arrives.

HANDLING MAIL DURING THE EMPLOYER'S ABSENCE

Executives spend a great deal of their time in travel. When they are away from the office, crises occur in handling the mail. Simply forwarding personal mail or sending photocopies of incoming business mail will not always meet the situations that arise. The secretary is in a decision-making role and *must* evaluate each piece of mail before giving it routine treatment.

For instance, an employer may be out of the country when the quarterly income tax falls due. If the necessary state and local forms that must accompany the income tax payments have not arrived before the executive departs, the secretary may be told to watch for these forms. When the forms arrive, the required checks, which had to be prepared in advance, would be enclosed with the forms so that the deadlines could be met. If the trip is an extended one, the secretary may be asked to watch for the rent, telephone, or utility bills and pay them with checks on which only the amounts are to be filled in. These bills should not be forwarded to a foreign country. Before the executive leaves, the secretary should get explicit instructions for such contingencies.

The same caution holds for business mail. The employer should not receive a photocopy, forwarded and reforwarded, of a letter about a major reorganization that may have personal ramifications. At times information should be transmitted by the most rapid service. The secretary must assume full responsibility for making the right decisions about handling mail in the employer's absence.

The Executive's Business Mail

In handling business mail, you will be expected to:

1. Communicate with the executive immediately when mail of vital importance arrives that no one else can handle. Executives on business trips may telephone their secretaries regularly, but occasions arise when the secretary must initiate a call.

2. Set aside those letters that can await the executive's return, but acknowledge their receipt if the answer may be delayed for several days.

3. Give to associates or superiors those letters which must have immediate executive action. Make a photocopy or typewritten copy of each one for the executive's information, noting to whom you gave it and stating the action taken.

4. Send copies (not originals) of those letters that contain information of interest or importance or that require the executive's personal attention, if they will arrive in time.

5. Answer or take personal action on letters which fall within your province.

6. Prepare a digest of mail and either send it to the executive or keep it in the office, depending on circumstances. (See illustration on page 168.)

7. Collect in a mail-received folder: (a) all the original letters awaiting attention; (b) copies of all letters given to others for action; (c) both the originals and answers of letters you have answered. Before giving the file to the executive, sort the letters into logical sequence, with the most important on top.

The Executive's Personal Mail

Before the executive leaves, ask what, if any, personal mail you are to open and attend to. Do not, however, open personal mail unless expressly asked to do so. Hold it in the mail-received folder. If

```
             DIGEST OF INCOMING MAIL

  Date    From              Description
  8/16    Clark Oil         Notice of Board of Directors
                            meeting 9/4 in Chicago at 9.

  8/16    Syracuse U.       Request to give telephone
                            interview to School of Business
                            students on 11/3 at 10.  Conflicts
                            with staff meeting.

  8/16    J. K. Smith       Wants conference on proposed budget
                            cuts.

  8/16    Forbes Mag.       Wants more info. on overseas operations.
                            Referred to MJB.

  8/16    Mary Mason        Requests conference on patent application
                            for Project 117.

  8/16    Helen Ball        Wants you to join husband and her for
                            dinner when in Chicago on 9/4.
```

forwarded mail will have time to arrive before the executive leaves a destination, forward it. It is usually better to forward a letter in a fresh envelope with your business return address rather than to add the forwarding address on the original envelope. Keep in the mail-received folder a running record of all letters mailed to the executive at an out-of-town address. Identify each forwarded letter by its postmark date and sender's name or by the postmark city if that is all that is shown.

The Executive's Advertising Mail

Hold the advertising mail in a separate large envelope. Sort it and give it to the executive when the press of accumulated work has lessened after the trip is over.

WORKING FOR MORE THAN ONE EXECUTIVE

When the secretary is working for more than one executive, the routine is basically the same. Probably a higher level of decision making is required because several employers' preferences and spheres of responsibility must be kept in mind and materials must be kept flowing to each one.

The secretary will, of course, keep the mail in separate piles for each executive. If one of them is obviously waiting, that principal gets the first delivery of processed mail.

The value of the mail register increases when the secretary is responsible for mail to several addressees, for it supplies proof of receipt for many different items of mail.

When one executive is more demanding than the others, the secretary's tact is called into play. Because several principals are sharing, many situations arise that require the display of impartiality.

SUGGESTED READINGS

Cook, Fred S., and Lenore Forti. *Professional Secretary's Handbook*. Chicago: Dartnell Corporation, 1971, pp. 41–42.

Dallas, Richard J., and James M. Thompson. *Clerical and Secretarial Systems for the Office*. Englewood Cliffs: Prentice-Hall, 1975, pp. 261–265.

Keeling, B. Lewis, Norman F. Kallaus, and John J. W. Neuner. *Administrative Office Management*, 7th ed. Cincinnati: South-Western Publishing Co., 1978, Chapter 7, "Written Communications in the Office" (correspondence cost reduction; handling incoming mail in large offices from the management standpoint).

Place, Irene, Charles Hicks, and Edward Byers. *College Secretarial Procedures*, 4th ed. New York: McGraw-Hill Book Co., 1972, pp. 76–91.

Winter, Elmer L. *The Successful Manager-Secretary Team*. West Nyack: Parker Publishing Co., 1974, Chapter 5, "How To Handle Your Mail," pp. 45–52.

QUESTIONS FOR DISCUSSION

1. If you were secretary to an executive who did not utilize your services in processing the mail as suggested in this chapter, what would you do?

2. In processing a morning's mail for the president of a corporation, decide what you would do if —
   (a) A letter refers to a letter the executive wrote nine months ago
   (b) A customer's letter complains about the actions of a salesperson who was discourteous
   (c) A letter asks that certain material be prepared and sent before the first of the month
   (d) A letter requests a photograph, the responsibility for which is in the public relations department
   (e) A letter contains information of importance to three department heads
   (f) An envelope obviously contains a bill from an engraver who recently supplied personal stationery for the executive
   (g) A letter requests duplicated materials available through your office
   (h) A letter refers to a package being sent as a separate mailing

3. The executive, Miss Alva Miller, is away on a two-week trip. Decide what you would do with a letter that —
   (a) Asks her to give a talk five months from now
   (b) Requires immediate management action
   (c) Is from her mother, whose handwriting you recognize

4. What steps could you take to obtain the address of a person who inquired about information and prices on a product when the

request was typed on a plain sheet of paper with no address given on either the letter or the envelope?

5. If the executive is out of town but expects to return tomorrow, what action would you take to record receipt of the following communications? How would you handle each situation?
   (a) A special-delivery letter requesting an estimate on a large quantity of coated paper
   (b) A telegram from one of your sales representatives sending in a rush order for a customer
   (c) A letter about a shipment of card stock complaining that one fourth of the blue is two shades lighter than the rest (Samples are enclosed as proof.)
   (d) A letter asking the length of time a Mr. Edwards was employed as a sales representative by your company, inquiring about his reason for leaving, and requesting a reference

6. Fill in the correct spelling in the following sentences. Then refer to the Reference Guide to verify or correct your answers.
   (a) Have no _____ about our determination to succeed. (illusions, allusions)
   (b) Honesty should _____ in all your relationships. (predominate, predominant)
   (c) The manager is an _____ authority on word processing. (eminent, imminent)

PROBLEMS

1. Mari Rodriguez is a secretary with responsibility for processing incoming mail. Type your comments concerning the steps she follows in performing this task.
   (a) The secretary arranges all of the mail in a stack and proceeds to open it and to remove the contents of each envelope in regular sequence.
   (b) She flattens out the letters and enclosures and discards the envelopes as useless items.
   (c) After all the letters have been removed, she checks the letters for stated enclosures. Pertinent enclosures she separates from the letters and sends to those concerned (such as orders for the order department). She discards the advertising.
   (d) She then time stamps, reads, underlines, and annotates all letters.
   She prepares a routing slip for letters requiring the attention of more than one person, and she fastens each routing slip to the proper letter with a paper clip.
   (e) She then places the letters, in the order in which they were processed, on the executive's desk face up for immediate attention.

2. Arrange the model desk in your secretarial practice room for opening and sorting incoming mail. Prepare a list of supplies needed. Have the instructor check the list and your demonstration of letter-opening and sorting techniques.

3. What action would you take to prepare the following four letters for your employer, Ms. Mary Jane Schmidt? Where would you locate the necessary information? Exactly what underlines and annotations would you make in each of the four cases?

W. W. KIM Engineer

Box 183,
Golden, Colorado
80401

March 15, 19--

M. J. Schmidt, Attorney
Anderson, Sakyo, and Harmon
Bank of Utah Plaza
2651 Washington Boulevard
Ogden, Utah 84401

Dear Mr. Schmidt

At the suggestion of Alger Holmes, I am
writing to inquire whether you would be willing to represent my interests in the uranium
mine near Provo that has now been closed and
is being liquidated. I understand that a
hearing is scheduled for May 4 and 5.

If you agree to accept this case, I will plan
to come to Ogden on March 28 and would like
an appointment with you then. What information would you like me to bring to such an
appointment?

I will telephone you at ten o'clock on March
18 to discuss this letter.

Yours truly

W. W. Kim

W. W. Kim

---

711 State Street
Madison, WI 54303
March 16, 19--

Ms. Mary Jane Schmidt
Anderson, Sakyo, and Harmon, Attorneys
Bank of Utah Plaza
2651 Washington Boulevard
Ogden, Utah, 84401

Dear Ms. Schmidt

When you spoke at the state meeting of the Business and
Professional Women's Clubs last Saturday, you referred
to a recently published book on management jobs for
women. All I can remember is that the word breakthrough
is in the title and that two women wrote it.

Several of my friends and I would like to purchase this
book to use in a discussion group we are forming. Will
you please give me the correct title, the names of the
authors, and the publisher? Do you think that it would
be available in local bookstores, or would we have to
order it from the publisher?

I want to thank you again for your very informative talk.
Everybody enjoyed it.

Cordially yours

Regina Gallatin

Regina Gallatin

---

340 Ocean Drive
Key Biscayne, FL 33149
March 15, 19--

Ms. Mary Jane Schmidt
Anderson, Sakyo, and Harmon, Attorneys
Bank of Utah Plaza
2651 Washington Boulevard
Ogden, UT 84401

My dear Ms. Schmidt

We want to invite you to speak at the Dade
County chapter of the League of Women Voters
in Miami on Friday, May 5.

Having a woman lawyer of your prominence
would be very inspirational to our young
career-minded members, some of whom are
studying law. At the same time our older
members would appreciate hearing your political opinions.

The choice of a topic is left to you, for we
know that you understand our objectives.
Will you please indicate the fee you would
expect in addition to travel expenses. Also
please tell us by March 30 whether it will
be possible for you to accept our invitation.

We look forward to hearing from you promptly.

Yours cordially

Theodora Menotti

Theodora Menotti
Chairperson of the
Program Committee

Howard Enterprises

940 OAK BOULEVARD OGDEN, UT 84401

Ms. Mary Jane Schmidt
Anderson, Sakyo, and Harmon, Attorneys
Bank of Utah Plaza
2651 Washington Boulevard
Ogden, UT 84401

Dear Ms. Schmidt

Will you please start collection proceedings against
Jerry Youngman for $354.82. This amount represents
two invoices, September 14 for $102.96 and October 8
for $231.86, copies of which are enclosed.

Mr. Youngman's last known address was 436 Maple Street,
Ogden, but we have received no answers to our telephone
calls to that address. Our letters, however, have
been delivered.

Thank you for your very efficient handling of the
overdue account of the Sports Shop. We received full
payment of this account, which we did not expect to
collect.

Yours truly

HOWARD ENTERPRISES

K. H. Howard

K. H. Howard, Credit Department

dd

enc. 2

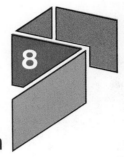

Taking and Giving Dictation

If an organization is structured along functional lines, the processing of written communications is assigned to specialized correspondence secretaries, and all other secretarial responsibilities are performed by administrative secretaries. Although the word processing center is gaining rapid acceptance, only a small percentage of all organizations have converted to automated word processing. It is highly likely, then, that the secretarial student will become a multifunctional secretary who transcribes from shorthand notes or from voice-writing equipment. Proof for this statement can be found in a 1975 survey of the membership of the National Secretaries Association (International) which indicated that three fourths of the secretaries who responded use symbol shorthand regularly as the medium of dictation.

This chapter discusses first the techniques required for taking symbol shorthand. Then it considers the responsibilities of the administrative secretary when dictation is given to voice-writing dictation machines, which usually record in locations remote from the dictator. Since secretaries, as well as executives, will probably dictate to these machines, instructions are included for giving easily transcribed dictation.

PREDICTATION RESPONSIBILITIES

Several of the secretary's predictation responsibilities apply regardless of how the dictation is given. Among them are preparing a list of items for today's attention and replenishing the executive's supplies.

Attention-Today Items

The first preliminary to dictation is the collection of *attention-today* items that the secretary prepares for the executive early each morning.

Some of the items will require dictation, while others may consume part of the executive's available dictation time. Overdue letters, reports, and shipments, or letters and reports that must meet

The secretary prepares a folder containing any carry-over correspondence and attaches to the edge of the folder a list of:
1. Any carry-over items in the folder
2. Items for the day from the office desk calendar and from the tickler file.

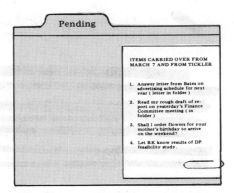

deadlines — all will require dictating attention. The day's appointments, conferences, and meetings will also affect the time available for dictation.

Type in brief form, in duplicate, the attention-today items, retaining a copy from which to take unfinished carry-over items each day. Clip the note (or separate notes for each item) to the edge of a portfolio or file folder. When an item has been attended to, the dictator can either tick it off the list or discard its note. Take the collection of items to the dictator's desk as early in the day as possible — definitely before dictation begins.

The Executive's Dictation Supplies

Another predictation responsibility is the daily checking and replenishing of the executive's supplies to see that these items are provided in sufficient quantity:

Sharpened pencils — An executive often dictates with pencil in hand, jotting down self-reminders on the letter being answered or entering items on the calendar as certain dates are decided on.

A scratch pad — For auxiliary notes, general outlines, or reminders.

A filled stapler, paper clips, pins

If the dictation will be given to a voice-writing machine, also include the following:

A supply of disks, belts, cassettes, or tapes, as appropriate

An empty file folder or portfolio in which the dictator can insert items related to the dictation

A wax pencil with which to date and identify the dictated units

A supply of printed forms for listing the material dictated on a unit, for special instructions regarding transcription, or for indicating any changes to be made

A supply of the special envelopes required for mailing a completed item (This item applies when the executive will be dictating while out of town.)

If the executive is dictating directly to the word processing center, always see that a supply of the usual pencils, paper, clips, and staplers is available at the desk. Also, provide a number of empty folders for the material related to the dictation. These folders of material do not go to the center. Retain them in your files for reference by you and the executive. Finally, provide the appropriate printed forms for listing special instructions to the center.

The Secretary's Dictation Supplies

If you take shorthand dictation, keep your supplies ready and waiting for instant availability. To avoid unnecessary clutter at the executive's desk, take adequate — but not excess — supplies.

A notebook — If you have a choice, use a notebook that has:
   a. Green pages ruled in green (easiest on the eyes, especially for transcription)
   b. Spiral binding so that the pages lie flat
   c. Stiff covers so that the book will stand alone for transcription. Take in only one book unless you are near the end of the current one.

A filled pen — Notes written in ink are easier on your eyes at transcription time. Violet ink is reputed to dry quickly and to be the easiest to read under fluorescent lights. A fine-point pen — not a ball point — is best. (An administrative secretary can insist on a high-quality pen.) The objections to using a pen are its running out of ink at crucial moments and the messiness of filling it.

Pointed pencils — Choose your favorite kind for size and shape, and for softness or hardness. Some secretaries prefer automatic, thin-lead pencils.

A colored pencil — The secretary most often uses red or blue.

Possibly an empty folder or portfolio with pockets on each side — Some secretaries clip notes to the portfolio as reminders to discuss the contents with the executive. If the executive wishes to put each answered letter in a file folder or portfolio, present it at each dictation session.

Answering the Call to Dictation

If the executive tries to dictate at approximately the same time each day, stay at your desk awaiting this call. Whenever you leave your desk, tell a co-worker or roll into your typewriter a note of your errand and the expected time of your return so that you can be located if necessary.

Before leaving your desk to take dictation — or for any extended time for that matter — cover, put away, or lock up all confidential papers and those of more than general interest. Ask someone nearby to take care of your telephone calls and visitors.

You may resent being called to dictation when you are engrossed in other work; but when the call comes, do try not to act annoyed at being interrupted. Go to the executive's desk with an attitude of willingness and helpfulness.

PERSON-TO-PERSON DICTATION

The new secretary may hesitate to ask questions about vocabulary or to make a tactful suggestion, even if it would possibly improve the transcript.

Yet for best results, dictation must be a cooperative effort. The secretary complements the dictator by catching omissions, errors, and ambiguities, and by either correcting them or pointing them out in a helpful way. Each person in the dictation situation has a role to play. The dictator's is the major, decisive role; the secretary's is a supporting but very important one.

At the Executive's Desk

During the actual dictation period, the secretary should adopt certain accepted practices. Seemingly unimportant details that often affect the success of the session are the secretary's location and attitude.

In the give-and-take of dictation, the executive and the secretary work together at very close range. Your dictation chair should be placed conveniently for the executive; but if you have a choice, sit where you have a generous-sized writing area. A dictator who paces the floor as thoughts are being organized should not be fenced in.

As a thoughtful, considerate secretary, you need to be as unobtrusive as possible during the dictation. Only then can the dictator be most productive while concentrating on the content and searching for the most effective phrasing. Self-effacement requires you to take the dictation without interrupting, to manage your supplies and papers with few motions, to refrain from unnecessary movements, and to avoid any indication of a critical reaction to the dictation.

Enlarging Your Dictation Vocabulary

A secretary has to experience only once the embarrassment of using *iniquity* for *integrity*, *impetuous* for *impervious*, or *ambitious* for *ambiguous* to learn the meaning, spelling, and pronunciation of such pairs of words that sound somewhat alike in dictation and look somewhat alike in shorthand.

To learn the executive's vocabulary quickly, read file copies of recent letters and appropriate technical and trade publications. From them make a list of words new to you. Alongside each one write its shorthand equivalent. Learn the meanings of the words, their spellings, and their pronunciations. In other words, compile your own glossary.

The several secretarial handbooks in the special fields of law, accounting, medicine, real estate, and so on, have word lists which can hasten the enlarging of those vocabularies.

Types of Dictation

In addition to business communications, the secretary's dictation probably includes instructions, reminders, requests, and mail to answer. The dictation may include first a letter, then an interoffice communication, then a telegram, then a request to go to the bank to get a check cashed, then another letter, then instructions on a tabulation of sales costs, then a request to copy certain paragraphs from a magazine article, and then a memorandum to arrange an appointment for the employer with the mayor. One of the annoying faults of an inexperienced secretary is reluctance to take notes of anything except transcription items. Instead of recording the instructions in black and white, the secretary relies on memory to carry them out — and sooner or later gets into trouble.

Dictation falls into the two broad categories of communications and instructions.

Communications. The bulk of dictation is in the category of communications. It includes all the dictation to be transcribed — letters, memos, telegrams, outlines, drafts, and so on.

Instructions. During the dictation period, numerous instructions are given to a secretary. *Take down all of these in your notebook:*

Directions for Transcribing. Often at the end of an item the dictator gives a direction for transcribing the communication; however, you should place it at the beginning if it:

Pinpoints the item for rush handling
Affects the kind of stationery to be used

Indicates the number of copies to be typed

Refers you to another person before transcribing the item

Use short abbreviations of your own devising and print them in oversized capitals, such as *RUF* for a rough-draft request, *RU* for a letter that requires immediate handling, and *5CCs* to indicate that six copies must be typed. For fast finding at transcribing time, turn back corners of pages that contain rush items or mark them with paper clips.

Directions for Composing. The executive often delegates to the secretary the composing of a letter. It may be a letter answering one at hand or a letter to be originated at the secretary's desk. For the former you are usually handed the letter and told, "Respond thus and so. . . ." Take such directions in shorthand verbatim, either in the notebook or on the letter itself. For an originating letter, take down the directions verbatim in the notebook. It is imperative to have complete, exact directions for each letter or memo to be composed in order to cover the points that the executive requested.

Specific Work Instructions. Take in shorthand in your notebook any specific instructions, such as to cancel one of the executive's appointments, to plan an itinerary, or to write and cash a check. Conspicuously key such instructions for easy finding. One secretary draws a rough box around each work instruction; another writes each one in the right column, which is left blank for instructions and insertions.

General Work Instructions. Take in shorthand in the notebook all instructions or explanations of office routines and executive preferences concerning procedure. Transcribe them when there is time and insert them in your desk manual for reference use.

Good Dictation Practices

Each of the dictation practices recommended below is a *good* one because it promotes efficiency. See how some of them are followed in the illustrated notes on page 181.

1. Write the beginning date of use on the notebook cover — the month, the day, and the year. When the notebook is filled, add the final date and keep the notebook for six months.

2. Reserve one place in or on your desk for the notebook. For convenience, keep an extra notebook and pencils in the employer's office, too.

3. Keep a rubber band around transcribed pages to help you find the first blank page on which to write.

4. Keep a filled pen, sharpened pencils, and one colored pencil under the rubber band around the notebook ready for instant use. While transcribing, keep these items together *in one specific place* where they can be quickly reached when you are called for dictation.

5. Keep a few paper clips around the edges of the notebook cover for possible use during the dictation session.

6. When the executive receives a personal telephone call during dictation, leave the office quietly; stay nearby so that you can return as soon as the call is finished. When a visitor comes in who will undoubtedly stay for a while, take your materials to your desk and start transcribing. When dictation is resumed, read the last several sentences in your notes without being asked, to help the dictator regain the thought.

7. During interruptions, write transcribing instructions in colored pencil and circle implied instructions, such as *attached* or *enclosed*. Use pauses and interruptions to read your notes, improve outlines, and insert punctuation.

8. Date each day's dictation on the first page with the month and day *in the lower right corner in red pencil*. Dictation notes are often the only source of valid reference. If the dictation load is heavy, add a.m. or p.m. to the bottom-of-page notation.

9. If you take dictation from more than one executive, you may choose to add the dictator's initials to each date or use a different notebook for each dictator.

10. Leave several lines between items of dictation or leave the right column blank to provide room for insertions, changes, and instructions. If the executive makes frequent or lengthy changes and insertions, leave six or eight lines or the full right column. If changes and insertions are rare, leave only three or four lines.

11. Should there be no lines available in which to write a transcribing instruction, print it in oversized capitals in abbreviated form diagonally across the beginning of the notes.

12. If there is the slightest possibility of inability to transcribe proper names, write them out during dictation.

13. Write uncertain words and unfamiliar terms in longhand if necessary to insure correct transcription.

14. To remind yourself to clear up an error, a question, an omission, an ambiguity, a redundancy, or the repeated use of words that occurred during dictation, put down some conspicuous signal such as a very large X.

15. Indicate the end of each item of dictation, *be it a communication or an instruction*, in some conspicuous way, such as with a quick

Editor Arthur Brisbane used to dictate his editorials. He spelled out everything, leaving nothing to his secretary's judgment. He even indicated punctuation by saying "Period" at the end of a sentence, "Quotation mark," etc.
It was not an easy habit to shake. Once, at the University of Chicago, Brisbane delivered an address to the faculty. After some minutes, he could see that his listeners appeared puzzled. Later, he asked one of the professors if something had been wrong with his speech. "No, it was fine," the other assured him, "except that you used too many commas."
Reader's Digest
September, 1976

swing line across the column or with a cross. You need a visual aid to assure that you are transcribing the item completely or carrying out the instruction.

16. Put each letter that the dictator hands you face down on top of the last one to keep the letters in the same order as the dictation.

17. If the executive assigns a number to each letter being answered (so that it is not necessary to dictate the name and address of the recipient each time), write only the number in the notebook. At transcription time, pair your numbered notes with the same-numbered letter; and write the name of the addressee in your notebook *above the numbered item* for later identification if necessary.

18. Tape a small calendar on the back cover of your notebook for quick reference during dictation.

Making Changes

You will have to recognize changes of thought during dictation. An executive often starts to dictate a sentence and, after a pause, begins again. Watch carefully to determine whether it is a new thought or a rephrasing of a previous one. An executive who habitually rephrases can be a problem, but through some sixth sense the beginning secretary learns to recognize which phrases are bona fide. When making a change, some dictators say, "Cross that out," and then begin to rephrase without mentioning what to cross out. They expect the secretary to know, and almost always their confidence is justified. When a long change is made far back in the notes, there is seldom enough time to go back, locate the notes to be deleted, and cross them out; nor is there likely to be enough room to write in the change. In such a case, treat the change as an insertion, taking down verbatim both the change and the instructions as to what is to be crossed out. Then go back and make the deletions later. *Do not rely on your memory to handle changes*.

The point has been made that you should be unobtrusive at dictation time. There are, however, at least three situations when interruptions may be helpful or even necessary.

1. When the executive is so far ahead of you that the thread of dictation is being lost, you must interrupt! Look up inquiringly and repeat the last words that have been taken down. The dictator much prefers that you get complete notes, interrupting if necessary, rather than leave the dictation session with words and phrases missing or incorrect.

2. When the executive repeats a conspicuous multisyllabic word or root word, mention the repetition — if you find that your help is

KEY TO THE PAGE OF DICTATION ➜

(1) A transcribing instruction is inserted as soon as possible in shorthand, in longhand abbreviations, or in king-sized capitals. Later, it is circled or underlined with a colored pencil for attention value.

(2) The swing line across the column indicates the end of an item.

(3) All instructions for composition are written in full so that they can be followed carefully.

(4) The personally devised abbreviation HW is used for Honeywell.

(5) This instruction signals that a tickler notation must be made.

(6) A transcribing instruction to make two carbon copies is inserted at the beginning of the item and later circled in color.

(7) The circled X indicates a question: Should the regional sales manager also get a copy?

(8) The corner is turned back to help locate quickly the page containing the rush item.

(9) The right column is left available for work instructions and insertions.

(10) A work instruction is always identified by a rough box.

(11) The initials of the executive, JR, are used instead of his whole name.

(12) The abbreviation *Ins C—3b* identifies the notes as Insert C to be used three pages back.

(13) Lines are drawn through notes to be deleted.

(14) *Hospitalization* was written in longhand because there was a mental block on the shorthand form. Rather than leave it out or waste time struggling to write it in shorthand, it was written in longhand.

(15) Slash lines are used to segregate an insertion from the surrounding notes.

(16) The date of dictation is always written at the *bottom* of the page.

These notes are keyed and signaled for efficient and accurate completion. The practices followed by this secretary are numbered and explained on the opposite page.

WHAT THE DICTATOR SAID:

Take a letter to J. K. Kelly at Smith-Keller. We have been disturbed, Jim, by the recent rise in the price of uranuim from blank dollars a ton to blank dollars a ton. Ask Henry to supply those figures. I think I am right, but I want to verify them before writing such an important letter. Since we are such a heavy user of your product, we wonder if you can't quote, no, offer, a better price on our next shipment, possibly a 5 percent discount on orders in excess of 2000 tons. If this is impossible, may I suggest that you agree to supply our needs for uranuim at the present price for the next ten months. Better send this over to Henry for approval before I sign it. If he thinks it is OK, make an extra carbon for the president. Yours truly

WHAT THE SECRETARY WROTE:

appreciated. If the executive said "*elaborate* plans" and then dictated, "They have *elaborated* upon this idea," you might mention, "We have just used *elaborate*." Usually another word is substituted, or you might simply be told, "Thanks, you fix it." From then on you would "fix it" and make a substitution when you go over the notes.

3. When a question comes to your mind about the dictation, insert a clear-up signal at the end of the line. Some dictators prefer to be interrupted immediately about such a question, others at the end of each item, and still others prefer to wait until all the dictation is completed. The executive will quickly learn your clear-up signal and at a propitious moment will often ask to what it refers.

Unusual Dictation

A secretary is often asked to take unusual kinds of dictation, such as those discussed below.

Highly Confidential Dictation. Transcribe highly confidential dictation when there is little likelihood of anyone being around. Give the original and carbon copies to the executive as soon as possible and destroy the dictated notes. If the carbon paper retains an imprint of the typescript, destroy it also.

Telephone Dictation. In taking telephone dictation, you have the use of only one hand and may have to ask for phrases to be repeated. Since the dictator cannot see how fast you are taking notes, it helps if you say "yes" after you have completed each phrase. To avoid errors, read the entire set of notes back to the dictator.

Occasionally the executive may request you to monitor a telephone conversation and take notes. Unless you are unusually speedy, you cannot hope to get every word, but you can take down the main points in the way one takes lecture notes. Transcribe such notes at once while they are still fresh in your mind.

Both sides of a telephone call can be recorded on a dictating machine placed near the telephone. Legally, however, the other person must be told that the conversation is being recorded. The recording may be kept for reference, or you may be asked to transcribe the entire conversation or to abstract the important points.

Taking dictation over the telephone requires exceptional care to insure the accuracy of the dictated material.

Xerox Corporation

During a conference, the executive has asked the secretary to come in and record comments on an advertising layout under consideration.

On-the-Spot Dictation. At times it is necessary to take dictation within a split second, while standing or working at a desk where there is no cleared space. You may even have to take the notes on scratch paper. Practice taking dictation with a notebook on your knee or while standing using a scratch pad, in order to become accustomed to the awkwardness of such rush work. The idea is to get it done quickly without fuss or commotion. After transcription, date the notes, fold them to less than page size, and staple them to the first blank page in the dictation notebook.

Dictation at the Typewriter. Occasionally the executive may ask you to type something as it is being dictated to you. It helps to ask before starting whether the dictation will be long or short to determine the placement of the item on the page. A retyping, however, is often required, because in the majority of cases the placement is unsatisfactory and insertions or corrections have been necessary. Do not stop to erase errors as they are made. It is better to correct the errors or retype the page when the executive has finished dictating and has left your desk.

Printed-Form Dictation. The answers to questions on a printed form are frequently dictated. The executive usually works from the form; therefore, the information given will seem sketchy and incomplete. If the dictator does not give the identifying numbers or letters of the items, ask for them so that you can type the information on the proper lines.

If only one copy is furnished, it may be well to make a photocopy of the completed form for the files.

MACHINE DICTATION

Dictation machines are not new. Dictators have for a number of years dictated to machines.

Dictation Equipment

There are three categories of dictation machines.

Portable and Desk Models. The portable dictation machine was and is a boon to the traveling salesperson or executive, who can mail the recorded material to the secretary for transcription. It is even possible to attach equipment to a telephone so that the telephoned dictation can be transmitted to the office for transcription without waiting for mail delivery.

Many executives who like to work at home find the dictation machine indispensable for originating communications. Others recognize that the time of one person is saved if they dictate to a desk-top machine in the office while the secretary is free for other tasks.

The media on which the dictation is recorded vary from cassettes to magnetically coated "visible" belts on which the recorded dictation is visible in grooves similar to those on a phonograph record. Usually the media hold from 30 to 90 minutes of recording time. It is possible to play back the dictation and to make changes and corrections. It is also possible to record instructions to the operator.

The multifunctional secretary has many opportunities both to transcribe from and to dictate to these dictation machines.

Dictation to the Word Processing Center. Dictation to a word processing center is transmitted from the word originator by some sort of telephone connection. Several recorders are located in the center, and with the more sophisticated systems a recorder not in use by another dictator is automatically selected and put into operation for the incoming dictation.

The use of dictation machines has proliferated at an amazing rate since the reorganization of the office has separated the word processing function from the administrative-support function. Today there are at least a dozen manufacturers of dictation equipment. Some of them are: Dictaphone, Fi-Cord, Memocord, IBM, SONY, Lanier, Phillips, Dictran, and DeJur-Amsco.

Endless Loop or Continuous Flow Systems. All of the dictation machines described up to this point are called discrete media equipment because they use a specific, removable recording medium. Such a medium can be stored, mailed, or switched from dictation machine to transcription machine.

Lanier Business Products

This dictating equipment, which combines tank and cassette technology, allows simultaneous dictation and transcription.

Much more functional, though, is the endless loop system. Loops of mag tape, which are sealed inside a case or tank, go round and round for hours of use and reuse. Dictation is recorded on one tape head, and another head plays out the dictation for the word processor to transcribe. It is possible, then, for the correspondence secretary to start to transcribe while the dictator continues recording and thus to speed up rush work. The other advantage is that the encased tape requires no monitoring to see whether it should be reloaded with new recording media. Monitoring panels with visible dials show the supervisor at a glance which tanks are in use, which are idle, and how much untranscribed dictation has not yet been assigned to an operator. The disadvantage of the endless loop machine over discrete media systems is in locating rush items and in assigning transcribing priorities.

Relationship of the Administrative Secretary to the Word Processing Center

In the organization of a typical word processing center, the administrative secretary will have these responsibilities for input and output from the center:

Assemble Attention-Today items that require dictation.

Research special names and addresses, sending them to the center to supplement its records.

Keep the backup materials from which the dictation originated organized for possible reference.

Receive the completed work and inspect it to the extent of the employer's wishes, possibly even proofreading.

Present the work to the dictator for signature.

Provide all appropriate enclosures and mail the material.

Return to the center any material to be corrected or revised.

Photocopy and distribute copies of signed material when the regulation number of copies provided is inadequate.

Follow up if the *turn-around* time (the time elapsed between dictation and delivery of transcript) is too long, requesting the completed material from the center.

Record and file the code numbers assigned to any material stored on permanent tape.

Dictate to the center.

Learning to Dictate

Both the multifunctional secretary and the administrative secretary will find that they can work more efficiently if they use dictation equipment. A deterrent to using dictation equipment is the reluctance of the dictator to organize both thoughts and materials before starting to speak. The principal also fears that the dictation will be imperfect, although all equipment provides for playback, correction of dictation, and an index slip with which to alert the transcriber to a transcription problem. Some secretaries, accustomed to transcribing and to speaking slowly and distinctly with logical phrasing, have less difficulty in dictating efficiently than do some executives.

To prepare for giving easily transcribed dictation, first study the instruction book for the equipment until you can operate all the controls. Dictate a practice item that contains tricky words and figures; wait until a later time; then see whether you can distinguish every word and figure.

An outline made before the dictation is a useful device in producing dictation of which you can be proud. And the more complex the letter, the more necessary the outline.

A large insurance company asked its transcribers to make a list of desirable dictation manners that were lacking in those from whom they took dictation.

Here are a few of their requests:

Before you start dictating
Identify the rush items and dictate them first.
Indicate immediately if it is a RUSH item.
First, mention the item to be dictated — letter, memo, report, and so on.

State the number of copies needed and to whom they are to be sent.
Give instructions about typewritten form — if it is unusual.

During the dictation
Spell out proper names and technical words.
Dictate figures very clearly.
Enunciate precisely.

After the dictation
Be gracious when the transcriber has a question.
Give praise once in a while.
Reject substandard work so that the transcriber maintains high
   quality standards.

Dictation by Number

Since many situations covered by the dictator are recurring ones,
it is a great time-saver to answer letters referring to a common situation by reproducing a numbered form letter, for example, Letter
19. If there is a slight variation in the circumstances, the dictator
may consolidate several form paragraphs into a satisfactory answer,
possibly adding an original paragraph or two.

In these circumstances, the originator, who has copies of form
letters and paragraphs at the desk, may dictate something like this:
Dear Henry, It was good to see you in Toledo last week. Paragraph
11, paragraph 67, and paragraph 3.

SUGGESTED READINGS

Becker, Esther R., and Evelyn Anders. *The Successful Secretary's Handbook*. New York: Harper and Row, 1971, pp. 62–63.

Blackburn, Norma Davis. *Secretaryship*. Pacific Palisades: Goodyear Publishing Co., 1974, Chapter 9, "Dictation," pp. 128–143.

Brunson, Evelyn V. *Professional Secretary*. Englewood Cliffs: Prentice-Hall, 1974, Chapter 8, "The Art of Dictation," pp. 133–146.

First Time Final. Franklin Lakes: Office Products Division of International Business Machines, 1973.

Place, Irene, Charles Hicks, and Edward Byers. *College Secretarial Procedures*, 4th ed. New York: McGraw-Hill Book Co., 1972, pp. 92–103.

South-Western Publishing Company *Century 21* textbooks in shorthand. Cincinnati: South-Western Publishing Co. (College and high school textbooks have hints on handling dictation.)

Standard Oil of Indiana. *Art of Dictation*. Reading: Addison Wesley Publishing Co., 1973. (A tape is also available.)

Wolf, Morris Philip, and Robert R. Aurner. *Effective Communication in Business*, 6th ed. Cincinnati: South-Western Publishing Co., 1974, pp. 176–190.

QUESTIONS FOR DISCUSSION

1. In what ways would your predictation responsibilities for supplies differ if your employer: (a) dictates directly to you, (b) dictates to a desk dictation unit, or (c) dictates to a remote dictation terminal in the word processing center?

2. As a new secretary to the director of an agricultural chemical research laboratory, how would you familiarize yourself with the highly technical vocabulary?

3. What would you do if during dictation the executive:
   (a) hands you a letter of invitation to speak at a professional meeting and asks you to reply stating that the pressure of business makes it impossible to prepare adequately for such a presentation and suggesting a substitute, Maria Savitsky?
   (b) dictates a telegram?
   (c) asks you to telephone for a plane reservation?
   (d) tells you to put all interoffice memorandums on a new form which is handed to you?
   (e) dictates a three-page monthly report and asks you to rough it out?
   (f) asks you to substitute another name for the one dictated in the first paragraph?
   (g) dictates an unfamiliar technical word?

4. How would you handle the situation if the dictator:
   (a) uses out-of-date stereotyped phrases habitually?
   (b) makes obvious errors in grammar?
   (c) repeats the same conspicuous word several times in one business letter?
   (d) refers to secretaries as *she* and executives as *he* in all dictation although your company has a model affirmative action program in operation?
   (e) dictates even the most obvious punctuation although much of it is questionable?
   (f) consistently uses passive voice?
   (g) mumbles?

5. What would you do if you were called to take dictation:
   (a) at 11:45 and you had a luncheon engagement at 12:10?
   (b) just as you were in the midst of giving instructions to an assistant who would have no other work to do unless you finished the explanation?
   (c) as you were putting the finishing touches on an important report that the executive had instructed you to complete before doing anything else?
   (d) as you were in the midst of reorganizing your card file?

6. Give the preferred plural for each of the following words. Then use the Reference Guide to verify or correct your answers.

attorney general	coming in	handful	spoonful
basis	court-martial	higher-up	trade-in
bill of lading	editor in chief	Jones	trade union
Chamber of Commerce	formula	knight-errant	trades union

PROBLEMS

1. Dictate to a dictation machine the letter called for in Discussion Question 3a. Ask either a classmate or your instructor to criticize your first effort in using this equipment.

2. As a multifunctional secretary, you usually rough out your compositions before typing a final copy. Your firm changes to a word processing center, and you fear you may be unable to dictate "perfect" communications to the center. Outline a plan of action for becoming more confident.

3. Take office-style dictation from your instructor or from a tape prepared by your instructor until you feel that you have mastered the special techniques required. (Dictation material is in teacher's manual.) Then take three letters from dictation or tape to be transcribed as Problem 5, Chapter 9.

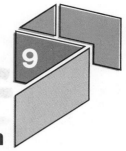

Quality Transcription

This chapter focuses on the final product, a quality transcript. No matter how carefully the dictation was prepared and recorded, no communication is going to receive the desired acceptance if it is not presented correctly and attractively.

First the chapter describes the techniques that a good transcriber uses. These techniques are valid whether the secretary is working from shorthand notes or from dictation equipment, either in the office adjacent to the executive or in a word processing center. Next the specialized techniques followed by the multifunctional secretary are presented. The final section is devoted to the transcription activities of the correspondence secretary and the responsibilities of the administrative secretary after receiving the completed transcript.

As you read the chapter, keep in mind that concern for cost reduction is bringing about today's changes in the methods of producing business communications. In whatever situation you expect to function as a secretary, vow to systematize your transcription practices so that your output will be of the highest quality and quantity. In this way you will contribute to a reduction in the spiraling costs of business documents.

YOUR FUNDAMENTALS

Your tool of the trade as a secretary is your facility with the English language — your spelling, punctuation, word usage, typewriting style, and use of reference books. You must master the fundamentals so that you can transmit the dictator's ideas flawlessly. You — not necessarily the dictator — are the expert in this area; you are responsible for perfection in communication mechanics.

To master your spelling difficulties, compile and maintain your own list of troublesome words, perhaps using the blank inside-cover pages of this book. If you will persistently write down each misspelling that occurs in your writing and each uncertainty that you have to check in a dictionary, you will have a custom-made list for instant reference.

It may help you also to develop your own mnemonic devices. Many a secretary has clinched correct spellings by word associations or parallelisms that are easy to remember: *calendar* ends with the *a* of *day*; *privilege* has the *leg* that comes from *legal; all right* parallels *all wrong*, and so on.

A secretary must know the rules of punctuation as they apply to formal writing. Some office work is at that level. A paper that is to appear in print or a report to the board of directors must be punctuated with formal correctness. In routine business writing there is a trend to reduce the amount of punctuation, especially those marks which indicate pauses. Such punctuation is often omitted in the customary places in sentences which are clear in meaning. But whenever you are in doubt, punctuate fully. Comprehensive punctuation rules are given in the Reference Guide.

Grammar and usage are based on the relatively fixed standards used in communicating at a formal or educated level. Since most of the executive's writing is at that level, the secretary must have a mastery of grammar — a knowledge of grammatical construction for speaking and writing correctly.

Dictionaries vary — from the very British and formal *Oxford English Dictionary* to *Webster's Third New International Dictionary of the English Language*, which aroused a great furor among scholars of the English language when it first appeared. It contains new words that have crept into the language through usage but have never before been listed. Those willing to accept such words as "finalize," who see a dictionary as a descriptive record of living language, will approve of the new *Third*. They will be guided by the designations *slang, substandard*, and *nonstandard* in their choice of a word. Those who look at a dictionary as a source of what the language *ought* to be, who believe that language should be a pure body of words revealed from on high, will believe that workaday forms are out of place. They will choose a more traditional reference.

Two recommended desk-size dictionaries that have recently been revised are: *The American Heritage Dictionary of the English Language (College Edition)* and *Webster's New Collegiate Dictionary*. A desk dictionary should be replaced every five years or so with a current edition.

Turning to the dictionary at transcribing time, you want to learn:

1. The correct spelling of a word — such as *neophyte*

2. The correct spelling of an inflectional form — such as the past tense of *benefit*

3. The preferred form of variant spellings — such as *acknowledgment* or *acknowledgement, judgment* or *judgement*

4. Whether to use one word or two words — such as *highlight* or *high light*

5. Whether to treat a word as a foreign one and underline it — such as *bon voyage* and *carte blanche*

6. How to divide a word at the end of a line — *committal*, for example

7. Whether to use a hyphen to join a suffix or prefix to a word or to form one complete word without a hyphen: such as *pre-Socratic* and *preview; selfsame* and *self-control; businesslike* and *droll-like*

Unfortunately, each of these seven situations is usually indicated in different ways in the entries in different dictionaries. The key to how they are indicated in your dictionary is given in the Explanatory Notes at the front of the dictionary. (Sometimes this section has a more explicit title, such as "Guide to the Use of the Dictionary.") One secretary hyphenated numerous words incorrectly because of confusing the mark denoting syllabication with the one indicating a hyphen. Careful reference to the Explanatory Notes will prevent such embarrassing mistakes.

When you do locate an important point in the Explanatory Notes, underline it or enclose it in a frame with pencil for easy finding the next time. You thus save considerable time on repeat hunts.

A current and comprehensive secretarial handbook will help you with many transcription problems. At the end of this chapter several preferred ones are listed. There are also secretarial manuals for special fields: law, medicine, science and technology, and so on. These aids are listed at the end of this chapter to help you in case your work involves specialization. Reference books are discussed more fully in Chapter 19.

TRANSCRIPTION PROCEDURE

To assure efficient transcription, first make certain that all is in readiness: the typewriter keys clean; the ribbon in good condition; the supply of letterheads, envelopes, and carbon paper adequate and carefully arranged for a flow of work without wasted motion; reference books within reach; a pencil for use in editing the notes and a colored pencil for identifying or emphasizing instructions at hand; and erasing and correcting supplies nearby.

Order of Transcription

Transcribe the rush and top-priority items in the order of their immediacy as indicated by your notes, the machine index slips, or the supervisor. Telegrams, mailgrams, or cablegrams get first attention. Special-delivery letters should be attended to next and, if urgent, presented immediately for signing and mailing. If there is an interoffice memorandum of great importance, it may take precedence over all of the rest of the transcription items. Show your employer that you can make the right decisions as to priorities. Store in one regular place any transcription items that must be carried over until the next day.

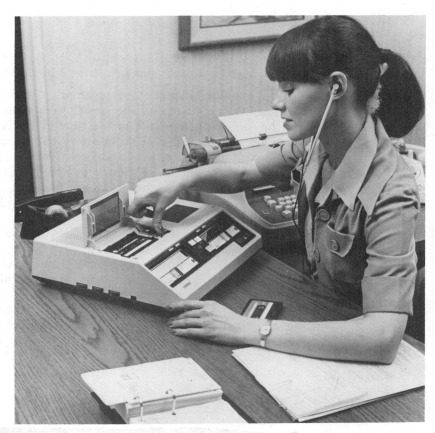

Lanier Business Products

The efficient secretary has priorities established and all materials at hand before beginning to transcribe dictation.

Editing and Completing Dictated Items

Before starting to type an item, read through it intently; then edit until it is letter-perfect and ready for smooth, continuous transcription. To read and rework your notes does not indicate incompetence but rather efficiency. As you read through each item:

Insert punctuation.	Make substitutions for repeated words.
Indicate paragraphs.	Rewrite poor sentences.
Correct errors in grammar.	Verify facts — prices, names, etc.
Correct errors in fact.	Write out difficult spellings.
Eliminate redundancies.	Fill in blanks left by executive.
Clarify ambiguities.	Find and insert needed information.

If the dictated sentence does not make sense to you, it probably will not be clear to the addressee. When in doubt, ask. If the dictator is in the next room, interrupt only at a propitious time. If your supervisor in a word processing center cannot clear up a transcription problem, telephone the originator.

Only valid, sensible changes should be made in the dictation, as illustrated below:

What the Executive Said	**What the Secretary Typed**
Let's meet in Chicago Wednesday morning, January 24. I'll arrive the night before the meeting. Please make a reservation for me at the Drake for the 24th.	Let's meet in Chicago Wednesday morning, January 24. I'll arrive the night before the meeting. Please make a reservation for me at the Drake for the 23rd.

It annoys a dictator for a secretary to change "We are sending you a selection of samples" to "A selection of samples is on its way to you," just because of a preference for the changed sentence. Don't be like the secretary who changed *criterion is* to *criteria is* because of unfamiliarity with the singular form and failure to check the dictated word.

The final step before the actual transcription of each item is to check any instructions in your notes or at the beginning of a machine-dictated item as to format, number of copies, distribution, additions on certain copies, and enclosures to be prepared.

Stationery

Give some thought to what is the most efficient arrangement for your stationery so that you can locate the correct letterhead quickly.

Choice of Letterheads. More than likely you will use a variety of letterheads. There will be at least the regular business one, the interoffice one, and the executive's personal letterhead. If the employer serves as an officer or member of the board of an outside organization, that letterhead will probably be used too.

Waste of Stationery. Letterheads are expensive, and the waste of them is appalling. Office wastebaskets are full of letterheads discarded because of careless work and slovenly corrections. Transcribe carefully and become skillful at correcting. One company reduced the cost and waste of hasty transcribing with a huge sign like that shown at the left.

IT TAKES LESS TIME
TO BE RIGHT THAN TO
REWRITE!

Number and Kinds of Copies

Some companies require two copies of every letter, one for the individual correspondence file, and another for a chronological file of all letters mailed each day. The materials in this chron file are kept at least a month for quick reference. This file often aids in locating an item that might otherwise be hard to find. In order to save filing space and supplies, other offices have a carbon copy typed on the back of the incoming letter. The majority, however, have one copy made on a second sheet for a correspondence file.

You will be asked to make and furnish certain individuals and departments with carbon copies of every letter you type that relates to subjects of mutual interest. List in your desk manual the persons who should receive copies for each general subject. You can then make the correct number of copies and distribute them properly each time. Before beginning to transcribe, always check the notations or oral instructions which precede the item. These will usually tell you the number of copies needed.

maître d'hôtel

résumé

garçon

señor

Diacritical Marks

Add any necessary diacritical marks (in pencil or ink) after removing the sheet from the typewriter.

The Matter of Dating

Date every paper. Use the date of transcription if it differs from that of the dictation. It may be necessary to edit the dictation to make it conform, as "your visit *yesterday*," rather than "your visit *this morning*." On casual typewritten matter use the abbreviated form, as *8/28/—*.

Letter and Envelope Styles

Many companies furnish form and style manuals for use with their correspondence. If you do not receive one, compile your own models from previous correspondence and from style authorities. Model letters and envelopes are shown on pages 736–737.

Keeping It Confidential

There are always several persons in a large office who are inquisitive as to what is currently happening in the executive offices. Transcripts on the secretaries' desks are often fruitful sources of information: finished letters waiting to be signed, the letter being typed, and carbon copies openly in view. If someone comes to your desk while you are transcribing, roll the letter back into the typewriter, making your action as unobtrusive as possible. Keep the group of transcribed letters covered with a sheet of paper, or in face-down order, or inside a file folder. Carbon copies are just as informative as originals, so treat them with the same respect. Many executives now use an electric wastebasket that shreds paper that might reveal company secrets.

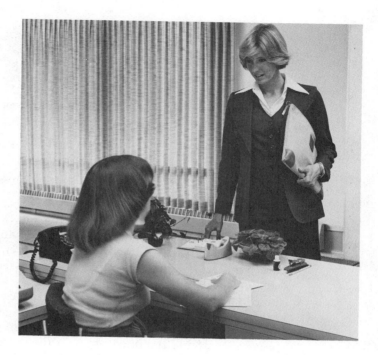

A secretary who works with confidential matters should form the habit of casually covering the work on the desk whenever someone approaches. This action can be so unobtrusive that the visitor is unaware of it.

Reference Initials

Reference initials may be treated in a variety of ways:

1. If the executive's name is typed in the closing lines, these initials may be omitted and only the transcriber's initials used.

2. Reference initials follow a carefully worked-out pattern whenever others compose letters for the executive's signature.

There are certain situations in which it is poor public relations to indicate that the executive delegated a letter to the secretary or to an associate to compose.

Envelopes

Before removing a letter from the typewriter, drop its envelope between the letter and the platen. When you remove the letter, the envelope will be positioned for addressing. After addressing the envelope and before removing it from the typewriter, check it against the original source document for accuracy. Then slip the addressed envelope, flap up, over the top of the letter and its enclosures. The accumulated stack of correspondence is easier to handle, and your employer will find it easier to read and sign the letters.

Identifying Copies

With a letter addressed to several persons but typed in one writing, type all the names in the address position. Treat each copy as an original, individual letter as indicated below.

1. Put a check mark above or beside the name of the person to whom the copy will be sent.

2. Address an envelope for that name; slip the envelope over that copy.

3. Present each checked letter with its addressed envelope for signing with the rest of the mail.

When carbon copies of a letter to a single addressee are to be sent to others for their information, type the names or initials of the carbon-copy recipients following the *cc* reference notation. Such copies are handled the same as multiple-addressee letters except that the sender does not sign each one.

When *blind copies* of a letter are to be sent, use the reference notation *bc* in the usual position for noting carbon copy distribution. Type the names or initials of the recipients on all copies *except the original letter* and handle them as if they were regular carbon copies. To reduce handling, use a piece of paper to cover the notation position on the original; type the notation before removing the carbon pack from the typewriter.

Enclosures

Whenever an enclosure is mentioned in a letter, there is an implied instruction to someone to obtain the enclosure and attach it to the letter before submitting it for signature. That someone is the multifunctional secretary in the traditional office and the administrative secretary if a word processing center is used. If possible, collect all enclosures at the same time. Do not use as an enclosure either the file copy of a letter or the original copy of a letter received. Instead, prepare a copy on a copying machine or type a plain, identified copy.

If an enclosure is small enough not to cover the body of the letter, it is attached to the face. If larger, it is put at the back of the letter.

Should it be necessary to send in a letter for signature without its enclosures, clip a note to it listing the enclosures missing. The note will serve a dual purpose: it will inform the executive that you have not forgotten the items to be enclosed, and it will remind you not to mail the letter until the enclosures are at hand.

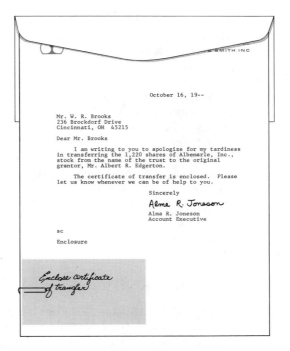

October 16, 19--

Mr. W. R. Brooks
236 Brockdorf Drive
Cincinnati, OH 45215

Dear Mr. Brooks

I am writing to you to apologize for my tardiness
in transferring the 1,220 shares of Albemarle, Inc.,
stock from the name of the trust to the original
grantor, Mr. Albert R. Edgerton.

The certificate of transfer is enclosed. Please
let us know whenever we can be of help to you.

Sincerely

Alma R. Joneson

Alma R. Joneson
Account Executive

sc

Enclosure

Enclose certificate of transfer

If an enclosure will be bulky or difficult for the signer to handle, the secretary attaches a note to the letter as a signal of awareness of the enclosure and as a self-reminder at mailing time.

Separate-Mail Items

Prepare or obtain material to be sent in a package or a mailing envelope and get it ready for mailing. If someone else is responsible for mailing, give complete instructions in writing to that person or department, and prepare a typewritten address label. Make a tickler item to check later on the material.

You may enclose a letter with a package sent by priority mail without additional postage. (See pages 237–238.) This procedure saves sending out a great deal of under-separate-cover mail and keeping track of it by tickler items.

Submitting the Correspondence for Signature

The secretary to only one executive submits the completed correspondence for signature; but in an organization with a word processing center the administrative secretary performs this function.

If rush items are involved, they are submitted as soon as completed. Some executives like to sign the mail at least twice a day. In other cases the mail is signed in the afternoon in time to meet the mail schedules (with which the secretary must become familiar). Learn and follow the executive's preferences in these matters.

The correct arrangement of transcribed material is: the letter and its envelope on top, then the extra carbons, and the file copy with its notations. If the executive is there, present the letters face up. If not, turn the top letter face down to keep it clean and to prevent its being read.

Most secretaries arrange to be at the executive's desk for the signing session, for there are often questions and comments about the items to be signed and about the work ahead.

A frequent point of irritation between an executive and a transcriber is the difference between what the executive thinks was dictated and what has been transcribed. There is only one gracious way to handle these differences of opinion as to who is at fault. The secretary accepts responsibility for making all corrections and changes. It really does not make any difference who made a mistake. The important thing is to go about correcting it at once, cheerfully and willingly.

Secretarial Signatures

Both the multifunctional secretary and the administrative secretary in a word processing setup are frequently given authority to sign the transcribed letter. Recently, both men and women in either the executive or the secretarial role have chosen a signature that does not identify their sex, possibly adopting initials rather than the given name. Some women select the increasingly popular Ms. that does not reveal their marital status.

Because it has become the prerogative of the person involved in producing correspondence to exercise personal preference in choosing a business signature, the secretary should be guided by this preference and follow it meticulously.

The customary ways for a secretary to sign mail in the executive's absence or upon request are:

Very truly yours

Helen Benton MW

President

Sign the executive's name in your own handwriting and add your initials. Use a readable script of generous size.

Very truly yours

Helen Benton

President

Imitate the executive's signature.

Sincerely yours

Max Williams

Max Williams
Secretary to Ms. Benton

Sign your name and then type your name, title, and the name of the principal.

Preparing the Correspondence for Filing

The transcribed dictation is prepared for filing by the multifunctional secretary or, if there is a word processing center, by the administrative secretary. Staple the carbon copy of each reply to the top of the incoming letter it answers. Staple the carbons of letters originating at your desk into sets if the letters are longer than one page. Place pertinent letters in the pending file or make tickler items from the carbon copies. Write each follow-up date on the carbon copy of the letter itself to show that the date has been set and recorded. Add the filing notation before laying the correspondence aside. The matter of designating *where* to file each letter is taken up in Chapters 14 and 15.

SENDING THE SIGNED MAIL

In some large offices secretaries are relieved of the final work of sending out correspondence. Mail clerks collect the signed letters and the envelopes and fold, insert, seal, and stamp them. In smaller offices the secretary attends to every step of the routine.

Modern office equipment such as the folding machine makes the routine faster and easier, but the secretary should know the most efficient manual procedures as well.

Folding and Inserting Letters Manually

A letter is ready for mailing when it is signed and all enclosures are assembled. A secretary often folds and inserts the letters while waiting at the desk for the executive to read and sign the rest of the mail. Every letter should be folded in such a way that it will unfold naturally into reading position. The proper methods are illustrated on page 202.

You can fold and insert a stack of letters very quickly at your own desk by developing a routine based on these steps.

1. Have a cleared space on the desk.

2. Then take a letter from the stack of signed mail; place it before you on the desk and fold it neatly; insert it into the envelope at once.

3. Lay the envelope aside in a stack with the flap out flat (not folded over the envelope) and with the address side downward.

The routine that proves most efficient for you must be worked out. Experiment with some 20 or 30 large and small dummy envelopes and letters until you have developed a routine free of wasted motions.

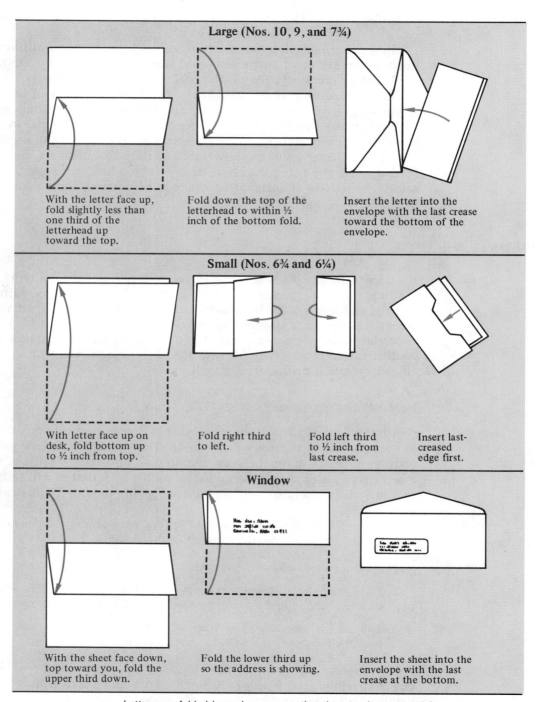

Large (Nos. 10, 9, and 7¾)

With the letter face up, fold slightly less than one third of the letterhead up toward the top.

Fold down the top of the letterhead to within ½ inch of the bottom fold.

Insert the letter into the envelope with the last crease toward the bottom of the envelope.

Small (Nos. 6¾ and 6¼)

With letter face up on desk, fold bottom up to ½ inch from top.

Fold right third to left.

Fold left third to ½ inch from last crease.

Insert last-creased edge first.

Window

With the sheet face down, top toward you, fold the upper third down.

Fold the lower third up so the address is showing.

Insert the sheet into the envelope with the last crease at the bottom.

Letters are folded in such a manner that they can be removed from the envelope and opened easily and quickly in position for reading.

Sealing Envelopes

When all the letters are enclosed, joggle the envelopes into a neat stack. All of the address sides will be down and the flaps will be opened out. Now pick up the stack, grasp the flaps, and bend them back in order to make them flatter. Holding the short edges of the stack of envelopes between the two hands, drop the envelopes off the bottom of the stack one at a time, onto the desk, so that only the gummed part of the flap of each envelope is visible. Then take a moistening tube, and with one swing of the arm start at the bottom and moisten all of the flaps at once. Lay the tube aside on a blotter and start sealing the envelope nearest you by folding over the flap. Continue up the column. As you seal each envelope, pick it up and lay it in a stack, flap side up.

In the ceramic wheel type of moistener, a wide wheel passes through a shallow reservoir of water at the bottom. To use this moistener, turn the stack of envelopes over so that the address sides are up. Take the top envelope and, with both hands at the short edges, pull just the gummed part of the flap over the rotating wheel. With the forefingers, fold the moistened flap down over the envelope and lay it aside, address side up.

Stamping

If the sealed envelopes are to be stamped by hand, first remove all those that require special stamping. Lay the rest of them out in columnar form with the address side up, leaving depth enough for the stamps to be pasted. Take a strip of stamps that are joined with the horizontal edges together, moisten a stamp at a time on a nearby sponge or moistener, and affix it to an envelope, working from the top envelope down. For strip stamps that are attached at the vertical edges, as rolled stamps are, lay the envelopes across the desk.

Envelopes requiring special stamping should be given individual attention. Those that are sent special delivery or to other countries and those that are too heavy for the minimum postage should be handled separately. Write in pencil in the stamp position the amount of postage needed. This penciled figure is later covered by the stamps.

Considerable loss is incurred from using excess postage. Also, many companies, notably the service industries such as banks or public utilities, will not pay postage due on mail with insufficient postage.[1] For these reasons, every office should have some kind of postal scale. Weigh every piece of mail. "When in doubt, weigh!" Small scales for first-class mail are sensitive to fractions of an ounce. Have your scales checked for accuracy periodically.

[1]The post office is not required to deliver unstamped mail but sometimes does as a convenience.

SPECIALIZED TRANSCRIBING TECHNIQUES FOR THE MULTIFUNCTIONAL SECRETARY

The following suggestions apply only to the multifunctional secretary transcribing from shorthand notes.

Positioning the Notebook

To hold your notebook in an upright position, attach a large button or tie a large knot at each end of a piece of string so that you can set the opened notebook between the buttons or knots.

Suggesting a Change

When you feel that a whole paragraph should be changed, type the dictated text on a separate sheet with your revision below. Take it in to the executive and say something like, "I roughed out a paragraph here. I thought you might want to change it because. . . ." If your revision is not approved, accept the decision matter-of-factly.

Transcribing a Rough Draft

To permit editing and polishing, make a rough draft of material that requires an especially effective communication — such as an important letter, a report to a superior, a speech, or a paper to be published. Strike over and "x" out; final-draft care on a rough draft is inefficient.

Single-space a rough draft of a *letter* on letterhead-size paper in exact letter form so that the draft will also serve as a guide to final placement on the page. Type a rough draft of a *report* or *paper* on legal-size substandard paper or on business-size colored sheets, thus getting both attention and reminder value among the other papers on the desk. Use margins of an inch or so, and double- or triple-space the lines to provide room for editorial changes.

Indicating Completed Work or an Interruption during Transcription

You may not transcribe items in consecutive order. As you complete each item, draw a diagonal line through your shorthand notes. In machine transcription mark the indicator slip according to instructions when each item is finished.

When shorthand transcription is interrupted, insert a conspicuous signal at the cutoff place in your notes or you may reread the whole page to find your place.

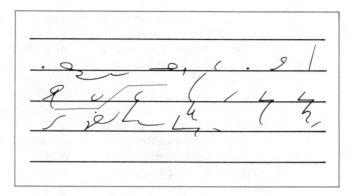

Dictation Page with Cutoff Signal

Systematizing Routine Mailings

You may be responsible for regular mailings to a specified list — 40 branch managers every Thursday, for instance. You can save time by following this routine:

1. Type stencils of the addresses, 10 to the page.

2. Run off 52 copies from each stencil, using gummed-back paper.

3. Cut individual labels from each sheet and affix them to the appropriate envelopes.

Envelopes for the year's mailings are ready in three operations.

SPECIALIZED TRANSCRIBING FUNCTIONS OF THE CORRESPONDENCE SECRETARY

The correspondence secretary performs three steps in transcribing the dictated material:

1. "Keyboarding in" the material dictated. (This phrase is part of the new vocabulary of word processing. It means typing the rough draft as rapidly as possible; not stopping for the correction of errors of any kind.)

2. Editing the copy and making the necessary corrections. Here is where your facility in spelling, punctuation, other English mechanics, and word usage is put into play.

3. Playing out the corrected copy into a usable document.

Keyboarding in the material is followed by correcting it. The most popular word processing typewriters have a visual screen similar to the one on a television set. On this screen, the operator can see the copy and the corrections as they are made.

Most correspondence secretaries perform the first two steps, but some of them specialize in playing out the corrected copy only, from a mag card or tape (usually a card) that has been filed in the center. When a filed letter is used in producing a new letter, the operator either types the dictated address or merges the address from a stored tape with the body of the letter. If several paragraphs are to be combined to form the finished letter, the operator knows the proper controls to push in order to call up the needed data.

The correspondence secretary needs great skill in English mechanics and word usage in order to perform the first two steps. Equally or more important, however, is an interest in and an understanding of machine capabilities. As Kleinschrod says:

> WP typewriters greatly reduce the consequence of error created by inaccurate keystroking, but they introduce errors of another sort. The machines come loaded with editing features, controls, and media whose electronic codings are there, but invisible, and not as easily deciphered as if they were visible. And a lot can go wrong.
>
> From a mechanical point of view, the prime mission in training a WP operator is no longer keyboard accuracy, but understanding the whole machine, the controls that format, assemble, send, retrieve, store, and do all manner of text manipulation at high speed. The mission is to get them to safely "drive" those dozen or more editing and directing keys to the left and right of the basic keyboard — the 40-odd alpha, numeric, and punctuation keys that were all the standard typist had to worry about.
>
> No, basic keyboard errors aren't worrisome; they're easily corrected. But functional WP system errors that could spew out hundreds of form letters inaccurately positioned on continuous letterheads because of a wrong format instruction could be very worrisome, especially if the addresses don't line up in window envelopes.
>
> And, yes, reasoning ability and skills in spelling and grammar do count for more than raw typing speed, for they are the qualities that help move the work forward thoughtfully, accurately, and unhampered by decision error. They are keys to effective throughput. Figure on it taking from nine months to a year before a WP operator achieves consistently high scores in final copy output.[2]

SUGGESTED READINGS

A basic reference that should accompany you to your first position is this textbook with its valuable reference section. The references which follow will also help the secretary in self-development.

---

[2]Walter A. Kleinschrod, *Management's Guide to Word Processing* (Chicago: Dartnell Corporation, 1975), p. 131.

GENERAL SECRETARIAL MANUALS

Becker, Esther R., and Evelyn Anders. *The Successful Secretary's Handbook*. New York: Harper & Row, Publishers, 1971.

Doris, Lillian, and Besse May Miller. *Complete Secretary's Handbook*, 3d ed. Englewood Cliffs: Prentice-Hall, 1970.

Engel, Pauline. *The Executive Secretary's Handbook*. West Nyack: Parker Publishing Co., 1970.

House, Clifford R., and Apollonia M. Koebele. *Reference Manual for Office Personnel*, 5th ed. Cincinnati: South-Western Publishing Co., 1970.

Janis, J. Harold, and Margaret Thompson. *New Standard Reference for Secretaries and Administrative Assistants*. New York: Macmillan Co., 1972.

A Manual of Style, 12th ed. Chicago: University of Chicago Press, 1969.

Schulz, Charles M. W. *A Secretary's Handbook*. New York: Holt, Rinehart & Winston, 1973.

Schweiger, Twyla. *Modern Secretary's Complete Guide*. West Nyack: Parker Publishing Co., 1971.

Webster's Secretary's Handbook. Springfield: G. & C. Merriam, 1976.

Whelan, Doris. *Secretary's Handbook*. New York: Harcourt Brace Jovanovich, 1975.

MEDICAL SECRETARIAL AIDS

Atkinson, Phillip S. *Medical Office Practice*, 2d ed. A practice set. Cincinnati: South-Western Publishing Co., 1976.

Bredow, Miriam, and M. G. Cooper. *Medical Office Procedures*, 6th ed. New York: McGraw-Hill Book Co., 1973.

Dennis, Robert L., and Jean M. Doyle. *The Complete Handbook for Medical Secretaries and Assistants*. Boston: Little, Brown & Co., 1971.

Root, Kathleen Berger, and Edward E. Byers. *Medical Secretary*, 3d ed. New York: McGraw-Hill Book Co., 1971.

LEGAL SECRETARIAL AIDS

Bate, Marjorie Dunlap, and Mary C. Casey. *Legal Office Procedures*. New York: McGraw-Hill Book Co., 1975.

Blackburn, Norma D. *Legal Secretaryship*. Englewood Cliffs: Prentice-Hall, 1971.

Miller, Besse May. *The Legal Secretary's Complete Handbook*, 2d ed. Englewood Cliffs: Prentice-Hall, 1971.

National Association of Legal Secretaries. *Manual for the Legal Secretarial Profession*, 2d ed. St. Paul: West Publishing Co., 1974.

Thomae, Betty K. *Legal Secretary's Desk Book — with Forms*. Englewood Cliffs: Prentice-Hall, 1973.

TECHNICAL SECRETARIAL AIDS

Laird, Eleanor. *Data Processing Secretary's Complete Handbook.* Englewood Cliffs: Prentice-Hall, 1973.

Lojko, Grace. *Typewriting Techniques for the Technical Secretary.* Englewood Cliffs: Prentice-Hall, 1972.

SUGGESTED QUICK REFERENCES

Dictionary (a recent one)

Leslie, Louis. *20,000 Words*, 7th ed. New York: McGraw-Hill Book Co., 1977. (Spelling and word division reference.)

Montoya, Sarah. Monthly column in *The Secretary* magazine called "Word Watching."

Sabin, William. *Gregg Reference Manual*, 5th ed. New York: McGraw-Hill Book Co., 1977.

Silverthorn, J. E., and Devern J. Perry. *Word Division Manual*, 2d ed. Cincinnati: South-Western Publishing Co., 1970.

ZIP Code Directory

QUESTIONS FOR DISCUSSION

1. Would any of the three following practices suggested in the chapter be unnecessary time-wasters for an experienced, competent secretary?
   (a) Prereading and editing notes before transcribing
   (b) Making a reading file of the day's transcription
   (c) Making rough drafts of items to be corrected as they are played out

2. Some executives dictate at the end of an item the number of extra copies wanted. How can the transcriber be sure that the required number of copies is provided? Do you have a suggestion for changing the dictator's habit?

3. In what ways do the responsibilities for a dictated item differ for the administrative secretary, the correspondence secretary, and the multifunctional secretary?

4. What kinds of changes should the secretary make in dictation? What kinds should not be made?

5. What implied directions would you follow in transcribing:
   (a) a personal letter to a classmate in charge of a college reunion?
   (b) a letter about a discount improperly taken if the invoice in question is handed to you along with the customer's letter being answered?
   (c) a reply to a letter of complaint about the service given to a customer by a branch office?
   (d) a proposed contract for the construction of a new plant?

6. Retype any of the following names and titles that are incorrect in form. Refer to the Reference Guide to verify your answers.
   (a) the Hon. Edith Romano
   (b) Frederick K. Ellman, Esq., M.A.
   (c) Professor Adam Lowenstein, ph.d.
   (d) Dr. Grace Borgman, M.D.

PROBLEMS

1. On the inside cover of your own collegiate dictionary paste a typewritten list showing exactly:
   (a) *How* the following are shown in the dictionary:
   Foreign words
   Hyphened words
   Inflectional forms
   Parts of speech
   Preferred spellings
   Syllabication
   (b) *Where* the following can be found in the dictionary:
   Abbreviations
   Adjective-and-noun phrases (such as *blind alley*)
   Biographical names
   Place names
   Prepositional phrases (such as *on hand*)
   Punctuation
   Noun-and-noun phrases (such as *band wagon*)
   Rules of grammar
   Having such a reference will save you much time in using the dictionary.

2. Be prepared to set up and demonstrate the following:
   (a) speed sealing of envelopes, using as many types of manual moisteners as possible
   (b) speed stamping

3. In typewritten form prepare answers to the following questions. Then correct your answers, using the reference books designated in the chapter and citing your authority.
   (a) What are synonyms for *agent, integrity, mediocrity*?
   (b) What is the correct salutation for a clergyman?
   (c) What are the approved regular and ZIP Code abbreviations for *Oregon*? *Connecticut*? *Nebraska*?
   (d) Should there be a space after the first period in writing *Ph.D.*?
   (e) How should the following sentence be punctuated?
   Did he say Are you going
   (f) Should *cooperate* and *reread* be hyphenated?

4. One of your greatest assets in producing quality transcripts is your ability to proofread accurately. As a pretest of your competency in this area, type this letter and check the errors, retyping a mailable copy if instructed to do so by your instructor. (You may need to refer to the Reference Guide.) Can you locate 15 errors?

   Johns & Simon
   1 Wall Street
   New York, NY 10005

   Ladies and Gentlemen

   We have no way of determing from your letter of February 10 you needs for additional display equiptment.

   We have asked our sales agent, Walter Johnson to telephone you for an appointment before Fridays conference opens, and see whether we can assist you in setting up your booth or in supplying other display materials.

   You should be warned that a city ordnance prohibits exhibitors from obstruct ing the street during the hours between ten a.m. and four p.m.; these being the hours of heaviest traffic.

   Last year several companies were fine for traffic violations; and we don't want you to meet the same fate.

   Yours Cordially

5. Transcribe your notes from Problem 3, Chapter 8.

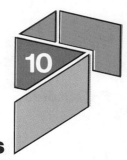

Composing Assignments

One area of written communications about which the new secretary may at first be uneasy is composing material for the employer's signature. Preparing effective written communication is difficult enough without the added dimension of writing in another person's style. Composing assignments test the educational background and experience of the secretary. Yet, composition enables the secretary to demonstrate the creativity which leads to recognition and promotion. A secretary, therefore, will perceive this responsibility to compose material as a challenge and will seek opportunities to demonstrate competence in this area.

To do a good job in this most important secretarial responsibility, you will want to become "letter perfect." This chapter presents in capsule form the principles involved in composing various kinds of business communications in a tone that produces favorable reader reaction and the desired response. Examples of typical letters a secretary may compose also are included.

A REVIEW OF THE BASICS

Writing ability is nine-tenths perspiration and one-tenth inspiration. Your employer knows this, so don't worry about the time you must spend at composing a letter; rather, worry about how well the letter accomplishes its purpose. Remember, in giving you a composing assignment, the employer is showing confidence in you. If you are not satisfied with your first attempt, try again.

Persons who write outstanding business letters have worked at it. They have learned how to organize ideas, how to weigh each word, and, most importantly, how to anticipate reader reaction. Underlying every written communication is the creation of goodwill — that is, a favorable reader response. As you write, you must put yourself in your reader's place. This is writing with the *you-attitude*.

Organize Before Writing

The effective writer doesn't just sit down and begin to write. Therefore, when you are asked to answer a letter, do these things before you put down one word:

1. *Read* the letter you are to answer, in its entirety. If it is a letter originating at your desk, read through the instructions you are to follow. Isolate the main purpose of the letter and develop your message around it. Know what action you want the reader to take, and *plan* how to make it easy to do this.

2. *Decide* on the answers to the questions asked and the information necessary to answer them. *Verify* all data you are going to include. *Collect* data needed before you start writing, so that you can give *complete* information.

3. *Make notes* of what you want to say. Organize the points you want to cover into the best sequence for reader understanding and response. Keep these points in plain sight as you compose.

Tone and Reader Response

The techniques of writing to win favorable reader response are analyzed in the following paragraphs.

Tone is that manner of writing that shows a certain attitude on the part of the writer. You want every letter you compose to create in the reader a sense of goodwill toward your office and to accomplish the purpose for which it was sent. To be successful, you must select warm and pleasant words to convey your message. Certainly, you will not want to write letters which cause feelings of annoyance, irritation, frustration, or confusion.

Writing in Anger. Never write in anger. No matter how hard you try, your words and expressions will give you away. Writing letters that destroy customer relations is something no business can afford. The best advice to follow is to cool off and wait a few days before responding. (If your employer violates this principle, you may take it upon yourself to hold the letter a few hours or even until the next day. Your employer knows this rule of thumb, too, and will appreciate and thank you for your good judgment.)

The Matter of Style. Each of us has an individual style of writing, a distinctive way of expressing ideas. If you are writing something for your employer to sign, make the message reflect your employer's style as well as ideas. This is not as difficult as it may seem. One way to capture another person's style of writing is simply to study previous dictation and letters in the file. With practice you may surpass your employer's skill in composition, and your letters may become the models for others to follow.

If you are writing letters to be signed "Secretary to . . . ," you, too, can develop a style compatible with your business personality — a step beyond the effusive communication of the novice.

Sentence Quality

Your writing will improve if you determine to let each sentence express one idea.

One-Thought Sentences. Letter-writing experts place much emphasis on simple, clear, direct writing. Such writing is achieved partly by writing sentences of only one thought and also by keeping sentences short and crisp. The average sentence length in a business letter is between 15 and 20 words.

A letter of all simple sentences (one subject and one predicate) could, however, become monotonous, even though it is easy to follow. It could imply low reader intelligence and limited ability on the part of the writer. Keep the reader in mind as you write.

Clarity. Writing letters that cannot be misunderstood by the reader is the goal in preparing the first draft. Rarely, however, is this accomplished by the new secretary on a first try. For this reason it is wise for the secretary to draft an important letter and then edit it for clarity. Exact, descriptive words help. Rephrasing confusing statements helps. Leaving nothing to be taken for granted helps. An important letter should be read aloud to catch any "fighting words."

Conciseness. A sentence that expresses a thought briefly and clearly is concise, stripped of superfluous words, and thus easy to read and understand.

Conciseness is a mark of finesse and skill. It is important because it is a saver. It saves time — the writer's, the typist's and the reader's — and it can save paper. To achieve conciseness, state a fact but once. Cut out the superfluous words and phrases in each sentence. Beware, however, of the brusque tone that can be created through *abrupt* conciseness. For instance, "Be here at five," lacks the graciousness of "I'm looking forward to seeing you at five."

In examples that follow, notice where conciseness is an asset and where it is a liability.

Forceful Sentences. To make a forceful impression, writers have found that the active rather than the passive voice is helpful. In the active voice, the subject is the doer of the action; whereas in the passive voice, the subject is acted upon. Therefore, passive voice tends to weaken a sentence. When *forcefulness* is not a factor, however, and the writer wants to concentrate on the you-attitude, passive voice may be used to avoid *we* and *I*. Passive voice is also effective in eliminating sexist pronouns (his, her) in describing occupations, life-styles, and so forth.

A verbal phrase at the beginning of a sentence may weaken the sentence. Substituting strong verbs enables you to write forceful sentences.

Less than Forceful	**Forceful**
Learning <u>your</u> reaction to our timer will be of great interest to us.	<u>We</u> are interested in your reaction to our timer.
<u>Your</u> letter is being forwarded today to Mr. Crane who is in Memphis this week.	<u>We</u> mailed your letter today to Mr. Crane in Memphis.
All errors in the final report will be corrected by the accountant.	The accountant corrects all errors in <u>his</u> final report.

Thank you, Miss Adams, for telling us ... you will be glad to know that ... You are right. We did ... Thank you, Mr. Graves, for asking us...

First Sentences. The tone of the letter is almost always set by the very first sentence. It is best then to start with thoughts that reflect the you-attitude, a genuine interest in the reader. Be gracious and courteous, and use words that are pleasant to the reader, such as those at the left. In the first sentence, establish friendly contact with the reader. The letter-writing situation is similar to a social meeting with a friend. On first meeting, you do not start by talking about yourself. You talk about something of interest to your friend. Note the letter openings at the right below.

I searched our records both in this department and in Sales to locate the information requested in your letter of June 6. I find that . . .

Your request was a real challenge. But I have the information you want. Here it is . . .

We have your letter of April 10 asking for a copy of our new folder. It was mailed to you.

The folder you requested is on its way. . . .

Importance of Words

Your choice of words in the body of the letter, as in the first sentence, is important in setting the tone. In business letters words are vitally important because of their effect on the reader. To assist you in selecting the right words, you should refer to the Reference Guide in this book. Letter-writing authorities have examined the impact of specific words and kinds of words and have made the following recommendations.

Short Conversational Words. The trend in business letters is toward short words that are used in conversation. They usually create a friendly, personal relationship between the writer and the reader; and they help the writer to relax and write naturally.

If a word is long or erudite, chances are you should change it to a shorter, more familiar one, so that the meaning is clear. Avoid the use of colloquialisms, slang words, and coined phrases. There are readers, however, who are scholarly and intellectual. Visualize the reader and use the kind of words suitable to the position and probable education of the reader.

In the list that follows, look over the words commonly used in business writing, and their short, conversational counterparts. Would you say that the short ones are always preferable to the long ones? that the long ones are always preferable to the short ones?

ameliorate	improve	endeavor	try
ascertain	learn	equitable	fair
cognizant of	aware of	initiate	begin
commitment	pledge, promise	modification	change
communication	letter	procure	get
consummate	complete	remuneration	pay, salary
determine	learn	submitted	sent
disseminate	spread	utilization	use
effectuate	bring about	verification	proof

A handy reference for the secretary's desk is *Roget's International Thesaurus in Dictionary Form*, a listing of synonyms, antonyms, and phrases.

You, I, and We. It is only human to want to hear about oneself and one's interests. For this reason, the effective letter writer focuses on what interests the reader by adopting the you-attitude. Each "you" and "your" and each word of direct address is pleasant to the reader when it is used in a natural, easy way. If, on the other hand, a sentence has been tortuously twisted to bring in the personal tone, the reader becomes annoyed.

It is also wise to avoid beginning the letter, and most paragraphs, with *I* — although using *I* as the first word in a paragraph *can* help the writer achieve simple, direct writing in some situations.

There is a technical point of interest to the secretary in choosing between *I* and *we* in letters. If a letter is signed THE JONES COMPANY, followed by the writer's signature and title, and *we* is used throughout, the legal responsibility of the writer is reduced. Today the letter writer frequently uses *I*, *my*, *we*, *our*, *me*, and *us* in correspondence, thus showing personal interest in the reader, as illustrated at the left.

We are pleased that you wrote us about the error we made in . . .

You will be pleased to know that we will be able to send you . . .

Negative Versus Positive Words. In every kind of letter, words of negative connotation are to be avoided. As one correspondent put it, negative words can turn a letter into a brink-of-war communiqué. Negative words in their kindest usage still have an unpleasant tinge. A starting list of negative-reaction words is given here. You can undoubtedly add others — and should!

alibi	claim	failure	reject
allege	complaint	fault	scheme
biased	criticize	impossible	so-called
blame	defend	insist	useless
can't	evict	regret	wrong
cheap			

Words of positive connotation are tone helpers. Use them whenever possible. Compiling your own reference list of positive-reaction words will help you to become alert to using them. Here are a few:

ability	good	pleasant
advantage	gratifying	please
benefit	happy	prominent
effective	help	recommend
enjoy	kind	responsible
fitting	lasting	thoughtful

Phrases or Words? Business-writing authorities recommend reducing wordy and hackneyed phrases to single-word or short equivalents. Oft-repeated phrases like those below make a letter commonplace. They imply that the writer is too indolent to find short, apt replacements by using a dictionary, thesaurus, or book of synonyms.

for the purpose of	for
preparatory to	before
in order to	to
make inquiry regarding	ask about
afford an opportunity	allow
for the simple reason that	because
at the present time	now
due to the fact that	because
experience indicated that	we learned
in a position to	can
meets with our approval	we approve
this day and age	today
until such time as	until
reason is because	because
in the course of	during
by means of	by
at this point in time	now
at all times	always
in the near future	soon

A civil tongue . . . means to me a language that is not bogged down in jargon, not puffed up with false dignity, not studded with trick phrases that have lost their meaning. . . . It is direct, specific, concrete, vigorous, colorful, subtle, and imaginative when it should be, and as lucid and eloquent as we are able to make it. It is something to revel in and enjoy.

Edwin Newman

With one possible exception, limit your use of such phrases because they are trite and tiresome. The possible exception is in a refusal letter, discussed later in the chapter.

Redundant Expressions. Avoid redundant expressions, those using two or more words when one will do. Their use indicates that the writer doesn't know better or doesn't care. Build a *Watch List*. Some examples follow.

baffling and puzzling	reiterate again
invisible to the eye	the only other alternative
new innovation	joined together
matinee performance	small in size
one and the same	true facts
free gratis	refer back

Length of Letter

Write a short letter instead of a long one when you can. Make a word do the work of a phrase; a phrase, the work of a clause.

The speaker, ~~who was~~ *known for verbosity*, attracted only a few listeners.
(Past participial phrase in place of adjective clause)

~~When you read~~ (*In*) the recommendations, you will find a surprising innovation.
(Prepositional phrase replacing a clause)

Mail early ~~so that you may~~ (*to*) be sure of delivery before Christmas.
(Infinitive replacing a clause)

The secretary approached the new assignment ~~with a great deal of caution~~ (*cautiously*).
(Adverb replacing an adverbial phrase)

Summary of Letter-Writing Basics

Before you mail a letter which you have composed, be sure it meets the following guidelines:

1. A friendly *tone* which will create goodwill in the reader.

2. A clearly expressed *purpose*.

3. *Short, one-thought sentences* which can be easily understood by the reader.

4. *Verbs in active voice* where possible.

5. *Short, conversational words*, positive in nature.

6. *Single words* instead of phrases and expressions, if possible.

7. The *you-attitude*, sincere and natural.

8. *Short*, yet complete, letter.

OPPORTUNITIES FOR COMPOSITION

The occasions when a secretary may be requested to compose material for the employer fall into two categories — assignments of a business nature and those of a personal nature. No matter what the orientation may be, a request to compose a letter for the employer's signature is to be regarded as a compliment — a compliment to your ability to do this high-level secretarial task.

Business Correspondence

Generally, experienced secretaries are asked to write drafts of reports, speeches, minutes of meetings, difficult letters, and memorandums. This material would probably require the employer's signature. Routine assignments, such as replies to requests for information, transmittal letters, special requests, Telex messages, reservations, appointment letters, or acknowledgments might appropriately be signed by the secretary or administrative assistant.

If you are just beginning to assume these correspondence duties, you may wish to type a suggested reply to a letter and give it to your employer for editing. This is a good way to familiarize your employer with your ability as a correspondent. In the course of transcribing your employer's dictation, you may find it necessary to correct errors in grammar, dates, amounts, repetition of words, and sentence structure. Of course, you will do so tactfully and courteously. This is another instance where your knowledge of English fundamentals can be brought to your employer's attention. If you become recognized as an expert in this area, you may find yourself putting the finishing touches on much of your employer's business correspondence!

Acknowledgments. In general, every letter should be *answered* or *acknowledged* promptly, preferably on the day it is received. In *answering* a letter, one discusses the points raised. In *acknowledging* a letter or material, one merely tells of its receipt and adds any other necessary information. An effective letter of acknowledgment is courteous, complete, and personal. Read the following examples as if they were addressed to you. Notice how their tone affects your own reader reaction.

Unacceptable	**Acceptable**
This will acknowledge receipt of your suggestion to improve our radio advertising. We are sending your suggestion to our advertising manager.	Thank you for taking the time to let us know your opinion of our radio advertising. Your suggestion will be considered by our advertising manager.
We acknowledge receipt of your letter of November 19 and thank you for it.	Thank you for your helpful letter of November 19 about Mr. Smith's credit experience with you.
This is to acknowledge receipt of your request of June 6, which will have Mrs. Stewart's attention upon her return to the office.	Mrs. Stewart is away from the office until next week. You should receive a reply to your letter of June 6 within the next two weeks.

Covering Letters. A universal business practice is to inform the recipient when money or material is being sent separately. Such a covering letter tells, with a touch of personal interest, what is being sent, why, when, and how.

A letter of transmittal is a form of covering letter also. This letter states that the material is enclosed and usually includes pertinent remarks about the material.

Covering Letter

Unacceptable	**Acceptable**
Under separate cover we are sending you a sample case of file folders. When they have served your purpose, will you please return the case, as they are difficult to replace.	Today we sent you a full stock of our samples of file folders in a convenient sample case. We are glad to lend you these materials and hope you will find something that will exactly fit your needs.
	When you are ready to return the case of samples, just use the enclosed address label.

Transmittal Letter

Enclosed herewith is a copy of our latest catalog. You will note that the lamp you described appears on page 121.	We are pleased to send you a copy of our latest catalog. The sale lamps in which you are interested are shown on page 121.

Requests and Inquiries. Every request or inquiry should be phrased courteously and should contain complete information. The following example is typical:

```
Will you please send us a copy of your report, "Word
Processing Works for Us." We are especially interested
in the operation of your satellite centers.

If you have additional information available about this
concept, we would be happy to receive it. We will, of
course, reimburse you for the cost of these reports.
```

Reminder Letters. Every secretary keeps a tickler file of items that have to be completed. Answers awaited, reports due, goods to be received — all are recorded. When an item is overdue, the secretary sends a reminder. This is a routine procedure and the secretary writes the note without being instructed to do so. Tactful phrasing is imperative, for no one likes to be reminded of negligence or lack of promptness. Here is an example:

```
On June 18 we asked you to send us detailed information
about several of your recent quotations. We are eager
to receive these details so that we can write directly
to the contractors.

Can you possibly send the data by the first of next
week? We don't want to impose a hardship upon you,
but we do need to complete this transaction soon.
```

Negative Letters. Often a letter must be written on an unpleasant subject: *complaints* or *claims, refusals, mistakes.* These require special care in composing.

Complaint Letters. As a company employee, you feel that a complaint letter which you receive is antagonistic to the company and must not be taken lightly. A prompt, thorough investigation of the complaint is necessary. Often a company does not even know there is a reason for dissatisfaction, so a genuine complaint letter is generally appreciated.

But what about the situation in which *you* have a complaint? A good formula to follow in writing your letter is to begin with a positive reference to the trouble, continue with a detailed explanation, and end with a courteous request for an adjustment. See if the following paragraphs meet these criteria:

```
The beautiful painting Dr. Stanley ordered for the
office came today. We noticed immediately that the
crate was cracked, and we feared that the painting
was damaged. Much to our dismay, our fears were
```

```
correct; the painting was torn at the upper right-
hand corner.

Would you please let us know what procedure we should
follow in filing a damage claim.  We will keep the
painting here until we hear from you.
```

Refusal Letters. Banks often have to reject loans; insurance companies have to refuse life insurance; employers have to turn down applications for positions; individuals must sometimes refuse to grant favors. All such refusals require tactful phrasing.

In a refusal letter, you will have to say *No*, but try to say it nicely. A *No* letter should be longer than the usual concise letter that communicates facts. A short *No* letter is like a curt dismissal. If possible, open with an alternative. If there is none to offer, start with a positive you-attitude sentence. Use *I* and *we* to indicate that you have a personal concern, as in the following opening paragraph:

```
It was very gracious of you to invite Ms. Howard
and me to show our slides of Alaska at your March
meeting.  Unfortunately, I have loaned them for
two months to a friend in Idaho.  We cannot,
therefore, show them again until late May.  If
you wish to select another date, we shall try
our best to come.
```

If you must apologize, do it in a few simple words — once. "We are sorry that . . . ." or "We sincerely regret that . . . ." can be used to express an apology. Nothing is gained by reiterating apologetic phrases.

Mistake Letters. When you must write a letter about a mistake — one of omission or one of commission — admit you are at fault. Do not beat about the bush with pompous phrases and long words.

Occasionally and unfortunately, mistake letters have to be written by the secretary. For example, you may neglect to put in an enclosure with a letter and discover the oversight the next day. You would draft and type a note of explanation, attach the omitted enclosure, and send the message in with the rest of the day's mail to be signed so that the executive learns about your error.

Psychologically, it is human nature to want to help a person who openly admits a mistake. Compare your reactions to the following:

```
We find on checking our shipping records that through
an unavoidable combination of circumstances we inad-
vertently delayed shipping the special gear you wanted.
It has gone out today by airmail.  We hope you have
not been inconvenienced.
```

```
This morning, when we discovered that the special
gear you requested had not gone out with yesterday's
shipment, we immediately had it packaged and sent to
you by airmail.  We are sorry for the inconvenience
and delay.
```

Personal Correspondence

Many employers delegate certain types of personal or business courtesy letter writing to their secretaries. Responding to invitations and writing letters of condolence, apology, appreciation and congratulation are typical. Here, it is especially important that your letter sounds like one your employer would write. Select the salutation, complimentary close, and phrasing your employer uses. For your first attempt, you may want to make a rough draft to be sure you are saying what your employer wishes to convey. Personal correspondence should be typed on executive-size or personal stationery, if available; otherwise, on plain bond paper.

Appreciation. A busy executive in the office is usually just as busy on the outside with community activities. For instance, after a year of work on a civic project, your employer may ask you to write a note to the committee members acknowledging the contributions they made to the project. You may want to say the following:

```
The work is finally concluded, and it is through
your efforts and those of the other members of
the committee that we can mark this project
"complete."

Watching our dream become a reality will be
gratifying to all of us.  I hope we will have
the opportunity to work together on another
project for the betterment of our community.
```

Recognition. In the course of your employment, you will come to know many of your employer's friends and will recognize their names when you see them in print. If one of them has an article in a current magazine, you may scan the article and draft a letter complimenting the friend, using the executive's writing style, as in the following example:

```
I have just read your interesting article in the
current issue of Dynamics.  The article is in-
formative and shows your skill in organizing
usually confusing ideas into a clear, pro-and-
con presentation that allows valid conclusions
to be drawn.  Your readers, I know, will commend
you for your treatment of this complex subject.
```

Congratulations. If there is publicity about the promotion or professional achievement of one of your employer's friends, you may want to draft a letter of congratulations, such as:

> Congratulations, Bob, on your appointment to the vice-presidency. I should like to add my sincere good wishes to the many others. From our years of association, I know that you will bring to the position the keen intellect and the fine personal qualities that the office requires.

Sympathy. If death or tragedy occurs in the family of one of the executive's friends, you can draft a sympathy note to be copied in longhand by the executive. A personal note is more meaningful than a commercial card. It is sincere, and usually brief. The words *die* and *death* are seldom used in sympathy notes, for they seem to be lacking in consideration. Euphemistic phrases such as *your bereavement, fatal illness, tragic happening,* and *the obituary in the paper* are kinder.

> I was sorry to read in this morning's paper of your mother's passing away. My thoughts are with you.

> It is difficult to find words to express my feelings about yesterday's events. Of course, I am thinking of you today, and my sympathy is with you.

Formal Acceptances and Regrets. When an invitation is received by letter or informal style from an organization, the answer should be made by letter or by telephone. A formal invitation, however, must be answered in handwriting in a similarly formal style on folded

Formal Invitation
(Printed or Engraved)

Mr. and Mrs. William Edwards
request the pleasure of

Mr. David Bender's

company at dinner in honor of
their silver anniversary
on Tuesday, the tenth of May,
at seven o'clock
Towne Club

stationery. When the employer receives a formal invitation, the secretary can help by drafting the answer in the proper wording and form. Center each line of the answer, and use attractive vertical spacing.

In answering, repeat only the last name (not the initials) of those who extend the invitation. In an acceptance include the day, date, and time as an assurance that they are correctly observed. In a regret it is obviously not necessary to include the time.

Formal Acceptance

Formal Regret
*(The reason in Line 3
may be omitted.)*

> Mr. David Bender
> accepts with pleasure
> Mr. and Mrs. Edwards'
> kind invitation for dinner
> on Tuesday, the tenth of May,
> at seven o'clock.

> Mr. David Bender
> regrets exceedingly that,
> because of a previous engagement,
> he is unable to accept
> Mr. and Mrs. Edwards'
> kind invitation for dinner
> on Tuesday,
> the tenth of May.

Guide Letters

You will soon discover that situations repeat themselves and that many of the letters you compose cover the same circumstances. When you find an especially effective phrase or sentence, preserve it for the next letter. You can do this by compiling a "guide-letter" reference manual containing letters which reflect your employer's language and typical reactions. Although the preparation of such a reference takes time, it will be one of your greatest time-savers. Here is how to do it:

1. Keep an extra carbon copy of all outgoing letters for a month.

2. Reread them at the end of the month, all in one sitting. As you reread them objectively, you will recognize words, phrases, and ideas that recur.

3. Separate the letters into categories, making extra copies of those that fit several classifications; underline favorite phrases and other keys to your employer's ways of handling situations; and set up a file folder for each group. Ask yourself the reasons for variations

among the letters in the amount of detail used, degree of cordiality, language, tone, and style.

4. Make an outline of the points usually covered in a letter in each category.

5. Pick out the best opening and closing sentences and the best key points tailored to specific situations.

6. Compile a letter guide, using a loose-leaf notebook. Type the model outline for the category on a heavy sheet to be used as the divider between categories of letters. Type model opening and closing sentences for the category on a separate sheet and model paragraphs on other sheets.

7. Code the index tabs for each section. For instance, "Congratulations" could be C and an especially good paragraph could be C4.

8. When you compose a letter, compare it with the outline to be sure that you have included all necessary parts.

9. Keep a record of the form used for each letter sent so that you will not again send the same letter to a person.

One of the capabilities of a word processing center is to store on magnetic tape or mag cards standard paragraphs which can be used in a variety of letters. It is the administrative secretary's responsibility to furnish paragraphs used often by the executive. When a letter is given to you for reply, and standard paragraphs apply, all you need do is signify by number the paragraphs required. The word processing center will do the rest.

Foreign Correspondence

Most corporations now do business abroad. Letter style for foreign correspondence is much more formal and traditional than for domestic correspondence. Such letters require a more "flowery" style of writing. Social amenities must be observed meticulously. Although you will probably not compose many foreign letters, you may be asked to have the message translated into the language of the recipient. Then you may have to retype it on your company's letterhead. That can be a real challenge even for the expert typist!

When addressing a letter to a foreign recipient, copy the address *exactly* as it is given. Here, too, style differs. In European and South American countries the street number *follows* the street name, as "Nassaustraat 7," not "7 Nassaustraat." In Japanese addresses there are many other designations in addition to the street name and number which are used to locate the prefecture and the section of the city; all are essential.

Interoffice Correspondence

Written communication among the staff of a company takes the form of an interoffice memorandum, a less formal style than the traditional letter. (See the illustration of an interoffice memorandum on page 737 of the Reference Guide.) The secretary will have many opportunities to compose messages for intracompany distribution, such as ordering supplies, requesting temporary help, or setting the time and place for a meeting. The writing approach for this correspondence is directness and conciseness. If your employer requests that you write a memorandum to the staff scheduling a meeting, your composition might be as follows:

```
The meeting of the sales staff will be held in
Mr. Breese's office at 10 a.m. on May 4.  The
items for discussion include the establishment
of sales districts and quotas.  Please bring. . .
```

News Releases

If in your company publicity is not the responsibility of an advertising department or an agency, you will at times be asked to compose or type brief articles for newspaper or magazine publication. News releases are unsolicited items which are sent to editors in the hope that they will be used. They must, therefore, be *newsworthy* and be of interest to readers.

Style. A good news item contains all the facts clearly stated *without* opinion. The italicized words in these expressions are opinions of a writer: *dire* emergency, everyone *should*, *noted* attorney, *signally* honored.

In composing a news release, answer the five W's — *who, what, when, where,* and *why* — plus the *how.* Get the most vital facts into the first sentence, the second most vital into the second, and so on. This journalistic style is for the convenience of the busy reader and the busy editor. If the release has to be shortened, the editor cuts out sentences beginning with the last one and works upward. This leaves the important news intact without rewriting.

Typewritten Form. A company that submits numerous releases uses a special letterhead form such as that shown on page 226. Otherwise, an item is put on a regular letterhead or on an 8½- by 11-inch sheet of good-weight paper. If a plain sheet is used, the name, address, and telephone number of the company are typed across the top. In every case a person whom the editor can call for additional information should be named. If the news stems from an outside activity of the executive, the secretary uses a plain sheet of paper and gives the executive's name as the contact. Other practices to observe are:

Give the date when the news may be published — the release date.

Type the release date near the top. Express it in either of these ways: *FOR IMMEDIATE RELEASE* or *FOR RELEASE TUESDAY, FEBRUARY 2, 19––*.

Give the article a title if possible. This gives the editor an idea of the contents at a quick glance.

Double-space the text. Leave generous margins for editorial use. Confine the release to one page, if possible.

Number each page after the first one at the top center.

Type "—more—" at the bottom of all pages but the last one.

Type # # # at the end of the release.

Send an original copy and type "Exclusive to . . ." on the release if it really is exclusive. A carbon copy indicates you are sending the same release to other publishers, and the editor may be one who will not use the release unless it appears to be exclusive.

Mail the release directly to the department editor.

For Release:
IMMEDIATE

IBM

International Business Machines Corporation
Office Products Division
Parson's Pond Drive
Franklin Lakes, New Jersey 07417
F. J. Steinberg   201/848-3448

NEW INFORMATION PROCESSING EQUIPMENT

FOR THE OFFICE ANNOUNCED BY IBM

FRANKLIN LAKES, N.J....A new series of information processing equipment has been introduced by the Office Products Division of International Business Machines Corporation. Called Office System 6, it utilizes advanced technologies to offer greater productivity for text editing, administrative record processing and electronic communications.

The new equipment features a functional display, high-density diskette storage, mag card reader/recorder, 96-character multilingual keyboard, high-speed ink jet printer, and automatic paper and envelope feeder and stackers. Electronic communications are optional on all models.

SUGGESTED READINGS

Bernstein, Theodore M. *Miss Thistlebottom's Hobgoblins*, The Careful Writer's Guide to the Taboos, Bugbears, and Outmoded Rules of English Usage. New York: Farrar, Straus and Giroux, 1971.

Buckley, Earle A. *How to Write Better Business Letters*, 4th ed. New York: McGraw-Hill Book Co., 1971.

The Bureau of Business Practice. *The Executive Secretary's Complete Portfolio of Letters*. Waterford: 1970.

Dallas, Richard J., and James M. Thompson. *Clerical and Secretarial Systems for the Office*. Englewood Cliffs: Prentice-Hall, 1975, pp. 210–236.

Eddings, Claire N. *Secretary's Complete Model Letter Handbook*. Englewood Cliffs: Prentice-Hall, 1965.

Krey, Isabelle, and Bernadette Metzler. *Principles and Techniques of Effective Business Communication*. New York: Harcourt Brace Jovanovich, 1976.

Wolf, Morris Philip, and Robert R. Aurner, *Effective Communication in Business*, 6th ed. Cincinnati: South-Western Publishing Co., 1974.

QUESTIONS FOR DISCUSSION

1. If your employer were promoted to a position involving international trade, how could you help to write overseas business letters that build goodwill for your company?

2. Your company has just established a word processing center. As an administrative secretary, you report to eight principals. You are asked to supply a list of the vocabulary used by your employers in technical correspondence. How would you go about obtaining this information, and what format would you follow in the report you give the center?

3. The executive says, "Subscribe to *Business Week* for me, please." These are the only details you have. How would you handle this task?

4. Your employer and family are out of the country on an extended business trip. In reading the morning paper you notice that one of your employer's business acquaintances is in the hospital. What action would you take in this situation?

5. What is your reader response to these first sentences in letters?
   (a) This is in answer to your letter of July 10. Your ideas . . .
   (b) We cannot send the merchandise you wanted until we receive payment for the last shipment.
   (c) Your ball-point pens are lousy, and we are sending back the whole kit and caboodle of them express collect!
   (d) It is with extreme pleasure we send you the catalog you so graciously requested in your welcome letter of May 7.

6. The following clauses have the fault of wordiness. Try to reduce them to the most concise phrases possible:
   (a) It is also of importance to bear in mind the following. . . .

(b) Consideration should be given also to the possibility of. . . .

(c) It is the consensus of opinion of the group that at the present time we should not endeavor to ascertain the reason for the change.

(d) We will all join together to make inquiry about the other possible alternatives.

7. Revise the following sentences to make them more euphonious. Then use the Reference Guide to check your answers.

(a) The letter was too abrupt and tactless.

(b) The job was just a job to the secretary.

With what euphemisms would you replace the italicized words in the following sentences?

(c) Her work is satisfactory, but she *is irritating* to others.

(d) He *was discharged* last August.

(e) He came from a *poor* neighborhood.

PROBLEMS

1. At a recent secretarial workshop the participants were asked to reduce the text of the following letter to the smallest possible number of words. One secretary got it down to eight words. Can you do as well?

Gentlemen

A copy of your pamphlet of "The Human Side" has been handed to the undersigned and in reading the contents we have been very much impressed and are wondering if this pamphlet can be secured by subscription and if so, what are the charges for such subscription. Might we hear from you in this regard at your earliest convenience?

Yours truly

2. Mr. Stanley intercepts the following two letters written by his assistant. He asks you to write acceptable replacements for them. Type each on a half-sheet simulated letterhead.

(a)

Dear Mrs. Gau:

Concerning our conversation of last week, we regret the delay of shipment of your order.

We are at a loss to explain why your merchandise has not reached you. The delivery truck picked up the package as requested.

We value your business. Naturally, we will do everything in our power to regain the confidence you have in our company and our products.

Very respectfully yours,

(b)

Dear Mr. Franklin:

We are indeed pleased to send you a copy of our recent catalog. In addition, we have alerted our sales representative in your territory, Janet Brinkley, to call for an appointment in your office. You should be hearing from her soon.

In checking our records, we see that we have not yet received your January order. Please let us have the opportunity to continue being of service to you.

Sincerely,

Part 3   CASE PROBLEMS

Case 3-1
CONFIDENTIALITY OF DICTATION

Ida Morgan was in a particularly sensitive position as secretary to Dr. Bryan Barton, director of research and development. She had been warned that the dictation she took often involved information about new processes or products, test results, analyses of competitors' products, and other confidential information.

She was shocked one day when Dr. Barton told her that information about a new product has been leaked to another corporation and would cause the loss of millions of dollars to her company. All employees, even she, were under suspicion. She was so shocked by the implication of her guilt that she could think of no reply.

In trying to assess the blame, she reviewed her relationships with the rest of the staff and remembered that when she returned from lunch one day, she surprised Al Johnson, a recently hired junior chemist, as he was rummaging through her desk. His explanation was that he had misplaced the schedule of projects and knew she had another one in her desk.

She also remembered that although she usually kept the top drawer of her desk locked and the key in her purse, she had neglected to lock the drawer that day. She was so sure that she knew the culprit that she decided to confront Al Johnson and insist that he tell Dr. Barton about his involvement and take full responsibility.

What steps would you have taken in this situation?

Case 3-2
CARELESSNESS IN MAILING CORRESPONDENCE

J. J. Payhos, branch sales manager of a large national corporation, was concerned about the disappointing performance of a salesperson under his supervision. He and the corporate sales manager had been discussing termination of the salesperson's employment.

Mr. Payhos then dictated a stern but courteous memo to the salesperson telling him that he must meet next month's sales quota and increase the number of daily calls if he hoped to stay with the company. At the bottom of the carbon copy which was to be sent to the corporate sales manager, he wrote in longhand, "Hope I wasn't too hard on him, but he has been goofing off long enough. I'll keep you informed of developments."

Two days later Herbert Prospy, the secretary who had transcribed the memo, was confronted by an irate Mr. Payhos: "Just look at this. See what you have done! You put the memos in the wrong envelopes. *This* is what happened." Herbert was handed the memo intended for the corporate sales manager with a second notation at the bottom: "I resign. I never 'goofed off' in my life."

Herbert remembers that when Mr. Payhos sent him on an emergency errand at 4:45, he gave the day's mail to the clerk assigned to him and asked him to insert the transcribed materials into the envelopes and see that they were dispatched.

What should Herbert say to his principal? How should he handle the error with the clerk? What principle is involved?

Case 3-3
DELEGATION OF CORRESPONDENCE RESPONSIBILITIES

Alice Barry, secretary to Edwin New, president of a large manufacturing company, was overworked. Her employer gave her heavy responsibility and regarded her as his strong right arm, never giving part of his work to others. Alice stayed long after 5 p.m. to finish each day's work and always felt hurried during the day as she tried to meet the expectations of her boss. Also, feeling indispensable, she carried in her mind much of the burden of her job after she finally left for the night.

She decided to discuss the situation with Mr. New, but three weeks passed before she could broach her problem. One evening just before five, she started to describe the problem and ask Mr. New's advice for its solution. After one sentence Mr. New broke in with, "Yes, Alice, I know you have too much to do. Why don't you get some of the people in the typing pool to help you on some of the routine jobs? I certainly don't want you to work so hard that you get ill. Just work things out and anything you do will be fine with me. I want to catch the 5:25, so I'll have to hurry."

With that Mr. New took his briefcase and rushed from the office. In fact, Alice felt that he was somewhat annoyed that she had brought up the problem.

The next morning Alice went to two young stenographers who had impressed her as competent and assigned 50 form letters to be completed by 4 p.m. Rather than being flattered to work directly for the president, they seemed annoyed and indicated that they would do the work — but only as a favor to Alice. At 4:30 they left the letters on her desk. In her usual check she found many errors that made the letters unmailable. She stayed after five to retype the letters, took a pill for her ulcer, and grumbled, "Well, *that* didn't help matters; I had to do the work myself after all. I don't know why these kids that we get in here can't do anything right."

What principles of supervision had Alice Barry violated? How could she have solved her problem?

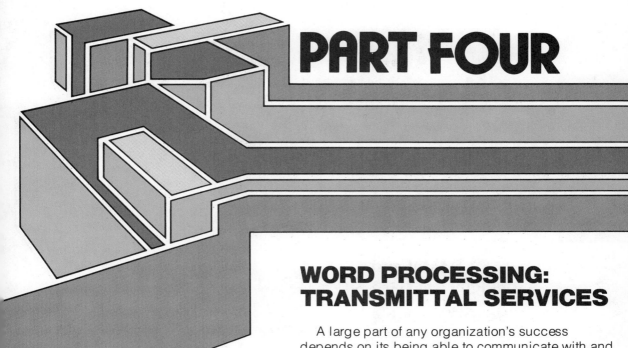

PART FOUR

WORD PROCESSING: TRANSMITTAL SERVICES

A large part of any organization's success depends on its being able to communicate with and exchange goods with other locations as expeditiously and as cheaply as possible. Technological advances are occurring at mind-boggling speed that make possible new modes of transmittal. Rates are rising so rapidly, too, that they are forcing new evaluations of alternative ways of sending products and information. Part of the secretary's expertise depends on acquiring a background of information about the telephone, postal, and shipping services available, the requirements for using them, and comparative costs. Only then can suitable telephone services be selected and appropriate instructions be given to the mail room and to the shipping department.

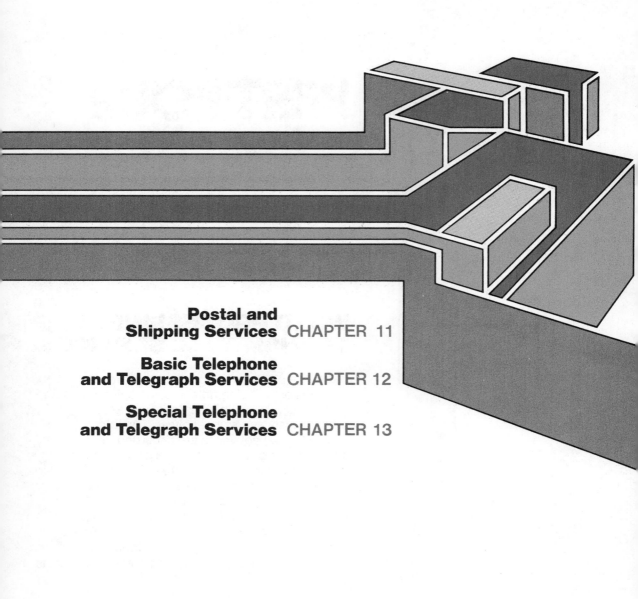

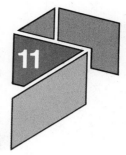

Postal and Shipping Services

Hardly a day goes by that a crisis does not develop in the office because a vital letter was not received or a package was delayed past its promised date. Yet since 1971, postage rates have doubled although the consumer price index has risen only 31 percent. More than half of the companies with over 1,000 employees pay more than $50,000 a year for postage.

The secretary frequently prepares and sends business mail, including packages. Transmittal expenses can be greatly reduced by a knowledgeable secretary — one who knows postal information and services.

THE MAIL SERVICE UNDER THE POSTAL REORGANIZATION ACT OF 1970

In 1970 legislation was passed to change the postal service, which had been a department of the federal government, into a quasi-independent corporation. It was hoped that this reorganization would lead to a self-sufficient service that would no longer require federal subsidy.

Unfortunately, these dreams have not been realized. Instead of increasing, the volume of mail has been steadily decreasing. In 1974 the postal service handled 90 billion pieces of mail; by 1979 it is estimated that the volume will be 84 billion pieces. Since 1971 parcel post has dropped from 968 million packages to fewer than 800 million pieces.

The plan of the Postal Reorganization Act was to mechanize mail handling, and 21 bulk mail stations were built in various parts of the country to expedite the sorting and dispatching of everything except first-class mail. As for first-class mail, the average delivery time increased from 1.3 days in 1969 to 1.6 days in 1976 because mechanization resulted in a higher percentage of missent mail.

Since the Postal Reorganization Act became operational, the average postal salary has increased 63 percent, twice as much as that of federal government employees. Naturally, decreased volume and higher salaries have resulted in postal budget deficits that grow larger every year. For instance, with a budget of 14.2 billion dollars in 1976, the postal service experienced a deficit of 1.4 billion dollars.[1]

Several factors account for the decrease in mail volume. Among them are a depressed national economy during the early years of the Act, increased use of the telephone instead of mail, development of alternative electronic media for sending messages, establishment of new services, and disenchantment with the quality of mail service. The alternatives will be discussed later in the chapter.

Undoubtedly, changes in mail services will have to be made, and interesting developments are in the offing.

DOMESTIC MAIL CLASSIFICATIONS

Domestic mail includes mail transmitted within, among, and between the United States and its territories and possessions; to Army-Air Force (APO) and Navy (FPO) post offices; to the United Nations in New York City.

The postal service divides mailable matter into the following general classes: *first class, second class, controlled circulation publications, third class, fourth class, priority mail, official and free mail, mail for the blind*, and *mixed classes*. There is no longer a higher rate for first-class airmail. First-class mail sent a considerable distance automatically goes by air. However, the airmail domestic mail classification is used when it is desirable to insure a piece of first-class mail.

General descriptions of each classification will be given in this chapter. Rates and fees will not be provided since they are subject to frequent change. For current information, consult the publications available from the local post office.

First-Class Mail

Among the kinds of mail sent by *first class* are: letters in any form (typewritten, handwritten, carbon copy, or photocopy); post cards; business reply mail; and matter partly in written form, such as bills and checks. Pieces less than 3½ inches wide or 5 inches long are nonmailable. For methods of sending first-class mail in combination

---

[1]These figures are taken from news articles in the *New York Times*, July 6, 1975; *Business Week*, March 29, 1976; the *New York Times*, February 3, 1976; and notes in various copies of *Administrative Management* magazine.

with a larger envelope or parcel of mail of another class, see pages 237–238.

The mailer who wants to send large envelopes first class should designate the class of mail on both the front and back of the envelope to prevent its being handled as third-class mail. Even better are envelopes with green diamond borders for first-class mail.

Second-Class Mail

Second-class mail includes printed newspapers and periodicals. Publishers and news agencies are granted second-class rates if they file the proper forms obtained from their local post office, pay the required fees, and comply with the regulations. Such mail must bear notice of second-class entry and be mailed in bulk lots.

Newspapers and periodicals that are mailed unsealed by the public are sent at a single-piece rate.

Controlled Circulation Publications

Publications of 24 or more pages which are circulated free, or mainly free, come under a special class called *controlled circulation publications*. Since only a limited number of secretaries will work with this class of mail, it is recommended that when information regarding such mailings is needed, the secretary consult the local post office.

Third-Class Mail

Third-class mail is used for matter that cannot be classified as first- or second-class mail and that weighs up to 16 ounces. The same matter in parcels of 16 ounces and over is considered fourth-class mail.

All sealed pieces mailed at the third-class postage rates must be marked THIRD CLASS (or BULK RATE if bulk rate has been authorized). This notation must be printed on the front of the envelope. It may be included in a permit imprint or meter stamp. Third-class mail which is unsealed does not require any endorsement.

Mail that may be sent third class includes merchandise, printed matter, keys, and so on. Special rates also apply to books, manuscripts, music, sound recordings, films, and the like.

Fourth-Class Mail

The more common term for *fourth-class service* is *parcel post*. It includes all mailable matter not in first, second, or third class which weighs 16 ounces or over.

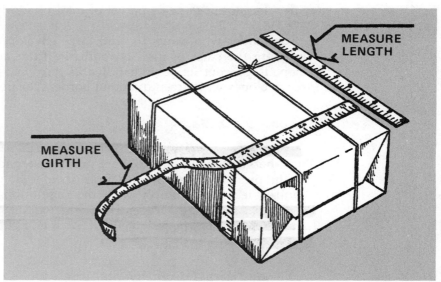

MEASURE
LENGTH

MEASURE
GIRTH

Postal Service Manual

To determine the size of a parcel, measure the longest side to get the length; measure the distance around the parcel at its thickest part to get the girth; and add the two figures together. For example, a parcel 10 inches long, 8 inches wide, and 4½ inches high measures 35 inches in length and girth combined (length, 10 inches; girth, 25 inches: 4½ inches + 8 inches + 4½ inches + 8 inches). A free pamphlet on "Packaging for Mailing" may be obtained from your post office.

Parcel-post rates are scaled according to the weight of the parcel and the distance it is being transported. Every local post office charts the country into eight zones. Zone charts showing the parcel-post zone of any domestic post office in relation to the sender's post office may be obtained free from the sender's post office.

There are both weight and size limits for fourth-class packages according to delivery zones. Size limits are given in total inches of length and girth combined, as shown in the illustration above. There are also special rates according to weight and zone for bound printed matter weighing 16 ounces or over. Size limits vary by class of post office at the destination. Consult your local post office.

Third- or fourth-class packages may be sent unsealed or sealed. Mailing of sealed packages implies that the sender consents to inspection of the contents. This silent assent replaces the old written endorsement: MAY BE OPENED FOR POSTAL INSPECTION. A sealed package is treated as parcel post by the postal sorters no matter what rate of postage has been paid unless the package is conspicuously marked FIRST CLASS.

Certain kinds of packaged mail are given special low rates as follows:

Special Fourth-Class Mail. Books without advertising that contain at least 22 printed pages are eligible for a preferential rate.

Library Materials. The *Library Rate* applies to materials sent to or from libraries, schools, and certain nonprofit organizations. The secretary may use this rate when returning qualifying material to any of the organizations that are permitted to use this rate. The rate is the same to all zones and applies to books, periodicals, theses, microfilms, music, sound recordings, films, and other library materials. The package may be sealed, but it must be marked LIBRARY RATE.

It is recommended that the sender consult the local post office before mailing special fourth-class mail or library materials.

Priority Mail

Priority mail refers to first-class mail weighing more than 13 ounces. When mail weighs more than 13 ounces a decreasing rate scale operates. Priority mail travels by air but does not involve a guaranteed delivery time.

Official and Free Mail

Federal government offices and personnel send out official mail without affixing postage. There are two kinds of official mail: franked mail and penalty mail.

A *franked* piece of mail must have a real or facsimile signature of the sender in place of the stamp and the words PUBLIC DOCUMENT — FREE on the address side. Only a few persons are authorized to use the frank, such as the Vice-President of the United States, members and members-elect of Congress, Resident Commissioners, the Secretary of the Senate, and the Sergeant of Arms of the Senate.

Penalty mail is used for official government correspondence. It travels in penalty envelopes or under penalty labels.

Free mail — mail sent without postage by the general public — is limited to a few items such as matter addressed to the Register of Copyrights, census mail, immigration and naturalization service mail, and absentee ballot envelopes from members of the Armed Forces. For further details, consult the local post office.

Mixed Classes of Mail

Sometimes it is expedient and reflects better judgment to send two pieces of mail of different classes together as a single mailing to

Congress of the United States
House of Representatives
Washington, D.C. 20515

OFFICIAL BUSINESS

Donald D. Clancy
M.C.

MR REX YOUNG
3788 WESTMONT DRIVE

UNITED STATES POST OFFICE

LOCKLAND BR.
CINCINNATI, OH 45215

PENALTY FOR PRIVATE
USE TO AVOID PAYMENT
OF POSTAGE, $300

U.S.MAIL

OFFICIAL BUSINESS
P-186

MR REX YOUNG
3788 WESTMONT DRIVE
CINCINNATI OH 45205

Notice the difference between an official franked envelope and penalty envelope. A franked envelope must show a real or facsimile signature and carry the words OFFICIAL BUSINESS. A penalty envelope must carry the penalty warning and the words OFFICIAL BUSINESS under a return address.

assure their arrival at the same time. For example, a first-class letter might be enclosed in a shipment of manuscript to an author. The material would be sent at the priority mail rate.

Mail for the Blind

Some kinds of mail to and from the blind may be mailed free; other kinds may be mailed at nominal rates. If, as secretary, your work involves sending letters and parcels to or from the blind, you will want to consult the local post office.

SPECIAL MAIL SERVICES

In addition to transmitting mail, the post office provides many special services. The sender should be aware, however, that fees for such services may be very expensive.

Registered and Insured Mail

A piece of important or valuable mail can be registered or insured, depending on its nature.

Registering Mail. First-class, airmail, or priority mail can be registered. The full amount of the value of the contents must be declared on a piece of mail being registered because the fee charged is based on the full value. There are two sets of fees. The one used depends upon whether the sender has commercial insurance covering the matter being mailed. The rates are slightly lower for values above $1,000 if the sender has such insurance. When the maximum liability of the post office is less than the value of the shipment, special private insurance is usually taken out by the sender for the specific shipment during transit.

Each piece of mail to be registered must be tightly sealed along all edges (transparent tape cannot be used) and must bear the complete addresses of both the sender and addressee. The sender takes it to the registry window where the postal clerk computes the fee.

The sender of the registered mail may instruct the postal service to change the address should it be necessary. For example, if you sent a registered letter to a company salesperson in St. Louis and then learned that the person had moved to Kansas City, you would telephone the St. Louis post office and request that the address be changed.

Insuring Mail. A piece of third- or fourth-class mail, or priority mail containing third- or fourth-class matter, may be insured up to $200. The package is taken to the post office window where the clerk makes out a receipt for it, stamps the package INSURED, and puts on it the receipt number, if any. An unnumbered receipt is given if the package is insured for $15 or less. After placing the regular and insured postage on the package, the clerk gives the receipt to the sender for filing. If the package is lost or damaged, the post office reimburses the sender according to the amount of the fee.

If a business frequently sends several insured packages at one time, it may be more convenient to use a mailing book rather than filing a separate receipt for each package. Mailing books, which are issued by the post office on request, provide pages for entering the description of parcels insured. The sheets of this book are officially endorsed at the time of mailing and become the sender's receipts.

Return Receipts and Restricted Delivery. The sender is always furnished with a receipt showing that the post office accepted the piece of insured or registered mail for transmittal and delivery. However, the sender often wants legal evidence that the piece of mail was also actually received by the addressee. For an added fee the sender may obtain a signed receipt, commonly called a *return receipt*, on any piece of certified or registered mail or on any piece of mail insured for more than $15. This service is helpful when the address used is one of several years' duration or when there is reason to believe that the addressee may have moved.

A sender who wants a return receipt fills in the number of the receipt, name, and address on a postal-card form supplied by the post office, and writes RETURN RECEIPT REQUESTED on the front of the mail.

This card is pasted (face down) along its two gummed edges to the back of the envelope or package. At delivery the letter carrier removes the card, obtains the addressee's signature on the un-gummed (reverse) side, fills in the information required, and mails the card to the sender.

For an added fee, delivery may be *restricted to the addressee* only if the piece of mail is registered, certified, or insured for more than $15. The charge for a return receipt is almost doubled if the receipt is requested after mailing.

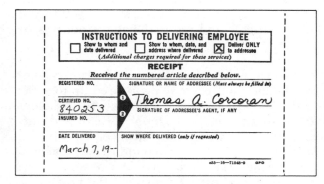

Ungummed Side

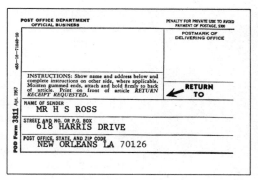

Gummed Side

Return Receipt

COD Service

Merchandise may be sent to a purchaser *COD* — that is, *collect on delivery* — if the shipment is based on a bona fide order or on an agreement made with the addressee by the mailer. The sender pre-pays the postage on the shipment and the COD fees, but they may be included in the amount to be collected if agreeable to the addressee. Otherwise, the addressee pays the amount due on the merchandise, plus the fee for the money order to return the money collected to the sender. The maximum amount collectible on one parcel is $300. If the sender alters the COD charges after the parcel is sent or desig-nates a new addressee, an additional charge is made. Information on mailing COD parcels is available from the local post office.

Certificates of Mailing

For a few cents a sender may obtain a very simple proof of having taken a piece of mail to the post office for dispatching. Such proof may be used for any kind of mail. The sender fills in the information required on a certificate blank, pastes on the appropriate stamp, and hands this certificate to the postal clerk with the piece of mail. The clerk cancels the stamp and hands the certificate back to the sender as evidence that the piece of mail was received at the post office.

This is an economical service for one who is mailing something that is of value to the addressee but who has no obligation or responsibility to pay the extra expense of having the material insured, registered, or certified. It also furnishes a sender with inexpensive proof of having mailed tax returns.

Special Delivery and Special Handling

The delivery of a piece of mail may be expedited by the use of special-delivery or special-handling services.

Special Delivery. *Special-delivery service* provides the fastest handling — from mailer to addressee — for all classes of mail. Mail must be marked SPECIAL DELIVERY above the address. Immediate delivery is by messenger during prescribed hours to points within certain limits of any post office or delivery station. Do not send special-delivery mail to post-office-box addresses, military installations (APO, FPO), or other places where mail delivery will not be expedited after arrival.

Special Handling. Most people are not aware of *special handling* for third- and fourth-class mail — a service that is less expensive than special delivery. It provides the most expeditious handling and ground transportation practicable. Parcels move with first class, but they do not receive special delivery at the destination post office.

Since all special-delivery mail (including packages) is handled and transported in the same manner as first-class mail, it is not necessary to include special handling on a package being sent special delivery.

Certified Mail

Certified-mail service requires that a record of delivery be maintained by the post office from which a letter is delivered. The carrier delivering the item obtains a signature from the addressee on a receipt form that is kept for two years. Certified mail is appropriate

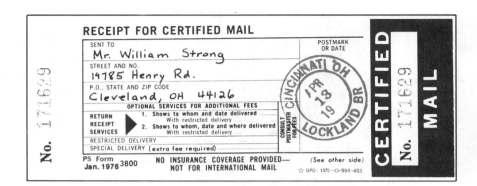

Receipt for Certified Mail

for first-class mail that has no real value (such as a letter, bill, or nonnegotiable bond). It carries no insurance. If a return receipt is to be sent to the mailer, an additional fee is charged.

Certified mail has the following advantages: (1) It provides the sender with a means of checking on the delivery of the letter. (2) It provides official evidence of mailing if a postmarked receipt is obtained. (3) It gives the letter the appearance of importance and urgency, and for that reason it is frequently used by many collection agencies.

Insufficient Postage

Formerly mail deposited without a stamp was delivered to the addressee and postage was collected at that point. Today such mail is not delivered.

Slugs for Hand Stamping

Bulky mail, called *slugs*, should be marked HAND STAMP in large red letters on both the front and back of the envelope. Unmarked slugs are often ruined during mail processing. Unless clearly marked for separation from other mail, slugs may be routinely placed in the canceling machine and may cause serious damage to it.

Stamps and Stamped Envelopes

Ordinary postage stamps are available in sheet, coil, or booklet form. Postage stamps can be exchanged at full value if stamps of the wrong denomination were purchased or if damaged stamps were received.

Precanceled Stamps and Envelopes. *Precanceled stamps* and *precanceled stamped envelopes* may be used only by those persons or companies who have been issued a permit to use them. Also, they may be used only on matter presented at the post office where the precanceled stamps or envelopes were purchased. Their advantage is the saving of canceling time at the post office.

Stamped Envelopes and Cards. Stamped envelopes in various sizes, kinds, and denominations may be purchased at the post office individually or in quantity lots. For a nominal amount, the post office will have the sender's return request and name and address imprinted on them when the envelopes are ordered in quantity lots. Two lines of advertising material may also be included.

First-class postal cards are available in single or double form, the latter kind being used when a reply is desired on the attached card. To facilitate in-company printing, government postal cards are available in sheets of 40.

Unserviceable and spoiled stamped envelopes and cards (if uncanceled) may be exchanged at postage value. Such exchanges are made in stamps, stamped envelopes, or postal cards.

Metered Postage

One of the quickest and most efficient ways of affixing postage to mail of any class is by means of a *postage meter* machine. The postage meter prints on each piece of mail the postmark and the proper amount of postage. Consequently, metered mail need not be canceled or postmarked when it reaches the post office. As a result, it often catches earlier trains or planes than does other mail.

The meter machine may be fully automatic, not only printing the postage, postmark, and date of mailing, but also feeding, sealing, and stacking the meter-stamped envelopes. The imprint is usually red and may carry a line or two of advertising. Some models can also print the postage on gummed tape which can be pasted onto packages. The meter registers the amount of postage used on each piece of mail, the amount of postage remaining in the meter, and the number of pieces that have passed through the machine.

The machine itself is purchased outright, but the meter mechanism is leased. In order to use a postage meter, a company must first obtain a meter license by filing an application with the post office where its mail is handled. The application must tell the make and model of the meter. A record of use must be maintained in a *Meter Record Book* supplied by the post office.

The meter is taken out of the machine to the post office where the meter is set and locked for the amount of postage bought. When that

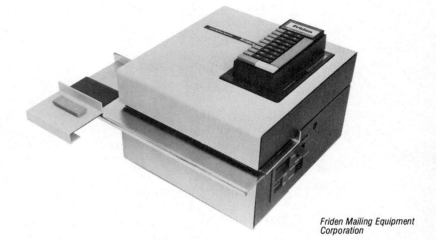

Postage meters simplify and speed the preparation of outgoing mail. The secretary who works for a smaller company with no central mail room may use a desk-top postage meter similar to this one.

Friden Mailing Equipment Corporation

amount of postage is used up, the meter locks. Then it is necessary to take it to the post office again and pay for more postage. Additional postage may be purchased before the meter locks. Unused meter stamps accompanied by an application and returned within one year from dates appearing in the stamps will be considered for refunds.

Forwarding, Returning, and Remailing

Unfortunately, mail does not always reach its final destination upon first mailing. Some pieces must be forwarded, returned to the sender, or remailed. Additional postage may or may not be required.

Forwarding Mail. The secretary is often required to forward mail. The following information indicates the extra postage or fee required.

First-Class Mail Up to 13 Ounces — No additional postage required. Change the address and deposit in mail.

Second-Class Publications — Full postage must be paid at a single-piece rate. Change address, affix postage, endorse SECOND-CLASS MAIL, and deposit in mail.

Third-Class and Fourth-Class Mail — Additional postage at applicable rate must be paid. Change address, affix postage, and deposit in mail.

Registered, Certified, Insured, COD, and Special-Handling Mail — Forwarded without payment of additional registry, insurance, COD, or special-handling fees; however, ordinary forwarding postage charge, if any, must be paid.

Special-Delivery Service — This mail will not receive special-delivery service at second address unless a change-of-address card has been filed.

Return of Undeliverable Mail. An undeliverable first-class letter will be returned to the sender free of charge. For undeliverable third- or fourth-class parcels, the sender must pay full postage for the return service. To assure that third- and fourth-class packages are returned, place RETURN POSTAGE GUARANTEED conspicuously below the return address.

Undeliverable letters and packages without return addresses are sent to the dead-letter office where they are examined. They may be opened to find a return address, so it is wise to enclose a completed address label in a package being mailed. Whenever an address is found, the mail is returned for a fee. Undeliverable dead mail is destroyed or sold.

Remailing Returned Mail. The secretary is always chagrined when mail is returned. Any piece of mail returned with the "pointing finger" rubber stamp RETURNED TO WRITER and with one of six reasons checked must be put in a fresh, correctly addressed envelope, and postage paid again.

Change of Address

The post office serving you must be officially notified by letter or by one of its forms when you change your address. The old and the new address and the date when the new address is effective must be given. Correspondents should be notified of a new address promptly by special notices or by stickers attached to all outgoing mail. The post office will supply new-address cards free for personal and business use.

Recalling Mail

Occasionally it may be necessary to recall a piece of mail that has been posted. This calls for fast action. Type an addressed envelope that duplicates the one mailed. Go to the post office in your mailing zone if the letter is local or to the central post office if the letter is an out-of-town mailing. Fill in *Sender's Application for Recall of Mail.*

If the mail is an undelivered local letter, on-the-spot return will be made. If the letter has left the post office for an out-of-town address, the post office (at the sender's request and expense) will wire or telephone the addressee's post office and ask that the letter be returned. If the mail has already been delivered, the sender is notified; but the addressee is not informed that a recall was requested.

Presorting Mail

To encourage large mailers to presort mail before depositing it in the post office, the postal service has inaugurated a reduction of postage on each piece when 300 to 500 pieces of mail (depending on the class) are presorted according to specifications. Because the secretary will rarely mail that many pieces at one time, details are not given here. The opportunity for postage reduction, however, carries the implication that every mailer in the organization must cooperate in enabling the mail room to secure such reductions. This means that mail should be sent to the mail room regularly during the day rather than following the practice now prevalent in which 75 percent of outgoing material reaches the mail room at some point in the late afternoon.

The secretary who is responsible for mailing material outside the company should presort mail for speedier handling by the post office. Before depositing mail, separate it into major categories such as local, out-of-town, precanceled, and metered. It can then bypass one or more preliminary handlings in the post office. Types of presorting vary with the types of individual mailings. For instance, if most of the mail goes to in-state addresses, this mail may be kept separate and identified as "all for (*State*)," thus eliminating one sorting operation and permitting immediate placement with the mail for that state.

Metered Mail. Postal regulations require bundling and identifying five or more pieces of metered mail.

Presorting by ZIP Code. Mail presorted by ZIP Code moves faster. Large mailers can presort and forward mail to a specific ZIP Code or to a specific company in one bag. The post office furnishes trays for presorting in preparing mail for deposit at the post office.

MAIL COLLECTION AND DELIVERY

A number of plans have been inaugurated by the postal service to improve service and to reduce operational cost.

ZIP Code and Optical Character Reader

The five-digit *ZIP* (Zone Improvement Plan) *Code* was designed to speed mail deliveries and facilitate use of automated equipment to reduce costs.

Type the ZIP Code, without a comma, one space after the state name. To permit the use of addressing equipment with limited line length for bulk mailings, the postal service has designed and approved a two-letter abbreviation for each state and abbreviations for cities with long names. The two-letter abbreviations can be used *only with a ZIP Code*. The list of approved abbreviations is presented on page 749 of this book.

Optical character readers that electronically read addresses are used in post offices in several major cities and will be used increasingly as more locations add new equipment. Post office optical character readers are programmed to scan a specific area on all envelopes; so the address must be completely within this read-zone, single-spaced, blocked in style. The two-letter state abbreviations, typed in uppercase, must be used. Acceptable placements for a No. 10 and a No. 6¾ envelope are shown on page 248.

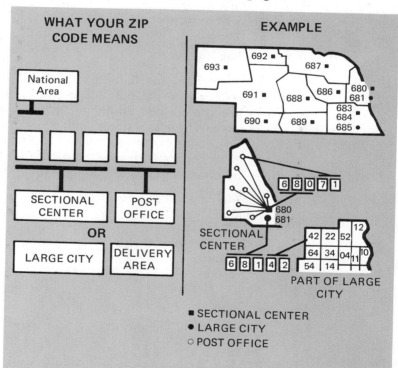

- Together, the *first three digits* of any ZIP Code number stand for either a particular Sectional Center *or* a metropolitan city.

- The *last two digits* of a Sectional Center ZIP Code number stand for one of the *associated post offices* served by the Sectional Center.

- The *last two digits* of a metropolitan city ZIP Code stand for one of the *delivery areas* served by the city post office, its branches and stations.

The experimental optical scanner scans the address and puts a dot-dash code on the envelope. This code can then be read by a relatively inexpensive mechanical reader at subsequent points in the distribution process.

All bulk mailers of second- or third-class mail are required to include the ZIP Code on the address. Failure to do so may subject the mail to a higher-postal-rate penalty. When the mail is being sorted, a letter with no ZIP Code goes into the reject slot, delaying the sorting operation.

A *ZIP Code Directory* can be purchased from the Superintendent of Documents, U.S. Government Printing Office, Washington, DC 20402. The cost is less than it may seem, for the directory is updated without charge. Other sources of ZIP Codes are the current edition of the *World Almanac and Book of Facts* and the directory placed in the lobby of most post offices.

Bar Codes

A series of bars and half-bars found on some letter mail represents an address to the post office electronic system. The series of bars below the address contains the ZIP Code and certain letters and numbers from the street address, city, and state. Envelopes bearing bar codes can be sorted mechanically at the rate of 42,000 an hour. Bar coding is most often used on business reply envelopes where the code is imprinted along with the address. The business reply envelope on page 249 is bar coded.

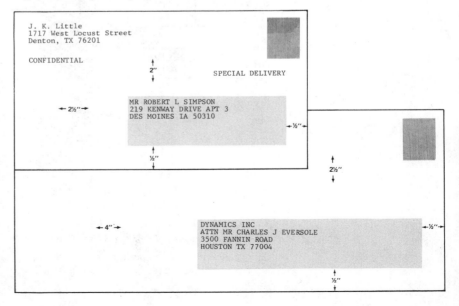

Post office optical character readers are programmed to scan a specific area on all envelopes. The illustration shows the read-zones within which the address must be typed on No. 6¾ and No. 10 envelopes.

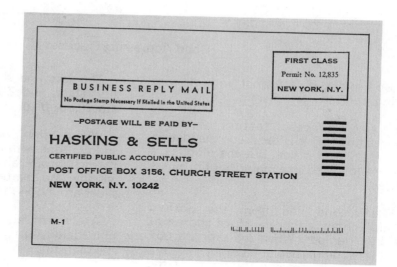

Business Reply Envelope Showing Bar Code

Post-Office Box

It is possible to rent a post-office box where mail can be picked up at any time that the post office building is open. Mail can be obtained faster from the box than from the carrier.

Experimental Express Mail Service

Experimental Express Mail Service is a rapidly growing system serving more than 600 cities in the United States. It is supplied to large mailers on a contract basis under four options:

1. On a regularly scheduled basis a postal driver picks up dispatches and takes them to a special airport agent. This agent dispatches them on the next aircraft to the destination city where another special postal agent gives them to a postal driver for delivery.

2. The same service except that the addressee picks up the mail at the receiving airport.

3. The same service except that the mailer takes the dispatches to the airport.

4. The same service except that the mailer and the addressee handle delivery to and from the airport.

Under Option 5 (available without contract) the mailer delivers the dispatches before 5 p.m. to a designated downtown outlet, which guarantees delivery to the destination post office for pickup by 10 a.m. the following morning.

Good Addressing Practices

Use a block-style format with all lines having a uniform left margin.

Use uppercase letters without punctuation. (This is the recommendation of the US post office, but the practice is not yet followed in a majority of business offices.)

The second line from the bottom should contain either the street address or the box number. When indicating a box number at a particular station, the box number should precede the name of the station.

The last line should contain only the city, state, and ZIP Code. The ZIP Code should not be placed on a line by itself.

When using window envelopes, the address zone within the window should be ¼ inch from all of the edges of the window, no matter how much the insert slides around in the envelope.

Apartment numbers should be placed immediately after the street address, on the same line.

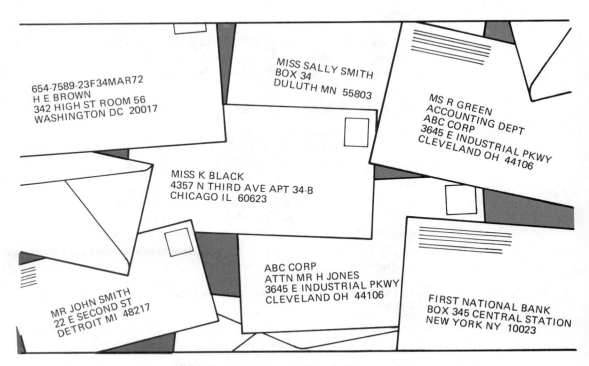

654-7589-23F34MAR72
H E BROWN
342 HIGH ST ROOM 56
WASHINGTON DC 20017

MISS SALLY SMITH
BOX 34
DULUTH MN 55803

MS R GREEN
ACCOUNTING DEPT
ABC CORP
3645 E INDUSTRIAL PKWY
CLEVELAND OH 44106

MISS K BLACK
4357 N THIRD AVE APT 34-B
CHICAGO IL 60623

MR JOHN SMITH
22 E SECOND ST
DETROIT MI 48217

ABC CORP
ATTN MR H JONES
3645 E INDUSTRIAL PKWY
CLEVELAND OH 44106

FIRST NATIONAL BANK
BOX 345 CENTRAL STATION
NEW YORK NY 10023

Reprinted from United States Postal Service, Guidelines for Designing and Printing Envelopes for Machine Processing, March, 1973.

Mailgram

The *mailgram* (described and illustrated on pages 286–287) is the result of cooperation between the postal service and Western Union. Western Union owns and installs in post offices equipment that receives messages on a continuous roll of paper. A postal service employee tears off the message, inserts it into a window envelope, and dispatches it for guaranteed delivery with the next morning's mail.

VIM

VIM (Vertical Improved Mail) is a mail distribution system installed in many new large office buildings. In essence, VIM is the reverse of the familiar mail chute that channels mail dropped from the upper floors into a collection box. Under VIM all incoming mail is delivered to a central mail room in the building. There postal employees sort it into lockboxes by floors. These boxes are then placed on a conveyor belt and keyed to be ejected automatically to the right floor. There the office personnel pick up and deliver the mail. By this process the offices on each floor of the building can have continuous delivery of incoming mail. In buildings where lockboxes are not feasible, call windows can be used for frequent pickup of mail.

General Delivery

Mail may be addressed to individuals in care of the *General Delivery* window of main post offices. This service is convenient to transients and to individuals who have no definite address in a city. Such mail is held for a specified number of days and, if uncalled for, is then returned to the sender.

The executive on a touring vacation or a sales representative who is driving for several days and does not have hotel addresses frequently asks to have mail addressed in care of GENERAL DELIVERY to a city en route. The address can also include the words TRANSIENT or TO BE CALLED FOR. This is the way the envelope address would look:

```
DELTA PI EPSILON
J. R. Sutton
7234 Miami Street
Mariemont, OH 45227

TO BE CALLED FOR

                    MS JERRI T MASTERSON
                    GENERAL DELIVERY
                    SALT LAKE CITY UT 84001
```

Such a letter would go to the main post office in Salt Lake City and be held at the *General Delivery* window for Ms. Masterson for 10 days or up to 30 days if the envelope bore such a request. If not picked up within that time, the letter would be returned to the sender.

Update of Mailing Lists

The mailer can do a great deal to secure information about changes of address by using first-class mail marked ADDRESS CORRECTION REQUESTED, RETURN POSTAGE GUARANTEED and paying a fee to the carrier delivering the returned mail.

The postmaster will correct any list of local mailing addresses at the expense of the mailer. Cards with the addresses of the "lost" addressees are distributed to the local carriers who fill in the correct addresses or explain other reasons why delivery cannot be made, such as NO SUCH NUMBER.

The list should be typed on cards about the size and quality of postal cards, with one address per card. The name of the owner of the list should be placed in the upper left corner of each card for identification purposes. Cards should be sent only to the post office that serves the address shown on the card.

Attempts to Bypass the Post Office

The United States Congress has invested the postal service with an absolute monopoly over the transportation of letters; if a *private* carrier is used, required postage must be affixed. To meet this stipulation, it is not uncommon for the mailer to affix the required postage and still transport the mail by private carrier. A large company may regularly send an air courier between offices to carry stamped letters.

Other companies use their own employees for mail delivery of unstamped letters between their offices and companies with whom they conduct a large volume of business. Another time- and money-saving operation is hand delivery of bills. Some magazines now send issues to their news dealers for hand delivery.

Probably the greatest cause of decreasing mail volume is the computerized transfer of money rather than sending checks by mail. The greatest user of the electronic transmission of funds is the vast Social Security system. Finally, facsimile document transmission is a worthwhile alternative to the vagaries of postal delivery.

Wiltek is an example of a complete electronic mail service. An advertisement in the *Wall Street Journal* describes it in this way:

Correspondence gets handled right at the source. With the new Wiltek electronic mail service, your secretary will no longer take your memo to a copier. Messengers will no longer carry your confidential management reports to the mail room. Or your sales order to the teletypewriter center. No postal employee will sort your correspondence, put it in a bag, carry it on trucks or airplanes. No one will delay it, misdirect it, or lose it.

The Wiltek electronic mail station right outside your office door will bypass all these old familar problems.

Simply compose your message as you do now. Your secretary types it on the Wiltek electronic mail station typewriter. Following your review and corrections, the correspondence is automatically picked up and routed swiftly by the Wiltek electronic mail service. At its destination, another Wiltek electronic mail station types it out at 450 words per minute. Beautifully. In executive type face on letterhead paper if you wish. It will look clean, accurate, crisp, impressive. The way you want it to look.

MONEY ORDERS

Money may be transferred from one person or business to another by use of a *money order*. There are instances in which money orders are the requested form of payment. They are also a convenience to individuals who do not have a checking account.

Domestic Money Orders

Postal money orders may be purchased at all post offices, branches, and stations. The maximum amount for a single *domestic money order* is $300. However, there is no limit on the number of money orders that may be purchased at one time. Money orders are also available at a low rate to depositors at savings banks.

International Money Orders

Money may be sent to a foreign country by means of an *international money order* procurable at the local post office. When buying such an order, you are given only a receipt for it by the postal clerk, who then arranges for sending the money order abroad. Exact information is required about the payee and the payee's address; if the payee is a woman, you must state whether she is a single, married, or widowed. The purpose of the payment should also be stated.

INTERNATIONAL MAIL

Information regarding the rates, services, and regulations covering international mail may be obtained from the local post office or from *The Directory of International Mail.*

Classifications of International Mail

International postal service provides for *postal union mail* and *parcel post.*

Postal Union Mail. *Postal union mail* is divided into *LC Mail* and *AO Mail.*

LC Mail (Letters and Cards) — letters, letter packages, air letters (aerogrammes), and postal cards

AO Mail (Other Articles) — printed matter, merchandise samples without salable value, commercial papers, small packets, matter for the blind.

The postage for letters and postal cards mailed to Canada and Mexico is the same as for the United States.

To all other countries the rates are higher and weights are limited. Letter packages (small, sealed packages sent at a letter rate of postage) are given letter treatment if they are marked LETTER. A customs label identifying the contents must be attached to each letter package carrying dutiable merchandise.

Parcel Post. Parcels for transmission overseas are mailed by *parcel post* and must be packed even more carefully than those delivered within the continental United States. These packages may be registered or insured. Special-handling services are also available. There is now no international COD service. A *customs-declaration* form must be attached to the parcel with an accurate and complete description of the contents. As rates, weight limitations, and other regulations are not the same for all countries, the secretary should obtain information from the post office about requirements for a particular shipment.

International Air Postal Services

Rates on letters by air to foreign countries are charged at a fixed rate for a half ounce (except to Canada and Mexico where rates are the same as in the United States — a one-ounce basis for a fixed rate).

Air Letters (Aerogrammes). The post office sells an *air-letter* sheet which may be mailed to any country with which we maintain airmail service. It is an airmail, prestamped, lightweight, single sheet that is folded into the form of an envelope and sealed. No enclosures, either paper or other kinds, are permitted. Firms engaged in international trade may print, subject to prior approval of the postal service, their own aerogramme letterheads.

AO Mail by Air. Many businesses are not aware of the cheapest and fastest of all international postal services — *AO mail by air.* No export forms are required for most shipments. This service is restricted to samples of such items as merchandise, maps, printed matter, and drawings; but it is ideal for shipping small articles and should be investigated by those companies using other air services.

International Air Parcel Post. A minimum of forms is required in shipping by *international air parcel post.* This service is available to nearly all countries and is rated on the first four ounces and each additional four ounces according to the country of destination.

Reply Postage

To enclose reply postage with mail going out of the country, use an international reply coupon, called *Coupon-Response International.* It is purchased at the post office and is exchanged for stamps by the addressee in the country where it is received. The stamps are then used for postage on the reply mail addressed to this country.

SPEEDING MAIL DELIVERY

- Type addresses within the OCR read-zone. Use single spacing and keep the address to three lines or, at the most, four.

- In addressing mail to multi-unit buildings, type the room, suite, or apartment number on the second line, *after* the street address.

- *ZIP Code* all mail.

- When the volume justifies the nominal expense, use the services of the post office to correct mailing lists and to add ZIP Codes.

- Bypass one or more preliminary handlings at the post office by presorting mail before depositing it.

- Mail early and often rather than all at once at the close of the business day. Establish an afternoon cutoff time for low-priority first-class mail (usually 2 or 3 p.m.) and send it to the post office before the evening rush. Low-priority first-class mail readied after this cutoff is then scheduled for deposit the following morning.

- Investigate the desirability of renting a *post-office box.* Box holders can obtain mail more often and at irregular hours. Mailgrams can be obtained by the start of the working day.

- When urgency is indicated, consider Express Mail Service, mailgrams, or facsimile mail (if available).

TIPS FOR REDUCING POSTAL EXPENSE

- Use paper and envelope weights that approximate the requirements for the class of mail involved. (One company that had been mailing first-class letters weighing slightly more than one ounce changed to a lighter weight of paper that reduced each piece to less than one ounce and cut its first-class-mail bill in half.)

- Send some mail by classes other than first when it is not imperative that the material be delivered immediately.

- When unsure of the correct amount of postage, weigh the mail to avoid wasted postage or mail delayed by insufficient postage. Have the scales checked for accuracy periodically.

- Except for urgent items, combine in one mailing at the end of the day all mail addressed to the same person or the same branch office. (In a large company the mail room will do this for you.)

- Obtain up-to-date rate charts from the post office. Consult your mail room for new rates and regulations secured from the local post office.

- Print reports and type long letters on both sides of the paper.

- Maintain up-to-date address lists, continually correcting all lists that may involve address changes.

- When sending reply-requested mail, use business-reply envelopes and postcards rather than stamped ones, thus paying postage only on those actually returned.

- Use *Special Handling* rather than *Special Delivery* for packages except in case of emergency.

- Send mail to the mail room regularly throughout the day so that it can be presorted for reduced postage rates.

SHIPPING SERVICES

Shipments are made by means other than the post office — by air, rail, ship, bus, and truck. The secretary needs to know the kinds of services rendered, the advantages of each, and the sources to investigate for current information. The following discussion deals with three shipping services — United Parcel Service, express, and freight.

United Parcel Service

United Parcel Service carries packages among all 50 states either by air or truck. The network of 28 eastern states is closely knit for surface transportation, and there is air service between points in these 28 states and the West, Alaska, and Hawaii. United Parcel provides pickup and delivery of packages up to 50 pounds in weight and 108 inches in length and girth. An added competitive feature is automatic insurance up to $100 without charge. Rates are zoned by the weight of the package and the distance traveled.

United Parcel is an accelerated service, not an express service. The standard, however, is next-day delivery to destinations within 150 miles, second-day delivery within 450 miles, third-day delivery within 900 miles, and fourth-day delivery within 1500 miles.

If a UPS driver is unable to make a delivery the first time, the driver will try twice more before a notice is issued to pick up the package at the local UPS office. Refused or undeliverable packages are returned to the sender at no extra charge.

Express Service

Express service is offered by air or bus. Each service offers advantages, and choice of service would depend on specific shipping needs.

Air Express. *Air express* is a highly competitive, growing service. It is expensive but it is the fastest means of transporting packages. Next-day delivery is assured to most points in the United States. Pickup and delivery service is provided.

Bus Express. If the executive wants speedy delivery of a package to a small town in another part of the state, the secretary should consider *bus express*. This service is particularly useful when destination points are located where there are no airports. Round-the-clock service is offered, including Sundays and holidays — and between many points, same-day service. Pickup and delivery service is available at an extra charge. Most bus lines offer this type of shipping, the most widely known being the *Greyhound Package Express*. Items such as films, optical supplies, foodstuffs, medicines, glass, and auto parts are insurable (free up to $50) with a weight limit up to 100 pounds per package and with a size limit of 24 × 24 × 45 inches.

Freight Services

Freight is generally thought of as a shipment sent by any method other than mail or express. It is the most economical service used to transport heavy, bulky goods in large quantities. Because freight shipping is the most complex of all methods, the secretary will probably not be required to select the carrier and to route the shipments. Still, it is good to know a few of the salient facts.

Railroad Freight. Ordinarily when goods are shipped by *railroad freight*, they must be delivered by the shipper (consignor) to the local freight office. When the shipment arrives at its destination, the addressee (consignee) must arrange for delivery or must call for the shipment. Many railroads, however, have instituted store-door delivery with trucks operated by the railway company in order to meet the competition of the door-delivery service of trucking companies. More and more, the shipper loads the goods into containers at the home location and takes them to the carrier, who transports and delivers the shipment to the consignee with no further handling. Containerized shipping offers the advantage of better security, also.

A service called *piggyback* is offered by the railroads to trucking firms for long-distance hauls. Here, loaded truck trailers are driven to the railway depot in one city, detached from the trucks and placed on railroad flatcars, and moved by rail to another city where they can be unloaded and driven to their destinations. Thus towns and areas not on the regular railroad lines can be reached by this service.

To provide a less-than-carload freight service at a special rate, *freight-forwarding companies* assemble from several consignors shipments that are less than a carload and that are going to the same destination. This service allows shippers of small quantities to gain a carload rate from the railroads.

Motor Freight. *Motor freight* is used for both local and long-distance hauls. Truck companies operate coast-to-coast service and have connecting services with local trucking lines. As described above, they often work in conjunction with railroads. Sometimes shipments are held by trucking companies until they have a paying load destined for the same locality. Specialized trucks also carry single commodities such as milk, gasoline, new cars, chemicals, sand, and gravel in truckload quantities.

Air Freight. Businessess find that the higher cost of air freight is partly offset by reduced costs in inventory and in warehouse space. There is also a saving in packing costs, as air shipments do not require the sturdy crating that surface shipments frequently demand.

Delivery service is provided without charge; however, there is a small charge for pickup service.

Water Freight. *Water freight* is usually considerably cheaper than any other means of freight transportation. River barges and other vessels on the inland waterways of the United States carry such commodities as lumber, coal, iron ore, and chemicals. Bulky items

The volume of freight being moved by cargo planes is growing rapidly as businesses discover this way to reduce costs of inventory, warehouse space, and packing.

The Port Authority of NY and NJ

for overseas shipment are carried in freighters, while passenger lines carry mail and items packaged in crates. Information on services and rates can be obtained from shipping companies.

Bills of Lading. For every freight shipment — no matter what kind of freight carrier — a bill of lading must be made out. Two types are used: the *straight bill of lading* and the *order bill of lading*.

When the freight shipment is sent on open account to the consignee, the straight bill of lading is used. It is also used when the freight carrier is to act as the collection agency for a COD shipment. The letters COD and the amount to be collected are written on the face of the bill of lading.

If a bank at the destination of the shipment is to act as the collection agency, an order bill of lading and sight draft are used. In this case, the consignee pays the bank the amount of the sight draft and obtains transfer of the bill of lading. The consignee then presents the bill of lading to the carrier and receives the shipment.

Comparative Costs. Savings in time and money can be obtained by comparing costs and delivery times of the various services.

If price is important but time is not, use parcel post. United Parcel Service is more expensive but provides quicker delivery. Because of the high rate for air express, a call was made to three air-express services requesting information for the same shipment. The responses indicated that charges vary widely. For instance, one company quoted $28.35 including pickup and delivery; another, $20.45. One service quoted $9.48 for two-day service and $19.50 for overnight service, all pick-up and delivery charges included. Obviously, it would be wise to check prices for air express and air freight by telephone before making a choice.

International Shipments

The market for American products is worldwide. International air cargo service makes it possible to deliver goods to most places in the world within a matter of hours. The bulk of tonnage to foreign markets, however, still moves via *surface* (ships).

International shipments present problems — special packing, complicated shipping procedures, marine insurance, foreign exchange — usually not encountered in domestic trade. The mere handling of communications with a foreign business firm can be a problem in itself.

Shipping Documents. A foreign shipment involves the preparation of a number of documents, such as forms to obtain an *export license* (some commodities), *ocean bill of lading, consular invoice* or *certificate of origin*, and *export customs declaration*. Large manufacturers doing extensive business abroad usually establish export departments: (1) to market the products, (2) to execute the required export and shipping forms, and (3) to arrange for the actual shipments.

Many smaller firms use the services of an export broker or CEM (Combination Export Management) firm. This firm performs the same functions as an export department; namely, marketing, processing, and shipping of goods.

Some businesses prefer to use the services of a foreign freight forwarder or cargo agent, who specializes in processing foreign shipments. The agent executes the required report and shipping documents and arranges for the actual shipment.

International airlines and steamship companies also maintain departments that assist customers with their overseas shipments.

International Air Cargo. To send a shipment by *international air cargo*, whether you are sending one package or a carload, contact the office of an international airline. The airline will provide instructions on packaging and addressing the shipment and completing the necessary documents such as *bill of lading* and *customs declaration*. In many cases, air freight or even express is less expensive than international parcel post.

SUGGESTED READINGS

Business Week, Administrative Management, The Office, Time, Newsweek, and the newspapers carry reports on the postal service as changes are made.

Davidson, Albert D. *Businessman's Guide to Reducing Mailing Costs.* New York: Arco Publishing Co., 1974.

Postal Service Manual. Washington: U.S. Government Printing Office. Leaflets excerpting sections are frequently available from the local post office. Pamphlets publicizing such services as Experimental Express Mail are also available, as well as current rate sheets.

World Almanac and Book of Facts. Published annually by Newspaper Enterprise Association, 230 Park Avenue, New York, NY 10017.

ZIP Code Directory. Available from the Superintendent of Documents, U.S. Government Printing Office, Washington, DC 20402.

QUESTIONS FOR DISCUSSION

1. Why has the Postal Reorganization Act of 1970 failed to live up to expectations? What is your prediction for the future?

2. What alternative services are available for transmitting information usually sent by first-class mail? second-class mail? third-class mail? for sending packages by fourth-class mail?

3. What considerations would influence you to choose certified mail over a certificate of mailing?

4. What precautions must be taken in the placement of the address on an envelope? Why?

5. In what three in-company ways can an organization speed the mail without increasing postage costs?

6. What improvements have been made within the postal service to speed the mail?

7. Your employer hands you an addressed and sealed envelope for stamping and mailing and says that it contains an income tax return. How would you go about obtaining legal evidence that the income tax return was mailed? (The federal government prosecutes a taxpayer whose return is not received, even though the taxpayer has a carbon copy of the return and makes a verbal claim that the return was filed by mail.)

8. You are sending a request for a free brochure published in Norway. How can you arrange to enclose with your request adequate postage for mailing the brochure?

9. There are three ways of sending a letter which tells that a parcel-post package is being mailed out: separately, enclosed with the contents, or in an envelope fastened to the outside of the package. Which do you think is preferable and why?

10. Your employer asked you to mail an important letter to Germany. You are chagrined when it is returned for insufficient postage. The letter weighed one ounce, and you had affixed domestic postage.

Why was it returned? How can you prevent the recurrence of such an error?

11. Mail from the home office reaches your city post office around 2 a.m. each morning. However, it is not delivered to your office until the time of the regular mail delivery at 10:30 a.m. Your employer would like to have the home-office mail as early as possible so that district sales representatives can be told of price changes. What would you suggest to solve this problem?

12. When would you choose Experimental Express Mail over priority mailing?

13. When would a company be willing to affix letter postage but use a private carrier? Do you think that the postal service should have a monopoly over handling letter mail?

14. What are the advantages of containerized shipping?

15. Fill in the blanks in these sentences. Then use your Reference Guide to verify or correct your answers. Tell which Reference Guide subheading entry applies to each point.
    (a) The company will be _____ years old tomorrow. (19)
    (b) We hope to have between _____ and _____ people attending the meeting. (80, 100)
    (c) A _____ basket of fruit will be given as a door prize. (55 pound)
    (d) Send us _____ _____ weights. (2, 12 pound)
    (e) We expect the temperature to reach_____ degrees above zero. (4)
    (f) We own less than _____ share. (⅓)
    (g) They will owe us over _____ by April. ($600.00)
    (h) I was in the military service for _____. (1 year, six months, and eight days)

PROBLEMS

1. Assume that your employer is out of the city on a business trip. How would you go about forwarding each of the following unopened pieces of mail? State whether additional postage is required.
   (a) A personal letter
   (b) A piece of registered mail requiring a signed return receipt
   (c) A letter mailed by your office to the employer but returned because of an insufficient address
   (d) A special-delivery letter you wish to have forwarded also by special delivery
   (e) A parcel-post package

2. Set up a three-column table with each column head indicating the information requested in (a), (b), and (c), below. In the appropriate columns, enter the information required by Items 1–21.
   (a) The class of postal service that should be used. If parcel post is chosen, indicate the zone.
   (b) The kinds of fees that must be paid in addition to postage.
   (c) Special requirements or secretarial procedures.
       (1) A carbon copy of a letter
       (2) A pen-corrected copy of a printed price list

(3) A library book you are returning by mail

(4) A letter addressed to a relative of the executive, enclosing bonds valued at $500 and registered for full value. Return receipt required showing address where delivery was made.

(5) A magazine addressed to a city 30 miles distant and sent at the personal request of the executive

(6) An 18-ounce sealed package containing a printing plate and addressed to a city 550 miles distant, with special-handling service.

(7) A 7-ounce unsealed package of candy sent special delivery

(8) A $20 money order addressed to a city which is 20 miles distant

(9) A box 3 feet long, 1½ feet wide, and 1½ feet high, weighing 40 pounds, addressed to a city 400 miles distant

(10) A sealed parcel weighing 5 ounces sent by priority mail

(11) A box of perishable bulbs weighing 8 pounds

(12) A monthly statement of a department store to a customer in the same city

(13) A postal card to a city 300 miles away

(14) A 1-pound parcel containing clothing sent to a city 95 miles distant and insured for $15 with a return receipt requested at the time the parcel was mailed

(15) A check for $45 to a city 300 miles away

(16) Sixty individually addressed unsealed envelopes containing 1-page mimeographed price lists

(17) A 5-pound box containing automobile parts addressed to a city 250 miles distant where your employer is stranded in a broken-down automobile

(18) A letter sent by certified mail with a postmarked receipt requested

(19) A 1-pound sealed parcel containing costume jewelry insured for $75 and being transmitted 2,500 miles

(20) A certified letter containing notice to an heir to an estate, with return receipt requested showing where the envelope was delivered

(21) Thirty mimeographed invitations in unsealed envelopes addressed to out-of-town members

3. What service would you recommend to someone living in a metropolitan area in sending the following goods?

(a) An engine part for factory equipment that has broken down

(b) One thousand copies of a convention program for distribution in two weeks

(c) An antique desk inherited by an heir in New Orleans from a relative in St. Louis

(d) Ten dozen summer shirts ready for shipment on March 3

(e) A year's supply of letterheads for a branch office in Osaka

(f) Photographs for a resident of a town 30 miles away; the recipient is to take them on a vacation trip the following day

(g) Ten dozen summer shirts to replenish stock during a sale

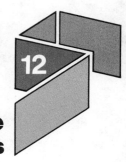

Basic Telephone
and Telegraph Services

An executive who frequently spoke by phone with an outstanding secretary described her in this way: "Gertrude is just perfect on the telephone. She always makes me feel good. Her voice always has a lilt, and she is willing to help me. Not only is she willing, but she does help me. She knows more about her company than most of the people who work there. She is worth thousands of dollars in good-will alone."

Any secretary who answers the telephone has an opportunity to make friends for the employer and for the company. The telephone is a vital link between you and the public and between you and your co-workers. It speeds up communication, often supplanting personal visits or letters. As a way of knowing and serving many people, it should challenge you to master its operation. You will need to choose the type of service to use in different situations, so you should know about the telephone equipment and services available.

Western Union, too, helps to accelerate business action and to get results when other means have failed. You must know how and when to use its services.

This chapter will improve your basic telephone and telegraph communication techniques.

TELEPHONE CONVERSATION

Some phase of at least 90 percent of all business transactions is conducted by telephone. That is why many personnel officers check the telephone performance of applicants before hiring them. It is also why companies frequently provide in-service telephone training for all office employees.

What the secretary says in carrying on the telephone conversation is important: tactful choice of words in contrast to blunt statements; offers of help in contrast to plain no's. Ease in conducting pleasant, effective conversations comes with experience and proper training.

The Voice with a Smile

Your voice over the phone reflects your personality. Make it attractive to whoever is calling. It may be a very important person, or it may be a nobody; you don't know so you cannot afford to answer indifferently. Here are seven simple rules to follow in developing a pleasant telephone voice:

1. Speak at a normal speed, with rising and falling inflections that avoid monotony.
2. Use a tone suitable for face-to-face-conversation, keeping the voice low-pitched.
3. Speak directly into the transmitter, which should be between half an inch and an inch from the lips.
4. Try to visualize and speak directly *to* the person calling — not *at* the telephone.
5. Try to convey a friendly, intelligent interest.
6. Show that you are wide awake and ready to help the person on the line.
7. Use simple, nontechnical language and avoid slang. The "bye-bye" at the end of a conversation leaves a distinctly bad impression.

Breaking Off a Conversation

Sometimes a secretary is required to terminate a conversation suddenly for any of several reasons. Use a plausible excuse — the truth, tactfully worded — for example, "I'm sorry, Mrs. Allen has just buzzed for me to come into her office"; or, "I'm sorry, someone is waiting for me in the reception room"; or, "I'm sorry, I must get out a rush letter for Mr. Barkley."

Even if you are busy and the office is so noisy that concentration is difficult when the phone rings, remember that when you answer it you are your company's and your employer's representative to the public.

Accuracy Technique

It is often necessary to give or take accurate information over the telephone — names, addresses, amounts, dates, and code words. Sounds can be mistaken as they travel over the wires. *F* and *S* are often confused, as are *P* and *B*, *T* and *D*, and *M* and *N*. *Five* and *nine* often get mixed up; and strange as it may seem, so do *zero* and *four*.

When word accuracy is needed, telephone spelling is used. To prevent mistakes, use any simple, easy-to-understand word to identify a letter, such as *D as in David*, *A as in Alice*, and so on. It is particularly important that the listener understand any numbers used in telephone conversation. The speaker should slightly exaggerate the enunciation, as "Th-r-ee" (strong R and long EE). Repeat the number; or, if there is still a question about one digit, give its preceding sequence, as "Three, four, FIVE," emphasizing the final proper number.

INCOMING CALLS

To handle incoming calls effectively, the secretary must understand the equipment in use as well as the techniques for answering, screening, and transferring calls and taking messages.

Equipment

The secretary will probably operate some kind of switchboard and possibly several types of desk telephones.

Dimension. Calls come into the office over a private branch exchange (PBX). The latest model of Bell System PBX, called *Dimension*, is an electronic system incorporating features not previously available on any PBX. One feature is a display board that shows the calling number and the class of service employed by the caller. The console also shows when a line is busy. On an outgoing call if the number called is busy, there will be an automatic callback when the busy phone is available. The Dimension can identify the telephone from which a call to a number outside the company originates so that toll charges can be assigned to that station. If the caller at that station abuses outward dialing privileges, the Dimension can indicate to the attendant that an attempt is being made to initiate a long-distance call from that phone. If a telephone is busy or is not answered, the call is automatically transferred to a previously designated line or to the attendant.

Dimension provides distinctive ringing patterns so that the person answering the call can automatically distinguish the type of

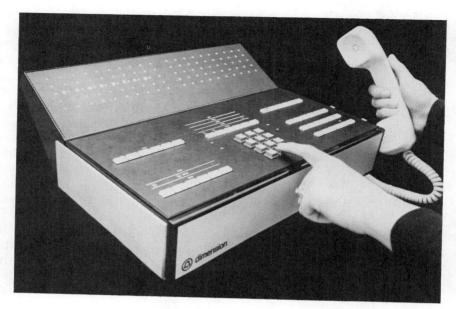

The Dimension provides a variety of information to the attendant so that the call can be handled efficiently. It controls unauthorized outgoing long-distance calls. It can make an automatic callback when a busy line becomes available.

American Telephone & Telegraph Co.

service being used by the caller (station-to-station, call through the attendant, call on the executive intercom, or an outside automatic callback). This equipment can handle all of the various types of extended service discussed in Chapter 13.

Com Key. Any secretary — and especially an administrative secretary reporting to several principals — may be supplied with a *Com Key*, which is practically a small desk switchboard. Com Key systems are replacing the desk Call Director because of their improved features.

With the Com Key the secretary can reach outside lines and intracompany phones as well as talk on the intercom.

American Telephone & Telegraph Co.

The Com Key comes with various capabilities, but the 416 is usually adequate for the secretary's desk. It gives an ultimate capacity of 4 central office lines, 16 stations, and 2 intercom paths. It has the distinctive ringing features of the Dimension so that the secretary is alerted to the type of call being answered. It is possible to set up multiline conferences among the phones in the system just by depressing the necessary buttons simultaneously. Two people may also converse with each other over the intercom.

When an in-company call is initiated, the buttons of the caller and the one being called on the Com Key are pressed down; and when the call is terminated, both buttons pop back up to signal that the lines are free. It is possible to summon personnel from any station in the system over wall-mounted loudspeakers. Incoming calls can be switched automatically to a predetermined alternate station. Background music can be piped to workers over the Com Key. If a message comes in while a phone is in use, the attendant can flash a light to alert the person at that phone to request the message.

Key Telephones. The secretary will probably use a desk telephone equipped with two to six lucite push buttons below the dialing mechanism. This *key telephone* enables a person to make or take a number of calls simultaneously from both inside and outside of the office. A key telephone in the hands of an inefficient secretary can create havoc with office procedure.

To answer a call:

1. Determine the line to be answered by the location of the ring, the tone, or the signal light on the bottom.

2. Depress the key for the line to be answered, remove the receiver, and speak.

To place a call:

1. Choose a line that is not in use (unlighted).

2. Push down the key for that line, remove the receiver, and make your call.

3. If you accidentally choose a line that is being held, depress the hold key to reestablish the hold.

To hold a call:

1. Ask the person to hold the line.

2. Depress the hold key for about two seconds to assure holding; both the line key and the hold key will return to normal position (with the light on).

3. Place or answer another call on another line. The person being held cannot overhear your other conversation.

This desk-top telephone of rectangular wedge design has a cradle at the left for the handset. It consists of a freestanding base designed with a row of 10 pushbuttons capable of handling 9 incoming/outgoing lines as well as rotary or Touch-Tone dial.

American Telephone & Telegraph Co.

The desk telephone may also be connected with the central transcription facility so that the executive can pick up the telephone and dictate an item to a voice-writing machine.

Centrex. One of the frustrations of the modern office is the difficulty of getting through the switchboard to the extension wanted. To circumvent this problem, many companies are changing over to *direct in-dialing* to the specific extension wanted (*Centrex*). After having been given the extension number and the company number, the frequent caller can dial the extension direct from an outside telephone in about one fifth the time normally needed to complete a switchboard-routed call. *After learning a Centrex number, record it in your directory*.

Additional features of Centrex are: identification of all outgoing calls so that the accounting department can apportion long-distance calls to the right telephone, and no-charge interoffice calls without attendant assistance. It is also possible to designate a centralized answering point so that one secretary can screen calls to several Centrex numbers.

Techniques

Four simple but effective habits will improve your skill in handling telephone calls.

1. Answer the telephone before the third ring, even if you are in the midst of an important job. This practice will not only establish a good relationship with the caller but will also reassure your employer about your competence.
2. Avoid implying by your tone of voice any feeling that the call is an intrusion.
3. *Listen* until you know definitely what the caller wants. If in doubt, ask for a confirmation of your understanding. Nothing is more annoying than telling someone the purpose of a call and then realizing by the response that you were not understood. The listening technique is one of the most important communication skills, and in no place can you demonstrate better your mastery of listening skills than in your telephone conversations.
4. Always be ready to take notes. As you answer your telephone, pick up a pencil and push a pad of paper into place.

Identification. The words with which you answer your telephone depend upon whether it is connected directly to an outside line or to the company switchboard; but you should always identify the company or the office and yourself. If your telephone is on an outside line, you may answer, "Allen and Lovell — Mr. ——." If the call comes through the company switchboard, you will answer, "Mrs. Allen's office, Miss ——," because the PBX attendant has already identified the company before ringing you. In no case do you say only "hello" or "yes."

When you can recognize the caller's voice and call him or her by name, you have made a very flattering gesture. In case of doubt, however, you should not risk the possibility of making an error in identification.

Screening Calls. Many executives prefer to answer their own telephones when they are at their desks. They feel that this practice saves time and builds goodwill. When the employer prefers to have you answer, is away from the office, or is obviously too busy to answer, you will, of course, answer all calls.

If you answer a call from someone whose voice you recognize as that of a VIP, you automatically put the call through without question. When the caller provides no identification or you do not recognize the voice, you may be required to find out who is calling. This procedure requires skillful questioning. The abrupt question, "Who is calling?" sounds rude and discriminating. Tactful secretaries phrase their questions somewhat like these:

May I ask who is calling, please?

or

May I tell Ms. Wong who is calling, please?

Always have writing equipment available for taking messages for others and for recording useful information for yourself.

American Telephone & Telegraph Co.

When you do not let the caller talk with the executive, you need to give a plausible explanation and to suggest a substitute person or time. A typical explanation might be:

> Mr. Graham, Mrs. Allen is holding an important conference. May I help you or transfer you to someone who can?

Executive Unavailable. The secretary has three responsibilities regarding incoming calls when the executive is not available for answering the telephone.

1. Giving helpful but not explicit information to the caller about the executive's time schedule and activities

2. Getting information from hesitant callers

3. Taking messages and keeping a record of incoming calls

Giving Information. When the executive is not available, the secretary is discreet about giving information. Definite information may be exactly what the executive does not want told to certain callers. *When in doubt, DON'T* be specific. Unless there is a known reason for being specific, the secretary tries to be helpful but not explicit. Note the differences in the following responses:

Specific	*Helpful but not Explicit*
Miss Ettinger hasn't come in yet.	Miss Ettinger isn't at her desk. I expect her at ten o'clock.
Mrs. Smith is in Chicago on business.	Mrs. Smith is out of the city today.
Mr. Hubbard left early today to play golf.	Mr. Hubbard won't be in again until tomorrow.

Getting Information. Getting information from an unidentified caller often presents a problem — and a challenge. How can you get both the name and the purpose of the call before the caller says, "I'll call back," and then hangs up? You may have to use a rather oblique approach. The conversation might develop something like this:

You answer the call and say, "Mrs. Allen is away today. I am her secretary; perhaps I can help you." Notice that you do not ask who is calling or what is wanted. If the caller is still hesitant, you might ask, "May I have her call you tomorrow?" If the answer is, "Yes, will you? This is Helen Fox, 621-6412," you might then ask, "Shall I give her any special message, Ms. Fox?" Or you might ask, "Will Mrs. Allen know what you are calling about?" A positive answer to any such question necessitates identification of the caller or the purpose of the call.

Tactful Requests	*Discourteous Requests*
May I say who's calling, please?	He wants to know who's calling.
He's in a meeting. May I take a message?	If you'll tell me who's calling, I'll see if I can locate him.
Will you please wait while I see if she is in?	Mrs. McDuff isn't taking any calls this morning.

Taking Messages. Always offer to take a message when your employer is out. Ask the caller to explain any details which you do not understand. Take time to repeat the message and verify all spelling and figures. Afterwards, complete the record by adding the date, the time the call came, the name and identity of the caller, and your initials. Some firms use small printed slips for this purpose. It is possible to buy books of telephone message forms interleaved with carbon sheets so that the original message can be put on the executive's desk and the carbon copy retained in the book for reference.

Even if there is no message to report, make a record of the call. When the executive is away, a helpful secretary keeps a complete telephone diary of all calls received and messages recorded.

TELEPHONE MESSAGE

FOR _Mrs. Mc Duff_ DATE _8/6/--_

M __r. E. Jones__ OF

PHONE NO. _301-921-4108_ TIME _9:15_

✓	TELEPHONED		PLEASE PHONE
	RETURNED YOUR CALL		WANTS TO SEE YOU
	CAME TO SEE YOU		WILL CALL AGAIN

MESSAGE _The meeting of the_
product managers has been
postponed until next week

BY _E J M_

Telephone Message
Form

Transferring Calls. When a call comes that someone else can handle better, transfer the call. The caller, however, may be justifiably annoyed if the call has already been transferred to you. Several techniques can be used to demonstrate that you and your organization want to be helpful. First, be sure that the person to whom you transfer the call can actually give the information sought. Here is an opportunity to demonstrate your understanding of your company's organization pattern, to show that you know who knows what. Second, tell the caller that you are transferring the call but if you are disconnected you can be reached again at ——. Stay on the line until you are sure that someone else has answered the call. Third, consider the possibility of getting the information for the caller yourself and returning the call. Nothing is more important than your company's (and your own) image, nor more exasperating than the "I couldn't care less, I have my own work to do" attitude.

Completing the Conversation. Every conversation should be closed courteously and graciously. Suggested wording of your last sentence might be:

Thank you for calling, Mrs. Levinson.

I'm glad I was able to help you. Goodbye.

You're welcome, Mr. Rogers. Goodbye.

Recording Complete or Summarized Telephone Conversations.
Your employer may wish to record crucial telephone conversations.
If so, the recorder must be equipped with a sound device that emits
intermittent beeps to warn the other person in the conversation
that the call is being recorded.

At other times you may be asked to summarize telephone conversations so that a less complete record is available. The transcript
can be summarized but should be typed in dialog form as indicated
on page 710 of the Reference Guide.

Receiving Long-Distance Calls

Occasionally, when your employer is absent, you will have to take
long-distance calls. If so, listen carefully and repeat your understanding of the message. Type a full report of the call immediately
so that there will be a correct and complete record for the employer.

If the executive is not available to answer a person-to-person call,
give the long-distance attendant full information as to when the call
can be returned. The attendant will ask you to have the executive
return the call and will give you those details of the call that will
help in completing the callback, such as: "Please ask Miss Downey
to call Operator 18 in Detroit and ask for 719-1380, Mr. Smith."

If the employer can be reached at another telephone, either locally or in another city, and you believe there would be no objection
to receiving a call there, you should tell the attendant where the call
should be transferred.

Message-Taking Services

New devices and services are available which assure that telephone calls are always answered, even when the telephone is not
covered.

Answering, Recording, and Switching Devices. Automatic answering equipment can deliver any message that the user records. Before
leaving the office, the executive (or the secretary) turns on the machine and makes a recording to tell callers the time of return and to
ask them to leave a message. The person calling hears the announcement and then records a message. An innovation made possible by
electronics is equipment that enables the executive to call in and
revise the previous recording. Small businesses, such as real estate
and insurance offices, find this service especially advantageous. This
equipment has also been expanded to attract larger users. For instance, up to six hours of recorded messages capture overnight
orders for a meat wholesaler.

Besides answering and recording devices, certain switching devices are also available. Practically all modern switchboards can be set to transfer incoming calls to a predetermined number.

Telephone Answering Service. Unlike the automatic recording device which merely recites impersonal messages, the attendant in a telephone answering service is able to exercise judgment and understanding in personally assisting the caller. Many business firms invest in such service as a way of personalizing their offices during the hours they are not open. The secretary in an office using such service should establish friendly relations with the answering service, check with the attendant immediately upon coming into the office after it has been closed, and provide complete information when the answering service takes over.

Taped Announcements. Almost every telephone user is familiar with taped announcements that may be dialed: time of day, weather, flight information, market information, movie schedules, and even prayers. It is possible for a business to develop such announcements.

Special Reverse-Charge Toll Service

A business can make its services easily available by telephone in cities where it has no office with a special listing in the telephone directory of each of the desired cities. These listings permit the caller to make the call as a local one, and the toll charge is billed to the listed number. For instance, a Yonkers company would have a New York City number listed in the New York City directory as:

Acetate Box Co
  263 AshbrtnAv Ynkrs ......NYC Tel No--292-2435

On such incoming calls, the secretary provides complete and cordial help — without waste of long-distance time. (See pages 277–278.)

OUTGOING CALLS

In addition to answering the telephone, the secretary will place local and long-distance calls. To do this well, you must know how to get maximum service from your telephone directories and telephone attendants and how to make the appropriate choices of service.

Using Telephone Directories

Before placing a call, the secretary must locate the telephone number, and sometimes that takes quite a bit of skill. The telephone directory has two parts: the *Alphabetical Directory (white pages)* which contains a complete list of subscribers, their addresses, and telephone numbers; and the *Yellow Pages (classified directory)* containing the alphabetic listings of names of businesses under headings which are also arranged alphabetically by product or service.

Both directories print, in the upper outside corner, the first and last names or headings listed on each page. The conspicuous location of these guide words makes it possible to locate the proper page quickly.

The telephone directory is a mine of information, especially one for a metropolitan area. For instance, the New York City alphabetical directory contains in its introductory pages: emergency numbers; instructions for dialing *Directory Assistance (Information)* in any locality; instructions for telephoning locally, nationally, and overseas; area codes for major cities in the United States; explanations of various types of service; zones for assessing message unit rates (see page 279); a map showing area code distribution; a local postal-zone map; long-distance rates to major cities and hours during which rates apply; two pages of facts about telephone service; helpful hints for finding numbers quicker and easier; and explanations of billing. Part of these explanations may be repeated in a foreign language if there are enough people in a particular geographical area to justify the translation.

A corporation may find it advantageous to keep in a central location a collection of telephone directories from cities in which it conducts a large volume of business. It is also possible to find out-of-town directories from the larger cities in some hotels and major travel terminals.

The Alphabetical Directory. In the *alphabetical directory* the numbers are usually located quickly, but the exceptions make it necessary for the secretary to know the rules followed in arranging names in alphabetical sequence in filing. For example, there are 21 columns of the surname *Miller* in one metropolitan directory. Alternate spellings are suggested as, *Also see MILLAR*.

Locating the various government offices and public services also requires a knowledge of the alphabetical listings. They are generally listed under their proper political subdivisions — city offices under the name of the municipality, county offices under the name of the county, state offices under the name of the state, and federal offices under *United States Government*. Public schools are usually listed under the municipality and then under *Board of Education*. Parochial schools are individually listed. Addresses of identical listings are in the alphabetical order of street names followed by numbered streets in numerical order. (*Eighth Street* would follow rather than precede *Second Street*.)

The Yellow Pages Directory. The *Yellow Pages* directory of business listings is a very helpful source of reference for the secretary. In metropolitan areas a separate Yellow Pages directory contains all classified listings. The executive may want to talk with "that air-conditioning firm on Church Street," but may not know its correct name. An alert secretary would look in the Yellow Pages under *Air-Conditioning Equip. & Supls.* and find *Tuttle & Bailey, Inc.*, the only air-conditioning firm on Church Street.

You should circle every frequently called telephone number in the directory for easy finding next time. You should also jot down the number you looked up just in case you get a busy signal when you first dial it. When a new number is obtained, it should be listed on the proper directory page or in a desk telephone directory.

Personal Telephone Directory. Every secretary keeps a *personal, up-to-date telephone directory*. In it are listed alphabetically the names of frequently called persons and firms and their telephone numbers. A thoughtful secretary places a condensed list of such numbers at the back of the executive's daily calendar pad.

Some kind of card listing or tab-insertion scheme is preferable to a solid-typed list which makes no provision for the addition of names and changes of personnel or telephone numbers. Any list becomes out of date quickly unless some system is devised that provides for additions and deletions. Most secretaries prefer a small rotary-wheel file for mounting this directory.

The time-and-motion-conscious secretary will be interested in the analysis by the telephone company: You can look up a number in your personal telephone directory in 10 seconds, about a third of the time required for a search of the large directory. A personal telephone booklet may be obtained from the local telephone company for the asking.

Some people prefer not to have their telephone number listed in the directory. This may cost them a few cents a month because of additional administrative costs. Usually, Directory Assistance (Information) will not have the number in its records. Only in exceptional circumstances, and with the customer's own consent, will the telephone company arrange to complete the call. Keeping unlisted numbers in the personal directory becomes doubly important since they cannot be looked up.

Telephone numbers of frequent correspondents may be taken from letterheads and entered in the personal telephone directory for possible use.

Business-Promotion Listings. A company may list its telephone number in several ways that will promote business.

One way is to list a special reverse-charge toll number. An example is the area code 800 number on which charges are automatically billed to the called party without any oral acceptance of charges being required. Newspaper and television advertising frequently carries an 800 number to call for further information, and hotels and motels often use this listing nationally. The listing looks like this and is explained on pages 297–298.

SHERATON HOTELS & MOTOR
INNS—
Reservation Office StLouisMo
No Charge To Calling Party   800 325-3535

Another way to attract business is to maintain a number in the city in which the directory is printed. From this number the call will be switched to the out-of-town subscriber's location. (The subscriber pays for the call.) Such a listing looks like this:

SAFECO INSURANCE CO OF
AMERICA—
Claims 175 GreatNeckRd
   GrtNk – – – – – –**NYC Tel No–895-7447**
Marketing 666 KindermackRd
   RiverEdgeNJ– – – –**NYC Tel No–524-2244**

Some companies also list their out-of-town numbers in the hope that they will promote business even if the caller has to pay for the call. An example of this listing is given below:

South-Western Publshng Co
925 SpringRd Pelhm   – – – –914 738–3600

Placing Local Calls

The procedure in placing calls varies with the kind of telephone equipment in use. If the desk telephone is a direct outside line, give the number to the telephone operator or dial it. If the line goes through the office switchboard, you either dial 9 for an outside line or ask the PBX attendant for a line by saying "Outside, please." When you get a dial tone, you dial the number.

You will regularly be making two kinds of local calls — reaching someone whom the employer will talk with and placing your own calls. In the first case, after getting the number desired, ask for the person wanted and immediately identify your employer as the caller, saying something like:

Mr. Norman, please. Mrs. Allen of Allen and Lovell calling.

To avoid making the person wait on the line, always determine if the executive is ready to take the call before placing it. If the answering operator or secretary asks you to put your employer on the line first, be gracious and follow the request. The person who must waste a few seconds waiting for the other to respond should be the one who originated the call.

In making your own calls, you will find it advisable to jot down what you want to say before you get the person on the line. This will help to avoid the embarrassment of having to call back for a point forgotten. You will speak with more confidence and effectiveness, and you will make a better impression by knowing in advance what you are going to say.

Introduce yourself properly. Upon being connected, give your own name, and, if desirable, your firm name. For example, "This is Miss Baer, Mrs. Allen's secretary, of Allen and Lovell." Making a good impression on people whom you telephone is just as important as making a good impression on those who call at your office.

Message Units

Within some metropolitan areas, calls between widely separated locations are not considered local calls or long-distance calls but are individually charged as *message-unit calls*.

A message unit is a telephone term describing a standard base rate used in determining the cost of a call. The table of rates in the front of the directory shows the *number* of message units chargeable between telephone exchanges and the length of the overtime period which is charged as a message unit. For instance, from Manhattan Zone 3 to Westchester Zone 6 is four message units (four times the base rate of 8.2 cents) or 33 cents. Message units are automatically charged and billed in total — not itemized.

Long-Distance Calls

Every time you pick up your phone, you enter a hundred-billion-dollar network that connects 160 million telephones in North America. Every day this network performs over a billion switching operations. The telephone network is truly a giant. Local or long-distance calls can be made to all telephones in a domestic system, as well as to most other countries and territories throughout the world.

Types of Long-Distance Calls. There are two general types of long-distance calls — *station-to-station* and *person-to-person*. The secretary is expected to know the relative costs, the recommended and permissible practices, and the situations in which to use each type.

Station-to-Station. Because of the time and money saved through direct distance dialing on *station-to-station* calls, businesses will probably tend to use this type of service more and more except in cases where there is a question of whether a specific person can be located readily.

The procedure for dialing a distant telephone number is discussed below. You would dial station-to-station when you are willing to talk with anyone who answers the call or when you are reasonably sure the person wanted is within reach of the telephone. Charges begin at the time the called telephone or switchboard is answered, even if the person wanted is not available. No charge is made if no one answers at the number called.

Sometimes valuable minutes are wasted by the efforts of the answering attendant to locate the person wanted. If you were trying to reach Mrs. Katz, registered at a hotel, the hotel operator might have to page her in the lobby and the hotel restaurants. If the operator was unsuccessful in finding her, the call would still be fully chargeable.

Person-to-Person. A person-to-person call is made when you must talk to a particular person or extension telephone. Charging begins when the called person or extension answers. The procedure for dialing a person-to-person call is given on page 281.

Placing Long-Distance Calls. Long-distance calls may be made by direct distance dialing or through the long-distance operator.

Direct Distance Dialing (DDD). Station-to-station long distance calls are dialed direct, without assistance from the operator except in case of difficulty. Usually, you dial 1 plus a three-digit *area code*, then the telephone number desired, except when you are dialing a number with your own area code.

Specific directions for DDD may be found in the front section of the telephone directory. The general procedures to be followed are described in the next two paragraphs.

Secure the area code from the company letterhead (where it is often included with the address), your personal telephone directory, the front of the telephone directory, or the operator. If you have the area code but do not know the telephone number of the person to be called, dial the prefix 1 (where necessary), the area code, and the number 555-1212. After you identify to the information clerk the city and individual or business you wish to call, you are given the number. If there is even a remote possibility of later calls, record both the area code and the telephone number in your personal directory.

Dial the number carefully; but if you reach the wrong number on any DDD call, obtain the name of the city you have reached and promptly report this information to the operator to avoid all charges for the call. If you are cut off before completing a call, inform the operator so that the charges can be adjusted. Sometimes you get a recorded message telling you that your call has not been completed and asking you to initiate it again. If it is evident that for some reason your call is not going through, dial the operator for help.

Operator-Assisted Calls. If you know the area code and telephone number to be called but you wish to call person-to-person, collect, on a credit card, or with the call to be charged to another number, you need only routine operator assistance. Follow this procedure:

1. Dial 0 (zero), the area code, and the telephone number.

2. When the operator answers, for a:

   Person-to-person call, give the name of the person you are calling.

   Collect call, say "Collect" and give your name.

   Credit-card call, say "Credit-card call" and give your credit-card number.

   Call charged to another number, say "Bill to" and give the area code and telephone number to which the call is to be billed.

If you require special assistance, dial 0, state your problem, and give the operator whatever information you have. One secretary had to call an official in Washington, D.C., at two o'clock for an employer who expected to be in the local courthouse near another telephone at that time. The secretary explained the situation to the operator, who placed the call at two o'clock to the courthouse telephone but charged the call to the employer's office telephone. Another secretary was asked to get in touch with A. J. Dearing, who was staying at a Pittsburgh hotel. The secretary told the long-distance operator that the only clue to Dearing's whereabouts was that lodging would be at one of the better hotels. The operator checked the hotels until Dearing was located. The secretary need not hesitate to ask for this kind of service.

Time Zones. Time zones are very important to the secretary in placing long-distance calls. A New York office would not call San Francisco before 12 noon because there would be little likelihood of reaching anyone in the San Francisco office before 9 a.m. Conversely, a secretary in Los Angeles, California, would not place a call for Boston, Massachusetts, after 2 p.m., for very likely the office in Boston would be closed around 5 p.m. The secretary who places overseas calls should learn the time differences for the cities called.

The map that appears on page 282 indicates time zones in the continental United States and adjacent Canadian provinces so that the person placing a long-distance call can plan the call to coincide with the business day in the place called. The time-zone map shows

This map shows telephone areas, area codes and time zones (Standard Time) in the continental United States and Canada.

the area code to be used with the desired long-distance number. The time at the place where the call originates determines whether day, evening, or night rates apply.

Relative Costs. A study of the tables on pages 283 and 284 shows that calls dialed directly are much cheaper than person-to-person calls and that having the number at hand and dialing the number yourself save a great deal of money. It also indicates that calling at night or on weekends is cheaper than calling during the business day.

Knowing relative costs of the different services enables the customer to use the telephone economically. For example, if an executive wanted to report a safe arrival in New York to the family in Seattle, a one-minute call could be made after 11 p.m. for 22 cents.

A table of long-distance rates to many cities is given in the front of every telephone directory. Rates to places not listed are obtainable from the long-distance operator.

You must often decide whether to use person-to-person or station-to-station service. You can arrive at the better choice only by considering every factor, including cost and whereabouts of the person called. If you were asked to reach a salesperson at the home office, you would choose a person-to-person call because the nature of a sales job requires field work, not office work, most of the time. On the other hand, the manager of a branch office is in the office most of the time and is readily available for a station-to-station call.

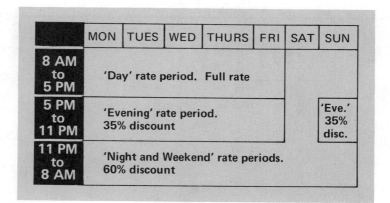

	MON	TUES	WED	THURS	FRI	SAT	SUN
8 AM to 5 PM	'Day' rate period. Full rate						
5 PM to 11 PM	'Evening' rate period. 35% discount						'Eve.' 35% disc.
11 PM to 8 AM	'Night and Weekend' rate periods. 60% discount						

Interstate Discount
Periods for
Long-Distance
Dial-Direct Calls

The Bell System wants to decrease the number of operator-assisted calls by emphasizing the advantages of direct dialing. An advertisement in a business magazine features a prominent executive saying, "On long-distance calling, I play the percentages. I've learned I'm ahead when I dial direct rather than call person-to-person, even if the odds are only 50–50 that my party will be there."

In another effort to reduce its labor force, the telephone companies in some localities give a small monthly credit if Directory Assistance was not called during that month.

Paying for Long Distance. The secretary may be responsible for accepting long-distance charges, accounting for them, reversing them, or securing for the executive a credit card on which to charge calls.

Obtaining Charges on Toll Calls. Charges for long-distance calls are referred to as *toll charges*. If you need to know the cost of a call, request the operator *at the time the call is placed* to report the charges. The operator will then notify you after the call has been completed and the cost has been calculated. This service is not available on DDD calls.

Cost Records of Toll Calls. For accounting purposes most companies charge toll calls in their records to specific departments, clients, or jobs. With memorandum records kept at the secretary's desk showing the date, point called, and the person calling, the correct toll charges can be checked against the bill and charged to the proper departments.

The federal government levies on long-distance calls an excise tax which the telephone company collects from the subscriber. The tax rates are shown on the customer's bill. If the secretary is required to keep a cost record of each long-distance call for accounting purposes, the tax must be computed and added to the toll charge.

CALLS FROM NEW YORK CITY TO:	STATION-TO-STATION										PERSON-TO-PERSON			
	DIRECT DISTANCE DIALED (Paid by calling party)						OPERATOR-ASSISTED							
	FULL WEEKDAY RATE Mon.–Fri. 8 AM–5 PM		35% EVENING DISCOUNT Sun.–Fri. 5 PM–11 PM		60% NIGHT & WEEKEND DISCOUNT Every Night 11 PM–8 AM; All Day and Night on Sat. to 5 PM Sun.		ALL DAYS & HOURS	OVERTIME			ALL DAYS & HOURS	OVERTIME		
								WEEKDAYS 8 AM–5 PM	35% EVENING DISCOUNT Sun.–Fri. 5 PM–11 PM	60% NIGHT & WEEKEND DISCOUNT Every Night 11 PM–8 AM; All Day and Night on Sat. to 5 PM Sun.		WEEKDAYS 8 AM–5 PM	35% EVENING DISCOUNT Sun.–Fri. 5 PM–11 PM	60% NIGHT & WEEKEND DISCOUNT Every Night 11 PM–8 AM; All Day and Night on Sat. to 5 PM Sun.
	Init. 1 Min.	Ea. Add. Min.	Init. 1 Min.	Ea. Add. Min.	Init. 1 Min.	Ea. Add. Min.	Init. 3 Mins.	Ea. Add. Min.	Ea. Add. Min.	Ea. Add. Min.	Init. 3 Mins.	Ea. Add. Min.	Ea. Add. Min.	Ea. Add. Min.
Atlanta, Ga.	.50	.35	.32	.22	.20	.14	1.80	.35	.22	.14	2.80	.35	.22	.14
Atlantic City, N.J.	.41	.26	.26	.16	.16	.10	1.35	.26	.16	.10	1.80	.26	.16	.10
Boston, Mass.	.44	.29	.28	.18	.17	.11	1.50	.29	.18	.11	2.10	.29	.18	.11
Chicago, Ill.	.50	.35	.32	.22	.20	.14	1.80	.35	.22	.14	2.80	.35	.22	.14
Cleveland, Ohio	.48	.33	.31	.21	.19	.13	1.70	.33	.21	.13	2.50	.33	.21	.13
Denver, Colo.	.54	.38	.35	.24	.21	.15	1.90	.38	.24	.15	3.10	.38	.24	.15
Detroit, Mich.	.49	.34	.31	.22	.19	.13	1.75	.34	.22	.13	2.65	.34	.22	.13
Hartford, Conn.	.41	.26	.26	.16	.16	.10	1.35	.26	.16	.10	1.80	.26	.16	.10
Houston, Tex.	.54	.38	.35	.24	.21	.15	1.90	.38	.24	.15	3.10	.38	.24	.15
Los Angeles, Cal.	.56	.40	.36	.26	.22	.16	1.95	.40	.26	.16	3.55	.40	.26	.16
Miami, Fla.	.52	.36	.33	.23	.20	.14	1.85	.36	.23	.14	2.95	.36	.23	.14
Milwaukee, Wisc.	.50	.35	.32	.23	.20	.14	1.80	.35	.22	.14	2.80	.35	.22	.14
New Orleans, La.	.52	.36	.33	.23	.20	.14	1.85	.36	.23	.14	2.95	.36	.23	.14
Philadelphia, Pa.	.40	.25	.26	.16	.16	.10	1.25	.25	.16	.10	1.70	.25	.16	.10
Portland, Maine	.46	.31	.29	.20	.18	.12	1.60	.31	.20	.12	2.30	.31	.20	.12
St. Louis, Mo.	.50	.35	.32	.22	.20	.14	1.80	.35	.22	.14	2.80	.35	.22	.14
Seattle, Wash.	.56	.40	.36	.26	.22	.16	1.95	.40	.26	.16	3.55	.40	.26	.16
Washington, D.C.	.45	.30	.29	.19	.18	.12	1.55	.30	.19	.12	2.20	.30	.19	.12
Wilmington, Del.	.42	.27	.27	.17	.16	.10	1.40	.27	.17	.10	1.90	.27	.17	.10

This table shows the differences in cost between directly dialed and operator-assisted calls, and between station-to-station and person-to-person calls of various lengths at different times of the day and night.

Collect Calls. A long-distance call (toll call) can be made *collect*. Charges on person-to-person and station-to-station calls can be reversed — that is, charged to the number called rather than to the one placing the call. The request to reverse the charges, however, must be made at the time of placing the call so that the person called can have an opportunity to accept or refuse the charge. Because collect calls are operator assisted, they are more expensive than direct-dialed calls.

Telephone Credit Cards. Executives who make a great many telephone calls away from the office may carry telephone credit cards on which they can charge these calls to their companies. These cards show a code number to be used when initiating a call through the operator. They also show the holder's name and business affiliation. Credit-card calls cost more than DDD calls because they involve the operator. Monthly telephone bills identify credit-card calls as such.

SECRETARIAL RESPONSIBILITY FOR WESTERN UNION MESSAGES

Frequently it is necessary in business to send an urgent but brief message. In such instances some form of Western Union message is appropriate because of: (1) its low cost, (2) the documentation that a written message provides, and (3) its attention-getting advantage over either a letter or a telephone call. The secretary will be expected to handle telegrams and mailgrams.

Telegrams

There are two classes of telegrams, the regular telegram and the overnight telegram. The regular *telegram* can be sent at any time, day or night, any day of the week. The minimum charge is based on 15 words exclusive of address and signature; an additional charge is made for each additional word. Messenger delivery is assured at most points within five hours, but a delivery charge is assessed. Proof of delivery, in the form of the recipient's signature which is sent to the sender, is available for an additional fee. Usually, though, delivery by telephone within two hours is assured. A written confirmation copy of the message is mailed to the sender for an additional fee.

The minimum charge for an *overnight telegram*, which costs considerably less than a regular telegram, is based on 100 words. Delivery of the overnight telegram is assured by 2 p.m. the following day.

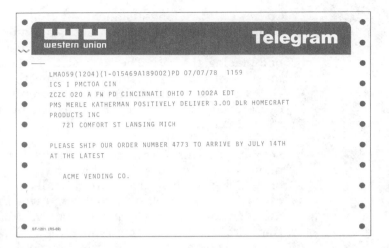

When for some reason a telegram must be delivered by messenger, there is a charge for the service. Note the words "Positively deliver" and the delivery charge notation immediately after the addressee's name.

If there is a chance that a telegram may be undeliverable at one location, an alternate address may be specified. If the message is of substantive importance, such as an order for bonds or confirmation of a contract, the sender may purchase insurance against an error in transmission.

Mailgrams

The *mailgram*, which was introduced in 1970, is a very popular service. It combines Western Union and post office services. Mailgram messages are sent over Western Union's microwave and satellite communications networks directly to the post office near the recipient's address. There the messages are typed by high-speed equipment on continuous rolls of paper. They are then torn off and inserted into distinctive blue-and-white envelopes for delivery the next business day by regular postal carriers. To receive Mailgrams even earlier than the first delivery, some organizations rent post-office boxes into which they are deposited as received.

Mailgrams offer several advantages over other forms of communication. They engender a sense of urgency and importance by their special envelopes and telegram format. They receive post-office priority. When received, they are usually opened before the other mail. They are relatively low in cost. (In June, 1977, the cost of a phone-originated mailgram was $2.75.) And finally, they are easy to send by telephone, by Telex or TWX (see pages 293–294), by computer, or by data terminals and facsimile devices.

Mailgrams may be sent to several people at different addresses simultaneously. For example, politicians use them widely to influence voters. They can be used to invite people to a function or to cancel one. They are often used in promoting sales. A recent business-promotion feature was introduced when it became possible to detach a reply form at the bottom of a mailgram message, fill it in, and fold it into a business-reply envelope to be mailed back to the sender, postage free.

Sending Telegrams and Mailgrams

If the message is to be written out for your communications center or delivered to a Western Union office, use either your company's or Western Union's form. Type the form, of course. Compose a message that is clear and brief. Use active verbs, avoid unnecessary adjectives, and use numbers instead of words when possible.

If you phone in the message, it will be typed by an operator as it is recorded. Collect complete information before making the call: correct spelling of all names, correct addresses (street, city, state, ZIP Code, and telephone number), and billing information.

If your office does not have Telex or TWX but the addressee's office does, you can reduce expenses by sending the message as a telegram to the recipient's teletypewriter terminal. (The Western Union operator can obtain the Telex or TWX number.)

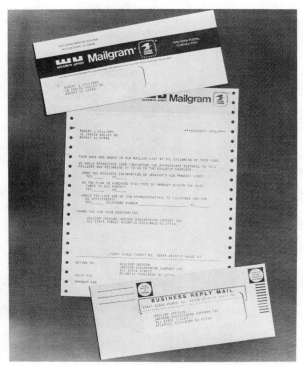

A Business-Reply
Mailgram

Western Union

SUGGESTED READINGS

Dallas, Richard J., and James M. Thompson. *Clerical and Secretarial Systems for the Office.* Englewood Cliffs: Prentice-Hall, 1975, pp. 151–182.

Griesinginer, Frank K. *How to Cut Costs and Improve Service of Your Telephone, Telex, TWX, and Other Telecommunications.* New York: McGraw-Hill Book Co., 1974. Also articles regularly in *Administrative Management* magazine.

Kuehn, Richard A. *Cost-Effective Telecommunications.* New York: American Management Association, 1974.

Telephone Company brochures obtained locally

Telephone Directory and *Yellow Pages* in your local community

Winter, Elmer L. *The Successful Manager-Secretary Team.* West Nyack: Parker Publishing Co., 1974, Ch. 8, "Suggestions to Help Your Secretary Better Handle Your Telephone," pp. 67–76.

QUESTIONS FOR DISCUSSION

1. Reword the following portions of conversations to reflect better telephone usage.
   (a) Sorry, I don't know where Miss Schwartz is. She should be at her desk.
   (b) We don't give that information out to the public.
   (c) You should have called the purchasing department for that information.
   (d) I don't know who handles employee insurance, but Mr. Wallenstein doesn't.
   (e) Mrs. Lombardi is in a conference with the tax consultant.
   (f) I haven't got time to look it up, Mr. Kenyon. I have to get this report ready for the committee meeting in 20 minutes.
   (g) I haven't the foggiest. I'll ask Marge to fill me in on what happened at that meeting.
   (h) Oh, I gave you the wrong information. I thought you were Professor Milligan of New State College who is writing a book on the same subject.

2. Think of business telephone calls in which you have taken part. Describe the techniques used by the other party that have pleased you and those that have annoyed you.

3. Examine your local telephone directory. What information is found in the introductory pages? in the Yellow Pages?

4. If your office is located in Philadelphia, between what office hours (yours) would you try to reach an office in Salt Lake City by long distance? If your office is in Salt Lake City, between what office hours (yours) would you try to reach a Philadelphia office?

5. What class of long-distance service would you use in trying to reach each of the following persons?
   (a) A buyer in a department store
   (b) A lawyer who is pleading an important case

    (c) A politician who is staying in a hotel at which you made the reservation

    (d) Your employer's son who lives in a college dormitory not equipped with Centrex

    (e) The city editor of a newspaper

6. Can you name a situation in which an overnight telegram would be preferable to a mailgram?

7. What class of service would you choose in sending a message to

    (a) quote a price change to 50 sales representatives in a national corporation?

    (b) accept the terms of a proposal to sell a farm?

    (c) inform a member who has received the annual award of a service club?

    (d) congratulate a colleague on retirement?

    (e) solicit orders for a new product which is described within the message?

    (f) inform a family member of the death of a close relative?

    (g) arrange an interview when you want proof that the message was received?

8. Assuming that the following words came at the ends of typewritten lines, indicate those words that you could correctly divide and show where you would make the divisions. Then use the Reference Guide to verify or correct your answers.

freight	profit-taking	science
Anderson	forgotten	February 26
half-brother	holiday	mailable
foundation	selling	into

PROBLEMS

1. Locate in the alphabetic section of your local telephone directory the numbers for the following. Type in tabular form a list showing for each item the organization or department wanted, the name under which the telphone is listed, and the telephone number.

    (a) City hall

    (b) Western Union

    (c) Fire department

    (d) Park or recreation department

    (e) Police department

    (f) Post office

    (g) Public library

    (h) The nearest hospital

    (i) Your college or university

    (j) The local office of the state employment service

    (k) Telephone repair service

    (l) Weather information

2. The purpose of this problem is to familiarize you with the organization of your Yellow Pages. Type a list showing the heading in the Yellow Pages under which you would find the names of subscribers for each of the following:

    (a) Agents for temporary help

    (b) Certified public accountants

    (c) Dealers in advertising stickers

    (d) Dealers in snap-out forms

3. Type the following excerpts of conversation in acceptable form. Then use the Reference Guide to verify or correct your answers.

   (a) The opening part of a telephone conversation which occurred this Monday, shortly before noon. Mr. Lawrence Bell called Mr. Thomas Green.

   Bell — Tom, have you come to a decision yet? Green — No, I'd like a day or two more to think it over. Bell — Time is getting short, Tom. I have to know by Wednesday at the latest. Green — I'll sleep on it and let you know the first thing in the morning.

   (b) A confidential memorandum to the president of the company, reporting on a conversation which occurred in the executive's office two weeks ago between Steve Douglas and Charlene Duncan:

   This is the conversation as I recall it. Steve said I talked it over with Nelson, very confidentially of course, and he thought he could arrange a meeting before the end of this month. Charlene said do you think it was wise to expose our hand. Steve said I don't think talking it over with Nelson can be called exposing our hand. He's trustworthy. Charlene said well it's done now. What about the meeting?

4. Rewrite each of the following messages, using not more than 15 words so that the message may be sent as a regular telegram.

   (a) THERE WILL BE A SALES MEETING SATURDAY MORNING IN THE OFFICE AT TEN O'CLOCK. PLEASE ARRANGE TO BE THERE. BRING REQUESTED ESTIMATES.

   (b) MR. WILCOX WIRED SAYING HE WOULD BE HERE TOMORROW. IS IT POSSIBLE FOR YOU TO COME BACK? MUST KNOW BY THREE O'CLOCK.

   (c) IN ANSWER YOUR TELEGRAM SUGGEST YOU OFFER A 40% DISCOUNT TERMS 2% 10 DAYS. DELIVERY TO BE MADE FOB NEW YORK.

5. Miss Mary Holmes, secretary to Harry Miller, handled the following telephone calls:

   (a) Mr. Miller was attending a Kiwanis luncheon meeting at the Terrace Hotel and expected to be back at his desk at 1:30 p.m. At 12:15 a long-distance call came in from his superior, who was in Boston. Miss Holmes said, "Mr. Miller will not be back until 1:30 and cannot be reached until then."

   (b) At closing time the long-distance operator had not reached a person with whom Mr. Miller must talk before the next morning. Mr. Miller was going to dinner at his brother's home but would be at his own home until 7 p.m. Miss Holmes said, "Operator, try that number again and keep trying until 7 o'clock. Mr. Miller will be at 734-8973 in half an hour and will be there until seven."

   (c) Mr. Miller was playing golf. The long-distance operator informed Miss Holmes that she had a call from Mr. Miller's New York broker, Mr. Adams, who wanted to talk to him as soon as possible. Miss Holmes said, "Mr. Miller is out of the office for the afternoon. If you will tell me where Mr. Adams can be reached, I will try to get in touch with Mr. Miller and ask him to call back immediately. I should be able to reach him within a hour."

   (d) Mr. Miller was writing copy for an advertising circular and told Miss Holmes that he did not wish to be disturbed under any circumstances before four o'clock. A call came in from George Herman, his assistant, who was in Baltimore attending a sales conference. Mr. Herman was to leave Baltimore on a three o'clock plane. Miss Holmes said, "I am sorry, but Mr. Miller can't be reached this afternoon. Ask Mr. Herman if I can help him instead. I am Mr. Miller's secretary."

(e) Mr. Miller wanted to make a long-distance call from the office telephone, 623-2219, to Dr. L. K. Holthaus of New Orleans on a personal matter. Miss Holmes did not know Dr. Holthaus' number but knew that he was a noted ophthalmologist. She dialed the operator and said, "Operator, this is 623-2219. I want to call Dr. L. K. Holthaus in New Orleans. I do not have the number, but he is a well-known eye specialist. Will you give me the area code and the number, please, so that I can dial him direct."

(f) Mr. Miller wanted to call Ms. Houston in the purchasing department of the Acme Company in White Plains, New York, area code 914. Mr. Miller wished to say that on Friday afternoon he would call on either Ms. Houston or her assistant about the new service contract. Could one of them be available for a conference? Miss Holmes made an operator-assisted call.

(g) Mr. Miller wanted to call his wife, who was visiting in Akron, Ohio. Her number was 864-0753 and the area code, 216. He said that it need not be a person-to-person call; but he wanted the call charged to his home number, 266-7106. Miss Holmes said, "Operator, this is 263-2219, Extension 62. I want to place a call to 864-0753 in Akron, Ohio. Don't charge the call to this number. It should be charged to 266-7106."

(h) Mr. Miller wanted to call Lawrence Taylor of the Lenox Supply Company in Los Angeles about the cancellation of an order. The number was 823-6501; the area code number, 213; the charges were to be reversed. Miss Holmes said, "Operator, this is 263-2219. I want to place a call to Lawrence Taylor of the Lenox Supply Company in Los Angeles. I don't know the number. Tell the switchboard operator there that Mr. Miller won't pay for the call because it is about an order he plans to cancel. Ask Mr. Taylor to pay for it."

(i) While Miss Holmes was on the button telephone, a second call came through. She excused herself and answered the second call, which was for Mr. Miller. She depressed the local button to ask Mr. Miller if he would take the call and then transferred it to his line. When she returned to the first call, she found that the caller had been disconnected.

Miss Holmes was surprised when Mr. Miller told her that he had arranged for her to take a five-hour course to improve her telephone techniques. She had always thought that she was unusually proficient in this area. Criticize Miss Holmes's handling of the 9 calls described above. Indicate what you would have done in the cases that were poorly handled.

Special Telephone and Telegraph Services

Breakthroughs in electronic word and number transmission have opened up completely new possibilities for the administration of an organization's business. No longer does a branch office mail weekly, monthly, or even annual reports to headquarters. All data can be collected at the home office from any arm of the corporation almost immediately. The communications manager's position has become an important one within the company, for this person is responsible for transmitting and receiving the information upon which management bases its decisions. Output from both word processing and data processing units is being merged into an *information system*.

THE STRUGGLE FOR CONTROL OF COMMUNICATIONS EQUIPMENT

The American Telephone & Telegraph Company had a virtual monopoly over telephone equipment until the 1968 Carterfone decision by the Federal Communications Commission. The Carterfone decision struck down the AT&T restriction against all "foreign attachments" (devices not owned by the telephone company) to the telephone system. Encouraged by this obvious motivation to competition, many companies arose to manufacture "interconnect" terminal equipment such as telephones, switchboards, and data transmission equipment. These companies did an 800-million-dollar business in 1975. During this period, however, users of foreign attachments were required to pay a service charge to the common carriers (telephone companies). This charge was for the installation and maintenance of a protective interface device that the telephone companies claimed was necessary to protect their equipment against damage by the attachment.

Other companies became "specialized common carriers" and offered big business and government customers special long-distance communications by microwave at lower rates than those of AT&T affiliates. In 1975 these companies grossed over 50 million dollars, cutting into the 1.2-billion-dollar long-lines business of AT&T.

With the scientific developments in the field of electronics, AT&T and the nearly 1,500 telephone companies that rent or lease their equipment to customers became very concerned. They mounted efforts both with the Federal Communications Commission and in Congress against the growing number of companies with electronic know-how, especially since such giants as IBM planned to enter the information systems field. In 1975 the FCC issued a decision allowing the use of ancillary devices, such as answering machines, without the protective circuit. Instead, users of such equipment would be required to register the equipment with the carrier. In 1976 the FCC ruled that protective interface devices would no longer be mandatory for PBXs, main switchboards, or key telephones; nor would users of the interface devices be required to pay a service charge to common carriers for installation and maintenance.

The federal court later issued a stay preventing the implementation of this decision. The stay was appealed, and in 1976 a federal court of appeals partially lifted the stay to allow Bell System customers to use data and ancillary equipment without the installation and maintenance fee for the interface device. However, the registration feature was retained. (Included under ancillary equipment are automatic answering machines, automatic dialers, conference-call devices, photocopiers, and computer terminals. The decision, however, required users to continue to insert the interface coupler for key telephones, PBXs, and switchboards.)

Unhappy with the decisions of the FCC and the courts, the telephone companies are raising an all-out political effort to secure Congressional legislation that will prevent further encroachment of competing long-lines companies and equipment manufacturers. Obviously, the battle is not over. It will be a fierce one, which you will want to follow both as a consumer and as a business employee.

THE NATURE OF TODAY'S INFORMATION SYSTEMS

With appropriate sending equipment, all forms of information can be transmitted from a point of origin to any distant point equipped with appropriate receiving equipment: handwritten or typed messages, processed or unprocessed data, charts, or voice messages.

The following section describes technical developments that are to a large extent informational. However, these developments have provided extended services that the secretary should be able to handle capably.

Teletypewriter Systems

The *teletypewriter* combines the immediacy of the telephone with the documentation and accuracy of the letter. It is a relatively inexpensive means of providing fast communication in writing, 24 hours a day, 7 days a week. There are two teletypewriter networks, *Telex* and *TWX* (both owned by Western Union), that can be interconnected. These systems vary only slightly in how they work and in what they can do.

In addition to Telex and TWX many large corporations also have their own teletypewriter systems for communicating with their branches. These systems can be used to back up oral decisions, to secure a written record of a two-way "conversation," and to remind the recipient of an agreed-upon action to be taken.

The teletypewriter is useful when an office in another time zone is closed, for the receiver can receive and act on the message the first thing the following morning. It should be used for a one-way call when you need no immediate response, when you want to ask for information that will probably require waiting for a later answer, when communicating statistical information which is more accurate in written form, or when you want to prepare the recipient of the message for a later telephone call involving an important executive decision.

In sending a teletypewritten message, always choose your own organization's teletypewriter over TWX or Telex. If the message is to be written out for the message center, type it on your company's forms for this purpose. After dialing Telex-to-Telex or TWX-to-TWX, you or the message-center attendant will get an automatic identification assuring you that you have reached the person wanted. The automatic identification may be repeated at the end of the transmission, confirming that the message has been received. In the actual sending process, messages are punched on a paper tape which can be corrected before transmission. Paper tapes should be retained for at least one business day in case the message must be resent because the lines were unavailable.

Teletypewriters are used in sending mailgrams, telegrams, and cablegrams. Special applications are possible for an organization which frequently sends mailgrams to the same list of people. The addresses can be fed to the sending equipment from an address tape to be merged with the tape containing the message. An address list can be stored in Western Union's InfoMaster computer system, from which it can be readily called into use.

Tone Transmission

Words and numbers can be sent long distances by transmitting *tones* to a terminal point on equipment that reconverts the sound signals into words and numbers. With a *touch telephone* a call can be dialed in half the time required for completing a dialed call. The touch telephone can be used for both regular-service and long-distance tone transmission of business information to compatible equipment that converts the electronic signals into printouts. In contrast to the ordinary dial telephone, the touch telephone provides small businesses with access to an entire communication system. The touch telephone inputs business information into either a company's own transmission system or a network used by numerous subscribers. (See Chapter 18 for a more complete discussion of data-communication systems.) Many companies use their information systems for regular voice communication during the day and for data transmission at night and over the weekend.

Data Communication

Communication systems provide the vital link between business machines; they speed information from where it originates to where it must go. A number of companies manufacture data communication equipment. The Bell System has several systems that use telephone lines to send data. They market various Data-Phone systems that transmit information from punched tape, punched cards, or magnetic cards a line at a time at high speed. Another Bell System product, Dataspeed, uses a display screen for projecting data received; or the data can be converted into hard copy from data stored

Data-Phones transmit large quantities of business data over telephone lines at high speed.

American Telephone & Telegraph Co.

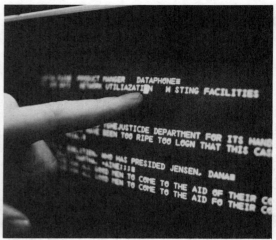

American Telephone & Telegraph Co.

The visual screen on Dataspeed enables the operator to correct errors before a message is sent. It also receives data for reading.

at the same location or sent from another point. Information can be sent at speeds up to 75 words per second.

Computer-Assisted Transmission

Computers are another important development in the transmission of both word and number communications. One example already described is InfoMaster which stores address lists. InfoMaster is at the heart of Western Union's operations. An incoming telegram is typed on a typewriter with a cathode ray tube so that it is immediately entered into the InfoMaster system.

Minicomputers are being used by a few large corporations to reduce telephone costs, sometimes by as much as $2,000 to $50,000 a month. The systems vary in degree of sophistication, but the overall aim is to reduce the costs of long-distance calling. All outgoing calls are funneled into the computer, which completes them through the least costly line available.

Microwave Transmission

Microwave transmission provides both voice- and data-grade communication by radio beams of ultrashort wavelengths. The great advantages of microwave transmission are economy, high quality, and the choice of purchasing a system or leasing lines for private use. For instance, a renter could lease enough voice-grade channels to meet its needs during business hours and switch to broadband data channels at night. (Broadband exchange service automatically links two subscribers over bands of greater width than are required for voice transmission, thus providing greater speed and capability for handling various nonvoice data.) Microwave Communications, Inc., is a leader in this field.

Transmission by Satellite

Several companies are transmitting or planning to transmit communications by satellite. Some of these companies are: RCA Global Communications, American Satellite, and Satellite Business Systems, a consortium of IBM, Comsat, and Aetna Life and Casualty Company.

Xerography

Equipment for the transmission of facsimile copies of documents through regular telephone circuits is available. The operator dials the recipient, positions a document in the long-distance facsimile unit, and places the transmitting device on the unit. Six minutes later a clear facsimile is reproduced 3,000 miles away by *Long-Distance Xerography* or other facsimile equipment.

The suffix *fax* refers to transmittal of facsimile copies. *Intrafax* is an interoffice transmittal system for sending pictorial, written, typed, or printed matter. *Ticket-Fax* reproduces an airplane or railroad ticket at a receiving center in eight seconds. *High-Speed Fax* can send a whole 20-page magazine, including illustrations, in a few minutes.

Although facsimile equipment is not necessarily part of a communications system, it will probably become more popular because it can eliminate time delays, thereby helping to balance peak-load problems.

EXTENDED SERVICES

In addition to basic telephone services, there are many additional communications services available that directly affect the secretary in today's office.

Wide Area Telecommunications Service (WATS)

Wide Area Telecommunications Service (WATS) provides reduced-rate long-distance service for subscribers with a high volume of voice or data transmission. Inward and outward WATS services are available. Two types of *outward WATS* may be purchased: Full Business Day (FBD), providing 240 hours of service a month with additional use charged by the hour; or Measured Time (MT), providing 10 hours a month with additional use charged by the hour. The country is divided, for WATS service, into five geographic areas ranging in size from Area I, which usually covers only neighboring states, to Area V, which extends from coast to coast.

One type of company may need expanded long-distance service to only one or two areas, while another may need WATS service covering all five areas. One company may want unlimited calls, while another may need only a limited number of calls and may want to restrict the length of calls.

Inward WATS is used for business promotion. The subscriber advertises a telephone number beginning with 800 and states that there is no charge to the calling party. (See page 278.) Since the call has already been paid for, there is no further billing.

The use of 800 numbers has increased to such an extent that there is a published directory of such numbers available from newsstands and from Toll Free Digest Company, Claverack, NY 12513. If you want to find the 800 number of an organization, you may dial toll-free 800-555-1212.

Automatic Identification of Outward Dialing (AIOD)

Unfortunately, many employees abuse the long-distance privilege. A check for a month in one company showed that 34 percent of its WATS calls were personal. *Automatic Identification of Outward Dialing (AIOD)* equipment in its simplest form enables a company to trace a dialed call back to the originating telephone station. This provides a control over unauthorized use of WATS and long-distance privileges.

Extended Area Service (EAS)

The concept of *Extended Area Service (EAS)* reflects the larger community of interest that exists in metropolitan areas. A business located in Washington, D.C., that needs "local" service to suburbs (such as Alexandria, Virginia, and Silver Springs, Maryland) could purchase reduced-rate EAS at a flat monthly fee. The extent of use of such service is shown by the fact that more than a third of the calls handled as long distance 20 years ago now go through as local calls.

Leased Lines

It is possible for a company to lease from the telephone company or from a private company telegraph and telephone lines for its exclusive use. The tie-line connects the various locations of a business complex in different parts of the same city or in different cities. It provides direct voice contact between separate units of a business and also transmits data. The tie line can connect switchboards, PBXs, key telephones, and regular telephones. It provides unlimited calling at a fixed monthly charge and is always reserved for the exclusive use of the subscriber.

Foreign Exchange Service (FX)

A local telephone number in a site remote from plant or company headquarters can be listed so that a call made to the listed number goes through as a local call. The New York City directory might carry the number of a firm located in New Brunswick, New Jersey, as New York City Tel. No. 987-6604. (See page 275.)

Conference Calls

The electronic Dimension PBX (see pages 266–267) has conference-call capability. If your organization does not have this equipment, however, it is still possible to set up conference calls. An executive may want to get a group opinion on an idea or to announce design or price changes or a policy decision. The secretary calls the number for long distance, asks for the conference operator, and gives the locations and names of persons to be included, sometimes specifying the time the call is to be put through. From 3 to 14 long-distance points can be connected for a *two-way* conference call. With specialized equipment such as a speakerphone or a loudspeaker, several persons may listen in on a call at any one location. Up to 49 points can be connected for a *one-way* conference call (one in which the voice of only the caller is transmitted).

With recent innovations in equipment, it is sometimes possible to set up conference calls without the services of the operator. Also, with the *Add-On* feature, a caller already engaged in a two-way conversation can add a third person to the call.

Mobile Service

More than 25,000 customers have mobile telephone service. These customers include trucks, news services, private automobiles, buses, planes, trains, and many other mobile users. Anyone can make a call to mobile equipment from any telephone, and any telephone can receive a call from mobile equipment. To place a call to a mobile telephone, either dial the number (which is listed in the telephone directory) or contact the mobile-service operator. The conversation travels partway by radio and partway by telephone wire.

Overseas Service

The extension of American business to foreign countries and the increased interaction between American and foreign companies has made overseas service increasingly common.

Telephone. If your company has the proper attachments for International Direct Distance Dialing (IDDD), you may now reach numbers in 36 foreign countries by dialing directly. If you know the local number (possibly from the letterhead of the company being called) and have a directory from the Bell System with key numbers for the countries that can be called, you can sometimes save hours in getting the number. The correct procedure is: Dial the international access code 011 (or 0011 if you dial 0 for long distance), plus the code of the country being called, plus the routing code, plus the local number. Since special reduced rates apply to United Kingdom calls, a portion of the folder for IDDD relating to that country is reproduced below. The chart indicates that to call an office in Edinburgh you would dial 011 + 44 + 31 + the local number. Because signals indicating ringing or busy differ somewhat from those in the United States, the folder also describes the tones you may hear after dialing the entire IDDD number. It also shows that the initial three minutes cost only $3.60.

Station-to-station international calls cost less than person-to-person calls. A directory of international long-distance rates is available from your local telephone company. IDDD calls to North American countries are charged a reduced rate.

If your telephone equipment is not capable of handling IDDD calls, dial the operator and give the country to be called, the name of the company wanted, and the name of the person to be reached. Of course, it is essential to consider the time zone (page 301) and to

IDDD information for calls to the United Kingdom. Complete IDDD information is available from your local telephone company office.

Country Code	City Routing Code		Phone No's	Audible Signals	Rates (tax not included)
44 UNITED KINGDOM	Belfast (N. Ire.)	232	three four five six or seven digits	**Ringing Signal** — two short tones followed by a pause; repeated more rapidly than U.S. ringing. **Busy Signal** — similar to U.S. but faster. **Circuits Busy Signal** — a rapid series of high-low tones. **Number Not In Use** — high-pitched continuous tone.	All Hours* **$3.60** first 3 minutes each add'l min. **$1.20** *There are no special reduced night rates.
	Birmingham	21			
	Bournemouth	202			
	Cardiff (Wales)	222			
	Durham	385			
	Edinburgh (Scot.)	31			
	Glasgow (Scot.)	41			
	Gloucester	452			
	Ipswich	473			
	Liverpool	51			
	London	1			
	Manchester	61			
	Nottingham	602			
	Prestwick (Scot.)	292			
	Sheffield	742			
	Southampton	703			

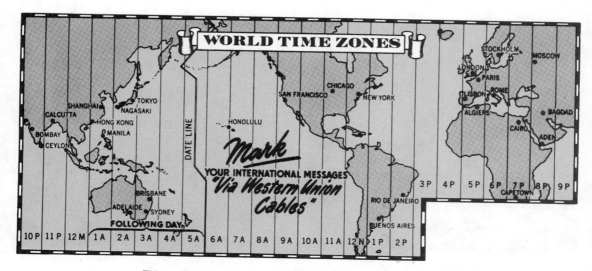

This world time-zone map will help the secretary in planning overseas communications. Refer also to page 282 for a time-zone map of the United States.

check with the local operator or directory for the charges and for the times during which the various rates apply.

Telegraph. Increased communication capabilities are available through Western Union International, Inc., which provides *Datel* services, high-speed combined message and data communications; *Telex* worldwide service between correspondents in 100 countries; and leased-wire voice-data circuits.

Ship-to-Shore Messages. A "ship-to-shore" (actually, *shore* to *ship*) radiogram should give the name of the addressee, the name of the ship, the name of the coast station through which the ship can be reached, and **DOM** or **FOR** following the address to indicate whether the vessel is of domestic or foreign registry.

NEW SERVICES

Special equipment of many types is available so that the telephone can be tailored to the user's needs. In addition to items discussed previously, the following supplementary services may be obtained from the telephone company for a surcharge or purchased from other vendors.

The Touch-a-matic Telephone

The *Touch-a-matic telephone* has an electronic memory in which up to 31 numbers can be stored so that they can be dialed at the

American Telephone & Telegraph Co.

The Touch-a-matic saves time in dialing frequently called numbers and in reconnecting with the last number called.

touch of a single button. The names of the persons most often called are displayed on the face of the instrument. There is also a Last-Person-Called button which enables the user to recall the person last talked to by touching the button before a new number is called. The multibutton version of this telephone includes five inside and/or outside lines, plus "Hold."

The Speakerphone

Although not a completely new service, the *speakerphone* should be included here. It has built-in transmitter and volume control so that both sides of a conversation can be amplified. The secretary can leave the telephone, walk to the opposite side of the office, look up information in a file, and read it to the caller from this location. The caller can be heard in various parts of the room; and vice versa, the caller can hear comments and discussions with others in the room. This equipment expands opportunities for full communication during conference calls. It is also possible to telephone lectures that may be amplified for delivery to class and conference groups.

Individualized Equipment

Color telephones, lightweight Princess telephones, and Trimline telephones with the dial embedded in the handset (especially attractive to those who see poorly) are available to the user who wants individualized equipment. With the influx of new equipment that permits individually owned telephones, we can expect many new designs.

INTERNATIONAL SERVICES

Overseas telegraph communications are sent by underwater cables (cablegrams), by radio (radiograms), or by satellite. International messages may be sent by Western Union International, RCA Corporation, French Cable, or one or two smaller companies. Since Western Union International has no connection with Western Union, if you send an international message to the domestic Western Union, it will be forwarded by TWX/Telex to one of the companies in the international field where compatible equipment will send it.

There are three levels of overseas service. The first is the telegram, used by individuals or companies sending few messages. The second level is for medium-volume users, who communicate by Telex. The third level is for large-volume users, who lease overseas communication channels.

Telegrams

There are two basic classes of international telegrams: *full rate (FR)* and *letter telegram (LT)*. These services are summarized in the table on page 304.

Because one code word may mean several plain-language words, code language is frequently used in cables. Code words are composed entirely of letters. They may be real or artificial words, but they must not contain more than five letters. In an international message the use of code words lowers the cost of the message. For example, the one code word KALOP may be used to cover the statements: "We authorize you to act for us. Will confirm this by mail."

A.B.C., Acme, Bentley's, and the Western Union codes are used most frequently. If you decide to use a private code, check with the telegraph company used in order to determine whether this code will be acceptable in the country to which the cablegram is sent.

Cipher words, used for secrecy, are usually composed of figures or of letters exceeding five per group. Cipher words do not fulfill the requirements of code or plain language. In a message that contains a combination of code, cipher, and plain language, the code and cipher words are charged at the rate of five characters to the word, while plain language is charged at the rate of fifteen letters to the word. Codes and ciphers are permissible only in the address and

	Full Rate (FR)	**Letter Telegram (LT)**
Indicator Preceding Address	No indicator necessary	LT
Charge for Indicator	——	*LT* chargeable as 1 word; position immediately preceding the address
Precedence of Transmission	Takes precedence over all other messages	Delivery at destination next morning
Language	Plain language, secret (cipher or code), or a combination	Plain language, but code may be used in address and signature
Word Length	Plain language: 15 letters to a word Cipher or code language: 5 characters to a word	15 letters to a word
Minimum Number of Words	5	22
Relationship of Rates	Based on distance message is sent	One half of full rate

signature of a letter telegram but may be used in all parts of full-rate messages.

Except for the destination country, each word in the name, address, and signature is counted as a chargeable word in a cablegram; therefore, a one-word cable address saves words in both incoming and outgoing messages. That is why one-word cable addresses are often printed on a company's letterhead. For a small annual charge a cable address may be registered at any telegraph office. It cannot duplicate another already on file.

Frequently a firm in this country and its foreign correspondent will register an identical cable address and restrict its use to the exclusive exchange of messages between themselves. This procedure, known as a reversible address, eliminates the need for a signature on messages, thus saving the cost of one word.

Telex

Telex has been described on page 294. Since Telex messages are charged by the minute in overseas communication, the sender should try to abbreviate the messages according to the suggestions for overseas telegrams.

Leased Channels

The user leases a channel for a large volume of communication. This is a dedicated (reserved) line between two points which is paid for at a flat rate. On the channel three types of messages can be sent and received: teletyped messages, voice messages, and high-speed data.

SUGGESTED READINGS

See Suggested Readings for Chapter 12, page 288.

QUESTIONS FOR DISCUSSION

1. What effect did the Carterfone decision have on the telecommunications industry?
2. Do you think that the telephone companies should have a monopoly over communications equipment, or do you tend to favor free competition?
3. When should you choose a teletypewriter message over a telephone message? Why?
4. How can a company cut down on unauthorized long-distance telephone calls, with special equipment? without special equipment? If the services are already paid for should an employee hesitate to make an unauthorized long-distance call?
5. Under what circumstances would an organization subscribe to outward WATS? inward WATS?
6. Name a situation in which an organization would choose EAS, leased lines, FX service.
7. For your office-procedures manual, develop a five-step procedure for placing an overseas call.
8. Give three examples of ways in which the computer has contributed to improvement in telecommunications.
9. What three levels of overseas communication are available, and when would each one be chosen?

PROBLEMS

1. If you were employed by a well-equipped corporation headquarters, which type of communication would you probably choose in the following situations? Tell why you chose the medium you did.

    (a) A message asking a governor to sign a bill

    (b) A message to three sales managers in different locations (A reaction is necessary from each.)

    (c) A message informing the payroll department in a branch office that data required for issuing paychecks have not been received

    (d) A message containing detailed information about production schedules of a branch factory for the next two months

    (e) A message to inquire about prices of a well-known office machine manufactured in a nearby suburb

    (f) A message (about an important interview in London) to the president of the company en route to Europe by ship

    (g) A message asking a salesperson 500 miles away to call on a prospective customer

    (h) A message to the production manager in a distant branch factory

    (i) A request for information from a bank in Englewood, New Jersey (across the Hudson River from your Manhattan office)

    (j) A message that must reach 12 sales representatives in different locations by the following morning

    (k) A message to the president of the company en route to Europe by ship (The message requires an immediate answer.)

    (l) A message to the manager of a restaurant for which you supplied building materials, expressing good wishes on opening day

    (m) A message that will be received after closing hours but must be available when the office opens the following morning

    (n) A graph to be used tomorrow in a national sales meeting

2. Develop a bibliography of ten articles published within the past six months describing innovations in data communication. Of what value was this investigation?

3. Visit the teletypewriter, Telex, TWX, or Data-Phone installation in one company. Report on the company's equipment usage to the class.

Part 4 CASE PROBLEMS

Case 4-1
ABSENTEEISM IN THE MAILROOM

Katherine McNamara was secretary to the personnel manager. At lunch with a group of co-workers, she heard a clerk from the mail room say to his friend,"Iz, I'm going to take this afternoon off. You sign out for me at five o'clock. Remember, I did the same for you on Monday."

Katherine had suspected that the mail department was loosely administered, but she had not believed it was possible to leave work without the absence being detected.

Since she worked in another department, she wondered about her responsibility.

Should she report the conversation to her employer? to the head of the mail department? Should she speak to the young employees herself? Not wanting to tattle, should she ignore the situation entirely because it does not involve her?

Case 4-2
HELP YOURSELF TO COMPANY EQUIPMENT AND SUPPLIES

Hashid Malik was a recently hired secretary to the head of the Transportation Department. He was also secretary of the neighborhood association that was planning a block party. Marina Maldonado, who had been secretary to the plant manager for the past ten years, was a friendly person who wanted to be helpful to new employees and had made a friend of Hashid.

When she went to the Reprographics Department with an order for Xerox copies of a report, she met Hashid, who said, "Want to see the posters we are distributing to every building on the block to advertise our block festival? I hope that you can come." A quick glance showed the job order for 50 posters. Marina replied, "They are very artisitic and should attract a crowd. I hope too that I can come. I think that it is wonderful that you are so interested in community work."

When she got back to her office, she questioned whether she should have told Hashid that it is dishonest to use company equipment and materials for personal use. After all, he was involved in a commendable project. She realized, too, that "Everybody does it." Did she have the authority to reprimand an employee at her own level anyway? She also wondered if she should report the violation of explicit company rules against using company equipment for personal use. If so, to whom?

**Case 4-3
TELEPHONE
EFFICIENCY**

Because of the frantic activity in the sales manager's office during the month before a new product was launched, Mary Malekos, secretary to the manager, was away from her desk a great deal of the time and asked Si Hills to cover her phone. The arrangement was that she would reciprocate when Si was not at his desk.

Several times callers told Mary that they had tried to reach her but got no answer, and she decided to check on the situation. One day she was approaching her desk when the phone rang. Si continued typing and did not answer. After approximately a minute, the ringing ceased. Mary said, "I thought you'd agreed to cover my phone while I'm away from my desk."

Si's answer was spoken accusingly, "It's just not fair. I've got my own work to do, and I haven't time to do yours. Answer your own phone. I haven't time to answer it. Besides, I'd have to answer for you about ten times oftener than you answer for me."

What suggestions do you have for Mary in solving the problem?

**Case 4-4
NECESSITY FOR
LEARNING
ABOUT
MAIL
SERVICES**

Louis Weldon had been secretary to an accounting firm for two weeks when he was given four items to mail on his way home from work: a signed quarterly income tax return of a client, a package of 200 handouts to be distributed by one of the partners when delivering a speech at a convention on Friday, a letter containing a check, and two magazines that had been borrowed from a colleague by a member accountant.

He sent the tax return and the check by first-class mail and the magazines and speech by special handling. When he was reprimanded by his employer for his decisions, he said, "You didn't tell me how you wanted the items sent, and besides I was working overtime to get them in the mail anyway."

How should the materials have been sent? Why?
What principles did Louis violate by his actions?

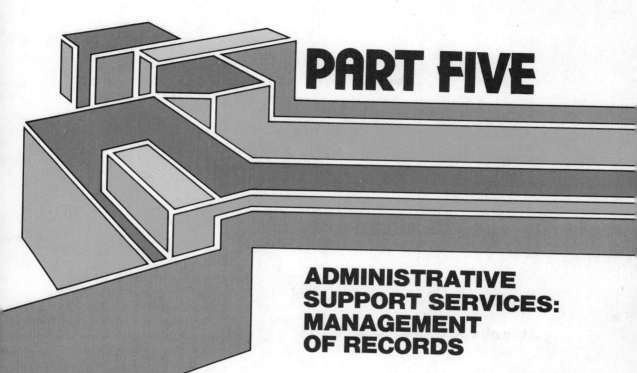

PART FIVE

ADMINISTRATIVE SUPPORT SERVICES: MANAGEMENT OF RECORDS

The automation tide that is sweeping over the office is having an impact upon the quantities of records produced, stored, retrieved, and destroyed. Furthermore, the records generated by today's office are on a variety of media: paper, tape, disk, belt, and film. They are in many forms: rolls, cartridges, cassettes, disks, mag cards, microfiche, microfilm, computer printouts, punched cards, sheets, and bound documents. All of these must be stored so as to be found when needed. Not only has technology expanded the variety of records, but it has greatly increased the volume of communications that flow in and out of the office. This volume would literally inundate the office with data if a records management program were not in operation; thus, records management is essential in today's office. The secretary is part of the records management team. This section will discuss the secretary's challenging role in records management.

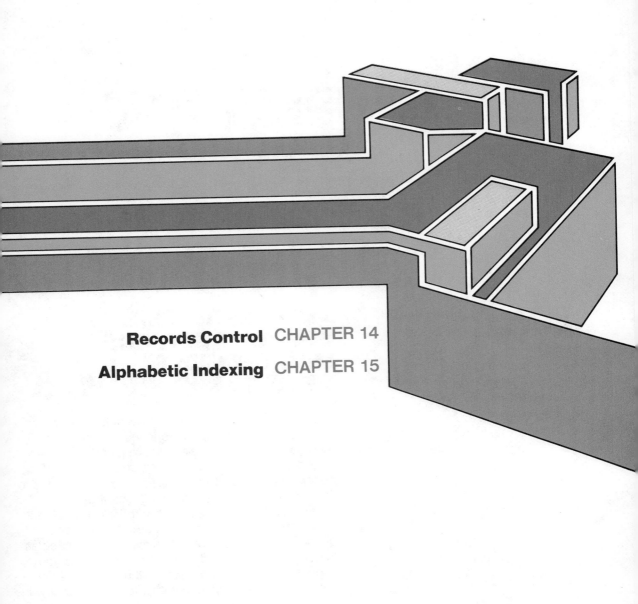

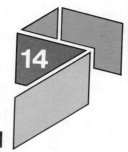

Records Control

Information is a prerequisite for sound managerial decision making. Supplying information when and where it is needed is the function of the secretary working with the office files. That is why files are maintained. Unless material put in the files can be found immediately, the decision-making process temporarily breaks down.

Since filing is done by people, the error potential is ever present. A mag card is put in the wrong folder. A folder is inadvertently attached to items in a related file. A microfiche is removed with no record of its withdrawal. A needed letter is buried in the mass of papers on the executive's desk. An important reference is snugly resting in the "Material to be Filed" folder in the secretary's desk drawer. When these things happen, the decision-making process is held up until the missing item can be located — a frustrating experience for the executive and an embarrassing one for the secretary.

All too frequently filing duties are left until the last minute and rushed through. Errors do occur. Sooner or later the errors will surface and the secretary cannot avoid responsibility for them. Filing errors cannot be avoided completely, but they can be greatly reduced through the application of sound filing procedures. Consequently, the secretary needs to observe good filing practices and to insist that others with access to the files also observe them.

THE SECRETARY'S FILING RESPONSIBILITIES

Files are the memory of a business. They may be *centralized* in one location or *decentralized* in various departments or branches. Administrative and multifunctional secretaries will probably maintain decentralized (in-office) files and also send materials to and secure materials from a larger central file. The executive and the secretary need to plan together the in-office files if they are to work well. Of course, the secretary will follow company procedures for borrowing and returning documents to the central file.

If the company has a records management program, the secretary will probably receive instructions about what materials are to be sent to the central file, what materials may be retained in the executive's files, and how long to keep certain records before destroying them or sending them to a low-cost storage area. Records managers are primarily concerned with reducing the amount of paper to be filed, and their work has been made more demanding by the accessibility of copying machines. The same document may be copied and filed in a half-dozen offices. Since it can cost as much as five cents or more a year to keep a piece of paper in the files, records managers want to prevent filing anything without reference value, to reduce duplication of copies in several locations, and to insure that superseded material will be destroyed when a current replacement is filed. To save space, they frequently try to reduce executive files. On the other hand, the executives, fearing that they cannot refer to items easily once the records have left their hands, build "little empires" that take up space and increase the expense of paperwork.

The secretary's task is one of reconciling the executive's habit of wanting to keep almost everything, with the need to reduce the executive's in-office files to a minimum. Consequently, the secretary needs to understand not only the executive's files but also the central filing system, so that material not available in the executive's files may be secured from the central file.

Designing the Files

There is a tendency to restrict one's concept of files to the typical vertical file cabinet conspicuous in every office. Actually, the secretary usually works with many types of files — card files, project files, files of catalogs frequently consulted, magazine files, blueprint or other outsized material files, tape-cassette files, transparency files, files of computer printouts, microform files, open-shelf files — in addition to the traditional drawer file with alphabetic, numeric, geographic, and subject captions. Each type of file has a unique function. The secretary's responsibility usually goes beyond maintaining existing files to include the designing and installation of various types of files that will best serve the executive's need for information. In planning files, three factors must always be considered: findability, confidentiality, and safety.

Findability. Unfortunately, files are thought of first as places to *put* materials, not places to *find* materials. Yet the criterion for judging any file system is findability. The efficient secretary makes decisions about where to put an item after considering, "How will it be requested?" or "How can I find it?" Materials must be located with dispatch and only those actually wanted must be selected from a complete file. To do this, the secretary must understand what the executive needs and not provide 250 pages when only 10 are wanted. Placing materials in safekeeping is important, but being able to find them promptly when wanted is *vital*.

Confidentiality. The secretary is also responsible for the confidentiality of the employer's files. The degree of security required varies from the tight surveillance required over files and papers marked "Confidential," "Secret," "Vital," or "Personal" to the exercise of reasonable protection for the less sensitive materials that constitute the major portion of most files. If the executive is working in a highly sensitive area or industry, there should be a company policy as to who may have access to confidential and secret materials. In the absence of a company policy, the secretary working with the executive should establish such a policy for the executive's office.

Safety. Allied to the need for security is the secretary's ultimate responsibility for the safety of the records in the executive's office. Many of them may be irreplaceable. A safe practice is to lock all confidential items in a filing cabinet or vault before leaving at night as a safeguard against prying eyes or fire damage.

Developing an Index

The secretary in a new position may find an index of file captions for the executive's files already prepared. Chances are, though, none will be available, and the development of an index telling where in the files to look for materials will have a high priority. Even after the secretary has become familiar with the files, such a guide will prove advantageous for it will help anyone (including the executive or a new assistant) to locate material. A simple table of contents that indicates where to look for all types of records is shown on this page. Do not underestimate its value.

	FILE INDEX NO. 89 CHEMICAL	
	Location	
	File No.	Drawer No.
Correspondence		
Company	2	1
Government	2	2
Patents	2	3
Personnel Work		
Applications	1	2
Medical	1	3
Security	1	6
Reports		
Company	5	1
Outside	5	3

A Table of Contents for Locating Filed Material

Communication between secretary and executive seems particularly weak in the filing area. Since the secretary is the one responsible for seeing that materials are placed in and retrieved from the files, there is the tendency to consider the files the secretary's private domain. Furthermore, there is a tendency not to involve the executive in the planning of the files. Yet the filing system is a joint secretary-executive responsibility. If they work together in planning the system, the transfer of either of them to another office will not destroy the continuity of the files. Obviously a new secretary should not attempt to reorganize the files until considerable insight into the informational needs of the office has been acquired.

Ideas for setting up files may sometimes be obtained from professional organizations and publications. For instance, suggestions might be found in an engineering magazine for filing blueprints. An educational secretary might find a model for pupil attendance records in publications of the National Association of Educational Secretaries. The Life Office Management Association has made studies of office systems for insurance records. Likewise, manuals of the legal profession give directions for developing numeric legal files. The American Municipal Association has developed a list of subject headings peculiar to municipal activities and problems. The American Institute of Architects has created a standard filing system and alphabetic index for information on the materials, appliances, and equipment used in construction and related activities.

It is also possible to buy prefabricated subject file systems for certain types of offices. For example, Shaw-Walker manufactures a prefabricated administration file containing main subjects and subclassifications printed on guide and folder tabs. The manufacturer claims this system will provide indexing applicable to 90 percent of all basic executive data.

FILING METHODS

Material should be filed according to the designation by which it will be sought and according to a method with an established procedure and set of rules which are understood by all who use the files. There are four basic filing methods — *alphabetic, subject, numeric,* and *geographic*.

Manufacturers of filing equipment have devised and patented improvements upon these four fundamental methods, such as color schemes to expedite sorting, filing, and finding procedures — or techniques for grouping names spelled differently but pronounced alike. Trade names such as *Variadex, Tell-I-Vision, Amberg-Nual,* or *Pendaflex* refer to commercial systems. The word *system* is reserved for any filing plan devised by a filing-equipment manufacturer.

Alphabetic Filing

Most, possibly as high as 80 percent, of all the filing done in the office is *alphabetical*; that is, the files are sequenced alphabetically. Furthermore, all filing systems are directly or indirectly based on the alphabetic system. Alphabetic filing is understood by everyone and the filing is *direct* (meaning that it is not necessary to consult a subordinate file before filing or finding). The method is based on the strict observance of the guides for alphabetic indexing that are presented in Chapter 15.

Phonetic indexing is a modification of alphabetic indexing. In phonetic indexing the names are arranged by their sound and not by their spelling. Thus, Burke and its variants — Burck, Berk, Berke, Birk, Bourke, Bork, Borck, and others — are filed together.

Subject Filing

The nature of some executives' work makes logical the filing of most of the correspondence, reports, and documents to be retained in the office under *subject headings* arranged in an alphabetic sequence in the files (actually, an alphabetic file except that all captions refer to subjects or topics rather than to names of people or names of organizations).

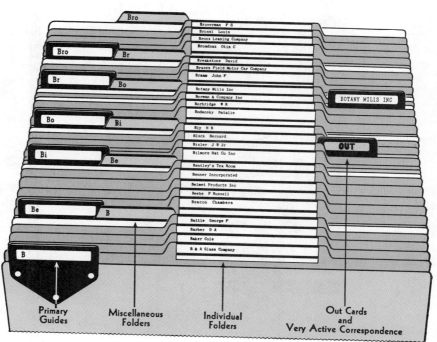

In this illustration of an alphabetic file, four positions are used for the captions.

Primary Guides

Miscellaneous Folders

Individual Folders

Out Cards and Very Active Correspondence

Remington Rand

Each piece of material is filed under *one subject caption*, but a *relative index* is prepared to support the subject file. This index is basically a cross-reference system. It lists all captions under which an item *may* be filed. To obtain an item from a subject file for which the subject caption is not known, the searcher first consults the relative index to identify all possible headings under which the item may be stored.

The executive and the secretary may profitably spend time in developing the relative index — time that will be saved later when the executive asks for the material under a number of captions. If the executive asks for the file on wage-incentive plans of a rival company, the Green Corporation, the secretary may have it filed under: (1) fringe benefits, (2) incentive plans, (3) personnel, or (4) Green Corporation. Reference to the relative index will help locate the pamphlet.

A description of a portion of the subject file pictured below will perhaps best illustrate the principles. This illustration shows only one of the major headings with its subdivisions.

Each main heading has a number of subheadings. For instance, **OFFICE EQUIPMENT** is subdivided into several categories such as:

OFFICE EQUIPMENT: Copying Machines

OFFICE EQUIPMENT: Duplicating Machines

OFFICE EQUIPMENT: Typewriters

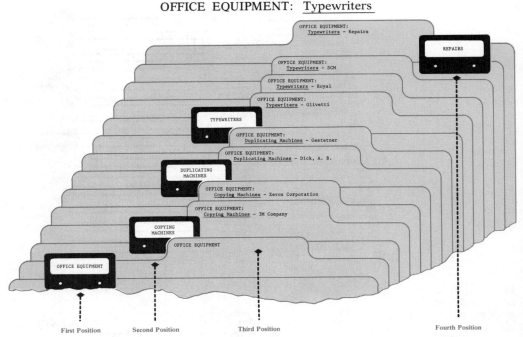

This subject file would be suitable for the purchasing agent or the office manager.

Some of these subdivisions are further subdivided. For example, OFFICE EQUIPMENT: Typewriters is subdivided into:

> OFFICE EQUIPMENT: Typewriters — Olivetti
> OFFICE EQUIPMENT: Typewriters — Royal
> OFFICE EQUIPMENT: Typewriters — SCM

The subdivision Typewriters is further subdivided by the special classification guide REPAIRS in the fourth position.

Subject filing presents special retrieval problems because material may be requested under any one of many titles. For this reason one management consultant said, "To do subject filing well, the secretary must think like the executive." No area of filing requires the exercise of better judgment on the part of the secretary than does arranging materials by titles that best indicate their content.

Numeric Filing

Lawyers, architects, engineers, accountants, realtors, insurance brokers and contractors may assign a number for each project; and that number becomes the basis for the *numeric file*. Case records and confidential material where anonymity is desired are commonly filed numerically.

A numeric filing plan has four parts:

1. Alphabetic card index
2. Main numeric file
3. Miscellaneous alphabetic file for correspondence
4. *Accession* or number book, a record of the numbers which are already assigned

In the numeric file, the alphabetic card index is first consulted to obtain the file number. The item is then located by number in the main numeric file. For a name or subject not shown in the card index, the miscellaneous alphabetic file is searched. Numeric filing is an *indirect* system, as one must refer to a card index before referring to the main numeric file.

Advantages and Disadvantages. Numeric filing has both advantages and disadvantages. It is easy to learn. Misfiling is reduced because individually assigned numbers are less confusing than are similarly spelled names. Furthermore, extensive cross-referencing is possible in the alphabetic card index. A disadvantage is the necessity of consulting the card index before locating the material — a very time-consuming factor. And when misfiling does occur, it is usually more difficult to locate the misfile than it is when an alphabetic file is used.

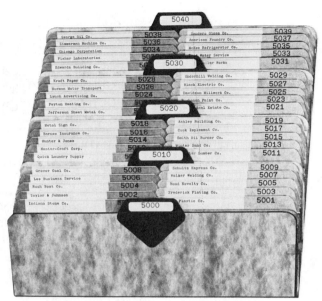

In numeric filing, misfiling is reduced because individually assigned numbers are less confusing than are similarly spelled names.

*Shaw Walker
Company*

Terminal- and Middle-Digit Filing. In straight numeric filing, as the files increase, the numbers assigned to them become higher. Because most of the filing work deals with the most recent dates, the work involves the highest numbers. In a numeric file of insurance policies, for instance, the most recent policies would have the highest numbers. Chances are that the file clerk would work mostly with the higher numbered files.

Terminal-digit filing avoids concentrating the bulk of the filing action in a small section of the files. This indexing method divides a number into pairs of digits. For example, insurance policy No. 412010 would be identified as 41 20 10. The last (terminal) digits would identify the drawer number; the second pair of digits to the left would indicate the guide number in the drawer; and the remaining digits would indicate the sequence of the folder behind the guide. Thus, policy No. 41 20 10 would be filed in Drawer 10, behind Guide 20, and in 41st sequence behind the guide (between policy No. 40 20 10 and policy No. 42 20 10).

To appreciate the advantage of terminal-digit filing, visualize 100 file drawers, each labeled with a two-digit number (00, 01, 02, and so on through 99). Policy No. 2 12 00 would go in Drawer 00, while policy No. 2 12 01 would go in Drawer 01, and so on. As consecutive new policy numbers are assigned, the policy materials will be distributed throughout the 100 drawers.

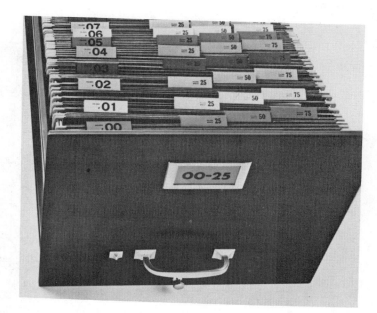

Oxford Pendaflex
Corporation

This illustration shows a portion of the 25 drawer of a terminal-digit file. The terminal-digit system assures easier filing and finding.

Research shows that terminal-digit filing saves up to 40 percent of file-operation costs by assuring a uniform work load, better employee relations, unlimited expansion facilities, and fewer misfiles. This system has been adapted and modified into the triple-terminal-digit system (using the last three digits as the drawer number).

In *middle-digit filing*, the two middle digits identify the drawer or section; the first two digits, the guide number in the drawer or section; and the final two digits, the sequence behind the guide.

Geographic Filing

Geographic filing keeps records by geographic units or territories. Divisions are made in some logical sequence: nations, states or provinces, cities, and so on. Guides are used for the larger divisions and subdivisions. Behind each guide, material is filed in miscellaneous folders alphabetically, usually by name of city and then by name of correspondent. Individual folders are filed alphabetically by location, then by name.

The geographic file is frequently supported by a card index in which names of companies are filed alphabetically. If the location of a company is forgotten, it may be obtained by reference to the alphabetic card index.

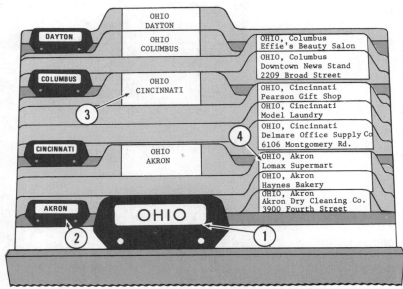

In this geographic file, papers are filed alphabetically by the geographical areas (see No. 1 and No. 2) indicated by the guides and folders. In the miscellaneous folder for each city (see No. 3), the papers are filed alphabetically by the names of the correspondents. Individual folders are used for correspondents who have enough communications to warrant a separate folder (see No. 4).

Selecting a Method

The basic filing methods used in your office should depend upon how materials are identified. If they are identified by name (either personal or company), an alphabetic file system would probably be used. If each client, job, or project is identified by number, a numeric system would be appropriate. When the identifying name for the item is a territory or a geographic location, the geographic method would be best. When items are categorized by subject, then a subject file would meet the needs. In practice, it is not unusual to find all four filing systems being used in the same office.

The Secretary's Chronological File

A secretary who must send material to a centralized file usually keeps a chronological file as a ready in-office reference. This file, sometimes called a *reading* or *chron* file, consists of a copy — carbon or photo — of each *outgoing* item of the day, filed in chronological order in a ring binder or topbound folder. Such a file can answer many questions — was a letter mailed, to whom was it addressed, when was it mailed, what price was quoted, and was an enclosure mentioned — all without the delay of consulting the central file.

To speed the locating of material in the reading file, some secretaries place a sheet with a date index tab between the carbons to separate each day's work. It is also recommended that a notation be placed on each carbon showing where the regular correspondence concerning that item is filed. The secretary retains materials in this file for a limited time only, perhaps six months to a year, each month discarding the materials for the earliest month.

FILING EQUIPMENT

Improved filing equipment and supplies are the result of the intense competition among manufacturers. Some of the new developments have significance for the secretary's files; others are important mainly to the larger centralized filing department.

Vertical Files

The most often used type of filing equipment is the vertical file (with papers filed on edge vertically) available in one- to six-drawer units in a wide range of colors. Opening the drawers of these units requires at least three to four feet of space in front of the cabinet.

Rock-a-File. The rock-a-file is a variation of the vertical file. The drawers rock or tilt open sideways, requiring less floor space in front. The rock-a-file may meet requirements in situations where space must be utilized efficiently.

Roll-Out File. The drawer in a roll-out file rolls out flat but sideways, thus exposing the entire contents of the drawer. It requires half the aisle space needed for a conventional vertical file drawer.

The secretary is using a file in which the drawers roll out from the side of the cabinet. This type of file, called a side, roll-out, or lateral file, offers the advantage of requiring less aisle space and 100 percent accessibility and visibility.

Photo furnished courtesy Browne-Morse Co., Muskegon, MI

This file combines the space-saving and ease-of-access features of open-shelf files with a suspension system. Each folder is suspended from two rods and always hangs in a vertical position, thereby eliminating sagging.

White Power Files, Inc.

Open-Shelf File. In open-shelf filing the folders are placed vertically on open shelves with no drawers involved. Access to the folders is from the front. Since the shelves can extend to the ceiling, they can accommodate more material per square foot of floor space than the drawer file can; they require less floor and aisle space; they cost less; and they require less time to file and find records.

Mobile File. Mobile files allow what is known as close-support filing — putting the records at the point of use. The concept is to bring the highly active file unit to the operations area rather than forcing the worker to go to the file. Some mobile files are single units that are pushed around like carts. Others are multiple modules that roll on a suspension system from the ceiling. Some are stationary, like the tub file, with trays rotating to give operators access to needed material.

Horizontal Files

Horizontal files store in a flat position materials such as maps, drawings, or blueprints that normally are much larger than the materials filed in a vertical file drawer. They are most commonly found in engineering and architectural offices.

Rotary-Card Files

The rotary-wheel file is designed to make a limited amount of information available within arm's reach of the operator. The wheel can be small for desk use or motorized to hold large trays of cards, such as accounts receivable, credit information, and key-punched cards.

Frequently referenced files may be placed in a file caddy that moves on casters. The caddy is stationed close to the user's desk, thereby saving the time and energy of repeated trips to file cabinets or shelves that may be several feet or offices away. The caddy may be moved from desk to desk thus expediting the work of several people.

This rotary-wheel file is designed for quick access to a limited amount of information. When the executive needs the addresses of several sales representatives, the secretary can furnish them quickly without leaving the desk.

The rotary file places a large volume of filed materials within arm's reach of the user. In this file the trays rotate independently.

Delco Associates, Inc.

Visible-Card Files

In a visible-card file, cards filed in a shallow metal tray or on upright stands show only the lower edge of each card. Flipping up the preceding card reveals the card desired. Cards can easily be inserted into and removed from holders that are fastened so that the backs of cards can also be used for record keeping.

Visible-card files are used extensively for perpetual inventories, accounting records of sales and purchases, personnel histories — those situations in which information must be available quickly, as in answer to a telephone inquiry. Colored signals provide a visible means of control; for example, a blue signal attached to the visible edge of a credit card may mean "Watch credit closely."

Keyboard-Access Files

Several highly mechanical or electronically controlled filing systems bring a high degree of automation to filing. In most of these systems, each stored item is coded. The operator enters the code number on a keyboard. The equipment either mechanically or electronically searches, locates, and retrieves the item bearing the code number. The most sophisticated equipment will find and deliver a document from a room-sized storage area within seconds.

Datavue Products

This visible-card file makes data quickly available. The lower border of each card extends below that of the card above it and shows the information necessary for quick identification.

Tape Files

Tape files use specially designed folders to hold punched tape, edge-punched cards, and magnetic tape.

Micrographics

Micographics involves transferring correspondence and records to film, destroying the correspondence and records, and storing only the film. The film is viewed with a microfilm reader, but a full-sized hard copy can be produced.

Initially, micrographics was used to record all inactive and semi-active files that would normally be stored. The space saving can be as much as 98 percent. However, the development of electronic devices that provide extremely rapid retrieval of microfilmed data and the decreasing per-frame cost of processing microfilm have made the system attractive for storage of current records. Furthermore, microfilm is now accepted by the Internal Revenue Service as a substitute for original documents.

The secretary is using a microfilm reader to recall material stored in cartridges. Each cartridge has an index of its contents. The secretary places the cartridge into the reader, keys into the keyboard the index code of the desired item, and the page appears promptly on the screen. The copy can be reviewed from the reader or a hard copy can be produced photographically from the screen image.

Microfilmed chronological or sequenced data, such as sales slips, checks, parts lists, newspapers, magazines, catalogs, and lengthy reports, are usually stored on rolls (reels, cartridges, and cassettes). Other types of data may be more convenient to use if the frames are clipped from the film roll and mounted on cards that have an opening that fits the size of a frame. These are called *aperture cards*. Data may be written on the card or coded by holes punched into the card to permit it to be filed and retrieved mechanically. Cards that provide for the mounting of several frames on the same card are called *chips*.

Microfiche. Another version of microfilm is called *microfiche* (pronounced *microfeesh*). "Fiche" is a French word meaning a card or a slip of paper. Although most microfiche contain from 60 to 98

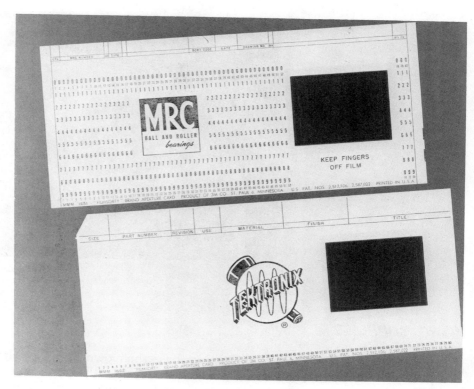

Microfilm Aperture
Cards

3M Company

frames, equipment is available to permit 269 images to be stored on
one card. Thus, a 269-page report can be recorded on one 6- by 4-
inch microfiche. Microfiche can be filed in a card file or in a specially designed book-type binder.

A number of electronic coding systems and devices permit aperture cards and microfiche to be stored and retrieved by use of electronic equipment. The console operator enters the identifying code
on a keyboard device and the card or microfiche is automatically
located, withdrawn, and presented to the operator in a matter of
seconds.

Computer Output Microfilm (COM). Computer-generated data can
be placed directly onto microfilm or microfiche by several methods.
The computer is capable of producing data at a much faster rate
than electronic printers can print. Thus, by bypassing the printing
operation and recording directly on film (COM), the computer-
generated data can be recorded faster. In addition, using COM provides a significant saving of space. For example, 200 feet of microfilm can carry the same amount of data as approximately 4,000
sheets of computer-printout paper.

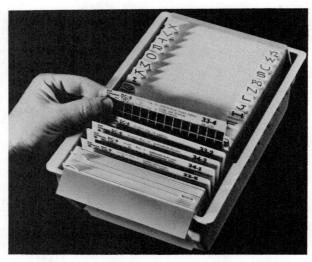

A Tray for Storing
Microfiche

Visu-Flex Company

FILING SUPPLIES

Some secretaries purchase their own filing supplies; some requisition them from the stockroom. In either case, a secretary needs to know what is available and how to describe each item correctly when ordering.

File Guides

File guides are rigid sheets that divide the file drawer into sections. They are frequently attached by a rod to the bottom of the drawer. They come in a variety of tab widths (tab *cuts*). A *one-fifth cut* means that the tab occupies one fifth of the top edge of the guide, permitting five tab positions. The positions are identified from left to right as *first position, second position,* and so on. An order for guides must specify the exact cut position or positions as "one-fifth cut in second position" or "one-third cut in staggered positions."

Some guide captions are printed directly on the tab (frequently the case with alphabetic systems), or the tab may be a metal or plastic holder into which small typed or printed captions can be easily inserted.

Alphabetic guides with printed captions are available in sets ranging from the 23-unit sets used by small businesses to the sets of several hundred units used by large businesses.

File Folders

File folders come in various styles, weights, cuts, colors, and materials. Tab cuts range from full width to one fifth with *single* or *double* captions (depth of the cut). At the bottom front of the folder two or more horizontal scores or creases permit folding to form a flat bottom surface to adjust to the thickness of the contents.

Folders come in light, medium, heavy, and extra-heavy weights; 11-point paper stock (a point is .001 inch) is medium weight. An innovation in this area is a folder made of thin, durable plastic. For bulky papers, pressboard folders with cloth expansion hinges at the bottom are best.

Also available are folders with built-in fasteners, with metal hooks for suspension from frames within the file drawer, and with printed captions. Folders come in a wide range of colors for color coding. Folders with pockets for holding punched tape, punched cards, or standard-size sheets can also be obtained.

Orders for folders must specify weight and color of stock and size, position, and depth of cut.

Folder Labels

Folder labels for captions come in continuous perforated rolls or in self-adhesive strips in a range of colors and in various widths to fit the tab cuts.

Colored labels and color-striped folders permit the use of a color code to divide the file into sections. Color coding increases filing accuracy, speeds the filing function, and reduces the time required to find misfiled folders.

Cross-Reference Sheets

Cross-reference sheets should be lightweight to conserve space. They should also be in color for easy identification in the folder. The secretary can purchase them or have them duplicated in the office.

FILING PROCEDURES

Many papers are filed that should have been destroyed. Letters of acknowledgment, letters of transmittal, announcements of meetings (noted on the desk calendar), forms and reports filed in another location, duplicate copies, and routine requests for catalogs and information fall into this category. (In some well-run organizations the original request is returned with the material.)

Any document that is superseded by another in the file should be removed. When filing a card giving a change in telephone number, remove the old one. When a new catalog is filed, destroy the old one.

A temporary file may be kept for materials having no permanent value. The paper is marked with a *T* and destroyed when the action involved is completed.

The government has developed this removal technique to a high level. In many departments of the government every document receives a date-of-destruction notation before it goes into the file. By continually purging the files of outdated material, the secretary can reduce the volume of material and keep the files up to date.

Preparing Materials for Filing

Routines for preparing materials for filing should proceed according to the following steps.

Conditioning Materials. In order to ready materials for filing, all pins, brads, and paper clips are removed, and related papers are stapled or welded together. Staple or weld in the upper right corner so that other papers will not be inserted between the sheets in the file. Clippings or other materials smaller than page size should be attached to a regular sheet of paper with paper cement. Damaged records should be mended or reinforced with tape. If they are not filed in special equipment, oversize papers should be folded to the dimensions of the folder and labeled to make it unnecessary to unfold them for identification.

Releasing Materials. When the secretary places an incoming letter in the filing basket, it should bear a *release mark* indicating that it has been acted on and is ready for filing. This mark may be the executive's initials, a FILE stamp and the secretary's initials, a code or check mark, a diagonal mark across the sheet, or some other agreed-upon designation. A check of all attachments will indicate whether they belong to the document. A release mark is not necessary on a carbon copy of an outgoing letter or on an original to which a carbon copy of a reply is attached. The file copy is usually of a distinctive color.

Indexing and Coding. The term *indexing* means deciding where to file a paper; *coding* refers to noting that decision on the face of the paper. The latter may be done either by underlining or coding the name or words that are to be used as a basis for filing or by writing the appropriate name, words, or number in a prominent place. A colored pencil is commonly used for this purpose. Coding saves time when refiling. If an uncoded paper is removed from the file, it must be reindexed each time it is refiled.

In alphabetic filing, correspondence is usually filed according to the most important name appearing on it. A letter to or from a business is usually coded and filed according to the name of that business. If the correspondent is an individual, that person's name is ordinarily used in coding. If, however, the person is writing as an agent of a business and the name of that business is known, the business name is used instead. Similarly, if a business letterhead is used by an individual to write a personal letter, the name of the individual is coded rather than the name of the business. Complete rules for alphabetic-filing sequence are given on pages 343–356.

In subject filing, the subject title must be determined from the body of the letter; the letter is then coded according to that title or a number that represents that subject. In numerical filing, the number to be used as a code is determined from a card-index file. In geographic filing, coding is done by underlining the city and state in the heading of an incoming letter or in the inside address of an in-house carbon copy.

Cross-Referencing. For correspondence or material that could be filed under more than one name, a cross-reference sheet or card should be prepared and filed. For instance, a letter from Allen Rothmore Company poses the problem: Is Allen a given name or a surname? In such a case a used file folder should be cut apart and only the back half used for the permanent cross-reference folder with the caption ALLEN ROTHMORE (*See* ROTHMORE ALLEN) and filed under *Al*. The regular file should be set up for ROTHMORE ALLEN and filed under *Ro*.

A cross-reference sheet should be prepared for material that could be filed under more than one heading or name.

CROSS-REFERENCE SHEET

Name or Subject *Modern Office Equipment Co. Baltimore, Maryland*

Date of Item *May 3, 19--*

Regarding *Exhibit – Eastern Office Equipment Assn. – Atlantic City, New Jersey, June 21-26*

SEE

Name or Subject *Eastern Office Equipment Association*

Authorized by *Joyce Replogle*

A letter may be received from the Modern Office Equipment Co. regarding an exhibit at the Eastern Office Equipment Association meeting in Atlantic City. The file clerk might file all correspondence about this meeting under EASTERN OFFICE EQUIPMENT ASSO-CIATION; however, a cross-reference sheet like the one in the illustration on page 331 would also be made and filed under MODERN OFFICE EQUIPMENT CO. Indicate that you have cross-referenced by placing an *X* (for cross-reference) near the name on the letter.

A photocopy or an extra carbon copy of the letter (usually on paper which is a different color from the file copy) can also be used as a cross-reference. In this case, it would be filed under MODERN OFFICE EQUIPMENT CO. and the cross-reference sheet would not be prepared.

Perhaps a letter should be cross-referenced by subject. If inquiries have been mailed to several printers asking for quotations on new letterheads, a cross-reference sheet labeled "Letterhead Quotations," listing the firms written, may be filed under *Le*. The correspondence with the printers may be filed alphabetically according to firm names.

Cross-reference forms may be colored sheets imprinted with blanks that are to be filled in; or they may be tabbed colored cards on which the reference information is listed. A good secretary follows the rule: "When in doubt, make out a cross-reference."

Sorting. Sorting is arranging the papers, including cross-reference sheets, in sequence for filing. When sorting material, the secretary should first make one or two preliminary sortings before the final one. For example, in the first sorting all A–E papers are placed in one group. In the second sort they are put in A, B, C, D, and E order. It is a simple matter then to put each of these letter groups in correct alphabetic sequence. Sorting for a numeric file should follow a similar efficient procedure.

Speed up the sorting process with a sorting device like the one shown here.

Typing Labels. The one rule that should be observed in the format for typing file labels is the rule of uniformity. The following are useful suggestions:

1. Type the caption uniformly two or three spaces from the left edge of the label. Position the labels uniformly on the folders (See the illustration). This practice will prevent captions from being hidden in the file.

2. Type the primary reference on the top line in uppercase and lowercase letters. Uppercase and lowercase letters are easier to read than all capitals. If the title is too long for the width of the label, indent the carry-over words on the second line. Omit punctuation marks.

3. Type the secondary reference, such as the city and state, on the second line blocked with the first line. If there is a street address, place it on the third line blocked with the preceding lines.

4. Spell out an abbreviation if the word is considered in filing. However, if the word is at the end of the name and is not needed for alphabetizing, it may be abbreviated.

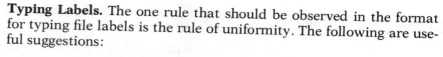

Achieve uniform placement of labels by premarking the folders.

Techniques for Drawer Filing

Use an *individual folder* for letters and other materials to, from, or about one correspondent or subject. For each section, use a *Miscellaneous* folder for those individuals and businesses with whom correspondence is infrequent. When five records relating to a person or topic have accumulated in the *Miscellaneous* folder, open an individual folder. File material in the *Miscellaneous* folder in alphabetic order; then, within the alphabetic order, file in chronological order with the most recent date to the front of the folder. Adopt the time-saving guides which follow.

1. Set a definite time for filing every day.

2. File records face up, top edge to the left, with the most recent date to the front of the folder. When material removed from the file is

The captions at the left are inconsistent in style, punctuation, capitalization, and placement. Captions should be typed in uppercase and lowercase letters as shown at the right.

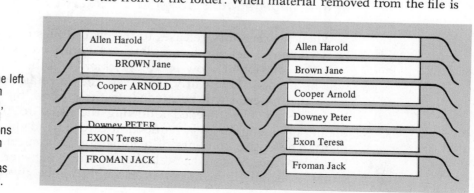

Allen Harold	Allen Harold
BROWN Jane	Brown Jane
Cooper ARNOLD	Cooper Arnold
Downey PETER	Downey Peter
EXON Teresa	Exon Teresa
FROMAN JACK	Froman Jack

refiled, it should be placed in correct chronological sequence and not necessarily to the front of the folder.

3. Place individual folders immediately *behind* the guides.

4. Place a Miscellaneous folder at the end of each section of the file, just in front of the next guide. Check the Miscellaneous folders frequently to determine if additional individual folders are warranted. Usually an individual folder is made for a person or firm when the accumulated papers amount to five sheets.

5. Use a guide for every 6–8 folders (generally about 1 inch of drawer space), about 20–25 guides to each drawer.

6. Leave one fifth of the drawer for expansion and working space.

7. Keep no more than 20–25 sheets in one folder. With heavy loads, use scored (creased-at-the-bottom) folders for expansion.

8. "Break" the files when the folder becomes crowded. Underscore the caption on the old folder in red so that all new material will be placed in the new folder. Date each folder and keep the folders filed together.

9. Use specially scored and reinforced folders for bulky materials such as catalogs.

10. Avoid accidents by opening only one file drawer at a time and closing it when the filing has been completed.

11. Lift the folder an inch or two out of the drawer before inserting material so that the sheets can drop down completely into the folder. When taking a folder out of the files for a short period, pull up the folder directly behind to serve as a marker in returning the folder.

12. Do not grasp guides and folders by their index tabs, or they will become dog-eared.

Requesting Materials from the Central Files

When the secretary releases to the central files material that will be needed at a definite future date, the item is marked or stamped with the notation "Follow-up" or "Tickler" and the date on which it will be needed. Frequently, however, the secretary will not know when the material will be needed. In these cases, the material will be requested when needed following the usual routine — by telephone, in person, or by a requisition card sent to the filing department. The entire contents of a folder or only specific items in a folder may be requested. A telephone request is faster than a requisition, especially if the information sought can be given verbally.

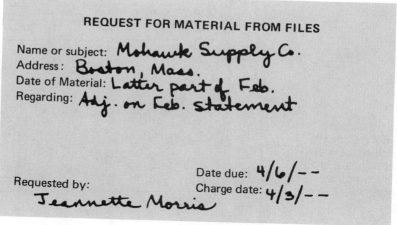

REQUEST FOR MATERIAL FROM FILES

Name or subject: *Mohawk Supply Co.*
Address: *Boston, Mass.*
Date of Material: *Latter part of Feb.*
Regarding: *Adj. on Feb. statement*

Requested by:
Jeannette Morris

Date due: *4/6/--*
Charge date: *4/3/--*

The secretary may request material from the central file on a standardized form such as this. The filing department records the two dates at the bottom of the card.

The more information the secretary can give the central files personnel about the wanted material (names, dates, subjects, addresses, file numbers, etc.), the faster the material can be located and delivered. Furthermore, the secretary who is familiar with the central filing system or systems can provide leads to the central files personnel as to where to locate what is wanted.

Materials should be returned to the central files promptly. A special problem arises when files that the secretary has received are transferred to someone in another department before they are returned to the filing department. In some companies, such transfers are to be reported to the filing department on a special form. In any case, the central files personnel should be informed of the location of the file.

Charge-Out Methods. When an entire folder is taken from the files or when separate items are removed from a folder, a record should be made so that others will be able to locate the materials.

Several charge-out methods are in common use. When an individual item is removed from the folder, a *substitution card* is usually put in its place in the folder. This card indicates the nature of the material, the name of the person who has the material, and the date it was removed. When an entire folder is removed, an *out guide* may be substituted for the folder; or an out folder with a substitution card may be placed in the drawer to take the place of the regular folder. Sometimes the regular folder is retained in the file drawer, and the contents of the folder are transferred to a special *carrier folder*. This practice does not disrupt the filing of new material.

In some companies the original requisitioned material never leaves the central filing area. A photocopy is sent to the person making a requisition, and the copy is destroyed when the requesting

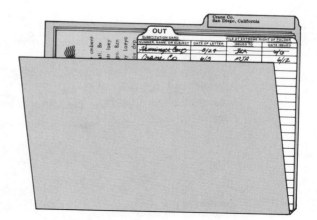

Out or substitution cards like this one are commonly used to replace one paper or a few related papers removed from a folder.

person is finished with it. As this practice is expensive and wasteful, it should be used only when it is essential for the original to remain in the central files.

Follow-Up Methods. The secretary may need to follow up on filed materials sent to other offices or departments. The daily calendar pad is frequently used for this purpose. The anticipated date for the return is jotted down as a notation on the future-date page of the calendar. Another method is to write or type the needed data on a card and place it in a tickler file.

MECHANICS OF GOOD FILING

The secretary who has mastered the proper filing techniques and procedures may still occasionally encounter the problem of the misfiled or "lost" item. The following information will assist you in reducing misfiles and will suggest ways of locating a missing item.

Reducing Misfiles

Manufacturers of filing equipment report it may cost as much as $80 in executive, secretarial, and clerical time to find a misfiled record. Furthermore, many companies experience a misfile rate of 1 percent. Obviously, the secretary should vow to avoid misfiles.

One cause of misfiles is carelessness — placing a record in a folder without scanning its contents to see if they are related to the paper being filed; fastening materials together with paper clips which often also pick up unrelated papers; or putting one folder inside another one. Another cause for misfiles is not using supplies and equipment as recommended — too many or too few guides; overcrowded folders that sag so much that their tabs are hidden;

HOW TO APPRAISE YOUR FILES

Open a file drawer and answer these questions:

1. How crowded is it?

A tightly packed file drawer slows filing, causes paper cuts and torn cuticles, and increases the physical work of filing. (See Guide 6 on page 334.)

2. How many file guides have been used?

The purpose of the file guide is to direct the eye to the approximate location of the item sought. (See Guide 5, page 334.) Too few guides result in time spent in pushing, pulling, and fingering through the file. If you can place your hand halfway between guides and find the desired folder no more than three or four folders away, you have used an adequate number of guides.

3. How uniform are the folders?

An efficient file must have folders of uniform size and weight, uniformly tabbed, logically and consistently arranged. A conglomerate of folder sizes and tab styles is a sure indication of a sick file.

4. How have the folders been labeled?

Labels typed in uniform style not only give a neat appearance but save finding time. Time is wasted in reading labels that are handwritten, crossed out and retyped, or carelessly positioned on the folder.

5. How much material is filed in a single folder?

A folder properly scored (creased) and filled will normally hold ¾ inch of material. More material than that will cause papers to "ride up" and become torn or mutilated. Furthermore the label will be hidden; and when labels are hidden, filing speed is greatly reduced.

---

drawers so overstuffed that there is inadequate work space; and miscellaneous folders crowded with papers for which individual folders should have been opened. The final cause of misfiles lies in coding — captions that are not mutually exclusive; the choice of a wrong title; or too few cross-references.

Places to Search

If only one paper is lost, it is probably in the wrong folder. Check the folders in front and in back of the correct folder, check between folders, and check the bottom of the drawer. Look in charge-outs and in file baskets, and don't overlook the employer's desk and your own. Look in the index of files transferred to storage areas. Look under alternate spellings and Anglicized forms of names and under similar numbers or titles. For instance, if the name is Brooks Allen, look under Allen Brooks. If 2309 is lost, look under 2390. Look in the relative index for other possible captions.

If an exhaustive search does not locate an item, type on a sheet of paper all the information known about the missing item and the date on which the loss was discovered. File the sheet (perhaps in a folder labeled *Lost*) where the missing item should be. This practice forestalls a later search for the same item. Consider the possibility, also, of obtaining a copy of the lost item from its sender or source.

GOOD RECORDS MANAGEMENT PRACTICES

The purpose of records management is to identify and protect the important papers and documents of the company and to eliminate the temporary, useless papers with the least possible delay. Experience has shown that a records management program usually results in 30 percent of the records being destroyed, 40 percent being transferred to a remote record (storage) center, and only the remaining 30 percent being retained in the office.

The emphasis, however, in records management is not only on the destruction of useless records but also on records preservation. The upsurge in government investigations of corporation, antitrust and price-fixing legal actions has made it necessary for companies to be certain they have retained adequate records and that there is no gap in their documentation.

Retention Schedules

The most efficiently operated companies often have an overall file-rentention plan which the secretary should follow. The retention schedule of a company specifies how long a document can remain in the office flow; if and when it is to be removed to a separate, low-cost records center; and when it should be destroyed.

From among the various professionally organized retention plans available, an adaptation of recommended practices is presented.

1. File one month:
     General correspondence requiring no follow-up

2. File three months:
     Incoming and outgoing correspondence with customers and vendors on routine, promptly settled business
     Bank statements
     Stenographers' notebooks
     Expired insurance policies

3. File two years:
     Work sheets for financial statements
     Internal reports and summaries, including printouts from data processing equipment, and all punched cards and tapes
     Physical inventories

4. File in order to comply with the statute of limitations in the states affected:

Canceled payroll checks and summaries
Invoices to customers and from vendors
Employee data, including accident reports
Completed contracts and leases, as well as other legal papers
Duplicate deposit tickets and checks, except as noted below

5. File permanently:

Books of accounts and minutes of stockholders' meetings
Capital stock ledgers and transfer records
Canceled checks, vouchers, and complete cost data on capital improvements
Tax returns and related papers
Perpetual agreements about pensions, group insurance, and other fringe benefits
All property records
Maps, specifications, plans
Organization charts and procedure manuals[1]

Because of the enormous volume of output materials, word processing centers usually have their own retention and disposal schedule. In one typical center these practices prevail:

1. Dictation belts are retained one day only.

2. Mag cards containing original letters that will not be repeated are kept for one week only.

3. Carbon copies of completed material are sent back to the originator without retaining a copy in the center.

4. Each prestructured paragraph that is to be merged with other paragraphs to form a complete letter is reproduced on a separate mag card and is retained until superseded.

Transferring Materials

Plans for storing files are made in relation to the importance of the material and the reduction of costs effected by storing infrequently called-for material in cheaper filing equipment and in cheaper rental areas. The possibility of destruction of vital records by a disaster has caused concern for safe storage — in mountain vaults and caves in some instances and in widely dispersed units in others. Some companies have built storage centers, and others have rented file storage space from companies that specialize in providing ready access to stored materials.

Certain types of files can be handled under a perpetual transfer plan. When a case is closed or a project finished, the file is closed

[1]Records Controls, Inc., Chicago, Illinois.

and transferred. In other cases periodic transfer is made. By the one-period method all material is taken at a designated time from the active files and sent to transfer files. Although active files are established, it is all but impossible to avoid consulting some old records. With a two-period transfer, however, the middle drawers are used for current materials; the upper and lower drawers, for semi-active materials. The semiactive materials are transferred in turn.

A variation of this plan is the maximum-minimum transfer. Only the inactive material is transferred at regular intervals. For instance, with a transfer date of June 30, 1977, materials filed from January, 1977, through June 30, 1977, would not be moved (they would remain in the active files). Materials dated from January 1, 1976, through December 31, 1976, however, would be transferred to storage. New materials would go into the active file until June 30, 1978. Then the files from January 1, 1977, through December 31, 1977, would be transferred, leaving the files for January 1, 1978, through June 30, 1978, in the active files. The secretary labels each transfer file with its contents, inclusive dates, and in some firms, the discard date.

SUGGESTED READINGS

Administrative Management, The Systems Magazine for Administrative Executives (Monthly). New York: Geyer-McAllister Publications. Select recent articles on records management and storage, micrographics, microfilm.

Dallas, Richard J., and James M. Thompson. *Clerical and Secretarial Systems for the Office*. Englewood Cliffs: Prentice-Hall, 1975, pp. 75–147.

Johnson, Mina M., and Norman F. Kallaus. *Records Management*, 2d ed. Cincinnati: South-Western Publishing Co., 1974.

Winter, Elmer L. *The Successful Manager-Secretary Team*. West Nyack: Parker Publishing Co., 1974, pp. 61–65.

QUESTIONS FOR DISCUSSION

1. In what ways has your concept of the filing work of a secretary changed since reading this chapter?

2. Filing and records management are commonly used as synonymous terms. What distinction would you make between the two terms?

3. Theorists predict that "technological advances will eventually eliminate the need for most paper files." What implications does this statement have for secretarial work?

4. Any communication having reference value should be retained and filed. What are some of the communications that come into or are generated in the office that should be discarded relatively promptly?

5. Companies centralize files for economy and efficiency. Executives, however, tend to resist releasing materials to the central files, preferring to build up their in-office files. What can the secretary do to help resolve this conflict?

6. Your employer asks you to get any correspondence with a Mr. Beal that is available in the central files. Neither you nor your employer is sure of the spelling of the person's name, nor do you recall the initials. Several years ago, however, there was a person with a similar name involved in an infringement of patent suit against the company. You recall that this person lived in St. Louis. How would you state your request to the central files?

7. If you were working for a company with no records-retention schedule, how would you proceed to establish one?

8. If you started to work in a position during a peak period and discovered that many materials were misfiled, the folders and drawers were overcrowded, the materials were not arranged chronologically in the folders, and the miscellaneous folders contained materials for which individual folders should have been opened, what would you do?

9. Suggest situations in which each of the following types of files would be advantageous:

alphabetic	subject	visible-card file
numeric	geographic	chronological

10. Type the following sentences in correct form. Then use the Reference Guide to verify or correct your typing of *yes* and *no*.
 (a) The answer is no we are sorry to say.
 (b) On second thought, we will say yes.

11. Some people feel that quoting an unusual word choice is uncomplimentary to the intelligence of the reader, and in some cases is sarcastic. Discuss the following italicized words. Would you use quotation marks with any of them in a business letter? Would you revise any of the sentences? Is any one of the italicized words an acronym?
 (a) We have your *so-called* revised chapter.
 (b) He is a *VIP* — an extremely important one.
 (c) The situation is completely *snafued* now.
 (d) Your *complaint* can be taken as a compliment too.
 (e) To save time we are sending you a rough draft in which deletions have been *X'd* out.
 (f) It looks as if we *goofed* on your order.
 Refer to PUNCTUATION; **Quotation Mark**; *Words different in tone* and to WORDS: COINED in the Reference Guide to check your answers.

PROBLEMS

1. You are administrative assistant and secretary to the sales manager. The following items have been seen by the manager and are ready for action. Indicate what disposition you would make of each one. For instance, a notice of an interoffice meeting would be entered on the desk calendar and then destroyed. If an item is retained, indicate under what name or subject

it would be filed. (A separate file is kept for the manager's personal items.)

(a) A reminder notice for the next weekly meeting of the Sales Executives Club

(b) A new catalog from Brown and Brown, a firm that provides sales-incentive plans (The old catalog is in the files.)

(c) An application for a sales position from Wanda Higel

(d) Copy for the *Weekly Sales Newsletter*, which is sent to the sales manager by Lloyd Giroux, editor, for final approval before it goes to the reprographics department

(e) A letter from an applicant for a sales position thanking the manager for the initial interview

(f) An announcement of fall courses at a local college (Employees who take job-related courses are reimbursed by the company for their tuition costs.)

(g) A notice that the executive's office subscription to *Sales Management* has expired

(h) A letter from Rosa Di Lorenzo asking to change her appointment from Wednesday to Friday at the same hour

(i) A completed chapter for a book on *Prognosis of Sales Ability* (The name of the chapter is "Psychological Testing.")

(j) A carbon copy of the manager's expense account for the preceding week

(k) A requisition for a new dictating unit for the manager's use

(l) A car-rental contract covering automobiles for sales representatives in the Chicago area

(m) A quarterly report of Xerox Corporation in which the manager holds stock

(n) An interoffice memo from the president of the company approving the manager's request to hold a sales-training conference at Lake Crystal on September 18–20

(o) A letter from an irate customer complaining about the treatment received from the Little Rock area salesman, Herman Beckwith

(p) A catalog from Hertz Company about its blanket quarterly service contract for company rentals

(q) Safety regulations applying to all departments in the home office

2. On July 18 your employer, Evelyn Forbes (Credit Manager), dictated the following letter to be sent to Mr. Frank W. Russo, 421 East Oak Street, Columbus, Ohio, 43210. "Dear Mr. Russo: On June 4 you wrote us that you had purchased the Oak Street Market in Columbus and that you would assume all the market's obligations. At that time the market owed us $86.15 on Invoice No. 3310. On June 13 you ordered more goods for $52.60 at 2/10, n/30. The old bill incurred by the Oak Street Market is now sixty days overdue and your own order of $52.60 remains unpaid. We wonder if something is wrong, Mr. Russo. Won't you write us at once, either enclosing your check for the two invoices or letting us know when we may expect payment. Yours very truly."

You are then told by the credit manager to follow up in 10 days with Form Letter 5 if the account is still unpaid. If no action has been secured in 20 days, you are to send Form Letter 8.

(a) Type the letter and one carbon copy in good form so you can prepare the carbon copy for filing

(b) Prepare a cross-reference sheet (see page 331–332) and cross-reference the letter

(c) Release the letter for filing

(d) Prepare the follow-up card for the tickler file.

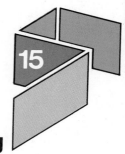

Alphabetic Indexing

Everyone has experienced the confusion of putting something away and then forgetting where it was put. Imagine the chaos that would exist in an office if no one could remember where needed materials were filed. No one person could remember unless that person followed a set of rules which determined where each item was to be put in the files. Thus, you file by rules to know where to find what was filed.

Order is achieved by following rules. There is general agreement on most of the rules for alphabetic indexing; but, unfortunately, they do not cover every filing situation. Occasionally an item may be filed under either of two rules. Thus, in addition to mastering the alphabetic indexing rules, the secretary must be able to handle the exceptions. Variations in the rules should be clearly written down and consistently observed. When either of two rules may be followed, the rule that best fits the needs of the particular office or organization should be selected. Consequently, the secretary must be a master of filing and, in a large organization, must work very closely and cooperatively with the filing supervisor.

On the following pages are rules for alphabetic indexing. The examples under each rule are listed in correct alphabetic order. In each example the underline indicates the first letter or letters used in determining the indexing sequence.

NAMES OF INDIVIDUALS

(1) Basic Order of Indexing Units

Each part of the name of an individual is an indexing unit. Consider the surname (last name) as the first unit, the first name or initial as the second unit, and the middle name or initial as the third unit. Arrange all names in A–Z sequence, comparing each letter in order until a point of difference is reached. *The letter that determines the order of any two names is the first letter that is different in the two names.* Consider first the first unit of each name. Consider the second units only when the first units are identical. Consider the third units only when the first and second units are identical. When

Nothing is more annoying to the executive nor embarrassing to the secretary than the inability to locate material readily in such a situation as during a telephone conversation.

further indexing is necessary to determine the relative position of two or more names that have exactly the same first, second, and third coding units, the relative position of the two or more names is determined by a further *identifying element*, such as *junior or senior*, or a part of the address. In such cases, the coder places a check mark above or at the left of the identifying element.

| Name | Index Order of Units | | | Identifying |
	Unit 1	Unit 2	Unit 3	Element
[1]Joan Ander	Ander,	Joan		
Joan E. Ander	Ander,	Joan	E.	
Louise Ander	Ander,	Louise		
Adam Anders	Anders,	Adam		
John C. Anderson, Jr.	Anderson,	John	C.	Junior
John C. Anderson, Sr.	Anderson,	John	C.	Senior
Anna Andersson	Andersson,	Anna		
Alma Lee Andrews	Andrews,	Alma	Lee	
E. Bennett Andrews	Andrews,	E.	Bennett	
[2]Soo On Bee	Bee,	Soo	On	
Eli J. Dorman, II	Dorman,	Eli	J.	II
Eli J. Dorman, III	Dorman,	Eli	J.	III

Note 1: *Ander* precedes *Anders* because the *r* in *Ander* is not followed by any letter. This is an example of the rule that *nothing precedes something.*

Note 2: An unusual or foreign personal name is indexed in the usual manner, with the last word considered to be the surname and therefore the first indexing unit.

(2) Surname Prefixes and Hyphened Surnames

(A) A surname prefix is considered to be a part of the first index-ing unit. Among the common prefixes are *D', Da, De, Del, Des, El, Il, La, Le, Les, Los, Mac, Mc, O', Van*, and *Von*. In some cases the first letter of a prefix is not capitalized. Spacing of the surname is not significant. (B) When compound (that is, hyphened) surnames, such as *Martin-Ames*, or given names, such as *Jo-Mar*, occur in filing, each part of the name is considered a separate unit.

Name	Index Order of Units		
	Unit 1	*Unit 2*	*Unit 3*
Catherine Lemate	Lemate,	Catherine	
Francis LeMate	LeMate,	Francis	
Ruth Martin-Ames	Martin-	Ames	Ruth
Wallace Martin	Martin,	Wallace	
Karen O'Bonner	O'Bonner,	Karen	
Jo-Mar Odell	Odell,	Jo-	Mar
[1]Edith St. Marner	Saint	Marner,	Edith

Note 1: Even though *St.* is abbreviated in the name *Edith St. Marner*, it is indexed as if it were spelled in full and is considered to be the first unit. (A variation of this rule is to consider the prefix *Saint* and the part of the surname that follows it to be one unit.)

Note 2: A variation of Rule 2B above is to consider hyphened surnames as one unit.

(3) Initials and Abbreviations

(A) An initial in an individual's name is considered as an indexing unit and precedes all names in the same unit beginning with the same letter as the initial. (B) An abbreviated first or middle name or a nickname is considered as if it were written in full.

Name	Index Order of Units		
	Unit 1	*Unit 2*	*Unit 3*
Paula Cameron	Cameron,	Paula	
D. D. Crawford	Crawford,	D.	D.
Dale Crawford	Crawford,	Dale	
Jas. E. Dackman	Dackman,	James	E.
Jane Dackman	Dackman,	Jane	
[1]Bob L. Davirro	Davirro,	Bob	L.
Robert Davirro	Davirro,	Robert	

Note 1: When the brief form of a given name is known to be used by an individual as her or his given name, this brief-form name is treated as a unit.

(4) Titles

(A) A personal or professional title or degree is usually not considered in filing. When the name is written in index form, the title is placed in parentheses at the end of the name. (B) A title is considered as the first indexing unit only when it is followed by the given name alone or by the surname alone.

Name	Index Order of Units		
	Unit 1	Unit 2	Unit 3
Miss Mary J. Fatam	Fatam,	Mary	J. (Miss)
[1a]Father Delbert	Father	Delbert	
Rev. A. O. Hanson	Hanson,	A.	O. (Rev.)
Ralph Hanson, D. D.	Hanson,	Ralph (D. D.)	
[1a]Father Robert O. Hanson	Hanson,	Robert	O. (Father)
Madame Mavis	Madame	Mavis	
Capt. Orrin Mason	Mason,	Orrin (Capt.)	
Mrs. Ann Jones Milton	Milton,	Ann	Jones (Mrs.)
Dr. Diana Miltson	Miltson,	Diana (Dr.)	

Note 1: For names including the religious titles *Father*, *Brother*, and *Sister*, Rule 4B may be modified as follows:

(a) To group together within a filing system all names bearing one of these titles, consider the titles themselves of first importance in indexing, regardless of the names that follow them. Names that do not include a surname are indexed in the order written: *Father Delbert*. Names that include one or more given names and a surname are transposed after the title, as explained in Rule 1: *Hanson, Robert O. (Father)*.

(b) To set up a separate section to include all such names in the files, consider the name or names following such titles as of first importance, and *disregard the title*. Names that do not include a surname are indexed in the order written. Names that include one or more given names and a surname are transposed. Indexing order for *Father Delbert* in such case would be *Delbert (Father)*; for *Father Robert O. Hanson* would be *Hanson, Robert O. (Father)*.

(5) Names of Married Women

The name of a married woman is indexed according to her legal name (her first name, either her maiden surname or her middle name or initial, and her husband's surname). The title *Mrs.* is disregarded in filing, but it is placed in parentheses after the legal name. The husband's name, if known, may be given in parentheses below a woman's legal name; but legally she assumes only the surname when she marries. If a married woman chooses to use her maiden surname, her name should be indexed as she signs it.

Name	Index Order of Units		
	Unit 1	Unit 2	Unit 3
Mrs. Becky Jones Fritts	Fritts,	Becky	Jones (Mrs.)
Mrs. Lucien (Becky Mae) Fritts	Fritts,	Becky	Mae (Mrs. Lucien)
Mrs. Becky Mae Jones	Jones,	Becky	Mae (Mrs.)

(6) Identical Names

When the names of individuals are identical, their alphabetic order is determined by their addresses, starting with the city. Names of states are considered when the names of the cities are also alike. When the city and the state names as well as the full names of the individuals are alike, the alphabetic order is determined by street names; next, house and building numbers, with the lowest first. When it is used, the address is an identifying element.

Name	Index Order of Units			Identifying Element
	Unit 1	Unit 2	Unit 3	
Janice Hess, 314 Elm Street, Toledo	Hess,	Janice		Elm
Janice Hess, 92 Plum Avenue, Toledo	Hess,	Janice		Plum
Edward Iglecia, Akron	Iglecia,	Edward		Akron
Edward Iglecia, Columbus	Iglecia,	Edward		Columbus
Edward Iglecia, Dayton	Iglecia,	Edward		Dayton
Edward B. Iglecia	Iglecia,	Edward	B.	

NAMES OF BUSINESSES AND GROUPS

(7) Basic Order of Indexing Units

(A) Usually the indexing units of a business or group name are considered in the order in which they are written. (B) An exception is made to the usual rule when a business name includes the full name of an individual, such as *Sam Martin Garage*. In that case the units in the individual name are considered in the same order as if the individual name appeared independently, as shown below.

Name	Index Order of Units		
	Unit 1	Unit 2	Unit 3
S. Martin Hats	Martin,	S.	Hats
Sam Martin Garage	Martin,	Sam	Garage
Nelson Lumber Company	Nelson	Lumber	Company
[1]Newsweek	Newsweek		
Jill Nobee News Corner	Nobee,	Jill	News
World Almanac	World	Almanac	

Note 1: The name of a magazine or book may be indexed according to these basic indexing rules for the name of a business.

(8) Articles, Conjunctions, and Prepositions

(A) Such words as *the, and, &, for, on, in, by,* and *of the* are generally disregarded in indexing and filing. However, they are placed in parentheses for coding purposes. An initial *the* is placed in parentheses after the last unit. (B) A word normally classified as a preposition but used as the first word in a business name, or as a modifying word, or as part of a compound name is considered to be a separate indexing unit.

| Name | Index Order of Units | | |
	Unit 1	Unit 2	Unit 3
By the Lane Inn	By (the)	Lane	Inn
Charles of the Ritz	Charles (of the)	Ritz	
Committee on Departmental Reorganization	Committee (on)	Departmental	Reorganization
Emery & Frank Shoes	Emery (&)	Frank	Shoes
End of the Mile Tavern	End (of the)	Mile	Tavern
The Favorite Music Shop	Favorite	Music	Shop (The)

(9) Initials, Abbreviations, and Titles

(A) An initial or letter that is not a common abbreviation precedes a *word* beginning with that letter. (B) A known abbreviation, even though the abbreviation consists of a single letter without a period, is treated as if it were spelled in full, except *Mr.* and *Mrs.*, which are filed alphabetically as they are written. (C) A business name including a title followed by a given name, a surname, or a coined name is indexed in the order in which it is written.

| Name | Index Order of Units | | |
	Unit 1	Unit 2	Unit 3
BB Brakes	B	B	Brakes
Ball Crank Co.	Ball	Crank	Company
B & O Railroad	Baltimore (&)	Ohio	Railroad
Bayard Co.	Bayard	Company	
C and C Dress Shoppe	C (and)	C	Dress
City Cleaners	City	Cleaners	
Dr. Footeze	Doctor	Footeze	
Monsieur Antoine Beauty Salon	Monsieur	Antoine	Beauty
Mr. Jim's Steak House	Mr.	Jim's	Steak
Mrs. Della Knits	Mrs.	Della	Knits

(10) Numbers and Symbols

(A) A number in a firm name is considered as if it were written as one word. It is indexed as one unit. Four-place numbers are expressed in hundreds (not in thousands) in order to consider a smaller number of letters in the indexing unit. (B) A symbol with the number is considered separately as a word.

Name	Index Order of Units		
	Unit 1	Unit 2	Unit 3
A 1 Garage	A	One	Garage
8th St. Bldg.	Eighth	Street	Building
1110 Choices Store	Elevenhundredten	Choices	Store
$5 Bargain Store	Five	Dollar	Bargain
Ft. Evans News	Fort	Evans	News
40th Avenue Laundry	Fortieth	Avenue	Laundry
Fortilair Food Shop	Fortilair	Food	Shop

Note 1: Some file manuals omit the words *hundred* and *thousand* in considering the indexing unit — examples: *fiveten* for 510 and *twelveseventy* for 1270.

Note 2: When several names differ only in numeric designations, the order of those names may be based upon the numeric sequence instead of the alphabetic order of those numbers written in words. For example, if several branch stores of the same company are numbered, it might be more convenient in an office to have the names arranged in numeric sequence.

(11) Hyphened Names

The hyphened parts of business names (including coined parts) are indexed and filed as separate words.

An exception is made to this rule when the hyphened parts are shown in the dictionary as a single word or as a hyphened word. Both parts are then considered together as one indexing unit.

Name	Index Order of Units		
	Unit 1	Unit 2	Unit 3
A-1 Retail Markets	A-	One	Retail
Read-N-Sew Studio	Read-	N-	Sew
Ready-Built Shelf Shop	Ready-	Built	Shelf
Reedy-Adam Corp.	Reedy-	Adam	Corporation
Charlene A. Reedy Corp.	Reedy,	Charlene	A.
Reedy-Miller Studios	Reedy-	Miller	Studios
Adam D. Reedy-Smith Corp.	Reedy-	Smith,	Adam
Self-Service Laundry	Self-Service	Laundry	
Self-Study Society	Self-Study	Society	
Selfton Voice Studio	Selfton	Voice	Studio

(12) One Versus Two Units

When separate words in a business name are shown in the dictionary as one word, the two should be treated as one indexing unit.

Name	Index Order of Units		
	Unit 1	Unit 2	Unit 3
Semi Trailer Rentals, Inc.	SemiTrailer	Rentals	Incorporated
Semi Weekly Cleaning Service	SemiWeekly	Cleaning	Service
Semiweekly Communication Review	Semiweekly	Communication	Review
Southwestern Machine Products	Southwestern	Machine	Products
South Western Office Supplies	SouthWestern	Office	Supplies
South-Western Publishing Co.	SouthWestern	Publishing	Company
Southwick Drug Service	Southwick	Drug	Service
Southwick Drug Store	Southwick	DrugStore	
Stephan's Super Repair Shop	Stephan's	Super	Repair
Stephan's Super Market Displays	Stephan's	SuperMarket	Displays

(13) Compound Geographic and Location Names

(A) Each English word in a compound geographic or location name is indexed as a separate unit. (B) A prefix or foreign article in such names is not considered as a separate indexing unit but is combined with the word that follows.

Name	Index Order of Units		
	Unit 1	Unit 2	Unit 3
Le Mont Food Products	LeMont	Food	Products
Los Angeles Actors' Guild	LosAngeles	Actors'	Guild
New York Central R. R.	New	York	Central
North Dakota Curios	North	Dakota	Curios
Old Saybury R. R. Station	Old	Saybury	Railroad
St. Thomas Island Home	Saint	Thomas	Island
Saintbury Publishing Co.	Saintbury	Publishing	Company
[1]San Diego Greenhouses, Inc.	San	Diego	Greenhouses
[1]Santa Clara Lithographers	Santa	Clara	Lithographers

Note 1: The words *San* in *San Diego* and *Santa* in *Santa Clara* mean *Saint* and are therefore indexed separately according to their spelling.

Note 2: When it is part of the actual name of a city (as *The Dalles*), *The* is considered to be the first unit.

Note 3: Some plans of filing treat each geographic name as one word regardless of the number of words in the name. *New Orleans* would be considered as one unit in such a filing system.

(14) Possessives

When a word ends in *apostrophe s* ('s), the final *s* is not considered as part of the word for filing purposes, except when the *s* is part of a contraction. When a word ends in *s apostrophe* (s'), however, the final *s* is considered.

Name	Index Order of Units		
	Unit 1	Unit 2	Unit 3
Girl Scouts of America	Girl	Scouts (of)	America
Girl's Sportswear	Girl('s)	Sportswear	
Girls' Short Stories	Girls'	Short	Stories
Harper's Restaurant	Harper('s)	Restaurant	
Harpers'	Harpers'		
Harperston's Apparel	Harperston('s)	Apparel	
Harperston Bank	Harperston	Bank	

(15) Identical Business Names

(A) Identical names of businesses are arranged alphabetically by address, with address parts treated as identifying elements. (For this reason the word *City* should not be used in place of the name of the city for local correspondents.) (B) If the names of the cities are alike, filing arrangement depends upon names of states. (C) When two or more branches of a business are located in the same city, the names of the branches are arranged alphabetically by street names.

Name	Index Order of Units			Identifying Element
	Unit 1	Unit 2	Unit 3	
Janicki Stationers, Decatur	Janicki	Stationers,		Decatur
Janicki Stationers, Eureka	Janicki	Stationers,		Eureka
Janicki Stationers, Sterling	Janicki	Stationers,		Sterling
Kastner's 531 Main Street	Kastner('s)			Main
Kastner's, 1024 Oak Street	Kastner('s)			Oak

Note 1: The name of the building in which the firm is located should not be considered unless the name of the street is not provided or is identical for both branches.

(16) Banking Institutions and Newspapers

(A) When only local banking institutions are involved, their names are indexed as written. (B) When banks or building and loan associations from several cities are involved, however, the names of the cities in which they are located are considered as the first indexing units with the words in the names of the institutions following. If the name of the banking institution contains the name of the city or state, that geographic location is not repeated in the indexed form. If several states are involved, the names of the states should be considered after the name of the city, as identifying elements. (C) Newspapers follow the same indexing rules as those used for banks.

| Name | Index Order of Units | | | Identifying Element |
	Unit 1	Unit 2	Unit 3	
Bloomington Trust Co. Bloomington, Illinois	Bloomington	Trust	Company	Illinois
Bloomington Trust Co. Bloomington, Indiana	Bloomington	Trust	Company	Indiana
First Federal Building and Loan Duluth, Minnesota	Duluth:	First	Federal	
Wenatchee Times Wenatchee, Washington	Wenatchee	Times		
Times Herald Williamsport, Pennsylvania	Williamsport:	Times	Herald	

(17) Elementary and Secondary Schools

A public elementary or secondary school name is indexed first by the name of the city and then by the name of the school. An individual's name within a school name is transposed in the usual manner. If a school name begins with a city name, the city name is considered only once. State names are treated as identifying elements if a city name is alike in two or more states. A parochial school is indexed by name.

| Name | Index Order of Units | | | Identifying Element |
	Unit 1	Unit 2	Unit 3	
Crispus Attucks High School Indianapolis, Indiana	Indianapolis:	Attucks,	Crispus	

| Name | Index Order of Units | | | Identifying |
	Unit 1	Unit 2	Unit 3	Element
Modesto Elementary School Modesto, California	Modesto	Elementary	School	
Muncie Central High School Muncie, Indiana	Muncie	Central	High	
Muncie Southside High School Muncie, Indiana	Muncie	Southside	High	
Newport Beach High School Newport Beach, California	Newport	Beach	High	
Newport High School Newport, Rhode Island	Newport	High	School	Rhode Island
Newport High School Newport, Washington	Newport	High	School	Washington

This secretary has discovered the convenience of hanging files for maintenance of bulky items, such as these data binders.

National Blank Book Co., Inc.

(18) Colleges, Universities, Special Schools, Hotels, Motels, and Other Organizations

(A) When, through common usage, one part of a name more clearly identifies the organization, that part is used as the first indexing unit. Otherwise, names of organizations are indexed as they are generally written. (B) A city or state name as part of the organization name is considered an indexing unit or units. When the name of an organization is the same in two or more cities, city names are considered last as identifying elements.

Name	Index Order of Units		
	Unit 1	Unit 2	Unit 3
[1]Howard Johnson's Motor Lodge	Howard	Johnson's	Motor
University of Idaho	Idaho,	University (of)	
Indiana University	Indiana	University	
Hotel Jolee Florists	Jolee,	Hotel,	Florists
Priest River Kiwanis Club	Kiwanis	Club,	Priest
Los Angeles City College	Los Angeles	City	College
Association of Lumbermen	Lumbermen,	Association (of)	
First Methodist Church	Methodist	Church,	First
[1]Martha Nelson Beauty College	Nelson,	Martha,	Beauty
[2]WLBC	Radio	Station	W
Venovich Motel	Venovich	Motel	

Note 1: An individual's name within the name of the organization is transposed in the usual manner unless the name is always considered as a unit.

Note 2: Preferable way to index a radio or television station is to consider *Radio Station* or *Television Station* as the first two units, followed by each call letter as a separate unit.

(19) Federal Government Offices

The name of a federal government office is considered for indexing in the following order: (1) United States Government (the first three indexing units), (2) principal word or words in the name of the department, (3) principal word or words in the name of the bureau, (4) principal word or words in the name of the division. Such words as *Department of, Bureau of,* and *Division of* are transposed, with the word *of* disregarded and so placed in parentheses.

When in doubt as to which United States government department a bureau, division, or office is attached, consult the *Government Manual.* This manual provides the latest available information on the administrative structure of the federal government.

Name	Unit 4	Unit 5	Unit 6	Unit 7	Unit 8
			Index Order of Units		
Bureau of the Census U.S. Department of Commerce	Commerce,	Department (of)	Census,	Bureau (of the)	
National Oceanic and Atmospheric Administration U.S. Department of Commerce	Commerce,	Department (of)	National	Oceanic (and) *Unit 9:*	Atmospheric Administration
Social Security Administration U.S. Department of Health, Education, and Welfare	Health,	Education, (and)	Welfare,	Department (of) { *Unit 9:* { *Unit 10:*	Social Security Administration
Bureau of Indian Affairs U.S. Department of the Interior	Interior,	Department (of the)	Indian	Affairs,	Bureau (of)
Federal Bureau of Investigation[1] U.S. Department of Justice	Justice,	Department (of)	Federal	Bureau (of)	Investigation

Note 1: The Federal Bureau of Investigation is so well known by its full name and initials that the name is often filed as known.

(20) Other Government Offices

(A) The name of any other government office is considered in the following order: (1) principal word or words in the name of the political subdivision, followed by its state, county, or city classification, (2) principal word or words in the name of the department, board, or office. Such words as *Department of* and *Bureau of* are transposed, with the word *of* placed in parentheses. (B) If two or more political subdivisions have the same first indexing unit, the state name as an identifying element is considered immediately after the first principal word in the political subdivision. This determines relative placement of items with identical first units.

Name	Unit 1	Unit 2	Unit 3
		Index Order of Units	
Department of Public Safety California	California,	State (of)	Public
Board of Health Cincinnati	Cincinnati,	City (of)	Health
Tax Collector Cook County	Cook,	County	Tax

(21) Foreign Governments

Foreign-language names are translated into English for indexing, and the distinctive English name of the foreign country is considered first. Next, divisions are considered in the same manner as are United States governmental units.

Name	Index Order of Units			
	Unit 1	Unit 2	Unit 3	Unit 4
Republique Francaise Armée de l'Air[1]	France	Air	Force	
Estados Unidos Mexicanos Secretaria de Industrio y Commercia	Mexico	Industry (and)	Commerce,	Secretary (of)

Note 1: The names of foreign countries may be uniformly filed according to the native spelling, rather than the English translation.

GENERAL GUIDES

The student of alphabetic indexing rules may find it helpful to think in terms of general guides and then to note variations of these general guides. The following items would be among those most important to remember:

1. An individual's full name is transposed, in either a personal or a business name; otherwise a business name is indexed as written.

2. Articles, conjunctions, prepositions, apostrophe addition in possessives, and titles are disregarded and placed in parentheses except where (a) a preposition or modifying word is a coined major part of a business name, or (b) a title is followed by a given name only or by a surname only.

3. Numbers and known abbreviations are spelled in full as one word, except *Mr.* or *Mrs.* or a nickname used as part of the individual's official signature.

4. Initials, hyphened parts of names, and separated words are treated as individual units except where hyphened or separated words are shown by the dictionary to be acceptable as one word.

5. A special organization is indexed first by that part of the name which common usage causes to stand out most clearly in identifying that organization.

6. Elementary and secondary schools, newspapers, and banking institutions may be indexed first by the name of the city.

7. Governmental offices are indexed first by the major governmental unit of which the particular office is a part.

. . . Information processing and record keeping are a major part of office work. Anyone, therefore, who expects to be an office worker must know something about developing and controlling a good workable information filing system. Records can be effectively controlled only when they are organized, safely stored, and handled by trained people.

Fundamental Filing Practice

The secretary or the file supervisor, in determining which of several possibilities of filing rules will best fit the needs of the office or organization, should keep in mind major criteria of serviceability: (1) What indexing procedure will provide for filing or refiling of materials with the least amount of error? (2) What indexing procedure will provide for filing or withdrawing materials and for refiling materials with least time waste?

Once such a decision is made, definite steps must be taken to assure that, through the office manual and whatever other means might be helpful, the procedure will be communicated successfully to all concerned and will be followed consistently.

QUESTIONS FOR DISCUSSION

1. If you are the only person with access to the in-office files, what difference would it make whether or not you follow an established set of indexing rules?

2. If all retained materials were stored on microfilm in a centralized filing department and no in-office files were maintained, would there be any reason for the secretary to be familiar with the rules of alphabetic indexing?

3. Why do rules for filing government units, banks, schools, churches, and other organizations differ from the other rules for indexing?

4. What is the major difference in indexing company names as opposed to indexing individual names?

5. Why should the word "City" not be used instead of the city name for local correspondents?

6. In what order are the units of a federal governmental office considered for indexing?

7. Refer to the Reference Guide. What salutation would be correct to use in a letter addressed to each of the following persons?
   (a) The wife of the President of the United States
   (b) The Vice-President of the United States
   (c) An American ambassador
   (d) Speaker of the House of Representatives
   (e) Governor of a state

PROBLEMS

1. Rewrite the following names of individuals in index form. Underline the first unit of the name once and the second unit of the name twice.
   (a) Wm. Mier, 381 Shady Lane, Louisville, Kentucky

   (b) Cheryl Mestes
   (c) Jas. C. Naber
   (d) Mrs. Mary Messino
   (e) Mrs. Robt. (Debra L.) O'Brien, Akron
   (f) Tom M. O'Connell, Sr.

(g) T. Kathleen MacNabb
(h) Wm. Mier, 29 Parkland Avenue, Louisville, Kentucky
(i) Mrs. J. Clarence Naber
(j) Sister Norita
(k) Mrs. Robt. (D. Lucille) O'Brien, Springfield
(l) Tom M. O'Connell, Jr.
(m) Thomas McNamara
(n) Joe Manendez
(o) J. L. Menio, Ph.D.

2. Rewrite the following business names in index form and alphabetical order. Underline the first unit of the name once and the second unit of the name twice.
   (a) Stoke's Paper Company
   (b) Mr. Tom's Fur Salon
   (c) The Las Vegas Novelty Shop
   (d) Tom & Joan's Bait Shop
   (e) Top of the Mount Restaurant
   (f) Russell Stone Camping Equipment
   (g) 8th Street Garage
   (h) Joanne Stokes and Daughters
   (i) S & T Delicatessen
   (j) Bureau of Labor Statistics U.S. Department of Labor
   (k) Stone's Grocery, No. 1
   (l) South West Auto Supplies
   (m) San Bernardino Rest Home
   (n) Stone's Grocery, No. 2

3. You are to set up a portion of a file for the Sales Promotion Department of Ohio Bell Telephone, which is planning solicitation of all business organizations in a small Ohio city for a new type of push-button telephone. Arrange the following names in the correct filing form and order:
   (a) First National Bank of Athens
   (b) Saint Joseph's Church
   (c) Martins' Service Station, Third Street
   (d) South-Eastern Ohio Freezer Co.
   (e) Bank of Ohio, Athens
   (f) First Baptist Church of Athens
   (g) Agricultural Extension Service (Federal Office)

(h) Board of Education, Athens
(i) Ohio University
(j) Rehabilitation Services Administration (Federal Office)
(k) Athens Chamber of Commerce
(l) State Highway Department
(m) C & O Railway
(n) Martin's Drive-In Theater
(o) Third National Bank of Athens
(p) Aaron Jones Retail Outlet
(q) Martins' Service Station, Elm Street
(r) Aaron-James Production Credit Corporation
(s) Cartinson Dress Shoppe

4. Group I is arranged alphabetically. File each Group II name in its proper position in Group I by placing the letter at the end of the line of the name it follows.

                    Group I
   1. AAA Answering and Office Service
   2. A & A Window Corporation
   3. ABC Vending Corporation
   4. A-1 Taxi Service
   5. Abbey Floor Waxing Company
   6. Abbott, A. C., Company, Inc.
   7. Abraham & Straus
   8. Abrahamson's Pharmacy
   9. Abrams, Norma J. (Dr.)
   10. Abrantes, Anthony (Jr.)
   11. Academy Auto Wreckers
   12. Accessory Shop
   13. Ace Auto Service
   14. Ackerman, Mary E.
   15. Ackermann, Andrew J.
   16. Acme Excavating Corporation
   17. Acme-Standard Supply Company
   18. Acorn Landscape Service
   19. Acousticon of White Plains
   20. Adam, Mary T.
   21. Adano, Loretta C., Company
   22. Addressograph-Multigraph Corporation
   23. Adelman, Murray P.
   24. Adelson, Maude
   25. Air Dispatch Incorporated
   26. Air-Way Travel Service

27. Al & Hazel's Restaurant
28. Albanese's Eastchester Inn
29. Albano Studio (The)
30. Alert Employment Agency
31. Alex's Radio & Television Service
32. Alfredo, A., Nurseries
33. Alitalia Airlines
34. All County Electric Service
35. Allen Brothers Incorporated
36. Allen-Keating Corporation
37. Allen's Supply Company
38. Allevi, Lillian (Mrs.)
39. Allied Van Lines, Incorporated
40. Allis-Chalmers Corporation

Group II

A. Accounting Associates
B. Addressing Machine & Equipment Company
C. A & A Automotive Company
D. Abrahamson Dress Shop
E. J. B. Allid
F. A-B-K Electric Company
G. Adler Shoes for Men
H. Acme Steel Company
I. Anita H. Alleva
J. Academy of Aeronautics
K. Air-Step Shoe Shop
L. Mrs. Elizabeth Abbott
M. Alexander Carpet Company
N. A & P Food Co.
O. Al's Glass Service
P. Paul Allen Incorporated
Q. Aladdin's House of Beauty
R. Julie B. L. Allen
S. First National Bank of Alden, New York
T. The Alice Ackermann Shop
U. The Allen-Andrews Mailing Co.

5. The following letters are filed in the individual folder for Elena Perez. Indicate the order, from front to back, in which the letters should be placed in this folder.
   (a) A letter of recommendation from Mr. Wilson, dated April 23.
   (b) Our request, dated April 7, to Anne Watson for a reference for Miss Perez.
   (c) A cross-reference dated March 27 to a letter with five suggestions for candidates, including Elena Perez.
   (d) Our reply to her on April 6.
   (e) A letter setting an appointment for Miss Perez's interview, dated April 27.
   (f) Anne Watson's recommendation for Miss Perez, dated April 10.
   (g) Elena Perez's application for a position, dated April 4.
   (h) Our second request to Mr. Wilson for a reference, dated April 20.
   (i) Our request to William Wilson for a letter of reference, dated April 7.

6. The purpose of this project is to bring your card filing to a skill level. You will need 75 cards (5- by 3-inch).

   Standards to try for:

   Type the cards in 15 minutes (approximately 15 words per minute).

   File the cards in 30 minutes — not more than 2 errors.

   With practice, reduce your time to 20 minutes — no errors.

   Type each of the following names in index form at the top of a file card. (a) Place the number of each name in the upper right-hand corner of the card. (b) Arrange the cards in correct alphabetic order.
   1. Paramount Theater
   2. K & D Statistics Bureau
   3. Mrs. Carl (Theresa L.) Saia
   4. El Dorado Saddle Shop
   5. Brother Edward Burke
   6. N.Y.C.R.R.
   7. Internal Revenue Service Department of the Treasury U.S. Government
   8. Richard Donaldson Camera Shop

9. No-Run Hose
10. North Western Printing Company
11. W. Walzak, Jr.
12. Union Trust Company
    Dallas, Texas
13. National Savings Bank
    Newark, New Jersey
14. Joseph Hall, LL.B.
15. Water Works Department
    City of Glendale
16. Nordell, Inc.
17. Yecch Sandwich Counter
18. National Park Service
    Dept. of the Interior
    U.S. Government
19. Acacia Mutual Insurance Co.
20. Mt. Carmel Welfare Center
21. Jane Le Doux
22. South Eastern Carloading Co.
23. Department of Health
    City of Rockdale
24. A & B Welding Co.
25. 19th Hole Restaurant
26. Walzak-Woody, Attys.
27. C. N. Walzak
28. Adam Salter
29. Paramount Shops, Inc.
    1000 Vine
    Cincinnati, Ohio
30. A 1 Letter Service
31. Edith Marie Beauty Shop
32. KDKA Radio Station
33. Bureau of Nursing Service
    City of Birmingham
34. Town of Ft. Mitchell
35. Wm. Walzak
36. Employment Service
    Department of Labor
    U.S. Government
37. Patricia St. Clair
38. Joan W. St. Clair
39. Bureau of Public Relief
    City of Rockdale
40. Paramount Shops, Inc.
    918 Glenway
    Cincinnati, Ohio
41. A B Furniture Co.

42. Jerome Rice Newman
43. La Mode Frocks
44. G. Laderman
45. East Hyde Park Market
46. Edith's Dancing Studio
47. Advance Laundry
48. Paramount Shops, Inc.
    Elder and Race
    Springfield, Ohio
49. Commission of Public Utilities
    City of Rockdale
50. South Norwalk Delicatessen
51. Maritime Administration
    Dept. of Commerce
    U.S. Government
52. Carla Walzak
53. Theresa Saia
54. Paramount Shops, Inc.
    2719 Erie Avenue
    Springfield, Ohio
55. Dr. H. F. Newman
56. Rev. Wm. J. Lekwin
57. J. A. Eckerle
58. Ad-Sales Corp.
59. Mountain Valley Water Co.
60. Newman-Rice Institute
61. B. A. Walzakman
62. Fire Department
    City of Rockdale
63. The J. H. Alcantara Co.
64. Paramount Shops, Inc.
    133 East 5th Street
    Springfield, Massachusetts
65. St. Charles Hotel
66. Christina G. Walzak
67. A & P Food Shoppe
68. Southern Pacific Lines
69. B. A. Walzaks, Sr.
70. The Abstract Co.
71. 9th St. Baptist Church
72. William E. Walzak
73. Paramount Shops, Inc.
    4220 Glenway
    Cincinnati, Ohio
74. Mrs. Anna Adamo
75. B. A. Walzaks, Jr.

Part 5   CASE PROBLEMS

**Case 5-1
BUILDING
A GOOD
RELATIONSHIP
WITH RECORDS
MANAGEMENT
PERSONNEL**

Marty Byrnes, secretary to Mark Janowitz, attorney in charge of shareholders' relations, was usually annoyed by the type of service she received from the records management administrator, Phyllis Downe. She felt that the department was inefficient and frequently slow in providing materials and often said so.

One day a crisis developed because of the possibility of a lawsuit instigated by a shareholder. Marty telephoned Mrs. Downe to request records that had not been referred to in ten years. Mrs. Downe told her that the files were, of course, on microfilm in the Records Center. It would be impossible to get them in fewer than four days because prior requests had to be taken care of first and she was shorthanded and had nobody to locate the records by reading the microfilm.

Marty said, "But this is an emergency. Mr. Janowitz wants those records by four o'clock today." Mrs. Downe replied, "Sorry, but that will be impossible unless Mr. Janowitz or you want to go 50 miles to the Records Center and get them yourselves."

What short-term action can be taken? What long-term action? What principles are involved?

**Case 5-2
CONTROLLING
THE FILES**

Jacques Grenadier had to cope with the "generosity" of Madame Jeanne D'Emelio, one of the principals for whom he was administrative secretary in a large cosmetics company. Madame D'Emelio frequently sent letters to colleagues with a penciled notation: "Please note and return" or "Let me have your comments please."

Few of the letters or reports were ever returned for the file. Frequently Madame D'Emelio wanted a letter immediately that could not be found. She would say, "But I must have that letter *maintenant*. It has to be in your files. Where have you misfiled it this time?"

What reply should Jacques make? What system would you suggest to avoid recurrences of this perennial cause of contention?

Case 5-3
SECRETARIAL
ETHICS

Elise Larson was secretary to Conrad Justasi, sales manager of the Jacobs Office Furniture Company. The company rented a list of sales prospects from Orville Evers, owner of a direct mail company, and used the list in a nationwide promotion.

In an independent personal effort, Mr. Justasi secured a patent for an electric wastepaper basket and started its manufacture in a small factory of his own.

Since distribution was his major problem, he used the sales prospect list rented by the Jacobs Office Furniture Company. He sent the advertising material out from his office, using the tapes containing the addresses that had been prepared for the Jacobs company. Elise, of course, knew of this mailing.

While Mr. Justasi was out of town, Orville Evers, owner of the direct mail company, stormed into the office with the advertising for the electric wastebasket and the envelope in which it had been mailed. He indignantly explained to Elise that one address on his rented list was fictitious and contained a key word used to detect just such unauthorized uses.

Mr. Evers demanded the return of the list on the spot. He also insisted that Elise give him the address tapes to take with him when he left the office.

What should Elise do?

What is her responsibility to Mr. Justasi? to the Jacobs Company?

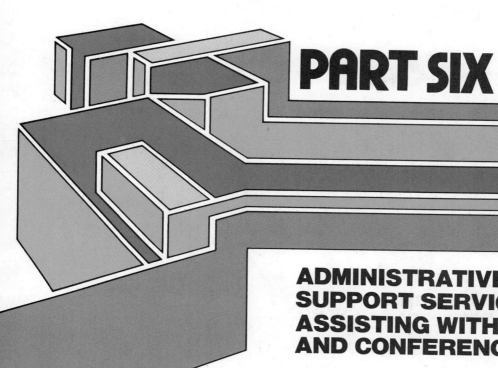

PART SIX

ADMINISTRATIVE SUPPORT SERVICES: ASSISTING WITH TRAVEL AND CONFERENCES

The business executive spends a large part of the working day in meetings. The secretary assists in scheduling these sessions, preparing for their smooth operation, recording them, and usually reporting the results. If the meeting requires travel, the secretary is involved in researching the most convenient schedules, procuring tickets, preparing necessary material to be taken on the trip, and following up after the trip is over. The secretary will enjoy these trips vicariously and can say, with Emerson, "I've traveled a good deal in Concord."

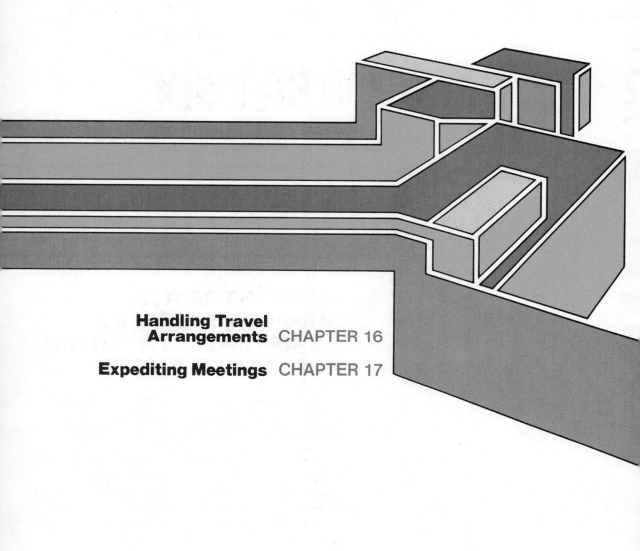

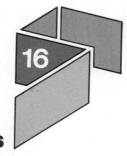

Handling Travel Arrangements

Today's business executive travels many miles a year while conducting company business. Even with the vast communication networks connecting the branch offices with headquarters and the management of one organization with the management of another, face-to-face contact is still essential in assessing a situation, in negotiating a deal, in exchanging ideas with the participants in a conference or convention. In fact, top executives spend more than a third of their time out of their offices, averaging more than 40 one- or two-day domestic trips and one or two foreign trips of about two weeks a year.

Much of the planning that precedes these trips and the follow-up activities required after their completion are performed by the secretary, either the multifunctional secretary or the administrative secretary who may be making travel arrangements for several principals simultaneously. In addition, the secretary is responsible for operating a smooth-running office while the executive is away.

Although a recent survey indicates that executives usually make their own decisions about the flight, train, or ship to be used, the secretary will probably research the information on which the choice is based and complete the details after the decision has been made. Because transportation is such a highly competitive field, changes in equipment, services, and fares are being announced constantly. You cannot handle travel arrangements efficiently unless you keep up with these changes and incorporate them into your arrangements for your employer's travel. You will also need to know your company's policies about travel arrangements, which may change often too. You will want to learn your employer's preferences as to airlines, hotels, rented automobiles, and all facilities that will make strenuous but necessary trips as pleasant and relaxing as possible.

COMPANY POLICIES REGARDING TRAVEL ARRANGEMENTS

The secretary's first concern in handling travel arrangements is to learn the company's policies. Who handles this responsibility? What airline, hotel, and other credit cards are issued, and what procedures are authorized for their use? How are tickets paid for? How are employees reimbursed for travel expenses? What restrictions does the company have as to per diem travel expenses? How are travel funds obtained?

Travel arrangements may be handled by a transportation department within the company, by an outside travel agency, or by the secretary.

Transportation Department

In a very large organization, actual reservations for travel are expedited by a transportation department or central travel service that maintains close contact with all carriers; has on hand complete official guides for airlines, railroads, and steamships; and deals with special reservation clerks (at unlisted numbers) serving only such volume buyers. The secretary informs the special department of a proposed trip; the department then suggests possible schedules to be approved by the executive and the secretary. When their decision is made, the department either issues or obtains the necessary tickets. The transportation department also secures and distributes credit cards for authorized personnel.

Travel Agencies

In recent years the business world has turned increasingly to travel agencies. Some agencies now work with business travelers exclusively. The know-how of the reputable agency is especially helpful to an overseas-bound customer; moreover, it is a convenience to the domestic traveler.

A travel agency charges the customer no fee; the transportation lines "pick up the tab." The agent plans the entire itinerary; handles all ticketing; and at times provides unusual services, such as car rentals, special discounts, and the like. The secretary provides the name, business and home address, business and home telephone, the cities to be visited, the hour at which the traveler must be in each city and the hour of departure, any hotel preferences, and any cost requirements.

The Secretary

If a business organization provides neither the services of an intracompany special transportation department nor the regular services of a travel agency, the secretary alone is responsible for handling all travel arrangements. The secretary deals directly with the transportation companies or enlists the services of a travel agency.

The alert secretary will soon discover the employer's preference of hotel chain, airline, or seat location. Consulting the executive about these preferences and remembering them from trip to trip can alleviate some of the mental and physical stress of the trip and thus contribute to its overall effectiveness.

AIR TRAVEL

Most people traveling on business prefer to fly, especially on long trips, because they save time. Today, a passenger can breakfast in Chicago, lunch in San Francisco, and dine in New York. The supersonic transport plane can cross the Atlantic from Washington to Paris in a little over three hours. The jet age has given the executive the advantage of keeping close contact with operations without being away from home base for too long a time.

Classes of Flights

Some people like to fly the jumbo 747's that connect the large cities of the United States with each other and with foreign cities. These planes are equipped with large away-from-seat lounges for both coach and first-class passengers. They also have in-flight movies and recorded entertainment. Other travelers prefer smaller planes, which also may provide movies and recorded entertainment in flight.

The major airlines are supported by regional lines that fly to cities too small for jet runways. A passenger traveling from a large city to a small one will probably fly on both jet planes and those of the regional airline.

Most planes have both a first-class and a coach section. Generally, the classes of flight are:

First class. Serves complimentary meals during conventional mealtimes and generous refreshments. Has several attendants. Seats are wider, farther apart, and provide more legroom than those in the coach section. Special airport lounges and in-flight meals at reserved tables are recent innovations designed to attract affluent passengers.

Coach. Serves a complimentary meal when the plane is aloft at mealtime and a snack at other times. Soft drinks are available without charge.

As an economy measure many organizations have a policy that only high-ranking executives may travel first class, possibly only presidents, vice-presidents, and department heads. The secretary should learn these rules before making travel arrangements. Even though the executive may be entitled to first-class accommodations, coach reservations will probably be adequate for short trips. On a longer trip, of course, the added comfort makes a first-class reservation desirable.

Meal services are diversified by competing airlines. Choices of up to three entrees in coach class are offered on certain domestic flights. Meals to accommodate special diets can be ordered.

Shuttle service is available between certain cities within the United States: New York/Boston, New York/Washington, and San Francisco/Los Angeles. Passengers board the plane without reservations, and the flights leave at frequent intervals or as soon as the plane is filled. Passengers pay their fares aloft with cash, credit card, or (with bona fide identification) personal check. Only carry-on baggage is accepted on shuttle flights.

On most domestic flights each passenger is allowed three pieces of luggage, one measuring not more than 62 inches in girth, another measuring not more than 55 inches, and the third not more than 45 inches. Some luggage may be carried aboard without charge if it fits under the seat in front of the passenger. To avoid waiting for checked luggage at the destination, some airlines provide compartments inside the boarding door for bulkier baggage. Luggage in excess of the weight allowed is charged excess baggage rates in addition to the regular fare.

Air Fares

Air fares are constantly being changed. In addition to first-class and coach fares, domestic airlines offer special rates for night flights, excursions that comprise a definite number of days, certain weekend trips, and tickets purchased a definite number of days before takeoff. The reduced-rate night flights and excursions are not appropriate for most business travel.

Formerly one-way fares between cities were shown at the back of the airline's timetable folder. For convenience, however, some airlines now publish these one-way fares right at the side of or directly above the schedules between two cities. These listings can become confusing if many fares are available, so other airlines continue to print the fares at the back of the folder.

Currently an 8 percent federal tax is added to the cost of domestic flights.

Flight Schedules

Airline flight schedules are not uniform in structure among airlines. Two sample schedules (not intended to be valid) are given on pages 369 and 370 to illustrate the ease with which they can be read. First is the schedule of all American Airlines flights between Phoenix, Arizona, and New York/Newark airports.

NEW YORK/NEWARK (ET) (Cont'd)

	Leave	Arrive	Flight No.	Stops or Via	Meals	Equip.	Freq.
To Phoenix	7:00a L	10:00a	103/107	Chicago	✕✌ ⊛	727/D10	Daily
F $297.00 Y $182.00	7:10a E	10:00a	451/107	Chicago	✕✌ ⊛	727/D10	ExSu
FN $182.00 YN $146.00	8:15a L	11:31a	295/159	Dallas/Ft Worth	✕✌	727/707	Daily
YE30 $309.00	8:20a E	11:31a	237/159	Dallas/Ft Worth	✕✌	727/707	Daily
YCHE40 $182.00	9:00a K	10:53a	117	NON-STOP	✕✌	707	Daily
YHE40 $309.00	9:00a L	1:04p	235/291	Chicago	✕✌	727/707	Daily
	10:00a E	1:04p	65/291	Chicago	✕✌ ⊛	D10/707	Daily
	11:00a L	2:18p	433/361	Chicago	✕✌	727/727	Daily
	1:00p L	4:49p	493/561	Chicago	✕✌	727/707	Daily
	1:45p E	4:49p	561	One-Stop	✕✌	707	Daily
	2:40p L	6:01p	249/535	Dallas/Ft Worth	✕✌	727/707	Daily
	2:40p E	6:01p	425/535	Dallas/Ft Worth	✕✌	707/707	Daily
	3:45p E	7:06p	581/617	Chicago	✕✌	707/707	Daily
	4:15p K	6:14p	187	NON-STOP	✕✌	707	Daily
	5:55p L	9:02p	375/69	Dallas/Ft Worth	✕✌	727/727	ExSa
	7:00p L	10:20p	259/157	Chicago	✕✌	727/D10	Daily
	7:15p E	10:20p	636/157	Chicago	✕✌	707/D10	ExSa
	9:25p E ★	2:18a	317/95	Dallas/Ft Worth	☂✌	D10/D10	Daily
	(Flt 95 Opts With 707 On Mo, Tu & We)						
	11:00p K ★	2:18a	95	One-Stop	☂✌	D10 ▰	Daily
	(Flt 95 Opts With 707 On Mo, Tu & We)						
From Phoenix	8:10a	4:55p L	618/98	Dallas/Ft Worth	✕✌	707/727	Daily
When in Phoenix,	8:30a	5:16p E	630/284	Chicago	✕✌ ⊛	D10/727	Daily
call 264-2654	8:45a	4:19p K	186	NON-STOP	✕✌	707	Daily
	10:40a	7:39p L	562/228	Dallas/Ft Worth	✕✌	707/727	Daily
	11:00a	7:46p E	142/182	Chicago	✕✌ ⊛	707/D10	Daily
	12:45p	9:55p E	66	One-Stop	✕✌	707	Daily
	12:45p	9:59p L	66/448	Chicago	✕✌	707/727	Daily
	2:20p	9:53p K	118	NON-STOP	✕✌	707	Daily
	2:20p	11:03p L	622/634	Dallas/Ft Worth	✕✌	707/727	ExSa
	10:40p ★	6:06a K	80	NON-STOP	☂✌	707	Daily
	12:25a ★	8:59a E	246/196	Chicago	✕✌	D10/D10	Daily
	(Flt 246 Opts With 727 On Tu, We & Th)						
	12:25a ★	9:55a L	246/430	Chicago	✕✌	D10/727	Daily
	(Flt 246 Opts With 727 On Tu, We & Th)						
	1:20a ★	10:17a E	258/90	Dallas/Ft Worth	✕✌	D10/727	Daily
	(Flt 258 Opts With 707 On Tu, We & Th)						
	1:20a ★	10:27a K	258	One-Stop	✕✌	D10 ▰	Daily
	(Opts With 707 On Tu, We & Th)						

SYMBOLS

✕ Meal	★ Nightcoach Fares, FN, YN	🎬 Astro-color Movie
☂ Snack	▰ Lower Deck	⊛ Short Subject
✌ Cocktail	Cargo Container Service	▮ Americana Hotel
	🚁 Helicopter Service	

AIRPORTS

E — Newark	S — San Francisco	D — Dulles	I — Baltimore/Washington
K — Kennedy	O — Oakland	N — National	International
L — LaGuardia	J — San Jose		

This schedule of all American Airlines flights between Phoenix, Arizona, and New York/Newark airports can be interpreted easily.

There are two nonstop American flights from New York/Newark to Phoenix, and three nonstop flights from Phoenix to New York/Newark, all on 707 planes. One of the nonstop flights (Flight 80) would probably be unattractive to an executive because it involves night travel. None of the nonstop flights have movies or short subjects. All flights except the night flight serve meals and cocktails.

The flights which stop do so either in Chicago or Dallas/Fort Worth where (except for Flights 561 and 95 westbound and Flights 66 and 258 eastbound) passengers must change planes, in some cases changing type of equipment.

The one-way first-class fare for these flights is $297; the coach fare, $182.

The Newark Airport is in New Jersey just across the Hudson River from New York and is the closest of the three New York terminals to the center of the city. Traveling through the Newark Airport takes a little over a third as much ground-travel time as is required by the executive using Kennedy Airport.

A Phoenix executive with business in New York would probably choose Flight 118 in order to be fully rested for the next day's appointments and still put in most of the day in the office. Conversely, a New York executive coming to Phoenix would probably select Flight 187 for the same reasons. This schedule does not indicate (as most do) that Phoenix is on Mountain Standard Time and that the passenger loses two hours in flying east from the mountain time zone and gains two hours flying west from the eastern time zone.

The second schedule shows the Trans World Airlines flights from Pittsburgh, Pennsylvania, to the airports in Chicago, Illinois. This schedule indicates the telephone number of the TWA reservations center in Pittsburgh, the local time zones for both cities, the time required for limousine travel from Pittsburgh to the airport, and the fares. It identifies the two airports serving the Chicago area, Midway and O'Hare, but it does not give the distances from each to the center of the city.

All of the flights listed use the O'Hare Airport. Since all of the TWA flights between Pittsburgh and Chicago are nonstop, there is no concern about changing planes or making connections between the two cities. Meals are served on four of the flights, and a snack is served on one flight. One of the flights operates on Sunday only, and another operates on all days except Sunday. The other flights operate on a daily basis. Music is not available on any of the flights probably because of the brevity of the flights. Carry-on luggage compartments, a special feature of TWA flights, are available on all domestic flights.

This schedule shows the Trans World Airlines flights from Pittsburgh, Pennsylvania, to the airports in Chicago, Illinois.

Leave	Arrive	Flight No.	Stops or Via	Freq.	Service
From: **PITTSBURGH, Pa.** (EDT)					Limousine 55 Min. $2.65
Reservations: Domestic: 391-3600 International: 391-2277 Freight: 771-4000					
To: **CHICAGO, Ill.** (CDT)					F-$87.00 Y-$56.00 YHE40-$95.00
AIRPORTS: M-Midway O-O'Hare					
7 30a O	7 46a	271	NON-STOP	Su Only	✕
7 55a O	8 15a	271	NON-STOP	Ex Su	✕
10 40a O	11 00a	25	NON-STOP	Daily	
12 15p O	12 39p	21	NON-STOP	Daily	◆ 1011
2 35p O	2 57p	235	NON-STOP	Daily	
4 45p O	5 14p	3	NON-STOP	Daily	✕
6 35p O	7 01p	261	NON-STOP	Daily	✕

SYMBOLS

✕ Meal   % Plane Change Enroute   Carry-on Luggage
◆ Snack   ♪ Music   Compartments are Available
♫ Movie and Music   † Arrival One Day Later   on All Domestic Flights.

An executive going to Chicago for business might leave Pittsburgh on Flight 271 in order to arrive early enough to spend a full business day in Chicago. This flight leaves Pittsburgh at 7:55 a.m., Eastern Daylight Time, and arrives in Chicago at 8:15 a.m., Central Daylight Time. The trip will actually take one hour and twenty minutes, not just twenty minutes, for the traveler gains one hour in flying west from a city in the eastern time zone to a location in the central time zone.

Flight Information

Because fares, services, and departure times change frequently, the secretary must be certain to use an up-to-date schedule. A call to the reservations and information number listed under the airline in the telephone directory will obtain information not only about flights on that line but on others as well. For infrequent travel planning, this is a quick, convenient method.

A transportation department — and in many cases an executive — with regular flights, however, will profit from a subscription to one of the airlines guides published by the Reuben H. Donnelley Corporation of Chicago: the monthly or semimonthly *Official Airline Guide*, the monthly *OAG Pocket Flight Guide*, or the quarterly *OAG Travel Planner & Hotel/Motel Guide*. Subscribers receive updated materials automatically. With one of these publications at hand, the secretary can research the most convenient flights available and present alternative plans for the employer's approval before initiating the actual reservations. These publications (according to their individual completeness) also give information about the airport facilities, the distance from the airport to the center of a city, limousine service (time, fares, and pickup points), hotels (Mobil ratings and rates), car rentals, and air taxi services available. The guides are simple to use, once you understand the general method of presentation. The opening pages provide keys to the abbreviations and symbols used. Flight information is listed alphabetically by the destination city, then alphabetically by the cities from which flights to that city are available. A brief discussion on the use of the *Official Airline Guide* follows.

Suppose your employer is to fly from Boston to Phoenix. You would turn to the *To Phoenix* section (listed alphabetically under *P*). Under *To Phoenix*, you would then locate the *From Boston* listings (listed alphabetically under *B*). There you would find a flight schedule similar to that shown on page 372.

Reading from the top of the table, you learn that:

Phoenix is on Mountain Standard Time.

PHX is the City/Airport code for Phoenix.

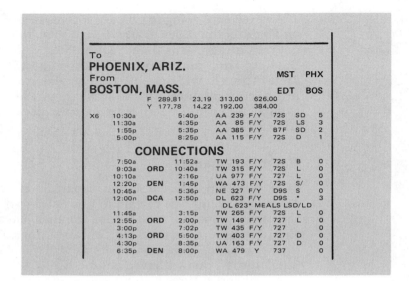

To						
PHOENIX, ARIZ.					MST	PHX
From						
BOSTON, MASS.					EDT	BOS
	F 289.81	23.19	313.00	626.00		
	Y 177.78	14.22	192.00	384.00		
X6 10:30a		5:40p	AA 239	F/Y	72S SD	5
11:30a		4:35p	AA 85	F/Y	72S LS	3
1:55p		5:35p	AA 385	F/Y	B7F SD	2
5:00p		8:25p	AA 115	F/Y	72S D	1

CONNECTIONS

7:50a		11:52a	TW 193	F/Y	72S B	0
9:03a	ORD	10:40a	TW 315	F/Y	72S L	0
10:10a		2:16p	UA 977	F/Y	727 L	0
12:20p	DEN	1:45p	WA 473	F/Y	72S S/	0
10:45a		5:36p	NE 327	F/Y	D9S S	0
12:00n	DCA	12:50p	DL 623	F/Y	D9S *	3
			DL 623* MEALS LSD/LD			
11:45a		3:15p	TW 265	F/Y	72S L	0
12:55p	ORD	2:00p	TW 149	F/Y	727 L	0
3:00p		7:02p	TW 435	F/Y	727	0
4:13p	ORD	5:50p	TW 403	F/Y	727 D	0
4:30p		8:35p	UA 163	F/Y	727 D	0
6:35p	DEN	8:00p	WA 479	Y	737	0

This schedule taken from the *Official Airline Guide* would be of help in planning a business trip from Boston to Phoenix.

Boston is on Eastern Daylight Time.

BOS is the City/Airport code for Boston.

The first-class (F) and jet coach (Y) fares are shown.

Under the flight schedules, you learn that for the first *direct* (no change of plane) flight of the day:

Except on Saturday (X6), you leave Boston at 10:30 a.m.

You arrive in Phoenix at 5:40 p.m. (Phoenix time).

It is American Airlines Flight 239.

First-class and jet coach classes are available.

The aircraft is a Boeing 727 super fan jet (72S).

You will be served a snack and a dinner en route.

The flight will make five stops.

Looking under the heading *Connections*, you learn that if a change in planes en route is acceptable, you can:

Leave Boston (every day) at 10:10 a.m. and arrive in Phoenix at 2:16 p.m. (Phoenix time).

You leave Boston on United Airlines Flight 977, first class or jet coach, on a Boeing 727 jet, and will be served lunch on this portion of the flight, which is nonstop to the connecting point.

You arrive at the connecting airport at Denver at 12:20 p.m. (Denver time).

You leave Denver at 1:45 p.m. on Western Airlines Flight 473, first class or jet coach, on a Boeing 72S super fan jet, will be served a snack, and will fly nonstop to Phoenix.

Using these facts and assuming that the departure times suited your employer, you would probably decide that the amount of time saved on the nondirect flight would offset the inconvenience of changing planes.

Flight Reservations and Ticketing

Reservations for air travel may be made by telephone or in person at the airport terminal, a ticket office, or a travel agency. After choosing a flight, the traveler asks the airline reservations clerk to check the availability of space in the desired section. This is done with electronic equipment that records and stores reservations made for a flight from all ticketing stations.

A ticket for an in-person reservation is issued at once; otherwise, it is issued and mailed to a specified address or held for pickup at the ticket office or airport. Messenger service is also available (for a fee) for ticket delivery and fare collection. Payment can be made by cash, by check, or with an acceptable credit card for later billing. An organization having a transportation department usually has authority and supplies for issuing tickets in-house.

This operator is entering an airline reservation into the equipment that will inform all other ticketing stations that the space has been reserved.

American Airlines Photo

Even with a trip involving several destinations and airlines, only one ticket is issued (by the airline on which the flight originates). A passenger who does not know the continuing flights required can purchase an open ticket and make reservations later. Data for any changes in ticketed flights are merely attached to the original ticket.

When checking in for some flights, the passenger may reserve an exact seat location or choose an aisle seat or a window seat; the smoking or nonsmoking section; or the front, back, or center section of the plane.

Tickets-by-Mail service enables the customer to make a telephone reservation and then pay the invoice mailed with the ticket in time for the check to clear before the actual flight. Some airlines, however, mail only the invoice, which must be paid before the ticket is mailed, a time-consuming system.

Air-travel credit cards are issued to key personnel by many organizations. Other companies maintain charge accounts with the airlines and are billed regularly for authorized travel by employees. Some airlines have special credit-card ticketing plans that allow a passenger to fill in the ticket after making a telephone reservation.

Reconfirmations

Although reconfirmation on domestic flights is not required, it is always wise to reconfirm reservations for each part of a continuing air trip after the first. This can be done on arrival at the airport. Giving the telephone number in that city at which the passenger can be reached is an assurance of a contact with the airline.

Redemption of Unused Plane Tickets

Unused tickets or unused portions of plane tickets can be redeemed by submitting them to the airline ticket office. Usually a check is mailed later.

Airport Services

An airport limousine is available for transportation between downtown locations and the airport, usually at a lower rate than taxi service. In some cities the limousine calls for passengers at key hotels; in others it leaves from either a downtown ticket office or a downtown airline terminal. The ticket often shows the location of the limousine pickup point and departure time for the airport. Sometimes it is necessary to reserve limousine space when making a plane reservation. If the limousine leaves from a downtown airport terminal, the passenger checks in at the terminal (checks in for the flight). On arrival in some cases the traveler has only to board the plane. If the limousine leaves from a point other than a terminal, the passenger checks in at the airport.

Limousine service is also supplied between airports serving one city and between airlines within the same airport.

The airline timetable indicates whether helicopter service is available between airports in cities served by more than one facility or from the airport to downtown points.

Each major airline operates a flight club which any traveler can join on payment of a moderate annual fee. The executive who travels frequently finds waiting for planes less tedious in the club atmosphere of the flight club lounge.

Company-Owned Planes

Many corporations own one or more planes. Business is taking to the air in its own craft to reduce travel time for executives even more than is possible by commercial aviation. Many companies, however, observe the precaution of limiting the number of top officials who can fly in the same plane (private or commercial) to protect continuity of management in case of an accident. Charter planes are also increasingly important, especially to areas not served by regional airlines.

TRAIN TRAVEL

Train travel for long distances is less and less attractive to business executives because of the time required and the reduction in services. Several federally subsidized reorganizations of the railroads have been attempted to improve services on long trips. At first *Amtrak* and later *Conrail* (in the northeast only) undertook to provide a higher type of service than was possible on the financially depressed individual railroads, especially on routes connecting cities with high population concentrations. The efforts have not been entirely successful but are continuing.

Metroliners are available between Boston and Washington, D.C., and points between, offering improved services and fast schedules that enable the railroad to compete with airlines. On these special trains a seat is reserved when the ticket is purchased. Because of heavy demand, tickets must be bought well in advance. On some trains parlor seats can also be reserved.

Overnight trains between East Coast points and Florida and between Chicago and Florida are available with various kinds of sleeper service; and extra-fare, extra-service trains are added during the winter season. Sleeper and dining-car service is also available between Chicago and the West Coast.

The secretary can become familiar with the rail services by consulting the *Official Guide of the Railways*, which contains schedules of all railway and steamship lines in the United States, Canada, Mexico, and Puerto Rico.

A railway timetable is simple to read, as can be seen from the partial schedule of the Conrail commuter train which operates between White Plains and New York City.

Executives who live in White Plains and work in New York City can commute to work by train. Notice the high concentration of trains marked E (Express) during the rush-hour times: 7:00 a.m. to 9:00 a.m. from White Plains to New York City, and 4:30 p.m. to 6:00 p.m. from New York City to White Plains. This demonstrates that the trains are designed to get the working commuter to and from the office as quickly as possible.

The Conrail commuter train which operates between White Plains and New York City is designed to get the working commuter to and from the office as quickly as possible.

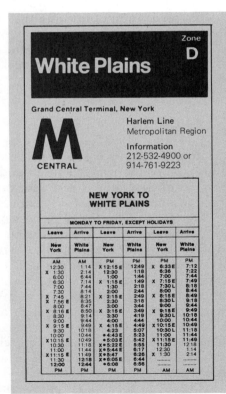

White Plains — Zone D

Grand Central Terminal, New York

M CENTRAL

Harlem Line
Metropolitan Region

Information
212-532-4900 or
914-761-9223

NEW YORK TO WHITE PLAINS

MONDAY TO FRIDAY, EXCEPT HOLIDAYS

Leave	Arrive	Leave	Arrive	Leave	Arrive
New York	White Plains	New York	White Plains	New York	White Plains
AM	AM	PM	PM	PM	PM
12:30	1:14	X 12:15 E	12:49	X 6:33 E	7:12
X 1:30	2:14	12:30	1:18	6:36	7:22
6:00	6:44	1:00	1:44	7:00	7:44
6:30	7:14	X 1:15 E	1:49	X 7:15 E	7:49
7:00	7:44	1:30	2:18	7:30 L	8:18
7:30	8:14	2:00	2:44	8:00	8:44
X 7:45 E	8:21	X 2:15 E	2:49	X 8:15 E	8:49
X 7:56 E	8:35	2:30	3:18	8:30 L	9:18
8:00	8:47	3:00	3:44	9:00	9:44
X 8:16 E	8:50	X 3:15 E	3:49	X 9:15 E	9:49
8:30	9:14	3:30	4:19	9:30 L	10:18
9:00	9:44	4:00	4:44	10:00	10:44
X 9:15 E	9:49	X 4:15 E	4:49	X 10:15 E	10:49
9:30	10:18	4:23	5:07	10:30 L	11:18
10:00	10:44	• 4:43 E	5:23	11:00	11:44
X 10:15 E	10:49	• 5:03 E	5:42	X 11:15 E	11:49
10:30	11:18	X • 5:22 E	5:55	11:30	12:18
11:00	11:44	X • 5:44 E	6:17	12:30	1:14
X 11:15 E	11:49	X • 5:47	6:26	X 1:30	2:14
11:30	12:18	X • 6:05 E	6:44	......	......
12:00	12:44	• 6:08	6:56	......	......
PM	PM	PM	PM	AM	AM

WHITE PLAINS TO NEW YORK

MONDAY TO FRIDAY, EXCEPT HOLIDAYS

Leave	Arrive	Leave	Arrive	Leave	Arrive
White Plains	New York	White Plains	New York	White Plains	New York
AM	AM	AM	AM	PM	PM
12:00	12:45	10:00	10:48	4:30	5:15
• 5:03	5:45	10:30	11:15	4:56 E	5:33
• 5:23 L	6:10	10:56 E	11:33	5:00	5:45
• 5:53 L	6:40	11:00	11:48	5:10 E	5:47
• 6:25	7:09	11:30	12:15	5:30	6:15
• 6:39 E	7:15	11:56 E	12:33	5:56 E	6:33
• 6:44	7:30	12:00	12:49	6:00	6:45
• 6:58 E	7:36	12:30	1:15	6:30	7:15
• 7:14 E	7:53	12:56 E	1:33	6:56 E	7:33
• 7:28 E	X 8:02	1:00	1:48	7:00	7:45
• 7:46 E	8:20	1:30	2:15	7:56 E	8:33
• 8:01 E	X 8:35	1:56 E	2:33	8:00	8:48
• 8:18 E	8:53	2:00	2:48	8:56 E	9:33
• 8:25	X 9:05	2:30	3:15	9:00	9:45
• 8:44 E	9:24	2:56 E	3:33	10:00	10:33
• 8:56 E	X 9:33	3:00	3:48	10:00	10:48
• 9:00	9:45	3:30	4:15	11:00	11:45
9:30	10:15	3:56 E	4:33	12:00	12:45
9:56 E	10:33	4:00	4:49	......	......
AM	AM	PM	PM	AM	AM

REFERENCES

Check displays in G.C.T. for departure tracks.
E-Express   L-Local
S-Saturdays and Washington's Birthday only.
X-All trains except those marked 'X' stop at 125th St. Station.
•-Economy off peak tickets are not valid on these trains.
HOLIDAYS- New Year's Day, Washington's Birthday, Memorial, Independence and Labor Day, Thanksgiving and Christmas.

RENT-A-CAR TRAVEL

At times a business executive finds it convenient to travel by air or train and then to rent a car. Both airline and railroad timetable folders indicate those cities with rent-a-car service. Automobile rental companies publish directories of their rental agencies both here and abroad, giving the daily rates and mileage charges of each station. Reservations for rental cars, specifying the make and type wanted, can be made along with the travel reservation or with the rental agency office at point of departure or pickup point.

One thoughtful secretary sends expected visitors an area map showing the employer's office location and the location of recommended hotels, motels, and restaurants nearby, as well as the approximate driving time.

Upon arriving at the pickup point, the traveler presents a driver's license and makes financial arrangements for renting the car. An especially attractive feature is the "rent-it-here-leave-it-there" policy of the agencies. The rental costs can be charged to any of a number of credit cards, a desirable feature because the deposit required can involve a heavy outlay of cash.

Rental agencies will help with local routes, where to eat and stay, and what to see.

The American Automobile Association provides its members with travel guides for any contemplated trip. Several oil companies and automobile insurance companies will map routes on request. Many handy dining and lodging guides are available at bookstores and travel agencies.

INTERNATIONAL TRAVEL

"Last week when I was in Rome . . ." is as common in business conversation today as a casual reference to a trip to a neighboring state used to be. A secretary to a top executive will probably plan international as well as domestic travel and will need to understand its many ramifications.

General Considerations

Planning for foreign travel differs in several ways from planning for shorter domestic trips. For instance, time changes can take a great toll on the executive. (See time zones, page 301.) Air Force medical experts suggest that important decisions should not be made either shortly before or shortly after a long jet flight. The business person who travels by plane should try to allow one day on arrival in Europe and two days on return to the United States to adjust both physically and psychologically to time differences. Leaving here on a morning flight which arrives overseas at night will force the traveler to rest before starting negotiations, and flying home on the first day of a weekend will provide rest before going back to the office. The travel planner should also keep in mind that passengers on overseas flights are expected to check in at the airport at least one hour before scheduled departure.

Another difference between domestic and foreign travel is in arranging appointments. Both because of possible difficulties in getting around in a foreign city and because of the slower pace at which European business is conducted, the American visitor will want to keep appointments to two or three a day.

Fares are standard with all airlines, so an airline can attract the lucrative American business travel only by providing special services. One airline arranges for conference rooms at the international airport and coordinates flight schedules of participants so that they can meet conveniently, sometimes without ever leaving the airport and going through customs. Other lines help to make business contracts, arrange for secretarial services and conference rooms, or make hotel reservations if they are given at least two weeks in which to provide these special accommodations and services.

The business card is an important adjunct to the business call, perhaps a card with English on one side and the appropriate foreign language on the reverse side. A card is always presented by a caller; therefore, a business visitor can easily use up a supply of 200 cards while attending a business fair. The European business fair has no counterpart in this country. An entire year's output of a product may be sold during such a fair.

Learning the mores of the countries to be visited is important to the success of a business visit. Most of the international airlines now publish guides for conducting business in Europe. These and *Business Week's Businessman's Guide to Europe* are useful references when planning a trip. In them are found dates of important trade fairs, holidays in each country, hotel and restaurant information, addresses of important business contacts in each country, currency information, and invaluable hints for improving business contacts.

Abroad it pays to bring gifts — judiciously. There are as many subtleties to the art of international gift giving as there are differences in customs and business methods around the world. What pleases a customer in London may be offensive to a Tokyo counterpart. A present to the wife of a business contact in Europe would be accepted gratefully, but a present to the wife of a Near Easterner would be most unacceptable. Asking advice of a resident of the country being visited may pay dividends.

Services of a Travel Agency

A company's travel department or a travel agency can be of great help in planning a foreign trip. In fact, without a well-established company travel department, the secretary will find the services of a travel agent almost indispensable to:

Make hotel and rent-a-car reservations

List available transportation

Suggest an itinerary or itineraries and procure tickets

Notify you of the required travel documents and how to obtain them

Give currency information and secure enough foreign currency for entering the first country on the itinerary

Explain baggage restrictions

Secure insurance for traveler and baggage

List port taxes levied (Most international airports charge from $1 to $3. An international transportation tax of $3 is imposed on each international passenger departing from the continental United States.)

Give information as to time limitations for visits

Supply free literature and services

Arrange for the traveler to be met by a representative or a limousine

Get visas, give advice about vaccinations and inoculations required in each country to be visited, and supply blanks for International Certificates of Vaccination

Foreign Business Contacts

Half the work of a successful trip abroad will take place before the executive boards the jet. Locating business contacts and other data must precede the trip.

One of the most helpful resources concerning foreign trade is the Domestic and International Business Administration of the United States Department of Commerce, with offices in the major cities of the United States. (Look in the telephone directory under United States Government listings to find the division office in your city.) This office will give information about any foreign country regarding economic developments, regulations, and trade statistics; costs and channels of distribution; key persons to contact both in the United States and in the foreign country; methods of protecting patent, copyright, and trademark rights; import and export restrictions; and national holidays, which can adversely affect an entire business trip.

Executives traveling to South America can get background information for their trips by consulting the Council of the Americas (680 Park Avenue, New York, NY 10021), which is run by United States corporations with South American holdings. The Council maintains local offices in virtually every South American location of economic significance. Dun and Bradstreet's reference service will provide subscribers with a card authorizing the holder to request credit information from any one of its foreign offices. The *Foreign Trade Handbook* (Dartnell Corporation, Chicago) covers foreign trade organizations, management, finance, technical procedures to follow, and legal considerations. A visit to the commercial attachés of the countries to be visited may uncover valuable data.

Passports

The first requisite for foreign travel is a *passport* issued by the Department of State. A passport is an official document granting permission to travel to the person specified in it and authenticating that person's right to protection. For travel in most countries outside the United States, a passport is necessary; but it is not required in Canada, Mexico, Bermuda, the West Indies, and Central American countries, although proof of citizenship may be requested. A visitor to Mexico who plans to stay longer than three days must secure a travel permit at the port of entry.

Passport application forms can be obtained from the travel agent, from passport offices (Department of State) in Boston, Chicago, Los Angeles, Miami, New Orleans, New York, San Francisco, and Washington, or from the passport office in local Federal buildings. For the first passport an applicant is required to appear in person before an agent of the passport office or a clerk of a federal court or a state court authorized by law to naturalize aliens. The applicant must present the following papers:

The completed application.

Proof of United States citizenship (birth certificate, baptismal certificate, or certificate of naturalization). If these proofs are not available, the applicant submits a notice by appropriate authorities that no birth record exists and such secondary evidence as census records, newspaper files, family Bibles, school records, or affidavits of persons with personal knowledge of the applicant's birth. An identifying witness may also appear with the applicant.

Proof of identification bearing signature and description, such as a driver's license.

Two signed duplicate photographs *taken by a photographer* within the past six months.

The passport fee.

If the applicant is going abroad on a government contract, a letter from the employing company is required showing the applicant's position, destination, purpose of travel, and proposed length of stay.

A person holding a previous passport issued in that person's own name within the past five years and meeting all of the requirements stated on the back of the form may renew the document by mail by completing Form DSP-82 and mailing the application. It is no longer necessary to appear before any official in person to renew a passport. The secretary may obtain the form from the nearest passport office. Then the applicant completes the form, signs and dates the application, attaches two signed duplicate photographs taken within six months of the date of the application, and encloses the expired passport and the passport fee. These materials are mailed to the nearest passport office.

A passport is valid for five years from date of issue. Since processing a passport application may take three or four weeks, anyone contemplating foreign travel should keep the passport in order. The secretary to a traveling executive can be of assistance by noting the passport expiration date in the tickler file.

As soon as the passport is received, it should be signed and the information requested on the inside cover must be filled in. During overseas travel, a passport should always be carried on the person and NEVER left in a hotel room, even in a locked suitcase. The business traveler should also carry a letter from the business organization represented — stating the where, when, why, and duration of the proposed visit.

Visas. A visa is a permit granted by a foreign government for a person to enter its territory. It usually appears as a stamped notation in a passport indicating that the bearer may enter the country for a certain purpose and for a specified period of time. Anyone in doubt as to the necessity of obtaining a travel visa for travel in any foreign country should consult the consul or a travel agent before leaving the United States. Consular representatives of most foreign countries are located in principal cities, and their addresses can be found in the *Congressional Directory* or in the Yellow Pages under "Consulates." A traveler who intends to work in the country to be visited should check to see whether a work permit is required.

Vaccination and Inoculation Requirements. The travel agent or the consulate of the country to be visited can give information about *vaccinations* and *inoculations* required by the country visited. A vaccination record is no longer required for reentry to the United

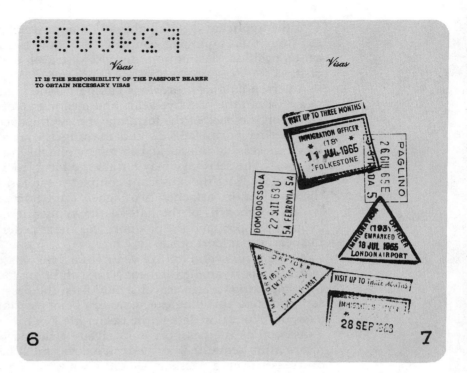

When a traveler enters a foreign country, an immigration officer of that country may stamp the immigrant's passport with a visa stamp (date of entry and allowable length of visit) and with an embarkation stamp when the visitor leaves the country.

States. Records of these vaccinations and inoculations are signed by the physican and validated by the local or state health officer on the International Certificates of Vaccination form obtainable from the travel agent, the passport office, or in some cases, the physician.

Overseas Flights

International plane travel is basically the same as it is for domestic flights, with a preponderance of jumbo jets that seat more than 200 passengers. Innovations in services include large passenger lounges, a choice among several entrees at mealtime, and containerized baggage compartments in which baggage is always stored in an upright position and unloaded swiftly by bringing the containers to the customs area.

There are two classes of flights on most planes — first class and economy or tourist. Gourmet meals and beverages catered by world-famous chefs such as Maxim's of Paris are served in first class. Beautiful china, crystal, and silver are used; and the service of flight attendants is outstanding. In tourist class, meals meet a lower quality standard, but the passenger has a choice among entrees on some flights. First-class passengers are allowed 66 pounds of luggage on overseas flights, and tourist-class passengers are allowed 44 pounds.

Fares vary with the season of year. They are constantly changing because of the competitive nature of the airline business. There are three seasonal variations in fares: summer or peak (highest), shoulder or spring (lower), and winter (lowest). During the peak period (eastbound during June, July, and August and westbound during July, August, and September) fares to and from Europe, the Middle East, and Africa are higher than they are during the rest of the year.

Fares also differ according to the length of stay: up to 14 days (highest), 14–21 days (lower), and 22–45 days (lowest). Obviously, the traveler on business is the one who usually pays the highest fares. The only way to keep abreast of air fares is to consult the airline reservation clerk or the travel agent for any available special excursion rates. An international flight schedule of a foreign airline is more complicated than a domestic schedule. The Scandinavian Airlines schedule from Chicago to Budapest illustrates the necessity for understanding the many codes used.

An international flight schedule of a foreign airline is more complicated than a domestic schedule. This Scandinavian Airlines schedule lists the flights from Chicago to Budapest.

From	Days	Air-port	Dep.	Arr.	Flight	Cl. A/C	Transfer At	Dep.	Flight	Cl. A/C	Note
CHICAGO							TEL 800-221-2350				
BUDAPEST											
	257	ORD	1840	*1345	SK 942	FY D10	CPH *1155	MA 751	Y	T34	68
	36	ORD	1840	*1505	SK 942	FY D10	CPH *1155	SK 783	Y	D9S	68
	1	ORD	1840	*1505	SK 946	FY D8S	CPH *1155	SK 783	Y	D9S	
	4	ORD	1840	*1345	SK 946	FY D8S	CPH *1155	MA 751	Y	T34	

The two pages of notes in small print are not reproduced here, but they enable the reader to know that the first trip on the schedule, SAS Flight 942, operating on Tuesday (2), Friday (5), and Sunday (7) leaves O'Hare Airport (ORD) at 6:40 p.m. (1840) and arrives in Budapest at 1:45 p.m. (1345) the following day (*). The equipment is a DC10 (D10) plane. There is no direct flight to Budapest on SAS, and passengers must change in Copenhagen to Malev Flight 751, which leaves at 11:55 a.m. using Tupalev (T34) equipment. The last number on the line (68) refers to a footnote saying that on Friday the Chicago-to-Copenhagen flight is made on a Super DC8 (D8S).

Timetables for foreign airlines are usually based on the 24-hour clock. Because of the frequency with which they are changed, fares are usually not listed in international schedules.

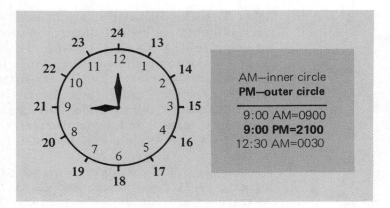

24-Hour Clock

Travel by Ship

Some travelers go to Europe one way by plane and the other way by ship so that they can combine business with vacation. An executive would choose either luxurious first-class or less glamorous but still very comfortable cabin-class passage. There is a trend today toward one- or two-class ships.

On many ships there are two seatings for dinner, so the travel agent should be told the passenger's preference in this matter as well as in the number of other diners preferred at the table. The agent can make the necessary arrangements before the ship sails.

Train Transportation

Most foreign railroads provide three classes of service: (1) *first-class* accommodations with four to six persons in a compartment, (2) *second-class* accommodations with six to eight persons, and (3) *third-class* accommodations where passengers sit on wooden, unupholstered seats. Seat reservations are necessary for first-class travel.

Sleeping cars are of the compartment type. Reservations well in advance of the trip are recommended, for it is often difficult to obtain sleeping-car (*wagon-lit*) accommodations. Extra-fare trains carrying first- and second-class sleepers only are available on the most important international routes. These deluxe trains with individual seats are also available for day travel.

Restaurant cars are attached to most express trains. Before the meal, the dining-car conductor comes through the train and takes reservations. The meal is served at an announced time at one seating only in most countries.

It is possible to buy a Eurail Pass *in this country only* that entitles the holder to unlimited train travel in European countries during the length of time specified on the ticket. Several foreign railway systems maintain ticket and information offices in major cities in America.

Hotel Reservations

Hotel reservations can be made through the travel agent either in this country or abroad or through the airline used. Business guides indicate whether secretarial services or meeting rooms are available in listed hotels. Breakfast is included in the hotel charge in Great Britain and frequently in the Netherlands. In other countries in Europe a continental breakfast, consisting of a hot beverage and a roll, is included.

Automobile Rentals

Rented automobiles are as readily available in larger foreign cities as in the United States. Flight schedules indicate whether this service can be secured at the airport. Rental can be arranged by the travel agent here, and it is usually possible to leave the car at a designated point rather than return it to the place of rental.

In most countries a United States driver's license is sufficient; but to be on the safe side, the traveler may obtain an American International Driving Permit from the American Automobile Association either here or in Europe for a small fee.

TRAVEL DETAILS HANDLED BY THE SECRETARY

The groundwork for planning a trip will probably be laid during a conference between the executive and the secretary. The executive will mention the places to be visited and the dates, and perhaps the names of preferred hotels. For example, if your employer in Omaha told you of a proposed business trip to visit the factory in West Chester on Monday, March 2, keep appointments in Brussels on March 4, meet with an executive in Paris on March 5, return to Omaha by way of New York, have a one-hour conference at the New York airport, and be back at the office on March 9, you would arrange all the details of the trip.

Planning the Trip

Planning a trip requires checking transportation schedules, researching hotel information, and making necessary reservations. In the case just given, you would route the executive by air to Philadelphia, from Philadelphia to Brussels, from Brussels to Paris, from

Paris to New York, and from New York back to Omaha. First you would obtain and study current timetable folders of airlines or discuss possible flights with airline reservation clerks or travel agents. You might also consult the transportation department in your own company. You would also list pertinent information about hotels or motels from a directory such as the *Hotel and Motel Red Book* (published annually by the American Hotel Association Directory Corporation), or *Leahy's Hotel Guide and Travel Atlas of the United States, Canada, and Mexico*, or regional directories published by the American Automobile Association or the oil companies. These directories give the number of rooms, the rates, and whether (in the case of a hotel) the lodging is operated on the European or the American plan. Under the European plan the rate represents the cost of the room only. Under the American plan the rate includes the cost of meals as well as the cost of the room. Most commercial hotels are European plan. A travel agency is especially helpful in choosing hotels.

Room rates quoted in a directory are for one night's lodging. Many hotels offer a reduced rate for occupancy of a room during the daytime only. This service is desirable for use as daytime headquarters when the traveler will be in the city for only a few hours. Since the time of arrival is often early morning, the executive may want to pay in advance and register a night earlier to be assured of accommodations before the midafternoon checkout hour.

If a rented automobile is to be used, a motel may be preferable to a hotel. In any case, you should check distances from the airport to the accommodations and to the meeting place. If a motel is chosen, it should be one that is near the destination. Nothing is more disconcerting than to find oneself across town from the appointment location.

Making Reservations

When the executive has selected the flights to be used and the accommodations preferred, you can make the actual airline reservations — without outside assistance (not recommended for overseas trips), with the help of the transportation department in your company, or in cooperation with a travel agency.

If you make the reservations for lodging yourself, the requests should be specific, including the items listed below:

Kind of Room Desired — one room or a suite (location away from elevator, above a certain floor, with a view, etc.)

Kind of Accommodations — twin beds; studio; tub or shower bath

Approximate or Relative Rate — medium-priced or luxury-priced room

Number of Persons in the Party

Date and Approximate Time of Registration (If Known) — after 6 p.m.; 9 p.m. (If the executive may be late in arriving, a "guaranteed-arrival" reservation can be made. The room will be held, but the guest will be billed even if the room is unoccupied).

Type of Transportation — because of uncertainty of time of arrival if by plane

Probable Length of Time Accommodation Is Needed

There are several ways of making a reservation. Hotels and motels in a chain such as Hilton or Sheraton have communication systems for making reservations with other member hotels. A telephone call to the local hotel or motel assures the reservation in a member hotel. Out-of-town hotels sometimes maintain in major cities local offices where the reservation can be made. Once again, check the Yellow Pages, where numbers can even be found for making reservations for hotels in Japan and Europe. A free world-wide directory can be obtained from American Express Reservations, Inc., Box G-10, 770 Broadway, New York, NY 10003. Most airlines also make hotel-motel reservations for their passengers. Some of them have a business tie-up with hotel chains. (Examples are United Airlines and Western International Hotels; TWA and Hilton Hotels; and American Airlines and Americana Hotels.) The secretary in a company with teletypewriter equipment may ask its operator to request reservations; large hotels have teletypewriters. The secretary can write for a reservation if there is sufficient time or telephone or telegraph if not.

In requesting a hotel-motel reservation, it is important to mention the business connection, as a special commercial rate may be involved. (Special rates are usually available to guests attending a convention.)

Confirmation policies differ; however, it is always safe to request a confirmation that the executive can have in hand when registering. Rooms are at a premium in many cities, and a confirmed reservation is a good precaution.

To simplify their accounting, some hotels and motels request that a deposit *not* be sent. Smaller operations may require a deposit.

Preparing the Itinerary

You can perform an important secretarial function by preparing a comprehensive itinerary for the executive to take on the trip. The usual itinerary (which is prepared by a travel agency if you use its services) covers only *when*, *where*, and *how* the traveler will go. An itinerary serves also as a daily appointment calendar. It contains helpful reminders and mentions the tickets and business papers taken along. The executive may request a number of copies for associates and family so that mail and messages can be forwarded and emergencies reported. Foresight and analysis are required to be able to prepare this type of itinerary.

A good way to start is to set up a file on the trip as soon as it enters the planning stage. In it, place the memorandum prepared on convenient flights and trains, the purchased tickets, the reservations made, the confirmations received, the appointments obtained, the factual material needed for scheduled meetings and appointments — in fact, everything that pertains to the trip. When it is time to prepare the itinerary, the items and notes can be sorted into chronological sequence according to the day and time each will come up. It is then an easy matter to list and describe each item in order. The sample on page 389 shows the detail and thoroughness with which an itinerary should be prepared.

Some executives prefer to carry two documents: the itinerary prepared by the travel agency and an appointment schedule, as shown below. The appointment schedule will show the time, persons having appointments, how to get in touch with them, location of the appointment, and special notes about the meeting or the person.

APPOINTMENT   SCHEDULE

City	GMT* Date/Time	With	Telephone	Address of Appt.	Remarks
London	Thursday, Aug. 6, 9 a.m.	Elizabeth Morse	Mansion House 3312	To be arranged	Telephone Mrs. Morse on arrival. Folder A contains papers for meeting.
	" 1 p.m.	Hubert Poling	Waterside Savoy 1113	"	Mr. Poling is arranging meeting with patent lawyer. Folder B contains patent information.

*Greenwich Mean Time

For an overseas (or extended) trip the executive may find it desirable to have two separate forms — (1) a travel itinerary prepared by a travel agent, and (2) an appointment schedule.

ITINERARY FOR J. B. KELLIKER

March 1 - 6, 19--

SUNDAY, MARCH 1 (Omaha to Philadelphia) No direct flights available

4:15 p.m. Leave Omaha on American Flight 23. Change in Chicago to United
           Flight 302 leaving at 6:15 p.m.
10:21 p.m. Arrive in Philadelphia. Guaranteed arrival reservation at Warwick
           Hotel (Confirmation attached)

MONDAY, MARCH 2 (West Chester Plant)

Take Southeastern Pennsylvania Transportation Authority Conrail commuter train
from Penn Center Station. Frequent service.
(Papers in briefcase)

TUESDAY, MARCH 3 (En Route to Brussels)

9 a.m.   Leave Philadelphia on American Flight 2 to LaGuardia Airport (New York)
         to connect with Sabena Flight 34 to Brussels.
11 a.m. Leave for Brussels.
5 p.m.   Arrive in Brussels. Reservation at Intercontinental Hotel (Reservation
         attached)

WEDNESDAY, MARCH 4 (Brussels)

9 a.m.   Interview at La Societe Generale, Room 913, with Johann Schmidt about
         development of European office in Brussels. (Prospectus in briefcase)
1 p.m.   Lunch at La Maison du Cygne with Madame Helene Moal and three colleagues
         for same purpose. (Confirm by telephone after 11 a.m.) (Prospectus in
         briefcase)
5 p.m.   Leave for Paris on Sabena Flight 711 to LeBourget Airport.
6:21 p.m. Arrive in Paris. Reservation at the George V Hotel. (Reservation
         attached)

THURSDAY, MARCH 5 (Paris)

10 a.m. Appointment with Martha Dillon at Citibank, 43 Rue de la Paix.
         (Financial statements in briefcase)
         Afternoon free.
8:30 p.m. Dinner at Maxim's with Roger Symonds. (Telephone 45-334)

FRIDAY, MARCH 6 (En Route to Omaha via New York)

12 Noon   Leave from Charles de Gaulle Airport on TWA Flight 803.
2:55 p.m. Arrive at Kennedy Airport where Tom McQuiddy will meet your flight with
          a car. Conference at International Hotel at airport. (Daytime reserva-
          tion enclosed) (Papers in McQuiddy folder)
4:45 p.m. Leave Kennedy Airport for Chicago on TWA Flight 347.
6:07 p.m. Arrive at O'Hare Airport in Chicago.
6:45 p.m. Leave Chicago on Frontier Flight 46 for Omaha.
7:51 p.m. Arrive at Omaha airport.

Carrying Travel Funds

Often you must ask the executive whether you are to get money for the trip from the company's cashier or the bank. If it is an overseas trip, you determine whether there are any restrictions in the amount of currency that may be taken into the countries to be visited. You can order a $10 packet of foreign currencies for each country through the bank, or you can remind the executive to purchase one at the automatic vending machines in most international airports. It is always a good idea to provide a number of convenient $1 bills.

Traveler's Checks. You should remind the executive who plans to carry *traveler's checks* that they must be purchased by the person who will use them and by nobody else. Traveler's checks are issued by American Express, Citibank, Bank of America, and Barclay's Bank in denominations of $10, $20, $50, and $100. Usually they cost $1 for each $100 of checks, but some banks issue them without charge especially during certain times of the year. An executive wishing to take $500 on a trip might take $100 in cash and the rest in traveler's checks.

Each traveler's check is numbered and printed on a special kind of paper. The purchaser signs each check on a line near the top before an agent of the issuing company. To cash one of the checks, the purchaser takes it to a business concern, bank, hotel, or American Express office and signs the check again at the bottom in front of the person paying out the money. Such checks are as acceptable as cash and constitute almost personalized money, because anyone other than the purchaser must forge the purchaser's name on each check in the presence of another person in order to cash it. The secretary should prepare a record in duplicate of the numbers and amounts of the checks issued, one for the files and one for the executive to carry so that reimbursement can be immediate in case the checks are lost or stolen.

It is now possible for an American Express card holder to obtain a special Personal Identification number. This number can be inserted along with the American Express card into a dispenser located in large airports and the holder can obtain automatically up to $500 in American Express traveler's checks. The holder of the Personal Identification number must authorize American Express to draw a bank check for the amount specified whenever the dispenser issues a traveler's check.

As a hedge against a decline in value of American currency while out of the country, a traveler can now buy American Express traveler's checks in some foreign currencies, such as Canadian dollars, pounds sterling, Swiss francs and West German deutsche marks.

Money Orders. Sometimes the secretary acts as an advance money agent who supplies the traveling executives of the firm with company funds through express money orders. Traveler's checks cannot be used for this purpose because they must be signed at the time of their purchase by the person who is to use them. In order to facilitate the cashing of express money orders the American Express Company furnishes identification cards which include the signature of the bearer.

The executive who is stranded without funds can always wire the secretary to send a money order by telegraph. The secretary takes the cash, cashier's check, or money order to the Western Union office, which in turn telegraphs the distant office to pay that amount to the designated person just as soon as an identification test is passed.

Letters of Credit. Sometimes a letter of credit is used when extensive travel is involved or when the amount of travel funds required is relatively large. The cost for a large amount of money through a letter of credit is considerably less than the cost of traveler's checks. A letter of credit can be obtained from the local bank. It indicates the person to whom it is issued, and that person is identified by signature on an identification card. It also states the amount the holder is entitled to draw on the issuing bank. To obtain funds, the holder presents the letter of credit to any one of the designated banks in the city being visited. The amounts drawn are recorded on the letter of credit so that the balance that can still be drawn is always known.

Credit Cards. A recent trend is toward extensive use of multipurpose credit cards. Airline, railway, telephone, hotel, American Express, VISA, MasterCharge, Diner's Club, and similar credit cards permit the holder to charge practically any service or goods to a personal or company charge account. Credit cards should be carried in the wallet, ready for presentation when needed. Your only secretarial responsibility for credit cards is in requesting renewals on those which expire and in keeping the serial numbers on file. Credit-card charges help the secretary in preparing expense reports and enable the executive to verify expenses.

Securing Insurance

The employing company sometimes buys blanket insurance policies covering executives while they are traveling on company business. In addition, it usually has rules governing the purchase of trip insurance at the airport. The secretary is expected to investigate company policy about travel insurance and follow through to see that the executive is appropriately covered.

Assisting in Departure

The secretary is frequently charged with packing the briefcase that accompanies the executive. This is an important responsibility, for the effectiveness of any business trip is determined by the accessibility of relevant material when it is needed.

When you learn that a trip is "in the making," start immediately to assemble materials to be taken along and to procure tickets and other papers necessary for the trip. Check the appointment book and ask how your employer wants to handle any scheduled appointments. Check on any personal items (rent, insurance, or income tax payments) that may fall due before the trip is over and get instructions for handling them. Write any preliminary letters that will increase the effectiveness of the trip. You and your employer will decide how expected mail is to be handled. Find out *who* is responsible for *what* during the trip.

Just before departure, hand the executive all of the documents procured, prepared, and kept safe:

Travel tickets (also a schedule of alternate flights)

Notes about reconfirming reservations for foreign flights at least 72 hours before departure

Hotel and motel confirmations

Travel funds (money packet of foreign currency for first stop, traveler's checks) and an American International Driving Permit (unless the secretary has determined that a United States driver's license is sufficient)

Car rental arrangements

Itinerary (both a detailed one and a thumbnail copy on a card)

Address book (including addresses of any people to be visited in the area)

Passport, International Certificates of Vaccination, and baggage identification labels for foreign travel

Papers to be taken along (Bulky materials may be sent air express on the same plane. A separate envelope for each appointment is recommended, including carbon copies of previous relevant correspondence, lists of people to be seen and their positions in their companies, and memorandums about matters to be discussed.)

A personal checkbook and expense-account forms

A supply of business cards for foreign calls

Personal items such as medication or extra eyeglasses

Typed address labels which can easily be attached to letters for known correspondents, such as the executive's family, secretary, or the president of the company

WHILE THE EXECUTIVE IS AWAY

While the executive is away, the secretary assumes greater responsibility for smooth operation of the office. But members of the management team also share the decision-making role involving problems usually handled by your employer. Sometimes it is better to discuss a perplexing situation with an executive who has been designated to handle crises than to assume too much authority. Routine matters, of course, should be taken care of promptly by the secretary.

The executive who wants to keep in touch with home base usually telephones the office daily, especially if the company uses WATS service. If you expect your employer to call you, you should keep notes about situations you want to discuss.

Your performance while the executive is away is just as important as (and sometimes more so than) when the executive is present. Other employees may be quick to notice whether you are busy or frittering away time, but the competent secretary will *automatically* have organized the work so that there is little time to be idle.

Upon return, the executive will be grateful and pleased if you have taken care of routine matters, kept records of office activities for review, and arranged the matters that require attention in terms of their importance. The materials that have been accumulated should be separated into two groups:

1. Matters already taken care of by you or others
2. Matters to be handled by the executive personally

You should place the first group in a folder marked "Information Only." The second group goes into a folder marked "Important." Just before presenting the folders, you should arrange the materials in each folder into logical order, with the most important on top.

The executive also likes to know who telephoned or visited the office, although in some instances this information is of more interest than importance. A list of future appointments and engagements should obviously be included in the "Important" folder.

If the trip is long, the executive may ask you to forward copies of documents that require personal attention (refer to pages 166–168 for proper processing of the mail). And the executive always appreciates a letter relating interesting developments in the office. Two copies of mail may be sent to the traveler — one to the destination on the itinerary and one to the next point to be visited, in case mail service is slower than expected.

FOLLOW-UP ACTIVITIES

After the executive returns to the office, a flurry of activity is required to wind up the trip. First are the expense accounts.

Expense Reports

Some firms advance funds for travel. Periodically or when the trip is over, the executive submits a complete report on the results and the expenses incurred. In other companies executives advance their own funds and are reimbursed later in accordance with the expense report submitted and approved. In either case the executive must keep an accurate record of the dates and times of travel, the conveyances used, and the costs. Some organizations require receipts for hotel and other accommodations and for any expenses above an established minimum. The traveler's word is usually taken for the amount of taxi fares, meals, and tips; but such items must usually be listed or itemized. If you realize that it takes well over $100 a day to keep a company salesperson on the road (and even more to finance an executive's travel), you will understand the importance of this facet of your work.

Expense-account forms are usually provided by the company and need only be filled in correctly and completely and totaled. The secretary should, however, check the executive's present accounting with previous reports to make sure that the amounts for such items as taxis and meals are reasonable and that the flight and rail fares are correct. Reimbursement is frequently held up until all items are in line and approved by the auditor's office.

Letters

Thank-you letters must be sent to show appreciation for favors during the trip. The need for other letters will be generated by the nature of the trip.

Files

Materials will be unpacked and returned to the files. Duplicate files can be destroyed. Files will be updated by the secretary to reflect any changes originated by the trip.

SUGGESTED READINGS

Several of the airlines publish special periodicals for the business traveler that are available without charge to possible business customers. In this highly competitive field of travel some airlines distribute complimentary handbooks on business travel and international trade: Japan Air Lines' *Executive Guide to the Orient*, Air France's *Business Travelers' Guide to Paris*, Sabena Airlines' booklet on business travel, and Pan American's *Frequent Traveler's Bulletins*.

Doing Business in Japan. New York: Japan Air Lines (Purchase only).

Flanagan, William G. *The Smart Executive's Guide for Major American Cities*. New York: William Morrow & Co., 1975.

The 1976 Guide to Traveling on Business in 160 Countries. Cambridge: Executive Publications (Revised annually).

The 1976 Guide to Traveling on Business in the USA. Cambridge: Executive Publications (Revised annually).

Winter, Elmer L. *The Successful Manager-Secretary Team*. West Nyack: Parker Publishing Co., 1974, Ch. 15, "Tips to Help You Prepare for a Trip," pp. 107–116.

World Trade with China. New York: Pan American Airlines (Purchase only).

QUESTIONS FOR DISCUSSION

1. What are the secretary's responsibilities for travel arrangements if there is an in-company transportation department?

2. In what ways can you inform yourself about current changes in air and rail travel? Just to show that you are alert to such changes, report any recent plan not described in the chapter.

3. If stranded without cash while on a business trip, what would a business executive do?

4. What air service would a business traveler probably choose between Los Angeles and San Francisco?

5. What criteria should the secretary use in determining what mail to forward to an executive away on a business trip? What procedures should be used in forwarding this mail?

6. What would be the procedure when the employer planning an overseas business trip requests the secretary to get a renewed passport, the necessary visas, and traveler's checks?

7. Just after your employer has left on a somewhat lengthy business trip by plane, you discover on your desk the itinerary, reservation letters, and appointment schedule. What would you do?

8. Why is it recommended that the services of a travel agency be enlisted in planning an overseas trip?

9. Your employer who is visiting a dissatisfied customer in a distant city telephones to ask you to mail at once the entire correspondence file relating to this customer. There is a strict company rule that no files can be taken from the building. What would you do?

10. If an employer delays in submitting expense reports, how can you make it easier to meet deadlines for such reports?

11. You are asked to write either of your two senators to request a certain report. How would you type the address and salutation? Refer to the Reference Guide to check your answer.

12. Type the following sentences correctly. Then refer to the Reference Guide to verify or correct your answers. Tell which Reference Guide entry you used for each reference.
    (a) The Case Western Reserve library is closed on Mondays.
    (b) Go to room 10 of the library this noon, please.
    (c) U.S. route 4 is within a half mile of our office.
    (d) All we know is: he is an american who upholds democracy.

PROBLEMS

1. Working individually, or as a member of a team as your instructor directs, use travel schedules provided in your classroom. Recommend the best services available for a trip to Miami, Florida, for a two-day student convention.

2. Referring to the American Airlines schedule on page 369, answer these questions:
   (a) What is the difference in cost between a first-class flight and a coach flight between New York and Phoenix?
   (b) What is the telephone number of the American Airlines office in Phoenix?
   (c) Which flights show movies? Which flights provide audio for short subjects?

3. You are secretary to T. M. Jonas, the sales manager of a corporation in St. Louis. You are to plan a visit to the five regional offices for your employer. The offices are located in Minneapolis, San Diego, Naugatuck (Connecticut), Portland (Oregon), and Birmingham (Alabama). It is your decision to establish the order in which the cities will be visited.

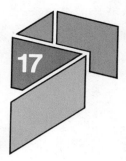

Expediting Meetings

Executives move from meeting to meeting in what seems like endless succession. As business leans more and more on the concept of participatory management, decisions are usually those of a group, not of an individual.

An executive participates in regularly scheduled meetings of long-term committees such as the financial committee, the employee-benefits committee, or the communications-media committee. Special committees, established to perform one specific function and then dissolve, also claim attention. The committee on recommendations for standardization of office forms, the committee on employee-performance appraisal, or the committee on avoiding a strike in the XYZ plant, for example, hammer out both policy and strategy before recommendations are made to the larger group. Top management is responsible for the annual corporation meeting where it accounts to the stockholders for results. Executives also hold meetings to explain procedures for instituting new practices or to acquaint other employees with a new product.

In addition to these job-related meetings, executives participate in many organizations in the outside community, often assuming a leadership role. They also attend numerous workshops, symposia, and conventions where they exchange ideas with people with similar interests and learn new developments that will improve their job performance. In fact, they are often speakers at such meetings.

All types of secretaries are involved, too, in the many activities required to make all of these meetings effective. The multifunctional secretary handles all of the tasks described in this chapter. The administrative secretary helps with many of the preliminary activities and with follow-up duties. The correspondence secretary may have responsibility for sending notices of meetings and processing the reports that emerge from meetings.

COMMITTEE MEETINGS OR INFORMAL OFFICE CONFERENCES

Many office meetings do not involve complicated arrangements. The secretary, however, may have to spend considerable time on the telephone with the secretaries of other executives in trying to schedule a possible meeting time. After the time is agreed upon, it is still a precautionary measure to send a confirming note reminding those who are to attend of the time and place. If the meeting takes place in the executive's office, the secretary makes sure that the room is in good order with enough chairs available for all members and that all the materials needed are assembled. One way to create an atmosphere of relaxation is to provide coffee — even if Styrofoam cups, plastic spoons, instant coffee, and powdered cream are used.

During the meeting the secretary may be asked to take notes. Recommended conference procedure suggests that the chairperson summarize the actions and consensus of the meeting. The secretary reporting a meeting for such a chairperson is lucky. Many office conferences, however, are informal discussions where opinions are exchanged, conclusions are reached, and recommendations are made with no observance of protocol. In these cases the secretary, working alone, is expected to make a summary — subject to the executive's revision, of course — to be distributed to all participants. Certainly, if during the meeting it is agreed that certain conferees take specific action, as a reminder the secretary should send each a copy of the report *with the agreed-upon action underlined*.

Informal business meetings may follow no protocol. The proceedings may be recorded for later transcription by the secretary, as shown here, or the secretary may attend and take notes.

Lanier Business Products

FORMAL MEETINGS

Just as soon as you know that a meeting is to be called, you should set up a file folder, listing on the caption the name of the meeting and its date. Into this folder goes every bit of relevant information that crosses your desk during the planning stages. When you prepare the agenda or later attend the meeting, you will derive much help from this folder.

If you are involved in planning a local meeting, the hotel personnel will make useful suggestions about facilities. For out-of-town meetings, you might inquire of the airlines and hotels involved whether they provide any type of planning service. Certainly they will coordinate the flight arrangements of the conferees and provide rooms, meals, and meeting rooms equipped with such necessary facilities as lecterns, chalkboards, or flip charts. Most international airlines provide conference facilities at airports for their passengers' use.

A hotel in which a convention is held customarily provides a complimentary room or suite for the president of the organization. The person making conference arrangements should also inquire as to whether or not meeting rooms are complimentary. These items should be included in the contract with the hotel.

Reserving the Meeting Room

The first detail to be taken care of by the secretary in making arrangements for a meeting is that of reserving the meeting room. This must be done before notices are sent out. What usually happens is something similar to this. The executive says, "Will you call a meeting on budget requests for next Wednesday afternoon at two?" Since these meetings have customarily been held in the conference room, you know that you are to check immediately to see that the room is available. You should also sign with the appropriate person for use of the room during the hours usually required for such meetings — and, as a safety measure, a little longer. Nothing is more embarrassing to the chairperson of a meeting — and more guaranteed to arouse animosity toward the secretary who is responsible — than to find that the room in which the meeting is to be held is already in use.

In case the meeting is to be held in a hotel, the secretary should be sure also that the meeting place and hour are posted correctly on the announcement board in the lobby and in the elevators. Usually, all participants have traveled a distance to the meeting, and it is annoying to reach the hotel at the last minute and be unable to locate the meeting.

Notices of Meetings

The secretary's responsibility for taking care of the notices of a meeting frequently involves the five steps listed below:

1. Making the calendar notation

2. Preparing the mailing list

3. Composing the notice

4. Typing and sending the notices

5. Handling the follow-up work

Making the Calendar Notations. The secretary must make follow-up notations on the calendar as a self-reminder to prepare and send the meeting notices. Make the notations on dates far enough ahead to allow time for the notices to be composed, reproduced, and delivered several days before the meeting. Notices that are too early may be forgotten. And while the notice for an office conference of staff personnel could be delivered the day before the meeting, an office conference of traveling salespeople might require two weeks' notice. You should also make a calendar notation for several days before the date of the meeting in order to confirm room reservations.

Preparing the Mailing List. Mailing lists of persons to receive notices of meetings are kept in several ways depending on the equipment available. If your organization has word processing equipment, the mailing lists can be put on one input medium and can be merged during the play-out with the notice itself from another input source. Even if the multifunctional secretary is outside the periphery of daily use of a word processing center, this is the type of routine work that might be handled in the center easily. Either the multifunctional secretary or the administrative secretary would be responsible for submitting alphabetized lists of names of those to receive notices for each type of meeting and for sending to the center changes in the mailing lists promptly as they occur. The correspondence secretary would be responsible for producing the properly addressed notices.

The multifunctional secretary and the administrative secretary should keep card files of the names and addresses of those who are to receive notices periodically. Type the addresses in either of two ways: Invert the name for easy filing (and follow with the address as it will appear on the notice), or type the entire item exactly as it will appear on the notice, perhaps underlining the last name as a filing aid. Type some sort of identifying signal beside each address, such as *AMS* to indicate that the addressee belongs on the Administrative

Management Society list. List or file by the last name of the addressee, using a systematic arrangement — straight alphabetic or alphabetically under geographic area, committee, group, or team.

If an addressing machine is available, the secretary may prepare plates for those who receive frequent notices. These plates are classified and filed in drawers marked for easy selection. For instance, tabs on plates for the total membership of an organization might be white; and tabs on plates for the heads of committees might be pink. An entire drawer is inserted into the addressing machine, and the list of notices can be quickly addressed. The machine can also be programmed to select only the pink-tabbed plates from among those in the drawer, thereby controlling a mailing to committee heads only. The plates are automatically replaced in the drawer after usage. Also, envelopes or cards can be addressed during slack periods so that one set is always ready for use. Where addressing-machine plates are impractical, run master copies of address lists on a duplicator.

An address list must be kept up to date. In addition to making changes as reported, once a year the secretary should send out double postcards for the membership to use in reporting their current addresses. When a change of address occurs, the secretary corrects the mailing list or makes a new addressing-machine plate and inserts it at the proper position in the drawer.

Composing the Notice. Simple notices can be composed by the secretary for approval by the executive. The notice of the previous meeting is a good model to follow if it specifies the day, the date, the time, the place, and either the purpose of a special meeting or the fact that it is a regularly scheduled one. The secretary who is required to prepare an agenda of items to be discussed at the meeting should send a request for agenda items along with the notice of the meeting.

Before a notice of an official meeting is sent out, the legal department should check the organization's bylaws for any stipulations of certain information necessary for an item to be acted upon at the meeting. For instance, the bylaws may require that the notice include a statement that no dividends can be voted upon unless the question of dividends is discussed at the meeting. Even in a less formal situation, it is desirable to indicate the agenda of the meeting in the notice.

In preparing a notice of a corporation meeting, the secretary should enclose with the notice a form on which the shareholder may execute a proxy. Signing a proxy authorizes someone else to vote the stock if the shareholder is absent from the meeting. Because this notice must include a detailed list of the business to be transacted,

```
MEETING     The Personnel Directors Club of Oklahoma City

TIME        Monday, October 3, 19--

PLACE       Sheraton-Oklahoma Hotel (Room 421)
            228 West Sheridan Street

PANEL       Kevin Schwartz, Phillips Petroleum; Sandra
MEMBERS     Krey, Peoples Insurance; M. M. VanHorst,
            Methodist Hospital

TOPIC       "Meeting Affirmative Action Standards"

LUNCHEON    $6.50   (Make checks payable to PDC.)

Please return your reservation card to reach secretary
by October 1.  You must cancel reservations by 11 a.m.
of the day of the meeting or be billed for the luncheon.

Telephone 834-5667 (Sarah Brown)
```

This notice is part of a double postcard. The return portion is preaddressed to the secretary and provides spaces for the recipient's name and number of reservations required for self and guests.

the reasons for soliciting the proxy, and other information specifically required by law, it is usually prepared by the corporate legal department.

Typing and Sending the Notice. For small groups the notice is either typewritten or telephoned. For large meetings the notice is printed or reproduced by some duplicating process.

Postcard notices should be typed attractively, with the message neatly displayed. A simple, double-spaced form is acceptable for short notices. Some secretaries underline the important words.

If the secretary is sending notices of regular meetings, a form may be printed or duplicated at the beginning of the club year so that the

```
                                        November 19, 19--

To the Budget Committee

    Donald Wang
    C. B. Newman
  ✓ Marian Sternberg

The Budget Committee will meet in the Conference Room at 10 a.m.
on November 24.

Please bring to this meeting comparisons of last year's budget
with actual results in your division as of October 31 so that
we can make preliminary estimates of changes that will be
necessary next year.
                                        J. J. Young
```

A duplicated notice of a meeting identifies all members of a committee with the name of the recipient checked off.

date, program topic, or other pertinent information is all that needs to be filled in to complete the form.

Some meetings or conferences are of such importance that the announcement is typed or duplicated on letterhead paper. If only a few names are involved, a tabular listing of the names of those to receive the letter may be typed in place of the usual single name, address, and salutation. With the tabular listing the salutation is a general one, such as "Dear Member," "Dear Committee Member," or "Dear . . . ," with the name to be filled in later. Modern usage permits the omission of the salutation entirely. An individual letter to each person is sometimes used, but that is a time-consuming procedure unless power typing equipment is available.

Because of the high cost of postage, many organizations have discontinued sending double postcards or return stamped envelopes that were formerly used to promote a high percentage of response.

Keeping a copy of the notice and the date of mailing is a precautionary measure that the secretary should adopt.

Handling the Follow-Up Work. The secretary's follow-up duties consist chiefly of recording who and how many will or will not attend the meeting. If return postcards have been furnished, the notice follow-up is merely a matter of sorting the cards into the *will's* and *will-not's*. But usually the follow-up means also telephoning several persons for a definite *yes* or *no*.

One executive who is secretary of a civic luncheon club in a large city sends out duplicated notices one week before the monthly meeting. Two days before the meeting the executive's secretary telephones to inquire of those who have not responded whether they plan to attend. An easy way to record attendance plans is to keep a three-column sheet on which names are listed along with acceptances and refusals. When this record is complete, the secretary telephones the hotel or restaurant, giving the number of reservations.

A helpful secretarial service, especially with a fairly small group, is to make reminder telephone calls to all persons expected or to their secretaries. A diplomatic way to do this is to inquire of the secretary if the executive plans to attend such and such a meeting called for such and such a time, adding in explanation that you are making a final check on probable attendance. Some members may be unable to attend for last-minute reasons; others may explain that they will be late. Fortified with such knowledge, the chairperson can call the meeting to order promptly.

Preparing the Order of Business

Every meeting follows some systematic program, which is planned and outlined before the meeting. In organized groups, this program is usually called the *order of business*. It is called the *agenda* in academic and business meetings and conferences. *Calendar* is the term used at meetings of some legislative bodies, such as a city council.

Several days before the meeting, you should remind the executive who is to preside over a meeting to prepare the order of business. If you know the purpose of the meeting, you can probably type this agenda in rough-draft form for later revision and polishing by your employer. It is definitely a secretarial duty to see that the order of business is ready on meeting day. A review of the bylaws and of the minutes of previous meetings (properly indexed for easy cross-reference) will be of invaluable aid in preparing the order of business and in helping the presiding officer to carry out the agenda in an effective manner.

In small discussion groups each person receives a copy of the order of business or program. Distributing the copies before the meeting is an especially helpful secretarial service in office conferences because it gives those attending the conference time to arrange their thoughts on the question to be discussed. If the meeting has been called to discuss a proposed plan, the secretary can distribute copies of the proposal prior to the meeting to facilitate action at the meeting.

The order of business may be set forth by the organization in its bylaws. If not, the usual order is:

Call to order by presiding officer

Roll call — either oral or observed by secretary

Announcement of quorum (not always done)

Reading of minutes of previous meeting (Sometimes the minutes are circulated before the meeting, and this step is omitted.)

Approval of minutes

Reports of officers ⎫
Reports of standing committees ⎬ Copies are usually given to the secretary.
Reports of special committees ⎭

Unfinished business (taken from previous minutes)

New business

Appointment of committees

Nominations and elections

Date of next meeting

Adjournment

A group that is meeting for the first time appoints a temporary chairperson to preside and a temporary secretary. Later in the initial meeting the group elects permanent officers or appoints a committee to nominate officers and to draw up the constitution and bylaws.

Last-Minute Duties

The secretary's first duty on meeting day is to check on the meeting room to see that the air in the room is fresh; that there are enough chairs, ashtrays, matches, paper, pencils, clips, and pins; and that any requested equipment such as a portable chalkboard or a tape recorder has arrived.

You should next assemble materials in a file folder for the executive, arranging them in the order in which they will be needed as indicated on the agenda.

You should take to the meeting the minutes of previous meetings, a list of those who should attend, a copy of *Robert's Rules of Order* for your employer's reference, the bylaws, a seating chart, blank ballots, and aids similar to those illustrated on page 406 for taking minutes.

Many small business meetings and conferences are recorded on tape. If this is the case, the secretary should make arrangements for setting up the recording machine. One of your responsibilities at the meeting may be to operate the tape recorder.

Unless you have previously done so, your next job is to gather together all the material that will be needed at the meeting —

The secretary prepares a conference room for a meeting. Preliminary duties include adjusting the lights to a level that insures good vision and checking the thermostat so that a comfortable temperature is assured.

Speaker's name _____

Identifying phrase _____

Speaker's name _____

Identifying phrase _____

Speaker's name _____

Identifying phrase _____

To identify the speakers at a taped meeting, this form is helpful. It not only allows space for the name but also for the first phrase or sentence of that person's dialog.

notebooks, pencils, a filled fountain pen, the minutes book, reports to be distributed to participants or perhaps a list of those attending, the companies they represent, and their addresses. It is most embarrassing to have to leave the meeting room several times for things that should already be there. It advertises that you are not very thorough. On the other hand, offering to get records or material on subjects that arise unexpectedly shows willingness to be of help. Before leaving a meeting room, however, the secretary must first get permission from the executive or the presiding officer. You are there to record data for the minutes, either through your own notes or though verbatim recordings of a professional reporter or a tape recorder (supplemented by your own notes taken as an aid in abstracting the important points from the mass of material later).

If you have noted beforehand from the order of business the names of those who are to present topics, you can record the names and topics easily at the meeting. You may also bring along or sketch a seating chart on which to fill in names as you hear them, thus being better able to match names with motions or discussions. If you miss a name, you can jot down some distinguishing characteristic of that person and ask your executive for help after the meeting.

Before the meeting opens, the secretary may have to make introductions, acknowledge introductions, or help with some last-minute arrangements.

Parliamentary Procedure

If you understand parliamentary procedure you can report meetings more accurately. You can also unobtrusively call the attention of the chairperson to any violations of parliamentary rules, such as voting on a motion before voting on an amendment to the motion. Therefore, you should review important points of parliamentary procedure before going to the meeting.

Parliamentary law has been defined as "common sense used in a gracious manner." Its purpose is to arrive at a group decision in an efficient and orderly manner. Parliamentary procedure is based on four principles:

1. Courtesy and justice must be accorded to all.

2. Only one topic is considered at one time.

3. The minority must be heard.

4. The majority must prevail.

Most business is transacted through main motions, which require a majority vote for adoption. A member addresses the chairperson, is recognized, and makes a motion. Another member seconds the motion. After the motion has been made and seconded, the chairperson states the motion, names both the one who made it and the one who seconded it, and calls for discussion. When the discussion ends, a vote is taken, usually by voice. The chairperson announces the result, "The motion is carried (or defeated)." If anyone calls "Division," the chairperson asks for a show of hands or a standing vote. If a majority demands it, the vote must be taken by ballot.

After a main motion has been made, a member of the body can propose an amendment to the motion. If the proposal is seconded, it is discussed. The proposed amendment must be voted upon before the main motion can again be considered. After announcing the action on a proposed amendment, the chairperson says, "The motion now before the house is . . ." and states the original motion plus the amendment, if the amendment carried. If the amendment lost, the original motion is acted upon.

If a motion involves two actions rather than one, a member can move that the question be divided for voting; then each part becomes a separate motion. If a motion is so bogged down that further discussion would seem to be a waste of time and if two thirds of the voting members agree, a member can "move the question," an action that forces an immediate vote. If the latter motion loses, discussion of the original motion continues.

A motion can be made to *table* a motion (to delay further discussion or action). A seconded motion to table must be voted upon at once. A successful motion to table permits the group to consider more important business and sometimes allows a motion to die — although a tabled motion may be taken from the table by a majority vote. (An even surer way to kill a motion is to move that the motion be postponed indefinitely.)

When it becomes obvious that further information is needed, a motion can be made to refer a matter to a committee, which is then named by the chairperson.

By unobtrusively calling the attention of the chairperson to a violation in parliamentary procedure, a secretary may prevent embarrassment to the employer occasioned by a member saying, "I rise to a point of order." When this statement is made, the presiding officer either must decide, without debate, whether the person raising the question is correct in claiming that the rules are being broken or must rely on the parliamentarian for advice. An error or omission in procedure can be pointed out by the secretary by a brief reminder note tactfully phrased.

Privileged motions have precedence over others. One of these is "to call for orders of the day," a motion that, without debate, forces the chairperson to follow the agenda.

The Secretary at the Meeting

The secretary's first duty at the meeting may be to report to the chairperson when a quorum is present. If you are to take full notes, concentrate on taking minutes as unobtrusively as possible. You should, however, ask to have everything repeated that you do not hear distinctly or are unable to get into note form. You may say, "I did not get that," or you may give a prearranged signal to the chairperson, such as raising your left hand slightly. Then the chairperson will ask that the point be repeated. The bylaws of some organizations require that the person making a motion submit the motion to the secretary in writing so that it will be exactly phrased in the minutes. Even here, though, you would be well advised to take the oral motion down verbatim to be sure that the written motion conforms to the oral one.

Too many notes are better than too few. No one turns to the secretary in a meeting and says, "Take this," or "You need not take this." You are simply held responsible for getting everything important in your notes, especially motions, amendments, and decisions. If you are afraid to decide at the instant whether statements are important, you should record them. They can be dropped from the final draft if they later seem inconsequential.

Some essential parts of the minutes may not be specifically recorded at the time of the meeting. The date, time, and place of the

---

BASIC RULES OF VOTING

The types of votes possible are:

1. Majority — a number greater than half the votes cast.
2. Plurality — the most votes cast regardless of majority.
3. Two-thirds vote — two thirds of the votes cast.
4. Tie vote — same number for and against, in which case the motion is considered lost.

The basic methods of voting are as follows:

1. By general consent — the chairperson states, "If there is no objection we will," etc. This method is used for routine decisions.
2. By voice vote — members vote "aye" or "no" by voice for a majority vote.
3. By a show of hands — members raise hands to "affirmative" or "negative." This method is usually used in small groups.
4. Rising vote — members stand to "affirmative" or "negative" for a two-thirds vote.
5. By roll call — each member's name is called and the member votes. This method provides a check on attendance as well as a careful vote.
6. By ballot — this method assures secrecy for the voter.
7. By mail or by proxy — this method can be used only if the bylaws so specify.

Observation: Members may waive their right to vote by abstaining. The bylaws of the organization should specify the vote required for legal action. Majority vote is the basic rule, but the bylaws should define "majority." A majority could mean a majority of those present and voting, majority of legal votes cast, majority of members, or the like.

From the book, *Business Etiquette Handbook* by Parker Editorial Staff © 1965 by Parker Publishing Co., Inc. Published by Parker Publishing Co., Inc., West Nyack, NY.

---

meeting and the name of the presiding officer may not be stated. The roll may be called; but if not, the *secretary is expected to observe and to record* all the details of attendance — who attended, who did not attend, who arrived late, and who left early. The last two items of information are important in recording action on measures voted upon. (Those not wishing to go on record with their votes may absent themselves from a part of the session for just that reason.) To report as present a person who left the meeting during important transactions could have serious consequences.

The secretary depending on a verbatim report of the meeting as the source of minutes will need to make notes of *items that are not likely to appear in the record*: the names of those attending, the official title of the speaker, the time of meeting and adjournment, the

Number present _____

Excused (Names) _____

_____

Absent (Names) _____

_____

_____

Things to do after meeting:

1.

2.

Motion _____

_____

Made by _____

Seconded by _____

Vote for _____   Against _____

Summary of discussion:

Skeleton forms similar to those above help you in taking minutes. These forms may be consolidated on one page or placed on slips to be clipped to shorthand notes. If you list each item on the agenda, leaving after each item plenty of space for notes, you already have a guide for your minutes when the meeting starts.

names of those voting *yes* and *no* to motions, the names of those coming in late and leaving early, and possibly any difficult names and words that may cause confusion in transcription. If you outline the proceedings during the meeting, you can more easily make necessary insertions when you work with the verbatim report.

If it is the secretary's duty to read the minutes of the last meeting, they should be read in a meaningful manner and in a voice loud enough that everyone in attendance will be able to hear what matters were considered and what decisions were made.

After the minutes are read, the presiding officer asks for corrections and additions. Usually this is a mere formality, and the vote approves the minutes as read. In some cases, however, corrections or additions are made. When this happens, the minutes should not be rewritten. The changes should be made in red ink on the copy of the minutes as they were originally written; and, of course, the corrections and additions become a part of the minutes of the meeting at which they are made. To save meeting time, some organizations have a Minutes Committee, whose function is to examine the minutes before the next meeting and report to the membership whether the minutes are in order or what changes should be made.

The order of business follows the agenda. The story of every motion, passed or defeated, must be recorded in the minutes. The name of the person making the motion, the complete motion exactly as stated, the name of the person seconding it, a summary of the pro's and con's given during the discussion, and the decision by vote — all must go into the secretary's notes. Motions written out by their originators and written committee reports are important source documents.

After the business of the meeting is completed, the date of the next meeting is announced, usually just before adjournment. After the meeting has been adjourned, the secretary collects copies of all papers read and all committee reports so that they can be made a part of the minutes. (The committee reports are attached to the minutes.) Before leaving the meeting room, the secretary should check and verify all doubtful or incomplete notes, such as the correct spelling of names and the correct phrasing of a motion.

Follow-Up Work After the Meeting

A great deal of work for the secretary always follows a meeting, aside from putting the meeting room back in order and writing the minutes or proceedings. Items that require future attention must be listed on both the executive's and the secretary's calendars. Individual letters must be written to those elected to membership and to those appointed to serve on committees or requested to perform certain tasks — even though they were at the meeting and are aware of the appointments or assignments. For expenses of participants to be paid by the organization, the secretary should see that necessary forms are completed and reimbursement made as soon as possible. (Many executives send a summary of the meeting to the entire group.)

Resolutions. Often an organization wishes to send an expression of its opinion or will (such as a resolution expressing sympathy on the death of a member or concurrence in a stated objective) in the form

```
                        RESOLUTION
                  Adopted October 11, 19--

WHEREAS, Judith Monique has been a member of the legal firm of
    Killian, Longhill, Paganne, and Monique for the past twelve
    years and during this time has contributed significantly to
    the professional prestige of our company as well as to its
    monetary success; and

WHEREAS, Ms. Monique is leaving the organization to accept an
    appointment as judge of the district court of New Jersey;
    therefore, be it

RESOLVED, that the members of this firm go on record as expressing
    their sincere appreciation of Ms. Monique's services at the
    same time that they wish her well in the judgeship for which
    she is eminently qualified; and be it

RESOLVED FURTHER, that our Secretary send a copy of this reso-
    lution to the Governor of the State of New Jersey.
```

Lucian Paganne
Lucian Paganne, Secretary

K. L. Killian
K. L. Killian, Senior Member

A resolution is usually presented as a formal statement. Each paragraph begins with WHEREAS or RESOLVED typed in capital letters or underlined.

of a resolution to a person or an association. A resolution may be presented at the meeting in writing, or the secretary may be instructed to prepare an appropriate resolution. After the meeting the secretary is responsible for composing or typing the resolution, having it signed and sent out, and incorporating it into the minutes.

Reporting the Meeting. The secretary sometimes encounters a problem in reporting what is *done* at a meeting, for the record reports only what is *said*. To winnow from the discussion the pertinent facts to serve as a record of *what has been decided* and as a guide to *what needs to be done by whom* challenges any secretary's best efforts.

Reports of meetings vary with the degree of formality required. For an office conference, the proceedings are compact and simple. For a meeting of an organization, the report customarily recognizes the efforts of individual members or refers to letters from former members, as well as recording the formal actions taken. The final minutes may not record the events in chronological order if the secretary finds that regrouping around a central theme is clearer. For *official minutes* of a formal nature, however, the proceedings are recorded in the order of occurrence in complete detail, including the exact wording of all motions or resolutions.

Sometimes the secretary records the minutes in the secretary's book only. In other cases, however, it may be desirable to duplicate and distribute the minutes after they have been officially approved by the chairperson. If the minutes are to be referred to at subsequent meetings, duplicated minutes are often prepared with the line numbers typed at the left margin. It is then easy for a speaker to refer to *Page 3, Line 17*, and have the entire group follow the discussion easily.

The secretary can aid the reader in locating each motion by typing in either of the following ways:

Professor Scott moved THAT A SPECIAL COMMITTEE BE ESTABLISHED TO RECOMMEND —

or

Professor Scott moved that a special committee be established to recommend —

The minutes should answer the journalistic questions: What? Where? When? Who? Why? The following suggestions apply to writing minutes of all kinds.

1. Capitalize and center the heading which designates the official title or nature of the group which met, as *Committee V; Student Personnel Services; Recruitment, Guidance, and Placement*.

2. Single- or double-space the minutes and allow generous margins. There is a preference for double-spaced minutes.

MEETING OF THE COMMITTEE TO STANDARDIZE OFFICE FORMS

February 17, 19--

The Committee held its organization meeting in the private dining room in the company cafeteria at 12 noon.

Those present were: Thomas Healey, L. D. Livovich, Margo Margolis, and Merville Perry. Madeline Marshall was absent.

By unanimous vote Miss Margolis was elected chairperson and Mr. Livovich was elected secretary.

The following actions were taken:

Collection of Forms Currently in Use. Using the corporation organization chart, Mr. Healey will assign each member of the Committee a definite number of departments from which to collect all forms presently being used. These forms are to be collected by March 1.

Research on Forms Control. Mr. Livovich will obtain from the company librarian a list of books already available in our library on forms control. He will bring these books to the next meeting of the Committee so that members can volunteer to study those of greatest interest to them. He will also research Books in Print and request that the librarian purchase new books that would be useful. Mr. Perry suggested that the number of new books requested be kept to five, and the group concurred.

Time Schedule. The Committee agreed that its report would be completed by June 1. Mr. Livovich recommended that weekly meetings be held during March. It can be decided later whether weekly or biweekly meetings will be more productive.

The next meeting will be held in the private dining room of the cafeteria at 12:15 p.m. on Monday, February 24.

The meeting was adjourned at 1:15 p.m.

February 17, 19--
Date

L. D. Livovich
L. D. Livovich

The secretary merely summarizes the major actions taken during a meeting that follows no regular order of business. Notice that the simplest typewriting form is used as a time-saver.

3. Prepare the minutes with marginal subject captions for the various sections to expedite locating information. Record each different action in a separate paragraph.

4. Establish that the meeting was properly called and members notified properly. Indicate whether it was a regular or a special meeting.

5. Give the names of the presiding officer and the secretary.

6. Indicate whether a quorum was present, and provide a roll of those present. At official meetings and committee meetings, list those absent.

7. Rough out the minutes with triple spacing for approval by your employer before preparing them in final form.

8. Transcribe notes while they are still fresh in your memory. If that is impossible, you may find it desirable to take the notes home and read through them, getting them in mind for accurate transcription the next day. If minutes for a meeting which you did not attend are dictated to you, be sure that you get all the pertinent data from your employer at the time of the dictation along with any answers to questions.

9. Capitalize such words as *Board of Directors, Company, Corporation*, and *Committee* in the minutes when they refer to the group in session.

10. Send official minutes to the secretary of the organization or presiding officer or both, for signatures. At the end of the minutes type a line for recording the date of their approval. *Respectfully submitted* or *Respectfully* may be used on formal minutes.

11. Do not include personal opinions, interpretations, or comments. Record only business actions, not sentiments or feelings. Such phrases as *outstanding speech, brilliant report*, or *provocative argument* are out of place in the minutes. Where gratitude or appreciation is to be expressed, it should take the form of a resolution.

12. Try to summarize the gist of the discussion about a motion, giving reasons presented for and against its adoption. A recently formed organization interested in improving business records for historical purposes decries the lack of helpful information contained in the minutes of company meetings at all levels. This organization stresses the value of such summaries when later discussions of similar proposals are held.

Indexing the Minutes. Because the composition of committees and organizations is constantly changing, sometimes groups find themselves in embarrassing situations because they do not know the regulations which they, as a body, have previously passed. They may take an action contrary to required procedure; they may violate their own regulations; or they may pass motions that contradict each other. The presiding officer may look at old minute books, which have been preserved since the beginning of the organization, and decide that it will be impossible to ferret out the separate actions on recurring problems. Nothing that you could do for the harassed officer could be more helpful than the preparation and maintenance of an index of the minutes by subject, giving the year

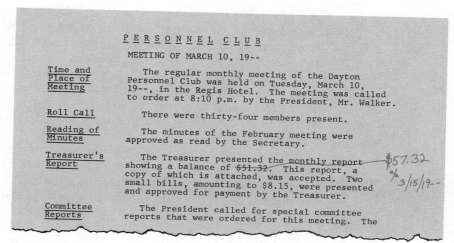

Minutes of a meeting follow the order of business given on page 404. They indicate whether the meeting was a regular or a special one. Marginal headings aid in locating items. The error was corrected by hand, initialed, and dated.

and page number of each action taken. Sometimes a separate volume is used for the minutes of each year.

Writing captions in the margin of the minute book beside the motions passed will facilitate preparing file cards for the index. The file cards should be captioned with the titles and possibly subtitles on which action was taken, along with the year in which the group acted and the page on which the decisions were recorded. For example, a card might show the caption <u>Affirmative Action</u> with references in 1974 on page 36, in 1976 on page 74, and in 1977 on page 93.

Other Duties. The secretary should be especially diligent in processing all forms necessary for prompt payment of honoraria, fees, and expense accounts to those who were part of the program and to those who attended the meeting. A check should also be made to see that appropriate thank-you notes and notifications of committee responsibilities resulting from the meeting are written.

Minutes of Corporations

Corporations are usually required by law to keep a minute book for recording the minutes of meetings of stockholders and directors. Stockholders usually meet once a year, but directors' meetings are held more frequently. Minute books are extremely important legal records. Recorded decisions must be carried out, for they constitute the regulations to which the management must conform.

The records of a corporation are kept by the corporation secretary, a full-time executive who is probably assisted by the secretary performing the type of duties described in this book. The stockholders' and directors' minutes are usually kept in separate books and are of immense legal significance. The minute books must be carefully guarded against substitution or removal of pages by: (a) the use of prenumbered pages, each signed and dated by the corporation secretary, (b) employing pages watermarked with a code symbol, or (c) a keylock binder that can be opened only with a carefully guarded key. Corrections resulting from the reading of the minutes at a subsequent meeting are written in and the incorrect portions ruled out in ink. These changes are initialed in the margin by those signing the minutes.

The minutes of a corporation identify the membership of the group, show the date and place of the meeting, tell whether the meeting is regular or special, give the names of those attending, and contain a complete record of the proceedings. The official secretary of the corporation has full responsibility for the completeness, accuracy, and legality for formal minutes even though a regular secretary may type them.

CONFERENCES AND CONVENTIONS

The executive is likely to participate in numerous conferences and conventions. A *conference* is a discussion or consultation on some important matter, often in a formal meeting. A *convention* is a formal meeting of delegates or members, often the annual assembly of a professional group. The executive's secretary is often involved in planning these events and in follow-up after the actual meeting.

Secretarial Preplanning Responsibilities

Some conferences and conventions require the full-time efforts of a secretary for an entire year. Weeks and months of painstaking work are required to:

1. Secure speakers and tell them explicitly what they are to do and how long a time they will have for their presentations

2. Obtain biographical material from speakers

3. Mail publicity material to prospective participants

4. Prepare menus and plan social activities

5. Prepare or maintain up-to-date mailing lists

6. Provide for the distribution of name tags

7. Possibly secure registrations by mail

8. Publicize the conference or convention

9. Iron out the thousand-and-one necessary details.

Duties at the Meeting

The secretary is challenged at every turn to perform efficiently during the meeting, for even with the best of preplanning, problems are bound to occur. You are responsible for seeing that an opaque projector is available if the speaker specified an opaque projector. Many a visual display has been ruined by the substitution of other visual equipment, such as an overhead projector, that is incompatible with the materials to be projected. You are responsible for finding out whether the hotel uses AC or DC current so that the speaker will not be disappointed because a film cannot be shown. You are the one to see that the projectionist is on hand at the very minute the speaker wants to show slides.

It is up to you to see that the microphones are operating and that repairers are on hand during any presentations. This may involve checking on union regulations. You are the one who remembers to send complimentary tickets for the spouse of the luncheon speaker, to have ice water at the lectern, to check the number of chairs on the platform, and to provide place cards for the speakers' table and arrange them with some sense of protocol. It is you who must follow through with the gracious gestures that send the participants home happy.

Conference Reporting

At many conferences, the proceedings are of such value that they are preserved in permanent form. For example, the American Management Association may hold a conference on employee appraisal and later publish the proceedings as a service to its entire membership and to outside purchasers of the report. These meetings are usually reported by specially trained reporters. Here your function changes from reporter to coordinator. If you work in a situation where outside conference reporters are regularly used, you are expected to locate persons who can do excellent work. Keeping a file of possible reporters, printers, lithographers, and artists — along with an appraisal of the quality of their services — will be an invaluable aid.

As a secretary, you are responsible for all the conference groundwork and probably for all the follow-up work, just as you would be for any other meeting. You should not, however, be concerned with the writing of the conference report — only with the processing of it.

Often registrants at the conference want a copy of the proceedings. This service might be paid for by the registration fee, or an additional charge might be made. In any case the secretary may be responsible for securing mailing addresses of those entitled to the publication.

If papers are read at the conference, each speaker is usually asked to submit the paper prior to (or at) the meeting so that it can be either printed in its entirety or abstracted. It is your responsibility to obtain a copy of this paper for publication. The conference reporter needs to report only the discussion following the presentation of the paper — either from a tape recording or from summary notes. Sometimes the speaker is asked to prepare the summary. Then the reporter has to organize the material; edit it for uniformity of style; and write proper introductions, conclusions, or recommendations.

A final task for the secretary might be to compose recommendations for subsequent meetings, based on experience gained from this one.

The effects of boredom can be disastrous for a meeting. The alert secretary, whether as chairperson of the meeting or as a pre-meeting planner, will find many ways to prevent participants from losing interest.

SUGGESTED READINGS

Auger, Bertrand Y. *How to Run Better Business Meetings*. New York: American Management Association, 1973.

Cromwell, Harvey. *The Compact Guide to Parliamentary Procedure*. New York: Thomas Y. Crowell Co., 1973.

Graham-Helwig, H. *How to Take Minutes*, 8th ed. New York: Beekman Publishers, 1975.

Maude, Barry. *Managing Meetings*. New York: Halsted Press, a division of John Wiley & Sons, 1975.

Robert, Henry M. *Robert's Rules of Order Revised: Seventy-Fifth Anniversary Edition*. New York: William Morrow & Co., 1971.

Snell, Frank. *How to Hold a Better Meeting*. New York: Cornerstone Library, a division of Simon & Schuster, 1974.

Winter, Elmer L. *The Successful Manager-Secretary Team*. West Nyack: Parker Publishing Co., 1974, Ch. 18, "How Your Secretary Can Help Make Your Meeting Go Off Better," pp. 127–130.

QUESTIONS FOR DISCUSSION

1. How could an efficient secretary have improved the last organized meeting you attended:
   (a) before the meeting?
   (b) during the meeting?
   (c) after the session?

2. When should you send notices for the following meetings?
   (a) an informal office meeting
   (b) a bimonthly meeting of a professional organization
   (c) the annual meeting of the board of directors of the American Association of University Women at which reports from all committees are due

3. How do the responsibilities for handling meetings differ when there is a one-to-one secretary-executive relationship rather than a word processing setup?

4. Contrast the methods of keeping mailing lists current when the secretary works alone and when the work is done by the correspondence secretary.

5. How can the secretary alleviate problems in preparing minutes of taped proceedings?

6. Why should the secretary submit a preliminary copy of the minutes before they are typed in final form?

7. What should the secretary do:
   (a) if an unidentified person makes a motion?
   (b) if a person makes a motion that lacks clarity and that is changed several times in phraseology before it is voted on?
   (c) if the chairperson entertains a new motion before the motion on the floor has been disposed of?

8. If a conference is being reported by a professional organization, what is the secretary's responsibility for the summary of the proceedings?

9. While taking notes at an office conference, you feel that the subject being discussed would be clarified by reference to a report in your employer's personal file in the next room. Would you
   (a) write a note to the chairperson asking if you should obtain the report?
   (b) leave the room to obtain it?
   (c) do nothing?

10. Capitalize words as necessary in the following sentences. Then use the Reference Guide to verify or correct your answers.
    (a) Attendance declines in the summer.
    (b) The atomic age brings its own wonders — its own terrible fears.
    (c) Mr. Lawson is the new president of our company.
    (d) We heard an address by president Lawson.
    (e) He hopes to become a professor of marketing.
    (f) The professor of mathematics spoke, too.
    (g) I know professor Lawson well.

PROBLEMS

1. Attend a formal meeting of an organization either inside or outside your college and take notes to use in writing the minutes of the meeting. Compose the minutes in acceptable format as shown in this chapter and submit them to your instructor for evaluation. On a separate sheet indicate any violations of *Robert's Rules of Order* or any deviations from recommended practices observed.

2. The Secretarial Department Club, which used to hold regular meetings every two weeks, has become inactive. You are one of a group of three students who have volunteered to reactivate the organization. You have invited Judy Joyce, secretary to the president of your college and an alumna of your department, to speak at the meeting, which is to be held in the North Lounge next Wednesday between 1 and 2:30 p.m. You and the other members of the committee have decided to contribute cookies and coffee. You want to allow 20 minutes for the election of permanent officers and establishment of the time of the meeting. Plan the meeting in detail.

Should Judy's presentation have a title? Should there be a question-and-answer period? Should the notice indicate that officers will be elected? Who should sign the notice? Prepare a notice of the meeting that will attract every student in the department, using either a double postcard or a full sheet.

3. After a recent conference for which you made most of the arrangements and wrote the minutes, the following complaints were made:
   (a) A participant from 500 miles away could not locate the meeting room, which had been changed the morning of the meeting.
   (b) Two participants were incorrectly identified in the minutes.
   (c) One participant complained that the motion she made was incorrectly worded in the minutes.
   (d) Two participants who were given specific post-conference responsibilities did not perform them and gave the excuse that they had forgotten what had transpired.

What should you do next time to prevent recurrence of these problems?

Part 6   CASE PROBLEMS

Case 6-1
AUTOCRATIC VERSUS PARTICIPATORY MANAGEMENT

Alice Knox, secretary to Laura Jennings, director of personnel, is appointed to a committee of secretaries with responsibility for revising the office style manual. The first meeting, a very informal one, is devoted to selection of a chairperson and establishment of a time schedule. To Alice's great surprise because of her relatively short time with the company, she is chosen as chairperson. Alice leaves the meeting with the statement, "Let's make this manual the pride of the company. Will all of you please come to the next meeting with lots of ideas to share with us."

Alice outlines the manual as she believes it should be arranged. She makes a list of the persons to do each part of the job. Then she compiles cost figures for three different formats for presentation so that the group can choose the one it prefers.

At her first meeting she presents her outline and appoints the persons to be in charge of different duties. When she presents the alternate formats for consideration and decision, she is surprised when a member of the committee says, "Well, I am surprised that you are giving us a choice. Seems to me that you have taken over and are running the show. I don't think that you have chosen the right people for the jobs either. I know, for instance, that I know a lot more about forms of address than Elsie, for we write lots of letters to dignitaries. Elsie knows more about grammar though. I thought that a committee is supposed to be democratic, not autocratic. Why not let us choose our own jobs? Oh, and another thing — I thought that our instructions were to bring in ideas to share with the rest of you."

Should Alice ask the members to shuffle the assignments according to their competencies, or would that action undermine her authority?

What management principle has she ignored?

How should she proceed with her responsibilities after this rebuff?

Case 6-2
HANDLING A SUPERVISORY PROBLEM

The office of the Regal Manufacturing Company has grown from a small office of three employees supervised by Mr. Thompson, president of the company, to an office staff of 20 employees. Up to now, the office staff was responsible to certain officials of the company; that is, certain staff members were responsible to the sales manager, others to the production manager, and so forth. Mr. Thompson has decided to reorganize the office and place the entire staff under the direct supervision of an office manager. Mary Adams has been Mr. Thompson's secretary for the past ten years and has grown with the company. She knows almost all of its operations and policies; she is company-minded and loyal. She knows all of the employees well and is well liked. Mr. Thompson decides that she would be the logical one to place in the newly created position of office supervisor. Mary accepts the position.

Mary's attitude is that she has not changed merely because her title has changed; therefore, she will continue her very close personal friendships with certain members of the office staff. It is Mary's plan to continue to identify with the secretarial and clerical staff, and not with the supervisory staff of the company. Thus, she will continue to eat lunch with the girls in the office and be concerned with their personal problems as she has in the past. The one thing she isn't going to be is high-hat or changed in her relationship with her fellow workers.

When a new employee comes to the office, Mary always makes it clear that, although she is technically the office supervisor, she wants to be treated and considered just as a member of the office gang. Her function is to help them, not to supervise them.

Mary is very hesitant to delegate difficult or unpleasant duties to other members of the staff. She feels that she should not ask others to do things that she herself would not like to do; as a result, she herself does many of the really tough jobs and more unpleasant chores. Whenever she assigns responsibilities, she always does it in the name of some other company official, such as "Mr. Thompson would like you to do this"; or "Mr. Franklin asked me to ask you to do this."

Working on the assumption that most problems will take care of themselves, if just given time, she plans to avoid becoming involved in arbitrating personality problems that arise among the office staff except when the situation becomes extremely serious. She is determined that she is not going to meddle in the petty frictions that are certain to arise when people work together.

How successful do you think Mary Adams will be as a supervisor?

Is Mary the kind of person for whom you would like to work?

Can a supervisor maintain close personal friendships with her working staff?

Should a supervisor ask a subordinate to do a task that she would not wish to do herself?

To what extent should a supervisor become involved in attempting to solve the petty personality problems of the office staff?

Case 6-3
LINES OF AUTHORITY

Ms. Elfverson came back from a trip complaining to her secretary, Lilli LiQuan, about the airline she had traveled on. Lilli had made the arrangements through Marie Koch in the Transportation Department. She knew that Marie usually chose the airline with which her principal had been displeased over others with parallel schedules.

Lilli had a friend who was an airline reservations clerk handling corporate travel accounts only, and she decided that she would discuss with him the best schedules and accommodations for a trip to Chicago that three company executives were to make the following week. She decided on the round-trip flights, telephoned Marie to give her specific requests, and asked her to make the actual reservations.

Marie said indignantly, "Don't tell me which flights to choose. What are you trying to do — take my job away from me?"

Lilli tried to appease her by saying, "But Ms. Elfverson didn't like her flight Wednesday and doesn't like to travel on the airline on which you always put our executives. I was just trying to be helpful."

What is the proper line of authority in this situation? What principle should Lilli follow in trying to handle the situation without troubling Ms. Elfverson?

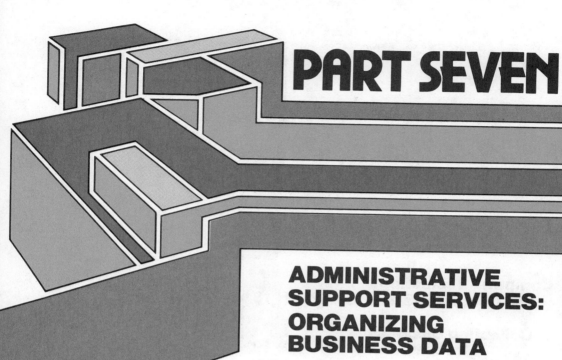

PART SEVEN

ADMINISTRATIVE SUPPORT SERVICES: ORGANIZING BUSINESS DATA

A challenging area of secretarial responsibility is the opportunity to assist in the research of information followed by the preparation of the material in typewritten reports, tables, charts, and other graphic presentations. In accomplishing these duties, the secretary may be working with new tools, such as the video display screen of a computer terminal or a microfilm reader. Systems and procedures in the office will continue to change as technology changes. The professional secretary, therefore, must keep informed on advancements that will affect the way in which data and words are processed in the office.

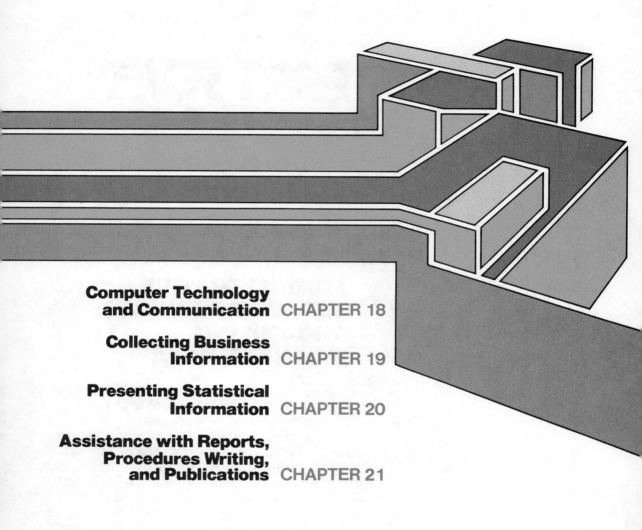

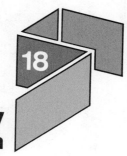

Computer Technology and Communication

For years the unit record (punched card) system accomplished the activities of reading, recording, classifying, sorting, calculating, summarizing, storing, and reporting of business data. For that period of time and at that point in our technological advancement, this system provided the means of processing numerical data rapidly. Today, this system is being replaced by a more sophisticated one — electronic data processing. Surely, this is the era of the computer. Computers are revolutionizing office procedures, as the unit record system once did. In today's office the computer is becoming as commonplace an item as the electric typewriter or the copying machine.

The computer offers an entirely new method of operation for the office executive and the office staff. In addition to processing data, the computer serves as a communication tool. For example, a computer communication network established between a main office of an organization and its branches makes it possible to transmit information in either direction in a matter of seconds. As a result, all decision making within an organization can be centralized; that is, all management decisions can be made from one location.

The secretary in a computerized office, while not expected to be a specialist in computer technology, must know its applications to secretarial duties and must be able to meet the challenges technology brings to the position. Certainly, as a key person on the office staff, the secretary must understand the concept of office automation, the functions involved, and the various methods of processing and communicating data.

ELECTRONIC DATA PROCESSING

An electronic data processing (EDP) system consists of input equipment, a central processing unit (the computer), and output equipment. In this system data are processed several hundred times faster than was possible with unit record equipment. The processing of data is a continuous chain of operations performed within the system rather than by separately operated machines. Information can be stored for immediate or future use in the computer's memory component. Operations are performed by entering a program of instructions into the computer system, and decisions and alternate courses of action are possible through the functioning of the logic unit of the computer.

The computer and its peripheral equipment are referred to as the *hardware* of the system. *Software* is the term used to indicate machine instructions, programs, procedures, rules, operator instructions, and other documentation concerned with the operation of the system.

This section discusses the basic components of the electronic data processing system — the input media and devices, the central processing unit, output media and equipment, and various computer applications.

Input Media and Devices

The term *input* describes the act of introducing data into an electronic data processing system. The input data may be any data upon which one or more of the basic data processing functions are to be performed — recording, coding, sorting, calculating, summarizing, storing, and communicating. An *input medium* is the machine-language form used by the system. Input media range from punched cards to voice recognition, which is still being developed and refined. An *input device*, considered peripheral equipment to the computer, is used to read the input medium into the system. Input devices vary with the types of input media used.

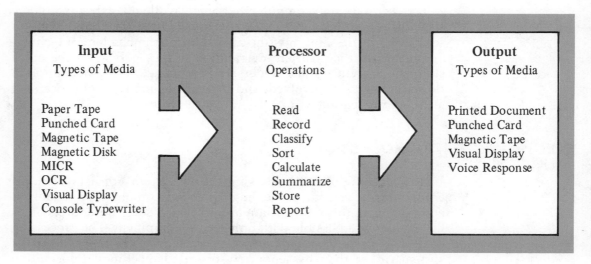

Input Types of Media	Processor Operations	Output Types of Media
Paper Tape Punched Card Magnetic Tape Magnetic Disk MICR OCR Visual Display Console Typewriter	Read Record Classify Sort Calculate Summarize Store Report	Printed Document Punched Card Magnetic Tape Visual Display Voice Response

The Three Components in a Data Processing System, Their Media and Operations

Punched Tape and Punched Cards. Punched tape and punched cards can be used to introduce source data to the computer system. High-speed readers convert the punched holes into coded electrical impulses which in turn are transmitted to the central processing unit.

To carry out its work, the central processing system must be given specific, step-by-step instructions as to what it is to do. These instructions are called the *program*. The program is usually recorded on punched cards or tape and fed into the central processing unit by the input equipment.

Magnetic Tape. A more sophisticated computer-system input medium than the punched card or tape is magnetic tape. Besides being a high-speed input medium, magnetic tape has the additional features of erasability, storage capacity for much more information (1,600 characters can be stored on 1 inch of tape), and security of information. Magnetic tape is also lower in cost than cards.

Magnetic tape is plastic, coated with a metallic oxide, and comes in widths of ½ to 1 inch and lengths of 2,400 to 3,600 feet per reel.

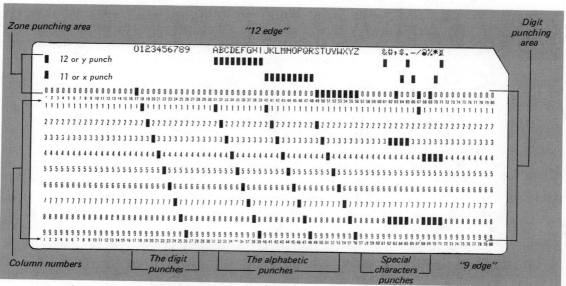

This 80-column card illustrates the meaning of the punched holes. Each letter has its own combination of two punches in one vertical column: one punch in one of three positions at the top of the card and the other punched in one of the figures in the same column. Note that the letter *A* is represented by a punch in the top position plus a punch in the figure *1* (in Column 31). The letter *W* is represented by a punch in the zero row (the lowest position at the top of the card) and in the figure *6*. A column with only one punch represents the actual figure punched, as shown in Columns 17–26 on this card. The cards feed through the machine and activate the equipment electrically.

Data are recorded on the tape as invisible magnetized spots that, when read into the system, create electrical impulses. As on punched tape, data are recorded in channels. A tape drive unit is used to read the magnetized spots into the computer.

Magnetic tape is considered a *sequential-access* medium; that is, what is first on the reel is read first, what is second is read second, and so forth. In other words, in order to locate information halfway through the tape, all the preceding material must be read first. For some business operations, such as periodic updating of customer accounts, the magnetic tape is ideal; but where information is scattered throughout a tape, the computer access time necessary to reach the desired data can delay the processing.

Error detection on magnetic tape is comparatively difficult; some installations, therefore, record source information on punched cards and then convert the cards to magnetic tape for reading into the computer system, thus combining the advantages of both media.

A recent trend is keying data directly to magnetic tape for reading to the computer, using a keyboard similar to that of an electric typewriter. Further, with recent technological advances, the operator can key data on miniature magnetic tapes in tape cassettes, which the computer can then convert to run-size tape for processing. This operation can even be a by-product of the original business typing. Key-to-tape input, with no time for converting cards to tape, cuts processing time as much as 20 percent.

Magnetic Disks. Magnetic disks are thin, circular, metal plates, coated on both sides with ferrous oxide. In appearance, a file of magnetic disks resembles a stack of phonograph records. Information is recorded and stored as magnetic spots on both sides of a disk, using various key-to-disk devices. Data can be transferred from the disk to a tape for processing by the computer.

Like magnetic tape, disks are durable and erasable. Depending on the nature of the information recorded on the magnetic disk or tape, a second copy may be made to ensure the information against accidental erasure or destruction. A major consideration in the use of a disk pack is its cost, which is nearly 100 times more than a single reel of magnetic tape.

While magnetic tape is a sequential-access medium (the computer must search from the beginning of the tape for desired data), magnetic disks are a *random-access* medium (the computer can go directly to any disk in the file and retrieve desired data). Thus access time to retrieve information is shorter with magnetic disks than with magnetic tape. Magnetic disks are used in computer installations for large-volume storage capacity.

MAGNETIC INK CHARACTER RECOGNITION CHART — E-13B type font

0	1	2	3	4	5	6	7	8	9
ZERO	ONE	TWO	THREE	FOUR	FIVE	SIX	SEVEN	EIGHT	NINE

AMOUNT SYMBOL	ON US SYMBOL	TRANSIT NUMBER SYMBOL	DASH SYMBOL

Magnetic Ink and Optical Character Recognition. Symbols and numbers imprinted in magnetic ink can be read and processed electronically by a Magnetic Ink Character Recognition (MICR) reader. This process is used in the banking industry where customer checks and deposit slips are numbered with magnetic ink in a standard type *font* (a complete assortment of type in one size or style). The use of magnetic ink has greatly automated banking transactions.

The Optical Character Recognition (OCR) reader reads and translates printed or handwritten characters into machine language and transfers the data directly into the computer system. Since no special ink is required, large billing companies like the petroleum industry, catalog houses, and utility companies commonly use this process for their credit account numbers. In the future it is likely that the OCR process may become as popular in business and education as the MICR is in the banking industry.

Visual Display. The *cathode-ray tube* (CRT) displays input data in much the manner of a television set. The unit contains a keyboard, a display screen, and a buffer storage area in which input information is retained while the operator verifies the information. Input data are directly submitted to the computer by using the keyboard or a light pen or by touching sensitized points on the tube.

Console Typewriter. Although the console typewriter keyboard can introduce data directly into the system, it is too slow for volume input and is used primarily for direct communication with the central processing unit, such as in asking questions. For example, the operator may use the keyboard to ask the balance of an account. The typewriter then receives and types the computer's responses.

Central Processing Unit

The heart of the electronic data processing system is the *central processing unit*. It consists of: (1) an internal storage or memory file,

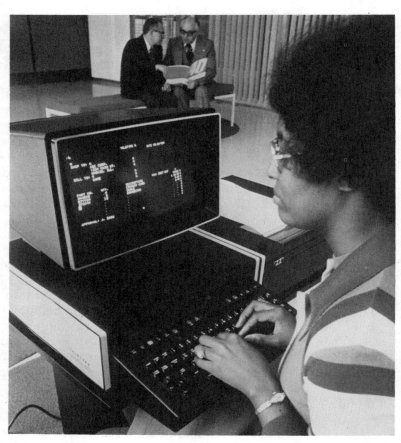

Teletype Corporation

Input data are stored in a buffer area while the operator verifies the data visually on the CRT display.

(2) an arithmetic-logic component, and (3) a control unit. The central processing unit accepts data from any of the various input devices, processes it according to the programmer's instructions, and sends results to storage or to the output device.

Storage or Memory File. *Storage* (frequently called memory, or memory file) is the place where computer data and programs are stored magnetically.

Storage is organized into thousands of individual locations, each with a unique address by which it can be located in the same manner that a house can be located by a street address. The speed with which the processing unit can locate an address in the storage or memory file and transfer the amount in the computer's address to the arithmetic component is referred to as *access time*. Since large processors can perform several hundred operations per second, the access time to stored data is critical; that is, slow access time uses up valuable computer time.

Most computers have two types of storage, internal and bulk (external). The internal storage is quick-access storage. The quick-access storage holds the program and the data that are being used at the time.

Arithmetic-Logic Component. The arithmetic section of the computer is like an electronic calculator which performs addition, subtraction, multiplication, and division. It can also make certain logical decisions concerning the data being processed.

Arithmetic Ability. The arithmetic component has two sections, the adder circuits and the accumulator registers. The calculations are performed in the *adder* section at lightning speed measured in *microseconds* (millionths of a second) and sometimes in *nanoseconds* (billionths of a second) of time. Naturally, this time varies with the size and complexity of the unit. A small computer might require .001 second (a thousand microseconds) to multiply a four-digit number by a five-digit number.

The *accumulator* is that portion of the arithmetic unit where results (answers) of the arithmetic operation are temporarily stored until the calculation is complete. The instructions may direct the equipment to:

1. Copy a number from a storage location into the accumulator.
2. Get a second number from a storage location and add it to the number in the accumulator.
3. Multiply the sum of the two numbers (in the accumulator) by 25 and return the answer to storage.

Decision-Making Ability. One of the distinctive qualities of the computer is its ability to select among alternate courses of action. This is frequently referred to as decision-making ability. The computer can be programmed to examine a figure and determine if it is above or below a certain amount. If it is above, the computer will follow one set of instructions. If it is below, the computer will follow another set. This decision-making ability makes it possible, once data and a program have been fed into the system, for the computer to complete a sequence of operations automatically. For instance, it can process a payroll without any further human intervention after data on the individual time cards are fed into the computer. It calculates the wage for each employee; searches out the payroll information, obtains the number of withholding tax exemptions, and then determines the withholding tax and social security tax; makes other approved deductions; determines the net pay; and prints the paycheck. In addition, it stores the payroll information, produces complete payroll information on each employee and prints the W-2 forms (Withholding Tax Statements). A payroll for several thousand employees can be completed within a few hours.

Control Unit. The control unit directs the many functions of the computer system. It seeks instructions from the storage files, interprets, and executes them. It internally controls operations of the input devices, the storage unit, the arithmetic-logic unit, and the output devices.

Output Media and Devices

Output refers to information processed by the computer. The *output medium* is the form in which the processed information appears. The *output device* is the equipment connected to the system that records or displays the processed data. The output information can be in the form of punched cards or magnetic tape for use in further data processing, or in the form of records, reports, visual displays, or voice responses for immediate use. By far the most common output medium is the printed document.

Punched Cards and Magnetic Tape. Data can be printed out on punched cards or magnetic tape and then stored. Output devices may include card punches and magnetic tape units.

Records and Reports. Processed data in the form of records and reports are printed on high-speed printing equipment that usually prints a whole line of characters at one time. Printers are of two types, *impact* and *nonimpact*. Impact printers print by means of a type bar that presses against a ribbon and paper. Nonimpact printers print information photographically. In terms of speed, many line (impact) printers can print at 1,000 lines a minute while nonimpact printers can produce up to 6,000 lines a minute. Although nonimpact printing requires special paper, impact printing does not and can be used with business forms and gummed labels.

The end product may be a sales analysis, payroll checks, utility bills, statistical reports, invoices, a cost distribution, and the like.

Visual Display. The cathode-ray tube (CRT) serves as both an input and an output medium.

Voice Response. For businesses like airlines, transportation companies, and banks, the most convenient means of data retrieval are voice-response terminals. For example, to check the credit reference of a customer, a bank representative can dial into the computer and a voice will respond with the requested information. A subscriber to the quotation service offered by the New York Stock Exchange can inquire and receive by telephone from the computer verbal quotations of the latest price and volume information on exchange stocks.

The words in a voice response come from a vocabulary stored in the system and are generally restricted to the basic type of information processed.

A GUIDE TO DATA PROCESSING TERMS

Access Time. The time required for the computer to locate data in its memory or storage section

Binary Number System. A number system using the base 2 (There are only two symbols: 1 or 0 — zero. In the electronic data processing system this is represented by "on" or "off" pulses.)

Common Language. A term used to describe punched paper tape, edge-punched cards, punched cards, or magnetic tape which may be read by and used to activate various office machines

Control Console. A panel through which the operator regulates the flow of data and instructions to the computer

Debug. To detect, locate, and remove errors in a program

Distributed Processing. A communication network made up of two or more minicomputers, each of which can also process data independently

Erase. To remove information stored on a magnetic drum, magnetic tape, magnetic disk, or other storage device

Floppy Disk. A key-to-disk system made of Mylar without the metal core, and thus a cheaper medium

Flowchart. A graphic technique used to analyze data flow and operations performed

Hardware. The components or configurations of machines (such as input, output, or power units) which make up a system of equipment

Input. Information (data) being transferred into the computer

Instruction. A coded symbol or word which tells the computer to perform some operation

Memory. Devices used for the internal storage of data such as magnetic tapes, magnetic drums, magnetic disks, and magnetic cores

Microsecond. One millionth of a second

Millisecond. One thousandth of a second

Nanosecond. One billionth of a second

Off-Line and On-Line Operation. The operation of peripheral equipment that is not in direct communication (off-line) or is in direct communication (on-line) with the central processing unit of the computer

Output. Information which is produced by the computer

Peripheral Equipment. Equipment used in conjunction with a computer but not a part of the computer itself; such as a converter, optical scanner, tape reader, printer, etc.

Printer. The machine that prints the output from the computer

Program. The specific, step-by-step, coded instructions given to the central processing system to carry out its work

Random Access or Direct Access. The ability to obtain or place information into storage independent of the sequence of the data being stored or retrieved

Read, Read In, Read Out. The operation of transferring information from one location to another

Sequential Access. The ability to obtain or place information into storage only according to the sequence of the data being stored or retrieved. For example, to locate information halfway through a medium, all the preceding material must be read first

Software. Programming aids, such as routines, applications, programs available to the computer

Storage. A general term used for the ability of the machine to hold information (This is frequently referred to as the memory.)

Terminal. A device used to communicate with a computer

Updating. The process of bringing data stored in the computer memory unit up to current value

Write. The operation of storing a number on the surface of a magnetic tape, or drum; transferring information to an output medium

Computer Services

In response to the growing need for computer access by business organizations, large and small, computer service centers and computer usage arrangements have developed. Examples of these services are discussed in this section.

Time-Sharing. A fast-growing practice by both small and large business organizations is time-sharing, a process by which a computer system serves many independent users at the same time. An input-output device in an individual firm's facility is connected by communication lines to a distant central processor. The computer receives data simultaneously from many users, and, by giving each user a small piece of its time, processes the data almost immediately. Generally each user has a set of computer programs and also has access to public programs.

Leasing. Another industry practice is to lease, from an independent leasing agency, computer equipment to be installed on the lessee's premises. Under this arrangement, the leasing agent buys the data processing equipment specified by the user and then leases it to the user at a lower cost than that offered by the manufacturer of the computer.

Data Processing Service Centers. Commercial data processing service centers provide computer service to small businesses and handle overflow loads for larger companies that have their own computer installations.

Considerable diversity exists among data processing services. Well-established centers may provide a complete data processing service: analyze customer requirements, offer consulting services, prepare computer programs, and implement the programs on their own equipment. Some centers have developed an area of expertise and industry specialization, such as processing pension plans, direct mail, or multi-plant operations.

Most service centers offer *batch* processing (periodic processing of data that have accumulated over a period of time, such as a monthly accounts receivable or a weekly payroll). The work is done on a fixed schedule. Some centers use time-sharing equipment, and some even provide batch processing from remote facilities.

Information Retrieval and Exchange. *Information service centers* have evolved to provide subscribers with business, scientific, and technical information by direct connection with computers over telecommunication facilities.

For example, a business can subscribe to a local credit rating service that in turn is affiliated with a regional or national credit service. One strategically located center can store the credit ratings of most businesses and millions of individuals in its area.

IMPACT OF EDP UPON BUSINESS MANAGEMENT

The advent of electronic data processing has made absolutely necessary the "systems approach" in all phases of business operation. The manager of today and tomorrow must have a higher quality of information upon which to base decisions — information which is timely, accurate, complete, and pertinent to business operations. The term *management information system* (MIS) is used to describe the combination and interaction of the people, machines, and procedures which produce the higher quality information needed by management. This section provides examples of the type of information which is available for management use.

Information Flow

Formerly it was impossible to communicate data from one location to another without an appreciable time interval. Because the flow of information was restricted to one physical segment of an organization (one plant, one location), it was necessary to decentralize operations and management. Decision making had to be delegated to management at the local level.

Improvements in the computer and in telecommunication allow the flow of information through the entire business organization. Corporate branches, regardless of geographical location, can be connected "on line" with a central computer. Thus, each branch has a direct connection and can feed data into and receive answers back from the computer.

An illustration of the on-line process is the reservation system used by some airlines. Each ticket sales office of the airline throughout the United States has an on-line connection with the computer center. In a matter of seconds, a ticket agent can question the computer on space available on any flight, receive the reply, and ticket (reserve) the space.

A department store with several branches accumulates data from the cash register in each department into a central processing center. When a sale is recorded on any register, it is automatically and simultaneously transmitted to the processing center. The center answers with voice response all requests for credit information, provides management with a daily report of sales in each department plus a comparison with last year's figures for the same day, analyzes sales trends, and compares the daily performance of each salesperson with previous records.

Centralization of Management

Telecommunication is bringing about important changes in management operational patterns. First, it is making all relevant facts immediately available to management. Management can now know what is happening inside the company as soon as it happens. Secondly, telecommunication is getting the information to management in "real time"; that is, in time to do something about it. For example, the production costs of a branch operation may be gradually increasing. Without the assistance of the computer, these costs could get far out of line before coming to the attention of management. With the computer, coupled with data communication facilities, however, any change in costs can be known at once and corrective action can be taken.

Management can now measure the immediate effect of its own decisions. This is known as "information feedback." A familiar illustration of the principle of feedback is the interaction between the thermostat and the air conditioner, which constantly work together to keep the room at a predetermined temperature. In a similar manner, the feedback through the computer permits management to regulate and initiate changes in costs, prices, profit margin, inventories, production, and so forth, in line with a predetermined plan.

Telecommunication is also making it possible to centralize management. Top management in the central office can now have access to everything important that is happening at any corporate outpost as soon as it happens. An executive in the central office can have data on each branch at the same time that the branch manager can have the data. Decisions can be made and fed back to the branch as rapidly as they could be made at the branch. Centralized control of decentralized operations is now a reality.

Informational Privacy

The technological capability to acquire data banks on individuals and the possibility of computer-related fraud with these data are factors which led to the enactment of the Federal Privacy Act of 1974. In general, this Act sets forth an individual's rights with regard to the information accumulated and prohibits federal agencies from misusing the information acquired. Violating any individual's rights under this Act may be subject to civil suit for damages. Therefore, managers of data processing installations, whether an information service center or a department within a business firm, are implementing policies for the control and use of the data available through computer networks. It is recognized that the data processing manager may be held directly responsible for the way in which information is used.

THE COMPUTER GENERATIONS

To illustrate the rapid changes in computer technology, one just has to look at the developments in the computer industry over the last 30 years. Computer historians tell us that the computer, as we know it today, is in its fourth generation of development, beginning in the 1940s.

The first computers were used primarily in scientific areas; however, business did utilize them as accounting tools. Calculating payroll and updating accounts receivable and payable are examples of early applications. These first computers had vacuum tubes for storage and experienced heat problems demanding a high rate of maintenance and repair time. They were soon replaced with the second generation of computers which, instead of vacuum tubes, used transistors, which are smaller, generate almost no heat, are less expensive, and require much less power than vacuum tubes. These computers offered more applications to business processing and requirements. The third generation, introduced in the mid-sixties, utilized integrated circuits containing the equivalent of many transistors. These computers were 900 times faster than the models used in the fifties! Further improvements were made in reducing cost and increasing storage capacity. The fourth generation, introduced in the early 1970s, can accommodate different types of input-output devices and offers greater speed in operations. The small business computer and the minicomputer, products of this period, have made spectacular advances in terms of lower prices, speed of operations, and applications to business firms, both large and small. Because of their impact on office technology, they are discussed in detail here.

The development of the *small business computer* has provided small business firms with high-speed, in-house data processing capabilities at a relatively low cost. This system offers the same opportunities to small business management as users with larger computer systems have — the capability of handling large volumes of data, readily accessible input-output devices, adequate storage capacity, and programming features. Depending on the software package, a clerical staff can operate a small business computer system with a minimum of training. Typical applications are accounts receivable, payroll preparation, invoice billing, inventory control, and sales analysis reports.

The *minicomputer* has smaller storage and slower output capabilities than the small business computer. Usually equipped with a

CRT screen, the minicomputer is suitable for some scientifically oriented and business applications and is priced considerably below the small business computer. For example, minicomputers can address a wide variety of different needs from industrial control in a factory to the computation of paychecks in the business office. A minicomputer with a *turnkey system* (prepared programs ready to go without alteration and the capability to communicate in English) provides the executive with tremendous potential to get the information needed at the time it is required.

In business, minicomputers are replacing manual or electromechanical data processing systems. They are being used as remote terminals to provide input to a larger computer and are serving as units in a network of minicomputers to substitute for a large computer system. A terminal combined with a minicomputer can perform many functions normally carried out by a central computer. This terminal is referred to as an "intelligent terminal," setting it apart from the terminal which serves only as an input-output device with the computer. The technological development which led to the intelligent terminal is the *microprocessor*, commonly called the computer-on-a-chip. The microprocessor is a tiny silicon chip which adds various decision-making, arithmetic, and memory functions to a machine.

Some experts in the field predict that the microprocessor-minicomputer will set off a second industrial revolution, one that will speed up automation in industrial areas of business. Some suggest an estimated 25,000 potential applications — including in the kitchen, at the sports desk, in traffic controls, and in major appliances. It is no surprise, then, that we can expect executives and secretaries to have access to computers.

AUTOMATION AND THE SECRETARY

Electronic data processing coupled with improved data and telecommunication have produced significant changes in office work. Machines have taken over the job of detailed computations and file maintenance. Routine clerical operations, once performed by the multifunctional secretary, are now accomplished by computerized equipment. Thus, the secretary has more time to devote to supervisory and administrative functions and tasks requiring imagination and initiative.

The computer has, in part, changed the secretary's role of compiler of data to one of screener of data — a role that involves decision making on an administrative level. The secretary may interpret, extract figures, and set up reports from computer output or set up material for input into the computer system.

The centralization of data — made possible through the computer with its connections with all the branches and divisions of a company — brings an abundance of information into the executive's office. These data are channeled through the top-level secretary. The secretary must perform the function of deciding what data are to be given to the executive. This screening task conserves the executive's time.

Earlier in this book, the impact of word processing equipment and word processing centers on the traditional secretarial position was discussed. Now, with the introduction of the computer to the word processing scene, it is very likely that data and word processing activities will integrate and be under the leadership of the data processing department of an organization. There will be new responsibilities for both the administrative and correspondence secretaries. The administrative secretary will take on a professional role and absorb more management responsibilities. This position will become an interface between management and the computer. Senior-level positions of the administrative secretary will require a college degree because of the expanded scope of responsibility and the opportunity for growth and advancement. The correspondence secretary will be a part of the mainstream of office activities. The assignments will vary between data processing and word processing, and the secretary will have the added dimension of being a computer technician.

There seems to be no limit to the opportunities for change and growth in the secretarial position. One thing is certain. The secretary must be prepared for the demands of the position. A broad understanding of economics, data processing, and business organization and management will provide a good background for success in the secretarial field.

SUGGESTED READINGS

Keeling, B. Lewis, Norman F. Kallaus, and John J. W. Neuner. *Administrative Office Management*, 7th ed. Cincinnati: South-Western Publishing Co., 1978.

Leeson, Marjorie. *Basic Concepts in Data Processing*. Dubuque: William C. Brown Co., Publishers, 1975.

Spencer, Donald D. *Introduction to Information Processing*, 2d ed. Columbus: Charles E. Merrill Publishing Co., 1977.

QUESTIONS FOR DISCUSSION

1. Why is accuracy so important in feeding input data into a computer system?

2. The statement has been made that businesses could not return to manual processing of data even if they wanted to. Why would this be true?

3. It has been said that although the computer has contributed a great deal to one segment of our society in making information accessible it has created a social hazard to the individual desiring privacy and the restriction of personal information. What are some situations in which an individual might feel that the right to privacy has been violated?

4. Give examples of ways in which electronic data processing and developments in telecommunications are revolutionizing management processes in business.

5. Predictions are that word processing functions and data processing functions will merge and be placed under the direction of data processing departments. What might be the reasons underlying this merger?

6. Why should a secretary entering the office force today have a background in data processing?

7. The microprocessor is said to be setting off a second industrial revolution. What are some applications you can see for this "smart machine"?

8. Will middle managers be replaced by computers and peripheral equipment?

9. Decide whether you would use the words italicized in the following sentences dictated by your employer. Then use the Reference Guide to verify or correct your answers.
   (a) The *balance* of the order was shipped this afternoon.
   (b) Ten committee members were present, but the *balance* had asked to be excused.
   (c) Mr. Downs acted as chairperson during the *remainder* of the meeting.
   (d) The *remainder* of the fund will be used for research.

PROBLEMS

1. Visit a computer installation in your community and prepare a report showing how the use of the equipment has reduced the amount of repetitive labor involved in the work of the office.

2. In the following bookkeeping applications, what are the step-by-step procedures in maintaining records, recording information, analyzing the data, and making decisions?

   Accounts Receivable
   Accounts Payable
   Payroll

   What types of input media for a computer would be appropriate?

3. Rewrite the following job description for a Secretary B to reflect the change in duties after the installation of a minicomputer in this company:
   SECRETARY B. Performs secretarial duties for the chief accountant. Responsible for posting payments and charges to accounts receivable and payable, preparing monthly statements, calculating interest payments, handling and distributing mail, office receptionist duties, filing, multiple mailings to customers, shorthand dictation and transcribing, and maintenance of personnel records.

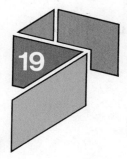

Collecting Business Information

A responsibility which gives the secretary an opportunity to show initiative and work without supervision (qualities which often lead to recognition and promotion) is the task of researching information for business reports. Knowing what information is available and where to find it represents a challenge even to the most experienced secretary. In this area the college-trained secretary should feel adept and thus should welcome the opportunity to demonstrate research ability.

Here are typical examples of assignments for research of business information:

Check out a proposal by gathering the pertinent data the executive will need in evaluation

Verify the accuracy of data submitted in support of a proposal

Gather the data the executive will need in preparing a proposal

Examine possible solutions to a problem, advantages and disadvantages, opinions of authorities, ways others solve the problem

Do the library research required by the executive in contributing to a project

Gather and organize information the executive will need in preparing a speech or an article for a professional magazine

In accomplishing these activities, the secretary locates the information and presents it in proper format. This chapter will assist you in becoming a knowledgeable researcher of business information. Chapters 20 and 21 discuss ways of organizing the data for effective presentation.

WHERE TO LOOK FOR INFORMATION

Needed information may be found in the *office of the executive or of the secretary*, in a *company library*, or in an *outside library*. An executive undoubtedly subscribes to technical publications; other materials are collected through memberships in trade or professional organizations. What the employer reads is often a clue to what the secretary should read. The executive often secures specialized reference books for a personal office library. The company also may provide reference materials for the desk of the secretary or office supervisor.

Many large corporations maintain a company library staffed with a technically trained librarian. In addition to a librarian, many companies have a research staff that locates information requested by each office. In this case the function of the secretary is to provide an accurate and exact request for information. In other situations the secretary must locate the information in the company library.

It may be necessary to go outside the organization for needed information. The first logical outside source is the public library. A number of cities have public libraries with specialized business departments and branches that provide invaluable assistance to the business interests in their area.

The *specialized library* is another source of information. *The Directory of Special Libraries and Information Centers*, published by Gale Research Company of Detroit, lists special libraries, their location, size, and specialty. A local Chamber of Commerce will frequently have a library on commercial and industrial subjects. Many business, technical, and professional societies or associations maintain excellent libraries, generally limited to use by members. Law libraries are often located in county and federal court buildings or at the local university or college of law. Many cities provide municipal reference libraries for the public as well as for city employees. Hospitals and colleges of medicine maintain medical and surgical libraries. Art, history, and natural history museums have specialized libraries, as do colleges and universities. Some newspaper offices have large library collections that they may open to limited public use. The United States Department of Commerce maintains regional offices in the principal cities, making available the files of the publications of the Department.

The public or special library (through its reference department) may answer questions over the telephone. Naturally, only questions that can be easily answered are accepted.

USING THE LIBRARY

When a subject requires extensive searching or considerable listing and copying, the secretary usually goes to the library to do the work. If the secretary is unfamiliar with the library, a brief stop at the information or reference desk and a statement outlining the purpose of the visit can save considerable time. The reference librarian is usually very willing to assist researchers in locating the information sources they need.

Finding the Information

The experienced researcher consults library indexes, guides, and catalogs as the first step in the process of finding information.

Books. The index of books is the *card catalog*. This is a card file that shows the contents of the library just as a book index shows the contents of a book. In the catalog there are at least three index cards for each book; one card is filed by the author's name, one by title, and one or more by subject classification. Many of the cards contain "See also" notes, which indicate where similar or related information may be found. The cards are usually uniformly printed and available to libraries from the Library of Congress.

An author's card in a library catalog shows: (1) classification and book number; (2) author's name; (3) title of the book, author or authors, edition, publisher, and date of publication; (4) text pages and size of the book in centimeters; (5) subject entry; (6) joint-author entry; (7) Library of Congress call number; (8) International Standard Book Number; (9) Dewey decimal classification number; and (10) serial number of the card.

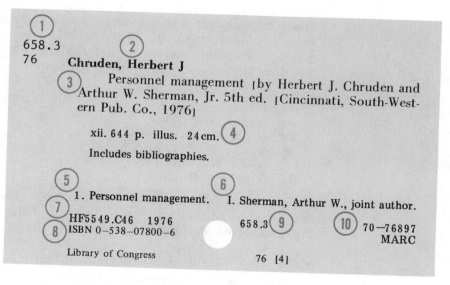

Dewey Decimal System. The Dewey decimal system, used in library classifications, is a type of subject filing. The subjects are divided into not more than ten general classifications numbered in hundreds from 000 to 900, inclusive. Each major class may be divided by units of ten, such as 100, 110, and 120. These classes may be further subdivided by units of one, such as 110, 111, and 112. Subdividing can be continued indefinitely by using the decimal point — for example, 126.1, 126.2, 126.21, 126.211. Under this system, business information is found in the 650 groups.

Library of Congress System. In libraries using the Library of Congress designations (combination of letters and figures), business information is found under the major category *H* (social sciences).

Published Indexes. An annual publication, *Books in Print*, lists all books included in publishers' catalogs, by author and title. This book is normally shelved in the reference section of the library.

The *Cumulative Book Index* (or the CBI as it is familiarly identified) is an index of most of the books printed in English all over the world and still available from publishers. The CBI lists each book in three ways — author, title, and subject. These extra-large volumes are normally shelved in the catalog department of the library.

Other indexes that will help the secretary to locate current information in special fields are: *Biological and Agricultural Index, Applied Science and Technology Index, Business Periodicals Index, Education Index, Social Science Index*, and *Engineering Index*.

Pamphlets and Booklets. Much valuable information is now published in pamphlet, booklet, or leaflet form. Such material is cataloged by subject and title in the *Vertical File Index* (a subject and title index to selected pamphlet material) which is published monthly. The following is a typical listing:

Personnel Management
Golden Rule Supervision;
practical ways to put the
Golden Rule in action on-the-job,
by Leonard J. Gordon 15 p '76
L. J. Gordon Associates
Box 395 Urbana, IL 61801

This source of information can easily be missed during research because the material may not be indexed in the library's card catalog nor shelved. It is usually stored vertically in file drawers.

News. *Facts on File* is a weekly world news digest published as a one-volume, loose-leaf booklet with a cumulative subject index.

For newspaper references the *New York Times Index* should be consulted. Supplements of this index are published monthly and cumulative editions, annually. Entries are arranged alphabetically under name of subject. *The Wall Street Journal* publishes a similar index.

Magazines. The best index on general magazines is the *Readers' Guide to Periodical Literature* — a cumulative author and subject index to articles appearing in periodicals that are on file in almost all main public libraries.

Preparing Bibliography Cards

The first consideration in selecting material for examination is its *date of publication*. If current information is desired, an article on laser beams published ten years ago would be of little value; but twenty- or thirty-year-old biographies of Benjamin Franklin would be worthwhile.

The second consideration is *content*. Some listings describe the types of information in the publications. Such descriptions help in selecting material to be researched.

For each reference selected for study, prepare a bibliography card. On a 5- by 3-inch card record the library call number, the author's name, the title of the publication (and article if it is in a periodical), the publisher, date of publication, and page reference.

Number the cards in the upper right corner in sequence, according to each new source used. The number that is thus assigned to a source is used to identify all notes that are taken from it. This method saves a great deal of time in identifying the sources when the references are copied or abstracted; besides, the bibliography cards serve as a permanent and detailed record of the sources used.

Taking Notes

The secretary is now ready to study, evaluate, accept or reject material, and record the references on individual sheets or on cards 6 by 4 inches or larger. By using cards or sheets of uniform size instead of a shorthand notebook, the complete set of references can be sorted for use in drafting the outline and the report.

Compiling Reference Cards. Each reference card should give the following information in a standard form similar to that in the illustration:

Page number — written in the upper left corner (Do this first to avoid omitting it.)

Source — indicated by the number on its bibliography card

Topic — described in a conspicuous position, giving the nature of the reference

Information — written either as a direct quotation or as a summary statement. It is important that you make a distinction for your employer between what is a summary statement and what is a direct

The bibliography card (left) identifies the book as source No. 6. The card at the right shows pertinent material, organized and easy to reorganize before the writing of the paper.

Chruden, Herbert J. and Arthur W. Sherman, Jr.   (6)

Personnel Management

South-Western Pub. Co.
Cincinnati, Ohio – 1976
pp. xii + 644

658.3
76
p. 193

pp. 793-804   (10)

Industrial and Labor Relations Review
Vol. 26 (No. 2) Jan, 1973
"The British Experiment with Industrial Reform," Joseph W. Garbarino
Brit. Industrial Relations Act described as combination of American Wagner, Taft-Hartley, + Landrum-Griffin Acts. Author sees perm. effect on Brit. ind. relations.

quotation from the information source. A direct quotation is written word for word and enclosed in quotation marks, and any omissions from the original are indicated by ellipses (. . .). Replication of the author's work without express permission is in violation of the copyright laws. (See also Chapter 25)

Abstracting. A reference in abstract form should be identified as such, with the source and page number from which it is taken. To prepare good abstracts, you must develop the ability to pick out the important points and to express them in summary form. A secretary who is skillful in doing this can save the employer a great deal of reading time.

Copying Material. Fortunately, most libraries provide researchers with typewriters and copying machines at a nominal cost. Because of the likelihood of errors in recording numerical data, statistical tables should be copied by machine.

Special equipment is required for researching information that is stored micrographically. This secretary is taking notes from the screen of a microfiche reader.

3M Company

When library publications can be borrowed, the material can be taken to the office and typed or reproduced on a copying machine. The librarian will, in fact, often lend the secretary a noncirculating copy for a limited time. Libraries are eager to cooperate with business people and to have them make the fullest use of the library collections.

SOURCES OF GENERAL INFORMATION

Information sources are being updated and revised constantly, and new materials are being published regularly. It is necessary, therefore, to update any guide (including this chapter) with current sources.

Atlases

An atlas is a collection of maps and statistical information regarding populations and geographic areas. *Rand McNally Commercial Atlas and Marketing Guide*, subscribed to by most libraries, contains not only geographic maps but also many economic maps with primary emphasis on the United States. The *Times Atlas of the World*, Comprehensive Edition, in addition to maps of every country in the world, includes sections on the solar system, world climate, and world energy resources.

Dictionaries

One would naturally expect a dictionary to be a frequently used reference source for the secretary. Even though the office has a large unabridged dictionary, the efficient secretary will want an up-to-date desk-size dictionary within arm's reach. *Webster's New Collegiate Dictionary*, for example, would be a valuable addition to the secretary's reference shelf. (See also Chapter 9.)

There are also innumerable specialized dictionaries: bilingual ones for use in writing and translating foreign correspondence; and technical ones such as *A Dictionary for Accountants; Dictionary of Business and Science; Dictionary of Computers; Dictionary of Insurance; A Dictionary of Occupational Titles; Dictionary of Education; Dictionary of Legal Words and Phrases; Black's Law Dictionary; Dictionary of Business, Finance, and Investment; Hackh's Chemical Dictionary; Modern Dictionary of Electronics; New Dictionary of Physics;* and *Black's Medical Dictionary*.

New developments outdate technical dictionaries rapidly. Only the most recent editions can be considered dependably up to date.

City Directories

A secretary to a lawyer or to an insurance agent may be asked to locate or trace the address of an individual by a search through city directories when the name of the person is not listed in the telephone directory. Current and back issues of city directories are kept at libraries for the convenience of business users. The library collection of directories might contain the local city directory and also directories of all the cities in the state and of the major cities over the country.

City directories are not published by cities but by commercial enterprises for profit. Some of the very largest cities, such as New York City and Los Angeles, no longer have city directories. The North American Directory Publishers print a *City Directory Catalog* annually.

Special Directories

There are also hundreds of classified directories serving many fields — so many, in fact, that a special guide to directories is published. The latest edition of *Guide to American Directories* lists more than 5,200 directories in over 300 major fields of public and private enterprise. Some of them are listed below.

1. Those that list individuals engaged in the same occupation — for example, the *American Medical Directory* which gives education and field of specialization of all physicians in the United States, Canada, Puerto Rico, and the Virgin Islands.

2. Those that provide biographical sketches of selected individuals. *Who's Who in America* is a biographical directory, reissued biennially, of notable living Americans prominent in science, politics, sports, or education. *Who's Who* is an international annual biographical dictionary. There are also many selective *Who's Who* references, such as: *Who's Who in Insurance; Who's Who in the Office Machine Industry; Who's Who in the South and Southwest; Who's Who of American Women; Who's Who in American Politics;* and *World's Who's Who in Finance and Industry*.

3. Those that list all the businesses or service institutions engaged in similar or related enterprises in the United States, such as *Thomas' Register of American Manufacturers*, and *Standard & Poor's Register of Corporations, Directors and Executives*.

4. Those that list businesses in foreign countries, such as *Jane's Major Companies of Europe, Japan Company Directory*, and *Directory of American Firms Operating in Foreign Countries*.

5. Those that serve as buyers' and consumers' guides. The best known is *MacRae's Blue Book*, a buying guide published annually. This

publication also lists trade names and firms owning such names. Of value to the consumer is *Where to Find Out*, a guide to consumer-interest publications.

6. Those that provide such information as the *Encyclopedia of Associations, A Banker's Guide to Washington,* and *The New Guide to Study Abroad.*

Encyclopedias

An excellent reference source is an encyclopedia. Only two are mentioned here. In addition to general information, the *Encyclopedia Americana* provides information on American cities and manufacturing and commerce. The *Encyclopaedia Britannica* is especially useful to secure information on European countries and cities.

Government Publications

The United States government is a prolific publisher and a major source of information for the business executive. Some government publications may be subscribed to or purchased. Others will be found on file in the reference department or business section of the public library or in the municipal reference library of a city hall — depending upon the subject matter. Larger cities usually have a depository library designated by law to receive all or part of the material published by the government.

In *The Monthly Catalog of U.S. Government Publications* the secretary will find a comprehensive list of all publications issued by the various departments and agencies of the United States government. Included in this list are those for sale by the Superintendent of Documents and those for official use only. A semimonthly list of *Selected United States Government Publications* is sent free to persons requesting the Superintendent of Documents to include their names on the mailing list.

Proceedings and debates of Congress are given in *The Congressional Record.* The official directory of the United States Congress, *The Congressional Directory*, provides information on the legislative, judicial, and executive branches of the federal government. The *Congressional Staff Directory* publishes the names of staff personnel of the members of Congress in Washington and those serving on committees and subcommittees. The *United States Government Manual*, the official handbook of the federal government, provides information on the purposes and programs of most government agencies and lists top personnel of those agencies.

Publications of the Bureau of the Census of the U.S. Department of Commerce are based on data from censuses taken in various years including information on population, housing, business, manufacturing, and agriculture. Full census reports provide complete information. *The Statistical Abstract of the United States* (annual), however, presents summary statistics about area and population, vital statistics, education, climate, employment, military affairs, social security, income, prices, banking, transportation, agriculture, forests, fisheries, mining, manufacturing, and related fields. Data on all cities over 25,000 in population are given in the *City Supplement* to the *Statistical Abstract*.

The U.S. Department of Commerce publishes a *Guide to Foreign Trade Statistics* that gives detailed records of the foreign commerce of the United States. *The Survey of Current Business* (issued monthly) reports on the industrial and business activities of the United States. Publications of the Department of Agriculture provide agricultural and marketing statistics and information for increasing production and agricultural efficiency. Department of Labor publications deal mostly with labor statistics, standards, and employment trends. The Department's official publication is the *Monthly Labor Review*.

Economic and agricultural data on many subjects may be acquired from various state governments. The secretary should address inquiries to the departments of health, geology or conservation, and highways; to the divisions of banks, insurance, and statistics; to industrial and public utilities commissions; or to the research bureaus of state universities. Pertinent information about executive, legislative, and judicial branches of state governments is given in the *Book of the States* which is published every two years by the Council of State Governments.

Yearbooks

Yearbooks are annual reports of summaries of statistics and facts. *The World Almanac and Book of Facts*, which is the most popular book of this type, contains many pages of statistics and facts preceded by an excellent index. One reference librarian has said, "Give me a good dictionary and *The World Almanac*, and I can answer 80 percent of all questions asked me." It covers such items as stock and bond markets; notable events; political and financial statistics on states and cities; statistics on population, farm crops, prices, trade and commerce; educational data; and information on the postal services. Because of its wide coverage and low price, the secretary might request the executive to purchase a copy of *The World Almanac* each year for office use. Another yearbook of this type is the *Information Please Almanac, Atlas, and Yearbook*, published by Simon & Schuster.

The *Statesman's Yearbook* provides factual and statistical information on countries of the world. Data are provided under the following headings: type of government, area and population, religion, education, justice, defense, commerce and industry, and finance. The *International Yearbook and Statesmen's Who's Who* (one book) includes biographical sketches of over 10,000 political leaders and general information on international affairs and foreign relations.

SOURCES OF BUSINESS INFORMATION

Sources of business information, like general information, are constantly being revised, and new materials are being published regularly. This listing of specific business sources, therefore, is to serve as a guide and should be supplemented with new sources as they appear.

Abstracting Services

So vast is the volume of technical literature published in many areas that engineers, scientists, and business executives find it difficult to keep abreast of new developments. To help bridge this information gap, some large companies subscribe to an abstracting service that specializes in a specific field. An example is the American Petroleum Institute's Central Abstracting and Indexing Service. Highly trained specialists abstract thousands of journals, publications, and scientific papers from all parts of the world. The abstracts are distributed to subscribers.

Some of the abstracting services feed abstracts and selected references into a computer. The computer arranges the material alphabetically by subject. A computer-driven phototypesetter prints out indexes periodically and can provide an immediate printout of all abstracts on a specific subject. The recipient can determine from the abstract whether to read the original and complete document.

General Subscription Information Services

Management often subscribes to information services relating to business conditions in general. These services present information from more direct and specialized sources than those found in the popular publications. A service may use loose-leaf form so that superseded pages can be destroyed and new and additional ones inserted easily. It may be the secretary's duty to see that the new material is filed in its proper place in the service, according to the instructions sent by the publisher. Services include the following:

Babson's Reports Inc. Two bulletins are issued: *Investment & Barometer Letter* (weekly) and the *Washington Forecast Letter* (weekly).

The Bureau of National Affairs, Inc. This privately owned company reports government actions affecting management, labor, law, taxes, finance, federal contracts, antitrust and trade regulations, international trade, and patent law. The bureau publishes a *Daily Report for Executives*.

The Kiplinger Washington Letter. This weekly confidential letter analyzes and condenses economic and political news for subscribers.

The Conference Board. Over 4,000 subscribers support research in the fields of business economics, financial, personnel, and marketing administration, international operations and public affairs administration. Included in the service is a monthly magazine — *Across the Board.*

Research Institute Recommendations. This weekly newsletter published by the Research Institute of America analyzes economic and legislative developments and makes tax recommendations.

Specialized Subscription Information Services

The secretary should be acquainted with the subscription services for specialized fields described below:

Credit. Dun & Bradstreet Credit Service. This service collects, analyzes, and distributes credit information on retail, wholesale, and manufacturing companies.

Financial. (Most brokerage houses provide investment information to prospective and present customers.) Moody's Investors Service. This service publishes *Moody's Bond Survey, Moody's Dividend Record, Moody's Bond Record*, and *Moody's Handbook of Common Stocks.*

Standard & Poor's Services. Publications include *Analysts Handbook; Bond Guide; Called Bond Record; Commercial Paper Reports; Corporation Records; Current Market Perspectives; Daily Basis Stock Charts; Dividend Record; Industry Surveys; International Stock Report; Daily Stock Price Records; Over-the-Counter Stock Reports; Register of Corporations, Directors and Executives; Review of Securities Regulations; Stock Guide.*

Labor. The Bureau of National Affairs, Inc. publishes a number of labor information services including the *Affirmative Action Compliance Manual for Federal Contractors, EEOC Compliance Manual, Fair Employment Practice Service, Labor Relations Reporter*, and *Manpower Information Service.*

Law, Tax. Commerce Clearing House Services. These services are especially useful to lawyers and accountants. The CCH Topical Law

Reports (over 100 loose-leaf publications) provide assistance on such topics as federal tax, labor, trade regulation, state tax, social security, securities, bankruptcy, trusts, insurance, and aviation.

Prentice-Hall Services. These loose-leaf current publications cover the latest laws, rules, and regulations with interpretations and comments. Most aspects of federal and state laws with respect to business and taxation are covered. In addition, *Accountant's Weekly Report, Insurance and Tax News* (a biweekly newsletter), *Lawyer's Weekly Report*, and *Executive's Tax Report* (weekly) keep subscribers up to date.

Office Administration. *Word Processing Report.* Published twice monthly, these reports cover industry trends, word processing equipment and systems, and analyses of case studies.

Real Estate. A Prentice-Hall loose-leaf publication, *Real Estate Guide*, covers all practical aspects of real estate operation. Monthly supplements and replacement pages keep the guide up to date.

Trade. The Bureau of National Affairs, Inc. In addition to providing general business services, this organization publishes *Antitrust and Trade Regulation Reporter, Federal Contracts Report, International Trade Reporter's Export Shipping Manual*, and the *United States Patents Quarterly.*

Newspapers and Periodicals for Executives

Periodicals coming into the office can be divided into two types — general and specialized.

General Periodicals. The alert secretary scans general business magazines received at the office for material that may be of immediate or possible interest to the executive.

Typical business magazines are:

Barron's. A national business and financial weekly published by Dow Jones & Co., Inc.

Business Week. A weekly periodical published by McGraw-Hill, Inc., covering factors of national and international interest to the business executive. Statistics reflect current trends.

Dun's Review. This monthly magazine which covers finance, credit, production, labor, sales, and distribution is published by Dun & Bradstreet Publications, Inc.

Finance Facts. A monthly publication distributed free by the National Consumer Finance Association on consumer financial behavior.

Forbes. A semimonthly magazine on corporate management for top executives published by Forbes, Inc., New York.

Fortune. This monthly magazine published by Time, Inc., features articles on specific industries and business leaders. It also analyzes current business problems.

Nation's Business. Published monthly by the Chamber of Commerce of the United States, this business magazine concerns political and general topics.

National Observer. Factual articles on world affairs and economic and political developments of special interest to the business executive are provided in this periodical published weekly by Dow Jones & Co., Inc. in newspaper format.

School of Business Publications. The executive may subscribe to the business magazines published by some of the larger university schools of business. Well-known magazines of this type are the *Harvard Business Review* (bimonthly) and the *Journal of Business* (quarterly) of the University of Chicago.

Special Articles. In the business sections of such weeklies as *Time* and *Newsweek* and the special articles in *U.S. News and World Report*, the reader can learn a great deal about current business trends.

Newspapers. *The New York Times* is a daily newspaper covering world, domestic, and financial news. *The Wall Street Journal*, primarily an investor's newspaper, covers current business news and lists daily stock reports.

Specialized Periodicals. It is common for a company to belong to several trade associations, each of which helps the company with a different aspect of its business. In addition, the executive may belong to several professional associations. These associations issue regular magazines to their members, publishing articles and statistics of current interest. *The Standard Periodical Directory* lists over 50,000 United States and Canadian periodicals.

The *Business Periodicals Index* is the primary source of information on a wide range of articles appearing in business periodicals.

When seeking data on a specific magazine or newspaper, the secretary might consult *Ayer's Directory of Publications* (newspapers and periodicals, annual) or *Ulrich's International Periodicals Directory* providing such information as name of publication, editor, publisher, date established, technical data, and geographic area served. Another source of specialized magazines is the *Readers' Guide to Periodical Literature*. More than 100 well-known magazines (such as the *Architectural Record, Changing Times, Consumer Reports, Foreign Affairs, Monthly Labor Review,* and *Time*) are indexed in each issue and their articles cataloged under appropriate headings.

Handbooks

Handbooks have been published in many areas of business. They are highly factual and are written to give a general survey of knowledge about a field (with the minimum use of time and effort). A few of the many handbooks that have been published include: *Handbook of Business Administration, Modern Accountant's Handbook, Handbook for Business and Advertising, Office Administration Handbook,* and the *Sales Manager's Handbook.*

Among a number of handbooks written for the secretary employed in a specialized office are those for the legal secretary, medical secretary, data processing secretary, real estate secretary, and others.

Secretary's Reference Shelf

In addition to the secretarial handbooks and reference materials needed for transcription, the secretary may collect other worthwhile reference books or may be asked by the executive to purchase them for the office. What is on the secretary's reference shelf should depend on the nature of the job and the background information needed. A useful, inexpensive reference is *How to Use the Business Library*. This manual is revised periodically and would be a valuable adjunct to the office library or secretary's reference shelf. Among other sources of information are the following:

Abridged encyclopedias — such as *The Columbia Encyclopedia* (one volume), comprised of very brief articles. It is particularly strong on biography and geography; or the *Lincoln Library of Essential Information* (two volumes), that classifies information into 12 broad subject fields, rather than alphabetically.

An annual book of statistics — such as the *Statistical Abstract of the United States, The World Almanac and Book of Facts* or the *Commodity Year Book. The Guinness Book of World Records* may be a valuable reference source.

An atlas or gazetteer — such as the *Rand McNally Illustrated World Atlas* or *Webster's New Geographical Dictionary.*

A thesaurus — such as *Webster's Collegiate Thesaurus.*

A book of quotations — such as *Bartlett's Familiar Quotations* or *The Home Book of Humorous Quotations.*

The secretary's reference shelf should surely include a technical handbook that covers the area of work of the executive.

SUGGESTED READINGS

Gates, Jean K. *Guide to the Use of Books and Libraries*, 3d ed. New York: McGraw-Hill Book Co., 1973.

Goeldner, C. R., and Laura M. Dirks."Business Facts: Where to Find Them." *MSU Business Topics*, Vol. 24, No. 3 (Summer, 1976), pp. 23–36.

Johnson, H. Webster. *How to Use the Business Library*, 4th ed. Cincinnati: South-Western Publishing Co., 1972.

Smith, George M., and Herbert J. Smith. *World Wide Business Publications Directory*. New York: Monarch Press (no publication date available).

Wasserman, Paul, *et al*. (eds.). *Encyclopedia of Business Information Sources*, 2d ed., 2 vols. Detroit: Gale Research Co., 1970.

QUESTIONS FOR DISCUSSION

1. You have just been named manager of the new word processing center in your company. What general categories of reference books would you select for use by the correspondence secretaries? By what criteria did you make your selections?

2. If your employer asked you to go to the public library to secure a copy of an article appearing in the *Journal of Business*, how would you locate the article?

3. In choosing a reference book, how can you be sure that you have the latest edition of the book?

4. Does the reference department of your public library render telephone service? If so, what limitations are placed on it? Is there a special business department or branch? Where is the nearest depository of government publications?

5. If your employer is involved in scientific research and gives highly technical dictation, where would you turn for help in learning the vocabulary?

6. It is difficult to determine how long reference material should be retained in an office. In each of these cases, what factors would determine your decision?
   (a) Catalogs from suppliers
   (b) Back issues of professional and technical magazines
   (c) Advertisements of competitive items
   (d) House organs of your company
   (e) Copies of *Who's Who in America*

7. In the following sentences insert the proper word for those enclosed in parentheses or rephrase the sentences so that there is no doubt as to the meaning. Then use the Reference Guide to verify or correct your answers.
   (a) New statistics are published (every two years).
   (b) Data are requested (twice a month).
   (c) Summaries are compiled (every two months).

8. Show how you could, in a piece of formal writing, avoid the use of *above* in the following sentences:

(a) The interpretation of the above statistics is important to any conclusion we reach.

(b) The above is subject to more than one interpretation.

PROBLEMS

1. For Problem 4 in Chapter 21 you will be asked to prepare a business report on one of the following subjects. In preparation, you are now to do the necessary reading, prepare bibliography cards, and take the necessary notes.
   (a) Professional organizations for the career secretary
   (b) Recent decisions in affirmative action cases
   (c) The contributions of text-editing machines to the reduction of correspondence costs
   (d) The era of the copier/duplicators
   (e) Orientation training for the new office worker
   (f) The use of job-related tests in the selection of office employees
   (g) The privacy law and office records
   (h) How the supervisor supervises workers effectively
   (i) How well "Management by Objectives" works
   (j) The feasibility study for a word processing reorganization

2. Your employer has asked you to prepare an annotated bibliography on the landscape office design, using only sources published within the last five years. Type the bibliography.

3. Assume that you are secretary to Randolph Parker, general counsel of one of the subsidiaries of a major manufacturing firm. Your employer has just been transferred to the home office and has just arrived in the office. He tells you that he has at least ten crates of books to be unpacked and arranged on his bookshelves. You are to supervise the arrangement of the books on the shelves. Also, he asks you to devise a system of control of these books, as he expects that many of the staff will want to use his material. What would be your plan of action for arranging the books on the shelves? What would be your system of control?

4. Assume that you are called upon to seek the following information. Prepare a list of your sources of information (identify by letter).
   (a) Who is the chairperson of the board of American Telephone and Telegraph Company? Where would you find biographical data about this person?
   (b) What is the address of the national headquarters of Kiwanis International? What is the total membership?
   (c) What was the population of Spokane, Washington, at the last official census?
   (d) Who are the members of the Washington office staff of a senator from your state?
   (e) What is the total circulation and the advertising rate of *Fortune*?
   (f) What is the annual crude petroleum production of Saudi Arabia?
   (g) What products are manufactured by Harold L. Palmer Company, Inc., Livonia, Michigan?
   (h) What are the five principal business centers located in the state of Arkansas?
   (i) What is the London address of NCR Corporation?

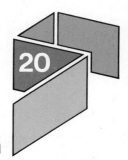

Presenting Statistical Information

Without a doubt, the most significant contribution to business decision making in recent years is computer technology. Through the use of the computer, business management has at its fingertips quantitative information which is pertinent to every facet of operations. Having these data available is only part of the decision-making process. For the executive or an assistant there remains the task of converting the information on the computer printout into meaningful and understandable form. Tables, charts, and graphs are used extensively for this purpose. A well-constructed table or chart can convey a picture of business operations more quickly and more clearly than words or numbers. Thus, management personnel rely heavily upon visual media to convey business information.

A good example is the annual sales conference of a company. Sales charts, graphs, and written communications including statistical data are commonplace. A speaker before the group would probably use overhead transparencies, flip charts, or a combination, to display quantitative information.

Giving life to figures, which well-planned tables and graphs really do, calls for a thorough knowledge of the techniques of table and graph construction, good planning, and imagination. The several steps involved in this type of work — compiling, classifying, and presenting data in tables and graphs — and the secretary's responsibility are discussed in this chapter.

THE SECRETARY'S RESPONSIBILITY

Chapter 19 pointed out that the secretary often has the task of gathering and organizing data for effective communication to others. This applies to both the multifunctional and administrative secretary. When a complicated chart, graph, or transparency is required, the person preparing it must know what has to be said and what type of graphic will best display the information. With these factors in mind, the secretary is better able either to (a) arrange for a graphic display to be made inside or outside the company or (b) prepare the graphic either freehand or with commercial materials. When simple tables, graphs, or charts are involved, the multifunctional secretary most likely would prepare them. In an organization utilizing the word processing center concept, the correspondence secretary using a composer or a phototypesetting machine should be able to produce very professional tables and graphs.

Throughout this chapter the general term *secretary* will be used to indicate the individual who actually does the preparation of the graphic.

COMPILING AND ORGANIZING DATA

The data with which the secretary works come from many sources. Some of them are compiled within the company. Other information, however, must be obtained from such secondary sources as magazines, yearbooks, and reports of outside agencies.

The data must be assembled onto a working form or forms so that totals can be obtained, averages and percentages calculated, and the information summarized. This process of transferring facts from the source documents to working forms is called *compiling* the data. The simplest compilation of data is a pencil-written tabulation similar to the one illustrated below.

A data work sheet should indicate the source, the compiler, and the checker. The work sheet should be filed with the completed tabulation, with the adding-machine or calculator tape attached as proof of totals.

The Leisure and Recreation Corp.
Summary of Operations
For the Year Ended December 31, 19--

Divisions	First Quarter	Second Quarter	Third Quarter	Fourth Quarter	Total for Year
Recreation					
Lawn and Garden	$25.6	$30.2	$39.4	$42.7	$137.9
Bicycles/Motorcycles	20.5	29.4	36.4	46.2	132.5
Sporting Goods	19.5	23.6	33.0	45.0	121.1
Marine Products	29.6	32.7	33.2	33.0	128.5
Total	$95.2	$115.9	$142.0	$166.9	$520.0
Recreational Vehicles					
Campers	$42.9	$45.2	$70.5	$90.2	$248.8

From Annual Report of the L+R Corp.
Compiled by R.C. 1/31/-- Checked by DN.

METHODS OF CLASSIFYING DATA

The objective in compiling data is to organize information into some type of meaningful classification. Data can be classified in any of five ways: (1) alphabetic sequence, (2) kind, (3) size, (4) location, or (5) time.

1. An *alphabetic sequence* of data is often used when the data are compiled for reference.

2. A *kind grouping* of data is used when the items are kinds of objects, characteristics, products, and so on. An example of kind grouping is a table entitled, "Retail Trade in U.S., 1978, by Kind Business." The number of stores and the year's sales are broken down into several main groups, such as food stores and apparel stores. Under each of these are listed the data for each of the types of stores included in the group.

3. *Size variations* may be shown in two ways: (a) in an *array* — that is, with the items listed in ascending or descending order, such as a table of the 50 greatest ports in the world with the ports arranged in the order of net tonnage in descending order; (b) in a *frequency distribution* — that is, according to the number in each size class. A frequency distribution is used instead of an array when the size classes can be grouped advantageously. Tables of age distribution are usually shown in this way; for example, the number of persons between the ages of 10 to 14, 15 to 19, and on as far as needed, instead of the number of persons 10 years old, 11 years old, and so on.

In many offices, machine tabulation has supplanted manual compilation of data. From punched cards or tape, the computer calculates and prints the data on perforated, accordion-folded sheets like that shown here.

ELECTRONICS, INC.

SALES & NET EARNINGS (IN MILLIONS)
FOR THE 5 COMPANY DIVISONS

1975-1978

DIVISION	YEAR	SALES	NET EARNINGS
AEROSPACE	1975	1,611	44
	1976	1,916	75
	1977	1,972	76
	1978	2,099	95
CONSUMER	1975	3,097	148
	1976	3,214	86
	1977	3,288	108
	1978	3,307	198

4. A *location listing* is used to show the data by geographic units — such as cities, states, and countries. Real-estate data are often listed this way, as are commodity sales on a national scale.

5. *Time-of-occurrence or time-series listings* are very common. The listing may be made by days, weeks, months, years, decades, and so on.

AVERAGE BUSINESS LETTER COSTS
FOR THE YEAR 1977[a]

Cost Factor	Average Cost per Letter	Percentage of Total Cost
Secretarial Time	$1.26	28.19[b]
Fixed Charges[c]	1.16	25.95
Dictator's Time	1.05	23.49
Nonproductive Labor[d]	0.35	7.83
Mailing Cost	0.28	6.26
Filing Cost	0.21	4.70
Materials	0.16	3.58
Totals	$4.47	100.00

[a]Based on data supplied by the Dartnell Corporation, Chicago.
[b]Expressed to the nearest 1/100 of 1%.
[c]Depreciation, overhead, rent, light, and similar items.
[d]Time lost due to waiting, illness, vacation, and other causes.

An array may list items in descending or ascending order. Vertical lines may be used to separate columns and the ends of the table may be left open. The footnotes are placed directly below the table and are identified by use of lowercase letters.

After data have been collected, they may be translated into either averages or percentages so that comparisons can be made. To say that sales in Dallas were 35 percent greater this month than last month is easier to interpret than to say that sales last month were $50,000 and this month, $67,500.

In some instances, it may be more helpful to know the average salary of clerks in the purchasing office than to know the highest and the lowest salary paid. The use to be made of the data determines which figures would be of most value.

Averages

One way to help the reader understand a set of figures is to compute averages of some type. (An average is a single value used to represent a group.) But which of the averages in common use should you choose? The one used most often is the *arithmetic average* or, more technically, *arithmetic mean*. It is determined by adding the values of the items and dividing that total by the number of items. If the weekly payroll for 120 employees is $30,000, for example, the average pay would be $250.

The *mode* is a second kind of average. It is the value that recurs the greatest number of times. The data are arranged in a frequency distribution to determine the mode. For example, the mode in the following distribution is the class interval $200.01 to $210.00, because the greatest number of earned amounts fall in that range.

Weekly Earnings	No. of Employees
$190.01–$200.00	2
200.01– 210.00	26 ←MODE
210.01– 220.00	19
220.01– 230.00	9
230.01– 240.00	5

The *median* is an average of position; it is the midpoint in an array. In order to determine it, the data must be arranged in an array; that is, in either ascending or descending order. Then it is necessary only to count the number of items and find the mid one, which is the median. For example, assume that five students have the following amounts in their checking accounts:

Student A	$500
Student B	190
Student C	175 ←MEDIAN
Student D	160
Student E	5

The median is $175; on the other hand, the mean is $206. Obviously, the mean is affected by extreme cases (the student with an abnormally large checking account and the one with almost nothing). This kind of influence is why the median is usually selected as the average that comes nearest to indicating the true state of affairs when there are extreme cases in the data.

Percentages

Percentages help in making numbers understandable and the relation of various items to one another and to the total more easily grasped. In the table on page 461, the last column shows the percentage each cost factor represents of the total cost. The statement, "The secretarial cost in producing a business letter is $1.26," has less meaning than "The secretarial cost in producing a business letter is $1.26 or 28.19 percent of the total cost of producing the letter."

Percentage relatives or *index numbers* are used to compare the extent or degree of changes. They are relative because they are based on a value at some specific time and that base must be clearly defined. For example, in 1929 there were approximately 20,000,000 telephones in the United States; in 1934, 17,000,000 telephones; in 1940, 22,000,000; in 1952, 45,000,000; in 1960, 66,500,000; and in 1973, 138,300,000. The percentage relatives, based on the 1929 figure as 100, are 85 for 1934, 110 for 1940, 225 for 1952, 332.5 for 1960, and 691.5 for the 1973 index.

PRESENTING DATA EFFECTIVELY

It is the secretary's responsibility to determine the most effective presentation of numeric data. Tables are preferable for exact representations and, when well constructed, are easy to read for making comparisons and reaching conclusions. Graphics (charts and graphs), on the other hand, are better when quick identification of relationships is important.

Tables

Three types of tables are used for writing business reports: *general-purpose* tables — those to be used for reference; *special-purpose* tables — those that direct the eye and mind to specific relationships of significance; and *spot* tables — unnumbered tables which appear within paragraphs of the report. General-purpose tables are usually placed in the appendix and numbered consecutively. Most of the tables of statistical data included in business reports are special-purpose tables. The tables on page 462 are spot tables.

A table should be self-explanatory. It should be kept simple and designed for rapid reading. The incorporation of too many elements in one table detracts from its readability and effectiveness. When planning a table, keep one question in mind: "Precisely what is this table to show?" All data that do not apply should be excluded.

After the table has been developed, it may be well to dramatize the material presented in it by a chart or graph. In other words, the chart does not replace the table; it supplements it. Tables provide details; charts present relationships but not minutiae and would not be satisfactory to the reader who seeks exact data.

Planning the Table Layout

A well-balanced table can be typed perfectly the first time if the work is carefully planned. The facts and the figures to be tabulated must be analyzed carefully before the various headings and column arrangements are determined. The best method of planning a table is to make a penciled rough draft.

After this plan is drawn, the secretary can save time by using the backspace-from-center method when tabulating.

Suggestions for Typing Tables

Additional suggestions will help you plan and type an effective table that first time!

Table Captions. Most tables include the following sections: main title, secondary heading, column or boxed headings, stub headings, and line headings. Only the main title is typed in all capital letters. The other headings are typed with initial capital letters only. The table below illustrates the important parts of a table.

Main Title. The title should be complete and clearly worded. The main title along with the other headings should make the table self-contained. If the data represent a period of time, the title or sub-headings should indicate the period covered. Include internal punctuation in the title, but no terminal period. Break a title too long for one line at the division of a thought.

POOR: The Annual International Convention of the National
          Secretaries Association (International), July 19–23, 1977, at
          the Hyatt Regency Hotel in Houston, Texas

GOOD: The Annual International Convention
          National Secretaries Association (International)
          Hyatt Regency Hotel, Houston, Texas, July 19–23, 1977

Abbreviations. In order to save space, abbreviations may be used in column headings; but they should never be used in titles.

Columns. For easy reference, the column headings may be numbered consecutively from left to right. Columns of related data

This table was prepared from the work-sheet compilation on page 459. Leaders and skipped lines have been used to improve the readability of the table. To avoid confusion in reading large figures, the amounts are shown in thousands. Thus, $95,200 is shown as $95.2.

THE LEISURE AND RECREATION CORPORATION
SUMMARY OF OPERATIONS
FOR THE YEAR ENDED DECEMBER 31, 19--

Divisions	Sales and Revenues (In Thousands)				Total for Year
	First Quarter	Second Quarter	Third Quarter	Fourth Quarter	
Recreation					
Lawn and Garden...........	$25.6	$ 30.2	$ 39.4	$ 42.7	$137.9
Bicycles/Motorcycles.......	20.5	29.4	36.4	46.2	132.5
Sporting Goods.............	19.5	23.6	33.0	45.0	121.1
Marine Products...........	29.6	32.7	33.2	33.0	128.5
Total	$95.2	$115.9	$142.0	$166.9	$520.0
Recreational Vehicles					
Campers...................	$42.9	$45.2	$70.5	$90.2	$248.8

should be placed closer together than other columns. Major divisions of groups of columns can be indicated by wider spaces or by double vertical rules.

Alignment. In tabulated words and phrases, the left margin should be kept even. In tabulated figures, the right margin must usually be kept straight. When decimal fractions involving different numbers of places to the right of the decimal point are listed, the decimal point must be kept in vertical alignment. Type +, −, and ± signs close to the number at the left. Use dashes, leader points, or a blank space to indicate omissions in a column.

	MULTIPLY	BY	TO OBTAIN (METRIC)
CORRECT ALIGNMENT:	Miles per hour	1.6	Kilometers per hour
	Pounds	0.45	Kilograms
	Square feet	0.09	Square Meters
	Ounces	28.35	Grams
INCORRECT ALIGNMENT:	Miles per hour	1.6	Kilometers per hour
	Pounds	0.45	Kilograms
	Square Feet	0.09	Square Meters
	Ounces	28.35	Grams

Amounts. A comma should be used to separate every three digits in amounts, but it should not be used with the digits after a decimal point. For example: *1,125.50* and *21.16184*.

For sums of money the dollar sign should be used with the first amount in a column and with each total. This also is true of columns of percentages or like symbols (pounds, kilograms, etc.)

Correct:	$1,456.26	*Incorrect:*	$1,456.26
	362.35		$ 362.35
	18.46		$ 18.46
	$1,837.07		$1,837.07

Readability. *Leaders*, or lines of periods, aid the reader by carrying the eyes across a wide expanse of space from one column to another. Leaders are usually typed with a single space between periods. Periods on successive lines should be in vertical alignment. When long columns are single-spaced, skipping a line every three, four, or five rows improves readability.

Rulings. Rulings may improve the appearance of a table. They may be typed with the underline key or made with pencil or a ball-point pen.

To rule lines on the typewriter, place the pencil or pen point at an angle in the cardholder notch. For horizontal lines, move the carriage from left to right. For vertical lines, release the variable line spacer and turn the platen forward or backward.

A double ruling is used at the top of the table two lines below the title. Single rulings should divide the stub and box headings from the rest of the table. A single ruling should also end the table. Vertical rulings should separate the columns. Rulings may be omitted at the sides.

Units. The unit designation of the data must be given (inches, pounds, and so forth). Generally, this information is provided above the columns as a part of the heading or subheading. Leave space above and below a column heading.

Special Notes. If the meaning of any item in the table is not clear or must be qualified, an explanation should be given in the form of a footnote. Footnotes are also used to indicate the source of secondary data.

To identify footnote references in numeric data, use symbols (24, 961*) or lowercase letters (24,961[a]). A number used to reference a footnote (24,961[1]) can be confused as being part of the numeric data.

Reference. The name of the person responsible for the preparation of the table should be indicated on the file copy at least. When the data come from a secondary source, such as a publication, the source should be indicated on the table.

Variety and Emphasis. Both variety and emphasis on relationships can be given to the typed copy by using italics, boldface, and type of different sizes and styles, or by varying the placement of the column totals. Two typewriters, one with pica type and the other with elite, can be used. Footnotes and column headings can be typed in elite type, and the body of the table typed in pica type. Changing the type elements on an element typewriter can provide even wider variations. Also, a wide-carriage typewriter and oversize paper can be used for a table that cannot be accommodated on standard equipment and paper.

Checking the Typed Table

Every typewritten table must be checked for accuracy. Proofreading requires the help of another person, who should read the original draft while the secretary checks the typed copy. Reading figures for checking is an oral technique that has a fairly definite prescribed routine, indicated by the examples given below. The words in the examples that are connected by a hyphen should be read as a group; the commas indicate pauses:

> 718 seven-one-eight
> 98,302 nine-eight, comma three-oh-two
> 24.76 two-four, point, seven-six
> $313.00 three-one-three even (or no cents) dollars
> 77,000 seventy-seven thousand even

For copy in columnar form it is usually advisable to read down a column rather than across the page. This procedure provides a double check because, in most instances, the typing work has been done across the page. If the table includes totals, the amounts in each column should be added and checked against the total.

After the accuracy of the typed table has been verified and errors corrected, the original draft of the table should be filed in a personal folder kept by the secretary or attached to and filed with the typed file copy of the final draft. If anyone who reads the typed copy discovers an error, the filed copy of the original data will enable the secretary to determine whether the error occurred in the original material, which may have been supplied to the secretary, or whether the error was made in the process of typing the table.

Graphic Presentation

A graph is a statistical picture. It presents numerical data in visual form, making them more easily analyzed and remembered. The average person can remember a graph yet is unable to remember the columns of figures upon which the graph is based. Taking the hard facts of business and organizing them in visual form to make comparisons easy, to emphasize contrasts, and to bring out the full force of the message is a challenging opportunity.

Graphic data processing equipment now permits people and machines to exchange graphic information at electronic speed. Some employees work directly with graphics, charts, curves, sketches, and drawings generated on a cathode-ray-display tube. The images can be recorded on film. Another form of business charting is the visual wall chart used for displaying numeric data and qualitative information, such as scheduling of personnel. An illustration of a wall chart is shown below.

You can construct graphs on your typewriter or with the help of commercially available aids, such as Chartpak or Zip-a-tone. These kits contain self-adhering bar and line tapes in various designs and colors. With these materials the amateur can make charts that are very effective — even dramatic. Then there are professional chart makers who can help with more complicated presentations.

Alphabet packs, such as Letraset, can also help the secretary produce an effective graphic presentation. The line graph on page 470 was prepared by a secretary untrained in art, using such materials. The secretary needs a basic knowledge of the various types of graphs. An "Idea" folder can be set up in which examples of each type (both typewritten and commercially prepared) can be placed, with notes concerning their suitability for certain data.

This visual wall chart is used for keeping track of jobs in process.

Visual Planning Corp.

Preparing Charts and Graphs

In making any chart or graph, no matter how simple, it is best to rough out a working copy first. The materials you will need include graph paper, protractor, ruler, compass, and a lettering guide. When the final copy is prepared, the graph should be framed on the paper. The bottom margin should be slightly larger than the top margin. The margins on the sides should be equal unless the pages are to be bound at the left. If the necessary guide points are marked lightly in pencil, they can be erased after the inking in is completed.

The title of the chart or graph should indicate its nature concisely. It should be centered above or below the chart, and its lettering should be the largest or the most heavily emphasized on the chart. The use of lettering guides is recommended. The source of the data and the date of compilation can be placed in one of the bottom corners at either margin. Even when this information is omitted from the presentation copy, it must be recorded on the working copy.

Line Graphs. A commonly used type of graph is the *line graph*. It is most effective in showing fluctuations in a value or a quantity over a period of time, such as variations in production, sales, costs, or profits over a period of months or years. Thus, the line graph is an effective way to depict a comparison of trends over a period of time.

The line graph on page 470 emphasizes the positive relationship that existed between the total sales of foreign and domestic branches of a company over a five-year period.

Follow these suggestions for preparing line graphs:

1. Prepare a working copy on printed graph or coordinate paper and the final or presentation copy on plain paper.

2. Place periods of time on the horizontal scale at the bottom of the graph; record variations in quantities or numbers on the vertical scale.

3. Always show the *zero* point. To prevent the curve from occurring too high on the chart, show a "break" in the chart with two wavy horizontal lines to indicate the part that you have omitted.

4. To avoid distortions, plan the size of your graph. It is good practice to make the width at least one and one-half and not more than one and three-fourths times the height. A rise can be made to appear very steep and thus sharp or quite gradual, depending upon the relation of height to width.

5. If possible, position all lettering horizontally on the chart.

6. Work with no more than four or five lines on a graph, giving each a legend or identification on the graph. Make each line distinctive in

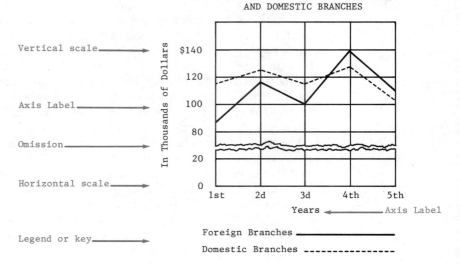

COMPARISON OF TOTAL SALES OF FOREIGN
AND DOMESTIC BRANCHES

This line graph shows the *zero* point, uses two wavy lines to indicate the omission that positions the significant data properly, and gives a key or legend identifying the two items being plotted. As many as four or five items can be plotted, provided the lines are not too close together.

character by using different colors or by using these lines: heavy solid (—), light solid(—), dash (———), dots (. . .), or dot dash (.—.—.—.).

Bar Graphs. The bar graph presents quantities by means of horizontal or vertical bars, both equally effective. Variations in quantity are indicated by the lengths of the bars. The bar graph is most effectively used to compare a limited number of values, generally not more than four or five. Bar graphs are used in time series and frequency distributions.

Follow these suggestions for preparing bar graphs:

1. For easy readability leave one-half to a whole bar width between single bars. Bars can be contiguous, having no spaces between them. This type of bar graph is called a *histogram*.

2. Except for time series, the quantities indicated on the chart should begin with *zero* (0). In a chart where starting at 0 makes the chart too tall or too wide, omit that portion after 0 on which all bars would appear and indicate the omitted portion by a pair of break lines.

3. When possible, arrange bars in ascending or descending order. If they are arranged according to time, chart the earliest period first.

4. Bars may be in outline form or solid. If the bars represent different items, shade or color them for contrast.

5. To type a bar, use uppercase letters (X, W, N, $), a heavy strikeover (X over 0), or a combination of letters and characters.

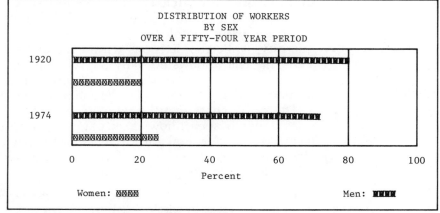

For this typewritten horizontal bar graph, the heavy bar was typed by striking over uppercase *M, W, A,* and *V.* The light bar was typed by striking over uppercase *X* and *O.*

Source: Bureau of the Census and Bureau of Labor Statistics, *Information Please Almanac,* 1976, p. 68.

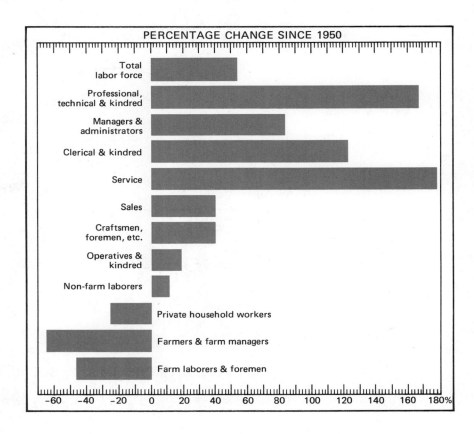

This horizontal bar graph was prepared using commercial materials.

Circle Charts. The circle chart is an effective way to show the manner in which a given quantity is divided into parts. In this type of illustration the complete area of the circle represents the whole quantity, while the divisions within the circle represent the parts. Thus, the chart shows not only the relationship of each part to the whole, but also of each part to every other part. A maximum of six parts is suggested so that all parts can be easily identified.

The circle chart may be used to present such data as how the sales dollar is spent; how taxes paid by a firm are divided among local, state, and federal governments; or the percentage of store purchases made by men compared with those made by women. Follow these suggestions for preparing circle charts:

1. Convert the data to be presented into percentage form. Let the circumference of the circle equal 100 percent.

2. Arrange the elements to be plotted according to size, largest first.

3. Mark the top center of the circumference of the circle, the "12 o'clock" position. From this point, moving in a clockwise direction, mark off that percentage of the total that each segment represents, beginning with the largest segment.

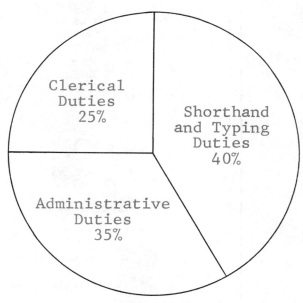

The partially typewritten circle chart shows the relationship of the duties of the multifunctional secretary by classification.

DAILY WORK DISTRIBUTION
OF THE
MULTIFUNCTIONAL SECRETARY

4. Determine the size of each segment. If a protractor is used, the circumference of the circle equals 360°, or a total of 100%; thus a segment representing 10% would be 36°. If a protractor is not available, divide the circumference of the circle into four equal parts (each part representing 25%). Each fourth part may in turn be divided into halves (representing 12½% segments). Follow this division plan until the size of segment desired is obtained.

5. If space permits, identify each segment by a caption inside the segment. Shade or color the segments to provide contrast and to dramatize proportions.

6. Type the titles of the sections horizontally.

Pictorial Charts. One of the more interesting developments in graphic representation is the use of pictorial charts. They are generally an adaptation of one of the other types of graphs in which drawn symbols are used to represent the types of data being charted.

For example, a bar chart showing fire losses may be illustrated with a streaming fire hose, the length of the stream varying with the amount of the loss. The growth of telephone service may be shown by drawings of telephones arranged in a line, each telephone representing so many thousand telephones. It is not considered good practice to represent increases by enlarging the size of the object symbolized, such as augmenting the size of the telephone to indicate an increased number; it is difficult to compare like objects of different sizes. It is easy to determine that one is larger than the other, but to estimate that one is twice or three times as large is difficult. Furthermore, the symbol frequently gives the impression that the item and not the quantity increased in size. Indicate size or growth by more symbols rather than larger symbols.

Map Charts. Maps are often used to depict quantitative information particularly when comparison is made of geographic areas. After the selection of the proper map, follow these suggestions in preparing the map chart:

1. Outline the geographic areas, by use of either color, shading, or crosshatching.

2. Provide a legend to explain the meanings given to the colors, shadings, or crosshatchings.

3. If quantities are involved, figures can be placed inside the geographic area. Other symbols representing quantities, such as dots, may also be used.

EMPLOYMENT IN SELECTED OCCUPATIONS

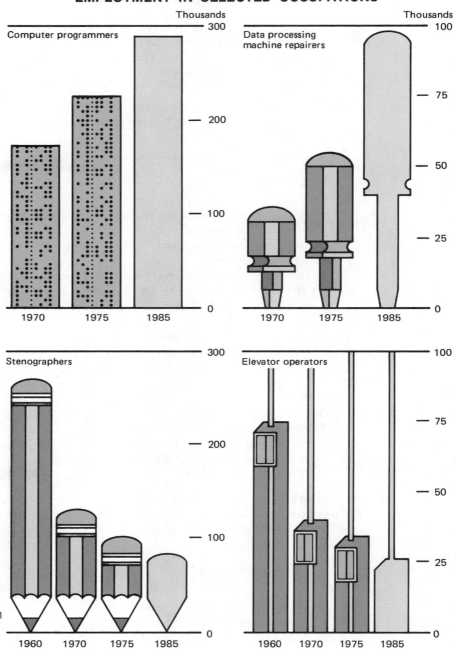

The secretary will not do the actual drawing of a pictorial chart such as this one, but will be responsible for planning the graphs and for the preparation of the drawings by a commercial artist.

Source: U.S. Department of Labor, Bureau of Labor Statistics Bulletin 1919, 1976.

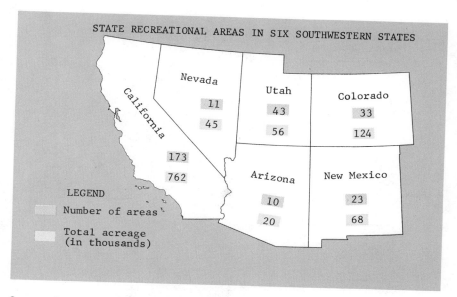

STATE RECREATIONAL AREAS IN SIX SOUTHWESTERN STATES

Nevada
11
45

Utah
43
56

Colorado
33
124

California
173
762

Arizona
10
20

New Mexico
23
68

LEGEND
☐ Number of areas
☐ Total acreage
   (in thousands)

To illustrate a report on recreational facilities, the secretary constructed this map chart, using color to give meaning to the figures presented on the chart.

Source: *Statistical Abstract of the United States*, 1975, p. 212. National Recreation & Park Association, Arlington, Va.

Limitations of Charts and Graphs

While charts or graphs are useful in presenting comparative data, they have certain limitations. The number of facts presented on any one graph is usually limited to four or five. It is best to use a table when six or more items are involved. A second limitation is that only approximate values can be shown on charts or graphs.

A third limitation is that it is possible for a graph to be drawn with mathematical accuracy and still give a distorted picture of the facts being presented. For example, the overall width of a line graph determines the angles of the plotted lines. A graph that is too narrow may indicate a much sharper rise and fall in the lines than the data indicate. In the same way, a graph that is too wide may tend to give the impression of a much more gradual fluctuation than may have actually occurred.

Flowcharts

One of the most widely used tools in office management is the flowchart. It traces a unit of work as it flows through the office. Symbols with connecting lines are used to trace a step-by-step sequence of the work from point of origin to point of completion. The basic symbols are shown on page 476. A template can be purchased

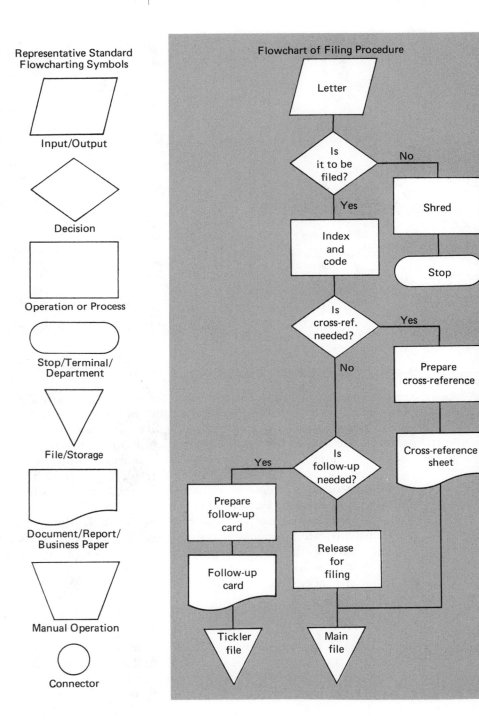

Representative Standard Flowcharting Symbols

Input/Output

Decision

Operation or Process

Stop/Terminal/Department

File/Storage

Document/Report/Business Paper

Manual Operation

Connector

Flowchart of Filing Procedure

Letter

Is it to be filed?

No → Shred → Stop

Yes

Index and code

Is cross-ref. needed?

Yes → Prepare cross-reference → Cross-reference sheet

No

Is follow-up needed?

Yes → Prepare follow-up card → Follow-up card → Tickler file

Release for filing → Main file

for drawing these symbols. While the meaning of each symbol has become fairly standardized, a key can be provided to prevent any misunderstanding.

Organization Charts

An organization chart is a graphic presentation of the organizational structure of a business. It points out responsibility relationships and answers two basic questions: (1) What are the lines of authority (who reports to whom)? (2) What are the functions of each unit (who is responsible for what)?

A business organization is seldom static. It is changed by new personnel, new divisions, new responsibilities, and realignment of old responsibilities. The organization chart, therefore, is frequently revised. The technique of preparing and updating an organization chart is part of the "know-how" that every secretary needs. Following are some suggestions for preparing an organization chart.

1. The chart should be simple. A complex chart can confuse more than it can help.

2. Responsibility should flow downward in the chart with each level clearly identifiable. Lines of authority should be easily identified.

3. When the intersecting of a line is unavoidable, the *pass symbol* (a half-circle "detour" in an otherwise straight line) is used.

4. Different symbols differentiate policy-making positions (line) from support positions (staff).

The organization chart shown on page 24 shows a line-and-staff relationship. Such a chart would be supplemented with a functions chart on which the responsibilities of each position would be identified. To show on one chart both authority relationships and functional responsibilities detracts from its visual simplicity.

SUGGESTED READINGS

Burtt, George. *Putting Yourself Across with the Art of Graphic Persuasion.* Englewood Cliffs: Prentice-Hall, 1972.

Dawe, Jessamon, and William J. Lord. *Functional Business Communication*, 2d ed. Englewood Cliffs: Prentice-Hall, 1974, pp. 340–348.

Famularo, Joseph J. *Organization Planning Manual.* New York: American Management Association, 1971.

Laird, Eleanor. *Data Processing Secretary's Complete Handbook.* Englewood Cliffs: Prentice-Hall, 1973, pp. 107–125.

QUESTIONS FOR DISCUSSION

1. Give two examples based on college enrollment figures to illustrate the necessity for extracting information from raw data so that appropriate decisions can be made.

2. What kind of graph should be prepared to present the data in each of the following?
   (a) Proof that a company has initiated affirmative action programs within the past three years
   (b) The total yearly cost of going to college during the past five years
   (c) Tuition rates at state-supported and private colleges over the past ten years
   (d) Amounts spent on research in the six divisions of a large corporation over the past three years

3. Corporations usually use graphs extensively in their annual reports to stockholders. Financial tables and statements, however, are generally used in presenting data to boards of directors and to banks. Why are graphs used in the one case and tables in the other?

4. What type of graphic presentation would you recommend for the following data?
   (a) Total sales in the U.S. by districts for one year
   (b) Sales by product in six districts for one year
   (c) Total company sales over a twenty-year period
   (d) Airline pilot work schedules
   (e) Steps in invoice processing

5. A consultant firm with a total of 50 employees reported in a community wage study that its average wage (arithmetic mean) was $15,000. An examination of the records revealed that the firm had ten high-paid executives, each receiving over $40,000 a year. What would be your criticism of the reported average wage figure?

6. In the printed copy of the lecture "The Care and Feeding of the Mind" by Professor Jacques Barzun there appears the following paragraph. Punctuate it as you would if it were dictated to you. Then use the Reference Guide to check your answers.

   The lesson is don't be afraid to *lend* your mind. It is a perfectly safe loan you are sure to get it back possibly with interest and in any case the very act of wrapping it around an alien thought will keep it in stretching trim. Give heed to any idea that is proposed to you and see where it leads. Don't judge by first appearances and don't fear a permanent imprint on the pure white page of your mind. You can always wind up with Euclid's favorite conclusion you remember how he starts by saying Let ABC be larger than DEF. You let him foolish as his idea appears from the diagram and pretty soon he reassures you by exclaiming Which is absurd!

7. Type the information in the blanks in the following sentences. Then use the Reference Guide to verify or correct your answers.
   (a) The typewriter is _____ years old. (8)
   (b) We are asking _____ for the typewriter which is _____ years old. ($20, 14)
   (c) To be exact, the mimeograph is _____ years, _____ months, and _____ days old. (15, 8, 4)

PROBLEMS

1. The total sales of four product lines of a women's wear company are $828,000 divided as follows:

Purses.................................... $250,000
Millinery............................... 125,000
Cosmetics............................. 275,000
Hosiery.................................. 178,000

(a) Convert the amount of sales of each line to a percentage of total sales.

(b) Prepare a circle chart showing these percentages.

2. From your knowledge of the personnel composition of a word processing center (see Chapter 1), prepare a line organization chart.

3. The following figures represent the sales volume for Innovative Products for one year. Prepare a line graph of the data. What implications can you give about seasonal fluctuations and general performance for the two years?

	First Year	Second Year
January....................	$86,857	$114,273
February.................	69,623	92,526
March	38,972	64,159
April	34,284	60,844
May	40,485	69,273
June.........................	37,737	76,294
July	40,852	74,858
August.....................	46,085	82,437
September..............	49,592	80,158
October	55,846	83,628
November..............	54,249	87,849
December..............	61,292	94,958

4. Your employer tells you that the company is considering the establishment of a new branch office. The proposed location has narrowed to:

Phoenix, Arizona
St. Petersburg, Florida
Grand Rapids, Michigan
Charlotte, North Carolina
Elyria, Ohio

He asks you to make a comparison of the 1960 and 1970 population reports for these five cities as one of the bases on which the Board of Directors will make its final decision.

(a) Prepare in pencil a tabulation of the data that you secure from a reference source. Compute the percentage of increase or decrease in population during the ten-year period, and arrange the table in descending order. In calculating your percentages, round your population figures to the nearest thousand.

(b) Type the table in good form, making one carbon copy. If necessary, prepare a pencil layout.

5. The following amounts are the April sales per day of a product.

Amount	Amount
$118.23	$ 9.61
41.32	18.23
91.73	107.16
63.24	26.31
36.74	83.17
18.92	67.92
87.65	74.26
27.11	68.31
16.94	17.08
78.26	10.66
124.36	94.33
97.08	101.09
	89.31

(a) Prepare in pencil a tabulation of the sales so that you can determine the median. What is the median sale for April?

(b) Calculate the arithmetic average or mean of the April sales.

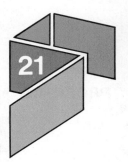

Assistance with Reports, Procedures Writing, and Publications

For every business, large or small, whatever the orientation, today can aptly be described as the age of reporting. The use of the computer has made much more quantitative information available to business than ever before, and this information has led to more and different types of reports. It appears that business is following this principle, "the more information, the better to function and make economic decisions."

In addition to reports involving strictly quantitative analysis, organizations thrive on reports of a qualitative nature; for instance, studies of specific projects and proposals. These reports may take the form of an interoffice memorandum or a bound report.

This chapter discusses the preparation and presentation of business reports, company procedures, and manuscripts for printing. It gives specific instructions for the organization of reports and illustrates techniques for making material attractive and interesting. This information is useful to secretaries in all job classifications.

REPORT WRITING

The primary purpose of a business report is to transmit objective information that in turn stimulates management action. A report is used to plan, organize, and implement business operations; it contains factual information presented in clear, concise language.

Reports are used within the company or outside the company. For internal use, reports are *vertical* (up and down the company ranks) or *horizontal* (across management lines). They are *formal* (written) or *informal* (both written and oral). As business becomes more complex, so do management problems; and the weight of report writing and reports themselves increases. Every year, millions of business reports are written — and generally it is management personnel who must digest and react to the information.

Report-Writing Routine

There is considerable difference in the routine for writing a report and the routine for writing a letter. The originator or an assistant follows this routine in preparing a business report:

Collects the information

Formulates an outline of the contents

Checks logic of content organization

Drafts the report for first typing

Rechecks the organization of material and edits sentence by sentence for clarity and correctness before the second typing

Checks again the organization and editing before final typing

Originators vary in their skill in writing reports. Every originator, however, edits and polishes successive drafts until the final report is as clear, concise, and logical as possible.

The Secretary's Responsibility

The multifunctional secretary, the administrative secretary, and the correspondence secretary play an important part in business report preparation. The multifunctional secretary's role follows closely the report writing routine discussed in the previous paragraph. It is not unusual for the secretary to be involved in each step of the report preparation, from collecting information to the final typing of the report. The administrative secretary may participate in all steps with the exception of the actual typing of the report. The correspondence secretary, on the other hand, would be responsible for the set-up and typing operations.

Naturally, all three secretarial roles include the responsibility for editing the report for clear language, for eliminating repetitive words and phrases, for checking spellings and meanings of words, and for double checking all figures. These are established contributions of the secretary to the report-writing process.

The Form of a Report

Some companies have developed style sheets for all or for special reports. If such is the case, the form indicated in the style sheets will be used as a standard practice. In other cases, the writer follows a consistent pattern.

A short report may consist of only the body or informative text. A long, formal report may have, in addition to the body, various introductory parts and appendixes, the order for which is as follows.

Introductory Parts: Cover or title page (or both)
                       Preface or letter of transmittal, including acknowledgments
                       Table of contents
                       List of tables, charts, and illustrations
                       Summary

Body of the Report: Introduction, including purpose of the report
                                    Main body of the report
                                    Conclusions and recommendations

Supplementary Parts: Appendix or reference section
                                    Bibliography
                                    Index

Notice that the summary *precedes* the main body of the report. This arrangement benefits the busy executive who may be interested in or have time to read only a synopsis of the report. Those who need or want complete information will read the entire report.

Of the three main parts of a report (introductory, body, and supplementary), the body is usually developed first and typed in all but final form before the other parts are prepared. For this reason, the development of the body of a report is discussed first here.

DEVELOPING THE BODY OF THE REPORT

Certainly the originator of a report is responsible for what the report says and what it implies. The writer who has access to a secretary will sensibly and logically work with that individual as a team member in the report preparation.

The Outline

A methodical writer first sets up a topic outline or framework of the report containing all the important points that will be covered. The outline is usually submitted to a superior for approval. This outline may later serve as the table of contents and the heading framework for the report.

No main heading or subheading in an outline ever stands alone. For every *I* there is at least a *II*, for every *A* a *B*. (When an outline contains a "single" heading, a thoughtful reading will usually reveal that the heading actually is part of another point, or misplaced, or irrelevant.) The main headings and subheadings should be phrased accurately and concisely *in parallel style*. They can be short constructions, long constructions that tell the story, or even complete sentences; but once the style is established, it must be consistent and parallel throughout.

In the following partial first-draft outline concerning the design of a business form, notice the parallel language (underscored) used in each category.

```
              DESIGNING A BUSINESS FORM

    I   PURPOSE OF THE FORM

        A.   Systems Analysis

             1.  Definition of the Problem
             2.  Discussion of the Facts
             3.  Analysis of the Results of the Study
             4.  Recommendation

        B.   Preparation of the Proposal

             1.  Rationale for the Study
             2.  Discussion of the Systems Analysis

    II  FORM DESIGN

        A.   Type of Information
        B.   Space Requirements
        C.   Sequence of Information
```

The Rough Draft

A carefully written formal paper is typed one or more times in rough-draft form. A rough draft is generously spaced and accurately transcribed with little thought of final form or appearance. The purpose of the rough draft is to get the writer's thoughts on paper — to provide something tangible to edit and improve. Rather than a waste of time, this is a vital step. In typing rough drafts, the secretary follows these practices:

1. The paper used is less than letterhead quality but is sufficiently strong to withstand erasing during the editing process. Many offices use colored paper.
2. Carbon copies are not made unless they are expressly requested. If an extra copy is needed for cutting into strips in reorganizing the material, a copy can be made on a copying machine.
3. Plenty of room for write-ins and transfer indications is provided by use of triple spacing and wide margins on all four sides.
4. Each successive draft is given a number and dated. Each page is numbered in sequence and sometimes carries the draft number and date also.

C. Brewer and Company, Limited

Preparation of a rough draft enables the writer or writers of a report to review it and make improvements before a final copy is typed.

5. Each successive draft is carefully checked and proofread so that subsequent drafts will contain valid material.
6. Typing errors are X'd or lined out unless the machine has a correcting mechanism.
7. Quoted matter, if several lines in length, is single-spaced and indented in the same form as in the final copy because changes in quoted matter are unlikely.
8. Footnotes are typed at the bottom of the page, or on a separate sheet, or as shown on page 485.

Save all rough drafts until the report is completed and presented, even though they have been superseded, because the writer may decide to use material from an earlier draft.

TYPING THE BODY OF THE REPORT

The final version of the report measures the originator's skill in concise, logical writing and the secretary's skill in sustained, attractive, meticulous typing and proofreading. To be sure that each page is uniformly typed, the secretary designs an attractive page layout for use in the final typing. If the secretary has a memory typewriter, instructions can be programmed into the machine. A dictionary and a punctuation guide must be within easy reach of the typist.

Most reports require multiple copies. Today the tendency is to type the original and photocopy for distribution or type the original on a master for reproduction.

A simple method of incorporating a footnote into a rough draft is shown

in this example[1]--that is, to type the footnote immediately

---

[1]J Marshall Hanna, Estelle L. Popham, and Rita Sloan Tilton, <u>Secretarial Procedures and Administration</u> (7th ed.; Cincinnati: South-Western Publishing Co., 1978), p. 513.

---

below the line in which the reference number appears, separated from the

textual matter above and below by lines across the page.

Footnotes typed in this style in a rough draft will automatically be retained in correct position if copy is rearranged during editing.

Page Layouts

There are two kinds of typed page layouts: the *traditional*, which looks much like a standard printed page of a textbook; and the *non-traditional*, in which the units of typing are creatively arranged and displayed. The successful secretary must be alert to ways of presenting facts in nontraditional layouts as well as in traditional ones. By varying margins, line spacing, indentions, capital and small letters, spacing between letters and words, underlining, placement of various parts, using white space generously, and devising charts, drawings, and graphs, the secretary can achieve results that will greatly enhance the effectiveness of a report.

Indentions. Paragraphs may be typed flush with the left margin or indented 5, 10, 15, or even 20 spaces. For single-spaced reports blocked or with paragraph indentions, double-space between paragraphs. In blocked double-spaced work, triple-space between paragraphs. Indentions make for easier reading regardless of the line space of the body.

Margins. The suggestions that follow will help the secretary maintain uniform margins.[1] Simplify the typewriting job by placing a *special guide sheet* directly behind the page being typed. Use ordinary bond or other serviceable paper (or onionskin, if carbon copies are necessary). The guide sheet, illustrated on page 486 for a left-bound manuscript, should be ruled with dark ink or colored pencil that will be visible through the top sheet.

1. In the *upper right corner* and *centered at the bottom* are short lines positioned so that a page number typed to rest on them will leave a ½-inch top and a 1-inch side margin or a ½-inch bottom margin, as

---

[1]Adapted from Erwin M. Keithley and Philip J. Schreiner, *A Manual of Style for the Preparation of Papers and Reports* (2d ed; Cincinnati: South-Western Publishing Co., 1971).

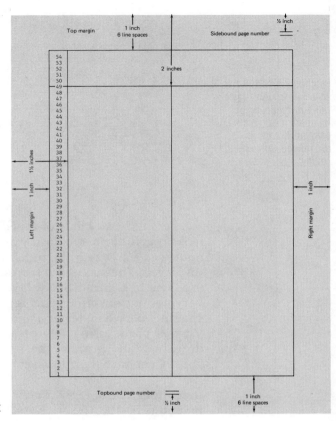

A Special Guide Sheet

desired. Usually only topbound manuscripts are numbered at the foot of the page; but if a first page of an unbound or leftbound manuscript is to be numbered, the number is centered at the foot of the page as for a topbound manuscript.

2. The vertical rule 1½ inches from the left indicates the left margin setting. The extra ½ inch is for binding.

3. The vertical rule 1 inch from the right indicates the right margin of the copy. Keep the right margin as even as possible. No more than two or three letters should extend beyond the vertical line. Use a word-division manual for speedy and correct decisions about end-of-line hyphenations. Avoid hyphenating words at the end of the first line on a page or at the end of more than two consecutive lines, and never end a page with a hyphenated word. Do not end or begin a line with a 1- or 2- letter syllable.

4. Two horizontal lines (1 inch and 2 inches from the top of the sheet) mark the top margins of the manuscript. The first page begins on Line 13, which leaves a 2-inch top margin. Subsequent pages start

on Line 7, which leaves a 1-inch top margin. (Position the typewriter cylinder to type on the first line of writing *below* the rules
shown.)

5. The horizontal line 1 inch from the bottom edge of the paper indicates the last line available for typing. Plan to leave at least two
   lines of a paragraph on the page and carry at least two lines forward to the next page. Plan the last line of the body of the material
   to allow for any footnotes that go on that page.

6. The vertical center rule shows the horizontal centering point of the
   page, the point equidistant between the marginal rulings at left
   and right.

Titles. An attractively arranged title or an unconventional display of
a title draws attention to the material, a respectable objective of a
title page. Several variations of title placement are illustrated
below.

1. Titles centered, optional underscoring:

```
           TRADITIONAL TITLE

        Uppercase  and  Lowercase

      S P R E A D    H E A D I N G

   EXTRA    SPACE    BETWEEN    WORDS
```

2. Framed titles, centered:

```
   .  .  .  .  .  .  .  .  .  .  .  .
   .        A   T I T L E         .
   .         F R A M E D          .
   . D I S T I N C T I V E L Y .
   .  .  .  .  .  .  .  .  .  .  .  .
```

3. Distinctive arrangements, centered:

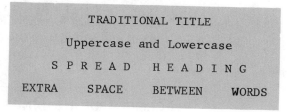

```
         - - - A n   U n c o n v e n t i o n a l
             A r r a n g e m e n t   o f
               t h e   T i t l e - - - - -

   ---An  Unconventional              ---An Unconventional
   Arrangement of the                   Arrangement
         Title---                         of the Title---
```

Every typewritten title is a part of a picture. Therefore, select a
style that is attractive in width and weight and that is in satisfying

proportion to the dimensions of the typed page. It is hard to *visualize* which form of title is best. But you can try them out for size, weight, and appearance by typing several experimental arrangements of the title, cutting them out, and laying each one on a full page of similar typing. The best one will become evident.

Headings and Subheadings. Headings and subheadings are used to guide the reader through the report. The criterion for their wording is: Does the heading clarify the content and increase readability, and is the construction parallel to other headings?

In general, headings and subheadings parallel the outline. Note their arrangement in this book and their usefulness in preparing the reader and in showing the relative importance of subject matter.

Both headings and subheadings can be varied by placement, by use of capitals and small letters, and by indentions. Before typing the report, the multifunctional secretary prepares a guide to the form and position of each heading and subheading, of each margin and indention, and of all line spacing. This plan, typed in a form easily referred to, is called a *style sheet*.

If the report is being typed in the word processing center and the originator prefers a certain format, the administrative secretary prepares a style sheet and sends it to the center with the manuscript.

A suggested placement guide for headings and subheadings is given below.

PLACEMENT OF HEADINGS AND SUBHEADINGS

Caption	*Placement*
Title of Report or Chapter Number	All capitals, optional underscoring. Two inches from top of paper. Each line centered horizontally. Four blank lines to first line of main heading.
A Main Heading or Chapter Title	All capitals, underscored, centered. Two blank lines to first line of typing.
First Subheading	All capitals, flush with left margin. One blank line to first line of typing.
Second Subheading	Initial capital letters, underscored, typed at paragraph indention point (five or more spaces).

Quoted Matter

Reports often quote material from other sources, either directly or indirectly, and must give credit to these sources. For indirect quotations or references, a footnote suffices. Direct quotations are handled in the following ways:

1. Quotations of *fewer than four lines* are typed in the body of the paragraph and enclosed in quotation marks.

2. Quotations of *four or more lines* are usually typed without quotation marks, single-spaced, and indented from the left margin or from both margins.

3. When a quotation of *several paragraphs* is not indented, quotation marks precede each paragraph and follow the final word in the last paragraph only.

4. *A quotation within a quotation* is enclosed in single quotation marks.

5. *Italicized words* in the quotation are underscored.

6. *Omissions* are shown by ellipses — three spaced (or unspaced) periods within a sentence, four periods at the end of a sentence.

7. *Inserted words (interpolations)* are enclosed in typewritten brackets using the underscore and diagonal: [ ]. Parentheses cannot be used, as they often occur naturally in the context and the reader could not identify matter enclosed in them as inserted matter.

8. A *footnote reference* showing the source should be made for the quotation unless the source is identified adequately in the text.

Permission to quote copyrighted material must be obtained from the copyright holder when reports are to be printed or duplicated and given public circulation. Material published by a governmental agency is not copyrighted. Full information should be sent with the request including:

1. The text leading up to the quotation or a copy of the page which includes the quotation.

2. The lines to be quoted, or lines underscored on the page as it will be published.

3. The credit line or complete footnote reference.

4. The title, publisher, and date of publication of the material in which the quoted matter will appear.

Footnotes

Footnotes are numbered in sequence on each page, throughout each section, or throughout the entire report. There is an advantage in numbering footnotes anew with each page or section — if footnotes are inserted or deleted, only the numbers on the page or within the section need be changed. Styles of typing footnotes may be reviewed in the footnote and bibliography style guide in the Communications Guide in Part 10.

Numbering Pages

Usually the typist saves time by waiting until the body is typed in final form before typing page numbers. If making carbon copies, the typist numbers the top sheet of each carbon assembly in pencil as it is completed, thus keeping unpaged copy in order. After the supplementary sections and the preliminary pages have been typed, page numbers can be typed for the body of the report.

Arabic numerals without punctuation are placed at the upper right corner of the body and supplementary parts of the report. Numbering the first page of a report is optional. If it is numbered, the number appears at the bottom center. The preliminary pages preceding the body are numbered in small Roman numerals at the bottom center.

PREPARING AND TYPING THE OTHER PARTS

The order in which the other parts of a report are prepared varies, but inserting page numbers on the table of contents must be one of the last steps. In the following discussion the concluding supplementary parts and then the introductory parts are considered.

Appendix or Reference Section

In a formal report an *appendix* or *reference section* devoted to supplementary information, supporting tables and statistics, or reference material follows the body of the report.

Bibliography

A report that is based upon a study of published materials frequently includes a bibliography listing the source material. Such a bibliography is called a *selected bibliography*. Many business reports are based on factual information within the company, and there is no need to refer to outside source material.

Sometimes the multifunctional or administrative secretary is requested to prepare a *comprehensive bibliography* listing all the material published on a subject for a selected period of time. An *annotated bibliography* contains an evaluation or a brief explanation of the content of each reference.

A bibliography reference is very similar in form to a footnote in that it cites the author's name, the title of the publication, the publisher, and the date. The name of an editor, a translator, or an illustrator may also be included. The price and complete details on the number of illustrations, plates, diagrams, and so on can be included if this information will be of value to those who will use the bibliography. Specific chapters or sections and their inclusive page numbers should be stated if the entry refers to only a certain part of the book or periodical; otherwise, page numbers are omitted.

Index

An *index* is included only when it is felt that there will be occasion to use it. A detailed table of contents usually suffices. When an index is necessary, the secretary uses a copy of the report for underlining in colored pencil each item on each page that should be included in the index. Each underlined item and its page number are written on a separate slip. The completed slips are then sorted into alphabetic order, and a typed index is prepared from them.

X
Transmittal, letter of, for a
X
report

491

The index slip for an item from this book is shown. The *X's* indicate that cross-reference slips were made and listed under *Letter of transmittal for a report* and *Report, letter of transmittal for.*

Letter of Transmittal

Frequently a *letter of transmittal* is bound into the report and performs a function similar to the preface of a book. It gives authorization for the report, details of its preparation, the period covered, acknowledgment of persons who contributed materials, and other such information to help the reader understand the depth and breadth of the report and arouse interest in studying it. (See page 495.)

The letter of transmittal is typed on the regular business letterhead and is signed in ink. It is reproduced on the same kind of paper used for the other pages of a duplicated or printed report, and the signature is duplicated rather than handwritten.

Summary

The summary is a concise review of the entire report and its findings. It includes a statement of the problem, its scope, the method of investigation, conclusions, and recommendations. It is objective in nature and is written to give the reader a clear understanding of the facts in the report. The length of the report determines the length of the summary; however, recommended style is to limit the summary to one page.

Title Page

Even a report of five or ten pages is improved with a *title page*. The title page designed by the secretary should be simple if the report is typed in traditional form. If the report is typed in nontraditional form, the secretary should try for distinction and artistic display of the information. Attractive borders can be made using the m, x,), (, *, ', or " keys or a decorative key.

The title page must contain the essential facts for identifying the report: the title, for whom it is prepared, by whom it is submitted, the date, and the place of preparation. The essential facts vary with the contents and the readers of a report. An interoffice report may require only the title and the date. The writer should approve the content and arrangement of the title page.

Table of Contents

After paging the report, the secretary prepares the table of contents that precedes the report. This table lists the main topics or chapter titles and page numbers, possibly conforming to the original outline. It may be useful to list subheadings and their page numbers as well. Rough out the table of contents to get an idea of its vertical length and the horizontal length of the items before deciding on the final style.

The next five pages present parts of a report typed in acceptable form.

```
**************************************************************************
```

A FEASIBILITY STUDY

OF

WORD PROCESSING - ADMINISTRATIVE SUPPORT CENTERS

```
*****************************
```

Prepared for

Electro-Mag Company
1606 North McVickers Street
Chicago, Illinois

```
*****************************
```

Submitted by

Management Research, Inc.
2500 Diversey Parkway, West
Chicago, Illinois

June 30, 19--

```
**************************************************************************
```

Title Page for a
Left-Bound Report

TABLE OF CONTENTS

Table of Contents Page
for a Left-Bound
Report

June 30, 19--

Mrs. Agnes B. Harper
Electro-Mag Company
1606 North McVickers Street
Chicago, IL 60639

Dear Mrs. Harper:

The feasibility study, authorized by you on January 1
of this year, concerning the establishment of the word processing
center concept in your organization is now complete.

The study included a thorough investigation of your company's
written communications requirements and a series of conferences
at random with management personnel and employees in the office.
An attitude survey of the clerical staff was also made.

It is recommended that the Electro-Mag Company establish
an experimental satellite word processing center in the Sales
Department and that a work measurement procedure be adopted for
this center. After a period of six months, it is suggested that
an evaluation be made of the center's productivity. This evaluation
will determine whether the concept should be implemented in the
Accounting and Manufacturing Departments.

Working with you and your staff has been a pleasure. Our
gratitude is expressed to the many employees of the Electro-Mag
Company who cooperated with us in making this study.

Yours very truly,

Jean J. Torres

Jean J. Torres
Director of Research

i

Letter of Transmittal
for a Left-Bound
Report

SUMMARY

The feasibility study of the word processing - administrative support center concept for the Electro-Mag Company indicated the desirability of implementation for the company. Immediate advantages will be realized in the rapid delivery of error-free sales proposals, in the capability of sending original copies of sales letters to prospective customers, and in the ability to meet the deadlines faced by the company in many of its written reports. The change to the system concept of producing written transcripts will result in long-term reduction of clerical costs in terms of personnel needs and supervisory time.

We recommend that:

1. The Electro-Mag Company establish an experimental satellite center in the Sales Department.

2. A work measurement study be made during the trial period of six months.

3. Six word processing stations be established in the center under the direction of two supervisory personnel.

4. An evaluation of the productivity of the center be made at the end of the trial period.

The results of the evaluation will determine whether additional centers should be established in the Accounting and Manufacturing Departments.

Summary Page for a
Left-Bound Report

<u>A FEASIBILITY STUDY</u>

<u>OF</u>

<u>WORD PROCESSING - ADMINISTRATIVE SUPPORT CENTERS</u>

INTRODUCTION

<u>The Problem</u>

The establishment of word processing - administrative support centers in the Electro-Mag Company is explored to determine whether the concept can meet the ever-growing communication needs of the company without an increase in per page costs. Random conferences with management personnel and surveys of the clerical staff are evaluated.

<u>Purpose of the Report</u>

Because of the increase in the written communication requirements of the Electro-Mag Company and the need for a reduction of clerical costs in this area, this feasibility study has been undertaken to determine whether the word processing center concept can accomplish these objectives. All factors involved in the output of written communications are considered. These factors are then studied in a cost analysis within each department of the company.

<u>Definitions</u>

The terms used frequently in this report are defined here.

<u>Word Processing</u>. The term used in a system whereby written communications are produced by power typewriters.

PROOFREADING, FINAL CHECKING, ASSEMBLING, AND BINDING

After all the typing is finished, four important steps remain: proofreading, final checking of mechanics, assembling, and binding. (All figures and computations would, of course, have been checked *before* the final typing.) If the report is typed in the word processing center, these activities would be performed in the center. The administrative secretary also proofreads the report.

Proofreading

Each typed page of the final copy of the report is proofread word for word and figure for figure. A practical plan is to use a copy for checking, boldly marking all corrections on it, and filing it permanently. The careful worker goes through the material at least twice — the first time comparing the copy with the original for accuracy of typing and for omissions, and a second time for consistency of style and form. If possible, proofread the copy with the help of another person.

Final Checking

Use a final-check sheet and go through the report once for each factor listed below. This final check has caught many an embarrassing error and is, in fact, a device that can well be used for all work involving detail and accuracy. Check the following items *on each set* of the report unless a copying machine has been used.

1. Indicated corrections made on every page

2. Correct references to page numbers, tables, or figures

3. Correct sequence of page numbers (necessary for each set even when a copying machine has been used)

Assembling

The final report is submitted in complete sets, with the ribbon copy on top. The typed pages are assembled in reverse order — that is, the bottom page is laid out first, face up. In this way, you can see any blank or mutilated pages during assembly. When you have collated a complete set, joggle the pages horizontally and vertically until they are exactly aligned.

Binding

Binding is the last step in preparing a report. The most popular form of binding is the staple. When only one staple is required, position it diagonally in the upper left corner. When a wider margin has been left for binding at the top or at the left, use two or three staples along the wide margin, parallel with the edge of the paper.

If a report that is to be stapled proves to be too thick, use double stapling, inserting the staples in proper position from the front and then inserting a second set in the same spots from the back.

Some offices prefer sturdier and more permanent types of binding. Some of these bindings require special supplies and equipment, such as metal eyelets, punches, wire spiral devices, or plastic combs. A convenient and attractive cover in transparent plastic with a snap-on spine is available.

PREPARING COPY FOR THE PRINTER

Most of the duties associated with preparing a manuscript for a magazine or an outside printer are part of the multifunctional and administrative secretary's responsibilities. If a word processing center is available, the actual typing would be done in the center. Since the copy is to be followed exactly, it is imperative that punctuation and spelling be correct. Of course, the office retains a file copy for ready reference.

If possible, the secretary should discuss styling with the person who is to be responsible for the work. Together they should develop a style sheet showing the type to be used for main headings and subheadings, for footnotes, for bibliography, and for captions.

Manuscript

A manuscript to be typeset must meet the following important specifications:

1. Type all copy double-spaced on one side of 8½- by 11-inch sheets, with one or preferably two copies. Leave generous side margins. Quoted material or other text matter to be set apart should be single-spaced and indented on both sides.

2. Key all typewritten copy to its exact position on a page layout.

3. Number all sheets in the upper right corner. Two or more compositors may work on the same assignment, so correct numbering is imperative.

4. Type incidental changes, or write them clearly in ink, between the lines or in the margins.

5. Typewrite a long addition on a separate full-sized sheet and give it an inserted page number, as 16a; indicate on page 16 the point at which the insertion is to be made.

6. Draw a heavy line through words to be omitted.

7. Give explicit directions. With the help of a compositor, specify size and style of type faces and amount of leading (space between lines) desired.

8. Use a single underline to indicate *italics*, a double underline for SMALL CAPS, and a triple underline for REGULAR CAPS. To indicate bold face, use a wavy underline.

9. Number footnotes consecutively. They may be typed on the page to which they pertain; between full-width rules directly under the line in which the reference occurs; at the bottom of the page but separated from the text by short line; or all in sequence on a separate sheet.

10. If a photograph is to be included, type the caption on a separate piece of paper and paste on the bottom edge of the picture.

11. Provide titles and number tables and illustrations consecutively with Arabic numerals. Send with the manuscript a full list of all tables and illustrations.

12. Include a title page showing the title, the author's name and address, and perhaps the date.

13. Include the author's vita sheet, if requested.

14. Send the original copy to the printer. Do not fasten the sheets together. Keep them flat by placing them between strong cardboards or in a strong box.

15. Send the manuscript by first-class mail.

Magazine Articles and Press Releases

At times an executive may be asked to submit an article for magazine publication. The secretary simplifies the editor's job of judging the space needed for the copy by typing a sample paragraph from a recent issue of the magazine line for line. In this way average line length and the number of lines to an inch of printed material is determined. Headings for the copy should be consistent with those used in the magazine. This information becomes the style sheet for the article. A covering letter giving the approximate number of words in the article also aids the editor.

If the approximate length requirements of the article are provided by the publisher, the secretary types a rough-draft version with double spacing in the average line length of the magazine copy. This copy is given to the executive with a close estimation of the amount of space presently accounted for. As revisions are made the executive can lengthen or shorten the article. Copies of the published material should be kept in a file so labeled.

Press releases should be addressed to the City Editor unless a definite person (such as the Financial Editor) is specified. Publicity and news releases are discussed in Chapter 10.

Reading Proof

It is customary for the printer to submit proofs. The secretary usually does the checking for errors, but the executive should be given an opportunity to approve revisions.

The first proof is usually in galley form — long sheets containing one column of printed copy, the column width as on the final printed page. Each kind of error or change to be made is indicated by a proofreader's mark (illustrated in the Reference Guide on page 741). The place of the correction is indicated in the text, and the kind of correction to be made is written in the margin on the same line. If there is more than one correction in a line, the proofreader's marks in the margin are separated by conspicuous diagonal lines.

The printer submits the second proof in page form. This new proof must be again meticulously read and corrected. Page numbers and page headings are shown in this proof and are usually checked as separate individual operations. This is often the final opportunity for the author to catch errors and to make changes.

PROCEDURES WRITING

Procedures writing has been called "verbal flowcharting." It lists step by step the logical sequence of activities involved in a given task so that an employee can perform an operation by following instructions. Procedures writing serves to control as well as to communicate. It controls how things are to be done as it instructs employees in the steps to follow in recurring operations.

Writing good procedures seems deceptively simple, but to eliminate extraneous material is extremely difficult. Effective procedures writing is one of the most valuable forms of business writing because it saves time and money.

Writing procedures is a sophisticated process — so much so, in fact, that some companies assign one person to write procedures, thus maintaining uniformity. It is important that procedures be written in a simple, direct style, using terms easily understood by all who will be expected to interpret and follow them.

Procedures for a department or for an operation are usually collected in a loose-leaf notebook that can be updated by adding and deleting pages as new procedures are issued. The notebook is commonly known as a procedures manual. It is helpful to include an index in the manual for easy reference.

A Sample Procedure

The establishment of word processing centers in most large corporate headquarters has necessitated the development of procedures for submitting work to the centers. As an administrative secretary, you might be asked to write some of the procedures which affect your office. Assume that your input is requested for the submittal of material to the center. There are at least four formats that you can use in writing the procedures: traditional, improved traditional, job breakdown, and playscript. These formats are illustrated on the following pages.

The traditional format features prose-style writing and uses little spacing variation.

```
The word originator who has a hard copy document to be typed
by the word processing center prepares the document in
readable form with complete instructions and attaches it
to Form 101 WP, Word Processing Center Job Ticket, and
sends to the Word Processing Center.

The Word Processing Manager enters the document on Form 102 WP,
Work Log, and notes the date and time on the Job Ticket.
The manager then assigns the work to one of the Correspondence
Secretaries.

The Correspondence Secretary types the final document in
appropriate form and makes the required number of copies
and then submits to the Word Processing Coordinator for
proofreading and distribution.  The messenger delivers the
completed work to the originator for signature and mailing.
```

The improved traditional format uses variations in spacing, underlining, and tabulations to emphasize appropriate points.

```
The word originator who has a hard copy document to be typed
by the word processing center

        1.   completes Form 101 WP giving detailed instructions
        2.   attaches Form 101 WP to the document
        3.   sends to the word processing center

The Word Processing Manager enters the document on the Work Log,
noting the date and time on Form 101 WP, and gives to a
correspondence secretary for typing.

After typing the document, the correspondence secretary submits
the work to the word processing coordinator for proofreading
and distribution.  A messenger delivers the work to the
originator for signature and mailing.
```

Job Breakdown. With the job breakdown the logical sequence of action is reflected in the *Steps*. The *Key Points* represent cautions to the worker at the points where mistakes are likely. The *Steps* tell the worker what to do; the *Key Points* tell how to do it.

Every *Step* does not have to have a *Key Point*, and there may be more than one *Key Point* for one operation.

Steps	Key Points
1. Prepare hard copy document.	1. Be sure that the document is in readable form.
2. Attach to Form 101 WP, Word Processing Job Ticket.	2. Include complete instructions and all necessary information.
3. Send to Word Processing Center by messenger.	3. Note the time the work was picked up.
4. Receive completed work from the Word Processing Center.	4a. Check to see that directions were followed and all information included.
	4b. Verify number of copies.
	4c. Check to see if envelope is included and is the right size.
5. Sign and mail.	5. Any changes would require the return of the document to the Center.

The Job Breakdown Format

Playscript. The playscript format answers the question, "Who does what?" It utilizes the team approach in completing office tasks. The actor is easily identified, and what the actor does starts with an action verb in the present tense. According to the developer of this technique, playscript is really a form of flowchart. Any step that backflows rather than proceeds by forward action can immediately be spotted, and gaps in the logical steps can also be quickly detected, just as backflow is revealed in a flowchart.

Responsibility	Action
Word Originator	1. Prepares document in readable form including complete instructions.
	2. Attaches Form 101 WP, Word Processing Center Job Ticket, and sends to the Center.
Word Processing Manager	3. Enters the document of Form 102 WP, Work Log, noting the date and time on the Job Ticket.
	4. Assigns the work to a correspondence secretary.
Correspondence Secretary	5. Prepares final document in appropriate form and number of copies.
	6. Submits to word processing coordinator.
Word Processing Coordinator	7. Proofs work and prepares for distribution.
Messenger	8. Delivers to originator for signature and mailing.

The Playscript Format

Selecting the Format

A traditional person or a traditional company would probably adopt the improved arrangement of the traditional format. A more venturesome author in search of eye-catching appeal would probably choose the job breakdown or the playscript. In a procedure involving one operator, the job breakdown might be chosen, for it has the advantage of cautioning against wrong moves. It looks more complicated than the playscript, however. The playscript would probably be selected for writing procedures involving more than one worker.

SUGGESTED READINGS

Archer, Robert M., and Ruth Pearson Ames. *Basic Business Communications*. Englewood Cliffs: Prentice-Hall, 1971.

Dawe, Jessamon, and William J. Lord. *Functional Business Communication*. Englewood Cliffs: Prentice-Hall, 1974, pp. 277–330.

Fulton, Ruth Coan. *Easy Guide to Report Writing*. Portland: Colonial Offset, 1974.

Keithley, Erwin M., and Philip J. Schreiner. *A Manual of Style for the Preparation of Papers and Reports*, 2d ed. Cincinnati: South-Western Publishing Co., 1971.

Matthies, Leslie H. *The New Playscript Procedure*, Management Tool for Action. Stamford: Office Publications, 1977.

Turabian, Kate L. *A Manual for Writers of Term Papers, Theses, and Dissertations*, 4th ed. Chicago: University of Chicago Press, 1973.

QUESTIONS FOR DISCUSSION

1. Assume that you and two other multifunctional secretaries will type the final copy of a formal report for your immediate supervisor. How will you make sure that all pages are uniform in placement and follow proper format? How will you proofread the work?

2. How do the responsibilities of the administrative secretary, the correspondence secretary, and the multifunctional secretary differ in business report preparation for one word originator?

3. Who and what determine the format of the company procedures manual?

4. In this age of sophisticated reprographic techniques, why should secretaries of all levels have training in the basics of printing?

5. If you had obtained all the data available on a certain subject and an executive had drafted a report based on this information, what would you do if in the morning's mail you received a business magazine containing an article which covers a new angle of the subject? Would you call the executive's attention to the new material, knowing that it would mean a rewrite job?

6. In what ways will a report differ if it is intended for individuals (a) who know little about the subject matter or (b) who are technicians of the subject matter? Give examples of types of reports written for each category.

7. Tell how you would indicate the following kinds of omissions in quoted matter. Then use the Reference Guide to verify or correct your answers.

> Research has barely begun, (words omitted here) and no fair estimate of additional time required can be given (closing words of sentence omitted here). We hope three months will be sufficient but can make no promises. (sentence omitted here) Two of the technicians begin new assignments October 1.

8. Tell how you would punctuate the following kinds of changes in quoted matter. Then use the Reference Guide to verify or correct your answers.

(a) To show a correction:
> This material is of excellent *actually inferior* quality.

(b) To show an uncorrected error:
> The *author's* styles are similar.

(c) To show an interpolation:
> Since publication *1975* the situation has changed.

PROBLEMS

1. Type each of the following titles twice (eight different arrangements). Divide the titles into two or more lines if necessary, and center each line horizontally on the page. Allow six line spaces between titles. Indicate your preference of the resulting styles.

(a) Career Paths in Word Processing Centers

(b) How Data Communication Creates Total Business Systems

(c) The Mature Woman Returns to Work in the Business Office

(d) The Increasing Ranks of the Male Secretary

2. As administrative assistant in a government procurement office, you are assigned the supervision of two young assistants. You have given them the responsibility of opening and sorting the office mail. You decide to prepare a procedural statement in playscript style covering this activity. Before you begin writing, you analyze the cycle of the operation, determine the actors involved (the two assistants, mail messenger, and yourself), analyze each action in the operation, and identify any office forms used in the process. Write the statement of procedures. (You may wish to refer to Chapter 7).

3. Type an outline of an article on the topic of word processing appearing in any recent issue of *Administrative Management* or *Word Processing World*.

4. From the bibliographical notes that you prepared for Problem 1 in Chapter 19, develop a business report on one of the ten topics given (or a topic of your own choice which your instructor has approved). Use graphs or tables if you think they will improve your presentation.

5. To provide some practice for yourself in using proofreader's marks, indicate the method of marking (both in the

text material and in the margins) the changes listed below. Set up three columns headed *Change Desired in Text, Proofreader's Mark in Text,* and *Proofreader's Mark in Margin.*

(1) Insert the word *more.*
(2) Change the word *readnig* to *reading.*
(3) Delete the word *usually.*
(4) Show a space in *ofthis.*
(5) Even up the left margin where the letters have been set a space too far to the left in one line.
(6) Write the word *think* in solid capitals.
(7) Show an apostrophe in the word *womens.*
(8) Capitalize the word *congressional.*
(9) Insert a hyphen in *selfemployed.*
(10) Indicate a new paragraph in the copy.
(11) Italicize the word *usually.*
(12) Use lowercase correctly for the words *History, Algebra, Social Studies,* and *English.*
(13) In marking the copy for the preceding question, you inadvertently indicated that the word *English* should be written in lowercase too. Show that you want the original capitalization to stand.
(14) Transpose *two only* to *only two.*
(15) Use less space between words.
(16) Use small caps for the paragraph heading, *Characteristics of the New Process.*
(17) Use quotation marks around *shot in the arm.*
(18) Indicate no paragraph.
(19) Indicate that type does not match.
(20) Delete the hyphen in *readily-available service.*
(21) Insert a comma between *pens* and *and.*
(22) Center and type in solid caps the heading: *Introduction.*

(23) Change *thimk* to *think.*
(24) Indicate leaving more space after a colon.
(25) Increase the amount of space between lines.
(26) Move copy to the right to align.
(27) Indicate correct spelling of *state room.*
(28) Delete the apostrophe in *it's.*
(29) In the title *A Manual of Style for the Preparation of Papers and Reports,* the words *and Reports* have been crossed out. Indicate that these two words should be retained.
(30) Delete the comma: *He finished the report, and got it on his superior's desk before leaving the office that afternoon.*

6. Using information in the Communications Guide, type correctly as a footnote and as a bibliography item the following information:
(a) An unsigned article, "A Prescription for Office Health," on pp. 53–55 of *Modern Office Procedures,* March, 1976.
(b) A book written by Margaret V. Higginson and Thomas L. Quick entitled *The Ambitious Woman's Guide To A Successful Career* published by Amacom, New York, in 1975. The footnote refers to page 85.
(c) A chapter entitled "Developing the Standard Operating Procedures Manual" in the *Handbook Of Modern Office Management and Administrative Services,* published by McGraw-Hill Book Company, New York, in 1972, Carl Heyel, Editor. This chapter appears on pages 9-126 to 9-140.
(d) An article by Gerald L. Hershey called "Education, Selection & Training of Word Processing Personnel" in the January, 1976, issue of *Management World.* The material is on page 13.

Part 7 CASE PROBLEMS

Case 7-1
DELEGATING
WORK

Carmen Reynolds was put in charge of producing a 78-page medical report. She met with each of the three typists assigned to the job, gave instructions as to style, handed them a prepared guide sheet, and requested each typist to read Chapter 21 of this book. The work had to be completed within two days so that Dr. Johanna Spector, her employer, could take it to a meeting at which she was to be the featured speaker. Carmen received the completed work for assembling for presentation to Doctor Spector just two hours before the deadline.

She was horrified to discover that one typist had used a typewriter with Imperial type although the other two had used elite type; one had put the footnotes in the center of the page following the material to which they referred; and one had typed paragraph headings in solid caps while the other two had capitalized only the important words in the title and had underscored the title.

She showed the variations to Doctor Spector and said, "I am just sick about the way this report looks. You would think that these typists could follow instructions. What can be done now?"

Doctor Spector replied icily, "Nothing, absolutely nothing. I will have to tell the people at the symposium that I will mail them a copy of the report next week. Heaven knows how I can get all of the addresses. But, Carmen, I am very unhappy with the way you handled this. After all, you are the one in charge. I had thought that you could handle a simple assignment like this one."

Was Carmen at fault? What did she do wrong? If she talked with you about the problem, what advice would you give her for handling such a situation?

Case 7-2
GETTING
COOPERATION
OF STAFF
AND
SUPERIORS

The office was relatively peaceful, and all workers were performing their regular duties with dispatch. Then the possibility of a merger loomed. Extensive reports would be needed immediately; and Henry Bronwell, the corporate treasurer, worked with his secretary, Ellen Burchard, through the whole weekend. They planned the work to be done before the crucial big meeting on Thursday. They roughed out the reports to be presented. Since some of the necessary information was not available in Mr. Bronwell's office, he told Ellen that she would have to get it from his colleagues.

Ellen's shorthand notes included the following work instructions:

"Because I'll be in meetings downtown all of Monday and Tuesday, you'll have to get the information necessary before you can complete the reports. Don't, though, intimate that there is any possibility of a merger. Pull Jerry and Rita off their regular jobs to get the report out."

Ellen reached home Sunday night exhausted, discouraged, and apprehensive. How, she wondered, could she enlist the cooperation of Jerry and Rita, especially since she was not free to tell the reason for their assignment to a special project? Mr. Bronwell had the authority to reassign them, but he did not realize that he had never officially given Ellen such authority, assuming that being his secretary carried the authority. Ellen, however, realized that Rita especially resented Ellen's giving her any work instructions.

She worried, too, about her relations with some of her superiors and wondered how to approach them to ask for data without appearing to be officious. On the other hand, she felt pleased and gratified by Mr. Bronwell's confidence in her ability to handle this difficult assignment and vowed to merit his trust.

What approach could Ellen take to get the support of those she must supervise? How could she get the cooperation of her superiors?

**Case 7-3
THE
SECRETARY'S
LOYALTIES**

Sheila Fong was secretary to Harold Roselli, sales manager of Brown-Haskins Manufacturing Company. During the five years since Mr. Roselli had joined the company, his career had been spectacular; and he had increased sales by 34 percent. He was out of the city about half the time and, because of his overly long hours, did not hesitate to take an occasional day off after a strenuous trip.

During the past two months, however, his unaccounted-for absences had reached alarming proportions. He had not come to the office at all the previous week although he was not on official vacation. He had telephoned from home every day and had dictated several letters and telegrams. On Monday he had asked Sheila to tell the president of the company that he was in San Francisco working on the Johnson order.

What should Sheila say to her employer? Where do her loyalties lie — with her employer or with the corporation?

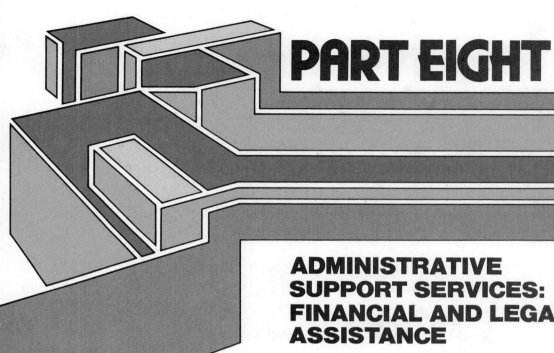

PART EIGHT

ADMINISTRATIVE SUPPORT SERVICES: FINANCIAL AND LEGAL ASSISTANCE

The extent to which a secretary is involved in the company and personal banking of the employer, in the employer's investment and insurance program, in payroll preparation, and in producing and processing legal papers depends upon a number of variables. Among such variables are the size of the business or office, the function of the division in which the secretary is employed, and the specific job title of the secretary. In addition, the financial interests of the executive or executives for whom the secretary works will determine the scope of the functions performed.

The topics in Part 8 not only contribute to the secretary's job performance but also have personal values. As a wage earner and a financially responsible individual, the secretary needs to understand banking services, ways to record and audit investments and insurance policies, how to organize data for the preparation of income tax returns, and the significance of certain legal terminology and forms.

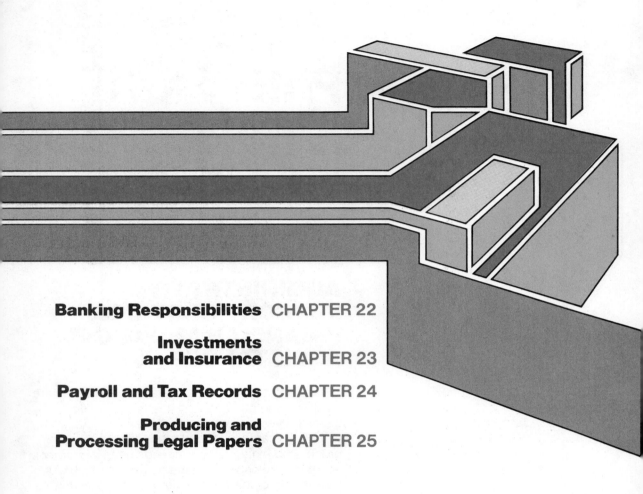

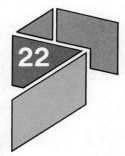

Banking Responsibilities

The extent to which the administrative or multifunctional secretary will be responsible for the office banking or the executive's personal banking usually depends upon the size of the office. In the small office, the secretary may keep all of the financial records and do all the banking. In a large office, these responsibilities are usually handled by others, but the secretary may keep the petty cash fund, use the special services provided by banks, approve bills for payment, arrange for foreign remittances, and perform other functions that relate to the company's bank accounts. In addition, many top executives expect their secretaries to assist with their personal financial records and banking. This assistance is justified on the basis that it frees executive time for company business.

Although the total time spent each day in performing these financial duties may be comparatively small, their importance must not be underestimated. They represent exacting and confidential responsibilities. They are exacting because they involve handling other people's money. They are confidential because financial data are always highly restricted pieces of information.

Whether your financial duties are extensive or limited, you may expect to perform some, if not all, of these functions: make bank deposits, write checks, cash checks, pay bills, reconcile bank statements, handle petty cash funds, and record incoming funds. Although specific practices and methods vary somewhat, the basic banking procedures of all banks are similar.

Although the correspondence secretary in the word processing center usually does not have office banking responsibilities, everyone needs training in personal finance. Much of the content of this chapter has as much personal use value as it has professional training value.

THE CHECKING ACCOUNT

The new secretary with financial responsibilities must be identified at the bank as representing the employer. If the secretary is to sign checks for the withdrawal or payment of personal or company funds from the bank accounts or to indorse and cash checks, the bank must be authorized to honor the secretary's signature. The bank may require the employer to sign a special authorization form or to arrange for the secretary's signature to be added to the signature card on file at the bank. Some banks require that the secretary be issued a power of attorney, described in Chapter 25, to perform these functions.

Accepting Checks

Accepting a check that is given in person or received through the mail requires precautions to assure that the check is valid — that it has been properly prepared. Examine these points: (a) date — to see that the check is not postdated (dated later than current date), (b) amount — to determine that the amount of payment is correct, (c) figures — to be sure that the amount written in figures agrees with the amount written in words, and (d) indorsement — to see that an indorsement, if required, has been properly made. To have a deposited check returned by the bank because it was improperly written is time consuming and inconvenient. Before depositing a check and while the details are still available, be sure to record the information needed for the accounting records on a receipt form or in a record book.

Depositing Funds

To make a deposit, the secretary presents to the bank teller a deposit ticket in duplicate listing the amounts being deposited (or a passbook). The deposit itself — consisting of currency, coin, indorsed checks, and money orders — should accompany the deposit ticket.

Preparing Coins and Bills for Deposit. Banks prefer that coins and bills, if in sufficient quantity, be put in the money wrappers that the banks furnish. Coins are packed in paper rolls as follows:

Denomination	Number of Coins to a Roll	Total Value of Coins in Roll
Pennies	50	$ .50
Nickels	40	2.00
Dimes	50	5.00
Quarters	40	10.00
Halves	20	10.00

Bills of each denomination are made into packages of $50, $100, and so forth. The packages are separated into all-of-a-kind groups with each bill laid right side up and top edge at the top. Torn bills are mended with tape. A paper bill wrapper — a narrow strip with the amount printed on it — is wrapped tightly around the bills and securely glued.

The depositor's name or account number should be stamped or written on each roll of coins and package of bills. Receiving tellers of banks do not stop to count packaged money when taking deposits, but someone counts it later in the day. If the depositor's name or account number appears on each roll or wrapper, mistakes can be easily traced.

Extra bills are counted and stacked, right side up, the largest denominations on the bottom and the smallest ones on top, and fastened with a rubber band. Extra coins are counted, placed in an envelope, identified, and sealed.

Preparing Checks for Deposit. In order to deposit a check or money order, the payee indorses it on the back; however, banks accept checks for deposit that are indorsed by a representative of the payee. In fact, a bank may accept an occasional check that lacks an indorsement. Some banks stamp the back of such a check with a statement such as, "Credited to account of payee named within — absence of indorsement guaranteed."

Notwithstanding the last sentence, it will be the secretary's responsibility to indorse every check for deposit. If the name of the payee is written differently on a check from the account name, indorse the check twice: first, as the name appears on the face of the check, and again, the exact way the account is carried. A rubber-stamp indorsement (showing the name of the bank, the name of the account, and the account number), obtained from the bank where the employer banks or from an office-supplies store, is the most time-saving method. Companies that receive a large number of checks can use a machine that will indorse checks at a high rate of speed. If a check is to be deposited, a pen signature need not be added to a rubber-stamp or machine indorsement.

There are several standard indorsements:

1. *A restrictive indorsement* is one in which some condition attached to the indorsement restrains the negotiability of the check or renders the indorser liable only upon a specified condition or conditions, such as "For deposit," or "Upon delivery of contract." A restrictive indorsement is commonly used when checks are being deposited. Checks indorsed "For deposit" need not be signed personally by the depositor but can be indorsed or stamped by the secretary. The "For deposit" qualification automatically keeps the check from being used for any purpose other than for deposit to the account of the depositor whose name appears in the indorsement.

2. An *indorsement in full* or *special indorsement* (bottom, page 514) gives the name of a specified payee, written before the indorser's

For deposit and
credit to the
account of
M and B Association
021-119085

No. __369__

ᴵLE, Oʜɪᴏ____May 17___19 -- ___ $\frac{56-105}{412}$

_____sociation_____$77.98____

-----------------------------Dᴏʟʟᴀʀs

ᵃ Wasserman

Indorsements are properly made across the back of the left end of checks and money orders, as is shown on the restrictive indorsement illustrated here.

signature. This indorsement identifies the person or firm to which the instrument is transferred. A check indorsed in this way cannot be cashed by anyone without the specified payee's signature. The words "Pay to the order of First National Bank" in the illustration identify the name of the bank to which the check is being transferred. For further transfer, the First National Bank must indorse the check again.

3. *A blank indorsement* consists simply of the signature of the payee, making the check payable to any holder. This indorsement, therefore, should never be used except at the bank immediately before the check is being deposited or cashed. A check should never be indorsed at the office or sent through the mail with a blank indorsement. If it is lost, the finder can turn it into cash.

The indorser of a check (unless stated otherwise in the indorsement) assumes three responsibilities: (1) that the check is genuine and valid, (2) that the indorser has received value for it, and (3) that, if necessary, the indorser will reimburse the holder of the check if it should be dishonored.

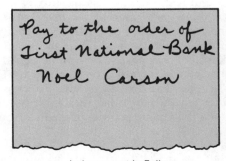

Indorsement in Full

Blank Indorsement

Magnetic Ink Numbers

Data processing equipment reduces the manual work involved in handling checking accounts. The American Bankers Association has adopted a uniform system of MICR (magnetic ink character recognition) that provides for preprinting the bank's transit number and the depositor's account number in magnetic ink characters in a uniform position at the bottom of the checks. When a check is received at the bank, the date, amount of the check, and other coded information also are recorded in magnetic ink characters at the bottom of the check. Optical character recognition (OCR) equipment sorts the checks according to issuing bank and account numbers, computes totals, and posts to the depositors' accounts. This sorting, totaling, and posting is done electronically at speeds of several hundred checks a minute.

A preprinted deposit ticket for an MICR system is shown below, and a check identified by magnetic ink characters is on page 516.

When an automated system is in use, the depositor can use only those deposit tickets and checks that have been specifically printed to show the account number. If a depositor does not have a deposit ticket or check at the time of a deposit or withdrawal at the bank, the bank clerk can handle the transaction.

Completing a Deposit Ticket. Many types of deposit tickets are used. Most banks have deposit tickets designed especially for use with automated equipment, usually in multiple sets with interleaved carbon or NCR coating. The deposit ticket shown below is designed for automated processing.

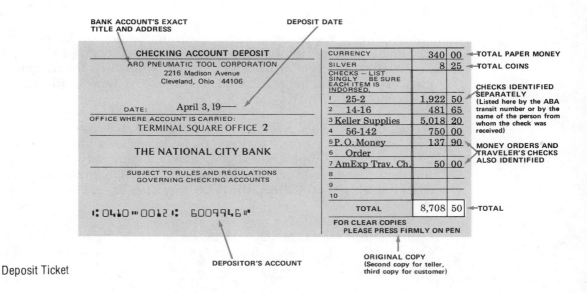

Deposit Ticket

Note that the series of magnetic ink identification numbers at the bottom of this check are the same as those of the preprinted deposit ticket on page 515.

No. _832_	$325.27	ARO PNEUMATIC TOOL CORPORATION		
Date _Apr. 15, 19—_		2216 Madison Avenue		NO. _832_
To _Apex Corp._		Cleveland, Ohio 44106		1-315
For _machinery parts_			Date _April 15, 19—_	260

PAY TO THE ORDER OF _Apex Corporation_ _____ $ 325.27

Three hundred twenty-five 27/100------------------------ Dollars

TERMINAL SQUARE OFFICE 2
THE NATIONAL CITY BANK
Cleveland, Ohio   _Marion L. Owen_

	Dollars	Cents
Bal Bro't For'd	8,604	81
Amt Deposited	913	40
Total	9,518	21
Amt This Check	325	27
Bal Car'd For'd	9,192	94

⑆ 0410 ⑈ 0012 ⑆ 6009946 ⑈

Account Numbers. Each depositor has an account number with which the bank's automated equipment identifies the depositor's account; therefore, the account number must appear on the deposit ticket. The bank provides the depositor with a supply of deposit tickets either printed with the account number in magnetic ink characters or with space provided for the depositor to record the account number.

Check Numbers. Each bank in the United States has been assigned an ABA (American Bankers Association) transit number. This number is usually printed in small type in the upper right portion of the check. It identifies the bank for clearinghouse functions. Illustrated, the numbers mean:

City or State $\dfrac{25\text{-}2}{412}$ Specific bank in the city or state
(4) Federal Reserve District
(1) Branch in the district
(2) Number of days required to clear the check

Some banks require each check listed on the deposit ticket to be identified by using the two top ABA transit numbers, in this case 25-2, unless the check is drawn on the bank in which the deposit is made. In this case, the check is identified by the name of the maker of the check.

Listing Checks. When a large number of checks are regularly deposited, common practice is to list the checks on an adding machine and to attach the tape to the deposit ticket, listing only the total on the deposit ticket. Some banks, however, which prefer that all checks be shown on the deposit ticket, provide "large" deposit tickets for such use.

Listing Other Items. Money orders, bank drafts, traveler's checks, and interest coupons are listed with the checks on the deposit ticket.

Certain government, municipal, and company bonds provide interest coupons attached to the bond. On the due date the coupon can be detached from the bond, placed with a deposit ticket in an envelope provided by the bank, and deposited. A separate envelope must be used for each class of coupon.

Banking by Mail

Depositing by mail has become very popular because of the time it saves. The secretary in a small office may make most or all of the bank deposits by mail. Various kinds of mail-deposit tickets and envelopes are provided by different banks. All checks must be indorsed "Pay to the order of (name of bank)" or "For Deposit Only," signed, and listed on the mail-deposit slip. The deposit ticket and indorsed checks are placed in an envelope and mailed to the bank. Currency should never be deposited in this manner unless sent by registered mail. By return mail, the bank sends the depositor a receipt, along with a new mail-deposit ticket and envelope.

After-Hours Banking

At many banks and bank terminals, deposits may be made and cash withdrawn after banking hours.

Night Depository. Some businesses use the *night* or *after-hour depository* for funds collected after banking hours. The bank provides the depositor with a bag in which to lock the deposit. The depositor then can drop the bag through a slot accessible from outside the bank at any time the bank is closed. On the next banking day, a bank teller unlocks the bag and makes the deposit. The depositor later stops at the bank to pick up the empty bag and deposit receipt. If the depositor prefers, however, the bank will leave the deposit bag locked until the depositor arrives to make the deposit personally. Branch banks and evening banking hours further add to the convenience of the depositor.

Automatic Tellers and Cash Dispensers. Many banks provide a 24-hour deposit and cash withdrawal service. The depositor is issued a plastic debit card and given a confidential code number. The card is called a debit card to differentiate it from the charge card. The simultaneous use of the card and code number with a terminal gives on-line entry into the depositor's computerized bank account. To make a cash withdrawal, the depositor inserts the card into the designated slot of the automatic teller or cash dispensing machine, keys the code number into the keyboard on the machine, pushes the key

A depositor making a cash withdrawal at an automated teller

Harris Bank

identifying the amount of cash desired, and receives the cash along with a printed record of the transaction. Deposits are similarly handled. A depositor may also obtain his or her account balance.

Usually these machines are located so the depositor can have access to them 24 hours a day, seven days a week. Some banks also install them in the bank as a convenient and fast service to depositors. Many are located in shopping centers, supermarkets, and department stores. Some banks issue one dual-purpose card. The one card is issued for both banking transactions at an automatic teller station and as a regular bank credit card.

Using the Checking Account

Banks provide a variety of check forms and checkbooks: one check with attached stub to the page; three or more checks to the page; pads with interleaved copy sheets or with attached *vouchers* (a form used to record the purpose and other details of the payment). Many businesses use prenumbered checks imprinted with the name of the business. The secretary is responsible for ordering a new checkbook before the old one is completely used. Banks usually bind an order sheet into the checkbook toward the back. The secretary merely mails the order sheet and receives a new checkbook shortly thereafter.

A voucher check consists of the check and a detachable stub that shows the purpose of the check and various data necessary for record keeping.

Completing Check Stubs. Complete the stub *before* you write the check. Failure to do so frequently results in the details of a check being forgotten. In addition to showing the number of the check, the date, the name of the payee, and the amount, the stub should provide other data for classifying or breaking down the disbursement in the accounting or tax records. For example, if the check is for a part payment, an installment payment, or a final payment, that fact should be noted. If the amount covers several items (such as payment for two or more invoices), each should be listed. If the check is in payment of an insurance premium, the name of the insured and the policy number should be listed.

Writing Checks. A check is a negotiable instrument and imposes certain legal responsibilities on the maker. Therefore, it must be written with care to insure that no unintended liability is created. For example, an altered check is not cashable. If a bank cashes such a check, the bank must assume any resulting loss. However, if it can be shown that the maker failed to use reasonable precautions in writing the check, thus making alteration difficult to detect, the maker must assume any resulting loss. Consequently, always type checks or write them in ink (never pencil). Follow these steps:

1. Be sure that the *number* of the check corresponds with that on the stub. If the checks are not numbered in printing, number all checks and check stubs upon starting a new checkbook.

2. *Date* the check on the exact date that the check is being written. Occasionally checks are postdated — that is, dated ahead to a time when sufficient funds will be in the checking account. This is a questionable practice, however.

3. Write the name of the *payee* in full and correctly spelled. For correct spelling, refer to bills, letterheads, or the telephone directory. Omit titles such as *Ms., Mr., Mrs., Miss,* and *Dr.* On checks written to a married woman, use her given name: *Ruth Hill*, not *Mrs. John R. Hill.*

4. In writing the *amount*, use large, bold figures written close to the dollar sign and sufficiently close together to prevent the insertion of other figures. In spelling out the amount, start at the extreme left, capitalizing the first letter only, and express cents as fractions of 100:

Three hundred forty and no/100—————————————————————Dollars

Two hundred thousand eight hundred sixty-four and 65/100 –Dollars

Two thousand seven hundred and 35/100 ——————————————Dollars

To write a check for less than $1, circle the amount written in figures and write "Only" before the spelled-out amount. Cross out "Dollars" at the end of the line.

5. Fill any *blank space* before or after the amount with hyphens, periods, or a line.

6. The *purpose* of the check, such as "In Payment of Invoice 6824," may be written in a corner of the check, if space permits, or across the end of the check.

Never cross out, erase, or change any part of a check. If you make an error, write "VOID" conspicuously across the face of both the check and the stub. Save a voided check and file it in numerical order with the canceled checks returned from the bank. Since it is easy to alter the impressions made by a worn ribbon, type checks with a fresh ribbon. Keep the checkbook in a safe place, and guard its confidentiality.

Writing Checks for Cash. A check for funds for the personal use of the account holder can be written to *Cash* as the payee and signed by the account holder. A check so written is highly negotiable. Anyone in possession of it can turn it into money. The cautious person, therefore, will use this form only when writing the check on the bank premises. (The bank asks the person receiving the money to indorse the check, even though the payee is *Cash*.)

The secretary may be expected to keep the executive supplied with cash. On banking days, the secretary simply asks, "Do you need money?" If so, the secretary writes the check and either presents it for the executive's signature or, if authorized, signs it. After cashing the check, the secretary should keep the currency separate from personal funds. Place the money in an envelope, seal it, and protect it until delivery.

As a special service some banks provide depositors with a check-cashing card. This card, which is a form of identification, guarantees that the bank will honor the card holder's check up to a specified amount. Check-cashing cards facilitate the cashing of personal checks at stores and at other banks.

Procedure to Stop Payment on Checks

After a check has been issued, payment can be stopped unless the check has been cleared by the bank upon which it was drawn. This procedure may be necessary when a check has been lost, stolen, or incorrectly written. Most banks charge for this service.

To stop payment, telephone the stop-payment desk of the bank and give the name of the maker, the date, number and amount of the check, the account number, the name of the payee, and the reason that payment is to be stopped. The bank clerk will search the checks on hand to see if the item in question has cleared. If it has not, the clerk will process the request for a stop-payment. Then you must dispatch either a letter of confirmation or a stop-payment form supplied by the bank. When you are sure that the stop-payment request is in effect, write a replacement, if necessary.

Reconciling the Bank Balance

Each month the bank returns to the account holder the *canceled checks* (checks that have cleared during the month) along with a statement that lists each deposit and withdrawal and any other items, such as a service charge or stop-payment charge. The account holder then checks the accuracy of the checkbook records and files the canceled checks as proof of payment.

When the statement and canceled checks are received, the final balance on the statement and the bank balance in the checkbook are compared and the difference between the two records accounted for. This process is called *reconciling the bank balance*.

Many banks print, on the back of the bank statement, instructions and a form for reconciling the bank balance. This printed form may be used, or the reconciliation may be typed on a separate sheet and attached to the bank statement.

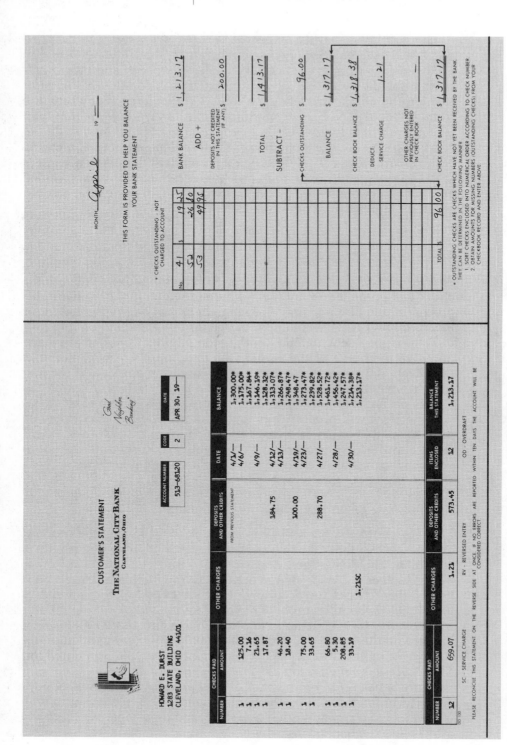

The monthly bank statement shows the checks paid, the deposits received, and any other deductions made from the account, such as the $1.21 service charge.

Printed on the back of many bank statements is a convenient form for reconciling the bank balance.

Procedure. The following is a systematic procedure for making the reconciliation:

1. Compare the amount of each canceled check returned by the bank with the amounts listed on the bank statement.

2. Arrange the canceled checks in numerical sequence.

3. Compare the returned checks with the checkbook stubs. Make a distinctive check mark on the stubs of canceled checks. Compare also the amounts of deposits shown on the stubs with those shown on the bank statement. List and total any that were omitted.

4. List the outstanding checks, showing the check number, the payee, and the amount. Total the outstanding checks.

5. Add the total unlisted deposits to the bank balance; subtract the total amount of the outstanding checks. The remainder is the corrected bank balance.

6. The bank will list any service charges among the withdrawals on the bank statement. Subtract the amount of the service charges and any other deductions made by the bank from the balance shown on the last checkbook stub for the period being reconciled. The resulting figure should be the same amount as the corrected bank balance. If so, you must deduct the amount of the service charges from the balance on the checkbook stub that is currently the last one used. The remainder will be the true *current* balance in the account.

As shown in the illustration at the left, an entry must now be made on the *current balance* (not the last stub of the reconciliation period) for any service charge or other charge by the bank.

Locating Errors. If the two adjusted balances — statement and stub — do not agree, first check the computation on the reconciliation sheet to make sure there is no error. If there is none, make sure that:

No check has been omitted in the reconciliation. Go through the check stubs (one by one) and see that each one is included among the checks either cleared or outstanding. Also make sure that each check has a stub.

No deposit has been omitted. Cross check the deposits in the check stubs with those on the bank statement.

A deposit made by mail on the date that your bank statement is prepared will not appear on the statement. Add this deposit to the bank statement balance on the reconciliation sheet.

If there is still an error, either the bank has made an arithmetical error in the statement, or more likely there is an error in the stubs.

First check the accuracy of the *amounts forwarded* on each check-stub page. If these are correct, the arithmetical computations for each stub should be examined. When the error is located, mark the stub where it occurs: "Error — should be $_____; corrected on Stub #_____." Then make the compensating adjustment on the last stub.

Enter the amount of the error on the reconciliation statement and show where the error occurs and where it is corrected in the check stubs. After the proper check stub (the last transaction covered by the bank statement), write "Agrees with the bank statement, *(date)*." Then you can easily find the starting point for the next month's reconciliation.

Filing Canceled Checks. File the bank reconciliation conveniently for the next reconciliation. You will need the records of checks now outstanding. Keep canceled checks inside the folded bank statements and file the statements chronologically, or file the bank statements chronologically and the checks numerically in a separate place. Save canceled checks, as they are evidences of payment; they constitute legal receipts. The retention period must be established by company policy.

Follow-Up on Outstanding Checks

Investigate any check that has not cleared through the bank within a few weeks of its date of issue. The payee may not have received the check or may have misplaced or lost it. A letter or telephone call to the payee will clarify the matter. If the check is apparently lost, cancel the old check in the checkbook, forward a stop-payment order to the bank, and issue a new check.

Bank Safe-Deposit Boxes

Frequently the employer rents a *safe-deposit box* from the bank. This is a metal box locked by two keys into a small compartment in the bank's safe-deposit vault. The bank has very strict rules about access to safe-deposit boxes. The customer must register each time entry to the box is requested. A bank employee accompanies the customer to the box, opens one of the locks with the bank's key, and opens the other lock with the customer's key. The box itself is then removed and taken by the customer to a private room. Securities, wills, insurance policies, notes, gems, and other small valuable articles may be protected by safe-deposit storage. Rent is usually billed annually and is deducted directly from the customer's checking account.

The executive must sign a special banking form if the secretary is to have access to the safe-deposit box. The secretary may have two responsibilities relative to safe-deposit-box work: (1) to maintain a perpetual inventory of its contents in duplicate, one copy to be kept in the box, the other in the office; and (2) to guard the key carefully.

Electronic Fund Transfer

Over 25 billion checks were processed by United States banks in 1975, and the number is increasing at an annual rate of 7 percent. A number of new procedures in the process of development by the banking industry may decrease the dependence upon checks and eventually result in a nearly checkless society. Most of the new procedures employ *electronic fund transfer (EFT)*. EFT permits amounts to be transferred from one depositor's account to another bank account or cash withdrawals to be made without the use of the check medium or the services of a bank teller.

Preauthorized Deposits. Direct payroll depositing is available in those areas where automated clearinghouse (ACH) facilities have been established. Instead of a payroll check and an employee pay statement being issued to each employee each payday, only the employee pay statement is prepared and given to the employee. The employee's net pay is deposited directly into the employee's bank account. The deposit is made electronically by means of magnetic tape or other machine-processable medium and processed through the facilities of the ACH which channels the deposit (net pay) to the employee's bank. Use of the automatic payroll-deposit plan saves the writing of millions of paychecks, relieves the employee of the inconvenience of having to go to the bank to make the deposit, and decreases the possible loss or theft of the paycheck. Social security payments are now made in many areas by direct deposit to the bank accounts of those recipients who so authorize. The goal of the government is eventually to process all payrolls and all types of government-to-consumer payments by the preauthorized deposit plan. Dividends may eventually be deposited to stockholders' bank accounts by this process.

Preauthorized Payments. In addition to deposits, bank customers in certain areas may make arrangements whereby a number of low-decision payments may be made by automatic withdrawal from their checking accounts. Low-decision payments include such items as utility bills, mortgage or rent payments, property taxes, and insurance payments: items that are fairly routine and are usually paid monthly. The utility company, for example, forwards the monthly bill to the customer's bank where the amount is directly subtracted from the depositor's account. A duplicate utility bill is sent to the customer for information.

In place of using the preauthorized payment system described in the preceding paragraph, the *bill check* is in use in some communities. The company sends the customer a monthly statement imprinted with the customer's bank routing number and the customer's bank account number. The customer fills in on the bill the amount to be paid, signs the bill, and returns it to the company. The bill information is transferred to some form of machine-processable medium and put through the automated clearinghouse where it is channeled to the customer's bank. The payment is then deducted from the customer's bank account. This procedure saves the writing and processing of a separate check.

Point-of-Sale Transfer. Point-of-sale (POS) terminals permit transfer of amounts from a purchaser's bank account to the store's bank account without the use of the check. The terminal is connected by telephone circuits to the bank's computerized accounting data center. When a customer makes a purchase at the store, the store clerk or cash register operator inserts the customer's bank-issued debit card into the store terminal. Using a telephone, the clerk dials the bank's computer storage facilities (this connects the store terminal to the bank's data center). The clerk then enters the amount of the purchase on the store's terminal keyboard. The customer keys in an individualized code number. The computer responds by authorizing the purchase, deducting the amount from the customer's checking account, and adding it to the merchant's account — all without a single piece of paper changing hands. The customer receives a monthly descriptive bank statement which describes checkless transactions in a form similar to the credit card statement.

This service may eventually be extended to include cash withdrawals and deposits, thus making it possible for a bank customer to complete all banking transactions at the supermarket.

The Telephone Transfer and One-Account System. Federal rulings have made it possible to transfer funds from a savings account to a demand (checking) account and vice versa by telephone. A depositor can thus move funds in and out of the savings account to maximize interest earnings. This procedure is expected to lead eventually to a one-account banking system. In the one-account system all funds would be funnelled into one account that would serve for both checking and savings. Interest would be earned depending upon the longevity of the balance kept in the account and the amount of activity in the account. At the same time, the full account balance would be available for a withdrawal by check or EFT.

A check given in payment of a bill may take several days in transit before it reaches the depositor's bank and is subtracted from the depositor's account. Since some businesses may have hundreds of outstanding checks, this can represent a large sum of money. Likewise, the bank-issued charge card usually gives the buyer a number of days before payment for a purchase is necessary. During this period the customer-depositor has the use of the money for interest bearing or other purposes. The establishment of electronic fund transfer and point-of-sale terminals means that there will be little or no "float," as amounts will be deducted immediately from the bank account. However, the use of electronic transfer of funds can decrease the number of checks that must be written and thus reduce office work loads and expenses.

PAYING BILLS

An executive seldom turns over personal bill paying to a new secretary. It is one of the responsibilities that a secretary acquires or, frequently, assumes. First, the secretary may be asked to address the envelopes. Then, when rushed, the executive may say, "Will you please write these checks for me." It is then that the secretary can demonstrate capability in handling this responsibility. *Bill paying* consists of:

1. Verifying the items and checking the computations on each bill.

2. Filling in the check stub. (Be sure to itemize and identify the payment in order to use the stub in accounting processes or in preparing income tax returns.)

3. Making out the check.

4. Writing on the face of the invoice or the statement the date, the number, and the amount of the check used in payment.

5. Addressing the envelope.

6. Tearing off the invoice or statement stub to be mailed with the check.

7. Attaching the stub from the bill to the check and inserting both under the flap of an addressed envelope ready for presentation to the executive for signature.

Verifying Bills

The secretary should verify the price, the terms, the extensions, and the additions on all bills. *Invoices* (itemized listings of goods purchased) must be checked against the quoted prices and terms or

TELEPHONE
703-598-2738

THE OLD DOMINION COMPANY
492 Broad Street   Richmond, Virginia 23219

MONTH	DAY	YEAR
1	11	--

SOLD TO W. R. BROOKS
1970 CAREW TOWER
CINCINNATI, OHIO 45202

YOUR ORDER NO. B-479
SALES REP J. LONG
SHIP VIA BEST WAY

QUANT.	COMMODITY	CODE NO.	PACK	SIZE	NET PRICE	EXTENSION
2	DESK MODULES, WALNUT	472A		6'6"	242.00	484 00
2	DESK MODULES, WALNUT	472B		5'4"	179.00	358 00
	SALES TAX					42 10
						884 10

Paid 2/8/--
Check No. 43

This invoice is ready for filing. The check marks indicate that the extensions have been checked. The number and date of the check sent in payment have been noted.

with records of previous prices paid. Monthly *statements* (details of accounts showing the amount due at the beginning of the month, purchases and payments made during the month, and the unpaid balance at the end of the month) can be verified by comparison with invoices and sales slips, check stubs, and other records of payments made on the account.

Bills for services (utility companies, for example) are usually accepted as they are, although the toll statement with the telephone bill is checked very carefully. You will wish to explore preauthorized bill payment service, if provided by your bank, to save your time in writing checks for utility bills. Before paying bills for professional services, the secretary should obtain the personal approval of the executive.

Credit Card Statements

To avoid carrying large amounts of cash or traveler's checks, many business and professional people use credit cards (such as American Express, Diners' Club, Master Charge and Carte Blanche) when traveling and when paying local entertainment expenses. Credit card statements also are helpful in preparing expense reports and in verifying travel and entertainment expenses for income tax reporting.

When making a purchase with a credit card, the purchaser signs a bill or receipt and receives a copy. A monthly statement for charges made to that card during the month is sent along with the

Rub the identification numbers on all credit cards with a heavy pencil. Lay all cards face down on the glass of a copying machine with space between them and make a one-page record. Write under each card on the copy the contact you must notify if the card is lost or stolen. File for ready reference.

signed receipts. The executive may delegate to the secretary the responsibility for checking the monthly credit card statement. This requires careful inspection of the signature on each receipt and a comparison of the amount on the enclosed receipt with that on the receipt given at the time of purchase.

Filing Paid Bills

Some logical system should be set up for filing paid bills, for they provide the key to the canceled checks. If there are only 10 to 20 bills each month, the secretary can place all of them in one file folder. If there are many, an alphabetic file may be set up for them; or a subject file may be used, keeping together all of the utility bills, the insurance bills, the bills for supplies, and so on. Whenever a question arises concerning the payment of a bill, the secretary should be able to locate the annotated bill giving the check number and then to get the canceled check from the files for evidence.

Making Payments by Other Forms

Although most of the payments handled by the secretary will probably be made by ordinary check or electronic fund transfer, one of several special checks or money orders that can be obtained at the bank (usually at a nominal charge) may be used on occasion.

Certified Check. A regular depositor's check that is guaranteed by the bank on which it is drawn is called a certified check. To obtain such a check, the secretary takes the employer's personal check to the bank and asks that it be certified. After seeing that sufficient funds are in the account to cover the check, a bank official stamps on the face of the check "CERTIFIED," adds an official signature, and immediately charges the account with the amount of the check.

No. 263 **The Southern Trust Co.** 69-371/515

Charleston _May 18_ 19 --

Pay to the order of _Penwood Supply Company_ $65.25

Sixty-five and 25/100 Dollars

CERTIFIED THE SOUTHERN TRUST CO. N. C. Clark CASHIER

L. R. Harris

⑈0515⑈037⑈: 9992⑈5207⑈

Certified Check

A certified check is used to accompany orders where cash is required and personal checks will not be accepted. A certified check may be required when bids or contracts are submitted for the purchase of state or federal property, for property settlements, and for other large purchases.

Official Check. A check written by the bank on its own funds is known as an *official check* (sometimes known as a cashier's or treasurer's check). Official checks may be used by depositors and by persons who do not have a checking account. The amount of the check plus a service fee is paid to the bank clerk, who then writes the check to the specified payee. Recommended practice is to have the official check made payable to the purchaser of the check who must then indorse it in full to the ultimate payee. The canceled check then is proof of payment.

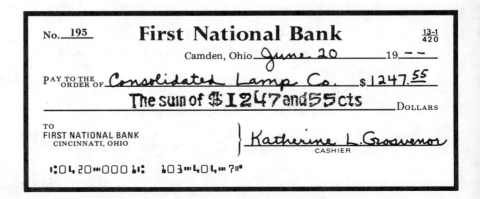

Official Check

Bank Draft

Bank Draft. A *bank draft* is a check written by the bank on its account in another bank located in the same or in another city. A purchaser pays the bank the exact amount of the draft plus a small fee for issuing the draft. Properly indorsed, the bank draft can then be cashed at the bank on which it is drawn. It differs from an official check only in that the bank draft is drawn by the bank on funds it has on deposit in another bank while an official check is drawn by the cashier on funds in the cashier's own bank.

The bank draft is used primarily for the transfer of large sums from one city to another specific city. The recipient of the draft can then be sure that the funds are in hand before taking certain action, such as releasing a shipment of merchandise, signing a deed, or starting work on a contract.

When there is need to transfer funds quickly, the bank can telegraph its corresponding bank in another city directing it to transfer funds to a designated person or company.

Bank Money Order. A *bank money order (personal money order* or *registered check)* is similar to that issued by the post office but less expensive. It is sold primarily to persons without a checking account who wish to send money through the mail. It can normally be cashed at any other bank — at home or abroad; it is negotiable and transferable by indorsement. The amount of a single bank money order generally is not more than $200, but there is no restriction on the number of bank money orders that may be issued to the same person to be sent to the same payee. The purchaser of a bank money order is given a receipt.

The bank money order is more frequently used than an official check or a bank draft when the amount of money transferred is relatively small. It differs from an official check in that the names of both the purchaser and the payee appear on the money order.

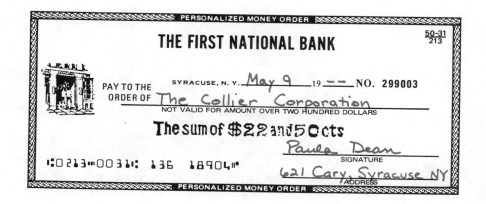

Bank Money Order

THE PETTY CASH FUND

Payments of small amounts for postage, bus and taxi fare, collect telegrams, donations, delivery charges, and incidental office supplies are frequently made from a *petty cash fund*. In many instances the fund is entrusted to the secretary.

The size of the fund will vary according to the demands made upon it. If the fund is large, it should be kept in a locked cash box and stored in the office safe or vault at night. If it is small, it can be kept in a small box or an envelope. In any event, the fund should be locked at night in a desk drawer, a file drawer, or the safe.

Petty Cash Records

The petty cash fund is usually set up with a stipulated amount, such as a $20 fund. Each replenishment of the depleted fund brings it up to $20 again. For example, after disbursements of $18.50 have been made from the fund, there should be $1.50 on hand. The reimbursement check to the petty cash fund is for $18.50. The employer may prefer to write a check for a full $20 each time or may give the secretary $10 one time and $15 another. A purely personal fund can be of any size desired.

Petty Cash Report

In replenishing the petty cash fund, the secretary should prepare a summary report of all payments made.

Each expenditure should have a voucher covering it for an accounting record. If vouchers are used consistently, the total money in the cash box plus the total of the vouchers should equal the amount of the fund.

Stationery stores sell pads of petty cash vouchers (or receipt forms).

PETTY CASH VOUCHER	No. 56
$ *3.00*	Date *January 4, 19—*
PAID TO *Post Office*	
FOR: *Stamps*	
	Received Payment *R. L. Reed*

Each item listed in the Paid column of a petty cash record requires a voucher.

Keep a record of the receipts and the disbursements. Balance the record whenever the funds get low — or periodically, if the employer prefers. Some of the expenses itemized in a petty cash record may be tax deductible; file the records and examine them at tax-return time. Make petty cash entries at once, for they are difficult to recall later. A practical form of a petty cash record is shown on page 532.

CREDIT AND COLLECTION INSTRUMENTS

The secretary's financial responsibilities may extend to such credit and collection instruments as notes, drafts, and certificates of deposit. Because these papers can be transferred or negotiated by the holder to someone else, they (together with checks and other substitutes for cash, such as bank drafts and money orders) are known as *negotiable instruments*.

Notes

A *promissory note*, more commonly referred to as a note, is a promise by one person (known as the *maker*) to pay a certain sum of

$ _660. 00_   _Phoenix, Ariz._ _August 7_ 19_—_

Four months ____ AFTER DATE _I_ PROMISE TO PAY TO

THE ORDER OF _James Bailey_

Six hundred sixty 00/100 _____ DOLLARS

PAYABLE AT _Second National Bank_

VALUE RECEIVED WITH INTEREST AT _6_ %

No. _13_   DUE _Dec. 7, 19—_   _Monica Shaw_

Promissory Note

money on demand or at a fixed or determinable future date to another person or party (known as the *payee*). A promissory note is illustrated above.

Frequently, collateral is requested to pledge the payment of a note. In this case the instrument is called a *collateral note*. Collateral can be salable securities (stocks, bonds), a real estate mortgage, or anything that represents ownership and is exchangeable. When an obligation is fully paid, the collateral is returned to the borrower. If it is not paid, the creditor can convert the collateral into cash.

Some notes bear interest, paid at maturity when the *face* of the note is due. On a noninterest-bearing note, the loan-making agency deducts in advance the "interest" (known as the *discount*) from the face of the note. The remainder is called the *proceeds*. For instance, a borrower who gives a bank a 3-month, noninterest-bearing note for $1,000 would receive $985 if the discount was computed at the rate of 6 percent.

The amount and the date of a partial payment on a note are written on the back of the note. When a partial payment is made on a note, the secretary should make certain the payment is recorded on the back of the note, for the note is held by the lender until it is paid in full. If payment is made in full, the indorsed note should be turned over to the secretary, for then it is a legal record that the obligation has been discharged.

Commercial Drafts

A draft is a written order by one person on another to pay a sum of money to a third person and is generally used as a collection device. In the commercial draft illustration on page 535, Ankromm and Son owe $539.62 to King and Wilson, who give this draft to their bank in Topeka for collection. The bank forwards the draft to its correspondent bank in St. Louis, which presents it for payment to Ankromm and Son. When the draft is paid, the proceeds are sent to the Topeka bank and then to King and Wilson.

$539.62   *Topeka, Kansas,*   *January 3,* 19--

At sight _____ PAY TO THE

ORDER OF *Ourselves*

Five hundred, thirty-nine and 62/100 DOLLARS

VALUE RECEIVED AND CHARGE TO ACCOUNT OF

TO *C. R. Ankromm & Son*) *King and Wilson*

No. *28*   *St. Louis, Missouri*) *L. B. King, Secretary*

Sight Draft

This draft is a *sight draft* for it instructs that it is to be paid "at sight." A *time draft* is payable at some future time and reads "thirty days after date" or some other stipulated period of time.

Drafts are frequently used as a means of collecting before delivery for goods shipped by freight. The merchandise is shipped on an *order bill of lading*, which requires that the receiver present the original copy of the bill of lading to the railroad company before obtaining possession of the merchandise. The bill of lading with the draft attached is sent to the bank in the town of the buyer. When the merchandise arrives, the purchaser pays the draft at the bank, obtains the bill of lading, and claims possession of the goods at the freight office.

Discounting Notes and Drafts

Business firms accept notes, time drafts, and installment contracts from customers in payment for merchandise and may convert these instruments into cash before they are due for payment. This is done by "selling the paper" to a bank or finance company. The bank deducts interest (discounts the paper) and gives the seller the cash proceeds. The bank, in turn, holds the paper until maturity and collects from the customer. The ownership of notes and drafts is transferred by indorsement in the same manner as that used for checks.

Foreign Remittances

When a payment or remittance is to be made to a person or business firm in a foreign country, the following forms of payment may be used.

Currency. United States currency, or foreign currency purchasable through your local bank, may be sent abroad. Most foreign countries regulate the amount of currency that may be so transferred. Your bank will advise you as to the legal restrictions. Currency payments, of course, would be sent by registered mail.

Cable Money Order. Either your bank or Western Union will cable money abroad for you. The cable money order is generally payable in the currency of the country to which it is being sent. Cable money orders are speedy but expensive.

American Express Money Orders. Money orders payable in a foreign currency may be purchased at any American Express Company office. Express money orders may be made payable to the purchaser or to another person or firm. American Express will arrange for the transfer of the money order to the person or firm in the foreign country to whom it is payable by cable, airmail, or mail; or the purchaser, if he or she elects, may receive the money order and transfer it by mail or some other means. Express money orders are payable in the foreign country at the office of the American Express Company or at the bank in the foreign country identified in the money order.

Foreign Bank Draft. A bank draft payable in a foreign currency can be purchased at your local bank. As with currency, most foreign countries limit the amount of money which may be transferred. The bank will arrange for the transfer of the draft, or the purchaser may transfer it by mail or by some other means. This method of payment or transfer of funds would be used when large amounts are involved.

SUGGESTED READINGS

Bank Services and You. American Bankers Association, 1975.

"Electronic Banking Is Here." *The Bankers Magazine*, Vol. 159, No. 7 (Spring, 1976), pp. 31–46.

"Get Ready for Cashless, Checkless Living." *Changing Times*, Vol. 28, No. 10 (October, 1975), pp. 6–10.

How to Manage Your Money. American Bankers Association, 1975.

Trust Services from Your Bank. American Bankers Association, 1975.

QUESTIONS FOR DISCUSSION

1. As Judith Hill was leaving for lunch, her supervisor, Edith Romero, asked her to deposit a customer's check in the bank. Mrs. Romero indorsed the check by writing the company name and her initials on the back of the check. Judith placed the check in her purse. During lunch and before the deposit was made, Judith's purse was either lost or stolen.
   (a) What poor business practices were evident in this situation?
   (b) Upon discovery of the loss, what should Judith do?

2. What precautions or safeguards should a secretary observe in writing checks? Explain why each precaution is important.

3. Many top-level executives expect their secretaries to assist them with their personal financial records and banking. This may include writing checks to pay personal bills, keeping the executive's checking account, keeping records of the executive's investments, and so forth. Is this use of company-paid secretarial time on the part of the corporate executive ethical? Is it the secretary's responsibility to conform or to refuse?

4. Your employer asks you to submit a plan for establishing and maintaining a petty cash fund in the office. What are the major topics or points you would include in your plan?

5. When a bank draft is purchased, it may be drawn in favor of the person or business to whom payment is being made or in favor of the person making the payment and indorsed by the purchaser to the creditor. Which do you think is the better method? Why?

6. Explain what shipping and payment procedure would be used to permit a fruit grower in California to receive payment for a rail shipment of fruit at the time of delivery to an Atlanta dealer. The fruit grower wants to permit the Atlanta dealer to be sure before making payment that the fruit arrives in Atlanta in accordance with the conditions of the order.

7. Your employer asks you to send $300 to a daughter at the University of Mexico, Mexico City. How do you send the money?

8. If necessary, correct the following. Then use the Reference Guide to check your answers.
   (a) An imminent ex-senator will be our choice for Vice-president of the company.
   (b) The signatures are both alike in the formation of the capitol letters.
   (c) I repeat again, the merchandise is depreciating in value every month.
   (d) Friction between the two employees resulted from their working together in such close proximity.
   (e) We had less people enter our store in the month of April than in the month of March.

PROBLEMS

1. You bank at the First Trust Company. Your checking account number is 202-8558. On a sheet of paper write the indorsement you would use on your paycheck under each of the following conditions.
   (a) You are depositing the check to your account by mail.
   (b) You are at the bank and are converting the check to cash.
   (c) You wish to transfer the check to Maas Brothers in payment on your charge account.
   (d) You wish to have a rubber stamp made so you can deposit checks by stamp indorsement. Specify what the stamp indorsement should state.

2. The following checks, bills, and coins are to be deposited.

Checks

ABA Transit Number	Amount
43-45	$ 225.80
18-24	18.50
63-785	1,346.00
2-77	7.50

Bills

5	$20 bills
12	$10 bills
35	$ 5 bills
16	$ 2 bills
110	$ 1 bills

Coins

21	Halves
42	Quarters
52	Dimes
36	Nickels
76	Pennies

(a) Determine the total amount of the deposit.

(b) Indicate specifically how the checks, bills, and coins in the deposit would be prepared for presenting to the bank teller.

3. You are asked to reconcile your employer's personal bank statement. You are given the canceled checks and the bank statement showing a bank balance on April 30 of $1,146.80. You compare the canceled checks and the deposits with the checkbook stubs and find the following:

The following checks were found to be outstanding:

#110	$86.90
#115	12.80
#120	7.40
#121	74.55

A deposit for $586.80 made by mail on April 29 was not listed on the bank statement but was listed on the check stub.

The bank had deducted the following charges from the account:

$15.00   Rent for safe-deposit box
$ 8.90   Printing of personalized checkbook

The checkbook balance carried forward at the end of check stub #121 was $1,575.85.

Prepare a typed bank reconciliation statement.

4. Your office has a $50 cash fund that is stored in a small metal box and locked in a file cabinet at the end of the day. Entries are made in a petty cash book that contains the following columns: Cash Received, Cash Paid, Postage, Office Supplies, Donations, and Miscellaneous. The largest single expenditure permitted from the fund is $5. Prenumbered petty cash vouchers are used.

Since you are turning the responsibility for the fund over to an assistant, you prepare written directions, specifying details for:

(a) Safekeeping of the fund
(b) Making payments from the fund
(c) Replenishing the fund

Prepare the instructions.

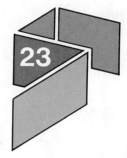

Investments and Insurance

All executives have insurance policies to protect their families and property. Many have extensive investments in securities and real estate. Both the administrative secretary and the multifunctional secretary may play an extremely important administrative support role in processing many of the insurance and investment transactions; furthermore, it is not unusual for the secretary to be solely responsible for maintaining the records related to these transactions. This responsibility takes on added importance when you consider that the secretary's records may be important evidence in determining tax liability and in assessing indemnity in case of loss. For example, the buying and selling dates for a security determine for tax purposes whether a long-term or a short-term capital gain or loss was realized. The amount of reimbursement for a fire or burglary loss may depend upon the availability, completeness, and timeliness of the property inventories maintained by the secretary.

While you need not share your employer's interest in the stock market or the financial section of the newspaper, the more you know about securities, property and insurance records, and other financial matters, the more valuable you will be in your administrative support role and the more satisfaction you will get from your work. And reading the *Wall Street Journal* can become a rewarding habit even for the correspondence secretary whose only interest in investments and insurance may be to invest and protect personal savings and to prepare for a sound financial future.

SECURITIES

A corporation can secure capital by issuing stock or by borrowing money through bonds. *Stocks* are evidence of ownership in the corporation; *bonds* are evidence of creditorship — that is, of a loan to the corporation.

Stocks

Ownership in a corporation is divided into units known as *shares of stock*. A stockholder is an owner of one or more shares of stock, and this ownership is shown by a paper known as a *stock certificate*. The stockholder receives *dividends* in return for the investment in the corporation. Dividends are paid from the earnings of the company either in cash or in additional stock referred to as a *stock dividend*.

Kinds of Stock. Stocks fall into two general classes, *common* and *preferred*. Holders of common stock are usually the only ones who have the right to vote in the stockholders' meetings. The rate of dividends paid on common stock is not fixed.

Preferred stock usually has a fixed dividend rate and a preference over common stock in first payment of dividends and in the first distribution of assets if the company is liquidated. Preferred stock may be *cumulative* or *noncumulative*. With cumulative preferred stock, any unpaid preferred-stock dividends accumulate and must be paid before any distribution can be made to common stockholders. Noncumulative preferred stock does not contain a provision to pay dividends in arrears.

Preferred stock also may be *participating* or *nonparticipating*. It is participating only if the stockholder is entitled to share with the common stockholders in any additional dividend disbursement after an agreed rate is paid on the common stock.

Some preferred stock is *convertible*; that is, the owner has the privilege of converting it into a specified number of shares of common stock at any time. Most preferred stocks are *callable*; that is, they are redeemable at the option of the issuing corporation at the redemption price specified in the stock certificate.

Stock may be *par-value* or *no-par-value* stock. *Par value* refers to a value ($1, $5, $10, $100) printed on the stock certificate. This printed value has no significance in determining the market price of the stock, which is measured by the stock's earning power — past, present, and future. Many companies today, therefore, do not print any value on their common stock. It is then known as *no-par-value* stock.

Stockholders' Meetings. Stockholders' meetings are held annually. Members of the board of directors are elected at this meeting by the stockholders present in person or by proxy. The board, in turn, elects the officers of the company at one of its regular meetings.

A notice of the stockholders' meeting, accompanied by a proxy form and a proxy statement, is sent to each stockholder entitled to vote. The notice gives a description of the business that is to be transacted. A *proxy* is a legal instrument assigning one's voting privilege to a specified person or persons. If directors of the corporation are to be elected, the proxy statement indicates the names of the persons nominated for whom the stockholder's proxy will be voted.

The stockholder may vote in person by attending the meeting or vote by mail by signing the proxy.

If the executive usually attends the stockholders' meeting, the date of the meeting should be recorded on the secretary's and executive's calendars. If the meeting is held out of town, the secretary may also be expected to make the travel arrangements.

Annual Reports. Most companies send annual, and usually also quarterly, reports to stockholders. Such reports usually include a review of the company's activities and its financial statements.

Some executives study these reports carefully and then keep them. If this is your employer's habit, file them with other such reports or in the separate folder for that stock.

Bonds: Regular or Coupon

A *bond* is a certificate containing a written interest-bearing promise to pay a definite sum of money at a specified time and place. The interest due must be paid to bondholders before stockholders can share in the profits of the company, and for that reason bonds are considered safer investments than stocks. The ownership of bonds does not give the investor voting rights in the company.

There are two general classes of bonds — coupon bonds and registered bonds. *Coupon bonds* are payable to the person holding them. If the bond or the interest coupons are lost or stolen, they can be converted into cash by the holder. Coupon bonds, therefore, present a security responsibility to the secretary who is entrusted to care for them. Bonds should be kept in a safe-deposit box.

Coupons are cut from the bonds on or after their due date and presented at a local bank for collection. Some banks make a small charge for this collection service. Bond coupons can be listed on a bank deposit ticket.

Registered bonds are decidedly less worry to the secretary. Such bonds are registered by the issuing corporation, which mails the interest and principal payments to the registered holders. If the bond is lost, the owner still receives the payments; and the bond certificate can be replaced.

Corporate bonds are usually issued in $1,000 units. The selling price, however, is quoted as a percent of the par value. Thus, if a $1,000 bond is said to sell at 97⅝, it actually sells at $976.25, a discount of 2⅜ ($23.75) from its maturity value.

Interest on bonds issued by a municipality, a state, or certain other political subdivisions is exempt from federal income tax. These bonds are known as *tax-exempt bonds*.

The best kept secret in the American economy is how it works.

Robert L. Hielbroner

Stock Market Trading

Most stocks and bonds are purchased and sold through a stock exchange, such as the New York Stock Exchange, the American Stock Exchange (Amex), the Midwest (Chicago) Stock Exchange, the Pacific Coast Stock Exchange, and the Toronto Stock Exchange. A number of smaller organized exchanges are found in different parts of the country in large cities. On the New York Stock Exchange only securities listed on the exchange are traded; the American Stock Exchange and other exchanges permit trading in unlisted securities.

Some stocks and bonds are purchased in the *over-the-counter* market, which is not a place but a method of doing business; that is, the transaction is handled privately through a bank, a broker, or a securities dealer and does not go through any of the stock exchanges. A buyer or seller of the security is located, and the sale price is arrived at by negotiation. Most over-the-counter transactions are limited to unlisted securities (stocks and bonds of relatively small local companies that are not listed on an exchange).

Buying and selling of stocks and bonds on the stock exchange is handled through a *broker*. Stock certificates sold through brokers are not passed from owner to owner; the seller turns in the certificates to the broker who sends them to the transfer agent for cancellation. The transfer agent employed by the corporation is usually a bank, which keeps a record of the specific owners of stock certificates by names and numbers. The agent fills in a new certificate with the name supplied, writes in the number of shares the certificate represents, has it signed and countersigned, and forwards it to the broker for delivery to the new owner or for deposit to the credit of the owner's account at the brokerage firm. As a service to investors, some brokerage firms will hold all stocks and bonds owned by an investor and send a monthly statement or inventory of holdings, listing the amounts received as dividends or interest that month.

The term *mutual funds* is used to identify investment companies (or investment trusts). These investment companies sell shares to individual investors and use capital raised in this manner to purchase additional securities. These stocks and bonds are known as the *portfolio* of the investment company. The individual with limited funds is offered a chance to own (indirectly) an interest in many companies and types of securities because these investments are diversified among bonds, preferred stocks, and common stocks, and also among many corporations.

Mutual funds are available to investors wanting to purchase specialized securities — for instance, insurance, chemicals, or other stocks offering growth possibilities or high income.

Stock Market Information. The financial pages of leading newspapers report daily the stock transactions at major exchanges. The number of shares sold and the selling price for all stocks listed and traded in that day on each exchange are reported. Sales and prices of bonds are also reported in separate tables.

Stocks on which there was no trading — that is, no sales were made of the stock on the day being reported — are printed under a special "Bid and Asked" section. This section gives the closing bid and asking price for the stock. For example, AmFinani bid 42½, asked 44½. This means no American Finance stock was transferred and that there was an offer to buy at 42½ and an offer to sell at 44½.

In addition to the daily stock market report and financial news that appear in the newspapers, information on security prices, trends, and business conditions may be obtained from such sources as *Wall Street Journal, Business Week, Barron's, Financial World, Forbes, The New York Stock Exchange Monthly Review, The Exchange, American Investor, Moody's Stock Survey,* and *Commercial and Financial Chronicle.* Several large brokerage firms and some banks also publish special reports on securities.

There are a number of investment advisory services, such as Moody's Investors Service Inc., Babson's Reports Inc., United Business and Investment Service, and Professional Investor. Most of these organizations analyze the stock market and for a fee provide investors with detailed information on companies, lists of stocks to watch, stocks that represent good buys, and stocks to sell. They also analyze the individual's stock holdings and provide other data that an investor may need. Such service is also available from the broker with whom an investor has an account.

Market Averages. A number of stock averages are designed to serve as barometers of the stock market — that is, to indicate whether the market is rising or falling. Probably the best known are the Standard and Poor's Index and the Dow-Jones Averages. The Standard and Poor's Index is based on the price of 500 stocks and is computed hourly each trading day. The Dow-Jones Averages include four separate averages — one for industrial (stocks of industrial corporations), one for rails, one for utilities, and a composite average of 65 stocks, intended to measure trends in all divisions of the market. The market averages are published in leading newspapers and are reported on television and by radio.

Market Terminology. Certain standard terminology is used in placing orders for the purchase or sale of stock.

Bid and Offer. The price at which a prospective buyer will purchase and the price at which a prospective seller will sell is called *bid and offer.* This quotation involves over-the-counter sales.

Day Order. The day order is good only for the day on which it is given; *GTW Order* is "good for this week"; a *GTM Order* is "good this month"; and a *GTC Order* (open order) is "good till canceled."

Discretionary Order. The discretionary order gives the broker the privilege of determining when to execute the order.

Ex Dividend. A company declares a dividend to be paid to all stockholders as of a given future date. Stock sold during the intervening period may be sold *ex dividend*; that is, the *seller* and not the *purchaser* of the stock will receive the unpaid declared dividend.

Limited Order. A limited order instructs the broker to buy or sell a security at a certain price only. If the transaction cannot be consummated at the designated price, the order is not executed.

Market Order. A *market order* instructs the broker to buy or sell a security at once. No price is indicated and the order is executed "at the market"; that is — at the best price obtainable.

Round and Odd Lots. Most stocks listed on the stock exchanges are traded in 100-share units, called *round lots*. An order for anything less than 100 shares is known as an *odd lot*. A small additional commission charge is made for handling *odd-lot* transactions.

Short Sale. The investor sells short — that is, sells securities that he or she does not own in anticipation of buying them later at a lower price. To negotiate the sale, the broker borrows the stocks temporarily.

Stock Rights. When a corporation plans to sell additional stock, each existing stockholder may be given a stock warrant indicating the number of shares that the stockholder is entitled to purchase at a designated price, usually slightly below the market. A stockholder who chooses not to exercise stock purchase rights has the option of selling the rights to another party.

Stock Split. A company may split its stock to lower the market price. In a *stock split*, the company issues to each stockholder a specified number of additional shares for each share the stockholder now owns. For example, if it is a three-to-two split, the stockholder will receive three shares in exchange for each two shares owned.

Stop Order. The investor using a stop order instructs the broker to buy or sell "at the market" whenever the security moves to a specified quotation.

NEW YORK STOCK EXCHANGE COMPOSITE TRANSACTION

19-- [1] High	Low	Stock [2]	P-E [3] Ratio	Sales [4] 100s	High [5]	Low [6]	Close [7]	Net [8] Chg.
55 1/2	37 1/4	AbbtLab 1	15	1357	46 1/4	45 1/2	46	– 3/4
53 1/4	36 1/4	AetnaLf pf 2	..	9	48 1/2	48 3/4	48 1/4	– 1/2
46 3/4	26 3/8	Boeing la	10	645	42	40 1/2	41 3/4	+1 3/8
7	5 1/2	CaroPw 1.72b	8	529	22 1/4	22 3/8	22 1/2	– 5/8
14 1/2	10 1/2	CloroxCo .52i	10	352	12 1/2	12 1/8	13 3/8	+ 1/8

Key

1 The price range (high and low) of the stock in the year to date

2 The name of the company and a description of the stock. The rate of annual dividend paid per share based on the last quarterly or semiannual declaration is listed next. Special and extra dividends are not included unless noted by a legend letter following the dividend rate. Check the legend at the end of the stock listing for interpretation of the letters. The following legend explains the letters used in the illustration above:

   a — Also extra or extras   b — Annual rate plus stock dividend

   i — Declared or paid after stock split   pf — preferred stock

3 Price-Earnings Ratio. The multiple shown in this column is the number of times the annual earnings per share that the current selling price of the stock represents.

4 The number of shares of stock sold during the day (in hundreds)

5 The *highest* price the stock reached during the day. Stock quotations are in eighths of a point (dollar). Thus 76⅛ means a price of $76.125 per share; 76¼ ($76.25); 76½ ($76.50); 76⅝ ($76.625).

6 The *lowest* price for which the stock sold during the day

7 The *last (closing)* price for the stock at the end of the day

8 The difference between today's last price and the last price of yesterday. The plus sign (+) indicates an increase in the last price of today over yesterday's last price; the minus sign (−) indicates a decrease.

The illustration shown above provides the following information: To date this year, Abbott Laboratories common stock has sold at a high of $55.50 (55½) and a low of $37.25 (37¼). The stock paid $1.00 in dividends in the past twelve months. The price-earnings ratio is 15, meaning that the current selling price of the stock is 15 times the annual earnings per share. During the day 135,700 shares were sold. It reached a high of $46.25, and the lowest amount for which it sold was $45.50. The last sale for the day was at $46. This was down ¾ ($.75) from yesterday's closing.

Stop-and-Limit Order. The stop-and-limit order sets the price at which the order may be executed after going through the stop. The limit price may be the same or different from the stop price.

Yield. The *yield* is the percentage of return for one year on one share of stock, computed at the current market price or at the price paid by an owner.

A Brokerage Transaction. To understand the procedure of a brokerage transaction, let us follow through a hypothetical one in which the secretary shares responsibility.

1. The purchaser or secretary places an order with the broker to buy 25 shares of U.S. Steel common "at the market" (generally by a telephone call). (The secretary makes a full memorandum of the order: the date, the time, and the order placed. The broker *executes* the order on that date — the trade date.)

2. When the broker has made the purchase through the stock exchange, an invoice called a *confirmation* for the purchase of the stock is sent to the buyer. (The invoice or bill for the purchase or sale of securities is called a *confirmation* because the broker is acting as an agent and is confirming by means of the invoice the instructions received. The confirmation lists the name of the stock and description, the number of shares purchased or sold, the price per share, extension, commission charge, tax, postage, and total. The secretary compares the confirmation with the memorandum of the order to make sure the order has been carried out correctly.)

3. The purchaser or secretary sends a check to the broker by the settlement date (which is five business days after the trade date).

4. The broker arranges for the transfer of the stock to the purchaser. (If the executive has the brokerage company retain the stock, the executive's account will be credited and the stock will be reported on the next monthly inventory statement. If the executive retains his or her own stock certificates, the certificate will be forwarded by registered mail. If delivery is made to the executive, the secretary, upon receipt of the stock, records the stock certificate number on the confirmation and transfers all the information from the confirmation to the executive's permanent record. The secretary may attach the confirmation to the stock certificate or file the confirmation chronologically under the broker's name so that it will be available when the stock is sold. The sales confirmation may be filed with the copy of the executive's income tax return.)

Delivery of Securities. When securities held personally by the executive are sold, they are ordinarily delivered to the broker's office by the secretary or by messenger or are sent by registered mail and insured, accompanied by a covering letter describing the securities

JAN	FEB	MAR	APR	MAY	JUN	JUL	AUG	SEPT	OCT	NOV	DEC

(Dividend Date)

STOCK: Detroit Edison, common
BROKER: Merrill Lynch   DIVIDENDS: Mar., June,
FILED: Safe deposit box, City National   Sept., Dec.

Date	Certificate Number	How Acquired	No. of Shares	Cost per Share	Total Cost*
1/18/--	H21601	Purchased	100	14 1/2	1,486.00
5/20/--	H29861	New cert. for H21601 after sale 40 shares	60		
12/4/--	H32504	5% stock dividend	3		

*Includes postage, insurance, and commission.

RECORD OF SALES						
Trading Date	Shares Sold	Selling Price	Gross Amount	Int. or State Tax	Commission Paid	Net Amt. Received
5/20/--	40	16 3/4	670.00	2.43	11.25	656.32

A separate record card or sheet for stock transactions should be kept for each lot of securities. Purchases and sales are recorded on the front of the card as illustrated. Dividends are recorded on the ruled form on the back of the card. A metal tab can be used to indicate the dates on which to expect dividends. The card should show where the securities are kept.

in full. Include the owner's name and such items as the company name, amount, and certificate number for each stock certificate or bond enclosed. Request a return receipt.

Records of Securities. One good rule for the secretary to follow in keeping financial records for securities is to use a separate page or card for each lot. The illustration above shows a convenient form and indicates the information that would be recorded on each group of securities.

The "where kept" notation is important information that should be recorded about any valuable paper. Papers tucked away in unusual safekeeping spots known only to the owner often remain hidden when they are desperately needed in the owner's absence.

Stock Certificate Numbers. When all the stock covered by one certificate is sold, the certificate is surrendered to the broker as part of

LIST OF SECURITIES (CURRENT AS OF 5/17/--)

Date Purchased	Security	No. of Shares	Price per Share	Total Cost
1/18/73	John Manville	240	28 3/8	$6,930.77
8/13/74	Mead Corp. Prf. 2.80	200	35 1/4	7,162.07
4/14/76	Pfizer	200	27 7/8	5,679.59

The executive should have at hand a typed alphabetic list of securities. Usually the list is typed in triplicate: one copy for the executive's desk, one for the files, and one for the secretary's records. Each purchase of stock for a given company made on different days or at different prices should be listed separately.

the sale. When only a portion of a block of stock covered by one certificate is sold, the certificate is also turned over to the broker; but the investor receives a new certificate for a total of the unsold shares. This procedure requires a change in the certificate number on the stock records. For example, in the stock record illustrated on page 547, the 40 shares that were sold were from the block of 100 shares covered by Certificate Number H21601. This fact was indicated. The new certificate number for the 60 unsold shares is also recorded.

REAL ESTATE

A secretary may be commissioned to do any or all of the tasks incident to the executive's real estate activities — to care for the valuable papers necessary to real-estate transactions, to do the banking work, and to keep simple, complete records of income and expenses.

Buying Property

When real property is purchased, the title of ownership is transferred by means of a properly executed written instrument known as a *deed*.

Deeds. There are two types of deeds — warranty deeds and quitclaim deeds. In a *warranty deed* the grantor or seller warrants that he or she is the true and lawful owner with full power to convey the property and that the title is free, clear, and unencumbered. In a *quitclaim deed*, the grantor quits claim to the property; that is, the grantor relinquishes claim but does not warrant or guarantee the title.

A deed must be signed, witnessed, and acknowledged before a notary public. It should be *recorded* — that is, entered on public record at the courthouse in the county where the property is located. Deeds, mortgages, and leases are valuable legal documents and should be kept in a bank safe-deposit box or in a fireproof vault or safe.

Legal Terms. Other legal terms frequently used when the title to real estate is transferred are:

Mortgage — a formal written contract that transfers interest in property as security for the payment of the debt (Mortgages must be signed, witnessed, and recorded in the public records the same as a deed. The law considers the mortgagor [the borrower] as owner of the property during the period of the loan.)

Junior (Second) Mortgage — a mortgage that is subordinate to a prior mortgage

Amortization — mortgage or loan repayment plan that permits the borrower through regular payments at stated intervals to retire the principal of the loan

Foreclosure Proceedings — legal process used to satisfy the claim of the lender in case of default in payment of interest or principal on a mortgage

Option — an agreement under which an owner of property gives another person the right to buy the property at a fixed price within a specified time

Appurtenances — rights of way or other types of easements that are properly used with the land, the title to which passes with the land

Easements — privileges regarding some special use of another person's property, such as right of way to pass over the land, to use a driveway, or to fish in a stream

Fixtures — those articles that are permanently attached to real estate, such as buildings, fences, and electric wiring in a building

Land Contract — a method of payment for property whereby the buyer makes a small down payment and agrees to pay additional amounts at intervals (The buyer does not get a deed to the property until a substantial amount of the price of the property is paid.)

Keep a property record similar to this form for each piece of property. At the end of each year all the income and expenses related to each piece of property can be conveniently organized for preparation of the income tax report.

Type and Location of Property	Commercial property 127 North Webster Avenue Tucson, Arizona 85715	
Title in Name of:	Robert C. and Mary K. Folley	
Date Acquired:	2/21/-- Purchase Price:	$97,500
Mortgage(s):	Main Savings and Loan First Federal Bank	$40,000 5,000
Assessed Evaluation for Taxes:	$59,000	
Remarks: Deed is filed in home safe		

Income from Rentals			Mortgage Payments Int. and Princ.			Expenses		
Date	Item	Amount	Date	Item	Amount	Date	Item	Amount
2/10	Rent	510.00	2/28	I.+P.	310.00	3/10	Taxes	500.00
3/10	Rent	510.00	3/31	I.+P.	310.00	3/10	Water	48.20
4/10	Rent	510.00	4/30	I.+P.	310.00	4/16	Plumb.	46.85

Property Records

Permanent records of property owned are kept for several reasons: to determine the value of the property, to show the outstanding debt, to use in tax reporting, and to use as a basis for setting a satisfactory selling price.

A separate record should be kept for each piece of property owned and should include information similar to that shown above.

Investment Property. Property held for rental income or to be sold at a hoped-for profit is *investment property*. The secretary's employer may own several such pieces, or the business may be employed to manage such property for other owners, for which a service fee is received. Managing property means negotiating with the tenants, keeping the building in repair, and handling certain of the finances — collecting rentals, paying expenses, and so on.

Tenants may be required to sign *leases* prepared by the secretary. Printed lease forms (see Chapter 25) are available in stationery or legal-supply stores. The pertinent facts must be filled in on the form and the signatures affixed. These forms should be checked with an attorney to be certain they set forth the exact conditions desired.

The secretary keeps detailed records of income and expenses on each piece of investment property because all income must be reported and all expenses are deductible on tax returns.

To keep accurate data on each unit, the secretary can follow the plan suggested here.

1. Set up an individual file folder for each rental unit, such as each suite of offices, each apartment in a building, or each house. As each unit would be identified on the file folder by the number or address, an alphabetic index of tenants' names giving their rental location would serve as a helpful cross-reference. File in this folder everything pertaining to the unit of rental, such as correspondence, the lease, bills for repairs or improvements, lists of any special fixtures or furniture provided, rental amount.

2. Use a miscellaneous folder (or folders) for the building in general to take care of the items that cannot be charged to a specific rental unit, such as janitor service, repairs to the exterior of the building or corridors, taxes, and other such items.

The record of all receipts and expenses paid can be written right on each folder, or on a card or sheet filed inside each folder. Preferably, such records are kept on separate sheets in a loose-leaf book where the chance of their being lost is considerably reduced.

The banking of money collected from investment property and the payment of bills for such property should be handled carefully. It is extremely important that the deposit slips be completed so that every deposit can be identified and that every check stub be labeled to be charged against a specific rental unit or building.

Personal-Property Records. To provide necessary information in event of death or other contingency, the secretary is often asked to keep a file of the executive's personal property, such as an inventory of household goods, a description and the location of family jewels and heirlooms, insurance policies, and the names and addresses of certain key people involved in the executive's personal affairs. Such information and materials should be placed in sealed envelopes, labeled, and kept in the safe-deposit box or fireproof office safe.

Tickler Card File

There are many recurring expenses on property, such as mortgage payments (usually due monthly), tax payments (due annually or semiannually), and insurance premiums (due quarterly). On income property, the rent is usually due on a certain day each month. To make sure that income is received when due and that recurring expenses are paid on time, a tickler card should be prepared for each item so that the card can be used continually — refiled under the next pertinent date after it comes to the front on the current reminder date.

In addition to interest and mortgage payments, use tickler cards for:

The tickler card for a monthly mortgage payment identifies the property, shows the file date, due date, amount of payment, to whom payment is to be made, and where the check is to be sent.

<u>File date</u>: 12th of each month

Mortgage payment due: 15th of each month
(Mail check no later than the 12th)

Duplex, 906 Seneca Street

Amount of check: $225.00

Make check to: Estate of Frank Foster
Send check to: Willis and Thompson
                148 Baker Bldg.
                110 W. 7th Street
                Fort Worth, TX 76102

Final payment date: April 15, 1983

Taxes — Indicate for each kind of tax payment: kind of tax, payment date, amount, to whom to make the check payable, where to send the check, and whether or not a return must accompany the payment.

Insurance Premiums — See the illustration at the bottom of page 555 for information to be shown.

Rent Receipts — For each rental unit show location, amount of rent, name and mailing address of tenant, and any special information regarding collection or interpretation of rent payment.

Source Materials

The employer who has extensive real estate holdings or is engaged in the real estate business may subscribe to an information service, such as the *Prentice-Hall Real Estate Service*. There are also a number of periodicals that specialize in providing current information on real estate, a few of which are *Real Estate Weekly, Builders and Realty Record, National Real Estate Investor, The Appraisal Journal, Journal of Property Management, Construction Digest,* and *Building Operating Management.*

INSURANCE

Insurance can be grouped into three general classes — personal, property, and liability. *Personal insurance* includes the many kinds of life, accident, and health insurance. *Property insurance* covers loss from impairment or destruction of property, such as fire, earthquake, burglary, and automobile collision. *Liability insurance* protects the insured against losses resulting from injury to another, such as public liability, workers' compensation, and employer's liability.

The individual or business purchasing the insurance is called the *policyholder*. The *policy* is the written contract that exists between the policyholder and the insurance company. The insurance company may be referred to as the insurer or the *underwriter*. The policyholder makes periodic payments to the insurance company for the policy. These payments are called the insurance *premium*.

The secretary has three responsibilities regarding insurance; namely, to see that the premiums are paid promptly so that there will be no lapse in protection, to keep summary records on each kind of insurance for the executive's information, and to store the policies and related correspondence in a safe place.

In correspondence, be sure to include the policy number. If the correspondence relates to a claim, include the claim number assigned by the insurance company.

Premium Payments and Renewals

Insurance premiums are payable in advance. Those on property insurance are usually paid annually or for a term of three or five years. Premiums on life insurance may be paid annually or in monthly, quarterly, or semiannual installments.

Many life insurance policies allow a 28- to 31-day grace period in making premium payments. If the premium is due and payable on August 16, payment of the premium may be made any time before September 16. If the premium notice does not specify the grace period, the secretary should inquire from the insurance company if a grace period is allowed.

Checks in payment of premiums must be drawn in sufficient time to have them signed and sent to the insurance company or agent before the expiration date. It is the secretary's responsibility to avoid any insurance policy lapse caused by failure to make premium payment.

In addition to seeing that premiums are paid, the secretary should also arrange for the cancellation of policies when the protection is no longer needed. A policy can be canceled by telling the insurance company or agent of the cancellation and returning the policy. The premium for the unexpired period of the policy is refundable. The secretary should place a follow-up in the tickler file to check on the receipt of the premium refund.

Insurance Records

A beginning secretary may be fortunate enough to inherit a summary record of the employer's personal insurance commitments.

The secretary must follow up on payment of insurance premiums, as well as cancellations and indorsements (changes in the policy).

More likely, however, no records will be available, and it will be necessary to compile the information from insurance policies on file in the office and from notices of premiums due as they are received in the mail.

Methods of keeping insurance records vary, but in general the records consist of an insurance register and a premium payment reminder, usually in the form of a tickler card. The register would contain information similar to that shown in the illustration at the bottom of page 555. Some secretaries record insurance policies on separate sheets in a small loose-leaf notebook. Thus, when a policy is no longer in force, the sheet can be removed. Others prefer to use a separate register for each type of insurance: life, property, and liability. Certainly, the executive's personal insurance and that of the business or office should be kept in separate registers.

Use a separate tickler card for each policy, and file the cards according to premium-payment date. This helps to avoid the lapse of a policy or a penalty for late payment of a premium. The insurance index card illustrated on page 556 provides all the information necessary.

TYPES OF INSURANCE

Personal Insurance — Protects against the results of illness, accident, and loss of income because of illness, accident, or death.

Life: Endowment
Limited payment life
Ordinary life
Term

Health: Hospital care
Medical fees
Surgical fees
Loss of income

Property Insurance — Protects from financial loss resulting from damage to insured's property.

Automobile collision
Burglary and employee theft
Fire
Fire — Extended coverage (windstorm, lightning, riot, strike violence, smoke damage, falling aircraft and vehicle damage, most explosions)
Plate glass
Standard boiler
Valuable papers
Vandalism

Marine: Barratry
Burning
Collision
Mutiny
Piracy
Sinking
Standing

Liability Insurance (Casualty) — Protects against claim of other people if insured person causes injury or property damage to others.

Automobile liability
Bailee insurance
Elevator insurance
Libel and slander

Premise and operations liability
Public liability
Product insurance
Workers' compensation

Credit, Fidelity, and Surety Insurance — Protects against losses from:

Bad accounts (Credit)
Title (Surety)

Employee embezzlement
(Fidelity)

Columns to provide appropriate information can be added to the insurance register as needed. When a policy expires, draw a line through the description to indicate the policy is no longer in force.

	INSURANCE REGISTER					
Company and Name of Agent	Policy No.	Type and Amount	Date Issued	Amt. of Premium	Date Due	Grace Period
N.Y. LIFE V. Getty	29 22 84	Ord. Life on Mr. B. $20,000	3/2/55	$284 Semi-an	2/2 8/2	30-day
N.Y. LIFE V. Getty	37 86 21 37 86 21	Term $10,000 on Mrs. B.	1/9/68	$175 Annual	5/6	30-day
CONN. GEN. T. Ramsey	H261 162	Fire on household goods $20,000	1/12/72	$249 Annual	12/12	

File an index card for each insurance policy in a tickler file. This provides a convenient record of the insurance and serves as a reminder notice for renewals and premium payments.

File date: December 26, 19--

Expiration date: January 4 each year

Type: Fire insurance on office furniture

Amount: $5,000   With: Mutual Insurance Co.
5352 First St., City

Policy No. X438832
Date of issue: January 5 each year
Premium: $97.20
Policy filed: First National Bank

Property Inventory

The importance of keeping an up-to-date property inventory can be fully appreciated only by someone who has experienced a fire or burglary loss. To present a claim for a loss, the insured must "furnish a complete inventory of the destroyed, lost, damaged, and undamaged property with cost and actual cash value." This is difficult to do after the loss has taken place. A property inventory also serves a second important purpose. It shows how much insurance should be carried. Property values change; and unless the inventory is updated periodically, property may be overinsured or underinsured.

The secretary in a small office can and should assume the responsibility for compiling an inventory of the furniture and equipment in the office. In addition, the executive should be encouraged to provide details for an inventory of the furniture and valuables at home. All inventories should be periodically updated.

Storage of Policies and Inventory Records

Since insurance policies must be examined occasionally for data on coverage, beneficiaries, rates, cash value, indorsements, and the like, the policies should be readily available — but in a safe place.

If the policies are kept in a file, you may find it convenient to remove them from their protective envelopes and place each policy in a separate folder. Identify the front of the folder with the name, address, and telephone number of the agent, and the policy number. Such a plan makes it possible to file with each policy any important

When insurance policies are stored in the office, there is always the possibility of their loss by fire. As a precaution, type a list of the policy numbers, insuring company, coverage, and amount. Your employer should store this list in a safe at home. Thus, if the office records are destroyed, they can be more readily reconstructed.

correspondence, itemized lists of property covered, indorsements, and other pertinent data that affect the conditions of the insurance contract.

Since an insurance policy *is* a contract, you can discard it when it has expired and keep your file cleared. First, however, you should call or write the agent to make certain that no claim on the policy is pending and that it has no continuing value.

Fidelity Bonds

A *fidelity bond* is insurance on an employee's honesty. Most employers carry such insurance on those employees who handle large sums of money. The bonding company investigates the employee's character and the supervisory and control methods in force in the employer's business. No bond is sold if the applicant's character is questionable or if office conditions would make it easy to embezzle company funds.

Blanket fidelity bonds covering the entire personnel are bought by banks and other financial institutions. They protect against losses by embezzlement, robbery, forgery, and so on.

To be asked to take out a fidelity bond is no reflection on your character. Actually it indicates that you are considered competent to be entrusted with company funds.

Action in Emergency

When disaster strikes, you will have an opportunity to prove that you are the cool-headed, responsible type that can think and act quickly. Others may be so excited and involved in the emergency that they fail to think of procedures. Insurance companies make these suggestions:

After a fire, as soon as the situation is under control, notify the insurance company immediately by phone and confirm the call by wire. The insurance company may be able to have an inspector on the scene to witness the damage and save a lot of paperwork later on.

Immediately report to the police any losses by theft.

Keep accurate and separate records for cleanup, repairs, and charges made by outside contractors. The items are all part of the insurance claim.

When an accident occurs, interview witnesses on the spot. Signed statements carry much weight and refresh memories in settling claims. If possible, take pictures at the scene.

WHERE-KEPT FILE

In the event of the sudden death of an executive, the family will need immediately certain financial information. The secretary can be of great assistance in such an emergency if a folder containing up-to-date information has been maintained. The following information might be included:

Bank Accounts — the name and address of each bank in which an account is kept, the type of account, the exact name of account, and the name of bank contact (if the executive has one)

Birth Certificate — where it can be found

Business Interests — list of the executive's business interests

Credit Cards — record of names and account numbers

Income Tax Record — where past returns are filed; the name and address of the tax consultant

Insurance Policies — location of insurance records (If these records do not contain detailed information on life, health and accident, hospitalization, and medical insurance policies, the information should be placed in the folder. The name and address of the insurance adviser should be filed also.)

Real Estate Investments — location of detailed property records

Passport — where it can be found

Safe-Deposit Box — the name of the bank, the box number, and location of key

Social Security — the social security number

Stocks and Bonds — location of detailed investment records

Tax Accountant — name

Will — location of the original and copies of the will; date of the latest will; name of attorney who prepared the will; executor's name and address

ADMINISTRATIVE FUNCTIONS

The secretary may be expected to perform a number of administrative functions related to the property, investments, and insurance coverage of the company and of the executive. The college-trained secretary has a background of courses in economics, accounting, business law, and, in some cases, real estate and insurance. All of these courses contribute to your competency.

As an administrative assistant you may be asked to:

1. Prepare an investment prospectus on stocks that are under consideration for investment. This activity would involve checking investment service reports for gathering data on products, past performance, background of company officials, forecasts for the area and for the company, comparison with competitors, and so forth. Such data are available in the business section of a public library and in special libraries.

2. Update the investment portfolio of the company or of the executive. The updating process would involve analyzing (1) the rate of yield on each investment, (2) profit trends, and (3) the outlook for the company. For some classes of stock, charts showing the fluctuations in the market may need to be prepared and updated at regular intervals.

3. Supervise and follow through on repairs and improvements made to investment property. Frequent visits to the location of the property and careful study of the repair or construction contract would be necessary.

4. Handle the details related to processing the sale or purchase of real estate. This activity involves such details as having the title searched for liens and mortgages, obtaining title insurance, and processing and recording the deed.

5. Review at regular intervals the insurance policies in force and arrange for revision in insurance coverage in keeping with changing values of the property. The responsibility includes canceling unneeded policies and being alert to new insurance needs.

6. Process an insurance claim. This responsibility involves compiling the records necessary to support a claim — cost records, appraisal of loss, and proof of loss.

SUGGESTED READINGS

Engle, Louis, and Peter Wyckoff. *How to Buy Stocks*. Boston: Little, Brown & Co., 1976.

"Know What Your Insurance Policies Really Say." *Changing Times*, Vol. 30, No. 1 (January, 1976), pp. 27–29.

Miller, Eugene. *Your Future in Securities*. New York: Richards Rosen Press, Inc., 1974, pp. 110–129 (glossary of stock market terms).

"Which Family Records Should You Hang Onto?" *Changing Times*, Vol. 28, No. 12 (December, 1974), pp. 37–40.

QUESTIONS FOR DISCUSSION

1. A secretary whose employer invests in securities must know a number of stock market terms. What does each of the following terms mean? (Refer to outside sources for the meanings of terms with which you are not familiar.)

bear market	market value
"blue-chip" stocks	mutual fund
book value	option
bull market	"over-the-counter"
ex dividend	rails
growth stocks	sleeper
industrials	stock dividend
investment companies	stock split
margin	utilities

2. If a stockholder is dissatisfied with the way a corporation is being managed, what can he or she do?

3. Your employer is considering an investment in Xerox Corporation. You are asked to compile a report on the stock. What type of information would you include in the report? What would your information sources be?

4. In addition to stock prices, what information does the financial section of the newspaper contain? Would you recommend that the secretary read this section regularly?

5. The suggestion is made in this chapter that the secretary establish a where-kept file. How would you organize this file? Where would you keep it?

6. In the event of fire or theft, all financial records (including stock certificates, bonds, and insurance policies) may be lost. What precautions should a secretary take or suggest to the employer that would minimize such losses?

7. An owner of a small grocery store with six employees wishes to be protected against all possible insurable losses. What types of insurance would be obtained? Include the building in which the store is located.

8. When the employer's automobile was involved in an accident, it was discovered that the insurance policy had lapsed because of nonpayment of premium. The employer was extremely critical of the secretary. The secretary's defense was that the premium notices and follow-ups had been placed on the employer's desk. Furthermore, this was personal business and the employer's failure to act was not the secretary's responsibility. Do you agree with the secretary's position?

9. Write the following years in Roman numerals:
    1920   1977   2000   Current Year
    Convert these Roman numerals to Arabic numbers:
    LD   XM   MMVIII

10. Show a shorter way of writing the following amounts. Consult the Reference Guide to verify your answers.
    $6,700,000 $5,100,000,000

PROBLEMS

1. Your employer owns all of the follow-ing securities:

   200 shares...American Natural Resources, common, (ANatR)

   100 shares...Coca Cola, common (CocaCol)

   75 shares...Consolidated Edison, 5% preferred, (ConE pf 5)

   5 bonds....New York Telephone, (NY Tel 4½s 91)

   200 shares...Standard Oil of Indiana (StOInd)

   500 shares...Union Oil of Canada (UnionOil)

   (a) Prepare a report showing the cur-rent market value of your em-ployer's security holdings. (Use the closing price of the security on the date of the report.)

   (b) Your employer purchased the shares of American Natural Re-sources stock at 25. A quarterly dividend of 66¢ per share is de-clared. Determine the rate of yield that is received on the investment and the rate of yield at the current market price.

2. Your employer has investments in stock and carries several insurance policies. The insurance policies are on the employer's spouse, son, home, and automobile. You decide to set up a tickler file to assist you in keeping track of the securities and the insur-ance premiums and policies. Make a list of the type of information you would include on the card about each (a) security, (b) insurance policy.

3. Your employer owns a professional building that cost $220,000. The build-ing houses 18 offices. Six offices rent for $450 per month, ten for $400, and the remaining two for $250 per month. All the offices were rented throughout the year except four of the $450 offices, which were each vacant three months while being redec-orated. The following expenses were incurred during the year in operating the building: management fee, 5% of the rental income; janitorial and main-tenance service, $880 per month; sup-plies, $2,150; utilities, $4,100; taxes, $9,560; repairs, $12,835; redecorating, $9,250; and miscellaneous expenses, $875. Prepare a report showing the in-come, expenses, and net income for the year and the annual percent of re-turn on the investment in the building.

4. On a sheet of paper construct a form that would be convenient for record-ing the income as received and the expenses as paid out during the year for the professional building de-scribed in Problem 3.

24

Payroll and Tax Records

Employers are required by federal and state laws to keep detailed payroll records. A business with a large number of employees usually centralizes payroll work in a payroll division. Unless employed in that division, a secretary would probably not be involved with payroll preparation. In the small office, however, the situation is different. The multifunctional, and in some cases the administrative, secretary may be in complete charge of the payroll. Thus, the payroll responsibilities of a secretary depend upon the size of the office, the function of the office, and the specific secretarial assignment in the office.

The second part of this chapter discusses the preparation of the personal income tax return. It is related to payroll because part of the data for the return is obtained from the payroll records. The preparation of an individual tax return requires the accumulation of income and expenses over a 12-month period. Usually, the compiling of this personal tax data is not an assigned secretarial responsibility. Consequently, the area offers the secretary the opportunity to exercise initiative and to play a very important assistance role — a role that the employer greatly appreciates.

PAYROLL PROCEDURES

Payroll work is detailed and demands mathematical accuracy. In addition, it requires an understanding of the forms and reports that are legislated by the Federal Insurance Contribution (Social Security) and Fair Labor Standards Acts, income tax laws, federal and state unemployment compensation acts, and any pertinent local legislation.

The payroll is also a security responsibility. Payroll information is confidential. The secretary, therefore, must guard all payroll facts. Not only must the actual payroll checks and records be secured, but all payroll computation sheets, carbon paper, and one-use typewriter carbon ribbons must be destroyed because they provide the inquisitive person with a source of information. If interrupted when working on the payroll, the secretary should place all information in a drawer before leaving the desk.

Social Security

Under the social security system most business, farm, and household employees and self-employed persons are provided an income in old age and survivor benefits in event of death. Social security also provides a nationwide system of unemployment insurance and hospital and medical insurance benefits (known as Medicare) for persons of age 65 or over.

To pay most of these social security benefits, both employees and employers contribute an equal amount. Medical insurance (for persons of age 65 or over) is optional and is financed jointly by contributions from the retired insured person and also from the federal government.

Social Security Numbers. Each employer and employee must obtain a social security number for identification in the government records. For the employer the number is called an *identification number*.

To obtain a number, file an application form with the nearest social security office or post office. You will receive a card stamped with your number. If the card is lost, a duplicate can be obtained. If you change your name or need to make other changes, report them to the Social Security Administration. The secretary may find it convenient to have the following social security forms on hand:

Application for a Social Security Number (or Replacement of Lost Card)

Request for Change in Social Security Records

Request for Statement of Earnings

The Social Security Administration recommends that every three or four years each employee request a statement of earnings to make sure that individual earnings have been reported properly.

The social security card shows the number assigned to each individual protected under the Social Security Act. The individual retains the same account number throughout life.

FICA Tax Deductions. Under the Social Security Act both the employer and employee pay *FICA* (Federal Insurance Contribution Act) *taxes* at the same rate. The present tax rates and those scheduled for the future (subject to change by Congress) are shown below.

PRESENT AND FUTURE FICA TAX RATES (Percentages)

Year	Employee	Employer	Self-Employed	Wage Base*
1978	6.05	6.05	8.10	$17,700
1979	6.13	6.13	8.10	22,900
1980	6.13	6.13	8.10	25,900
1981	6.65	6.65	9.30	29,700
1982	6.70	6.70	9.35	31,800

*Maximum earnings subject to FICA tax.

The FICA tax is deducted from the employee's wage each payday; these amounts are accumulated and forwarded together with the employer's FICA tax payment to the Internal Revenue Service Center for the region. To illustrate, assume that an employee earns $200 a week and is paid at the end of each week. At the rate of 6.05 percent, $12.10 is deducted for the employee's FICA tax and the employer contributes an equal amount. At the end of the quarter (13 weeks) the employer must remit to the government a total of $314.60.

Self-employed persons (such as farmers, architects, and contractors) are required to pay at a rate that is approximately three fourths of the total paid by the employer and the employee on the same income. Self-employed individuals report and pay their FICA tax simultaneously with their income tax.

Unemployment Compensation Tax Deductions. Under the Social Security Act, employers of four or more workers must pay a federal tax levied to pay the administrative costs of the state unemployment laws.

Most employers are also subject to a state unemployment tax. This tax, in most states paid by employers only, provides funds from which unemployment compensation can be paid to unemployed workers. The tax rate in most states is 2.7 percent of earnings up to $6,000 yearly on each employee. The employer's contributions to state unemployment compensation funds are reported on special forms filed quarterly.

In some states the unemployment tax is levied on employees as well as employers. In these states, the tax is deducted by the employer from the employee's wage. The employers submit quarterly to the state amounts deducted along with their contributions.

Withholding (Income Tax) Deductions

The federal government requires employers to withhold an advanced payment on income tax from the wages paid to an employee. The amounts withheld are remitted to the regional Internal Revenue Service Center at the time the FICA taxes are paid. The term *wages* used in this connection includes the total compensation paid for service, such as wages, salaries, commissions, bonuses, and vacation allowances.

The amount of income tax withheld depends upon the amount of wages received and the number of personal exemptions the taxpayer claims. Each employee must file with the employer, immediately upon reporting to work, an Employee's Withholding Allowance Certificate (Form W-4) to indicate the number of personal exemptions which the employee claims. The following exemptions may be claimed:

An exemption for the employee

An exemption for the employee's spouse (unless the spouse claims his or her own exemption)

An exemption for each dependent (unless the employee's spouse claims them)

An additional exemption if the taxpayer or spouse is 65 years of age or more or is blind

The amount of tax withheld is then computed from a table provided by the Internal Revenue Service.

A number of cities and states tax personal income. The percentage of deduction and the form of payment vary; for example, one city may have the employer deduct 1 percent from every payroll check issued and remit the total deductions at the end of each quarter of a calendar year. Some states and cities require individuals to file annual income tax returns.

The following forms are needed for payroll records:

W-2......................Wage and Tax Statement

W-3......................Transmittal of Income and Tax Statements

W-4......................Employee's Withholding Allowance Certificate

501 ....Federal Tax Deposit

940 ....Employer's Annual Federal Unemployment Tax Return

941 ....Employer's Quarterly Federal Tax Return

State Unemployment Return; other state and city report forms as required

CALENDAR OF PAYROLL PROCEDURES

On Hiring a New Employee:

Have the employee complete Form W-4 (Employee's Withholding Allowance Certificate). Record employee's social security number and number of exemptions. File the certificate in a safe place.

On Each Payment of Wages to an Employee:

Withhold the proper amount of income tax and FICA tax (refer to the instructions and tables supplied by the Internal Revenue Service and also to city and state information, if necessary). Make all other deductions.

As part of the payroll check or as a separate statement, a record of total wages, amount and kind of each deduction, and net amount should be given to the employee.

Within 15 Days after the Close of Each of the First Two Months of Any Calendar Quarter:

If income and employees' and employer's FICA taxes withheld total $200 or more, but less than $2,000, by the last day of the first month and/or by the last day of the second month in a calendar quarter, the full amount must be deposited in a Federal Reserve Bank or authorized bank by the 15th of the next month. Use Form 501. (Federal Tax Deposit).

If the total amount of undeposited taxes is less than $200 by the last day of the second month of a calendar quarter, the full amount may be paid with the employer's quarterly tax return (Form 941).

On or Before Each April 30, July 31, October 31, and January 31:

File *Form 941 (Employer's Quarterly Federal Tax Return)* with the regional Internal Revenue Service Center. Remit with it the full amount due; that is, the total amount of income and employees' and employer's FICA taxes withheld during the quarter less total of Federal Tax Deposits Receipts (Form 501).

The *State Unemployment Return* is usually filed at this time.

On or Before January 31 and at the End of an Employee's Employment:

Prepare *Form W-2 (Wage and Tax Statement)* showing the total wages, total wages subject to withholdings for income tax, the amount of income tax withheld, the total wage subject to FICA tax, and the amount of FICA tax withheld.

The government-prepared Form W-2 consists of four copies — two copies given to the employee; one copy for the Internal Revenue Service Center, one copy for the employer's record. To save paper work, many large firms print their own W-2 forms with five or six copies. The additional copies are given to the city and state (that is, for records of income tax withheld) if they require them.

On or Before January 31 of Each Year:

File *Form 940 (Employer's Annual Federal Unemployment Tax Return)* to report payment of federal unemployment taxes under the Federal Unemployment Tax Act.

File *Form W-3 (Transmittal of Income and Tax Statements)* to provide a summary statement that enables a comparison of the total income taxes withheld as reported on all Form W-2s and the total amount of income tax withheld as reported on the four quarterly Forms 941.

Retain payroll records for a period of FOUR YEARS.

Other Payroll Deductions

In addition to the deductions required by federal and state legislation, other payroll deductions — such as hospital care insurance (hospitalization), group insurance premiums, stock and bond purchases — may be made. In most firms these deductions are voluntary, and usually the authorizations may be canceled by the employee at any time.

Most employers furnish with each wage payment an itemized listing of all deductions made from the employee's wage. This information is usually provided on a form attached to the check, to be removed and retained by the employee when the check is cashed. At the end of each year, the employer is required to furnish each employee with a Wage and Tax Statement (Form W-2) that shows the total earnings and tax deductions. One copy of Form W-2 is attached to the individual's income tax return form.

Fair Labor Standards Act

There are primarily two classes of remuneration — *wages* at a rate per hour and *salaries* at a rate per week or month. Persons receiving wages are usually paid only for the hours they work; persons receiving salaries are usually paid for the full pay period even though they may be absent from work for brief periods. To differentiate, employees are called "hourly" and "salary" employees respectively. Office employees are almost always paid salaries, although record-keeping requirements at times may make practical the payment of office employees on an hourly basis.

Most hourly and salaried employees come under the provisions of the *Fair Labor Standards Act*, which sets a minimum hourly wage and requires that each employer keep a record of the hours worked by each employee and that each employee be paid at a rate at least 50 percent greater than the employee's regular hourly rate for all time over 40 hours during a workweek. Professional workers and executives are excluded from the provisions of the act.

Some companies pay overtime for all work beyond a specific number of hours a day. In other companies no overtime is paid salaried workers, but compensatory time off is given instead.

The Fair Labor Standards Act does not require the filing of overtime reports to any governmental office, but records must be kept on file for four years in the employer's office on nonexempt employees for perusal at any time a government examiner chooses to look them over. Detailed information about this legislation may be obtained from the nearest office of the Wage and Hour Division, Department of Labor.

SOC. SEC. NO.	696-44-2878			
			PAY PERIOD ENDING 4/30/--	
CLOCK NO. 12			WITHHOLDING TAX EXEMPTIONS 1	
NAME Nancy Daniels				
REG. HOURS	RATE	AMOUNT	F.I.C.A. TAX	TOTAL EARNINGS
35½	4.10	145.55	9.95	170.15
O.T. HOURS	RATE	AMOUNT	INC. TAX WITH.	TOTAL DEDUCTIONS
4	6.15	24.60	26.80	40.60
TOTAL HRS.		AMOUNT	GROUP INS.	NET PAY
39½			.50	129.55
			HOSP. 3.35	
			OTHER	

Days	IN MORNING	OUT	IN AFTERNOON	OUT	IN OVERTIME	OUT	TOTAL Hours
1	Σ 8⁰⁴	Σ 12⁰¹	Σ 12⁴⁸	Σ 4³²			7¼
2	⊇ 7⁵⁴	⊇ 12⁰²	⊇ 12⁵²	⊇ 3⁵⁸			6¾
3	≽ 7⁵⁸	≽ 11³⁰	≽ 12⁵⁴	≽ 4³⁶			7
4	Ŧ 7⁵⁹	Ŧ 12⁰³	Ŧ 1²⁸	Ŧ 4³¹			7
5	℞ 7⁴⁶	℞ 12⁰²	℞ 12⁴⁹	℞ 4³⁰	℞ 5⁰⁰	℞ 9⁰⁵	11½
6							
7							
	IN MORNING	OUT	IN AFTERNOON	OUT	IN OVERTIME	OUT	39½

Time Card

Time Records

Hourly workers, such as factory and department-store employees and some salaried workers, "punch in" and "punch out" each time they enter and leave their places of employment. The time is stamped on a time card. At the end of the payroll period the cards are collected and the pay is computed from the time stampings. A time card is illustrated above.

Instead of using a time clock, salaried employees may sign in and out on a ruled sheet; or the secretary may be responsible for checking each person in and out daily on such a time sheet. Time records are not necessary in computing salaries, but it is advisable to keep them as such records may be the basis of paying overtime earnings or balancing time off with overtime worked. Then too, there are various reports that require records of the overtime or time off of salaried employees.

Payroll Records

Federal legislation requires employers to keep payroll records. These usually include a form similar to that on page 570, to be completed each pay period. In addition, an employee's earning record is usually kept for *each* employee. Data from payroll records are transferred periodically to the employee's earning record, preferably each pay period. The employee's earning record form illustrated on page 570 provides quarterly totals for the required quarterly tax reports, as well as the annual total. Even though the laws affecting payroll taxes are changed from time to time, a comprehensive record similar to that illustrated will provide the basic data from which to compile almost any type of payroll tax report.

Requesting Salary Check

If a secretary is the lone employee in a firm, it may be necessary to remind the executive that it is payday — a somewhat embarrassing necessity for the new or young secretary. A not-so-obvious way is to ask, "Shall I write out my salary check for your signature?" or "Do you want me to cash a check this noon for my salary?" Never wait until two minutes before leaving time and meekly and hesitatingly say, "This is payday." The lawyer, doctor, or branch-office representative under whom the secretary is likely to be the only employee is a matter-of-fact business person who wants the secretary to be paid promptly but who may forget that important day and may not wish to be delayed at the last minute.

Administrative Responsibilities

The secretary may be involved in salary administration. For example, a secretary may be asked to perform such administrative functions as to recommend promotions and salary increases for members of the office staff, to assist in determining compensation for office personnel, to determine work standards, to examine and propose incentive plans for the office, to evaluate office employees, and to make recommendations for transfers and dismissals. The manner in which these functions are carried out plays an extremely important role in determining office morale.

An essential to a sound salary-administration plan is that each employee be paid a fair and reasonable compensation for work done. This requires some form of job analysis. Before making recommendations involving salary administration, the secretary needs to be thoroughly familiar with the competencies required for each position and to have some measure of the quality and quantity of the work produced by each staff member. Job analysis and employee evaluation are two administrative areas in which the secretary may need to obtain background knowledge.

The secretary also may find an awareness of union and legislative regulations regarding labor to be helpful.

PAYROLL REGISTER

FOR PERIOD ENDING *March 15, 19__*

	EMPLOYEE	S M	EXEMP.	EARNINGS			DEDUCTIONS				NET PAY	CHECK NO.
				REG.	OVER-TIME	TOTAL	F.I.C.A. TAX	WITH-TAX	HEALTH INS.	TOTAL	AMOUNT	
1	Allen, Joanne	S	1	500.00	36.50	536.50	31.39	93.30	16.00	140.69	395.81	123
2	Bauer, Thomas	M	2	520.00		520.00	30.42	68.60	26.00	125.02	394.98	124
3	Cowan, Rhonda	S	1	460.00		460.00	26.91	79.60	16.00	122.51	337.49	125
19	Scott, Martha	M	2	500.00		500.00	29.25	65.20	26.00	120.45	379.55	141
20	Weyer, Louis	S	1	420.00	45.75	465.75	27.25	79.60	16.00	122.85	342.90	142
	TOTALS			8,340.00	954.00	9,294.00	543.70	1,246.80	400.00	2,190.50	7,103.50	

Shown above is a partial page from a basic payroll register. According to the needs of the specific situation, the secretary may either purchase standard forms at a stationery store or design and duplicate a form with the number of columns and lines required. If requirements are large enough to justify having the form specially printed, the company will likely have a payroll department.

EMPLOYEE'S EARNINGS RECORD

	19-- PERIOD ENDING	EARNINGS			DEDUCTIONS				NET PAY
		REG.	OVER-TIME	TOTAL	F.I.C.A. TAX	WITH-TAX	HEALTH INS.	TOTAL	AMOUNT
1	1/15	500.00		500.00	29.25	65.20	26.00	120.45	379.55
2	1/31	500.00		500.00	29.25	65.20	26.00	120.45	379.55
3	2/15	500.00	18.75	518.75	30.35	65.20	26.00	121.55	397.20
4	2/28	500.00		500.00	29.25	65.20	26.00	120.45	379.55
5	3/15	500.00		500.00	29.25	65.20	26.00	120.45	379.55
6	3/31	500.00		500.00	29.25	65.20	26.00	120.45	379.55
QUARTER TOTALS		3,000.00	18.75	3,018.75	176.60	391.20	156.00	723.80	2,294.95
YEARLY TOTALS		12,000.00	86.00	12,086.00	707.03	1,564.80	624.00	2,895.83	9,190.17

NAME	ADDRESS	SOC. SEC. NO.	KIND OF WORK	DEPT.
Scott, Martha	261 Rose Avenue	561-245-4800	Secretary	Sales
NO. DED. 2	Atlanta, Georgia	MARITAL STATUS M		

In addition to the payroll register shown at the top of the page, the secretary must keep an individual record for each employee involved. Specific requirements will determine the number of columns and the data to be recorded.

THE EXECUTIVE'S INCOME TAX

The secretary can assist the executive in the preparation of his or her annual income tax return by:

Being alert to items that the executive must report as income and items that may be taken as deductions

Accumulating such items throughout the year with supporting papers and records for use at income tax time

Following up to see that returns are filed and payments are made

The performance of these duties demands certain basic understandings as to what constitutes taxable income, what deductions are allowable, and how to organize the material to make it readily accessible.

Income Tax Files

The *income tax files* generally consist of income and deduction records, supporting computations and memorandums, previous years' tax returns, and a current income tax file folder or portfolio. To avoid the possibility of filing current tax materials with those of previous years, large expansion portfolios may be used and all the income tax material related to a given year filed in that portfolio and labeled "Federal Income Tax, 19—." All supporting records of income tax returns should be retained for several years.

At the beginning of each year a portfolio should be set up for income tax materials for the year, and all tax data (bills, canceled checks, reports, itemized listings, receipts) should go into it. Thus, when it is time to prepare the executive's tax return, all the essential records and reference materials will have been accumulated.

Records of Taxable Income

A record of the executive's personal income may be maintained in a special record book where each item is individually recorded. In most instances, however, no separate record book will be kept. The tax information will consist mainly of deposit slips to which identifying notations have been attached, copies of receipts, statements of earnings and deductions, dividend distribution statements, statements of interest income on savings accounts, and other notations which the secretary files in the income tax portfolio. As personal income may be derived from many sources and be received at irregular intervals, the secretary must be able to identify taxable income and must be alert in seeing that a notation on each income item gets into the tax portfolio.

The following items are *taxable income*:

Wages, Salaries, and Other Compensation. The gross amount (amount before deductions for such items as income tax, retirement contributions, employee pensions, hospitalization, and insurance) received from wages, salaries, commissions, fees, tips, and similar sources is taxable. In addition to these items, awards and prizes of money or merchandise, amounts received in reimbursement for expenses that are in excess of the actual business expenses incurred, and bonuses are also taxable income.

Dividends. Cash dividends over $100 per year on stock when paid in cash are generally taxable. Stock dividends, however, may or may not be taxable. Since some dividends may be wholly or partially exempt from taxation, a complete record of all dividends received should be maintained. Those dividends which are not taxable can be eliminated at the time the tax return is prepared.

At the beginning of the year, corporations usually send stockholders a form (Form 1099) stating the total amount of dividends paid to the addressed stockholder the previous year. Watch for and file this information in the income tax portfolio.

Interest. With the exception of interest on tax-exempt securities, all interest received is taxable. Thus, interest received from corporate bonds, mortgage bonds, notes, bank deposits, personal loans, accounts in savings and loan associations, and most U.S. government bonds should be itemized and recorded.

Gains on Sale or Exchange of Property. Profit from the sale of property (including home) is fully or partially taxable depending upon the length of time the property was owned and upon other circumstances. In order that the exact profit may be determined, it is essential that detailed property records be kept on each property item. Real estate, stocks, and other securities are property items.

Proceeds from Annuities and Endowment Life Insurance. A portion of income from annuities and endowment life insurance is taxable.

Rents Received. Income received from rents is taxable. The owner of property from which rents are received is entitled to deductions for depreciation, mortgage interest, taxes, repairs, insurance, agent's commission, and other ordinary and necessary expenses of operating the property. Property records should be kept on each rental unit owned. (See pages 550–551.)

Accuracy is of great importance as the secretary compiles the employer's income tax records.

Royalties. Royalties include income received from writings, works of art, musical compositions, and inventions and patents. All expenses incurred in producing property (such as patents and books) that provide a royalty income are deductible.

Income from a Profession or a Personally Owned Business. All income from a profession or a personally owned business is taxable after deductions for all ordinary, necessary operating expenses have been made.

Nontaxable Income. Even with nontaxable items, the secretary should strive to keep as complete a record of all income as the working situation permits. The data will then be available when the tax return is being prepared. Incomes which are not taxable or incomes from which deductions are allowable can be examined and properly excluded or recorded by the tax consultant at the time of preparation of the tax return. The secretary should not assume the responsibility for excluding income items from the tax data.

Records of Tax Credits and Deductions

A detailed record of each of the following allowable tax credits and deductions should be kept in the tax portfolio for aid in the preparation of the income tax return.

Alimony. Alimony or other payments in lieu of alimony under a decree of divorce or of separate maintenance are allowable as a personal deduction. Such deductions are taken in the year of payment by the spouse making the payment but are taxable income to the spouse receiving the payment. Child support payments, however, are neither deductible nor taxable.

Bad Debts. Nonbusiness bad debt losses are deductible as short-term capital losses if they are supported by document and are non-family loans.

Casualty and Theft Losses. Losses resulting from fire, storm, flood, or theft are deductible if not reimbursed by insurance. Damage to the taxpayer's automobile resulting from an accident would be deductible to the extent not covered by insurance. The taxpayer must absorb the first $100 of each casualty and theft loss.

Child and Dependent Care Credit. A tax credit for expenditures for child care (when parents are working) and for disabled dependents is allowed up to a designated amount and under certain conditions.

Contributions. Contributions to organizations or institutions devoted primarily to charitable, religious, educational, scientific, or literary purposes are deductible. Examples would be contributions to schools and colleges, churches, hospitals, American Cancer Foundation, Girl Scouts, Salvation Army, and United Appeal. Charitable gifts to individuals, political organizations, social clubs, or labor unions are not deductible. Limited contributions to political parties are deductible.

Nonreimbursed expenses (use of automobile, postage, out-of-town telephone calls) incurred while serving in a campaign to collect funds for a charitable, religious, or educational organization are considered a contribution to the organization and are deductible as such.

Education. The cost of improving job-related competencies may or may not be deductible depending upon meeting criteria established by the Internal Revenue Service. This includes expenses for tuition, books, and professional journals.

Interest. All interest paid on personal debts may be deducted. This deduction includes interest paid on such items as bank loans, home and property mortgages, and installment loans on the family automobile.

Medical and Dental Expenses. Medical and dental expenses are not restricted to those of the taxpayer but may also include the taxpayer's family and dependents. Medical care insurance up to a certain amount and medical expenses over a certain amount are deductible. To claim this deduction, the taxpayer is required to furnish the name and address of each person to whom such expenses were paid, the amount, and the approximate date of payment.

Taxes. Such personal taxes as the following are deductible: state or local income taxes, personal property taxes, real estate taxes, state or local sales taxes, state and local gasoline taxes, and state transfer taxes on securities.

The Executive's Business Expenses. *Traveling expenses* incurred when away from home in connection with one's business or profession and for which reimbursement is not received are deductible. These expenses include such items as airline tickets, excess-baggage charges, airport transportation services, car rentals, automobile expenses, bus and subway fares, taxi fares, meals (only if away overnight), hotel/motel expenses, tips, telephone/telegraph expenses, and laundry.

Travel expenses may be forgotten if they are not recorded promptly. At the completion of each business trip, the secretary should obtain from the executive the data needed to complete a report of travel expenses. Unless the expenses are reimbursed by the corporation, the report should be filed with attached receipts in the income tax portfolio.

```
                        TRAVEL EXPENSE REPORT
       From/to   Houston to Chicago          Date(s) Feb. 5-7, 19--
       Purpose   To attend convention of National Dental Trade Ass'n

                                                        Cost
       Transportation  Air/coach                       $186.00
       Hotel           Conrad Hilton - 2 nights          64.00
       Meals           2/5      $ 9.00
                       2/6       15.50
                       2/7       12.80                   37.30
       Other           Tips            $ 8.00
                       Taxi             12.50
                       Convention reg.  10.00
                       Airport parking   8.00            38.50
                                               Total    $325.80
       Receipts attached
           Hotel
           Braniff
           Convention registration
```

Entertainment expenses for business purposes (customers, agents, clients, professional advisers) are deductible. The spouse of an out-of-town guest may also be included. Meals, including tips, theatre and other tickets are recognized entertainment costs. Even club dues are deductible provided the club is used primarily for entertaining business guests. Deductions for entertainment, however, are subject to detailed examination by the Internal Revenue Service. A detailed record similar to the one illustrated below should be prepared, identifying each guest and the business connection, and supported by receipts if the total cost is $25 or more.

Gifts up to $25 in value per recipient per year are deductible when given for a business purpose. Each gift deduction, however, must be supported by a record showing date, cost, reason for giving, and the name and business connection of the recipient.

Many executives use credit cards in paying for travel and entertainment expenses. The secretary should identify each travel and entertainment expenditure on the monthly credit card statement and file it, or a copy, in the income tax portfolio.

GRILL	36234

Maketewah Country Club

2	Onion soup	2.00
3	Shrimp cocktail	6.00
2	Special salad bowl	6.00
2	Filet sole	8.00
1	Small steak	6.00
5	Coffee	3.00
3	Pecan pie	2.70
2	Lemon sherbet	1.20

SUBTOTAL		34.90
SALES TAX		1.75
TIP	+15%	5.25
TOTAL		41.90

SIGNATURE *Betty Randall*

GUEST LIST

(Business Entertainment)

Date   April 10, 19--

Guest(s)   George Snyder
            Frank Fletcher
            Mary Lossi
            John Malinowski
            (All of the V. M. Massey Co.)

Explanation   Lunch at the country club
               to discuss contract renewal

Total cost $36.65 plus 15% tip, $41.90
              Receipt attached.

A record must support each entertainment expense. If the total cost is $25 or more, a receipt must be attached. At the end of each day, the secretary should check the appointment book and flag any appointment that has involved deductible expenses. The next day the needed information can be obtained from the executive, the report prepared and filed with attached receipts in the income tax portfolio.

Other Deductions. Other allowable deductions that apply in specific cases are: safe-deposit-box rental when income-producing items are stored in the box, subscriptions to investment publications, cost of uniforms and their upkeep when they are essential, union dues, moving expenses (within certain limitations), and cost of repairs to business property. The secretary should add to the master list of deductible items those items that are pertinent to the executive's situation.

Tax Guides and Forms

The secretary can be of more assistance to the executive in handling income tax materials after studying an income tax guide. The secretary should also become familiar with the various tax forms, know how to choose the proper ones, and know where to find them.

FORMS USED FOR FILING INDIVIDUAL INCOME TAX RETURNS

File on or before April 15 Following the Close of the Calendar Year:

Form 1040 (U.S. Individual Income Tax Return) — a two-page return (called the "long form") that may be used for *any* amount of income. All deductions can be listed in full, and all of the computations are made by the taxpayer.

Form 1040-ES (Declaration of Estimated Tax for Individuals) — filed by every citizen who can reasonably expect to receive more than $500 from sources other than wages subject to withholding; or can reasonably expect gross income to exceed —

(1) $20,000 for a single individual, a head of household, or a widow or widower entitled to the special tax rates;
(2) $20,000 for a married individual entitled to file a joint declaration with spouse, but only if the spouse has not received wages for the taxable year;
(3) $10,000 for a married individual entitled to file a joint declaration with spouse, but only if both spouses have received wages for the taxable year;
(4) $5,000 for a married individual not entitled to file a joint declaration with spouse.

The estimated unpaid tax may be paid in full at the time of filing the declaration form; or it may be paid in four equal quarterly installments (payable on April 15, June 15, September 15, and January 15). The first installment payment must accompany the declaration.

A CHECKLIST FOR COMPUTING INCOME TAX

As you keep a tax portfolio or prepare the income tax return, check this list of common items that are deductible or nondeductible from adjusted gross income.

	Deductible	Nondeductible
Alimony and separate maintenance payments taxable to recipient	✓	
Automobile expenses (car used exclusively for pleasure)		
State gasoline taxes imposed on consumer	✓	
Interest on finance loans	✓	
License fees		✓
Ordinary upkeep and operating expenses		✓
Burglary losses (if not covered by insurance)	✓	
Casualty losses not covered by insurance (fire, flood, windstorm, lightning, earthquakes, etc.)	✓	
Charitable contributions to approved institutions	✓	
Domestic servants (wages paid)		✓
Dues, social clubs for personal use		✓
Employment fees paid to agencies	✓	
Federal income taxes		✓
FICA taxes withheld by employer		✓
Fines for violation of laws and regulations		✓
Funeral expenses		✓
Gambling losses (to extent of gains only)	✓	
Gift taxes		✓
Gifts to relatives and other individuals		✓
Income tax imposed by city or state	✓	
Inheritance taxes		✓
Interest paid on personal loans	✓	
Life insurance premiums		✓
Medical Care Insurance Premiums (including Blue Cross and Blue Shield). Limited to 50% of premium cost with a $150 maximum	✓	
Medical expenses in excess of 3% of adjusted gross income (including the cost of artificial limbs, artificial teeth, eyeglasses, hearing aids, dental fees, hospital expenses, premiums on hospital or medical insurance) to extent not covered by insurance	✓	
Political campaign contribution up to prescribed limits	✓	
Property taxes, real and personal	✓	
Residence for personal use		
Improvements and street assessments		✓
Insurance		✓
Interest on mortgage loan	✓	
Loss from sale of		✓
Rent paid		✓
Repairs		✓
Taxes	✓	
Sales taxes, state and local	✓	
Traveling expenses attending professional meetings	✓	
Traveling expenses to and from place of business or employment		✓
Uniforms for personal use including cost and upkeep, if not adaptable for general use (nurses, police officers, jockeys, baseball players, etc.)	✓	
Union dues	✓	
Use taxes imposed on consumers under state law	✓	

Tax Guides. The following publications can be obtained from the office of the Internal Revenue Service free or for a nominal charge: *Your Federal Income Tax; Employer's Tax Guide* (Circular E); *Farmer's Tax Guide; Tax Guide for U.S. Citizens Abroad;* and *Tax Information on Disasters, Casualty Losses, and Thefts.* Inexpensive tax guides can also be obtained at bookstores.

Tax Forms. One set of blank forms is mailed to each taxpayer; additional copies needed for drafting the return may be obtained from the local office of the Internal Revenue Service and usually from banks and post offices or reproduced on a copying machine. The Internal Revenue Service has ruled that reproduction of tax forms, schedules, and supporting data on office copying machines is acceptable. Forms may be prepared in pencil and reproduced on a copying machine, thus avoiding the necessity of recopying or typing the form.

Copies for the files should be made on a copying machine of all supplementary information and supporting data such as receipts, statements, expense reports, and other items that may be attached and mailed with the tax return.

Typing and Mailing Tax Returns

The tax return contains confidential information. It should be typed by the secretary, not by an assistant. Before typing, each figure must be checked for accuracy; then the return must be typed and proofread carefully. Before mailing the form, the secretary should check to see that it has been properly signed and that materials to accompany the return have been securely attached to the finished form as directed.

At the foot of the first page of the federal tax forms, space is provided for "Signature of preparer other than taxpayer." This does not mean the signature of the secretary who has merely collected tax data or typed the form. The signature is to be that of a tax consultant or attorney who has prepared the return and who assumes responsibility for its validity.

As the mailing of all tax returns is a very important responsibility, the secretary should mail them personally. Do not put them in the regular office mail, send them through the mailing department, or trust them to a clerk or anyone else to post. The secretary should note on the file copy the exact time and place where each return was mailed. A certificate of mailing may be obtained from the post office as legal proof that the return was mailed. If such a certificate is obtained, attach it to the file copy of the return.

If a Declaration of Estimated Tax has been filed, the secretary must remind the employer when quarterly tax payments are due (June 15, September 15, and January 15). A good idea is to place cards in the tickler file at appropriate points.

Late Filing

The taxpayer who is late in filing a return is assessed a penalty. An individual, however, may obtain an automatic two-month extension for filing the return after the April 15 deadline by submitting an Application for Automatic Extension of Time to File U.S. Individual Income Tax Return. Further extensions are granted only under very unusual circumstances.

SUGGESTED READINGS

Bower, James B., and Harold Q. Langenderfer. *Income Tax Procedure*, issued annually. Cincinnati: South-Western Publishing Co.

Keeling, B. Lewis, and Bernard J. Beig. *Payroll Records and Accounting*, issued annually. Cincinnati: South-Western Publishing Co.

QUESTIONS FOR DISCUSSION

1. Does it build employee morale to make available to all employees the salaries paid employees in the company? Support your answer.

2. Why should a secretary not employed in the payroll department be familiar with payroll procedures and payroll taxes?

3. Why is the self-employed person taxed at a higher FICA tax rate than employees?

4. One of your assistants, who is your senior in age and tenure in the company, has the habit of arriving at work a few minutes late each morning. As a corrective measure you ask each member of your staff to sign in and out each day on a register sheet. There is opposition to your regulation by the other members of your staff on the grounds that they are salaried, not hourly employees. What is the difference between a "Salaried" and an "Hourly" employee, and how would you respond to this objection?

5. What is the relationship between salary administration and job analysis, and why may a secretary need to have training in job analysis?

6. Assume you are employed in a small office (four employees) and your employer asks you to take complete charge of the payroll records including preparing and submitting all payroll tax reports. Where could you obtain assistance to help you prepare for and carry out this assignment?

7. It is said that the secretary should play an "assist" role in the preparation of the employer's income tax return. What does this mean to you?

8. The Internal Revenue Service requires a taxpayer to document all traveling and entertainment expenses for which a tax deduction is claimed. What is the secretary's role in compiling all of this important information?

9. What precautions should the secretary observe in typing and mailing the employer's income tax return?

10. Insert the information in the blanks in the following sentences. Then consult the Reference Guide to correct your answers.
   (a) We received your letter on the _____ day of October. (18)
   (b) Please send us _____ for postage. ($1.16)
   (c) Interest will be charged for _____. (1 year, 6 months, 18 days)
   (d) She received a clear majority of votes from the _____ Ward. (4th)
   (e) They owe us _____ on the property. ($600.00)
   (f) The stock is selling at _____. (101¾)
   (g) Over _____ of the employees are dissatisfied. (¼)
   (h) The record low temperature for this date is _____ degrees below zero. (eight)
   (i) You should jog _____ mile each day. (½)
   (j) One and one half quarts _____ enough. (is, are)

11. What terminal punctuation mark is used after each of the following enumerations?
   (a) Tabulated words or phrases
   (b) Tabulated sentences
   (c) Run-in words or phrases
   (d) Run-in clauses
   (e) Run-in sentences

12. When do you use a semicolon to separate units in a series?

PROBLEMS

1. Obtain one of the following payroll forms, study the instructions for completing it, and be prepared to present to the class a description of the form and the method of completing it.
   SS-4......Application for Employer Identification Number
   SS-5......Application for a Social Security Number
   941........Employer's Quarterly Federal Tax Return

   W-2........Wage and Tax Statement
   W-4........Employee's Withholding Allowance Certificate
   OAAN-
   7003 ..Request for Change in Social Security Records

2. To accumulate information for a tax file, a secretary must have some understanding of taxable income and allowable deductions. From the following list, select those income items

that are taxable and those expense items that are deductible. Arrange the items alphabetically and type them in a form convenient for reference. You may need to check reference sources to identify the tax status of certain items.

Income Items

Payment for writing magazine article

Interest from municipal bonds

Bonus from employer

Prize — paid vacation to a resort as a prize for the "Best Idea" contest

Rent received on property inherited from a relative

Dividends on corporation stock

Interest on U.S. government bonds

Merchandise received from employer

Interest on deposits in savings and loan association

Payments from accident insurance

Property inherited from a relative

Payment for a speech to a service club (not related to business)

Royalties received from a patent

Profit from sale of building lot originally planned for home

Expense Items

Contribution to an old friend

Tips paid for service while on business trip

Federal income tax paid during year

Interest on loan on family automobile

Contributions to Girl Scouts

Contribution of $25 to a political party

Interest on loan on home

Driver's license fee

State income tax

Property loss resulting from theft (not covered by insurance)

Federal Social Security tax

Retail sales tax (state)

Employment fees paid to agency

Life insurance premiums

Traveling expenses to and from the place of employment

Union dues

Repairs on home

Gift costing $25 given to a customer

Expenses incurred in acting as chairman of United Appeal fund drive

3. John Sekosky is paid $4.20 per hour and an overtime wage of one and one half times his hourly rate. All hours over 36 are considered overtime. He worked 39 hours during the last week in March.

(a) What are his gross earnings for the week?

(b) If the FICA tax rate is 6.05 percent and there is a $15.30 federal income tax deduction and a 2 percent state income tax deduction, what are his net earnings?

Producing and Processing Legal Papers

25

The scope and amount of legal work that the secretary performs obviously varies from office to office. The secretary in the corporate office dealing with the nonlegal aspects of a business may have only an occasional legal-related function. On the other hand, the secretary in a legal office works full time in an environment where legal terminology, documents, and procedures are the core of the activity. The work is so specialized that legal secretaries have their own association that administers a training and certification program to give preparation and prestige to their profession. In the larger legal offices, word processing technology is having a dramatic impact on the functions of the legal secretary. Much of the repetitive typing, copying, and proofreading that formerly constituted a significant part of the work of the legal secretary is now being done via automatic typewriters, computer printout terminals, and copying machines. This makes legal secretarial work less clerical and more professional and enables some legal secretaries to be upgraded by becoming legal assistants or researchers.

This chapter is designed to introduce the secretary to legal-related work. It describes some of the more commonly used legal documents, discusses the secretarial procedures related to preparing them, and suggests reference sources to which the secretary may turn for assistance.

You may find legal work attractive and decide to become a trainee in a law firm, the legal department of a large corporation, or the government. In that case, you can build upon the content of this chapter with a specialized training program to become a certified legal secretary or legal assistant; both are rewarding and challenging fields. You may even decide to study law and prepare for the bar.

FREQUENTLY USED LEGAL DOCUMENTS

Business transactions frequently involve parties from different states. Complexities and problems arise in preparing the legal documents to cover conflicting laws of the federal government and the 50 states. To expedite legal procedures, a number of uniform statutes (laws) have been enacted, the most recent and most important one from the business standpoint being the Uniform Commercial Code. The legal documents described here conform to this code.

Contracts

Many people are concerned with the legalities of buying and selling goods, property, and services. Every buying and selling activity constitutes a contract between or among those concerned. A *contract* is an enforceable agreement, either oral or written, which involves legal rights and responsibilities. A contract may be in the form of an oral agreement, sales slip, a memorandum, a promissory note, a letter, or a contract form. Some contracts, such as those for the purchase of real estate, must be in writing; but *all* important contracts should be written, although this is not a legal requirement.

Content. In typing a contract, the secretary should see if the following essential information is included:

Date and place of agreement

Names of parties entering into the agreement

Purpose of the contract

Duties of each party

Money, services, or goods in consideration of contract

Time element or duration involved

Signatures of the parties

Prepare enough copies of a contract so that each party will have a file copy. (If the contract is prepared in a law office, an additional copy is made for the law office files.) When the executive sells his or her services by contract (as do engineers, architects, builders, and real estate representatives), the secretary may have a standard form to use as a model; but usually there are items peculiar to each contract that make it necessary to vary the fill-ins each time. Printed forms are available for most common legal documents. Since some contracts must follow a statutory model or must contain specified provisions, it is recommended that the secretary use a printed form or follow legal advice when preparing specified provisions.

Care Before Signing. All contracts should be carefully read by all parties before they are signed. Not only will mistakes, misunderstandings, and fraud be avoided but also content will be clarified with regard to: (1) what responsibilities are assumed by each party,

(2) exactly what is offered at what price, (3) how payment is to be made, (4) whether or not material can be returned, and (5) when and how the contract can be terminated.

Contracts Made by the Secretary. As has already been pointed out, the secretary often acts (in a legal sense) as the deputy of the executive; that is, the secretary knowingly — and sometimes even unknowingly — executes contracts. This situation places responsibility on the secretary to exercise caution in making commitments, in requesting work to be done by outside agencies, in quoting prices or making offers to purchase, and in signing purchase or repair orders, sales orders, or agreements on the secretary's own initiative, for such commitments may be contractual.

When signing a secretary-generated agreement (contract), the executive usually relies on the secretary's recommendation. The mere fact that the secretary presents the contract for machine repair service for signature implies the secretary's indorsement of its content. For example, the secretary may make all the arrangements for redecorating the office or for the purchase of a new machine. The executive signs the contract on the presumption that the secretary has checked all details and has verified that the contract is correct, understood, and proper. By attaching an annotation of the important points to a contract, the secretary can save the employer the time of reading "the fine print."

Filing Contracts. A contract copy should be filed carefully, for it is a legal instrument necessary to prosecuting any deviation from the contract. It is well to place the contract in a No. 10 envelope and mark plainly on the outside, "Signed contract between . . . ." The contract can be filed permanently in the company's or person's file, in a separate "Signed-Contracts" file, or, if it is important enough, in a safe-deposit box. In some companies, such legal papers are kept in asbestos envelopes as a protection against fire.

Wills and Codicils

The requirements regarding the drawing of wills and codicils are rather technical and vary among the states. Hence, they should not be drawn without proper legal supervision or direction.

Wills. A *will* is a legal instrument whereby a person provides for the disposition of property after death. A *testator* (man) or *testatrix* (woman) is the one who makes the will. One who dies without having made a will is said to die *intestate*. A *nuncupative* will is an oral one and is valid only as to personal property; land may not be devised by a nuncupative will. A will in the handwriting of the testator is called a *holographic* will.

A will may be *revoked* by mutilation, cancellation, destruction, or the execution of a new will. Every will should contain a provision stating that any and all previous wills are revoked even though the testator does not remember ever having made another will.

To *probate* a will is to prove its validity to the court for the purpose of carrying out its provisions. An *executor* (man) or *executrix* (woman) is the one named by the testator to carry out the provisions of a will.

Codicils. A *codicil* is a supplement that makes a change in the will, deletes or adds something to it, or explains it. It must be signed and witnessed with all the formalities of the original will.

A person asked to *attest* (witness) a will or codicil need not read the provisions and, of course, does not try. The attestant is merely witnessing the signature of the testator and assuring the beneficiaries that the testator was in sound mind when the will was signed. A will presented for witnessing should have only the signature area visible, thus preventing any chance reading of the contents.

Copyrights

Creative work reproduced for sale or public distribution may be *copyrighted*. Copyrighting applies not only to printed matter, such as books and periodicals, but also to photographs, pictorial illustrations, musical compositions, maps, paintings, and movies.

To copyright is to register a claim with the federal government to a piece of original literary or artistic work. A copyright grants the exclusive right to reproduce a creative work or to perform it publicly. Registering is done either by the originator of the work or the one reproducing and marketing copies. Copyrighting tends to prevent a dishonest or careless person from stealing another's creative work and marketing it as his or her own. The increased use of photocopying equipment increases the necessity for the protection of a copyright.

Recent changes in the copyright law extend the duration of a copyright for a term consisting of the life of the author plus 50 years after the author's death, insures that public broadcasters and others cannot use the work of writers without their consent, and provides guidelines under which classroom and library copying of material is permitted. A copyright can be obtained by filing an application for copyright with the Register of Copyrights in Washington, D.C.

Patents

A *patent* may be obtained by a person who has "invented or discovered a new and useful art, machine, manufacture, or composition of matter, or any new and useful improvement thereof — not known or used by others in this country before...." Literature on the procedure for securing a patent can be obtained from the Superintendent of Documents, U.S. Government Printing Office, Washington, DC 20402.

Legal specialists usually are employed to prepare the patent application, the first step in negotiations between the Patent Office and the inventor.

A patent grant gives the exclusive right to make, use, and sell the patent. A patent must be applied for by the inventor. After the patent has been granted, it can be sold outright or leased, in which case the inventor is paid a royalty for its use. A patent expires at the end of 17 years and can be renewed only by an act of Congress.

Trademarks

The Patent Office also registers trademarks for goods moved in interstate commerce, giving evidence of the validity and ownership of the mark by the registrant and of the right to use the mark. The registration term covers 20 years. However, during the sixth year of registration, an affidavit must be filed with the Patent Office showing that the trademark is being used or that its nonuse does not signify intention to abandon the mark.

Affidavit

An *affidavit* is a written declaration made under oath that the facts set forth are sworn to be true and correct. The word itself means "he has made oath." An affidavit, made by an *affiant*, must be sworn to before a public officer (such as a notary, judge, or a justice of the peace).

For example, evidence of citizenship is required before an applicant can obtain a United States passport. If the person seeking a passport has no birth certificate, an affidavit from a relative declaring that the passport applicant was born in the United States may be used.

Power of Attorney

A legal instrument authorizing one to act as agent for another is known as *power of attorney*. Often a secretary may be given power of

```
                              AFFIDAVIT

    STATE OF WEST VIRGINIA )
                           ( ss.
    County of Kanawha      )

              Before me, the subscriber, a notary public for the County of
    Kanawha, State of West Virginia, personally appeared Ruth Ellen Houser
    of Charleston, Kanawha County, West Virginia, who being duly sworn deposes
    and says that
              (1) she was employed as a public health nurse by the
              Department of Health, State of West Virginia, from April 10,
              1962 through March 24, 1977.
              (2) she received no severance pay at the time of termination
              of employment nor has she received any severance pay since
              that date from the State of West Virginia.
    Sworn and subscribed this 24th day of April, 1977.

                                        Margaret H. McDaniel    (L. S.)
                                            Notary Public
```

An affidavit may be typed on ruled legal paper, as illustrated here, or it may be typed on unruled paper. It must be signed by a notary public, judge, or justice of the peace.

attorney by the employer to act in the name and on behalf of the employer in performing certain specified functions set forth in the document. For example, the secretary may be authorized to sign checks and other legal documents for the executive. It may be made for an indefinite period, for a specific period, or for a specific purpose only. Only a tried-and-true secretary whose business integrity is unquestioned earns this decidedly weighty responsibility of acting as the employer's agent.

Should the executive have power of attorney for someone else, the secretary sets up a special file and records all executions.

POSSIBLE RESPONSIBILITIES FOR LEGAL PAPERS

The secretary may type legal papers, fill in printed legal forms, and witness the signing of the completed papers. To complete the work, it may be necessary to have the papers notarized; that is, acknowledged by a notary public. A notary public acknowledges that a document was actually executed by the person or persons who sign it. For convenience, it may be practical for the secretary to become a notary public thus avoiding the inconvenience of having to go outside the office for this service. Finally, the secretary may be responsible for the recording of the legal paper.

Power of Attorney
Know All Men By These Presents

That   Henry Thomas Aske of the City of Akron, Summit County, State of Ohio

ha s   made, constituted and appointed, and by these presents do es   make, constitute and ap-

point Raymond Henry Petroskey of the City of Seattle, State of Washington true and

lawful attorney for   me   and in   my   name, place and stead   to

negotiate for the purchase of the structure and property situated at

112 West Third Street, City of Seattle, Kling County, State of Washington

known as Hidalgo Towers ——————————————————————

giving and granting unto   Raymond Henry Petroskey   said attorney full power

and authority to do and perform all and every act and thing whatsoever requisite and necessary

to be done in and about the premises as fully, to all intents and purposes, as   I   might or

could do if personally present, with full power of substitution and revocation, hereby ratify-

ing and confirming all that   Raymond Henry Petroskey   said attorney or

his   substitute shall lawfully do or cause to be done by virtue hereof.

In Witness Whereof,   I   have hereunto set   my   hand and

seal the   Third   day of   October   , in the year one thousand nine

hundred and   seventy eight.

Sealed and delivered in the presence of

....(L. S.)

The legal form *Power of Attorney* would be notarized in a form similar to that shown on page 590.

Notary Public

Notarial commissions are issued by the secretary of state, the governor, or other designated official in the various state capitals. Application blanks will be furnished upon request by the appropriate official in the state in which the commission is sought, or they may be bought at a stationery store. There are usually a fee, an examination, and certain citizenship qualifications. Most states also require bond, which may be applied for on forms obtained along with the application. A notary public can purchase Error and Omission insurance to protect against financial liability.

The notary's appointment states the county or counties in which the notary is authorized to perform and the date of expiration of commission. It is necessary to buy a notary-public seal and a rubber stamp. The former is used to press into the document the seal showing the name of the county in which the notary is commissioned to act and the seal of the state. The rubber stamp shows the date when the commission expires. Each notary receives local rules and instructions which must be observed.

A notary does not scrutinize the document being certified. The notary gives the oath and verifies that the signature or signatures are genuine. If you should become a notary, remember not to be curious about what is in the paper you are certifying.

If the secretary is not a notary public, a responsibility may be to arrange for the details related to having papers notarized. The names of two or three notaries public convenient to the office should be obtained. Sometimes it may be necessary to arrange a meeting time with the notary public and to notify all parties involved.

The notary public witnesses affidavits and signs *acknowledgments* and *verifications* which are executed under oath. In an acknowledgment the person swears that the signature appearing on a document is genuine and was made of free will. A verification is a sworn and signed statement of the truth and correctness of the content of a document. All necessary signatures must be completed before the notary public signs the document.

Preparation of Legal Papers

Legal papers can be divided into two classes:

1. *Court Documents.* These vary considerably and must follow the specifications of the particular court in the city, county, state, and federal government. They include such documents as *complaints, answers, demurrers, notices, motions, affidavits, summonses,* and *subpoenas.*

2. *Noncourt Legal Documents.* These include such legal papers as contracts, wills, leases, powers of attorney, agreements, and many others. They give formal expression to legal acts and are legal evidence if court action or litigation becomes necessary.

```
STATE OF OHIO      )
                   ( ss.
County of Summit   )

         On October 3, 1978, before me, a Notary Public, in and for

said County and State, personally appeared Henry Thomas Aske, known to

me to be the person whose name is subscribed to the within instrument,

and acknowledged that he executed the same.

         IN TESTIMONY THEREFOR I have hereunto subscribed my name and

affixed my seal of office the day and year last above written.

                     Stephen C. Gill          (L. S.)
```

An Acknowledgment of a Notary Public.

The form of legal papers is standardized in some respects; in others, it varies with the wishes of the court and with the personal preference of the employer.

Paper Size. Traditionally, all legal documents were typed on 8½- by 13- or 14-inch hard-to-tear white paper called *legal cap*. Legal cap is printed with a red or blue vertical double rule 1⅜ inches from the left edge and a single rule ⅜ inch from the right edge. *Brief* paper, 8½ by 10½ inches, also with ruled margins, was used for legal briefs and memorandums; for some documents each line on a sheet was numbered. Although some courts still require legal cap for court documents, there is a trend toward using the standard 8½- by 11-inch sheet because this size can be microfilmed for storage in court files. Before typing a court document, the secretary should learn the requirements of the particular court.

Copies. Multiple copies of legal documents are usually required. For example, all parties to a contract receive a copy, file copies are necessary, and the attorney retains one or more copies for the office. Before the copying machine came into common office use, multiple copies were made with carbon paper. Sometimes two or more typings were necessary to provide a sufficient number of legible copies of a document. Now the copies can be made on the copying machine; and, if so, the secretary types only the original and makes the copies from the original on the copier. In some offices the secretary types the original and, on color-coded tissue-weight paper, a file copy. All other copies are made from the original on the copier.

Copies can be used and referred to as *duplicate originals* if they are signed and made to *conform* in all respects to the original (to contain all the copy shown on the original).

After the paper has been *executed* (the original and duplicate originals made valid by necessary procedures, such as signing, witnessing, perhaps notarizing, and recording), all the distribution copies and the office file copy must be *conformed* by typing in the signatures, dates, and all other data that were added in executing the paper.

Type. For legal papers, pica type is preferred and may be required for court documents. In any case, do not use the "fancy" typefaces like script, italic, or gothic.

Margins, Spacing, and Centered Titles. On paper with printed marginal rules, type within the rules by one or two spaces. On unruled paper, use 1½-inch left and at least ½-inch right margins. Top margins are 2 inches on the first page and 1½ inches on subsequent pages. Bottom margins are 1 inch.

TIME-SAVER. To insure that no line of the original copy of a legal document has been omitted in retyping, hold line-for-line typed copy beside the original — or align the copy over the original and hold them up to a bright light.

For most legal papers, use double spacing, with a triple space above side headings. Some legal secretaries recommend that a triple space be made between paragraphs to provide flexibility for limited changes on any page without making it necessary to retype the entire instrument. Very long documents are sometimes single-spaced to avoid exceptional bulkiness.

Two inches from the top of the first page, type the title of the paper in all capitals, centered between the rules. Divide at a logical point and double-space a heading that is too long for one line. Leave two blank line spaces below the title.

Hyphenation. Learn the preference for your particular situation. Sometimes the last word on a page must not be hyphenated; sometimes a divided last word is recommended to make the unwarranted insertion of pages more difficult. Avoid dividing words at the end of other lines.

Paragraphs. Indent ten spaces for paragraphs. To make difficult any unwarranted insertion of pages, do not end a page with the last line of a paragraph. Carry over two or more lines to the next page.

Quoted Matter and Land Descriptions. For quoted matter and land descriptions, indent five to ten spaces from the left margin; retain the right margin if desired, or indent five spaces. Indent another five spaces for a new paragraph in the quoted material. Indented quotations may be single-spaced.

Page Numbers. Legal documents frequently go through a series of drafts before the final one. Number and date each draft; the first typing, "First draft," the second, "Second draft," and so on. Keep all drafts until the final document has been typed and processed.

Center page numbers one-half inch from the bottom edge. Always number the first and last page of every document.

Dates. Spell out single-digit ordinal dates and type the year to conform: *the first day of June, nineteen hundred and seventy-eight* (but *the 15th day of June, 1978*). Date every legal paper. If the last paragraph does not include the date, type the date on the last line immediately preceding the signature lines.

Numbers. Numbers with legal significance (amounts of money, periods of time) have traditionally been written in both words *and* figures. For example, *Five Thousand Dollars ($5,000)* or *Ten (10) barrels of oil* or *Sixty (60) days* (but a *six-month period*). (For general number usage, follow the style preferred by your employer.)

CONTRACT

THIS CONTRACT made and entered into this 4th day of January, 1978, by and between ROBERT LEYLAND ROBINS of the City of Tampa, County of Hillsborough, State of Florida, doing business under the name of ADORN MANUFACTURING COMPANY, and referred to as the firm in this contract, and JANICE WEBBER LOGAL of Bradenton, Manatee County, State of Florida, WITNESSETH:

1. JANICE WEBBER LOGAL shall enter the services of the said firm as a products representative for them in their business of manufacturing cosmetics for the period of one year from the 12th day of October, 1977, subject to the general control of said firm.

2. The said products representative shall devote the whole of her time, attention and energies to the performance of her duties as such representative, and shall not either directly or indirectly, alone or in partnership, be connected with or concerned in any other business or pursuit whatsoever during the said term of one year.

3. The said products representative shall, subject to the control of the said firm, keep proper books of account and make due and correct entries of the price of all goods sold and of all transactions and dealings of and in relation to the said business and shall serve the firm diligently and according to the best abilities of all respects.

4. The fixed salary of the said products representative shall be ten thousand dollars ($10,000) per annum, payable in equal semi-monthly installments.

Date: January 4, 1978   /s/ _____
                                      Adorn Manufacturing Company

                                /s/ _____
                                         Janice Webber Logal

Observe that pica type has been used, copy is double-spaced and paragraphs have been indented ten spaces, names of the parties to the contract are in all caps, and dates conform to suggested patterns for legal papers.

Use the dollar sign with a number in conformity with the spelled-out version: *Sixty Dollars ($60)*, but *Sixty (60) Dollars*. Capitalize all words of an amount except *and: Three Hundred Seventy-Five and 45/100 Dollars ($375.45)*. Some offices type dollar amounts in all capitals.

Reference Notations. On the first page of the file copy in the upper left corner, type the full names of the recipients of all copies of the document.

Names and Signature Lines. If you know the exact signature that is to be used, type it in the body of the document in exactly that way. If you do not know the form of the signature, use the legal name — the full two or three names of the person without abbreviations or initials. The legal signature of a married woman preferably combines her maiden name with her married name, such as Dorothy Keller Brown — not Dorothy Ann Brown. Personal titles *(Mr., Mrs., Ms., Miss)* are not used; ordinarily neither are professional titles. To permit easy reference and identification, it is common practice to type in all capitals the names of individuals, businesses, agencies, and institutions named in a legal document.

At the end of a legal paper, type three lines for required signatures. These signature lines cannot stand alone on a page; arrange the body of the instrument so that at least two lines of text will appear on the page with the signatures. The lines extend from slightly right of center to the right margin, with two or three blank line spaces between them. Signature lines for witnesses begin at the left margin and extend to the page center.

Some secretaries lightly pencil in the respective initials at the beginnings of the lines on which each is to sign. Other secretaries use a small "X" to mark the spot. In some jurisdictions the names must be typed under the signature lines. Names are typed on file-copy signature lines after some indication for *signed*, such as *Sgd*.

Seals. The abbreviation *L.S.* *(locus sigilli,* meaning "place of the seal") frequently appears at the end of lines on which parties to a paper sign their names. These letters have the legal significance of a wax seal. State laws determine whether or not a legal paper requires a seal.

Insertions. At the time of signing a legal paper, an insertion may be requested. An insertion is valid if the signers indorse it by writing their initials in ink near it. At the time of typing, however, an omission may not be inserted between the lines to avoid retyping the page.

TIME-SAVER. After preparing multiple copies of a legal paper that requires many signatures, attach a colored file flag at the appropriate point for each signer, using a different color for each one.

Erasures and Corrections. Each page should be typed accurately, for an erased and corrected error can cast doubt on the validity of an item if it occurs in a vital phrase. For example, *"four* thousand acres" erased and changed to *"forty* thousand acres" (or "June 6" changed to "June 5") might raise a question of validity. An error in a single word in the straight text can usually be erased and corrected without question, but avoid erasing figures, dates, names, and places. If they must be erased, have the correction initialed.

Proofreading. The secretary unfamiliar with legal work should be particularly careful in proofreading, questioning terms that are not understood. Novices have typed "the plaintiff praise" for "the plaintiff prays" and referred to the "Court of Common Please" or the "Court of Common Police" rather than the "Court of Common Pleas." They have embarrassed themselves by referring to a "notary republic." If you are not sure of your ground, find out!

Property descriptions, quoted material, and all figures and dates that appear in legal documents should be proofread twice because a minor discrepancy can be the basis of a litigation. Read a second time aloud to another person. Identify all capital letters, punctuation marks, and abbreviations.

Standard Legal Forms

Undoubtedly your employer will engage legal counsel when preparing important legal papers. If, however, certain types of papers are often used, such as leases or deeds, the forms given in legal reference books can be used as guides. Avoid indiscriminate copying of such forms because the laws vary from state to state, and laws also change.

Legal Forms. Stationery stores that supply legal offices carry printed legal forms that concur with local laws. These are called *legal forms* or law blanks. Look in the Yellow Pages under the heading *legal forms* for sources of supply for printed blanks of such common documents as affidavits, agreements, deeds, leases, powers of attorney, and wills.

Many printed legal forms consist of four pages, printed on both sides of one sheet of 8½- by 28-inch paper and folded once to make four pages of 8½ by 14 inches. The form for the indorsement is printed on the fourth page. With this arrangement, binding of the pages at the top is unnecessary, and a cover is not used. When the front page (page 1) is turned, pages 2 and 3 will read as one continuous page down the full inside length of the document.

REMINDER
Some legal forms are purchased in pads. Insert a reorder reminder approximately three fourths of the way through each new pad.

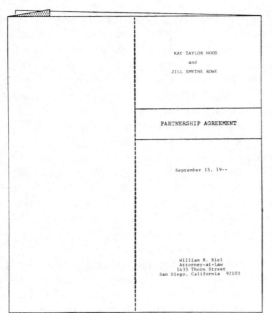

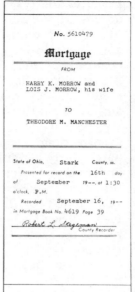

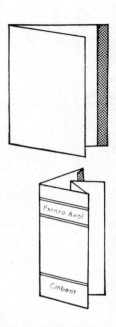

The *indorsement* (a description of the legal paper within) is typed on the outside of a cover as illustrated at the left above, or on a printed legal back as shown in the center. The correct folding of a legal back is shown at the right. Some offices file the folded documents in tall, narrow files with the indorsements in view; others use file drawers 16 inches wide and file unfolded legal papers with the first page to the front and the indorsements not visible.

To protect a legal document, use a single backing sheet ("legal back" or "cover") with dimensions that are about 1 inch wider and 1½ inches longer than the instrument. This sheet is usually blue and of tough, heavy-quality paper. After the back has been properly folded and reopened, the indorsement is typed. The typed pages are then inserted under the inch fold at the top of the backing sheet, and an eyelet or staple is placed at each side (about 1 inch from the top and the sides). Backing sheets may be color coded to differentiate types of documents.

PARTNERSHIP AGREEMENT

THIS AGREEMENT, made in the City of San Diego, State of California, on the 15th day of September, 19--, between KAY TAYLOR HOOD and JILL SMYTHE ROWE, both of San Diego, California,

WHEREIN IT IS MUTUALLY AGREED, AS FOLLOWS:

1. That the parties hereto shall, as partners, engage in and conduct the business of worldwide travel agency.

2. That the name of the partnership shall be THE WORLDWIDE TRAVEL-EASE AGENCY.

3. That the capital of the partnership shall be the sum of Twenty Thousand Dollars ($20,000); and each party shall contribute thereto, contemporaneously with the execution of this agreement, the sum of Ten Thousand Dollars ($10,000) in cash.

4. That at the end of each calendar year the net profit or net loss shall be divided equally between the parties hereto, and the account of each shall be credited or debited as the case may be, with her proportionate share thereof.

_____
Kay Taylor Hood

_____
Jill Smythe Rowe

Signed and delivered
in the presence of

Fill-Ins on Legal Blanks. Fill-ins may range from a single letter or figure to words, phrases, or long lines of text. Printed lines are usually not provided in the blank spaces; the typist, therefore, must align the typing line with the printing line. Use the printed margins for typing full lines. As a precaution, rule a Z in ink to fill deep unused space.

Carbon Copies of Legal Blanks. To insure the best possible alignment on carbon copies of printed forms, check the forms to be sure that all copies were printed at the same time. The legend 60M 7/6/-- indicates that 60,000 copies were printed on July 6, 19--. Roll the matched set carefully into the typewriter and then insert the carbons (as shown on page 103). Because aligning is difficult, you may prefer to type each blank individually, checking each one against the source document. If you do this, type *COPY* on all but the one to be used as the original.

Riders. When the space allotted for filling in conditional clauses or other provisions in a legal blank is not large enough for the typewritten material, leave sufficient space after the last line to permit a slip of paper containing the rest of the typewritten material (called a *rider*) to be pasted to the document. Use legal cap for the rider, and cut off any unused part of the sheet. Fasten the rider securely to the document and fold the rider to fit neatly within the backing sheet.

Forms File. Many legal documents that the secretary types are adaptations of previous ones. A forms file of commonly typed legal documents, therefore, can be an important time-saver. Accumulate this file by making an extra carbon or copying-machine copy of representative legal documents at the time of the first typing. In the margin, add helpful notes such as the number of copies to be prepared, the distribution of the copies, and other pertinent data. In time, the file will contain most, if not all, of the legal documents produced in the office. You can then consult the file to determine the exact procedure for any document contained therein. Legal secretaries consider their forms file to be their most valuable reference source.

WORD PROCESSING AND THE LEGAL OFFICE

Most large and many small legal offices are equipped with automated word processing equipment. There are several reasons why this is the case.

This secretary is consulting the file of legal forms that he has compiled. On each form he has noted all the facts pertinent to completing and filing it.

Standard paragraphs that have been court tested make up a significant portion of many legal documents. By having these paragraphs on magnetic media and by using magnetic-media-activated typewriters, the paragraphs can be typed automatically, quickly, and error-free. This leaves the operator the task of filling in the variable materials only.

Typographical errors and erasures in certain critical places in a legal document can disqualify the document for court purposes. Automated typewriters produce error-free typing. This saves many hours of proofreading time.

Computer networks have been established to service legal offices. These networks have large banks of stored legal material — cases, decisions, opinions, and reviews — carefully indexed. For a fee a legal office can have access to this vast amount of stored information and save hours of research. For example, the computer network can be instructed to print out all the court decisions dealing with a specific point of law. This information usually comes into the legal office to subscribers via some form of computer terminal. In many cases, this terminal is an automated typewriter that serves a dual purpose: reproducing materials stored on magnetic media within the legal office and receiving output from the legal computer network in response to a request.

SOURCES OF INFORMATION FOR THE LEGAL SECRETARY

The legal secretary may obtain helpful information from the legal secretarial handbooks listed at the end of this chapter and from the following publications. Most of these publications are available in local libraries.

Martindale-Hubbel Law Directory. A four-volume reference published annually listing lawyers and their addresses, as well as a digest of the laws of the 50 states and patent, copyright, and trademark laws.

Legal Secretary's Concise Dictionary. Compiled by the Louisiana Association of Legal Secretaries and distributed by Claitor's Book Store, Baton Rouge, Louisiana.

The Lawyer's Handbook, Black's Law Dictionary, and *Weihofen's Writing Style.* Published by West Publishing Co., St. Paul, Minnesota.

Legal Secretary's Complete Handbook, 2d ed., and *Sletwold's Manual of Documents and Forms for the Legal Secretary,* 2d ed. Published by Prentice-Hall Inc., Englewood Cliffs, New Jersey.

NALS Docket. A bimonthly magazine published for members of the National Association of Legal Secretaries, 3005 E. Skelly Drive, Suite 120, Tulsa, OK 74105.

Local Law Bulletin (daily or weekly). A record of court calls and current news about meetings of interest to the legal profession.

Catalogs of printing companies that provide legal forms.

The National Association of Legal Secretaries provides a contact with other legal secretaries and promotes interest in professional development. Those who qualify for and pass its seven-part examination become Professional Legal Secretaries (PLS), certified by NALS.

SUGGESTED READINGS

Bate, Marjorie Dunlap, and Mary Casey. *Legal Office Procedures*. New York: McGraw-Hill Book Co., 1974.

National Association of Legal Secretaries. *Manual for the Legal Secretarial Profession*, 2d ed. St. Paul: West Publishing Co., 1974.

Oran, Daniel. *Law Dictionary for Non-Lawyers*. St. Paul: West Publishing Co., 1975.

Reilly, Theresa M. *Legal Secretary's Word Finder and Desk Book*. Englewood Cliffs: Prentice-Hall, 1973.

Thomae, Betty K. *Legal Secretary's Desk Book — With Forms*. Englewood Cliffs: Prentice-Hall, 1973.

QUESTIONS FOR DISCUSSION

1. Answer the following questions relating to the preparation of a power of attorney.
   (a) What variable data are usually typed on a power of attorney form?
   (b) What may be done to prevent the fraudulent insertion of additions after the power of attorney form has been signed?
   (c) If the power of attorney is to authorize the bank to accept checks drawn on the company bank account when signed by the secretary, how many copies should be made of the document itself?
   (d) How can you be sure that all copies of a printed legal form are identical?

2. How does legal typing differ from manuscript typing in (a) the use of the hyphen in dividing words? (b) numbering of pages? (c) ending of a page with the last line of a paragraph? (d) acceptability of erasures and corrections?

3. Assume you are a notary public. In what way do your responsibilities differ when you sign an agreement for monthly machine repair service than when you notarize an affidavit?

4. The secretary in an adjacent office asks you to witness the signatures on a contract. When you reach the office, you find that the signatures have already been affixed and you are asked to sign as a witness. What would you do?

5. Your employer asks you to rush out a legal paper that must be signed by persons waiting in the office. You type it quickly, check it even more quickly, and hand it in. After the signers leave, you notice you have made a serious error in a date. What would you do?

6. What precautions are required regarding signatures to legal documents?

7. One reference source states: "When making photocopies of the Will or Codicil, IT IS NEVER TO BE UNSTAPLED OR TAKEN

APART." What is a codicil? Why should not the will or codicil be unstapled when preparing copies?

8. Many Latin words and phrases are used in legal documents. What is the English translation of each of the following Latin terms?

corpus juris
de jure
loco citato
prima facie
pro tempore (*or* pro tem)

quasi
quod erat demonstrandum (Q.E.D.)
scilicet (ss)
sic

If necessary, consult one of the references given on page 599 for the correct translation.

9. A conversion is the unconventional use of a word, such as using a noun as an adjective or a verb as a noun. Select the words in the following sentences that have been converted to unconventional parts of speech. Consult the Reference Guide in order to check your answers.
   (a) That swimmer will be a blue ribbon winner!
   (b) The general master-minded the whole sordid affair.
   (c) They say the new lawyer has a textbook degree and a gunboat personality.
   (d) You sweet talked your way out of an embarrassing situation.

PROBLEMS

1. It has been recommended that a secretary should accumulate a file of legal forms for reference purposes. Prepare a typing instruction sheet that could be inserted in the front of such a file. Include typing instructions for:
   (a) Margins
   (b) Spacing
   (c) Paragraph indention
   (d) Writing dates
   (e) Paging
   (f) Writing figures
   (g) Typing names
   (h) Typing quoted matter
   (i) Preparing forms for signatures
   (j) Fill-ins in legal blanks
   (k) Correction of errors

2. Assume that you wish to become a notary public in your state.

   (a) From your library, from a notary public, or from some other source obtain the name and address of the designated official in your state who issues notary public commissions.
   (b) Obtain from the designated official the specific requirements for the commission in your state. Type a summary list of these various requirements.

3. You are a notary public commissioned in Storey County, Nevada. Mr. Toni Nuvamsa asks you to prepare an affidavit for his signature stating that he, Toni Nuvamsa, is a member of the Apache Indian tribe and has resided for the past eighteen years at 2323 North Canyon Drive, Reno, Nevada. Prepare the affidavit using the one

shown on page 588 as a guide. Use the current date. You are to sign the form as the notary public.

4. Mr. Edward Thomas Stanek, who lives at 134 North 10th Street, Cleveland, Ohio, owns a building located at 3150 North Platt Street, Orlando, Florida. Mr. Stanek wishes to give Rebecca Mary Ploeger of 86 Professional Drive, Orlando, authority to sell the building and land for him and to execute in his behalf all papers necessary for the transfer of the property. Prepare the power of attorney. Use the form on page 589 as a guide. Your form, however, will be typewritten in place of using a printed form as illustrated.

Use the current date. Complete the notary public statement that constitutes part of the power of attorney.

5. Using the partnership agreement shown on page 596 (bottom), type an original and two carbons of the partnership agreement for Helen Bates Royzet and Martin Charles Cassi, both residents of Columbia, South Carolina. They are forming a partnership to operate a tax accounting service to be known as the Star Tax Service. Each agrees to invest $25,000 in the business. Profits and losses are to be distributed annually and divided equally between the partners. Use the current date.

Part 8   CASE PROBLEMS

Case 8-1
CHECK AND
DOUBLE CHECK

John Sanchez was recently transferred from the personnel department to become secretary to Jeff Winters, manager of the accounting department. John was responsible for duplicating the quarterly financial report for the board of directors' meeting on Friday from rough-draft copy handed him on Wednesday morning by his employer. On Thursday afternoon he typed the multilith master and took it to the reprographics department along with an order form for the duplicating job.

First thing Friday morning he put the copies on Mr. Winters' desk. Ten minutes later — and just fifteen minutes before the meeting — Mr. Winters stormed up to John's desk, shouting, "Look at this! Didn't you proofread this before you had it run? Don't you know that you always have to check your totals? Every good accountant does! You'd have seen that the total of every single column is wrong. The complete report is worthless, and the board is due in the conference room right now. You've made me look stupid! What can I do at this late date?"

Referring to the original rough draft, the two men discovered together that Mr. Winters' 1's had a tail on them which John had read as 7's, a mistake that was repeated throughout the statement.

What can be done? Whose fault was the error? What changes should John make in his procedures?

Case 8-2
WORK
ORGANIZATION

Norma Wilson was secretary to the dean of the School of Business at XYZ University. The dean was to present a paper on Friday in a distant city, and the 30-page paper was then to be submitted for publication in the proceedings of the symposium.

On Thursday Norma planned to type the final draft of the paper, for which she had done much of the research herself. As she settled down to the typing, the registrar called to remind her that all teaching schedules for the following semester were due by five o'clock that day. On Monday she had sent a rough copy of proposed schedules to all members of the division with a request from the dean that each member initial the schedule if approved or submit by Wednesday evening a request for revision and the reason for asking for the change. In checking the returned schedules, she found that Professor Lawler, a usually dissident faculty member, had not been heard from. She called his secretary, who said, "Professor Lawler is never in on Thursday. That's the day he works at the Research Council. It's on his class schedule filed in your office."

Norma then telephoned the registrar that the dean's material would be delayed until Monday at 10:30 because all of the faculty members had not responded. Just as she was starting on the report, the dean called an emergency meeting involving a disciplinary matter; and, as was customary, Norma was asked to take notes. Since both the meeting and the report were short, Norma transcribed her notes as soon as she returned to her desk.

At 11:30 Norma started on the research paper again. She discovered that she had omitted two page references on footnotes when researching the information. Instead of taking her lunch hour, she made a quick trip to the library to secure the missing information. Before resuming her typing, she telephoned to ask Professor Lawler's secretary to bring the missing schedule to her office just as soon as the professor came in on Friday. Then she placed a note on the dean's desk that the schedules would be delayed until Monday and asked if the schedules should be approved before she typed them. (The dean attended the Council for Deans at ten o'clock every Monday.)

A constant stream of faculty and student visitors delayed the report even more. At three o'clock the dean rushed to Norma's desk saying, "May I have the manuscript so that I can familiarize myself with it this afternoon? I want to read it smoothly tomorrow, and that requires practice."

Norma had to admit, "It's not ready yet, dean. There's just too much work in this office for one person. I can give you a rough draft in about twenty minutes, and I can mail the final corrected manuscript tomorrow afternoon if you give me the name and address of the editor of the proceedings."

The dean, visibly annoyed, retreated, muttering, "I gave it to you on Wednesday morning. You knew I had to have it today. Maybe you should try to plan your work better."

What errors in work organization did Norma commit?

Case 8-3
THE SECRETARY
AS CONFIDANT

Olga Grimaldi was secretary to the chief lawyer in a small legal firm. She joined Romano Conradi, a recently employed clerk, at the table where he was eating lunch alone and asked, "How are things going?"

Sensing that he had found a friend when he needed one, he said, "Everything I do seems to be wrong. I think I'll quit on Friday." As she pressed for details, Romano said, "I don't like Mr. Grosso. He expects too much and never tells you anything. This morning he told me to take a lease he had just completed to the First National Bank building and get the signature of Mrs. Thomas. There wasn't any Mrs. Thomas listed on the building directory so I brought it back. He yelled at me that Mrs. Thomas is the owner of the Acme Employment Service and that I could have found the name of the company if I had just read the lease. Well, it was in a sealed envelope, and I didn't think I had any right to open the envelope. Don't you think that I did the right thing, Miss Grimaldi? You don't like Mr. Grosso either, do you? Nobody does."

How do you think Miss Grimaldi should have replied? Should she have listened to Romano's complaints about a member of the firm? Should she have maintained a "hands-off" attitude?

Should she regard herself as the ears of her employer and report to him the problem that arose?

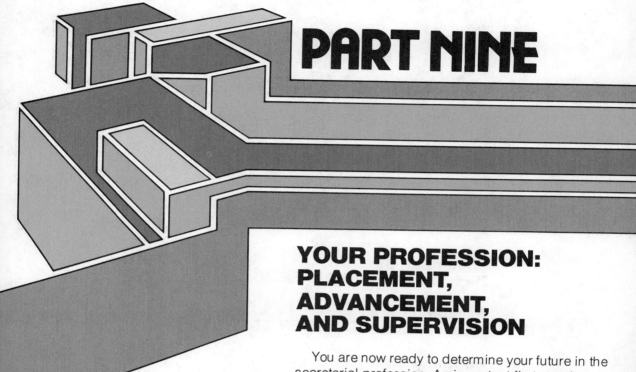

PART NINE

YOUR PROFESSION: PLACEMENT, ADVANCEMENT, AND SUPERVISION

You are now ready to determine your future in the secretarial profession. An important first step is obtaining the right position, one that offers both job satisfaction and opportunity for advancement. Growing in the secretarial profession comes with time, experience, and study of an organization and its functions. By making significant contributions to your job and to your employer, you may soon earn an administrative position, a post many proven secretaries occupy today.

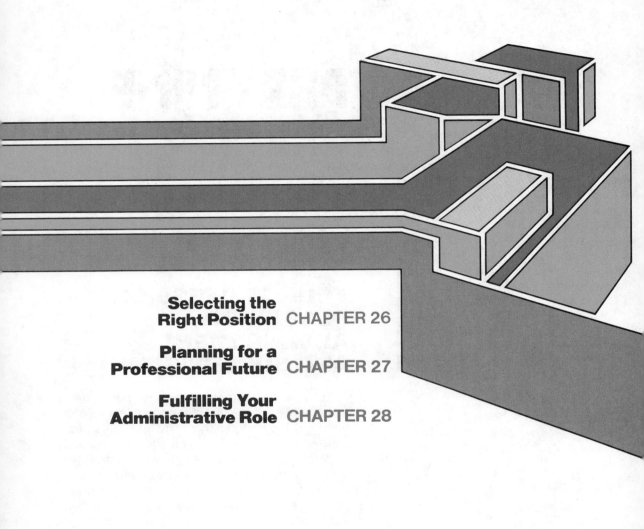

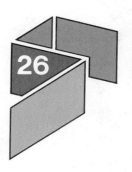

Selecting the Right Position

The secretary preparing for employment today has many career options and many decisions to make in selecting that right position. In large organizations, for example, new technology has provided two new career paths, as a secretary in a word processing center or in the administrative support area. In addition to fields of specialization, such as legal, medical, or engineering, the secretary can consider the merits of being a private secretary or one that serves several individuals. Another decision is whether to work in a large or small office, in the heart of downtown or in the suburbs. An even more basic decision might be geographic location. All these decisions are yours. As a well-qualified secretary, you will have no difficulty in getting the secretarial position you want, in the right office, location, and specialization of your choice.

This chapter will prepare you to make some of these decisions. Steps in the employment process—preparation of the personal data sheet and application forms and interview techniques are discussed. The chapter concludes with a section for the older job seeker, giving useful suggestions for job hunting and preparing a personal data sheet.

TYPES OF OFFICES

The size of an office and its location will determine the type and extent of the benefits afforded employees. Although many secretaries work in the downtown areas of cities, where salaries are usually higher than in outlying districts, attractive positions are open in the suburbs and in small outlying towns. From a secretary's viewpoint each type of office and location offers certain benefits. In a labor market in which 1.5 million additional secretaries are needed to manage the communications and paperwork in the office, the well-qualified secretary can make the final selection.

Small Offices

Many secretaries prefer to work in a small office because they are able to perform a wide variety of duties. There is no one else to do the filing, handle the petty cash, duplicate materials, sort and send out the mail, and purchase supplies. Examples of one-secretary offices are those maintained by attorneys, architects, engineers, accountants, doctors, dentists, insurance agencies, schools, and company branches.

Personnel Policies. One of the advantages of working in a small office is the freedom offered. The hours of work are usually established, but the secretary knows the volume of work and when time permits may take longer lunch hours, leave early, or take a day off.

Small offices usually have general personnel policies rather than clearly defined ones. This may or may not be to the advantage of the secretary. There may be no limit to sick leaves and emergency absences, or there may be no provision at all for them.

There are, however, a few definite disadvantages to working in a small office. Generally, there is a limit to the amount of salary a small office can pay. The ceiling may be set by circumstances of the business and not by the competence of the secretary. Instead of giving specified salary increases at definite intervals, the employer is likely to consider each salary increase individually. Another disadvantage is the absence of social opportunities in the work situation.

Administrative Opportunities. In some small offices, the secretary must assume a great deal of administrative responsibility but rarely is given an administrative title or status. The employer, depending upon the nature of the work, may be out of the office much of the time and then the responsibility for running the office falls upon the secretary.

An office with three and four secretaries frequently provides excellent opportunities to gain supervisory experience. In such situations, the senior secretary may supervise the work of the office staff in addition to other duties of the job.

Large Offices

The work of the secretary in the large office tends to differ in many respects from that of the secretary in the small office. In the large office many of the business routines are performed by special departments. Telephone duties are handled by switchboard operators; postal and shipping chores, by the mailing and shipping departments; the purchasing department orders supplies — to mention a few. On the other hand, in addition to communication responsibilities the secretary in the large office may handle travel details, research business information for the executive, draft reports, sit in on conferences and write the proceedings, and perform many other important services.

In some offices the typing and nontyping duties of the secretarial position may be separated, with the word processing center assuming the correspondence responsibilities. The secretary may choose whether to follow the career paths available in the center or those in the administrative support areas. In both options the secretary enjoys the benefits of membership in a large organization.

Personnel Policies. Personnel policies must be clearly defined and followed in large offices. Singling out an individual employee for special privileges can be damaging to office morale. The personnel policies of a large company usually cover such matters as:

Hours of work, lunch hour, and rest periods

Overtime pay or compensatory time off

Eligibility for vacation; length of vacation

Number of days allowed annually for emergency sick leave

Days considered as holidays (days off with pay)

Salary range for each job; frequency and extent of salary increases

Fringe benefits

Job Classifications. There is opportunity for advancement in a large organization. Supervisory and administrative positions exist to which the secretary can advance. Secretaries to top management are frequently administrative assistants both in duties and title.

Fringe Benefits. Many businesses and government agencies offer fringe benefits to their employees. They are called "fringe" because they are outside the realm of salary, and sometimes outside the realm of taxable income. In some instances, these benefits cost the organization an additional 25 to 30 percent of the wages paid.

The most common benefits are:

Group life insurance

Medical and hospitalization insurance

Company stock-purchase plan

Pension fund

Bonuses

Employee credit union

Company educational seminars and conferences

Membership expenses in professional organizations

A company may pay for all or part of the insurance premiums, make substantial contributions to the pension fund, and provide office space for the employee-operated credit union. In addition, some companies provide numerous outside recreational facilities for employees and their dependents. Generous vacation and sick leave periods are becoming more and more common. Liberal maternity benefits have been written into many company policies. Finally, firms dealing in a product or service, such as retailers and commercial airlines, offer attractive purchase discounts or travel plans to their employees.

OPPORTUNITIES FOR SPECIALIZATION

There are unlimited opportunities for the qualified secretary to specialize in a particular field. For most secretaries, a decision to specialize usually comes after some experience in general office work. Some office experience, training in business fundamentals and secretarial skills, and an interest in the area of specialization are necessary prerequisites for making this decision. While there are many areas of specialization, this book can discuss only a few of them. In each field the typical duties of the position are mentioned.

The Medical Secretary

A long-established and rapidly growing area of secretarial specialization is that of the medical secretary. You may work in a doctor's or dentist's office, or for a clinic, a hospital, a pharmaceutical company, a public health facility, or even an insurance company.

While desirable, special training is not essential; learning on the job is always possible. A knowledge of Latin, however, is a distinct help in understanding the terminology. Courses in German, likewise, will prove helpful. Independent business schools, community colleges, technical colleges and institutes, and some four-year colleges and universities offer programs for training the medical secretary. Besides training in the office skills and medical dictation, curriculums include a number of science courses, the study of medical terminology, records management, and accounting procedures common to medical offices. A rich variety of handbooks are available to the medical secretary and to the secretary who is contemplating this specialization.

In the one-doctor office, the secretary may serve as receptionist, bookkeeper, transcriber of case histories, secretary, and office manager. Routine technical duties like sterilizing instruments or taking temperatures may be required. The secretary, if the only employee in the office, must perform all of the office duties and must assume responsibility for running a smooth office. In the process, the principles of medical ethics are followed by keeping patients' medical records confidential.

In larger offices and in hospitals, the work will consist of transcribing patients' records, either from shorthand or machine dictation, and of the myriad details involved in smoothly, pleasantly, and comfortingly handling the patients in today's busy medical office. But regardless of the size of the office or organization, the secretary must be familiar with medical terms — both the meaning and the spelling — and with professional office procedures as well as medical and hospital insurance forms.

To keep current in the field, the medical secretary should join the American Association of Medical Assistants, a professional organization for the office staff, nurses, technicians, and assistants who are employed by a physician or an accredited hospital. This organization sponsors a certification program (Certified Medical Assistants, Administrative), publishes a bimonthly magazine called *The Professional Medical Assistant*, and holds an annual convention.

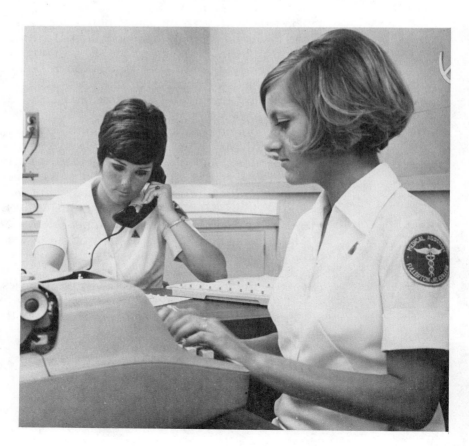

A medical secretary must be familiar with medical terminology. The American Association of Medical Assistants sponsors training programs for the medical secretary in which specialized duties and vocabularies are stressed.

To be eligible to take the certification examination, candidates must meet certain requirements of training acquired in a medical assisting program or experience in the field. The examination consists of two divisions:

Division I (General) — covers medical terminology, basic anatomy and physiology, psychology, and medical law and ethics

Division II (Administrative) — covers oral and written communications, bookkeeping and insurance, and administrative procedures

The Legal Secretary

Legal secretaries are among the highest paid in the profession, and rightly so. The work of the law office is exacting; an inaccurate record can be extremely expensive. The secretary must have a command of the English language and high typewriting and shorthand proficiencies. Working long hours — most of them under pressure — the secretary must have a thorough knowledge of legal procedures and a real interest in the law.

The title *legal secretary* comes only after considerable experience in the field, and in many instances after receiving training from the senior secretaries in the law office. To give professional status to the legal secretary, the National Association of Legal Secretaries (International) sponsors, through its chapters, free training programs, an employment service, and a Professional Legal Secretary examination and certification program.

To be eligible for the PLS examination, an applicant must be a member of NALS, must have had at least five years' experience as a legal secretary, and must present letters from five reputable persons, one of whom must be a member of the American Bar Association and another, the applicant's present employer.

Founded in 1929, NALS holds an annual convention and offers its membership a bimonthly publication, *NALS Docket*.

Many of the peculiarities of the work of the legal secretary were described in Chapter 25. Actually, the legal secretary's work is highly varied and involves extensive contacts with people — the clients of the law office. Occasionally, secretaries become so fascinated with the profession that they study law at evening classes, pass the bar examination, and proudly change the desk plate from "Secretary" to "Attorney."

The Educational Secretary

Every community offers employment opportunities for educational secretaries in work that varies widely among positions. The secretary to the top school officials of a large city system will have duties similar to those of the secretary in business and industry. On the other hand, the secretary in the office of the small local school will perform vastly different duties. Some examples are taking dictation, keeping records, ordering materials and supplies, supervising student aides, scheduling facilities, working on master schedules, and planning group meetings. The secretary will also meet school visitors and have close contacts with students, teachers, and parents.

The National Association of Educational Secretaries is the professional organization for secretaries in this field. The organization upgrades the profession by sponsoring a continuing academic program, conducting conferences, and distributing three publications (*The National Educational Secretary, Beam,* and *Crossroads*) and pertinent information. The NAES also sponsors a Professional Standards Program that issues seven kinds of certificates (basic, associate professional, advanced I, II, III, professional, and master) based on education, experience, and professional activity. A college degree is required for the professional certificate and a master's degree for the master certificate. To be eligible for the examination, an applicant must be a member of NAES.

The Technical Secretary

The technical secretary serves the engineer and the scientist — those who are at home in the laboratory but not in the office. To conserve the time of the highly paid scientific and engineering personnel, many companies provide each top-level scientist and engineer with assistants to perform routine functions and free the scientist for creative work. The secretary is the member of this team who assumes the office burden and minimizes the distractions and interruptions necessitated by office responsibilities.

The technical secretary is probably as much an administrative assistant as a secretary. The work includes not only the usual secretarial duties but such additional responsibilities as handling all or most of the correspondence from composition to mailing, maintaining the office technical library, at times gathering materials from other library resources, and proofreading and frequently editing scientific papers, as well as handling all details incident to their publication. The secretary prepares engineering reports, checks materials against specifications and standards, and orders materials in compliance with specifications. The work is demanding and exacting, but the pay is exceedingly rewarding. A strong background in mathematics and science is a definite asset, and advancement in the position requires continued study.

The technical secretary takes on additional responsibilities according to the employer's line of work. This technical secretary has a strong background in mathematics. He is using a programmable calculator to check statistical information.

Hewlett-Packard

When you work as a technical secretary, you may expect to undergo security clearance if you are to be employed in a company having contracts with the U.S. Department of Defense. The maintenance of strict security control is becoming important to other companies as well, because of the possibility of the pirating of formulas, research findings, advanced designs, and so forth. The secretary must know how security is maintained for each classification from restricted data to top secret.

The Public Stenographer

As the title implies, the public stenographer works for the public — that is, for anyone who comes along with secretarial work to be done. For this reason, the office is usually located in a hotel, off the main foyer of a large office building, or at an airport facility. The public stenographer charges by the hour or job and may work for as many as a dozen persons each day. The work ranges from taking highly technical dictation to recording speeches and testimony of witnesses, to typing legal documents, to running errands for a busy executive. A public stenographer is usually a notary public as well.

The secretary who is an expert may find public stenography gratifying and exciting. A word of caution is needed, however: Only a secretary with a broad education, a wealth of office experience, and the highest level of skills should attempt to enter the field.

In the right location, the income is high; but much of the work is performed under time pressure.

Word Processing and Administrative Secretaries

The concept of word processing has provided two distinct career paths for the secretary employed in most large organizations. The word processing specialist or correspondence secretary (see Chapter 1) enjoys being a part of the most innovative change in today's office. Armed with the basic skills of typing and English facility, the specialist operates the newest of text-editing machines in a teamwork environment. Word processing specialists tell of their fascination with the equipment and the daily challenge in learning the capabilities of the machine. The production of perfect typewritten lines and the assignment of confidential material or an entire job from start to finish are means by which the secretary is given more responsibility. Some center secretaries are paid additional premiums for line production work.

In addition to the basic skills, particular attributes for success in the center include the ability to think logically, to work with others to get the job done, and to organize work, completing it in order of priority.

Since the concept of word processing is relatively new, the experienced word processor is in demand. Experience can lead to advancement to word processing coordinator or manager as new centers are opened up in a company. The word processor who intends to move up the career ladder must be equipped with managerial ability. This training can be acquired independently or as part of a company training program.

The traditional nontyping activities of the secretarial position are accomplished by administrative secretaries (see Chapter 1). These secretaries handle the work required of several employers and coordinate the material sent to the center. They may also dictate to the center.

Administrative secretaries must enjoy meeting the public in person and over the telephone. The ability to organize work and determine priority is crucial when a number of principals are served. Advancement opportunities may be greater than those of a multifunctional secretary because of the opportunity to work with a variety of executives.

The Temporary Service Secretary

One of the fastest-growing services today is that of providing part-time office help. Kelly Services, Inc.; Western Girl, Inc.; and Manpower, Inc. are but a few of the organizations specializing in this service. Others are listed in the Yellow Pages and are widely advertised in general publications. These organizations offer a corps of temporary workers to be deployed wherever required. They help the office that experiences intermittent periods of heavy workload, they fill in for employees who are on vacation or ill, and they provide the one-half secretary for the one-and-a-half-secretary office.

In addition to providing a service to business, these organizations provide a means of organized part-time employment to a large number of persons who are unable, because of family obligations or other duties, to devote themselves to year-round, full-time jobs.

The work of the "temporary" is as varied as is business. Calls for assistance come from all types of offices. The agency attempts to match the requirements of the job with the competencies of the temporary worker. Many a secretarial trainee in college has found that being an office temporary for the summer has been profitable both financially and experience-wise. This is one way to cram a wide variety of experience into a short summer period.

The Civil Service Secretary

More secretaries work for the government than for any other type of business or organization. Government positions offer certain advantages, such as assured annual increments, job security, a sound retirement system, and the opportunity for advancement based on merit. A college-trained secretary who has initiative and ambition can advance to a position of great responsibility in government service. The increasingly large number of women in high-level government executive positions attests to the opportunities there.

Being a civil servant does not necessarily mean working in Washington, D.C., or for the federal government. Wherever there is a military installation, veteran's hospital, weather station, or federal bureau office, there are federal employees, including secretaries. State and local governments (combined) employ far more office workers than does the federal government. Thus, government jobs are found in towns and cities in America and in foreign countries.

The federal government, all states, and many municipal governments have a civil (meaning civilian) service merit system, which means that jobs are classified and appointments are made on examination results. Stenographic posts are classified in the federal government as GS3 (General Schedule 3) through GS6, and it is possible for a secretary to advance to GS7 and 8. There is a standard base salary, with annual increments, for each GS rating.

The United States is divided into ten regions with a U.S. Civil Service Office in each. To obtain information about a position, write to the regional office in which you wish to obtain employment. In major cities, information regarding federal employment can be obtained by calling a local telephone number. If you are interested in working in Washington, D.C., write to the U.S. Civil Service Commission, 1900 E Street N.W., Washington, DC 20415. You can also obtain information about federal civil service examinations from your local post office.

The Foreign Service Secretary

Does the prospect of serving as a secretary in the American Legation in Beirut, Tokyo, Paris, Buenos Aires, or Copenhagen excite you? If so, you should examine the employment opportunities in the Foreign Service of the Department of State, United States Information Agency (USIA), Agency for International Development (AID), and the Departments of Army, Navy, and Air Force.

Working in a foreign country can be thrilling, but also exacting, and calls for a special kind of person — one who is willing to live in an exemplary fashion, for our foreign service personnel are on display 24 hours a day. Each staff member represents the United States and contributes to the success of our program. The Department of State, USIA, and AID, therefore, carefully screen all foreign-service personnel; and requirements are high. The basic requirements for a secretarial position in the Foreign Service of the Department of State are as follows:

21 years of age

U.S. citizen

High school graduate or equivalent

High score on a qualifying examination covering clerical ability, spelling, typing, shorthand

Good health

Minimum of one year of continuous general experience and one year of continuous office experience using shorthand (A year in college is usually considered equal to a year of work experience; however, a minimum of one year of full-time shorthand experience is always required.)

Competency in a foreign language is not required. If, however, you should have ambitions to advance to the position of a Foreign Service Staff Officer in the Department of State, ability to speak and write a foreign language is required. Extensive study of a foreign language in college would be a strong plus factor when your application is evaluated.

The pay is comparatively good, with additional allowances for housing, cost of living, and special compensation for hardship posts.

A booklet entitled *Assignment: Worldwide Foreign Service Secretaries with the U.S. Department of State* can be obtained by writing to the Employment Division, Department of State, Washington, DC 20520.[1]

SURVEY OF EMPLOYMENT OPPORTUNITIES

A review of the help-wanted advertisements in most newspapers will show that the highly qualified, college-trained secretary is in a position to pick and choose. The problem, then, is one of job selection. There are many dimensions to the selection process, as these questions reveal:

Do you want to work in your local community, or do you hope to find employment in a new location — a large city, a different part of the country, or abroad?

How well does the business relate to your special interests in art, music, sports, medicine, accounting, social work, research, writing, politics?

Are you likely to be satisfied in the position a year from now? five years from now?

Would you prefer to work in a one-secretary office or in a large group surrounding?

Are you fascinated with the new text-editing machines, and would you consider working with machines a challenge?

What are you looking for in a job? Security? No pressure? Competition? Responsibility?

Psychologists say that the key items in job satisfaction are a sense of responsibility, satisfaction of achievement, opportunity for growth, recognition from employer, and a feeling of being needed. The right choice is not the result of luck but of careful analysis and action.

Before you begin your job search, take a few minutes to prepare a job prospect list. Decide how you will evaluate a company. Set goals and objectives for yourself. Then, begin to execute your plan.

Developing a Job Prospect List

No good sales campaign is ready for action without a *prospect list*. Your job prospect list should include potential employers who could

---

[1]Information about foreign employment through the U.S. Information Agency and the Agency for International Development can be obtained by writing to these agencies in Washington, D.C.

offer the kind of employment opportunity you are seeking — location, size, interest appeal, permanence, and job satisfaction.

School Placement Office. The placement office of the school you have attended for your secretarial training can give you expert help in developing your prospect list and can assist you in making job contacts. Complete all forms necessary for registration promptly. Get acquainted with the placement office personnel. Discuss your employment needs with them freely and often. If they arrange a job interview for you, always report to them after the interview. Solicit their advice and let them know you appreciate their assistance.

Free Employment Agencies. Employment agencies are a good source of prospective positions. Any person seeking employment may register without charge with one of the state employment offices. Registration includes a comprehensive interview and a skills test so that you can be properly classified according to your abilities, personality traits, training, and experience. In order to keep on its active list, you must communicate with that office regularly.

Other free employment services are available in some metropolitan areas. Consult the classified section of your newspaper for their listings.

Private Employment Agencies. A private employment agency performs three functions. It acts as an agent for the job seeker, as a recruiter for the employer, and as a job market information center which charges a fee for these services. In some states, regulatory bodies set limits on fees charged by agencies. Applicants registering with an agency sign a contract in which the fee terms are stated. A major advantage of a good agency is that it carries out a complete job hunt for the applicant, thus relieving the job seeker of much of the repetitive detail work involved in job hunting. Another advantage is that the agency serves as a third party representative for the applicant with prospective employers.

Private employment agencies perform a valuable service for the employer as well. The staff of the agency can expertly screen, test, and interview each applicant. The company then interviews only those who meet the company's specified qualifications. Because many businesses use private agencies exclusively, keep in mind that many desirable positions are available only through such an agency.

A private employment agency should be selected carefully. Don't hesitate to interview the agency to determine its professionalism. For a directory of reputable agencies, write to the National Employment Association, 2000 K Street, N.W., Washington, DC 20006.

Agencies listed in the directory subscribe to a code of ethical practices. The directory will be especially helpful in locating an agency in a distant city where you would like to obtain employment.

Newspaper Advertisements. The classified section of the newspaper is an excellent source of information for the job seeker. Besides the employment picture of the community, skill requirements and the "going" pay rates for secretarial positions are often stated.

In reviewing the help-wanted section, you will soon notice that these advertisements do not specify male or female or in any way indicate a preferred age of an applicant. Federal law prohibits employers and employment agencies from classifying jobs by sex (unless a realistic occupational qualification) or by preferred ethnic group or age level. If a particular advertisement appeals to you, follow to the letter the directions given for making an application.

Firms that advertise for help in the classified columns sometimes use a *blind advertisement* like the one below. A blind advertisement is one in which a key or box number is used for your reply and the firm name is not mentioned. A legitimate blind advertisement is usually inserted that way because the firm does not want to be bothered with interviewing large numbers of applicants. On the other hand, blind advertisements are sometimes used just to get names of sales prospects by someone who has something to sell.

Friends, Relatives, and Associates. You may wish to include friends, friends of your family, business people with whom you have had some kind of contact, student alumni groups, and your instructors

---

EXECUTIVE SECRETARY

If you are seeking a position which offers:

Responsibility for your judgment
Challenge for your ambition
Superior starting salary for your desires
A chance to exercise your creativity
An opportunity to use your personality to meet and work with people

With a company that offers:

An outstanding growth record
Excellent benefit programs
Newly decorated offices
Highly qualified professional staff

And you offer the following qualifications:

Excellent typing and shorthand skills
Superior level of maturity
Preferably at least 1 yr. secretarial experience and a 2-yr. secretarial course

Then please send brief resume in confidence to Personnel Dept., P.O. Box 10313, Milwaukee, WI 53203.

A Blind Advertisement

on your job prospect list. Inform all of them that you are in the market for a position and that you would appreciate their help. Naturally, you will be sure not to make a nuisance of yourself. Another source of information is a professional organization, many of which have referral services. For example, the National Federation of Business and Professional Women's Clubs maintains a "Talent Bank" of members for referral to employers seeking women to fill middle to top-level management jobs. If someone refers you to an opening, it is a matter of courtesy to give that person feedback concerning the outcome.

Other Sources. The Yellow Pages provide a classified list of the local businesses to which you might apply. For instance, if you are interested in a position in an insurance company, you would find listed under *Insurance* all of the local companies.

Become an avid reader of the daily newspaper and watch all news items that would give you a clue to a possible job contact. New businesses are constantly opening, and items relating to jobs, changes, or expansions in business often appear in the newspaper.

Job Prospects in Other Locations. There are a number of information sources you may use to obtain job prospects in a distant city or area. The names of reputable private employment agencies in the city or area can be obtained from the directory of the National Employment Association. (See page 619.) Copies of the leading newspapers in the city or area can be examined at your local library. Names of companies can be obtained from the Yellow Pages. Telephone directories for major cities are kept in many public libraries.

Learning About a Company

You should exhaust all means of getting information on each of the firms on your prospect list. Telephone to find out the employment manager's name. Inquire of your friends, acquaintances, and instructors about the firm. Examine the company's advertisements that appear in papers and magazines. Study the annual report of the firm. A copy can usually be obtained by sending a request to the company.

Many large companies publish brochures describing job opportunities and employment policies of the company. Your college placement office may have them on file. If not, send a request to the company. If it is a small firm, you may inquire of its reputation from the Chamber of Commerce and the Better Business Bureau. Use separate file folders to accumulate pertinent material on each company.

Many firms will be eliminated as you proceed in this information-gathering campaign. When your prospect list is as complete as you can make it, check it and group your prospects by jobs you are best fitted to fill. Select the prospects with which you think you have the best chances for employment and which would provide an interesting future.

Evaluating a Company

How do you judge a company as a potential employer? There is no sure test, but answers to the following questions may help.

What is the reputation of the company in the community? The community image of a company is the sum of many things — employee relationships, reputation for progressive management, sponsorship of community projects, fair employment practices, and general leadership in civic and business activities.

How satisfactory are the employer-employee relationships (company morale)? Do the employees seem to have a common bond of enthusiasm, or are there undercurrents of distrust and backbiting?

Is the business financially stable? A business that is not economically sound cannot give its employees a feeling of financial security. Its wage policies and employee benefits will always depend on the profit picture. Are any lawsuits pending?

Is the company expanding? A growing organization usually offers opportunities for advancement.

What opportunities for training and advancement are provided? Companies that provide special training programs or pay tuition in local universities and colleges merit special consideration.

Don't overlook the opportunities in the small office — you may be happier there — or in the new company that is just getting under way. Being on the beginning team can be exciting and rewarding.

PREPARATION OF AN APPLICATION

A fundamental step in preparing to make an application for a position is to take an inventory of your knowledge, skills, strengths, and weaknesses in terms of the requirements of that particular position. What skills, understandings, and special qualities will the employer be seeking? What type of experience background will be expected? Do you have unique qualities that would be an asset in the position? What weaknesses in your preparation or background might the employer note? What plan do you have to correct these weaknesses?

The preparation of your personal data sheet will assist you in making this analysis.

Your Personal Data Sheet

Sometimes called a *résumé* or *personal history*, a personal data sheet is a concise, positive presentation of your background and abilities. Because your purpose is to gain a personal interview with the employer, your data sheet must arouse interest in your unique qualifications — must be an "appetizer." It must be short, preferably one page; if too long, it dulls the appetite.

There are two types of personal data sheets: a *chronological data sheet*, which is a record of your work history (illustrated on page 624), and a *functional data sheet*, which emphasizes job titles and job descriptions (shown on page 637). In the latter, experience related to the job in question is fully described, and the names of employers and dates of employment can be omitted.

You will use your data sheet in a number of ways. Send it with your letter of application (discussed in the next section). Give copies to friends, relatives, and business acquaintances to pass on to a prospective employer. Your college placement office will need one or more copies. Always take a copy to an interview. Use it to list accomplishments and some of the extras that wouldn't be included in an application form.

Make sure that your data sheet is expertly typed on good quality paper. Use wide margins and leave plenty of blank lines between sections. These techniques add to the readability of your data sheet. Its appearance says as much about you as does the content. Many an applicant has lost the opportunity for an interview because of messy corrections, poor set-up, misspelled words, or grammatical errors on the data sheet or accompanying application letter.

Type each copy individually, and include these fundamentals (the order of which can vary).

Personal Data. Every data sheet must have the name, address, telephone number, and permanent address, if appropriate, of the job seeker. This identification should appear as a heading for the information that follows.

It is no longer necessary to provide such personal information as age, height, weight, gender, marital status, or social security number. If, however, you consider it to your advantage to include this information, then do so.

DATA SHEET

Lee M. Palmer
2925 Miramar Street
Dayton, OH 45432
(513) 426-9309

Career Objective: A secretarial position with opportunities to use shorthand skills, display initiative, and assume responsibility

EDUCATION

Sinclair Community College   Associate Degree   Major: Secretarial Studies
444 West Third Street   June, 1978
Dayton, OH 45430

Major Courses:		
Accounting	Data Processing	Office Management
Business Communications	Economics	Secretarial Procedures
Business Law	Office Machines	Word Processing I

Secretarial Skills: Shorthand dictation rate, 120 words a minute
                     Shorthand transcription rate, 35 words a minute
                     Typewriting straight-copy rate, 75 words a minute

Office Machines: Mimeograph, direct-process, and offset duplicators;
                     key-driven and electronic calculators; adding
                     machines, and Wang text-editing typewriter.

Belmont High School   Diploma (5th in class of 174), June, 1976
2323 Mapleview
Dayton, OH 45430

WORK EXPERIENCE

Summers   Defense Electronic Supply Center   Correspondence Secretary
1976-77   Dayton, Ohio   (Word Processing Center)

1977-78   Office of the Dean,   Stenographer (typing,
(part-time)   Division of Business   shorthand, filing)
                   Sinclair Community College

EXTRACURRICULAR ACTIVITIES

President   Office Education Association Club
Member   Future Business Leaders of America

REFERENCES   Available upon request

A Chronological Data Sheet

2925 Miramar Street
Dayton, OH 45432
April 10, 1978

Mr. Howard Edmunds, Personnel Director
Harmon Manufacturing Company
1604 Stanley
Dayton, OH 45432

Dear Mr. Edmunds:

<!-- margin note: tells why you are writing -->

The Placement Office at Sinclair Community College has told me of the opening in your office for an associate degree graduate with some stenographic experience. I understand that the position requires a large volume of dictation in addition to routine office duties and provides an opportunity to assume administrative responsibilities. I believe I have the necessary qualifications; therefore, I would like to be considered for this position.

<!-- margin note: tells why you are interested in this company -->

While taking secretarial training at Sinclair, I had the opportunity to tour a number of industrial firms in our city. Of those that I visited, your company offices, your operations, and the friendliness of the staff impressed me the most. My hope is to become a part of that organization.

<!-- margin note: refers to data sheet -->

You will see from the enclosed data sheet that I have acquired a high level of stenographic skills and have the ability to operate a number of office machines including the Wang text-editing typewriter. You will also note that I have supplemented my course work at Sinclair with on-the-job experience during the summers.

<!-- margin note: requests action -->

Since it may be difficult to reach me by telephone during working hours, I shall take the liberty to call your office for an appointment next Tuesday. I am looking forward to discussing this position with you.

Yours very truly,

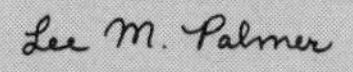

Lee M. Palmer

Lee M. Palmer

Enclosure

Letter of Application

Attaching a photograph to the data sheet is not recommended. If your qualifications match the requirements of the position, the hiring officer will want to set up an interview.

Objective. A statement indicating the position that you seek projects your positive view of your qualifications and also provides the reader with an instant knowledge of the sort of job that you seek.

Education. Include complete pertinent information about your educational background. Begin with facts about your most recent educational experience.

Schools Attended. List all the colleges and universities that you have attended and the high school from which you were graduated. List the most recent schools first and give dates of graduation, diplomas received, degrees conferred, awards, and scholarships.

Major Subjects. The business courses that you completed should be listed. Include also courses related specifically to the position for which you are applying. For example, in applying for a secretarial position in an advertising office, you would list the English, art, and psychology courses taken.

Secretarial Skills and Abilities. Give your speed in shorthand dictation and transcription. List separately the business machines that you can operate, stating your operating ability. Say, for example, that you have operating knowledge on a machine, or expert ability if you have had considerable experience and can operate a certain machine well. Overrating your ability, however, may give your application a tone of superiority which may impress your potential employer unfavorably.

Work Experience. List your work experience in the order of recency (on a chronological data sheet) or in the order of its importance to the position in question (on a functional data sheet). For example, in applying for a secretarial position, list office experience (full and part-time) first, giving inclusive dates of employment, the name and address of the employer, the title of the position held, and a brief description of it. If your work involved the supervision of others, be sure to include the fact. And don't forget to mention promotions.

If you are like most college students whose experience is limited to part-time and summer employment which is not office work, you should include the dates and description of the work on your data sheet.

Special Interests, Abilities, and Accomplishments. Your extracurricular activities, special interests, and achievements may give the prospective employer an indication of what kind of person you are and how you would fit into the office; therefore, you should list:

1. *The extracurricular activities in which you have participated and the offices you have held.* Holding responsible offices in one or more activities or groups may be more impressive than parading evidence of membership in virtually every organization on the campus.

2. *Special honors received.* Recognition by awards and scholarships is evidence of your ability and perseverance.

3. *Special achievements if they have implications for the position you are seeking.* Your ability to read or speak a foreign language, awards for English composition or original writing, or special training in some field of science may be the specific point that influences the employer in your favor.

References. You will need to have at least three references in mind when you begin your job search. The longer and better they have known you, the more valid will be their evaluation of your abilities.

If you have had no experience, consider using instructors of business subjects or administrators who know you well. You must secure permission to use anyone's name as a reference before submitting it to a prospective employer.

On the data sheet indicate that references are "available upon request." The names and addresses of your references are to be furnished during the interview or when you are completing an application blank.

Other Information. You may also wish to include on your data sheet when you can be available for employment and also whether you are willing to relocate. Save for the interview matters concerning salary and your reasons for leaving previous employment.

Your Application Letter

An application letter is another document used by the job seeker to obtain a personal interview. It may be the only document to describe your qualifications, or it may be a two-part document — the application letter with the data sheet attached. Like the data sheet, the application letter should be individually and faultlessly typed and limited to one page. Bear in mind, too, that your letter is but one of many that the employer received. Thus, it must be unique or individualistic enough to set it apart from all the rest.

Solicited and Unsolicited Application Letters. An application letter is *solicited* if you are responding to a help-wanted advertisement or are writing at the request of an employer (frequently a part of the screening process). A personal data sheet should accompany a solicited letter. The letter will expand on your special qualifications for the position vacancy and will indicate why you are interested in the company (if known).

Unsolicited application letters can be written as "feelers" to discover a vacancy or to follow up a reported vacancy. The same unsolicited-letter form can be used repeatedly with carefully made adaptations to meet special requirements. An unsolicited application letter need not include the data sheet. The letter should include a summary of your previous experience and a discussion of your capabilities and how they relate to the position you are seeking. If you are granted an interview, then you can present your data sheet tailored specifically to the position available.

Basic Parts of an Application Letter. Whether solicited or unsolicited, your letter should include the following parts:

1. An interesting first paragraph which tells why you are writing

    The position of secretary described in your advertisement in today's issue of the <u>Sentinel</u> is a challenging opportunity. May I be considered for the position?

    Mr. Grant Lehman of your Sales Department suggested that I write to inquire whether you have. . . .

    Have you a place in your office for a college graduate who possesses good stenographic skills, who majored in English, and who participated in . . . .

    Mr. Ron Radtke, Head of the Secretarial Science Department at Eastern Community College, tells me that you have a secretarial position open for a graduate with stenographic and word processing training. Will you please consider me an applicant.

2. A statement indicating why you are interested in joining the company (if the name of the company is known), or in lieu of that, an expansion on what you know about the requirements of the position you are seeking

    Your company is well known in our community for its superior products, recent plant expansion, and the benefits to employees. From what I have learned about LKM Company, I would be proud to be part of your future growth.

    Words such as "responsible" and "administrative ability" in the description of the position available immediately appealed to me. These words mean that you are looking for an individual who can show initiative, work without supervision, and assume some of the administrative tasks of the employer. I believe that my training at Madison Technical College has qualified me to say "I am up to the tasks."

3. A closing ("selling") paragraph suggesting an appointment and definite action

> Because I cannot be called by telephone during business hours, I shall telephone your office on Friday morning to ask for an appointment for an interview.

> I should like very much to come to your office to talk with you about the position. When I telephone you on Wednesday morning, will you please let me know a time that would be convenient for you to see me?

Guides for Writing Application Letters. There is no one formula for writing an effective application letter, but observance of these guides will be of great aid.

1. Address Letter to an Individual. A letter directed "To Whom It May Concern" may never concern anyone. Find out the name and title of the person in charge of employment and use them. This information may be obtained from the switchboard operator of the company. The use of the name (correctly spelled) and title personalizes the letter and makes a favorable first impression.

Obviously you cannot address your letter to an individual when you are replying to a blind advertisement. The correct address form and salutation for such a letter is shown at the left.

Box H-816
Charlotte Observer
Charlotte, NC 28202

Ladies and Gentlemen:

2. Use "You" Approach. Your application letter is a sales letter and the product is you. You must convince the reader, the prospective employer, how you can serve that company. Certainly you do so by telling about yourself, but this must be done from the perspective of the employer. Avoid phrases such as "I want," "I did this," and "I did that." Show that you understand the requirements of the position and demonstrate how your qualifications meet the employer's needs.

3. Be Honest and Confident. Your application letter can show a proper but not overemphasized appreciation of your ability. Above all, be *honest.* Your letter should be neither boastful nor begging. Employers are experts in detecting insincerity. Be specific about the position you want and the things you can do, but do not exaggerate. You may be called upon to prove your claims.

Do not be apologetic. If your experience is limited, you need not call attention to the fact. Concentrate on your positive qualities.

4. Be Concise. If you enclose your personal data sheet, omit in your letter a detailed treatment of your education and experience. Your letter then must be an invitation to read the data sheet. The statement, "I am enclosing information about my training and experience," does little to persuade the reader to continue to your data sheet. Stimulate interest by such statements as, "An examination of my personal data sheet will show that I am well prepared by training and experience for secretarial work," or "My extracurricular activities, described in the enclosed personal data sheet, have prepared me to work with other people."

5. *Make Action Easy.* You are more likely to win an interview by saying, "I shall call you on Friday morning to see if you wish to arrange a personal interview," instead of saying "May I hear from you?" The purpose of the application letter is to get an interview. If you obtain one, your letter has done as much as you can expect it to do.

6. *Give the Letter Eye Appeal.* Make your letter attractive and absolutely faultless in conformity with the best rules of business-letter writing. Anything you say will be worthless if your message contains a typographical error. There must be no flaws in spelling, grammar, punctuation, typing, arrangement, spacing, placement, or wording. You should use a good quality of white bond paper of standard letter size. Your envelope should match the paper in quality. Letterhead paper should not be used, but your complete address (but no name) should be typed in the heading.

7. *File a Copy of Each Application Letter That You Write.* It is a good idea also to keep records of the companies you interviewed, with whom you interviewed, and your evaluation of your performance.

THE INTERVIEW

In a company's hiring process, there are usually two interviews — the first takes place in the personnel department, and the second within the department where the position is available. An invitation for the initial interview gives you an opportunity to learn more about the company and the position, as well as to discuss your career aspirations, training, and specific skills related to the position available.

This first interview typically lasts half an hour which is ample time to exchange information and questions. During this period you must make a good impression. The interviewer will form opinions based on your general appearance, your voice, diction, posture, attitude, and personality. Your enthusiasm for your career will be noted. Certainly, the interviewer will evaluate how you answer questions and how your abilities match the company's requirements. In short, your performance during this first interview, plus your data sheet and application form, provide a volume of information about you. If you are interested in the position, you will want an invitation for the second interview at the departmental level.

A successful interview doesn't just happen. The job seeker must prepare well to make that good first impression. This section will help you do just that.

Guides to a Successful Interview

Tend toward the conservative side in dress and appearance. Men should wear business suits; women, a suit, dress, or skirt and blouse combination. Nails should be clean and well manicured. Hair should be clean, trimmed, and styled simply. Make sure that you are satisfied with your appearance before you leave for the interview. It is a good idea to hold a dress rehearsal prior to the interview.

A card, a letter, or a note of introduction to someone in the organization can be helpful. It may be a referral card from your placement or employment agency office or a note on the back of a personal card. This communication should put you in contact with the one you want to see.

If the preliminary interviewer is impressed with your presence and credentials, you will be invited back for an interview with the person to whom you would report on the job.

Anticipate the questions the interviewer may ask. If you have thought through the possible questions, you will be less likely to be caught off your guard during the interview. So plan your answers to talk not too much nor too little; strive for the happy medium.

Before the interview, use the pre-interview checklist to be sure you are well prepared.

The Application Blank. You may be asked to complete an application blank before you are interviewed. The application blank is as vital a part of your application as the interview. Many applicants are eliminated entirely on the basis of the way they fill out the application. Therefore, never treat it casually. Read it through carefully before you begin to fill it out.

A PRE-INTERVIEW CHECKLIST

Are you properly dressed and groomed for an interview?

Have you gathered all the information you need about the company — its products, its policies, its status in the community?

Do you know the interviewer's name? If not, obtain it from the receptionist before the interview.

Have you mentally formulated answers to the usual factual questions and also to possible unusual questions that the interviewer may ask?

Are you prepared for an interview? Be sure to take —

Your personal data sheet
Your social security card
A complete school record showing "To" and "From" dates
A tabulated summary of your college courses
A record of your business skills and personal accomplishments (unless included on personal data sheet)
Letters of reference (Some personnel experts question the value of open letters of recommendation. You may decide to omit them.)
List of personal references
Your employment record, including dates, names, addresses of employers, duties performed, and name of immediate supervisor
List of questions you wish to ask the interviewer
A pen and well-sharpened pencils
A small notebook for dictation (you may be asked to take an employment test)
A good pocket-size dictionary
Correction materials

Application blanks are usually planned with care. Every question serves a purpose for the interviewer. Although by law you need not reveal your age, marital status, number of dependents, and so forth, many applications still ask for this information. You will be told that you need not complete those blanks.

In completing an application, be careful that you follow instructions. For instance, print your name when the instructions tell you to print; put your last name first if you are so requested. The way you fill out the blank reveals far more about you than you realize.

The general neatness of the blank is important. Good handwriting is desirable because there is always need for longhand writing in office work, and no one in any office wants to decipher a scrawly, illegible hand. An application blank to be typed may be a disguised part of the typing test, so it should represent your best work.

The Interviewer's Method. The employment director of a company or a member of the staff conducts the preliminary interview. If you make a favorable impression, the interviewer sends the applicant to the immediate supervisor of the available position. In talking with applicants, the initial interviewer follows a set pattern:

Establishes rapport with the applicant

Indicates who will make the final selection

Reviews the applicant's work-experience record

Asks questions related to the available job

Leads into the closing of the interview

For a successful interview, keep in mind the interview pointers listed below.

INTERVIEW REMINDERS

Refrain from smoking and chewing gum during an interview.

Keep your voice well modulated.

Look directly at the interviewer when speaking or listening.

Control your nervous actions and maintain good posture.

Refrain from overtalking or undertalking.

Be pleasant to everyone you meet in the office.

At the end of the interview, thank the interviewer for the time and consideration and leave at once. Thank the receptionist also when you leave.

Some things
interviewers dislike:

Messy application
Untidy appearance
Weak handshake
Exaggerations
Irrelevant questions
Incessant talker
Job pleader

The interviewer will question you to encourage you to talk. Many of the questions will be routine and, although answered on your personal data sheet, may be asked again merely to put you at ease and to give you an opportunity to express yourself.

Some of the usual questions are:

What is your education?

What is your special training for this work?

What business experience have you had? By what firms have you been employed? Why did you leave them — particularly the last one?

Why do you want to work for this company? (What an opportunity to show that you know something about it!)

Recognizing that the law prohibits the interviewer from asking certain questions of a personal nature, you may wish to volunteer this information. Doing this may give you the leverage you need to obtain the position. A good rule to follow is to provide those facts which are to your advantage in gaining employment.

In addition to the typical questions, the interviewer may include a few that will take the applicant off guard. Some of these questions may seem to be unusual and perhaps presumptuous, but they are all part of the interview technique and have a purpose. Some questions of this nature are listed below:

If you were starting college over again, what courses would you take?

How much money do you hope to make by the age of 30?

What do you plan to be doing in your career 5–10 years from now?

Do you prefer to accomplish work with others or by yourself?

Do you feel you have done the best scholastic work of which you are capable?

What special interests do you have?

What have you learned from some of the positions you have held?

What are your future educational plans?

What personal characteristics do you believe are important in your field?

What do you think determines a person's progress within a company?

Why did you choose the secretarial field?

What do you consider your strengths? Your weaknesses? (Hint: give positive weaknesses, such as impatience, exacting, etc., which are terms often used by employers to describe good workers.)

If you have had business experience, it is quite logical that your previous employment will be a point of discussion in the interview. You will probably be asked why you left your last position. Be prepared to answer this question and be sure to emphasize positive — not negative factors. Be truthful but brief. It is tactless and unethical for you to say anything detrimental about any former employer or firm for which you have worked, regardless of any personal feelings you may have. Always speak well of former employers. Nothing is gained by doing otherwise.

The Salary Question. Salary is always important, but don't pass up an interesting position for one that pays a few dollars a week more. If your work is challenging and interesting, your performance will soon merit a salary increase.

Your college placement office can obtain information about salaries. The Administrative Management Society publishes an annual survey of office salaries, fringe benefits, and working hours. The United States Department of Labor makes an annual occupational wage survey in the larger cities. The survey reports may be obtained from your Regional Office, Bureau of Labor Statistics.

Most large businesses have a salary schedule about which you can become informed before applying for a position. When the salary question comes up in the interview — and it usually does — the best response is "I am willing to start at your scheduled salary for a person with my background."

If, before leaving the interview, you are not told what the salary would be, it would be appropriate to inquire "What would be the starting salary for this position?" If the application blank asks "Salary Desired" and you do not wish to state a salary figure, write "Open" or "Your Schedule" in the space.

Asking Questions. An interview is a two-way street, and you will be expected to ask questions. In fact, your failure to do so may be interpreted as indicating a lack of genuine interest on your part. What will be the scope of your work? With whom would you be working? What opportunities will the position provide for advancement? Does the company promote from within? Is there a company training program for self-improvement? These are all thoughtful, intelligent questions that concern you. Questions about working hours, vacation schedules, coffee breaks, and so forth are appropriate *if* you take care to give the impression that you are more interested in giving than in what you will get.

Concluding the Interview. You will probably know quite definitely when the interview is coming to an end. If the interviewer has shown interest and in any way has encouraged you but has not made a definite commitment about a position, it is permissible to ask directly, "When will your decision be made?" If this does not seem to be a fitting question, you might ask, "May I call you on Friday at two?"

The interviewer may rise, and that will indicate that the interview is at an end. You should rise too and thank the interviewer for the opportunity to discuss the position. Make no attempt to prolong the interview. Leave at once, pleasantly and with dignity. Remember to thank the receptionist as you leave.

Tests for Selecting Employees

If you have gained favorable consideration, you may be asked to take some form of test. By law, any test must be job related. For a secretarial position, a job-related test may be merely a letter or two to ascertain your ability in shorthand, typewriting, and spelling. It may be the operation of sophisticated equipment, as a text-editing typewriter or telephone equipment. It may be a test to determine your mathematical ability. Some employers request a more general test or one designed to detect a wide variety of abilities. The main thing to remember is that you know how to do what is asked and to do it quietly, confidently, and efficiently.

You may be asked, however, to take a psychological test or a lie detector test. You can refuse to take the test; but if you do, for all practical purposes you have removed yourself from any consideration for the position.

Evaluation of the Interview

A good practice after the interview is to evaluate your performance and attitude.

Were your answers logical?

Did your conversation ramble?

Were you completely honest with the interviewer?

Were you convincing in your sales approach?

Did you keep your eyes directed to the interviewer?

Were you always courteous and positive in your replies?

What did you learn about the position?

Which questions did you handle well? Poorly?

Can you do anything else to increase your chances of obtaining the position sought?

Each interview can be a valuable learning experience. If you feel you did not make a favorable impression, consider why and begin now on a program of improvement.

Besides evaluating your own behavior, it is important that you decide whether this is the "ideal" job for you. Refer to the section *Evaluating a Company* on page 622 to assist you in your decision.

Follow-Up of the Interview

If you decide you are interested in the position, a follow-up letter, arriving within two or three days after the interview, may put your application on top. A good follow-up letter includes an expression of appreciation for the interview, a statement reaffirming your interest in the position, and additional selling points, such as qualifications not completely covered during the interview.

For some reason you may decide not to accept a position that has been offered. Certainly this situation demands a prompt, courteous, and straightforward letter of explanation. The day may come when you need the goodwill of that company or person.

TERMINATION OF EMPLOYMENT

As you grow in your career, if you are like many office workers, you may decide to terminate a position. Perhaps you become unhappy with your job or your salary is not commensurate with your responsibilities. Once you decide to resign, do so the right way by following the written or understood rules of convention. If the company has a manual, you will find the proper procedures given there. Otherwise, give notice first verbally and then in written form (if requested). A resignation letter specifies the date of notice, the last day of employment, and the reason for leaving. It should also include a summary statement about the pleasant associations you have enjoyed with the firm. While still on the job, inquire about any benefits to which you are entitled, such as insurance options or unused vacation. After the notice period (usually two weeks unless you have made special arrangements), simply go pleasantly.

In the event that your employer initiates the termination you should be entitled to advance notice or severance pay. Before you leave, determine what benefits you have and whether you can expect a good reference from the company.

Regardless of the reason for termination, your exit should be an amicable one. Avoid expressing ill will against the company or attempting to make fellow workers dissatisfied with the company and their jobs.

FOR THE OLDER JOB SEEKER

The Age Discrimination in Employment Act of 1967 protects those workers in the 40–65 age bracket. Basically, employers cannot discriminate against workers or applicants because of their age.

The older job seeker has much to offer a company: work experience, the prospect of a good attendance record, and the ability to learn as well as younger persons. Probably the only reservation lies in the cost of benefits of the older recruit. Retirement fund benefits, for instance, begin much sooner than with a younger person.

```
                              RÉSUMÉ

                          Pat L. Swenson
                       8209 West 13th Street
                       Vancouver, WA  98661
                         (206)  693-2247

CAREER OBJECTIVE        A secretarial position requiring a high level
                        of stenographic skills and administrative abilities

SUMMARY                 Five years of full-time secretarial experience in
                        the paper industry and three years of part-time
                        stenographic experience in the medical field

EDUCATION               Associate Degree, Secretarial Studies, Santa Rosa
                        Junior College, Santa Rosa, California

EXPERIENCE
   Secretary to         As secretary to the Administrative Vice-President of
   Executive            St. Regis Paper Company, I coordinated the efforts
                        of the clerical personnel in the section in addition
                        to accomplishing the varied duties of the position.
                        In a typical day it was not unusual for me to
                        type fifty letters from shorthand dictation.  Routine
                        recordkeeping was necessary to control the volume of
                        mail entering the office each day.  Maintaining
                        confidential files was a responsibility of this
                        position.

   Stenographer         During my college training, I held a part-time
                        stenographic post at the Santa Rosa Medical Clinic.
                        My major responsibilities included transcribing
                        medical records from a voice recording machine
                        and assisting with posting charges and credits to
                        patients' accounts.

SPECIAL QUALIFICATIONS  Ability to handle a wide variety of secretarial
                        responsibilities and supervise clerical workers.
                        Especially capable in the area of human relations.
                        Health and stamina to work under pressure of time.

MEMBERSHIPS             National Secretaries Association (International)
                        Word Processing Society, Inc.
                        President, Parent-Teachers Assn., John F.
                           Kennedy School

REFERENCES              Can be provided upon request
```

This functional data sheet gives no dates of employment and places emphasis on the duties of former positions and the applicant's accomplishments.

None is so old as the person who has outlived enthusiasm.
Henry Thoreau

The returning secretary must devote a period of time in preparation for employment. Dormant office skills must be revitalized by taking a refresher course or an individualized instructional program. The next step is to make a survey of employment opportunities. Temporary service agencies and companies that require part-time workers should be included. These avenues may lead to eventual full-time employment, while providing the means for rebuilding office knowledges and skills. Finally, the older job seeker should prepare a personal data sheet and letters of application. Include all your work experience, both paid and volunteer.

As a last word of advice, don't be in a hurry to accept your first job offer. Evaluate each company and position in terms of your own goals and interests. Accepting an interim job may prevent your later accepting the very job that you were seeking. The next interview just might be that right position for you.

SUGGESTED READINGS

Bostwick, Burdette E. *Resume Writing*, A Comprehensive How-To-Do-It Guide. New York: John Wiley & Sons, 1976.

Erdlen, John D. (ed.). *Job Hunting Guide*, Official Manual of the Employment Management Association. Boston: Herman Publishing, 1975.

Fregly, Bert. *How To Get a Job*. Homewood: ETC Publications, 1974.

Taylor, Phoebe. *How To Succeed in the Business of Finding a Job*. Chicago: Nelson-Hall Co., 1975.

U.S. Department of Labor, Employment Standards Administration, Women's Bureau. *A Working Woman's Guide to Her Job Rights*, Leaflet 55. Washington: U.S. Government Printing Office, 1975.

QUESTIONS FOR DISCUSSION

1. Although there are many fine opportunities for employment in the suburbs of large cities, why is it that most young secretaries prefer to work in offices located downtown?

2. As a secretary in a business office, do you feel that you have a right to dress as you wish?

3. After carefully considering your training, interests, and special aptitudes, would you choose a specialization in the secretarial field (for example, legal, medical, technical, or educational)? If so, give the reasons for your choice.

4. What advantages can you give for working as a secretary for a temporary employment agency?

5. What circumstances would make it desirable for a secretarial applicant to register with a private employment agency?

6. Some authorities say that references should not be listed on the personal data sheet, but a statement such as "References available on request" should be included. What reasons, if any, are there for including the references?

7. What personal information, if any, would you provide on a personal data sheet if you are
   (a) male, 26 years old, married, one son, height 6'1", 170 lbs., willing to relocate?
   (b) female, 40 years old, divorced, two small children at home, 20 years of office experience?
   (c) male, 52 years old, divorced, excellent health?
   What data sheet format would you select in each example?

8. A highly qualified job counselor recommends that if, at the time of the interview, you are offered the position, you should ask for time to think it over — even though you definitely plan to accept. The delay is suggested so that the company will not think that you make hasty decisions. Do you agree? Why?

9. Is it ethical to accept, without advising your potential employer, a position which she or he considers to be permanent but which you consider to be temporary? Examples are a position for the summer only, a position you intend to keep only until another position comes along, or a position to gain experience to qualify for a position in another company.

10. In terminating employment, why is it good practice to avoid creating ill will against your employer and the company?

11. A compound word may be written as a solid word, joined with a hyphen, or written as individual words. Explain why the following groups of words are written as shown. Then consult the Reference Guide to verify or correct your answers.
    (a) shell-like, heel-less, re-employ, pre-establish
    (b) twenty-five, eighty-four, one-fourth, fifty-five
    (c) re-collect, re-form, fruit-less diet, re-count
    (d) S-curve, X-ray, U-turn, T-square, H-bomb
    (e) a make-believe plan, a two-hour session, a well-known enemy
    (f) ex-President, pre-Easter, semi-Dutch, anti-Freudian

12. Show which words you would capitalize in the following sentences. Then use the Reference Guide to check your answers.
    (a) I am sorry that I have not studied biology, chemistry, or physics; perhaps I can take a night course in one of them.
    (b) I received straight A's in secretarial practice and also in human relations in business.
    (c) I majored in languages: french, german, russian, and spanish.

PROBLEMS

1. Assume that you are seeking a position as a secretary. Prepare a data sheet and an application letter in reply to one of the following newspaper advertisements.

CORRESPONDENCE SECRETARY
Busy nationwide company is looking for a secretary for an entry-level position in the word processing center. Typing minimum 50 wpm. Excellent

benefits. Send letter and data sheet to Box 1853, JOURNAL.

SECRETARY

Needed: a secretary with better-than-average communication skills; shorthand 100 wpm; typing 60 wpm. Position involves maintaining a large volume of correspondence, telephone work, and customer assistance. Salary commensurate with ability. Reply Box 2100, JOURNAL.

2. When applying for a specific position, you are asked the following questions. Type your replies on a sheet of paper. In preparing your answers, try to analyze the motive behind the question.
   (a) What are your career plans?
   (b) How do you spend your spare time?
   (c) Why do you want to work for this company?
   (d) Are you willing to relocate?
   (e) Do you like to work with office machines?
   (f) Do your interests lie in the area of data processing?
   (g) What do you consider a good starting salary for this position?
   (h) Do you think your college grades reflect your true ability?
   (i) Are you willing to work overtime when the situation warrants?
   (j) What qualifications do you have that you feel will make you successful in your chosen career?
   (k) Do you plan to join a professional organization?

3. Just before completing your secretarial training, you decide to survey the secretarial openings in your community by sending out a number of unsolicited letters of application. Using your own data and the names of local companies, prepare the letter, making sure that it is appropriate for each of the companies.

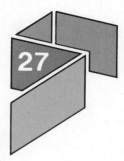

Planning for a Professional Future

Throughout this book you have been exposed to the many different duties of a secretarial position. You also have become aware of the new career paths within the secretarial field and the responsibilities of each. In Chapter 26 you learned how to find the position of your choice. Now you should begin to consider a long-range goal — to become a successful secretary.

This chapter will discuss three areas which are basic to your success in your first position and ultimately to your entire career. They are what *you* personally bring to the office, the *office* itself, and the quality of your *work*. As you read this chapter, place yourself in your first position, in a new office with new people to meet, and with duties and responsibilities that you need to assume. Rate yourself on your personal contributions, consider how you will make a good start, and finally decide how you will succeed in your work.

YOU AND YOUR PERSONAL CONTRIBUTIONS

New secretaries enter the job market with varying degrees of competence in the skills necessary to perform the job. The same is true of personal qualities. One secretary may have all the characteristics which contribute to a successful career, while another may be weak in one or more of them.

Successful secretaries, those who are proficient in their work and who enjoy satisfaction and recognition in their career, suggest certain traits as prerequisites to secretaryship. Some are innate to the individual, and some can be learned on the job. They are:

1. Display your *initiative*.

2. Develop *flexibility* in your approach to office needs and operations.

3. Develop *awareness* of the business and your employer.

4. Build *positive human relationships*.

5. Grow in your *profession*.

Displaying Initiative

A new secretary may be reluctant to do work without being told or to assume new responsibilities not understood as part of the job description. Displaying initiative comes with confidence in one's ability to do the job. Taking initiative, unfortunately, means taking risks. Use your judgment in taking action. Then review what you have done with your employer. Nine times out of ten you will be correct. If you are not, you can profit from what you have learned and apply this new knowledge to a similar situation.

There are many opportunities in the secretarial position to use initiative. In fact, making independent decisions and taking actions soon become a daily exercise. A secretary who composes a reply to a letter without the employer's requesting it is displaying initiative. A secretary who obtains information for an employer before being asked to do so is using initiative. You, the college-trained secretary, should feel comfortable in displaying your initiative. You have the background to be successful in making decisions on your own.

Being Flexible

You probably have heard the phrase, "Nothing is more certain than change." For years the functions of the office were accomplished in the same way and with the same equipment. Today, technology has revolutionized the way we communicate, the way we calculate, and even the way we send correspondence in the office. Secretaries in today's offices have had to learn to cope with change. The look of the office has changed; and, for some secretaries, a choice has had to be made between specializing in correspondence or in the administrative-support tasks of the secretarial position. A person entering the office who has ambition must be flexible. That person must be able to adjust to tomorrow's office and tomorrow's duties quickly.

Offices usually have their own routine, their own way of working with information and getting jobs done. A new secretary must be willing to learn from others. On occasion the employer may request that you work a half hour later or on a Saturday. Although this is a disruption of your regular schedule, if you are flexible you will be willing to make alterations in your work schedule and personal life schedule.

One very sensitive area in an office community is the promotion or shift of personnel. The secretary may be transferred to another department with a new set of co-workers and tasks or may be assigned a new employer or employers. These changes are a way of life in all organizations. Whether you like or dislike, approve or disapprove, you must maintain a positive attitude. As one of the ten commandments listed on page 644, remember the boss is the boss, and that person is responsible for the economic health of the organization. This responsibility often requires instituting changes in personnel, systems, and procedures. An employee who is flexible will make the most of these changes.

Developing Awareness

Being able to look at the office and its operations is one thing, but seeing what is there is quite another matter. Awareness is this "seeing" capacity — an alertness in drawing accurate inferences from what is seen, heard, and learned. A secretary must be aware of how each person fits into the work scheme. Naturally, as a secretary, you must see quickly the part your employer plays and thus how your work contributes to the organization. "Listen and watch" may be a good motto for you to follow during your initial weeks on the job.

A college-trained secretary should have little difficulty in developing this trait. In college you studied business principles and organization, you understood office costs, and you learned the meaning of profit. With this background, *see* what you can do to assist the growth of your company, your employer, and yourself. (A word of caution is needed here: Temper any feelings of superiority you might have over your co-workers because of your college training.)

Building Positive Human Relations

To be happy and to grow in your secretarial position, you must feel good about going to the office each day. One reason a secretary may feel content about being in an office is the people in it. Good working relationships with one's supervisor, co-workers, and subordinates play an extremely important role in the well-being of a secretary. Expect to like everyone whom you work with and expect to be liked in return. One may have the highest of secretarial skills to offer the employer. Yet without the ability to maintain good working relationships this same secretary can soon become dispensable.

The golden rule approach with co-workers and office visitors is worth considering. If you have been successful in establishing friendships throughout your life, you will be sensitive to the needs of others. For instance, you will play your part in making a new office colleague feel a member of the group. You will cooperate with others. You will treat each person courteously.

TEN COMMANDMENTS FOR THE SECRETARY

1. The company's business is no one else's business.

2. Your executive calls the plays.

3. Smile.

4. Be time conscious.

5. You're not the boss (your boss is).

6. Every office visitor is important.

7. Cheerfully go beyond the call of duty.

8. Develop initiative.

9. Be the voice with the smile.

10. Be a human reminder system.

Elmer L. Winter, *The Successful Manager-Secretary Team*. (West Nyack: Parker Publishing Co., 1974), p. 54.

All other aspects of an office may change but not the necessity for positive human relations skills. These skills have no age. They never seem to go out of style.

Growing Professionally

Your activities while you are in your initial position will determine your development toward professional status. You will need to learn all that you can while you are in the office, but you can also make your out-of-office activities contribute to your growth.

Certification programs for areas of secretarial specialization — medicine, law, and education — are offered through the professional organizations in these fields. The certification programs of the American Association of Medical Assistants, the National Association of Legal Secretaries (International), and the National Association of Educational Secretaries were described in Chapter 26. Secretaries who do not choose to specialize, however, can work toward becoming a *Certified Professional Secretary*.

In addition, management training programs are available to the secretary. A secretary who advances to a management position may wish to take the examination for the Certified Administrative Manager certificate. (See page 647.)

Certified Professional Secretary. A Certified Professional Secretary (CPS) is one who has successfully passed an examination administered by the Institute for Certifying Secretaries of the National Secretaries Association (International).

The CPS rating is the sign of achievement of the profession. It indicates that the secretary has a wide background in the field of business. Many employers offer CPS encouragement programs in the form of monetary assistance or company-sponsored courses.

Many organizations, such as Liggett Group Incorporated and Murray State University, view the CPS rating an achievement which merits a salary increase or promotion. Some colleges and universities grant college credit to those secretaries who hold the certificate. A listing of the companies and organizations which sponsor CPS encouragement programs and the colleges and universities which grant college credit for this achievement can be obtained by writing the Institute for Certifying Secretaries.

The CPS examination is divided into six sections: Environmental Relationships in Business, Business and Public Policy, Economics of Management, Financial Analysis and Mathematics of Business, Communications and Decision Making, and Office Procedures. The two-day examination is given only once each year in May in more than 100 testing centers in the United States, Canada, and Puerto Rico.

The examination is open to anyone who meets the qualifications, and membership in NSA is not required. There are certain educational and experience requirements, but it is possible to take the examination before meeting the secretarial experience requirements. (A student planning to graduate by August 31 of a given calendar year can take the CPS examination in May of that year. Those who graduate after August 31 must wait until the following year; however, to meet eligibility requirements, they must take the exam within 12 months of receipt of the diploma or degree.)

Candidates with Previous Work Experience. Secretaries with work experience must meet *one* of the following sets of requirements:

1. High school graduation or equivalent, plus a minimum of three years' verified secretarial experience (one of which must have been a continuous 12-month period with one employer and within the past 5 years). All experience must have been within the past 25 years.

2. Two years of post-high-school formal education, plus a minimum of two years of verified secretarial experience (one of which must have been a continuous 12-month period with one employer and within the past 5 years). All experience must have been within the past 25 years.

3. College degree plus 12 months' cumulative verified secretarial experience within the past 5 years.

Candidates meeting one set of these requirements and passing all six parts of the examination are issued the CPS certificate.

Candidates Without Previous Work Experience. Candidates who take and pass the examination before acquiring work experience must meet *one* of the following sets of requirements before certification as a CPS:

1. Two-year certificate, diploma, or associate degree from an accredited school of business, two-year college, technical institute, or four-year college; then two complete years of verified secretarial experience.

2. Baccalaureate or advanced degree; then one complete year of verified secretarial experience.

To prepare for the examination, obtain a study outline and bibliography, at no cost, by writing the Institute for Certifying Secretaries, NSA Headquarters, 2440 Pershing Road, Suite G-10, Kansas City, MO 64108. You should plan now to include the coveted CPS rating in your professional development program.

Seminars for Secretaries. Several professional organizations offer seminars of interest to secretaries. The local chapters of the National Secretaries Association (International) conduct workshops and seminars for secretaries. The Dartnell Institute of Management and other private organizations sponsor series of secretarial training seminars in major U.S. cities; the Administrative Management Society and the American Management Association also offer seminars.

Many companies have sent secretaries to these workshop seminars. If you are interested in attending any of them, you must request financial support from your company through your immediate employer. If your request is granted, arrangements for time off from work and payment of registration can be made with your employer.

Management Training Programs. Large businesses offer management training programs to deserving and talented employees. To be considered, you must prove yourself in every secretarial position you hold. You must also make known your commitment to your career and to the company. Your employer must know that you have long-range goals for yourself and your career.

Other management training programs are available through colleges and universities. Specialized courses to develop managerial abilities for those in office occupations are offered during the evening or on the weekends. Some companies will reimburse employees for tuition and book expenses as a fringe benefit.

Certified Administrative Manager. The secretary who advances to a management position can apply for a Certified Administrative Manager (CAM) certificate. The Administrative Management Society, an international organization, sponsors the CAM program. Candidates must pass a five-part examination on personnel management; financial management, control, and economics; administrative services; systems and information management; and an in-depth case-study analysis. The examination is given twice each year.

Complete information about eligibility can be obtained from the Administrative Management Society, Director of Professionalization, Administrative Management Society Headquarters, Willow Grove, PA 19090.

YOU AND THE OFFICE

That first week on the job can be overwhelming. Everything will be new to you — the people, the office, and the work. This section gives you some clues on how to survive this first week of getting to know the office staff and learning about the company.

Making a Good Start

Some companies have a well-planned program for inducting new employees into their positions. If you obtain a position in such a firm, someone will be assigned to welcome you, introduce you to your colleagues, show you your work area, perhaps take you to lunch, tell you something of the history of the organization, possibly show you a movie about your new company, and provide you with booklets describing company policies and benefits.

Many companies, however, have no organized induction program. If you are fortunate, the secretary whose place you are taking will remain on the job for a few days to train you. In many cases, though, you will report to an employer whose secretary has already left, and you sink or swim alone.

First Impressions. Everyone in the office will form first impressions of you, just as you will of them. The very same things you considered important when you made your application for the position will continue to be important as you try to succeed on the job. Because you were hired, you can assume that you made a satisfactory first impression on your employer. Now you must make a satisfactory first impression on those with whom you work — and strive to make this impression a permanent one.

You will be under critical and detailed inspection that first day. Your dress, your grooming, and everything you do and say will be observed. At this point, exercise good judgment by first being an attentive *listener*. It is a human trait to be defensive toward an outsider or a newcomer until that person wins one's goodwill and approval. Don't be disconcerted by this; if you understand it, you will be encouraged to make your associates like and accept you. Remember that their approval is most important to your future welfare and your happiness.

Begin your first day on time, allowing plenty of time for the things that fate seems to have in store for that first trip to a new job! Being even a few minutes late will require an explanation to your employer, a situation that you will find uncomfortable.

Learning Names. Certainly one way to create a good first impression is to learn promptly and pronounce correctly the names of those with whom you work. Associate the name with a mental picture of the person, as you are introduced or as soon as possible. An effective plan is to write the name and practice pronouncing it. Then address the person by name at every appropriate occasion. Drawing a floor plan to show the location of the desks and the names of their occupants will help you through that first week.

Observing Ground Rules. New employees are expected to learn quickly the company's regulations relative to rest periods, lunch hours, personal telephone calls, coffee breaks, smoking, and other similar activities. Some of these rules may be in writing; others will

Your orientation to the office will probably include introductions to the other members of the office staff.

have been established by custom but are nonetheless binding. One of the surest ways to get off to a poor start is to be a rule breaker. Ignorance is a poor excuse. The only safe policy is to find out the rules and customs of the office and observe them.

The Secretary's Code. In addition to observing company rules and policies, you will want to observe an unwritten work code. This code includes an appreciation of what belongs to your employer. For instance, you have agreed to work a certain number of hours a week. You have agreed also to the length of the work day. Any abuses of this time which is to be devoted to your work would be in violation of your work code. You may be surprised to learn that employee tardiness and absenteeism costs one employer an average of $300 per year per employee. In addition, you have respect for the equipment and supplies which belong to your employer. This means a concerted effort to reduce waste and to maintain the security of these materials within the office.

These aspects of working in the office are considered so important that the 37,000 members of the National Secretaries Association adopted the following Code of Ethics at its international convention in 1967:

> Recognizing the secretary's position of trust, we resolve in all of our activities to be guided by the highest ideals for which THE NATIONAL SECRETARIES ASSOCIATION stands; to establish, practice, and promote professional standards; and to be ethical and understanding in all of our business associations.
>
> We resolve to promote the interest of the business in which we are employed; to exemplify loyalty and conscientiousness at all times; and to maintain dignity and poise under all circumstances.
>
> We further resolve to share knowledge; to encourage ambition and inspire hope; and to sustain faith, knowing that the eternal laws of God are the ultimate laws under which we may truly succeed.

Office Friends. Many secretaries make a distinction between their work lives and their personal lives. They try to avoid socializing with members of the office staff outside office hours. They believe this separation makes them immune from office gossips and office cliques.

Of course, these same secretaries recognize that office friendships are beneficial. Certainly, the secretary who has friends throughout the company is better able to serve the employer. Through these friendships the secretary also gains a better understanding of the company and the functions of the various departments as parts of the total unit, the company.

Friendliness should extend to all employment levels — the good-will of the office messenger, the custodian, and the duplicating machine operator is important to your success.

Learning About the Company

From the first moment, your overall program will be to learn as much as you can, about everything you can, as soon as you can. This is a sizable order for the new employee, but it can be done.

In some companies a job analysis, job description, or job specifications for your new position will be available in a company manual and will give you an idea of the scope of your duties. To serve your employer effectively, you need to learn about the organization quickly so that you can interpret any request and carry out directions without asking for elementary information.

Learn as quickly as possible the names of customers, the names of your employer's close associates, the most frequently used telephone numbers, the most frequently used phrases in dictation, and the technical language of the company. The more you know and the more ready you are with the information, the quicker you will become valuable to your employer and the organization.

Company Manuals. Most organizations have one or more company manuals or instruction sheets for office routine. A general office manual will usually explain the organization of the company, the relationships of the various offices and departments, the general rules and regulations, and information that affects all employees — the date and method of distributing paychecks, descriptions of company benefits, and a list of the holidays observed by the company. Some manuals give directions for the work of all departments (or merely one department); others are procedural manuals for initiating and completing specific activities of the company.

Operating manuals are often available for the various machines and equipment in the office, and most large companies have style manuals or other forms of direction for setting up correspondence and company forms. If your office has such a manual, spend many of your spare moments studying and thoroughly digesting everything that has a bearing on your work — almost to the point of memorizing important facts.

If it is permissible for you to take some of these materials home for study, you should do so. Devoting an hour or so of quiet time at home may reduce considerably the amount of learning time required in the office.

The Office Files. The office files offer a wealth of information to the new secretary. Previous correspondence, incoming and outgoing, will indicate the type of correspondence you can expect and will also be an excellent source of terminology and technical language. As you look through the files, list the terms with which you are unfamiliar. Note your employer's letter-writing style and proper title, and where and how to file letters and records. Become familiar with the various forms and types of stationery of the company.

Other Sources of Information. Special types of records are often available to the secretary: Scrapbooks or collections of clippings about the executive, the company, or its products are sources of background information. Many organizations publish a periodical (known as a *house organ*) written by and about its employees. Back issues of these will tell you a great deal, as will journals of the particular industry.

One way to determine the actual scope of your position is to acquaint yourself with the duties of other company employees. Seeing how your job relates to theirs will help you understand not only your own job but also the total functions of the office.

Questions. Of course you must ask questions; but make them few and make them count. There are two kinds of questions. *Learning* questions help you find out things you need to know; they are excellent questions. *Leaning* questions are those about something you really should know or could research for yourself; they are the kind that you should avoid.

The new secretary should learn where to find information about company policies and procedures and make every question count.

F. W. Woolworth Co.

There is a time and place for questioning. During the first few days of your work, whenever possible, accumulate your problems and questions by making notes, and ask them all at a logical time in one session with the employer or with your temporary mentor. As you compile your list, however, be sure that it does not include a problem that you could have solved for yourself.

The other employees will usually be helpful in answering questions, but you must remember that they have full-time work to do themselves. Sometime later you will probably have an opportunity to repay those who have helped you by returning the favor when they need extra help.

YOU AND YOUR WORK

In assuming a new job, the secretary may not have the luxury of a training session with the previous job holder. It may be that the position has been vacant for a week, two weeks, or even a month. The new secretary walking into this situation may have to bring order out of the chaos, and do so quickly.

One of the first decisions you will have to make on the job is to determine priorities of the many duties of the position. You will have to decide what work must be done immediately, what must be done by the end of the day, and what can be done at some later time. You will want to set up tickler, pending, and chronological files, and acquire desk reference manuals if none are available to you.

The Secretary's Desk Manual

A helpful organizer for the secretary in a new job is the desk manual. If you have inherited one at your desk, you will find in this loose-leaf notebook explanations of company procedures, examples of company forms, and instructions for handling the duties peculiar to your job. If one is not available to you, begin at once to compile the information for your desk manual.

You can start some sections, such as correct letter form and mailing procedures, immediately. Accumulating others will require time and experience. You may want to prepare a breakdown of your duties by time periods: daily, weekly, monthly, and annually. If you are always busy during the day, take the time to do the bulk of the preparation after office hours. The first draft will be the most time-consuming; once written and thoughtfully indexed, the manual can be updated quickly and easily.

Procedures Sections. Undoubtedly one of the first sections you will prepare is the one that explains how to handle various secretarial duties. The topic outline on pages 654–655 is suggested in organizing this part of the manual. If you are an administrative secretary in a company with a word processing center, you will add to Section II the Part D given in the Insert (see page 656, bottom). The correspondence secretary will want to prepare a desk manual also. A suggested format appears on page 656, top.

In addition to these procedural sections, the secretary will include information of a general nature concerning the company, directories of important employer contacts, customers, or projects. A personal data section giving information about the employer is appropriate for the manual. If a secretary reports to several principals, it is a good idea to have specific information for each in the manual.

Company Information. One section of the manual will consist of pertinent company information, such as an organizational chart showing the lines of authority and the person in each executive and supervisory position. In addition the following information should be helpful to the secretary new on the job:

Addresses and telephone numbers of branch offices and subsidiaries

Names and titles of supervisory personnel at the branch offices and subsidiaries

Company rules and regulations — hours of work, lunch hour, coffee breaks, and the like

Company policies (vacations, sick leave, insurance, and other fringe benefits) in summary form

Telephone numbers of specific office services

Who's Who Directory. Another section of the manual will likely be a directory of the persons with whom the employer has frequent contacts. Individual circumstances will determine whether to subdivide into *in-company* and *outside* listings. At any rate, the list should include the following:

1. Those with whom the employer frequently corresponds

2. Those with whom the employer frequently talks on the telephone

3. Frequent office visitors

4. The names of professional or service people (attorney, doctor, broker, automobile service agencies)

TOPIC OUTLINE FOR PROCEDURES SECTION
OF THE DESK MANUAL

I. INCOMING MAIL
    A. Mail register
        1. Explanation of posting procedure
        2. Sample form
    B. Distribution of the mail

II. CORRESPONDENCE
    A. Interoffice correspondence
        1. Model interoffice memorandum forms
        2. Number and distribution of copies
    B. Outside correspondence
        1. Model letter forms
        2. Stationery examples
        3. Number and distribution of copies
    C. Mail schedules

III. COMPANY FORMS
    A. Models of all forms
    B. Instructions for completing
    C. Number and distribution of copies

IV. FILING
    A. Centralized filing system
        1. Materials that go to centralized file
        2. Procedure for release of materials for filing
        3. Procedure for obtaining materials from filing
    B. Secretary's file (full explanation of filing system)
    C. Transfer and storage policies

V. FINANCIAL DUTIES
    A. Bank account
        1. Procedure for making deposits
        2. Procedure for reconciling the bank statement
        3. Disposition of canceled checks and bank statements
        4. Location of bankbook and checkbook
    B. Payments of recurring expenses like membership dues and miscellaneous
        fees
        1. Dates of payments
        2. Procedures for payments
    C. Petty cash
        1. Location of fund
        2. Regulations covering expenditures from fund
        3. Filing of receipts
        4. Procedure for replenishing fund

VI. COMPUTER TERMINALS
    A. Locations
    B. Instructions for usage
    C. Input/output
        1. Preparation of input information
        2. Distribution of output information

VII. OFFICE MACHINES
A. Inventory (serial numbers and purchase date of all machines)
B. Repair services (service contracts, name and telephone number of each service)

VIII. SUPPLIES
A. List of supplies to be stocked
1. Quantities of each to be ordered
2. Names and addresses (or telephone numbers) of suppliers
B. Procedure for obtaining supplies
C. Procedure for controlling supplies

IX. SUBSCRIPTIONS TO PUBLICATIONS
A. Names, number of copies, renewal dates
B. Procedure for renewal
C. Routing of publications in office

X. PUBLIC RELATIONS
A. News releases
B. Announcements

XI. TELEPHONE PROCEDURES
A. Placing a toll call
B. Recording toll charges
C. Accepting collect calls
D. WATS lines
E. Leased lines
F. Conference calls

XII. TELECOMMUNICATIONS
A. Examples of telegrams, TELEX, TWX, FAX
B. Number and distribution of copies
C. Procedure for sending
1. Determination of method used
2. Time restrictions
D. Procedure for recording charges

XIII. TRAVEL
A. Notes on employer's travel and hotel preferences
B. Names and telephone numbers of persons in travel agency or airlines office
C. Location of timetables
D. Model itinerary
E. Method of ticket pickup
F. Expense report form
1. Number and distribution of copies
2. Receipts required

XIV. REFERENCE SECTION
A. Form letters
B. Guide letter paragraphs
C. Vocabulary list

```
              WORD PROCESSING CENTER

Every word processing center will have a
procedures manual which applies to all the
operations and all the correspondence
secretaries.  In addition, the correspondence
secretary may compile a desk manual that
will include
     I.  MACHINE OPERATIONS
         A.  Machine codes (Menus)
         B.  Machine capabilities
    II.  CORRESPONDENCE AND REPORTS
         A.  Distribution of copies
         B.  Filing
         C.  Storage
         D.  Standard proofreading marks
   III.  DIRECTORY OF CUSTOMERS, CLIENTS
         A.  Names and addresses
         B.  Selective salutations and
             complimentary closings
    IV.  COMPANY INFORMATION
         A.  Organization chart
         B.  List of administrative
             secretaries
    VI.  COMPANY FORMS
         A.  Signature authorizations
         B.  Distribution of copies
   VII.  WORD PROCESSING REPORTING PROCEDURES
         A.  Production report
         B.  Transcription report




              Administrative Support

The administrative secretary's desk manual
may include all of the sections given on
pages 654-655.  In Section II the following
addition would be appropriate:

         D.  Word processing center
             1.  Dictation instructions
             2.  Forms
                 (a)  dictated material
                 (b)  hard copy
                 (c)  review sheet
                 (d)  rush work
                 (e)  form letters
             3.  Proofreading/copying
                 responsibilities
             4.  File retention procedures
```

To build the set of names for the directory, jot down each one as it comes to your attention. Then prepare a card for each name, listing the following information:

1. The correct name of the person

2. The company affiliation and its address

3. The telephone number (area code, extension number)

4. The salutation and complimentary close for correspondence, if not standard

5. The way the employer signs his or her name, if other than the usual way

6. The identity of the person in relationship to the executive (such as relative, school friend, attorney)

There are always a few favored correspondents with whom the employer uses more friendly and intimate forms of salutations and closings. To know who is so treated and what forms to use is of real help to anyone unfamiliar with handling the executive's dictation. A person customarily addressed "Dear Charles" or "Dear C. J." does not relish receiving the formal salutation, "Dear Mr. Giles."

To be of the most use, the manual should include generous cross references of affiliations and identifications. For example, if you have Mr. Ericson's name as sales manager of Acme Metal Company and Ms. Curry's name as advertising manager of the same company, make up a cross-reference slip for Acme Metal Company and list on it the address of the company, and the names of Mr. Ericson, Ms. Curry, and any others in that company with whom the executive has contacts.

Likewise, if Mr. Robert Nolan is your employer's attorney, make out a slip for "Mr. Robert Nolan, Attorney," and a cross-reference slip headed "Attorney, Mr. Robert Nolan."

When all the name and cross-reference cards have been made out, sort them alphabetically. Type the names and cross-references on the loose-leaf pages. For alphabetic letters that frequently begin names, leave a full page. Insert the pages, with an appropriately tabbed divider page, into the manual. Later, type and paste or staple any change of address over the permanent entry until time permits retyping the page. (Some secretaries prefer a card file.)

Clients and Projects Directory. When your employer works with a succession of important clients, customers, projects, or jobs, a special section in the manual is necessary. Provide a page for each person or project, listing such information as the title of the job, the work to be performed, pertinent data, terms, and special procedures that the secretary must follow. A list of all persons importantly connected with the job is also helpful. Here too, cross-referencing should be freely used.

Personal Data Section. In addition to the major items that comprise the basic desk manual, many secretaries add a personal section. This section contains the unusual reminders — dates and events of special significance to the employer or employers and any personal information known by the secretary, such as:

Biography of employer or a complete listing of educational achievements, employment records, awards, and community services

Important numbers — Social Security, passport, and credit cards

Insurance policies — numbers, amounts, and payment dates (unless already in an insurance register)

Memberships in professional and civic organizations — offices held, meeting dates, dues, committee assignments, and so on

Compiling and updating a desk manual will help the secretary in every aspect of the job.

Work to Get Ahead

The secretarial profession is exactly what you make it. If you stay in your own little niche, doing only the work that has been assigned to you, you are likely to remain in the same position and at about the same salary indefinitely. Advancement is very much up to you. Each time you find a way to free your employer of some task, you will become more valuable. Each time you assume a new responsibility and prove yourself equal to the task, you will be better qualified for that coveted advancement.

This statement does not mean that you barge in before you are sure or that you muscle in or infringe on the work of your co-workers — a sure way to insure your being thoroughly disliked — but it does mean that if you expect to get ahead, you must be a "self-starter," alert to opportunities to prove your value by assuming more responsibility.

In your rush to get ahead, don't overlook the fact that there is no substitute for competence. Competence comes at a high price — a price paid in hard work, study, and dedication. A capacity for growth must be coupled with the self-discipline necessary to carry out a sustained effort toward growing with a job.

Build an impressive record of service to your employer and to others. Continue to promote your own individuality by maintaining a wholesome balance between business and social life, by developing interests and hobbies, and by cultivating friendships. Be well informed on the topics that interest you. Most of all, be *yourself* during each work day. A highly respected bank president who started as a secretary has this advice: "You reach the executive suite by the road called Hard Work, a trail often littered with carbon paper and typewriter ribbons. Prove your worth, and someone in the organization will discover you."

Promote Your Employer

The more important your employer appears in the eyes of others — company executives, customers, clients, friends — the more important you appear too. Here are some suggestions which will help in keeping you both in the limelight.

1. Keep your employer's personal data sheet up to date. Many employers have a prepared data sheet which they may submit when applying for membership in a professional organization or when supplying a biographical sketch prior to a speech or publication. This sheet needs to be updated regularly.

2. Watch the newspaper and magazines for press notices that mention your employer. See that they are clipped, identified, and filed. They

can be rubber cemented into a scrapbook. Many people are too modest to handle or supervise such a task, so the secretary should take the initiative. Incidentally, posting clippings about your employer on the bulletin board is one way of letting everyone in the office know that your boss, too, is important.

3. Keep your employer's committee folders in good order and up to date. This important assistance will ensure that your employer presents a good image in the eyes of other company personnel.

4. Watch the news for items concerning your employer's business associates and friends. When they are honored or promoted, draft a letter of congratulations for your employer's signature and submit it with the clipping.

5. Look for news reports about new firms or plants that might be potential customers. Your employer will be watching for these items also, but it does no harm for you to say "Did you happen to see this in yesterday's paper?"

As a secretary, however, do not forget that there is no better way to promote the image of your employer than to see that all work going out of the office is flawless and is turned out with dispatch. Mistakes, delays, and sloppiness are not the marks of a professional secretary.

Identify Yourself with Management

The position of secretary to a major official of the business is not one that you step into or inherit because you have completed a degree or technical program. These positions must be earned and are usually filled from the inside. Therefore, you will probably start on a lower level, but your goal is eventually to associate yourself with top management.

To work effectively on this level, the secretary must develop the ability to look at problems from the management point of view. This trait requires an orientation into management thinking through reading the same magazines that management reads, such as *Fortune, Nation's Business, Business Week, Wall Street Journal, Forbes, The Office, Administrative Management*, and others; through becoming concerned with management problems; and through studying management books and taking management courses, if available.

The emphasis of much of your secretarial training has been on following instructions, observing directives, carrying through on decisions that have been made, and assuming the initiative in a relatively narrow range of operation only. The management point of view, however, involves determining courses of action, making decisions, giving directions, and delegating authority and responsibility.

To shift to the management outlook, the secretary must view problems basically from the "other side of the desk." This transition requires a carefully planned program of self-education, orientation, and discipline.

You will need to grow every day of your working life. If the time comes when you cannot keep up with your employer, be assured that you will be replaced by someone who can. If you continue to grow with the job, you will have a position as long as you want it; and the possibilities for advancement become limitless.

As you grow into your management role, you will gradually be performing more supervisory functions. The higher up the management ladder you climb, the greater your supervisory responsibilities will be. Chapter 28, the final chapter in this text, will discuss management and supervisory problems.

SUGGESTED READINGS

Dallas, Richard J., and James M. Thompson. *Clerical and Secretarial Systems for the Office*. Englewood Cliffs: Prentice-Hall, 1975.

Ellenson, Ann. *Human Relations*. Englewood Cliffs: Prentice-Hall, 1973.

Simpson, Marian G. *Tested Secretarial Techniques for Getting Things Done*. Englewood Cliffs: Prentice-Hall, 1973.

Winter, Elmer L. *The Successful Manager-Secretary Team*. West Nyack: Parker Publishing Co., 1974.

QUESTIONS FOR DISCUSSION

1. What recommendations would you make to a co-worker who asks your advice on how to grow in the secretarial profession?

2. In what ways can a secretary profit from joining a local chapter of a professional organization?

3. Assume that you are employed to replace the secretary to a department manager in a large company and that the secretary has already left when you report. Where would you obtain the following information?
   (a) Your job description
   (b) Your employer's proper title
   (c) The lines of authority in the office
   (d) The letter style preferred by your employer
   (e) The name of the company president's secretary
   (f) The branch offices of the company
   (g) Your employer's professional memberships

4. Do you think a new secretary should be willing to take company manuals and work material home for study when first learning a new job? Why or why not?

5. As a new employee, you are asked to learn the functions of other closely related jobs in your office. What are the advantages of this practice? Are there any disadvantages?

6. What do you think about the theory of some secretaries that professional work life should remain separate from personal life?

7. In today's office, why should a secretary have a code of ethics, while some other employees may not?

8. Personnel changes in company organization have resulted in your being assigned a second employer. In your own mind you question whether you can handle the work of another person. What attitude should you take with your present employer and the new one?

9. Many secretaries have been successful in being promoted to management positions. Given the opportunity to interview one of them, what questions would you ask?

10. Explain the difference in meaning between the two words in each set, and illustrate the correct meaning of each word in a sentence. Then consult the Reference Guide to check your answers.

advice; advise	disillusion; dissolution
allude; elude	disinterested; uninterested
amount; number	illusion; allusion
appraise; apprise	ingenious; ingenuous
complement; compliment	practical; practicable
descendant; descendent	predominant; predominate

PROBLEMS

1. Prepare a report on one of the following topics:
   (a) What you believe are the personal contributions a secretary makes to the office, to co-workers, and to secretarial work.
   (b) How you plan to meet the challenge of new office technology in secretarial work.

2. Select a professional organization which has a chapter in your area. Make arrangements to attend one of the meetings or interview one of the members. Give an oral report to the class which will include a description of the organization, its objectives, activities, membership requirements, and services to members.

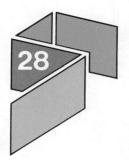

Fulfilling Your Administrative Role

"Dynamic" is the word that aptly describes the secretarial profession today. Practically every aspect of the secretarial position is changing — from procedures to the equipment used in the office. You have chosen this field because the work, the office environment, the benefits, the salary, and the opportunities to advance are to your liking. You recognize, too, that the average worker will be in the office 25 to 35 years.

After a year or two in your first full-time position, you should begin to plan the rest of your years in the profession. Ask yourself: "Where do I plan to be in my career in five years? in ten years?" Then, begin a development program for self-fulfillment in your chosen profession.

This chapter sends you on your way with ideas — ideas to make you ready to seize every opportunity to advance in the profession. Projections are that the office will require an additional 411,000 secretaries each year through 1985.[1] Without a doubt, you have selected a profession on the move. To advance with it, you must be able to make your contributions. In this final chapter of the book are suggestions to help you prepare for your administrative role.

Four areas of responsibility are discussed: how to recruit, orient, and train employees; how to maintain a communication network; how to develop your administrative potential; and finally, how to continue your own development so that you become increasingly capable of managing and supervising.

RECRUITING, ORIENTING, AND TRAINING EMPLOYEES

As a supervisor or administrator, you will need to work *through other people* to accomplish your goals. That is why some people who are excellent practitioners themselves are not good supervisors or administrators — although a person who is not a natural leader may, through effort and education, develop competencies for these responsibilities. The importance of learning how to work through people accounts for the increasing emphasis on the behavioral

---

[1] *U.S. News and World Report* (March 31, 1975), pp. 66–67.

sciences in college curriculums in business administration, in business books and magazines, and in management seminars.

In the first place, it is necessary to recruit the best possible people for the jobs to be filled. After that, ways must be found for developing those selected so that they can realize their greatest potential.

Recruiting the Best Possible People

The actual recruitment is usually the responsibility of the staff of the personnel department. Before they begin any recruiting, however, they study the complete job description and the educational, work-experience, and skill requirements for the position. Later, potential employees who have met screening standards are sent to the immediate supervisor for final approval or rejection. (Note the word *rejection*. The supervisor, being close to the job, may recognize valid reasons why the proposed candidate would not be effective in the work situation. It is best to say no now and avoid later trouble.)

An objective of every company is promotion from within; as an effective supervisor or administrator, you should include as one of your objectives the development of replacements and personnel for new jobs. In fact, without a well-trained replacement, you may not be considered for a promotion.

Assisting employees in reaching their potential begins with the orientation to the job. The better the orientation process, the less supervision is required and thus, the more time you have to accomplish your work.

Developing the Employee's Potential

If the employees under your supervision achieve optimum performance, they will thereby multiply tremendously the human resources in your segment of the organization. All of your supervisees' capabilities, not just yours alone, will be at work for you. And your success depends on their growth as well as your own.

The way in which you supervise these employees and how they perceive their jobs will affect their job performance. It is important to generate in every employee the feeling: I MATTER. As a supervisor, it is your responsibility to evaluate and assist each employee in reaching full potential.

The Orientation Process. Large organizations have a formal orientation program for new employees. Films, slides, and lectures acquaint the new employee with the history, products, and fringe benefits of the company. Information related to the specific job, however, is left to the immediate supervisor. As this supervisor, it is your responsibility to explain and demonstrate the tasks of the job.

We can see, already developing, an era of people-centered management. I see signs that management is recognizing that in this age of complex systems and equipment, the major variable — the difference between satisfactory and superior performance — lies in how well people are utilized and allowed to contribute. The need is to employ the *whole* person usefully — the mind as well as the body.

The Sohioan

Included in your discussion must be how and when the employee will be evaluated and how this evaluation is tied to salary increments. The supervisor also introduces new employees to the office workers and conducts a tour of the office facilities. In a small organization, the secretary-supervisor provides the entire orientation program — from general information about the company to specific information about the job.

Many supervisors develop an induction checklist to follow in orienting a new employee to the company and to the position. This list may include 50 to 100 items, whatever it takes to explain the job. Supplementary materials such as an organization chart and the office telephone directory are useful in outlining the office hierarchy and office procedures.

Effective Supervision. The amount of supervision needed depends upon the quality of the orientation process and subsequent training on the job. If the employee has received an in-depth orientation and adequate training, the need for supervision is considerably lessened. After the initial training period, the right dosage of supervision becomes important — too much gives the employee the feeling of being policed; too little leads to confusion.

As a secretary-supervisor, you direct the work of your subordinates and are accountable for the work that they produce. You must:

The secretary-supervisor recognizes that effective communication is a two-way street. The secretary shown here is discussing a new office procedure with her subordinates. By doing so orally, she invites questions or comments on matters of concern to them.

See that each individual receives the necessary on-the-job training.

Assign, schedule, coordinate, and approve the work of the office force.

Provide the employee with objectives and a sense of direction.

Set and maintain high personal and professional standards for all office workers, including yourself.

Establish an office climate of cooperation and confidence.

Relate well to employees under your direction.

Sufficient Training. In training employees you must create and maintain a climate for learning. An impatient teacher who is abrupt in explanations does not provide the atmosphere for learning. The supervisor may find a list of specific duties and responsibilities of the job, like the induction checklist, helpful in training new employees. It is also suggested that the supervisor follow these guidelines:

1. Focus attention on what the employee is to do. First, have the employee observe as you complete a task. Then check the employee's understanding by having the trainee work through the process step by step. Allow more time for the more difficult concepts.

2. Discuss the purposes behind each task and encourage questions. Explain the WHO, WHAT, WHERE, WHEN, WHY and HOW of each task. Suggest that the employee compile a list of instructions. For more complicated tasks it is a good practice for the supervisor to provide a written set of instructions. Use materials and office forms which are part of the job in your explanations.

3. Allow the employee some quiet time to digest this information.

4. Assist the employee in seeing what tasks are important and those which are not so important. Emphasize the key steps in each job task.

5. Provide feedback to the employee on the work that has been done. You may have to reteach certain points which may have been misunderstood by the employee or overlooked in your explanation.

After an employee has been in the office long enough to learn the assigned job, continue your teaching responsibility by training the employee to do other jobs in the department. This technique is called *cross training*. Cross training has merit for the supervisor and for the employee. When employees are absent because of sickness or vacations, another employee can assume the duties of the position. Cross training makes the employee more valuable to the department in addition to increasing the employee's job skills.

An example of cross training can be found in the administrative support/word processing center concept. Many companies train the administrative support secretaries on word processing equipment to provide for better understanding of the center's function as well as to provide greater flexibility of personnel. Within the center itself, correspondence secretaries, while being assigned to one specific piece of equipment, might be trained on all equipment available for the same reason — staff flexibility.

Delegating Work. One of your supervisory responsibilities is to delegate the work of the office.

Rose H. Scott, office administrator in the department of scientific development at A. H. Robins Company, suggests six principles for the successful delegation of work.[2]

1. Select the jobs to be delegated and get them organized for turnover. Try routine jobs first. Break down the job into logical steps and sequences and define the procedure in writing, if possible.

2. Pick the proper person, a person who will be able to understand the work and be capable of doing it along with the present workload.

3. Prepare and motivate the delegatee. Make the employee want to cooperate by building confidence.

4. Turn over the work and make sure it is fully understood. Explain the job yourself, using every written and graphic aid at your disposal.

5. Encourage independence. Give the delegatee a chance to learn.

6. Maintain control. Don't abdicate responsibility for the job.

You may find that some supervisors are reluctant to delegate work. There are a number of reasons why this could be true. A supervisor may lack confidence in the employees, lack teacher training, or suffer from personal insecurity. As a secretary-supervisor, you will be judged on your ability to develop productive employees. Examples of work that can be easily delegated are:

Filling out reports, requisitions, standard forms

Follow-up operations which may require only verifications of results

Materials and supply checks

An Approach to Analyzing Behavior. A theory being recognized by supervisors as a tool in analyzing the behavior of subordinates (and superiors as well) is Transactional Analysis (TA). This discussion is merely an overview of the concept, as a number of books are available on the subject (*I'm OK — You're OK* by Thomas A. Harris and

---

[2]Rose H. Scott, "You Owe It to Yourself to Delegate," *Administrative Management* (December, 1972), p. 77.

Born to Win by Muriel James and Dorothy Jongeward, to mention two popular ones).

TA is widely used in business, schools, and government. It is relatively easy and fun to learn and can be applied immediately, on the job or off, to understand yourself and others, subordinates and bosses. According to TA, everyone's personality is composed of three ego states (child, adult, parent) which relate to feelings and behavior a person develops in the stages of growing up. In addition, there are four possible ways in which people feel about themselves and others. They are OK or not-OK attitudes which can take any one of these psychological positions: I'M NOT OK — YOU'RE OK; I'M NOT OK — YOU'RE NOT OK; I'M OK — YOU'RE NOT OK; I'M OK — YOU'RE OK.[3] Understanding ego states, the OK and not-OK attitudes, and the personal communications (words and behavior called transactions) of what people do and say to one another can assist supervisors in their relations with their subordinates, their bosses, and their friends and family.

To learn more about this theory and its successful application to the office, the secretary-supervisor may attend TA seminars which are being offered throughout the country.

Job Motivation. When an office is plagued with a whole range of problems, such as tardiness, absenteeism, carelessness, and poor work, invariably the reason given is unmotivated employees. The problem for the supervisor, then, is to determine the cause and, as well as possible, attempt to remedy the situation.

There are a number of principles which can assist you in helping your subordinates to be successful in their work. A few of them are given here.

Make the employee feel that the job is important.

Make the employee feel that you believe the employee is important.

Allow the employee a voice in how to do the job tasks (see the employee job analyzer on page 671).

Stretch the employee's knowledge and performance.

Be an example of the performance requirements expected.

Invite creativity and inventiveness on the job.

Show what other employees can do and are doing.

Allow some freedom in the accomplishment of job tasks.

Remember, the immediate supervisor is the catalyst that generates motivation in employees and inspires them to work to their full

---

[3]Thomas A. Harris, *I'm OK — You're OK* (New York: Avon Books, 1969), p. 66.

capacity. You recognize and reward those who do reach their fullest potential. You realize that how you motivate your subordinates will determine whether they achieve the goals for the office.

Job Satisfaction. Closely allied to job motivation is the need for job satisfaction. Each individual has a set of needs applying to the job situation that must be satisfied.

Research studies by behavioral scientists such as Abraham Maslow have helped management personnel to determine the needs of employees. Maslow identified a *hierarchy* of human needs: physiological (food, clothing, shelter), safety, belongingness, esteem, and self-actualization.[4] He indicated that once a lower need is fairly well satisfied, a worker can be motivated only by a desire to satisfy the next-higher need. His work suggests that managers must help employees to realize their upper-level needs (belonging, esteem, self-actualization) before complete job satisfaction — and thus higher productivity — can be obtained. In the office, *belonging*, the third level, refers to acceptance and achievement of status with one's peers. The fourth level, *esteem*, is the need for prestige, recognition, and achievement. *Self-actualization*, the highest level, emphasizes becoming whatever a person must be, reaching one's fullest potential.

The secretary-supervisor can assist subordinates in achieving a degree of the higher level needs by:

Giving each employee complete responsibility for the preparation of one section of a report or one unit of work

Granting increased authority in the accomplishment of office tasks

Allowing employees to participate in making decisions that affect their work

This chart, based on Maslow's research, shows not only the importance of self-actualization but the fact that it must follow the achievement of more basic needs in a well-defined hierarchy.

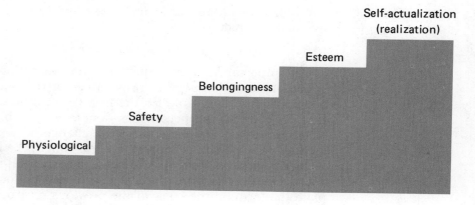

Physiological

Safety

Belongingness

Esteem

Self-actualization
(realization)

---

[4]A. H. Maslow, adapted in Herbert J. Chruden and Arthur W. Sherman, Jr., *Personnel Management* (5th ed.; Cincinnati: South-Western Publishing Co., 1976), p. 242.

Job Enrichment. Increased automation, the lack of diversity in many office jobs, and perhaps the monotony of some office tasks have brought a new challenge to the supervisor. More managers are beginning to give attention to the concept of job enrichment — an attempt to bridge the gap between the employee's capabilities and job responsibilities. This is done by providing greater challenge, more of a sense of accomplishment and wider latitudes of decision making. Techniques such as flexible hours (employees choose within limits when to begin working hours), job rotation, full responsibility for an entire project, and pleasant working environment are being used in many organizations to provide job enrichment. In many companies jobs are being redesigned to fill this need.

After all is said and done, however, unless actual benefits accrue to the worker, job enrichment techniques will become ineffective. Artificial measures, unfortunately, cannot replace the need for training and promotion procedures designed to move employees through the hierarchy of an organization.

Evaluation of Supervisees. Periodically, the secretary-supervisor must evaluate subordinates' work. In addition to being an organization's requirement, your evaluation is wanted and needed by the employee. Your evaluation can be either formal or informal (See Chapter 2).

In order to assess an employee's job performance you must:

Be thoroughly familiar with the work involved.

Have a set of job-performance criteria.

Be aware of individual differences in performing the tasks required by the position.

Consider such factors as accuracy, neatness, and quantity of the employee's production.

Be able to communicate your evaluation.

The importance to an employee of an evaluation cannot be overstated. Assume that you are responsible for the yearly evaluation of a subordinate. It is time for the first-year evaluation, and you feel that, in general, the person has done a good job. In the past few weeks, however, you have noticed a change in performance and in attitude. The person is cooperative but sullen; the work is not up to former standards. Reluctant to make negative statements on record, you decide to disregard the last few weeks' performance and complete the form on the basis of the previous record, feeling sure that something personal is bothering the person and that it will work out in time. Also, you decide not to mention these points in your conference with the person.

14 IMPORTANT WORDS AND 1 UNIMPORTANT WORD

The 5 most important words:
That was a good job.

The 4 most important words:
What is your opinion?

The 3 most important words:
Will you please?

The 2 most important words:
Thank you.

The 1 least important word:
"I"

EMPLOYEE JOB ANALYZER

      Employees should answer the following questions, keeping their own work in mind. This is not a test nor is it meant to evaluate performance. It is merely an aid to help people do their jobs better — — and to improve departmental performance overall.

What part of your job takes the most time to do? Can this part be done in less time, more easily, using less material, etc.? _____

_____

_____

Is there any part of the job you would like to change to get better results?

_____

_____

_____

Your job is a part of other activities. Is the sequence of work organized in the best way?

_____

_____

_____

Are you doing tasks unrelated to your basic responsibilities? Specify. Should you continue to do them or can you suggest some constructive changes? _____

_____

_____

_____

Do you have any suggestions for improving any aspects of your department's operations?

_____

_____

_____

Taken from The Research Institute of America, Inc., *RIA Supervisory Alert,* February 10, 1976, p. 34. There is no copyright and supervisors are encouraged to copy and use.

Is this the best course of action? Surprisingly, many supervisors in this situation would react in exactly the same way, tending to avoid possible unpleasant incidents and, in general, not wanting to become involved in the personal problems of their employees. Yet it is the supervisor's responsibility to maintain the work level in the department or group and to assist the employee in every way to be a happy and effective worker. An unpleasant situation should be faced and an attempt made to resolve any problems as soon as possible.

A supplement to a formal yearly evaluation of employees is a list to determine an employee's cooperativeness at specific points during the year. Such a checkup may point out problem areas for you to investigate. For example, here are some activities you can review.

Does the employee accept instructions and assignments willingly?

Does the employee perform as directed?

Does the employee assume responsibility for work, inform the supervisor if something goes wrong, call relevant matters to the supervisor's attention?

Does the employee volunteer for special assignments?

Does the employee give the job better than average attention?

The result of such an approach might be to commend the high performers, encourage the average group, and possibly work more closely with those who appear to need it.

MAINTAINING A COMMUNICATION NETWORK

It is estimated that 85 percent of a successful manager's job lies in the area of interpersonal communication skills. The ability to communicate effectively with employees is essential to the productivity of the office and to the well-being of its staff. This qualification is also important for the secretary-supervisor. The secretary must develop and maintain open channels of communication between and among subordinates, other supervisors, and company executives. Within an organization a communication network must be available for work instructions, problem solving, and work and information flow. Basic to the establishment of this network is the understanding of how communications are generated in the office.

Organizational Communications

Very little work can be accomplished in an office without communication. Through communication information is furnished to management for use in decision making and control. Communication also serves to motivate and influence employees to higher productivity with which to meet the goals of the company.

Organizational communication takes many forms. It can be oral on a one-to-one basis or in a group. It can be written in correspondence, reports, forms, a company magazine, newsletters, an employee suggestion system, or bulletin boards.

Organizational communication can take several different directions. It can be upward to the company hierarchy; it can be horizontal to those on the same managerial level; and it can be downward to supervisees.

Office communicators, and everyone in the office qualifies, have an obligation to speak, write, and listen as the situation dictates so that the message is understood. This is the only way interpersonal communication activities can be of benefit to the company and to its employees.

Barriers to Communication

No two people enter the office with exactly the same educational, economic, and ethnic background. Yet many office managers, and secretaries as well, make the assumption that if an individual has the skills to do the job, adaptation to the work, people, procedures, and equipment will come in due time. The fallacy in this assumption, of course, is with the important variable, people, and whether they communicate successfully with each other.

There are a number of reasons why communication between two people in the office can fail. Perhaps the most important one is *semantics*, the meanings of words and the changes in the meanings of words. *Lack of common knowledge* is another. A secretary who uses words that can be easily misinterpreted or uses technical jargon with a new employee is essentially wasting training time. Miscommunication can occur also because of the mere fact that the employee is new and the secretary represents rank in the company.

Other barriers to effective communication are physical distance between desks or between offices and the noise level and distractions in an office. The secretary must recognize these as potential barriers and attempt to make changes or overcome them.

Communicating Effectively

In order to be successful in your supervisory role, you must communicate honestly, sincerely, and directly with your subordinates. Employees tend to be more responsive to the manager who creates an atmosphere of understanding and trust.

Effective communication is a two-way street. The sender and receiver must come away from the discussion or the written message with an understanding of what was related. In your supervisory capacity you will learn quickly the advantages of listening to employees. By doing so, you can establish a common ground on which to base further communications. You can also learn to know your subordinates so that a climate of mutual respect is possible.

Two areas in which the secretary can demonstrate interpersonal communication skills are the explanation of work instructions and the interpretation of personnel policies to subordinates.

Work Instructions. Work instructions can be given orally or in writing. Oral instructions have certain advantages over written ones in that the secretary knows immediately whether a subordinate understands the instruction, using facial expression and the employee's questions as clues. If the instructions are complicated, it is recommended that they be given both orally and in writing.

Often the secretary-supervisor needs to write job instructions or work procedures in order to update a procedural manual or to see that instructions are available, understood, and followed. Here the important points are:

How to perform a certain procedure

Why that specific type of performance is desirable and important

Personnel Policies. As a supervisor, you will be responsible for interpreting management policy to workers in such a way that whatever conformity is needed is secured. Usually this means explaining the reasons behind such policy and the benefits that will accrue from its enactment. Whether you are in sympathy with the policy or not, you have an unavoidable obligation to support all company personnel policies. Conversely, you have an equal obligation to communicate to management suggestions for change — either your own or those of your supervisees.

DEVELOPING YOUR ADMINISTRATIVE POTENTIAL

In addition to being competent in the selection and supervision of employees, a manager must be able to plan, organize, and control office activities. The secretary should begin now to understand what makes an office function efficiently and how to achieve administrative status.

Recognizing the Need for Goals

All successful organizations must operate with a set of goals and specific plans for accomplishing them. These goals may be identified in five- or ten-year intervals or annually with interim checkpoints when corrective action can be taken.

A style of management that involves an entire organization from the top echelon to departmental employees is Management by Objectives (MBO). In its true form MBO is a technique for integrating goals, plans, and performance evaluation for the entire company. When this theory is practiced, at least three steps are followed:

1. A superior meets with a subordinate, and together they work out realistic performance objectives concerning the subordinate's work.

2. They agree on the means by which the employee is to reach the specified results.

3. At the end of a given time period, the superior and the employee compare actual results with expected results and then make appropriate decisions concerning future action.

If you are working in such an environment, you will be required to establish with your employer goals concerning your area of responsibility. The goals agreed upon will be specific, measurable, and time-bounded. Once the goals are identified, you begin to make plans to achieve them. Then, as a secretary-supervisor, you meet with your subordinates to determine their objectives. After a specified length of time, you may be evaluated in terms of the results you and your subordinates have achieved.

The secretary-employer team takes advantage of the first few minutes each day to discuss work priorities and administrative matters and, in general, to plan their work day.

Westinghouse Electric
Corporation

Setting goals, developing plans for action, and evaluating performance based on one's success in reaching these goals make employees accountable for how they perform their work. This participation has been effective in raising employee morale and making employees feel that they and the job they are doing are important. All of these activities fit into the needs pattern discussed earlier in this chapter.

One weakness to the MBO system is that people can mutually agree upon lower standards or lower results than are actually feasible. This is particularly true when MBO is tied to salary increments. Another weakness is that some areas of work cannot be measured equitably. For instance, the difficulty of and the time required to research information for one company report may be distinctly different from that required for another report. An astute supervisor who knows the quality and quantity of an employee's work and who knows what the work entails can combat both weaknesses. This same supervisor is thus able to assist the employee in setting realistic objectives upon which both can agree.

Whether or not your company follows a formal MBO procedure, you will want to set realistic goals for yourself and for your subordinates. How else will you know if you and your subordinates are making contributions to the organization?

Using Systems and Procedures Analysis

Developing your administrative potential requires that you continually be alert to better ways of completing office tasks. By analyzing the flow of work in your office, you can pinpoint areas where better organization is needed. In your study ask yourself the following questions:

Does the work move in a systematic fashion?

Can employee work stations be rearranged to facilitate the flow of work?

Are there any delays in the work process?

Are there any gaps in the information provided?

Are there peaks and valleys in the workload which can be remedied by a different procedure?

An analysis of office forms may indicate that there is an overlap of information on several of the forms. You may find that the instructions are not clear, or you may discover that some of the forms can be eliminated, reduced, or consolidated.

In many companies a systems and procedures staff is available for the scientific study of problems in individual offices. Although these specialists may be called upon for studies of a particular problem, the secretary will want to become familiar with recent developments in this field and learn to apply them to the office.

Controlling Office Costs

Another managerial responsibility is control of office costs, ranging from work productivity to such items as heat, electricity, and insurance. The secretary, being at the pulse of office work, can contribute to the control of office costs and to the application of work measurement techniques.

Office Costs. Every time the secretary destroys a no-carbon-required (NCR) form because of a careless mistake or because the correction may be difficult, the secretary is adding to office costs. When the secretary places a person-to-person long-distance call instead of using direct distance dialing, office costs go up. A package sent first class when fourth class will do adds to office costs. When the secretary is tardy, absent, or adds an extra ten minutes to a coffee break, office costs rise. And the list goes on. Be mindful of how you can reduce the needless waste of costly paper products in your office and how you can cut other costly office misdemeanors.

When you come across an idea that will save your employer money (and you will eventually), initiate the practice and call attention to your discovery. Let your employer know that you recognize office efficiency in terms of lower costs and higher productivity.

Applying Measurement Methods. In evaluating your work and that of your subordinates, you will need a set of criteria upon which to base your judgments. Output in highly repetitive office operations has been successfully measured, and realistic quantitative standards have been established. In word processing centers line and page count are commonly being used to measure worker productivity and the success of the center concept itself. In the management literature you can find standards for such processes as straight-copy and letter typing, addressing envelopes, filling in form letters, or cutting stencils. Your own systems and procedures staff will help you in setting standards. Qualitative standards are not as easy; just remember that the quality of all the work from your department is your responsibility.

Making Sound Business Decisions

Sound decisions are usually based on facts, and facts are secured through reading about research conducted by others or through conducting your own. After a certain procedure has been followed in a

> Nothing is easier than being busy and nothing more difficult than being effective.
>
> *R. Alec Mackenzie*

project, the outcomes should be evaluated. Objective analysis of results is essential to sound business decisions — application of research techniques to business problems, in other words. Using research as a basis for sound business decisions, though, requires the ability to read, develop, and interpret *raw* data as well as classified or statistical data such as that found in charts and graphs.

Computers are helping in the collection of business data upon which to base management decisions. The latest applications lie in the field of business simulation: If we take this action, what will be the result? By feeding into the computer various proposed courses of action, management can secure a quantitative estimation of results.

Recommendations to Superiors. One of the first evidences of management potential is your reluctance to dump your problems in the lap of your superior for solution. On the Army staff, all problem interviews are handled on a "staff-work-accomplished" basis. The person with the problem is required to present all data along with a recommendation of at least one solution, but preferably several alternate ones — not a bad technique for business to follow too. After a problem is identified, the person closest to it should be in the best position to work out a solution and to recommend action.

The Decision Formula. Decision making is a part of the secretary's job. This is the reason why you have been provided with so many decision-making activities throughout this course. Routine decisions can be made quickly and with relatively little mental exercise; but important decisions take considerable time, thought, and effort. Making the *important* decisions is the responsibility of management personnel. In arriving at the proper course of action, successful decision makers:

Determine exactly what the problem is and write it down.

Develop a list of alternative solutions to the problem.

Examine the advantages and disadvantages of each possible solution.

Select the best solution and review all the ramifications of this choice.

Implement (and later evaluate) the chosen course of action.

You can train yourself to be a successful decision maker (and problem solver) by following these steps in even the routine decisions you face in the office.

Your Own Decisions. You will have to learn what decisions to make on your own initiative and which ones you should refer to your superior along with all pertinent supporting data needed to make a wise choice. Experience will guide you, for employers vary. Some

My advice to managers is try leadership. Take one step forward. Think, and say what you think. Be out front. You may fall flat on your face. You may be wrong. You may take some outrageous slings and arrows, but you will never know the job of leading until you have stopped following.

H. Justin Davidson,
Cornell University

like to delegate as much work as possible and will give a free hand once you have proved your capability. Others just naturally cling to authority and their prerogatives in decision making. Learn to adjust to the type of employer with whom you find yourself working. In general, though, you should make routine decisions, keeping the employer informed of them. Your freedom to make decisions will probably increase as your employer develops confidence in your decision-making ability.

CONTINUING YOUR PROFESSIONAL GROWTH

In this chapter you have studied suggestions on how to succeed in the selection and supervision of employees. You have become aware of the importance of human relations and the ability to communicate with your subordinates, peers, and supervisors. Finally you have been introduced to the techniques managers employ to attain satisfactory worker productivity. In concluding the secretarial training offered you in this book, you should now consider where you can go from here, and how you can continue your professional growth.

THIRTEEN CAREER COMMANDMENTS

1. Remember that good performance is the basic foundation of success.
2. Manage your career by actively influencing decisions about you.
3. Strive for positions that have high visibility.
4. Find a senior executive who can be your sponsor.
5. Learn your job quickly and train a replacement.
6. Nominate yourself for other positions.
7. Accept promotions that draw on your strengths, not weaknesses.
8. Leave at your convenience and on good terms.
9. Don't be trapped by formal, narrow job descriptions.
10. Recognize and work within office politics.
11. Get out of management if you can't stand dependency on others and having them dependent on you.
12. Recognize that you may face ethical dilemmas.
13. Stick to your personal values.

Source: Ross A. Weber, "The Three Dilemmas of Career Growth," *MBA* (May, 1975), p. 47.

Nurturing Creativity

Many people believe that only a chosen few, those in artistic fields, are creative. They feel that creativity is a talent and that one must be born with it to have it. Every day in this business world of ours these people are proven wrong.

Creativity can be present in many people in many occupational fields and can take many forms. Anyone who has an idea and develops it is being creative. Successful business people had to be creative to be successful. You can be creative, too. You can become a contributor in the business office, a creator of ideas and actions.

Where to begin? Start by having an open mind. Ideas are born in imagination, perhaps in nonconformist alternatives to office problems. Build a kit of ideas; and as you do, experiment with them. Consider that a little idea can be expanded to a bigger or better idea.

Be an active observer of the office functions. Look for *questions* surely, but also seek *answers*. Look for ways to improve office work and information flow. Be a sounding board for your superior, and let the ideas happen.

Most people have a certain time of the day when they operate at their best level. For some people it may be the early morning hours; for others, it may be at twilight. Determine when you operate best, then set your mind to action. A mind can be alert only if it and its physical home are well rested. Adequate leisure time and proper eating habits are stimulants to creative brain activity.

A last note on creativity is a suggestion that you welcome new office experiences. In themselves, they are found to enlarge your visionary powers from which ideas and actions will come. There seems to be little question — a secretary who wants to can be creative. It is, therefore, up to you.

Improving Your Communication Skills

You will try to improve your communication skills, for even presidents of companies and countries continue to search for clearer and more persuasive ways of telling their story.

You will find yourself on committees where you will want to influence the actions of others. Keep in mind the "staff-work-accomplished" approach, and make sure that when you speak you are making a constructive suggestion.

Plan what you are to say: Your well-presented communication will reduce your superior's reading time. Write and rewrite to reduce verbiage. Abstract material and present it graphically. Arrange material to highlight all the salient points. Become a master at presenting the heart of the matter in one succinct paragraph.

One way to continue your professional growth is to accept committee assignments in a professional organization, such as the National Secretaries Association (International). Here the secretary is contributing to her professional development by mastering the techniques of chairing committee meetings.

Consider the possibility of expressing your ideas in articles and talks. Too many people are afraid to attempt public speaking or writing for publication. Yet these are tremendous aids to personal development and creativity; they make you clarify and organize your thoughts effectively. Public speaking teaches you to think on your feet. You can learn to judge the reactions of your listeners and emphasize or rephrase a point according to your interpretation of your listeners' reactions.

Developing Personal Specialties

Work to develop one or more specialties for which you are known throughout the organization. For instance, you may be an expert in sentence structure and grammar. Through your training of subordinates in your office, your reputation as a superior teacher may be known. Because of this recognition, you may be asked to develop and teach a company-sponsored secretarial training course. Your desk manual may lead to the development of an office procedures manual. You may be considered a resource person, the person who knows the answers to questions frequently asked in the office. Or, if you have become acquainted with the word processing concept through the Word Processing Association, you may be asked to participate in a feasibility study for your office. Whatever your inclination, your specialty or specialties can work to the company's advantage and to your own.

Meeting the Challenge of Technology

While you are in the work force, the equipment you use and the procedures you follow in the office will change many times. In fact, it is estimated that $10,000 or more will be spent on capital equipment per year for every office worker by 1985.

As a professional in your field, you must keep up with the technological developments that will affect you and your office. You must think positively and see the applications which can be put into effect. No other behavior is acceptable for the professional. Read these magazines religiously: *Administrative Management*, *The Secretary*, and *Modern Office Procedures*. Attend office equipment exhibits. While you do, put your creative mind to work. This is the way to meet the challenge of the eighties.

SUGGESTED READINGS

Blicq, Ronald. *On the Move*, Communication for Employees. Englewood Cliffs: Prentice-Hall, 1976.

Broadwell, Martin M. *The New Supervisor*. Reading: Addison-Wesley Publishing Co., 1972.

Hegarty, James (ed.). *How to Succeed in Company Politics*, 2d ed. New York: McGraw-Hill Book Co., 1976.

Higginson, Margaret V., and Thomas L. Quick. *The Ambitious Woman's Guide to a Successful Career*. New York: American Management Association, 1975.

Lynch, Edith M. *The Executive Suite — Feminine Style*. New York: American Management Association, 1973.

Simpson, Marian G. *Tested Secretarial Techniques for Getting Things Done*. Englewood Cliffs: Prentice-Hall, 1973.

Winter, Elmer L. *The Successful Manager-Secretary Team*. West Nyack: Parker Publishing Co., 1974.

QUESTIONS FOR DISCUSSION

1. Why might a secretary who does not have a well-trained replacement not be considered for a promotion?

2. Why is the orientation process for a new employee so important?

3. Your company usually follows the policy of promoting from within. As the office supervisor, you find it necessary on one occasion to recruit a replacement from outside the company. What is your responsibility to the employees in your office?

4. What is meant by the term "cross training"? How is it of benefit to the employer? to the employee?

5. As a secretary-supervisor, what contributions can you make to assist subordinates in reaching their full potential?

6. What qualifications must a person have in order to evaluate the job performance of another employee?

7. Why is job enrichment so important in today's business office?

8. Communication is said to be a two-way street. What is meant by this statement with reference to the office?

9. Assume that you are working as a secretary in an organization which follows the MBO leadership style. How would this affect your position?

10. In what ways can the secretary contribute to the reduction of office costs?

11. Why is creativity so important to the secretary who seeks promotion and advancement in the profession?

12. What specialty do you have that might be developed into a plus factor in your job?

PROBLEMS

1. In developing a feasibility study for a word processing center, your employer requests that you compare letter costs in your office with those reported in the national study shown in the table on page 461. Your employer asks that you collect and report the data.

   To obtain data, you keep a production record for one week for Miss Wright, who devotes full time to taking dictation and transcribing. She recorded and transcribed 120 letters during the week.

   The cost division of the Accounting Department provides you with the following cost information:

   Miss Wright's salary.............. $200 a week

   Dictator's time...................... 14 hours, costing $10 an hour

   Fixed charges (depreciation, supervision, rent, light, interest, taxes, insurance, pension, and similar overhead)............... 40% of labor cost

   Labor cost: Miss Wright's salary plus cost of dictator's time

   Nonproductive cost (time lost by Miss Wright and dictator due to waiting, illness, vacation, and other causes)..................... 15% of labor cost

   Materials (amount used during week)........................... $22.60

   Mailing cost for 120 letters (postage and labor)........... $28.40

   Filing cost for 120 letters (labor and materials)......... $22.60

   Prepare a memo containing the total cost of producing the 120 letters and the cost per letter with a breakdown showing the amount and percentage of the cost that each factor represents. Include in your memo a discussion of the experiences of other companies that have word processing centers.

2. Your employer, Mr. Luna, is concerned about the loss caused the company by employee absenteeism. He gives you the following chart and asks you to compute cost figures. Further, he requests that you include

in your report (for his investigation) general categories for some possible causes of excessive absenteeism (such as inadequate recruitment procedures).

Total sick days paid
 previous 12 months   _____
Average daily pay
 multiplied by total
 sick days   _____
Annual cost   _____
Total accrued 5-yr.
 expense   _____

You learn from the Accounting Department that in the last year 2,450 sick days have been paid and that the average daily pay is $30.

3. Assume that in your current secretarial position you have learned all that you can about the job and you see little possibility for advancement. You decide to seek another position. Before you begin, develop a career plan by compiling the following data:
(a) A description of the next job you wish to hold
(b) Status of the job market
(c) The size of the organization that will best assist you in your professional development now, three years from now, and six years from now
(d) The working conditions of those organizations listed in (c)
Type your analysis in memorandum form.

Part 9　　　　**CASE PROBLEMS**

Case 9-1
FLEXIBILITY

When Joanne Nelson applied for a position at Beacon Industries at the end of her secretarial training program, she took an extensive series of tests in English mechanics, typewriting, and transcription from a dictating machine. After the tests were checked, the personnel director told her that her scores in spelling, grammar, and punctuation were superior and offered her a position as a word processor in a newly created center.

Joanne said that she really expected to work as a secretary for one principal and that she felt that word processing centers are just a new term used to describe typing pools. She also said that she wanted closer association with management than she could get in the position offered.

The personnel manager presented the arguments that secretarial work is being automated, that the best opportunities for advancement probably lie within the new organizational pattern, and that she would have an opportunity to work with several executives and have better opportunities to attract attention that could lead to advancement. The personnel manager also pointed out that flexibility and acceptance of new equipment and new methods are probably the most important qualifications of today's employee.

Joanne asked for time to think over the offer but promised to report her decision three days later.

What factors, personal and related to modern business practices, should Joanne consider? How should she proceed to reach the decision? What do you think her decision should be?

Case 9-2
STAFF WORK
ACCOMPLISHED

Karl Tremont was a new supervisor in the word processing center. He had had little experience in supervision and had been chosen because of his interest in the machine capabilities of the equipment and for his facility in English grammar. Things were not going well, and he decided to go to his superior who was director of administrative services, Morton Pope, lay his problems on the table, and ask for help.

When Mr. Pope asked what the difficulty was, he replied, "Just about everything. The word processors need more training in English mechanics. Only one of them has reached my production goals. Three of the principals don't like to dictate to a telephone and are continuing to use their secretaries for dictation although these employees have been given new titles as administrative secretaries. I am having a dreadful time, too, in getting service from the manufacturers of our equipment. I guess I am just not cut out for supervision. I thought maybe you would work out my problems and tell me what to do."

Mr. Pope, who believed that developing the people under his supervision was one of his most important functions, said, "You know, Karl, I am an old Army man. One of the first things we learned was the concept of 'staff work accomplished.' Now all of the problems you have reported are really your problems, you know. In the Army we were required to bring along with every problem one or two solutions and an analysis of the consequences of each solution. We would present the problem and then discuss these possible solutions with our superior officer. It worked out pretty well for the Army, and I have found that it works well for me here. Suppose you go back to your office and think through your situation. Come back on Monday with staff work accomplished, and maybe I can help you. Anyway I'll be glad to try."

Assuming Karl's role, work out a plan for the next visit to Mr. Pope.

Case 9-3 UPWARD MOBILITY

Greta Kruger was ambitious to advance to the management level. She took a secretarial position with the idea of using it as a stepping stone and let it be known among her co-workers that she intended to get ahead.

She attended all in-company training courses. She enrolled in college courses in business administration provided at company expense. She read the management magazines and participated in professional meetings and workshops. She used her lunch hour to study and preferred to sit alone while she ate. She volunteered for extra work, often assigning it to an assistant and presenting it for approval as her own. She suggested a new system for distributing supplies that was superior to the current method, but the office manager rejected the idea. She was always available to her employer, even if she had to work overtime to complete the work. Naturally, he thought highly of her.

At the end of eight months she applied to the Personnel Department for a position there that represented a promotion. When she did not receive the job, she asked a college friend who worked in the same company, Angela Abovoci, for suggestions.

What do you think Angela told her? What factors are most important in achieving a job objective?

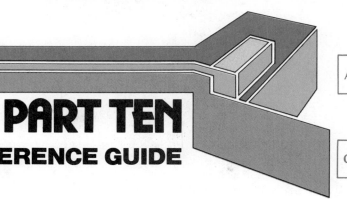

PART TEN
REFERENCE GUIDE

How to Use the Guide

This Reference Guide is divided into nine main divisions. The headings for these divisions are boxed in heavy rules at the right. In direct alignment behind each heading is the visible rule on the part that starts the material of the heading. These pages will start *main divisions*. The main divisions are arranged alphabetically, as are the items within them. (The Communications and Postal Guides, however, are presented last — out of alphabetical order.)

In the items in this Guide, the styles of type have special meanings. Headings of the main divisions always appear in color in all capital letters. Headings for the next order are in **boldface letters**. Items under these secondary headings are in ***boldface italics***.

Example: You want to know whether or not to set off by commas the word *too*.

Step 1. Turn to PUNCTUATION (using the visible rule aligned with the boxed heading for PUNCTUATION at the right).

Step 2. Find the subdivision **Comma**, listed alphabetically under PUNCTUATION.

Step 3. Under **Comma**, find *too*, listed alphabetically under **Comma**.

Cross-references within the Guide will use the type styles as shown above. For instance, in the main division ABBREVIATIONS, you will find the listing shown below.

Degrees — See CAPITALIZATION; **Degrees**.

Because CAPITALIZATION appears in all capitals, you know it is one of the main divisions. Because **Degrees** appears in boldface type, you know that you will find the item listed alphabetically under CAPITALIZATION.

INTRODUCTION

The English language in all its forms (usage, vocabulary, punctuation) is ever changing. Its study is fascinating and challenging. No part of this book will be of more value to a secretary than the English-usage section of this Reference Guide.

Handbooks and dictionaries *report* usage at different levels but are not arbitrary authorities. Nor does this Guide presume to be authoritative. It, too, *reports* current acceptable business usages.

When more than one usage is reported in this Guide, it is because there is *divided* usage — dictionaries and handbooks do not agree. A secretary, therefore, cannot assume that one reference book stands alone as supreme authority on usage. But once a selection of form has been made, that form should be used consistently.

Formal English usage is followed in reports, dignified letters, papers for publication, and the like. Colloquial English usage often occurs in friendly business letters. A word marked *colloquial* in the dictionary means that it occurs in spoken English, in conversation at an educated level. Because most spoken English is informal, colloquial usage suggests the informal level. In this guide, colloquial expressions are labeled *informal*.

Standard business English may be used in business correspondence because the nature of business writing is distinctly different from that of other writing. Standard business English is direct and to the point; its economy of words saves time for the writer and for the reader. Frequently, the purpose of a business letter is to obtain a favorable result or to create a friendly reaction. These purposes can often be realized by a conversational, spoken-English tone. Thus colloquial English can be appropriate to and desirable in business writing.

Business English often gives a new meaning to an old word — or uses it as an unusual part of speech, such as *to power your engine*. Business people often coin needed words (like *finalize* and *know-how*, both of which have been accepted into the language — by business writers and by the publishers of *Webster's Third New International Dictionary*). When confronted with a coined word or expression, the secretary must decide whether to call attention to it by quoting or underlining it. If a word as used appears in the dictionary, neither quotation marks nor italics are needed.

Punctuation practices are always changing. The trend is toward less punctuation at the informal level although full, correct punctuation is still required at the formal level. Keep in mind that the purpose of punctuation is to help make your meaning clear to your reader. Use the punctuation that will fulfill this purpose.

GENERAL RULE: In formal typewritten text, spell out all words that would be conspicuous if abbreviated. Use abbreviations in informal writing and in tables, footnotes, records, billing, and technical writing. In formal writing, use periods after any abbreviations although periods are often omitted in informal writing.

Ampersand

Use *and* unless you know that the company in question prefers the ampersand.

Building and Loan Association
American Telephone and Telegraph Company
Norfolk & Western Railway

At the beginning of a sentence

Even in informal writing, spell out or move from the beginning of the sentence.

Procter & Gamble officials announced today that . . .
The announcement by P & G officials that . . .

Capitalization of

Follow the style of the unabbreviated form of the word.

versus, vs.   Fahrenheit, F.
ante meridiem, a.m.   Associated Press, AP

Coined verb forms

Add an apostrophe and *s, d,* or *ing.*

She c.o.d.'s everything.
We are o.k.'ing the payment.
The committee n.g.'d the proposal.

Degrees — See CAPITALIZATION; **Degrees.**

Dimensions and weights

a. Spell out in formal writing; use abbreviated designations in informal; do not use periods at end of abbreviations; use symbols in technical writing and business forms only.

Formal: An area six miles by two miles . . .
Informal: Please refer to item No. 3 . . .
Technical: Test #27 showed 12° less variation . . .
Business forms:
  62 #474, 8' × 12"   8 cu ft   1 qt   6 qts

See Weights and Measures with Metric Equivalents for abbreviations.

b. In the metric system, do not use periods at the end of abbreviations. Singular and plural forms are alike.

1 m   1 meter
10 m²   10 square meters

Esq.

This title of courtesy, always in abbreviated form, follows a man's name. No other title or college degree is used with it.

Alan R. Lane, Esq.
  not:
Mr. Alan R. Lane, Esq.
Alan R. Lane, Esq., Ph.D.

Geographic names

In formal text, do not abbreviate County, Fort, Mount, Point, and Port.

He was born in Mount Pleasant, Michigan.
  but:
Mr. Herbert Hazelton
622 Grand Avenue
Mt. Pleasant, MI 48858

Government agencies, labor organizations

Government agencies, international organizations, and labor groups are often abbreviated with neither spaces nor periods.

WHO   World Health Organization
ICC   Interstate Commerce Commission
AFL-CIO   American Federation of Labor-
          Congress of Industrial Organizations

Honorable

Do not abbreviate when preceded by *the.* See USAGE; **Honorable.**

the Honorable A. R. Lane

Jr., Sr.

These designations may be used with titles and academic degrees with or without comma.

Mr. Alan R. Lane, Sr., President
Prof. Alan R. Lane, Jr.
Alan R. Lane Jr., M.D.

See PUNCTUATION; **Comma;** *Jr., Sr.* and USAGE; **Jr., Sr.**

Months

Do not abbreviate names of months or days of the week except in tabulations, citations, references, and the like.

Names of companies

Follow the style of the company in the use of abbreviations and symbols.

Wm Taylor & Sons   Saks Fifth Avenue

Names of persons (initials, contractions)

a. Follow the style in which the persons sign their names. Space after initials.

Lee R. Penske   R. Floyd King   E. A. Fox

b. With more than two initials, internal spacing may be omitted.

A.R.J. Simms   *or:*   A. R. J. Simms

c. When a letter is not actually an initial, follow the style used by the person.

J Marshall Hanna   Harry R Turner

d. Do not use a period with contractions of names. (Use contractions only when necessary to meet space requirements in tabulations, forms, etc.)

Rob't Riemenschneider   Dan'l Falkenhausen

Organizations

Abbreviations made up of single initials, all capitals, usually require no periods and no internal space.

AFL-CIO, PTA, YWCA, IBM, AMA, ABC

Exceptions: Retain the periods in abbreviations of geographic names, and academic degrees.

U.S.A., U.K., U.S.S.R., A.B., M.S., M.A.

Periods with abbreviations

Follow with a period each part of an abbreviation that represents a word unless common usage is without periods.

c.o.d.	*not:*	cod
i.e.		ie

but:

AFL-CIO, cc, FM, IOU, PBX, UFO, VHF, UHF

See ABBREVIATIONS; **Time (b)**.

Period with other punctuation

a. A period ending an abbreviation precedes other punctuation.

If you call at 10:15 a.m., we . . . .

b. Use only one period when an abbreviation ends a sentence unless the abbreviation is enclosed in parentheses.

Please call at 10:15 a.m.
Set the thermostat at 77°F.(25°C.).

Plurals of abbreviations

a. For most, add *s*.

gals, yds, Drs., bbls

b. For abbreviations in all caps, add *s*.

C.P.S.s   CPSs   R.N.s   RNs

c. For abbreviations consisting of single lowercase letters, add *'s*.

c.o.d.'s   btu's   cc's

Possessives of abbreviations

To form singular possessive, add *'s*; to form plural possessive, add *s'*.

CPS's salary   CPSs' salaries

Publications, parts of

Spell out in typewritten text. Abbreviate in references and footnotes. Follow the capitalization of the spelled-out form or the one used by the organization.

Vol. II: Vols. II and V   p. 17; pp. 17–26
Ch. 3; Chs. 3 to 6   Art. VII; Arts. I–VI

Reverend

Do not abbreviate when preceded by *the*.

Rev. A. B. Lane   the Reverend Mr. Lane

II, 2d, or 2nd

When known, the form that the person uses should be followed.

Mr. A. B. Lane, II   Mr. A. B. Lane, 2d
Prof. B. F. Lane, II   Prof. B. F. Lane II

See PUNCTUATION; **Comma; *Jr., Sr., II, III***

Spacing within abbreviations.

See ABBREVIATIONS; **Organizations**.

States and territories

a. Do not abbreviate in typewritten text.

b. Abbreviate in tabulations, footnotes, business forms, and the like.

c. In letter addresses, use the special 2-letter abbreviations with the zip code.

d. *United States* may be abbreviated when used with names of federal agencies, programs, or policies. Spell out when used as a noun.

Street addresses

a. Do not abbreviate *Street, Building, Road, etc.* in typewritten text. Abbreviate in inside and envelope addresses only to achieve balanced line lengths.

b. Do not abbreviate one-word compass designations that apply to the street name.

210 North State Street   210 Plaza North
but:
210 First Street, N.W.

Time

a. Abbreviate *a.m.* and *p.m.* in expressions of time, preferably in lowercase letters.

b. Abbreviate standard time zones in all caps without periods or spaces.

EST, EDST, CST, MST, PDST, GMT

c. A.D. precedes the year; B.C. follows the year.

A.D. 1973   79 B.C.

See NUMBERS; **Time of day**.

Titles

a. Abbreviate courtesy titles.

Mr., Mrs., Ms., M., MM., Mme., Mmes., Mlle., Messrs.

b. In textual matter or addresses, do not abbreviate business titles (*president, general manager, etc.*) if a courtesy title is also used. Trend is to omit title if it creates an address of more than four lines.

Mr. Howard Hansen, President
Uniflex Corporation
788 East 17th South
Salt Lake City, UT 84104

c. Designating titles in addresses may be abbreviated.

Prof. A. B. Lane   Dr. M. P. Wolf

CAPITALIZATION—Page 691

GENERAL RULE: When you can find no rule or example to guide you, do not capitalize.

Abbreviations

Capitalize if the words they represent are proper nouns or adjectives.

Ages (eras)

a. Lowercase most period designations (including numerical ones) and latter-day designations.

romantic period, eighteenth century, nuclear age

b. Capitalize cultural periods recognized by archeologists and anthropologists and some historical periods by tradition or to avoid ambiguity.

Stone Age, Middle Ages, Renaissance

Astronomical bodies

Except *earth, moon,* and *sun,* capitalize the specific names of astronomical bodies.

Mars, the North Star, the Southern Cross, the Big Dipper

Bible

Capitalize the word *bible* and its derivatives when they refer to the Scriptures but not when they refer to a handbook.

a Biblical reference, the Bible
That dictionary is my bible.

Buildings

a. Capitalize names of office buildings.

the Stowe Building, Carew Tower

b. Capitalize names of public buildings only when used as a proper name.

Go to the Kent County Courthouse.
I'll be at the courthouse until two o'clock.

Compound words

See WORDS; COMPOUND.

Congress

Capitalize when the word or its derivatives are used as proper names.

the Congress of the United States, the Senate, the House, the Eighty-Ninth Congress, the second session of Congress

Countries, regions and compass points

a. Capitalize names of countries, continents, and their derivatives.

the United Kingdom, the Continent, the continent of North America, European travel, French cuisine

b. Capitalize regions used as proper nouns or adjectives.

He lives in the West on the north bank of a river.
He flew to the Coast on business.
the people of the Far East (the Near East)

c. Do not capitalize points of the compass when they merely indicate direction.

They live east of Grand Rapids.
They live in East Grand Rapids.

Courses of study

Capitalize a specific course name but not the names of fields of knowledge unless they are proper nouns.

He passed Algebra III.
A secretary must excel in spelling.
She majored in French.

Degrees

a. Capitalize abbreviations of degrees. Capitalize a spelled-out degree that immediately follows a name; otherwise do not capitalize.

Professor J. W. Knapp, Ph.D., will . . .
Dean John W. Knapp, Doctor of Philosophy, . . .
The degree of doctor of education is . . . .

b. Type abbreviations of degrees with periods and without internal spaces. Set off with commas.

Alan J. Lane, B.S., will . . . .
Fran Santos, B.A. in Ed., will . . . .

c. In biographical references, list all degrees in chronological order — or give all earned degrees chronologically, then honorary degrees chronologically.

d. In letter addresses, the only degrees commonly used are M.D. and D.D.S., and then only if *Dr.* is omitted.

Michael Gavlak, M.D.   *not:*
Dr. Michael Gavlack   Dr. Michael Gavlak, M.D.
Dr. Ray Stevens

e. In textual matter, for a degree that follows a name, use only the highest degree in each field. With it, before the name, you may use any title except *Mr.* (and *Dr.*, if one of the degrees is a doctorate).

Professor Grace Weber, Ph.D., is . . . .
Dean Russell Olderman, M.B.A., is . . . .
Mrs. Margaret Linderman, B.S.'73, is . . . .
              not:
Mr. A. J. Black, Ph. D., is . . . .

Epithets

Capitalize when used with a proper name or as a proper name.

They called him Golden Rule Smith.
He gave all the difficult jobs to Mr. Nice.
Cincinnati's Big Red Machine won the World Series in 1976.

Federal, government, national, state, etc.

a. Capitalize these words when they are part of a proper name. Otherwise, follow your own preference. The style trend is toward noncapitalization.

the Federal Reserve Bank, a federal tax, a Federal tax, the state capital, the State Capitol

b. Capitalize *administration* and *government* when they are applied to a particular government in power.

the Administration seeks, the Carter Government

First words

a. Of direct quotations, capitalize as follows:

He said, "That's fine."
"That's fine," he said, "for you."
"That's true," he said. "You're right."
He explained: There is a reason . . . .

b. Of clause-type questions, do not capitalize first words and leave only one typewriter space.

What will happen if you are not ready? if you fail?

c. Of phrase-type questions, use same style as for clause-type.

How is the sailing? the swimming? the fishing?

d. Of internal independent clauses or phrases, capitalize as follows:

The problem is, How can we do it?
The fact is — Too little, too late!

e. Of lines of poetry, capitalize first word of each line.

I ask of thee, beloved Night —
Swift to thine approaching flight,
Come soon, soon!
                                    — Shelley

f. Of sentences, always capitalize.

g. Of thoughts, capitalize as follows:

I thought: He knows now.

Freshman, sophomore, junior, senior

Capitalize only when used as a proper name.

As a senior you will . . . .   The Junior Class plans . . .

Governmental agencies

a. Capitalize names of specific bureaus, departments, commissions, etc., and the shortened form of a specific name.

the Civil Service Commission   the Commission
the Internal Revenue Service   the Service

b. Do not capitalize when used generally.

He asked me which bureau handled such matters, and I replied that the Bureau of Labor Statistics would help him.

Holidays, holy days

Capitalize all holidays and holy days.

Christmas, Easter, New Year's Day, Mother's Day, Passover, Yom Kippur, Fourth of July, Labor Day

Hyphenated words

a. Capitalize any part that is a proper noun or adjective.

the North-South game, mid-August, pro-American

b. Handbooks do not agree on the capitalization of hyphenated words in headings. Use one style consistently.

The Internal-Combustion Engine
or:
The Internal-combustion Engine

Locations with identifying numbers

Capitalize unless the designation *No.* is used.

Room 10, Column 3, Figure 72, Table 4

Exceptions: Do not capitalize *page, verse,* or *line.*

See page 18, verse 6, line 3.

See NUMBERS; **Room numbers, Serial and policy numbers.**

Measurements

Do not capitalize units of measurement.

6 ft   3 qts   4 lbs   5 tons

Military units

Capitalize.

Lieutenant Colonel Karen Benoit heads the Twenty-first Division, Corps of Engineers.

Months, names of

Always capitalize.

Nation

Capitalize *nation* only when used as a synonym for the United States (or a specific country).

This great Nation will long endure.

Organizations and clubs, names of

a. Capitalize the proper name of an association, club, order, etc.

the National Association of . . .
the University Club of Akron
the Urban League

b. Capitalize words like *club, organization,* etc., only when used as a proper name.

Mr. Vincent will meet you at the Club for lunch.
Children enjoy forming clubs and holding meetings.
They belong to a bowling league.

Persons, names of

Follow the style, if known, used by the person.

Anne Obrien, Mr. de Rossett, Mr. DeGraff

Political groups

Capitalize as follows:

> the Democratic Party, a Democrat, the Republican Party, a Republican, the Communist Party, a Communist, the Labor Party, a Laborite

> *but:*

> a republican form of government, a democracy, a communistic government

Public Places

Capitalize when essential elements of specific name.

> Golden Gate Bridge, Holland Tunnel

Races and peoples

Always capitalize.

> Caucasian(s), Negro(es), Polynesian, Micronesian, Asian

Relatives

Capitalize when used as a designation with a name or alone as a proper noun.

> Have you seen Uncle John, Mother?
> My father enjoys playing golf, but my uncle does not.
> Thank you Dad for the delicious candy.

Religious faiths and denominations, sacred books, religious figures

a. Capitalize all such words and their derivatives.

> Roman Catholic(s), Jewish, Protestantism, the Bible, the Scriptures, Allah, the Old Testament, the Koran, the Blessed Virgin, Buddhism, Methodists

b. Handbooks vary on capitalizing pronouns referring to the Deity. Usually they are not capitalized when the noun form precedes them in a sentence.

> God commanded his people.
> We know He loves His children.

River, lake, ocean, mountain

Capitalize when part of a proper name (but not when used with more than one name).

> the Atlantic Ocean, Lake Cumberland, the Smoky Mountains, the Missouri River

> *but:*

> the Atlantic and Pacific oceans, the Ohio, Mississippi, and Missouri rivers; Spring, Torch, Houghton, and Higgins lakes

> The Great Lakes are sometimes called "inland seas."

Roads, routes, streets, and thoroughfares

Capitalize when part of a proper name.

> State Route 17, Lincoln Tunnel, the Ohio Turnpike, Interstate 75, the Oakland Ferry, Madison Road, Fifth Avenue, Brockdorf Drive, Brooklyn Bridge

> *but:*

> The streets and highways were clogged with traffic.

Schools

Capitalize *school, high school, college,* or *university* only when part of a proper name.

> Mrs. Isabelle Knapp, who taught at South High School, was an excellent English teacher.

> From among many fine universities, he chose to attend the University of North Carolina.

Seasons, names of

Do not capitalize.

> We had a rainy spring but a dry summer.

Ships, names of

Capitalize and underline or merely capitalize.

> Wayne and Edith sailed on the France.
> We cruised the Caribbean on the Mermoz.

Shortened names

Capitalize well-known shortened forms of proper names.

> the Street [Wall], the Continent [of Europe], the District [of Columbia], the Gulf [of Mexico], the Coast [Pacific]

State, county, city, district, ward, etc.

a. Capitalize when part of a proper name unless they *precede* the proper name.

> New York State, the state of New York, the Second Ward, the County Clerk of Courts, Boone County, Fountain Square

b. Capitalize or not when they stand alone or are used as adjectives.

> File your state (State) tax return.
> There was a county (County) election.

The as part of a title

a. In textual matter, capitalize *the* if it is actually the first word of the title but not if it occurs internally in the title.

A statement in The New York Times . . . .
We read An Economic History of the United States.

b. The trend in informal writing is to lowercase an initial *the* of titles.

Titles of books, magazines, newspapers

See PUNCTUATION; **Special Element, Titles of Published Matter.**

Titles of persons

a. When used alone, capitalize *president* and *vice-president* and other high federal government officials.

the President's speech, the Vice-President's speech, the President of Mexico, the Secretary of State

b. Capitalize titles that are used as designations preceding a name. (Some handbooks also capitalize any title used instead of the person's name.)

Please read President Lane's letter.
A letter from Mr. A. B. Lane, president of . . . .
A directive from the president (President) states . . . .

c. Although most authorities hyphenate *vice-president*, common usage tends to omit the hyphen in a title designation before a proper name.

Vice President Albert Andrews reports that . . . .

d. Do not capitalize the following titles when they are used alone in a general way.

priest, rabbi, pastor, cantor, superintendent, minister, rector, judge, consul, professor

Trademarked names

Capitalize unless the trademark uses lowercase letters as a distinctive style or the word has become a generic term.

Vaseline, Coca-Cola, Dacron, Thermo-Fax, Scotch tape, Pyrex, Xerox, Crisco, mimeograph, cellophane

Weeks of special observance

Always capitalize.

There was widespread observance of Holy Week.

Whereas; Resolved

Use one of these styles:

WHEREAS, The	Resolved That . . . .
WHEREAS the	RESOLVED, That . . . .
WHEREAS, THE	Resolved, That . . . .

NUMBERS—Page 695

GENERAL RULE: In typewritten text, spell out all numbers under a certain specified one; usage, however, varies as to what this number should be. Follow the rule of your office or select one of those below. Make it your General Rule to be followed consistently.

SPELL OUT:

- Numbers under 10 (all agree on this)
- Numbers under 11 or 13
- Numbers under 100 that do not require hyphens
- Numbers under 101
- All numbers under 100 plus those over 100 that can be written in three words or less (as *one hundred nine, twelve hundred eighteen*)

Addresses

a. House numbers: Spell out the number *1*. (Some handbooks spell out numbers *1* through *10*.) Otherwise use figures.

One Fifth Avenue
Ten Park Terrace *or* 10 Park Terrace
182 Dearborn Street

b. Street numbers: Follow your general rule in spelling out small-numbered streets. There is no consensus on the use of ordinals with street numbers and on the style of separating house and street numbers. In forming ordinals, *2d* and *3d* are favored in current usage over *2nd* and *3rd*; or the cardinal number may be used. To separate the house and street number, use a compass indication, if possible, or one of the styles shown below.

Preferred:
22 North 72d Street (72nd Street)

Without compass indication:
22 Seventy-second Street (Seventy-Second Street)
22–72d Street   22–72 Street
22, 72d Street   22, 72 Street

Ages (in years)

a. Spell out approximate ages.
Sally is nearly twenty-one.
Her brother is about twenty-five.

b. Use figures for exact ages (without commas).
He is 19 today.
I am 22 years 3 months 11 days old.

c. When an age precedes a noun, follow the General Rule.
A two-year-old child is full of energy.
The 20-year-old house was in good condition.

Approximations

a. Usually, approximate numbers are written out when they can be expressed in one or two words.
Approximately eighty people attended.

b. If other numbers will occur in the same paragraph that will be written in figures, be consistent and use figures for all.
Between 90 and 125 people attended.

At the beginning of a sentence

Spell out, even when other numbers will be written in figures.
Sixty-three students passed the test.
Fifty years ago, only 575 people lived in that village.

Centuries

Spell out, according to most handbooks.
The twentieth century has been a dramatic one.

Chapters, sections, pages, paragraphs, verses, lines, etc.

Use Arabic or Roman numerals according to the way the unit is numbered. (Note the style of capitalization.)

Chapter IX	Paragraph 2
Chapter 6	lines 3–11 (3 to 11)
Volume II	page iv, page 1002
Volume 3	verse 18
Part 7	Section 4(b)

Commas with figures

a. The comma may be omitted in four-digit numbers in typewritten text.
We sent 1475 units by motor express.

b. Use a comma between two adjacent numbers.
Regarding yesterday's test, out of 22, 18 passed.
In 1973, 493 students took that course.

Compound numeric adjectives

a. Hyphenate a number-noun combination preceding a noun. Follow the General Rule for expressing numbers.
a 768-page book, a 54-inch map, 40- and 50-yard bolts *or* forty- and fifty-yard bolts

b. Dimensions written before a noun are hyphened, using the singular form, but dimensions written after the noun are not hyphened and use the plural form.
a 40-foot line, a line 40 feet long

Congress, sessions of

Spell out and capitalize as follows:
Ninety-first Congress, first session
or:
Ninety-First Congress, first session

Consistency within a sentence

a. Treat alike all numbers in a group unless one begins a sentence.
Your three orders of 8, 25, and 110 dozen . . . .
Eight, 25, and 110 dozen were . . . .

b. Spell out only one of two consecutive small numbers (usually spelling out the shorter word).
We need two 8-foot boards.
We need 8 two-foot boards.

c. Spell out a small number that is different in context from a large number.

We sold 625 units in nine months.

Dates

a. Express and punctuate dates as shown in the examples. (A comma in parentheses shows that its use is optional.)

On May 22, 1979, we . . . .
On May 22 (,) we . . . .
On May twenty-second (,) we . . . .
On the 22d we . . . .
On the twenty-second we . . . .
On the 22d of May (,) we . . . .
On the 22d of May, 1979, we . . . .

b. Express two or more consecutive dates as follows:

On May 22, 23, or 26 we . . . .
In May, June, and July 1979 we . . . .
In May, June, and July of 1979 we . . . .
From May 4 to May 11 the . . . .
In our letters of May 4 and 7, we . . . .

c. In legal documents dates are often spelled out as follows:

On this tenth day of May in the year of our Lord one thousand nine hundred and seventy-nine . . .
. . . this tenth day of May, A.D. 1979 . . . .

See NUMBERS; **Years.**

Decades

Express in numbers or spell out as follows:

the 1970s, the 1970's, the seventies, the mid-seventies, the '70s, the 70's

Decimals

a. Express in figures. With numbers less than *1*, use a cipher before the period except when the decimal begins with a cipher. In columns of numbers that include decimals, align the numbers at the decimal point.

22.33
0.56
.045

b. Do not use commas after a decimal point.

Degrees of temperature or angles

Express in figures.

8 degrees below zero, 4° above zero, a 45-degree angle, an angle of 45 degrees

Distances

Express in figures except for fractions.

an 825-mile flight
a distance of 825 miles
about a mile and one half away
a three-quarter-mile stretch of highway

Dividing numbers at end of line

Figures should never be divided at the end of a line. Avoid dividing spelled-out numbers except for hyphened numbers, which may be divided at the hyphen.

Enumerations

See PUNCTUATION; **Special Element, Enumerations.**

Fractions

a. As a noun or adjective, a fraction takes the singular or plural form according to the noun or pronoun that follows it.

Half the work is checked.
Half the tests are checked.
Half of it is checked *or* half of them are checked.

Exception: In a mixed fraction of one, the *noun* following is plural and the *verb* is singular.

Probably one and one half tons is enough.

b. Spell out fractions of less than one, but hyphenate only when used as an adjective; do not hyphenate if either element is already hyphenated.

a one-third share
one third of the shares
a seven twenty-fifths share

c. In typing fractions in multiple-copy work, *make* the fractions for greater legibility 1/2 (not ½). Key fractions may be illegible on the carbon copies. (In a writing, use all made or all key fractions.)

1/2 and 3/4 (not ½ and 3/4)

d. In typing fractions in figures, do not use commas in four-digit numbers.

1/1000   1279/10000

e. In typing mixed fractions, space before a made fraction but not before a key fraction.

46 1/4, $46\frac{1}{4}$

Hyphenated numbers

Hyphenate all spelled-out compound numbers between twenty-one and ninety-nine.

Market quotations

Express in figures.

He bought 4s at 102 3/8.

Measurements

Express in figures except for fractions under *1* and sometimes small whole numbers that would usually be spelled out. Note that an exact measurement, like an exact age, is written without commas.

8 ft 10 in by 12 ft 6 in
36 miles on two gallons of gas
$8\frac{1}{2}$″ by 11″ paper *or* $8\frac{1}{2}$ - by 11-inch paper
three-fourths bushel of tomatoes

Millions and billions

Million and *billion*, spelled out, may take the place of the ciphers in a number.

7.9 million, $25 million, 6 billion

Money

a. For amounts in *even dollars*, express in figures and omit ciphers for cents. Spell out a small amount if preferred — or if it ends a sentence.

a cost of $600, a saving of $125
It cost two dollars. It cost $22.

b. For amounts in *dollars and cents*, always express in figures.

Our quotation is $1.13 each.

c. For amounts in *cents*, spell out *cent* or *cents*. Use figures or spell out the number.

a 2-cent tax, 6 cents, six cents, 88 cents,
a one-half-cent increase, a $\frac{1}{2}$-cent increase, an increase of one-half cent

d. Amounts in *legal documents* are usually spelled out and followed with the amount in figures in parentheses. Words are usually capitalized.

price of Two Hundred Dollars ($200)
price of Two Hundred (200) Dollars

Percent

Dictionaries vary on the usage of figures, the % symbol, and the spelling of *percent*.

6 percent, six percent, 6 per cent, six per cent, 6%

Periods of time

a. Express exact periods of time (those that include year, month, and days) in figures without commas.

They paid interest for 1 year 6 months and 12 days.

b. In informal writing, periods of time may be expressed in possessive form. In formal writing, reword to avoid the possessive form.

After six weeks' intensive research, we found . . . .
After intensive study for a period of six weeks, we found . . . .

Plurals of numbers

a. Form plurals of numbers by adding either *s* or *'s*.

1900s *or* 1900's
20s and 30s *or* 20's and 30's

b. Form plurals of spelled out numbers in the usual manner, as *tens*.

Political subdivisions

Spell out and capitalize, as *the Fourth Ward*.

Possessives of numbers

Form singular possessive by adding *'s*; form plural possessive by adding apostrophe to plural form. Except for informal writing, reword to avoid the possessive form for inanimate objects.

a 60-day option *or* 60 days' option
$25's worth, ten cents' worth

Roman numerals

a. Roman numerals are numbers expressed in letters, usually uppercase.

b. Arabic numbers and their equivalents in Roman numerals are shown below. Note that the Roman numerals are aligned at the right.

1	I	4	IV	10	X	500	D
2	II	5	V	50	L	1,000	M
3	III			100	C		

c. Repeating a letter repeats its value. (This is done up to three times.) Placing a letter of lesser value before another subtracts its value; this is done rather than repeating a letter four times.

20 = XX, 30 = XXX, 40 = XL, CM = 900

d. Placing a letter of lesser value after one of greater value adds the values.

13 = XIII, 14 = XIV, 16 = XVI

e. A dash over a number multiplies it by 1,000.

5,000 = $\overline{V}$, 1,000,000 = $\overline{M}$

Room numbers

a. Always express in figures. Do not use commas in room numbers of 1000 and over.

The class met in Room 8.

b. The designations *room* and *suite* are omitted when the name of the building immediately follows.

1948 Carew Tower, 2006 John Hancock Building

See CAPITALIZATION; **Locations**.

Round numbers

In typing large round numbers, use figures, spell out in the fewest possible words, or combine words and figures.

1500 *or* 1,500   62,000 *or* sixty-two thousand
520,000,000 *or* five-hundred-twenty million *or* 520 million

Serial and policy numbers

Express in figures. Copy internal spacing if known. Do not use commas, but you may use internal spacing to aid the reader.

No. 3718960, Policy 3 718 960, #3 71 89 60

Sequential numbers

The hyphen may be used to indicate the omission of the word *through*.

on pages 37–65   during August 21–26

Time of day

a. Express *even* hours as follows:

11 a.m., 11 o'clock, eleven o'clock

b. Express other times as follows:

a quarter to ten, (*of* ten), 1:20 p.m.

c. Write 24-hour-clock time as follows:

0045 (12:45 a.m.), 0715 (7:15 a.m.), 1530 (3:30 p.m.)

Years

Express as follows:

A.D. 1973, 400 B.C., class of '75, mid-1974

PLURALS—Page 699
POSSESSIVES—Page 700

PLURALS

GENERAL RULE: Dictionaries give irregularly formed plurals of words. Given a choice between a foreign and an English plural, use the English.

Exception: Use the plural that is most familiar for the subject matter.* For instance, people in the advertising field use *media* in referring to modes of advertising. In the following list, the *preferred* usages (according to *Webster's Third New International Dictionary*) are shown in italics.

English Plural	Foreign Plural
appendixes	appendices
criterions	*criteria*
*curriculums	curricula
focuses	foci
gymnasiums	gymnasia
indexes	indices
maximums	*maxima*
mediums	*media
memorandums	memoranda
minimums	*minima*
radiuses	*radii*
referendums	referenda
spectrums	*spectra*
tempos	*tempi*
ultimatums	ultimata

Abbreviations, plurals of

See also ABBREVIATIONS; **Plurals and compound words and phrases.**

a. Pluralize the main word.

> attorneys general, major generals, judge advocates, notaries public, trade unions, assistant postmasters general

b. Pluralize the main word in a compound that ends in a prepositional phrase.

> chambers of commerce, commanders in chief, attorneys at law, powers of attorney, points of view, bills of lading

c. When a preposition is hyphened to a noun, pluralize the noun.

> lookers-on, passers-by, hangers-on, runners-up, listeners-in, goings-on

d. When *neither word is a noun*, pluralize the last word.

> also-rans, come-ons, follow-ups, go-betweens, higher-ups, trade-ins

Cupful, handful, etc.

Add *s*, as *cupfuls.*

Letters used alone

a. With capital letters, add *'s* or *s.*

> B's *or* Bs

b. With lowercase letters, add *'s.*

> a's, b's, c's

Numbers, plurals of

See NUMBERS; **Compound numeric adjectives (b)** and **Fractions (b)**, and **Plurals of numbers**.

Proper names

a. Add *es* to names ending in sibilants.

> the Jameses, the Morrises, the Foxes, the Perezes, the Lorches, the Marshes

b. To other proper names (even those ending in *y* or in a vowel), add *s.*

> the Americas, Eskimos, the Alvarados, the Johnsons, the Bachs, the Lillys, the Montessoris, the Murrays, the Randolphs

Word used as a word

Add *'s* or form plural regularly.

> 10 yes's and 3 no's *or:* 10 Yeses and 3 Noes

POSSESSIVES

GENERAL RULE: If a possessive form looks or sounds displeasing, reword the sentence to avoid it. For instance, *the climate of Kansas City, Kansas*, is more pleasing than is *Kansas City, Kansas' climate.*

Ordinarily, possession is not shown for inanimate things. Avoid: *a contract's terms, a pen's top.* Acceptable in business writing: *the company's, the corporation's.*

Abbreviations

See ABBREVIATIONS; **Possessives**.

Alternative possession

Each noun should be possessive.

> Is it a child's or an adult's handwriting?
> Did he go to the mayor's or the commissioner's office?

See POSSESSIVES; **Joint possession**.

Appositives

To indicate possession when an appositive is used, add the possessive ending to the appositive or reword the sentence.

> It is Mr. Lane, our manager's, idea.
> It is our manager, Mr. Lane's, idea.
> It is the idea of Mr. Lane, our manager.

Compound words

Add the possessive ending (usually *'s* for both singular and plural) to the last word.

> He read his son-in-law's letter.
> My sons-in-law's gifts arrived today.
> A passer-by's hat blew into the street.
> Three passers-by's heads turned in unison when the cars collided.

Else phrases

Add *'s.*

> I saw no one else's grade.
> Matthew took someone else's coat inadvertently.

Gerunds

Gerunds take the possessive form.

> Allen's thinking was confused.
> The girls' singing was well received.

See USAGE; **Gerund (b)**.

Joint possession

To indicate joint possession, add the possessive ending to the last of two or more nouns (unless a lack of clarity would result).

Bob and Rita's dinner party was a success.
but:
They saw Jim's and Patty's daughter at the pool.
not: They saw Jim and Patty's daughter at the pool.

Money's Worth

Use possessive form with this idiom, as *five dollars' worth, $20's worth*.

Multiple and compound proper names

a. In proper names of several words, add the possessive ending to the last word according to POSSESSIVES; **Sibilant sounds,** or reword to avoid the possessive form.

Haskins & Sells's report *or* the report from Haskins & Sells
the Scott Company's letter
John, Jr.'s graduation
the Senator from Michigan's speech

b. In proper names some words are considered *descriptive* rather than possessive. Follow official style, if known.

Artists Supplies, Inc.
Citizens National Bank

Numbers, possessive forms for

Form the singular possessive by adding *'s*. Form the plural possessive by adding the apostrophe to the plural form or by rewording to avoid the possessive form.

$12's worth, four days' work, 30 days' option, a 30-day option

See NUMBERS; **Possessives of numbers.**

Plurals of possessives

Form the plural of a word first, then add the possessive ending.

The children's toys were lost.
The women's decision was announced.

Separate possession

See POSSESSIVES; **Alternative possession.**

Sibilant sounds

a. For one-syllable words and those whose last syllable is accented, add *'s*.

Mr. Jones's car, Mrs. Mendez's report

b. For two-syllable words (singular or plural) whose last syllable is not accented, add only the apostrophe.

Mr. Roberts' office, the Joneses' house

c. For words not ending in sibilant sounds, add *'s*.

the senator's vote, the people's choice

Time phrases

Form possessives regularly or convert to adjective phrases.

They returned from a three weeks' trip.
They returned from a three-week trip.

See NUMBERS; **Time of day** and **Years.**

PUNCTUATION—Page 701

Punctuation elements are listed separately as shown, headed in **boldface** type. Items under these headings are listed alphabetically in ***boldface italics***.

Punctuation Marks

• Apostrophe

a. Use an apostrophe to indicate possession. See PLURALS AND POSSESSIVES (POSSESSIVES) and ABBREVIATIONS ; **Plurals**.

b. Use an apostrophe to form the plural of abbreviations, letters, and figures.

See PLURALS AND POSSESSIVES (PLURALS) and ABBREVIATIONS ; **Plurals** and NUMBERS ; **Plurals**.

c. Use an apostrophe to indicate omitted letters. Do not use a period after a contraction.

> ne'er   Rob't *not:* Rob't. (with a period)

• Brackets

Type brackets using the diagonal and underline key [thus].

Inner parentheses

Use brackets for a set of inner parentheses.

> It is in her textbook (Secretarial Reports [2d edition only], page 7).

Quoted matter

a. *Copied errors (sic):* Use brackets to enclose the Latin word *sic*, meaning *thus*, to indicate that an error has been copied exactly.

> "The Rosevelts [sic] came to America . . . ."

b. *Corrections:* Use brackets to enclose a correction in quoted matter.

> "Mr. Willson [Wilson] stated that . . . ."

c. *Interpolations:* Use brackets to enclose an interpolation (matter inserted to clarify or question) in quoted matter.

> "They [his brothers] claim the property."

• Colon

Use a colon to indicate that some closely related matter follows.

After a clause

a. A colon after a clause indicates that a restatement or amplification follows:

> This much is certain: We must act within a week.

b. A complete sentence following a colon may or may not begin with a capital letter, depending on the emphasis that is desired.

> To succeed is not easy: it takes constant effort.

c. A quoted sentence after a colon always begins with a capital letter.

Before an enumeration

a. Use a colon before a run-in enumeration when the introductory words are an independent clause.

> They will use three criteria: (1) the importance of the topic, (2) the purpose of . . . .
>
> *but:*
>
> The three criteria are (1) the importance of the topic, (2) the purpose of . . . .

b. Use a colon before tabulated enumerations.

> The three criteria are:
> 1. The importance of the topic
> 2. The purpose of the study
> 3. The scope of the findings

c. With *namely, i.e., for instance*, and the like, substitute a semicolon. If the items are tabulated, use no introductory word.

> . . . a number of aptitudes; namely, loyalty, honesty, and vitality.
>
> Without *namely:*
>
> . . a number of items were missing:
> 1. An antique jug
> 2. A complete set of Shakespeare . . .

Before a quotation

Use a colon before a quotation of a sentence or more.

See PUNCTUATION ; **Special Element, Quoted Matter;** *Poetry,* and *Several paragraphs* and *Several sentences* .

Before a series or list

Introduce a series or list with a colon, a comma, or a dash.

See PUNCTUATION ; **Special Element, Series**.

With other punctuation

The colon follows a closing quotation mark.

● Comma

Because the use of the comma is often necessary to clarify an intended meaning, the rules for comma usage cannot be stated to cover all situations.

Custom and accepted style, however, do dictate certain usages for formal writing. Therefore, in formal writing, observe all the comma rules.

Appositives

An appositive adds information about the word that precedes it.

a. Set off nonrestrictive appositives with commas.

> Janice, the star of the play, became ill.

b. Do not set off one-word appositives.

> My partner Clark is out of town.

c. Do not set off an appositive that is quoted, underlined, or typed in all capitals.

> The phrase "by your leave" is . . . .
> The warning mail early appeared in . . . .
> The book TIME WILL TELL reveals that . . . .

d. Set off an emphatic appositive with a dash. See PUNCTUATION; **Dash;** *Appositives* .

Breaks in continuity

Use the comma to set off words that break the continuity of a sentence.

> It is the most unusual, if not the most difficult, problem that we face.
> It is best, we believe, to approach the . . . .

But

a. Use a comma before *but* when it joins two independent clauses that do not have internal commas.

> They planned to go skiing this weekend, but they changed their plans when the snow melted.

b. Use a comma before *but* when it joins short independent clauses only if they are contrasted in meaning.

> The idea is good, but it is costly.
> It was raining but we didn't stop playing.

c. Use a comma with *but* only when it is a conjunction.

> The idea is good but costly.
> The idea is not only good but also practical.

d. When *but* begins a sentence, no comma is used unless a parenthetical phrase follows it.

> This was true in the past. But in view of . . . .
> But, as you know, we agreed . . . .

Cities and states

In textual matter, set off the state name as you would an appositive.

> He was born in Salisbury, North Carolina, in 1956.

Clauses, independent

a. A compound sentence consists of two or more independent clauses that may or may not be joined by a conjunction. If one of the independent clauses contains a comma, use a semicolon between independent clauses.

> Your órder for chairs, tables, and lamps was received July 12; the items were shipped on the 15th.

b. The comma may be omitted between two brief independent clauses joined by a conjunction.

> We have tried the product and we are satisfied.

Clause, dependent (subordinate)

a. When a subordinate clause precedes an independent clause, set it off with a comma. Subordinate clauses begin with such words as *although, when, if, unless, because, who, that,* etc.

> If you have not heard by the 12th, please wire.

b. Set off *nonrestrictive* clauses with commas. Whether a clause is restrictive or nonrestrictive depends on *what you mean*. In the nonrestrictive clause below, the writer is considering only one book; and the book happens to be lying on the desk.

> She needed the book, which was lying on the desk.

The same sentence written *without* a comma indicates that among two or more books, the one on the desk was the one needed. Thus the clause is *restrictive*.

> She needed the book which was lying on the desk.

Clarity, commas for

Use a comma to avoid misreading or ambiguity.

> After all, the effort is secondary.
> Please call in, in a few days.
> Inside, the office was full of activity.

Commands within a sentence

Set off with commas a mild command within a sentence.

> In this case, remember, it is important to . . . .

Contrast or emphasis

a. Use commas to set off elements that are in emphatic contrast to the rest of the sentence. They usually begin with *not* or *but not*.

> It is to be used, not abused.

b. Commas set off single emphatic words.

> Many insist, rightfully, upon being heard.

Dates

See NUMBERS; **Dates.**

Degrees, academic

See CAPITALIZATION; **Degrees.**

Dimensions, weights, etc.

Do not separate the parts with commas.

> 10 feet 2 inches by 12 feet 6 inches

Direct address

Commas set off words in direct address.

> Thank you, Miss Canter, for helping.

Etc., et cetera

Commas set off *etc., and so forth, and so on,* or *and the like* in a sentence. (Abbreviate *et cetera* only in technical or informal writing.)

> Art, drama, music, and the like, are well supported.

Exclamations, mild

A mild exclamation within a sentence is set off with commas.

> The plane, thank goodness, arrived on time.

Gerunds

A gerund is a verb form used as a noun. Unless its noun usage requires a comma, do not set off a gerund. Do not confuse gerunds with participles (verbal phrases used as adjectives).

> *Gerund:* Observing their reactions was amusing.
> *Participle:* Observing their reactions, we were amused.
> *Gerund as an appositive:* His hobby, collecting stamps, is a rewarding one.

Inc., Ltd.

Set off with commas *Inc.* and *Ltd.*

> Perhaps Tressel, Inc., stocks it.

Infinitives

An infinitive is a verbal phrase that can be used as a noun or an adjective. Do not set off unless its noun usage requires commas.

> To act on your proposal, we must first . . . .
> To act on your proposal requires that we . . . .
> We intend to act on your proposal.

Introductory phrases

a. Long prepositional phrases or verbal phrases that begin a sentence are set off with commas.

> At the earliest possible date, will you please . . . .
> Beginning with Question 4, will you write . . . .
> *but:*
> At the moment we do not anticipate . . . .

b. An introductory phrase as the subject of the sentence is not set off by a comma.

> To go without permission is wrong.

Jr., Sr., II, III

a. Use a comma *before* any of these seniority designations if the person uses a comma in his signature. In a sentence, use a comma after the designation if it is preceded by one.

> Write Robert Lane, II, about it.
> Notify Ralph Miller Jr. to come to the meeting.

b. Do not follow the possessive with a comma.

> Call Richard Adams, Jr.'s home.

See ABBREVIATIONS; **Jr., Sr.**

Like

When *like* introduces a nonrestrictive phrase, set off the phrase with commas.

The future, like the weather, is unpredictable.
A spectator sport like football can be enjoyed either at the stadium or on television.

Myself, himself, yourself, etc.

Do not set off intensive pronouns with commas.

Mr. Lane himself approved it.

Numbers, commas with

See NUMBERS; **Commas, Decimals, Measurements, Periods of time, Round numbers, Serial and policy numbers.**

Of (before locations or affiliations)

A comma may precede *of*.

Mr. Robert Krause, of Haines & Hamby, wrote . . . .
Mayor Albert Flick, of East Burlap, announced . . . .
The mayor of the city announced that . . . .

Omitted words

A comma can replace omitted words that are clearly understood.

Mr. Lane left on Sunday; Mr. Baker, on Tuesday

Opinions, introductory expression of

A comma follows introductory words like *fortunately, naturally, obviously,* etc. A semicolon precedes them if they join two clauses.

It was raining; fortunately, I had my umbrella.

Parenthetical expressions

If a pause is required, set off with commas such parenthetical expressions as *however, therefore, nevertheless, accordingly, consequently, moreover,* etc. When these expressions join two clauses, a semicolon precedes them.

The trend, however, is to use fewer commas.
We should, nevertheless, know the rules.

Participial phrases

Use a comma after an introductory participial phrase.

After studying your proposal, we feel . . . .

Questions within sentences

See PUNCTUATION; **Question Mark**.

Restrictive and nonrestrictive elements

a. A *restrictive* element defines, limits, or identifies the noun that it modifies. It indicates that the noun is one specific, individual thing. Do not set off with commas.

The person *who composed that letter* needs to develop tact.

b. A *nonrestrictive* element describes or amplifies the noun that it modifies. It can be dropped without changing the *basic* meaning of the sentence. Set it off with commas.

The writer of that letter, *which is a prize example of how to lose customers,* needs to develop tact.

Such as

When *such as* introduces nonrestrictive elements, set off the element with commas. Do not use commas with restrictive elements.

We order office supplies, such as paper, pencils, and typewriter ribbons, from them.
An excuse such as this cannot be accepted.

Too

When *too,* meaning *also,* occurs within a sentence, set it off with commas. Informal writing omits the comma when *too* ends a sentence.

We believe, too, that the plan is good.
We believe that the plan is good, too.
We believe that the plan is good too.

Transitional expressions

See PUNCTUATION; **Comma;** *Opinions* and *Parenthetical expressions* and **Semicolon;** *Clauses*.

Transposed elements

Set off with commas sentence elements that are out of their natural order.

That he talks convincingly, we agree.

Two consecutive adjectives

Set off with commas two consecutive adjectives if the words can be reversed or if *and* can be inserted with no change in meaning.

> Red is a brilliant, intense color.
> It was a long, difficult journey.
> We have a new alkyd paint.
> That is a good secretarial procedure.

Verbal phrases, introductory

See PUNCTUATION; **Commas;** *Gerunds* and *Infinitives* and *Participial phrases*.

With other punctuation

Place the comma inside closing quotation marks but outside a closing parenthesis. Do not use a comma before an opening parenthesis.

> ''Getting that order,'' he told me, ''will assure your getting a bonus.''
> The order was the largest this year (as far as I know), and it will need a good follow-up.

Words that answer

Set off with commas such words as *yes, no, certainly, well,* etc. as follows:

> Certainly, we plan to send a delegate.
> Well, we have finally finished that project.
> *but:*
> We certainly are looking forward to seeing you.
> We asked them and they said Yes.

Yet (conjunction)

Use a comma or a semicolon before *yet* when it joins two clauses. (*Yet* can be an adverb.)

> We approve it, yet we wish it were better designed.
> We approve it; yet we wish it were better designed.
> We have not approved it yet.

• Dash

Appositives

Set off with dashes an emphatic appositive or one with internal punctuation.

> Speed — the desire of all typists — comes with practice.
> Even though the facts — the local labor market, the new tax law, and our long-range plan — seem valid, we cannot take action until . . . .

See PUNCTUATION; **Comma;** *Appositive*.

Change in thought or structure

Set off with dashes an abrupt change in thought or sentence structure. The dash goes after internal punctuation.

> The typist turned in thirty perfect letters — Isn't that amazing? — on the first day.

Credit lines, reference sources

See PUNCTUATION; **Special Element, Quoted Matter;** *Credit lines and reference sources*.

Emphasis

For special emphasis, set off a word or phrase with dashes.

> These are the newest — and the best — available.

Incomplete sentence

Use a dash to indicate that an unfinished sentence trails off into nothingness or that the omitted part is obvious.

> Your kindness so overwhelms me that —
> Telephone Mr. Lane today or — !

See PUNCTUATION; **Special Element, Ellipses**.

Placement at end of line

In typewritten text, type the dash at the end of a line of typing rather than at the beginning of the next line.

> Although the main problem — the local labor market — remains unsolved, we . . . .

Repetition of a word or phrase

Use a dash before an emphasized repetition.

> We are introducing a new plan — a plan that . . . .

Series, lists

See PUNCTUATION; **Special Element, Series**.

Summation

A dash precedes the summation of a series.

> Her hard work, her friendliness, her attitude — all tend to inspire us.

• Exclamation Point

Exclamatory elements

a. Use an exclamation point after a forceful remark or command.

Mail it today! You'll be glad.

b. Use a comma after expression of mild force or surprise.

Truly, it is not to be taken so lightly.

Extreme emphasis

Indicate the extreme in emphasis with an exclamation point. Note the decreasing emphasis in these examples:

This means a 200% profit!
This means a 200% profit.
This means a 200% profit.

Irony

Use an exclamation point enclosed in parentheses to indicate that a word or expression is used ironically.

Your conscientious (!) follow-up caused us to lose the order.

O, Oh

a. With *Oh* use an exclamation point or a comma, depending on the degree of forcefulness you intend.

Oh! what a surprise your letter was.
Oh, that reminds me. You are to be here . . . .

b. *O* is always coupled with a name in direct address (in solemn or poetic writing).

O Hamlet, what a tragic day . . . .

Rhetorical questions

Use an exclamation point for emphasis.

How can we ever convince him!

With other punctuation

Place the exclamation point inside or outside closing punctuation marks, depending upon the relation of the enclosed matter to the sentence.

''Don't be a litterbug!'' is a worthy slogan.
What a clever ''riposte''!

• Hyphen

Capitalized compound words

a. If the base word is capitalized, hyphenate to form a compound.

pre-Christmas, anti-American, pro-French, un-American, ex-Republican party leader

b. In titles and headings, capitalize words that you would capitalize without the hyphens.

An Off-the-Record Report
A Middle-of-the-Road Leader

See CAPITALIZATION; **Hyphenated words** and **Titles of persons.**

Clarity

Use the hyphen to clarify your meaning.

A *little-used car* is not the same as a *little used car.*

Compound words as adjectives

a. Hyphenate two or more words used as a single modifier when they *precede* the noun. In most instances no hyphen is needed when the modifier follows the noun.

He received on-the-job training.
That company provides training on the job.

b. In modern usage the hyphen is omitted in frequently used, one-thought modifers that are instantly clear to the reader without the hyphen.

the civil rights movement, a long distance call, the data processing equipment, the post office workers

c. Do not hyphenate:

1. An adverb-adjective combination

a highly technical report, an unusually warm day, a barely legible copy, a frequently used word

Note, however, that some adjectives end in *ly* and therefore would not come under the rule.

a surly-looking person, the friendly-appearing clerk

2. An adjective-possessive combination

a six months' vacation

3. A two-word proper adjective used before the noun.

of Scotch Irish descent, the Mason Dixon line

4. A modifier that is a foreign phrase

our per diem rate

5. A modifier enclosed in quotation marks

That is a "brain trust" idea.

6. Comparative modifiers — unless required for clarity

He is the highest ranking officer present.

but:

I have never seen a slower-moving van.

I have never seen a slower moving van.

See NUMBERS; **Compound numeric adjectives.**

Identical words with different meanings

Use a hyphen to prevent misreading a compound.

We plan to re-cover the furniture.

Will we recover damages for that?

Letter prefixes

Hyphenate a compound with a letter prefix.

L-shaped, U-turn

Numbers

Hyphenate spelled-out compound numbers, as *thirty-second, twenty-two, ninety-nine.*

See NUMBERS; **Ages, Consistency within a sentence, Fractions, Sequential numbers.**

Prefixes, hyphenated

The following prefixes are almost always hyphenated.

self	self-sufficient
ex	ex-champion
vice	vice-consul

Prefixes, joined

Compounds with the following prefixes are usually written as one word.

anti	antifreeze
bi	bimonthly
co	coplanner
dis	disaffect
extra	extracurricular

fore	foreknown
hydro	hydrochloride
hyper	hypertension
in	incapable
inter	international
mis	misread
non	nonconductor
out	outdistance
over	overanxious
pre	premeeting
pro	proexercise
post	postdate
re	restyle
semi	semicircular
trans	transcontinental
tri	tricity
un	unsuitable
under	underestimate

See PUNCTUATION; **Hyphens;** *Compound words as adjectives (b).*

Prefixes with mixed usage

Some prefixes are either hyphenated or joined to a base word according to the part-of-speech usage.

air   half   high   ill

a. Noun compounds are usually written as two words.

an air mass, a half frown, a high spot

b. Most adjective compounds are hyphenated.

an air-mixed liquid, a half-sincere offer

c. Most verb compounds are hyphenated.

to air-mix, to half-approve, to high-hat

Series of hyphenated words

In a series of repeated compounds, the hyphen is repeated but the base word is used only in the last compound.

There were two-, three-, and four-time winners.

Suffixes

The following suffixes are joined to the base word unless the resulting word is long.

like	a childlike look, a gasoline-like odor
hood	childhood, widowhood
free	carefree, frostfree, complication-free
proof	fireproof, burglar-proof
wide	nationwide, statewide, worldwide

• Parentheses

Capitalization within

Within parentheses, capitalize only proper names. A complete sentence is not initially capped if it is within another sentence.

> We played bridge (do you play it?) all evening.

Function of parentheses

Enclose in parentheses any words, phrases, clauses, or sentences that explain, verify, illustrate, define, identify, and so on.

See PUNCTUATION; **Special Element, Enumerations;** *Parentheses* .

Inner parentheses

Enclose in inner parentheses or brackets any parenthetical matter *within* parenthetical matter.

With other punctuation

a. No punctuation is used before an *opening* parenthesis.

b. Appropriate punctuation precedes and follows a *closing* parenthesis.

> At the meeting (April 2) we . . . .
> At the last regular meeting (April 2), we . . . .
> Were you at the last meeting (April 2)?

• Period

Use the period after declarative and imperative sentences, commands phrased as questions, abbreviations, initials, and numbers or letters in enumerations. See:

ABBREVIATIONS

CAPITALIZATION; **Degrees**

NUMBERS; **Decimals, Money, Time of day, Years**

PUNCTUATION; **Quotation marks;** *With other punctuation* and **Special Element, Ellipses,** and **Special Element, Enumerations.**

• Question Mark

Direct and indirect quotations

Use a question mark at the end of a direct question, a period at the end of an indirect question.

> *Direct:* When did you order it?
> *Indirect:* He asked when you ordered it.

Doubt or conjecture

Use a question mark in parentheses to question the accuracy of a statement or to indicate that it is but a conjecture.

> He worked there for five (?) years.

Question within a sentence

a. Use a question mark at the end of a sentence that contains a clause questioning the whole sentence. Set the clause off with commas.

> She promised, didn't she, to call?

b. If a clause questions only the part preceding it, use the question mark after the clause and set the clause off with dashes.

> As a graduate of Yale — or is it Harvard? — she has . . . .

c. Use a question mark immediately after a quoted question or one in apposition to the word *question*.

> One question "Can you finish it in time?" must be asked.
> The question, Can you finish it in time?, must be asked.

Requests phrased as questions

Use a period after a polite request in question form to which no direct answer is expected.

> *Direct question:* Can you come on the 29th?
> *Polite request:* Will you please send me your latest catalog.

Series of questions with a sentence

See CAPITALIZATION; **First words (b), (c).**

With other punctuation

Refer to the specific mark (listed alphabetically in this division, PUNCTUATION).

• Quotation Mark

Conversation

a. In literary writing, narration is often interspersed with a person's spoken words.

> "I see what you mean, Jan. This will change our plans," Lou said, turning the pages of the report. "I'll have to think about it."

b. Dialogue or direct conversation is punctuated as follows:

> He said, "That's fine."
> "That's fine," he said, "for you."
> "That's true," he said. "You're right."
> "When can you come?" he asked.

c. A word-for-word personal or telephone conversation is typed in any quickly typed, easily read style. All speakers must be fully identified at the start.

> Telephone call — 6/10/78 — 2:50 p.m. Mr. Alan King
>   called Mr. Willis Burt
> K Hello, Willis, how are you?
> B Fine, Alan. What can I do for you?

Familiar sayings

Quoting or underlining a familiar saying (although unnecessary) can enliven a typed text. If the saying is used as an adjective, however, hyphens are sufficient.

> If "good things come by threes," I am especially blessed,
>   for I have four to report.
> This is a good-things-come-by-threes report.

Quoted matter

See PUNCTUATION; **Special Element, Quoted Matter**.

Titles of published matter

See PUNCTUATION; **Special Element, Titles of Published Matter**.

With other punctuation

a. Place closing quotation marks: after a comma or period; before a semicolon or colon; before or after other marks according to usage.

b. Other than the quotation mark, use only one punctuation mark at the end of a sentence even though the sentence structure suggests two.

> I read that article "Why Punctuate?"

c. With a double question, use only one question mark — either inside or outside the quotation mark.

> Have you read "Why Punctuate?"
> Have you read "Why Punctuate"?

Words different in tone

a. Enclose in quotation marks (do not underline) words of a different tone, like popular terms, unusual meanings, and slang.

> A "man of distinction" like you . . . .
> Your "invitation" arrived and . . . .

b. Omit the quotation marks if *so-called* is used.

> Your so-called invitation arrived and . . . .

Words used as words

Enclose in quotation marks or underline words that are defined or pointed out.

> The term coffee break means . . . .
> Her favorite word is "dynamic."

• Semicolon

Clauses in compound sentences

a. If a main clause contains commas, use a semicolon between clauses.

> A good dictionary, they say, is a secretary's best friend; and
>   a good grammar is a loyal pal.

b. When two long main clauses are not joined by a conjunction, use a semicolon between them.

> I wrote him about the Baker order last Monday; his reply
>   didn't get here until this morning.

c. If a transitional word or phrase joins main clauses, use a semicolon before and a comma after it. Some transitional words are:

also	namely	nevertheless
hence	for example	therefore
then	consequently	whereas
thus	furthermore	that is
yet	moreover	for instance

> The need is pressing; therefore, we must . . . .

d. When a very short transitional word joins two main clauses, the comma may be omitted.

> The need is pressing; thus we must have . . . .

e. With transitional words or phrases, the comma can replace understood words.

> We have one matter to discuss; namely, a pension plan.

Run-in enumerations

With a series of enumerated clauses, use a colon before the first figure and a semicolon before the following figures.

> The agenda for the meeting includes these items:
> (1) We will choose a replacement for Bob Jones; (2) we will vote on two tabled motions; and (3) we will set the date for the sales meeting.

See PUNCTUATION; **Special Element, Enumerations**; *Capitalization of units*, at the right.

With other punctuation

A semicolon arbitrarily follows a closing quotation mark.

> He said, "There will be no increase"; however, we hope he is wrong.

Special Elements of Punctuation

• Ellipses

Ellipses (omission marks) consist of three spaced or unspaced periods within a sentence. If the omission is at the end of a sentence, the period ending the sentence makes a fourth period in the ellipsis.

Ellipses are used:

a. To indicate an omission of a phrase, a sentence, or more from quoted matter

> ". . . because it is so well written . . . and so timely . . . we should like to reprint . . . ."

b. To show that a series continues (in place of *et cetera*)

> Answer every third question (3, 6, 9 . . .).

c. To show passage of time in narrative

> He rose slowly . . . tried to steady himself . . . fell forward.

d. To show that a statement is unfinished or dies away

> Your reason makes us wonder . . . .

See PUNCTUATION; **Dash**; *Incomplete sentence*.

• Enumerations

Capitalization of units

a. *Run-in enumerations of complete sentences:* If a main clause introduces a series of complete sentences, capitalize and punctuate in one of the following ways.

> We cited three objections: (1) Time is limited. (2) The cost is excessive. (3) We lack the trained personnel.
>
> *or:*
>
> We cited three objections: (1) Time is limited; (2) the cost is excessive; and (3) we lack the personnel.

b. *Run-in enumerations of words and phrases:*

1. With introductory main clause:

> We cited three objections: (1) limited time, (2) excessive cost, and (3) lack of trained personnel.

2. With introductory sentence fragment:

> Our three objections are (1) limited time, (2) excessive cost, and (3) lack of trained personnel.

c. *Tabulated enumerations:*

1. With complete sentences, use conventional capitalization.

2. Common usage is to capitalize the first word (and any proper words) with words and phrases.

> The colors are:
> 1. Light beige
> 2. Pale yellow
> 3. Charcoal gray

Introductory colon

A *run-in* enumeration introduced by a complete sentence takes a colon; a *tabulated* enumeration always requires a colon, as shown in the example above.

Punctuation after items

Run-in independent clauses: Use semicolons or periods and a terminal period.

Run-in words or phrases: Use commas and a terminal period.

Tabulated sentences: Use terminal periods.

Tabulated words or phrases: Omit terminal punctuation.

• Quoted Matter

To identify the exact words of a speaker or a writer as such, enclose them in quotation marks, set them off by indention, or both.

Copied errors (sic)

See PUNCTUATION ; **Brackets;** *Quoted matter* .

Corrections

See PUNCTUATION ; **Brackets,** *Quoted matter* .

Credit lines and reference sources

The source of quoted matter is given (1) in the text, (2) in a footnote, or (3) in a credit line following the indented quotation.

> The article "Facsimile Equipment" in the July, 1972, The Office says:
> "In the coming year, our economy will continue to grow stronger,"[1] states a leading . . . .
> Four be the things I am wiser to know:
> Idleness, sorrow, a friend, a foe.
> — Dorothy Parker

See COMMUNICATIONS GUIDE ; **Footnote construction.**

Inserted words (interpolations)

Enclose in brackets any words inserted into quoted matter.

See PUNCTUATION ; **Brackets;** *Quoted matter* .

Omissions

Use ellipses to show omission of words or sentences in quoted matter.

See PUNCTUATION ; **Special Element, Ellipses** .

Poetry

Introduce quoted poetry with a colon. Separate it from the text by line spaces and centering. Copy line lengths, indentions, and capitalization.

Quotation within a quotation

Enclose the inner quotation in single quotes.

> "He needs more 'get up and go' if he is to succeed," the manager commented.

Quoted sentence fragments

Enclose them in quotation marks.

> The letter said that she is "pleasant and conscientious" but that she "lacks initiative."

Several paragraphs

Indent quoted matter of several paragraphs and introduce with a colon; identify the source. Omit quotation marks with indented matter.

Several sentences

a. Use a colon to introduce several quoted sentences.

b. Indent from both margins four or more quoted lines, usually without quotation marks.

c. Type quotations of fewer than four lines in run-in style with quotation marks.

Single sentences

Enclose a single quoted sentence in quotation marks. Introduce with a colon. See PUNCTUATION ; **Quotation marks;** *Conversation* .

Words in italics

When typing from printed material, underline words that are printed in italics.

• Series

a. Use commas between units in a series if none contain internal commas.

b. Use semicolons between units if one or more contain internal commas or if the commas would confuse the meaning.

> Please send copies to James Martin, president, Anco, Inc.; Peter Andrews, treasurer, Peerless Foundry; and Bruce Parish, treasurer, Mills and Johnson.

c. Some writers omit the comma before the final connective in a series.

> a choice of tan, ivory and gray.

d. Omit punctuation if all units are joined with connectives.

> It comes in tan or ivory or gray.

e. Set off with commas the expressions *and the like, and so forth,* and *etc.*

> He is reading books, reports, and the like, for information.

f. To introduce a series or list, use either introductory words properly punctuated or punctuation alone, as follows:

> many colors; for example, beige, ivory, and cream.
> many colors — for example, beige, ivory, and cream.
> many colors, such as beige, ivory, and cream.
> many colors: beige, ivory, and cream.
> many colors — beige, ivory, and cream.

See PUNCTUATION; **Dash;** *Summation*.

• Titles of Published Matter

Books, magazines, newspapers

Type in all capitals, or capitalize the important words and underline the entire title. Even when *the* is a formal part of the title, it is often disregarded.

> in yesterday's NEW YORK TIMES
> in the New York Times of
> in The New York Times of

Parts of published works

Enclose in quotation marks the title of any subdivision or unit of a published work (chapters, articles, features, columns, etc.)

> In the "Reference Guide" of SECRETARIAL PROCEDURES AND ADMINISTRATION . . . .
> According to "Review and Outlook" in the Wall Street Journal . . . .

Movies, songs, lectures, plays, sermons

Capitalize important words and enclose title in quotation marks.

Titles with hyphenated compounds

See CAPITALIZATION; **Hyphenated words** and PUNCTUATION; **Hyphen;** *Capitalized compound words (b)*.

• Underlining

Underline two or more words as follows:

a. With closely related words (a title, phrase, or clause) use a solid underline.

> Send the items by parcel post if they will arrive by May 7; if not, use first-class mail.

b. With a series of distinct items, underline each word but not punctuation or spaces.

> We desperately need your cooperation, loyalty, and friendship if we are to complete this project.

Emphasis

Underline any words to be emphasized.

Foreign words or phrases

To indicate that a word or phrase is from a foreign language, underline it.

> His manner has a certain je ne sais quoi.

Italics

In preparing copy for a printer, underline words that are to be printed in italics.

Titles of published matter

See opposite column.

Words used as words

See PUNCTUATION; **Quotation marks;** *Words used as words*.

> USAGE—WORDS AND PHRASES —Page 713

The entries in this division of the Reference Guide consist of common *acceptable* usages for words or phrases that are often misused and about which information is not commonly available in standard dictionaries.

GENERAL RULE: Devote some time to becoming familiar with the items in this division. After that — *when in doubt, look it up.*

A or *an* before the letter *h*

Common usage is as follows:

> a historic (*or* historical) event, an honor, a hotel, a habitual trait, a humble (if you pronounce the *h*), an humble (if you do not)

Ability to

Ability *to*, plus verb (ability to influence), not *of* (ability of influencing)

About, at about

Use one or the other — not both.
> Leave at noon. Leave about noon.

Above

a. In all levels of writing, this word is used as a preposition and an adverb.
> Her office is two floors above mine.
> It is as blue as the sky above.

b. In business writing it is sometimes used as a pronoun or adjective.
> Consider the above carefully.
> The above price is f.o.b. our factory.

Absolve

To *free from*, as to *absolve from blame*.

Accept, except

a. *Accept* means to agree or to receive; it is always a verb.
> I accept your offer. She accepted the gift.

b. *Except* as a preposition means but.
> Everyone replied except Mr. Slade.

c. *Except* as a verb means to exclude.
> Once that clause was excepted, the motion passed.

Accompany

To be accompanied *by someone or in association with* something.
> Mr. Slade was accompanied by Ms. Howard.
> The report was accompanied with a letter.

Acquiesce in

To acquiesce *in*, not *to*.
> He acquiesced in the matter of the bonus.

Acronyms

Acronyms are words from the initial letters or syllable of two or more words. They are not enclosed in quotes nor underlined. Plurals, possessives, and tenses are formed regularly. (WAC, snafu, HUD)

A.D.

See NUMBERS; **Years**

Adapt, adopt, adept

To adapt (change or make suitable), to adopt (to accept or put into practice), to be adept (expert)
> They adapted the device to their needs.
> They formally adopted the proposal.
> He is adept in (*not* at) training beginners.

Adhere, adherent

To adhere (hold fast) *to*, as *adhere to our policy;* an adherent *of*, as *an adherent of that policy*

Advice, advise

Advice is a noun meaning a recommendation; *advise* is a verb meaning to counsel.
> I can advise you, but will you follow my advice?

Adverse, averse

Adverse means antagonistic; *averse* means disinclined and is milder.
> The proposal met adverse reactions.
> Joseph is averse to manual labor.

Affect, effect

a. *Affect* is a verb meaning to influence.
> The weather affected our sales.

b. *Effect* as a noun means result.
> The weather had an adverse effect on our sales.

c. *Effect* as a verb means to accomplish or produce.
> The delegates effected a compromise.

A la or à la

Except in formal or in specialized writing, the accent is dropped in typewritten text.

All, all of

Use *all* with nouns, *all of* with pronouns.
> Check all the reports; check all of them.

All, any none, some, more, most

These words may be either singular or plural, depending on intended meaning.

None of the money has been collected; none of the bills have been paid.

All right

This is the only correct spelling. *Alright* is incorrect.

All together, altogether

All together means in the same place; *altogether* means entirely.

The correspondence is all together in one folder.
He is altogether too casual in his manner.

Allude, elude

Allude (to refer indirectly); elude (to avoid)

They alluded to a possible wage increase, but eluded making a positive statement.

Allusion

See USAGE; **Illusion, allusion**.

Already, all ready

Already is an adverb meaning previously, *all ready* is an adverb-adjective compound meaning completely ready.

Are you all ready to go? Ms. Adams has already left.

Altar, alter

Altar is a noun referring to worship; *alter* is a verb meaning to change.

They decorated the altar.
The tailor altered Mr. Davis' suit.

Alumna, alumnae, alumnus, alumni

An *alumna* is a woman graduate or former student (plural, *alumnae*).

An *alumnus* is a man graduate or former student (plural, *alumni*).

Graduate or *graduates* is a good substitute word.

Among, between

Generally, *between* implies *two; among, more than two*. In choices, comparison, distinctions, and interrelationships, however, *between* is used with more than two.

Games between the six schools have been scheduled.
Differentiate between *to, too*, and *two*.

Amount, number

Amount is commonly used of money and of that which cannot be counted; *number*, of things that can be counted.

The unusually large number of speculators accounted for the large amount of speculation.

See USAGE; **Number, numeral, figure**.

Amounts, quantities

An amount or quantity takes plural forms unless it refers to one unit.

A unit: Ten yards makes one slipcover.
                    but:
Ten teams are participating.

And in compound subjects

Compound subjects of two or more words joined by *and* take plural verbs and pronouns unless the words together comprise one thing.

Our sales manager and our advertising director have sent in their reports.
Our sales manager and advertising director has sent in his report.
A pen and a pencil were found after the meeting.
A matching pen and pencil makes a welcome gift.

And/or

This informal phrase indicates a three-way choice. *Come Monday and/or Tuesday* means to come Monday or Tuesday or both days. In formal writing, say: *Come both Monday and Tuesday or both days.*

Angry

One is angry *at* or *about* things, *with* or *at* people.

He is sure to be angry with (*or* at) Mr. Lane about the oversight.
He is sure to be angry at having to wait.

Any

Use singular or plural verbs and pronouns according to intended meaning.

Was any of the dessert left?
Are any of the students eligible for the prize?

See USAGE; **All, any, none, some, more, most**.

Anyone, any one

a. *Anyone* (with accent on the first syllable) is written as one word. *Any one* (with accent on the *one*) is written as two words and is usually modified by a prepositional phrase.

> Anyone is welcome to register. (*Anyone*)
> Any one of your men can do the job. (Any *one*)

b. This hint also applies to *anyway, any way; everyone, every one;* and *someone, some one.*

Anxious, eager

Both *anxious* and *eager* mean earnest desire, but *anxious* denotes worry.

> We look forward eagerly to your visit.
> We are anxious to meet your requirements (but worried that we may fail).

Appraise, apprise

Appraise means to set a value on; *apprise* means to inform.

> The adjuster will appraise the damage and will apprise you of the estimate.

Appropriate

To appropriate (take) *something*; to appropriate (set aside) *for*; to be appropriate (suitable) *to* or *for.*

> The city appropriated the land.
> They appropriated money for the land.
> The cover is appropriate to the book.
> A suit is appropriate for office wear.

Apropos

To be apropos *to* or *of* (pertinent to)

> His remark was not apropos to the occasion.

Apt, likely, liable

a. Do not use *apt* for *likely* or *liable*; *apt* means suitable or qualified (*apt phrasing*).

b. *Likely* means probably (*likely to refuse*).

c. *Liable* means susceptible to something unpleasant (*liable to break*) or responsible (*liable for damages*).

As, usage of

> *Adverb:* Write as often as possible.
> *Preposition:* He said it as an afterthought.
> *Conjunction:* The students took notes as I read to them.

Do not use *as* for *because* or *since.*

> Because (*not as*) you were late, we missed the plane.

As — as, not so — as

In regular comparisons use as . . . as; in negative comparisons in formal writing use not so . . . as.

> This design is as attractive as that one.
> This design is not so attractive as that one.

As to

Usually a single preposition like *in, for, of, on, about, whether* etc. is preferable.

> She commented on (as to) your idea.

As well as, together with

Because the noun or pronoun *preceding* either of these phrases is the subject of the sentence, subsequent nouns or pronouns do not affect the verb.

> The report, as well as the schedules, is finished.
> The schedules, together with the report, are finished.

B.C.

See NUMBERS; **Years**.

Bad, badly

Use *bad* with a linking verb because it is an adjective. *Badly* is an adverb and is used with regular transitive and intransitive verbs.

Linking verbs and predicate adjectives:

> He feels bad about losing. She looks bad.
> The news tonight sounds bad. The weather is too bad for a picnic.
> > *but:*
> He played badly in the tournament. He was injured badly in the accident. The home team played the game badly and lost, which made them feel bad.

Bail, bale

Bail means something pledged for security or to dip a liquid from a vessel. *Bale* is a bundle or a package.

Balance, remainder

Balance means the amount of money in an account (the bank account or credit account with a firm). To use *balance* for *remainder* is colloquial.

> Send the remainder (*or* rest) of the order.
> Colloquial: Send the balance of the order.

Bases, basis

Bases is the plural of *base* and *basis*.

Because of

See USAGE; **Due to**.

Between

See USAGE; **Among, between**.

Biannual, biennial, semiannual

Biannual means twice a year; *biennial*, once in two years; *semiannual*, every half year.

Bimonthly, semimonthly

Bimonthly, every two months; *Semimonthly*, twice a month.

Blond, blonde, brunet, brunette

Blond and *brunet* are masculine; *blonde* and *brunette* are feminine.

But that, but what

But that is formal; *but what*, colloquial.

> We never dreamed but that they would accept our offer.
> We didn't know but what they might refuse.

Can, could, would

Could is the past tense of *can*. *Can* and *could* imply ability. Use *would* with *could* in a related clause.

> If you would meet with us, we could select the items.

Can, may

In formal writing, use *can* for ability; *may*, for permission, doubt, or possibility.

> This model can be used for . . . .
> This model may be discontinued.
> You may find that . . . .
> Tell him that he may leave when he is finished.

Cannot, can not

Cannot is more generally used. Some writers feel that *can not* is more emphatic.

> I can *not* believe it!

Cannot help but

This phrase is unacceptable. Use instead:

> We can but advise you (*or* we cannot but) . . . .
> We can only advise you . . . .

Cannot (can't) seem to

This phrase is informal. Use *seem unable* to in formal writing.

> They seem unable to decide.
> They can't seem to decide.

Canvas, canvass

Canvas is a noun (a cloth). *Canvass* is a verb meaning to survey or solicit.

> The cartons were covered with canvas.
> Mr. Lindsay will canvass the employees for the United Appeal drive.

Capacity

Capacity is a noun meaning ability or measure of content.

> A capacity to listen will help you make friends.
> He has a capacity for making friends.
> The tank has a capacity of five hundred gallons.

Capital, capitol

Use *capital* unless you are talking about the building that houses a government. Capitalize *capitol* only when it is part of a proper name.

> We visited the State Capitol in Lansing, Michigan.

Cite, sight, site

Cite means to quote; *sight* means vision, *site* means location.

> She cited some good examples in her lecture.
> They sighted another ship on the horizon.
> We chose the site for our new branch plant.

Claim

As a verb, *claim* has an antagonistic overtone. *Say* and *feel* are more tactful.

See USAGE; **Euphemisms**.

Coincidence, coincident, coincidental

Coincidence is a noun meaning a series of apparently unrelated events. *Coincident* is an adjective meaning "in the same space or time" or "of a similar nature." *Coincidental* means "as a result of a coincidence."

Colloquial

A word or meaning marked *colloquial* in a dictionary is used in the conversation of educated people. Colloquialisms are acceptable in informal writing and friendly business letters.

Comedian, comedienne

Comedian is masculine; *comedienne*, feminine.

Complected, complexioned

Always use *complexioned*, as *light complexioned*.

Complement, compliment

Complement means to complete, fill, or make perfect; *compliment* means to praise.

> He complimented Miss Shelley on her good work.
> Her attention to detail complements his energetic salesmanship.

Confidant, confidante

Confidant is masculine; *confidante*, feminine.

Congress, sessions of

See CAPITALIZATION; **Congress** and NUMBERS; **Congress, sessions of**.

Connected with, in connection with

These wordy phrases usually can be shortened to *with* or *in* — or omitted entirely.

> We received your bill for services in (*not* in connection with) the study of our plan.

Consensus of opinion

Purists object to this phrase as redundant, but Webster says it is now accepted.

See USAGE; **Redundancy**.

Considerable

As a noun, *considerable* is colloquial. Use the word as an adjective.

> There was a considerable amount of waste.
> *Colloquial:* We had considerable to discuss.

Consist of, consist in

To *consist of* means composed of; to *consist in* means to be comprised of.

> The mixture consists of four herbs.
> Experience consists not only in doing things repeatedly but also in learning from them.

Consonant

To be *consonant in* or *with* means to be in agreement in or with.

Consul, council, counsel

Consul means a representative; *council* means an assembly; *counsel* means advice or to advise.

Consult

To consult *about* something or merely to consult (Usually *with* is redundant.)

> The heirs consulted the lawyer about the will.

Contact

Dictionaries label the use of *contact* as a verb colloquial; handbooks, a business usage.

> *Noun:* We wish to establish a business contact in Brazil.
> *Verb:* Please contact our Denver office soon.

Contingency, contingent

Contingency is a noun meaning a fact that depends on the existence of another fact or event. *Contingent* is the adjective form.

> There is one contingency: The strike may delay our plans.
> Our plans are contingent upon (*or* on) settlement of the strike.

Continual, continuous

Continual means constantly repeated with only small breaks between; *continuous* means constantly without break.

> There were continual interruptions.
> The machine has been in continuous use since May.

Contractions

See PUNCTUATION; **Apostrophe (c)**.

Conversation

See PUNCTUATION; **Quotation marks;** *Conversation*.

Conversions of word usages

See WORDS: COINED; **Conversions**.

Correlate

To correlate (connect systematically) *one thing and another thing*; to correlate *with*.

> This course correlates study and on-the-job training; it correlates learning with doing.

Could

See USAGE; **Can, could, would**.

Credible, creditable, credulous

Credible means believable; *creditable*, praiseworthy; *credulous*, ready to believe on weak evidence.

Data

Data is the plural form of the Latin *datum*. Business usage gives *data* plural forms when the thought is plural, singular forms when reference is to a unit.

> Data are processed electronically at incredible speeds.
> The data supporting our conclusion is enclosed.

Date (chronological)

> It dates from (*not* back to) 1970.

See NUMBERS; **Dates and Years**.

Date (appointment or engagement)

This usage is variously termed *informal, slang, familiar, colloquial* in the meaning of a social engagement with a member of the opposite sex.

Degrees, academic

See CAPITALIZATION; **Degrees**.

Descendant, descendent

Avoid possible misspelling by using *descendant*, which can be either a noun or an adjective. (*Descendent* is only an adjective.)

Differ

One thing differs *from* another; Persons differ *with* each other.

> One author's style differs from that of another in many ways.
> He differs with us on that point.

Different from

Different *from* is always correct. Different *than* is sometimes used when followed by a clause.

> This shipment is different from the last one.
> The circumstances were different than (*or* different from) those he recalled.

Dimensions

See ABBREVIATIONS; **Dimensions and weights**.

Discriminate

To discriminate *against* or *between*

> They were unjust to discriminate against the worker for those reasons.
> We must be careful to discriminate between the new dress codes for business and actual poor taste.

Disillusion, dissolution

Disillusion means destroying an illusion; *dissolution* means dissolving.

> We were disillusioned to learn his true character.
> The dissolution of the company forced cancellation of many contracts.

Disinterested, uninterested

Disinterested implies an unbiased, unprejudiced interest; *uninterested* implies the absence of any interest.

> Ethics requires a CPA to be disinterested in the success of his clients.
> He is uninterested in books of fiction.

Distinguish

To *distinguish* between (even if more than two); to distinguish one from another; to be distinguished *for*

> It is difficult to distinguish between the three sizes of type.
> This form can be distinguished from that one by noting its form number.
> She is distinguished for her speaking ability.

Doubt

a. To express doubt, use *if* or *whether*.

I doubt if there is time.
He doubts whether she will attend.

b. To express the lack of doubt, use a negative and *that*.

I do not doubt that there is time.
I have no doubt that there is time.

See PUNCTUATION; **Question mark;** *Doubt*.

Due to

a. The use of this phrase as a preposition is controversial. Purists strenuously object to it. Use *owing to* or *because of*.

Owing to (*or* because of) faulty brakes, we drove slowly.
not:
Due to faulty brakes, we drove slowly.

b. In the usage below, *due* is correct as a predicate adjective followed by the infinitive phrase *to arrive*.

Flight 72 was due to arrive at 9:05 p.m.

Each

As a pronoun, *each* is singular; as an adjective, it does not affect the verb.

Pronoun: Each of the plans has its advantages.
Adjective: They each have their good points.

Eager

See USAGE; **Anxious, eager.**

Effect

See USAGE; **Affect, effect.**

Either, neither

These words as adjectives or pronouns take singular forms.

Adjective: Either day is convenient.
Pronoun: Neither has replied to my letter.
Neither of them has replied.

Either — or, neither — nor

a. When these connectives join subject words, the *word that is nearer the verb* determines the use of singular or plural verbs and, in some cases, the person of the verb. Usually, place the plural word nearer to the verb.

Either Mr. Lance or his associates are going.
Neither the reports nor the book is here.

b. Reword to avoid awkwardness.

Either he is coming or I am.
not:
Either he or I am coming.

Else's

See POSSESSIVES; *Else* phrases.

Eminent, imminent

Eminent means high, lofty, distinguished; *imminent* means impending or threatening.

Enthuse

This verb, a back-formation from the noun *enthusiasm*, is labeled informal by most dictionaries. Do not use *enthuse* in formal writing.

He enthused at great length about the plan.
He was enthusiastic about the plan.

Enumerations

See PUNCTUATION; **Special Element, Enumerations.**

Equivalent

As an adjective, *to* or *in*; as a noun, *of*

Her position is equivalent to that of director.
The value of these items is equivalent to that of the items you ordered.
The two machines are equivalent in quality.
The contents are the equivalent of three pounds.

Errors in quoted matter

See PUNCTUATION; **Brackets;** *Quoted matter (a)*.

Etc., and so forth, et cetera

If *et cetera* is dictated, the secretary usually transcribes it as *and so forth* or *etc*. To avoid them, substitute *and the like*.

We must have all sales reports, expense reports, budgets, and the like, by the tenth of each month.

See PUNCTUATION; **Special Element, Series.**

Ethics

This word takes singular verbs and pronouns when it means a set of practices; plural forms when it means individual ones.

Professional ethics prohibits our advertising.
In some instances his ethics have been questionable.

Euphemisms

Euphemisms are softened, tactful phrases for blunt or harsh facts. Some common ones are:

For *buried:* laid to rest
For *discharged:* left our employ
For *died:* passed away
For *claim:* say *or* feel
For *is:* seems

Euphony

Euphony (pleasing speech sounds) can be achieved by:

— Avoiding the harsh or ugly sounds (*f's, b's, ch's, t's, ug's, og's*)

— Repeating pleasant sounds

— Using rhythmically accented syllables

Choppy: We are glad indeed to be able to advise you . . . .
Euphonious: We are pleased that we can tell you . . . .
The record of all receipts and expenses . . . .

Everybody, everyone

a. These take singular verbs and pronouns.

Everyone is asked to wire his or her opinion.

b. For the distinction between *everyone* and *every one*, see USAGE; **Anyone, any one.**

Except

See USAGE; **Accept, except.**

Exclusive

To be exclusive *of* or *with*

The price mentioned is exclusive of tax.
That line of apparel is exclusive with our shop.

Excuse

See USAGE; **Pardon, excuse.**

Explicit, implicit

To be *explicit in* or *on* means to explain or to "spell out"; to be *implicit in* or *on* means to imply but not actually state something that can be understood or inferred.

Catalogs are explicit in describing items.
The president's approval of that point was implicit in his approval of the full report.

Farther, further

In formal English, *farther* is used for distances (far way); *further*, for advancement or degree, often with *into*. At the information level, however, *further* is used for all.

The airport is a mile farther on this road.
We can go into the matter further tomorrow.

Federal

See CAPITALIZATION; **Federal.**

Female

Female is used in records and statistics but is not acceptable as a synonym for *woman, lady,* or *feminine.*

Few

As a subject, *few* is a collective pronoun that takes a plural verb and a singular modifier.

A few are ready now. Only a few plan to come.

Fewer, less

In strict usage, *fewer* refers to things that can be counted; *less*, to things that must be measured.

Fewer persons attended the conference this year.
Less time and effort are required to do the work with this appliance than with that one.

Fiancé, fiancée

Fiancé is masculine and *fiancée* feminine for a betrothed couple.

Flaunt, flout

Flaunt means to wave; to display boastfully. *Flout* means to treat with contempt or insult.

Follow-up, follow up

Follow-up is a noun or adjective; follow up is a verb.

> A follow-up will be necessary on this order.
> Write a follow-up letter on May 2.
> Be sure to follow up on this tomorrow.

Fractions

See NUMBERS; **Fractions**.

Further

See USAGE; **Farther, further**.

Gerund

a. A gerund is a verbal (ending in *ing*) used as a noun. Gerunds can be used in all noun usages.

> *Subject:* You learn that editing takes time.
> *Object:* She learned editing from the senior editor.

b. In formal writing a possessive is used with a gerund.

> His editing included Chapter 10.
> The team's winning made the crowd happy.

Exception: The possessive form is not necessary with a compound or inanimate modifer.

> The No. 2 mill breaking down caused a delay.
> The mill (*or* mill's) breaking down caused a delay.

Good, well

To *feel good* and to *feel well* are not synonymous. Both *good* and *well* are adjectives and *feel* (in this usage) is a linking verb. Use *well* to mean *in fine health*; use *good* to mean pleasant or attractive.

> Usually, when you feel well, you look good.
> I feel well and energetic.
> She feels good about her promotion.

See USAGE; **Linking verbs**.

Got, gotten

Both words are the past participle of *to get*.

Government

This word takes singular verbs and pronouns.

> The government is setting up its budget.

Graduated

Use either *graduated from* or *was graduated from*. In letters of application, use the latter form — in case your reader is a purist.

> *Formal:* He was graduated from Indiana University.
> *Informal:* He graduated from Indiana University.

Honorable

In an address the first name or initials and surname follow *Honorable* or *Hon*. In text, use the styles below.

> *Address:* Hon. Alan Lane, Honorable A. R. Lane
> *In text:* the Honorable Alan Lane, the Honorable Mr. Lane
> *not:* the Honorable Lane

See ABBREVIATIONS; **Honorable**.

Hope phrases

Do not use *in hopes of* and *no hopes of*. Use the singular form.

> We sent the letter to Fairbanks, Alaska, in the hope of reaching Dr. Hanna.

However

Avoid starting a sentence with *however* as a transitional word. Used as an adverb, *however* can start a sentence.

> *Transitional:* We waited for hours; however, he . . . .
> *As adverb:* However you advised him, he did not . . . .

Identified with

This term, when it means *associated with*, is colloquial according to some sources.

Idioms

a. An *idiom* is an expression or phrase that is somehow peculiar — an arbitrary grouping of words that is often illogical in construction or meaning but is acceptable in usage. Some common American idioms are *to make ends meet, to take pains, laid up with a virus, by and large*, and *to catch a cold* or *bug*.

b. A prepositional idiom is one in which the combination of words has a special meaning. Some common ones are *to live up to, to live down* something, *to put up with* something, *to set up, to set about* something, *to hand over, to bring up* a point.

If clauses

See USAGE; **Subjunctive mood**.

Illusion, allusion

Illusion means a deceptive appearance; *allusion*, something referred to.

Imply, infer

To *imply* means to give a certain impression; to *infer* means to receive a certain impression.

> Your question implies that you don't understand.
> I infer from your question that you don't understand.

In, into, in to

In implies a set location; *into*, movement to a location; *in to*, the adverb *in* and the preposition *to* (usually with a verb).

> She is in her office; she went into her office; she went in to answer the telephone.

In connection with

Use *connected with*.

In person

See USAGE; **Personally, in person**.

Inc.

See PUNCTUATION; **Comma;** *Inc., Ltd*.

Incidence, incident, incidental

Incidence means the occurrence of; *incident*, pertaining to (as an adjective); *incidental*, occurring by chance or unrelatedly.

Inconsistent

To be inconsistent *in* or *with*.

> He is inconsistent in his arguments.
> Her statements were inconsistent with her record.

Increase

For business usage, see USAGE; **Raise, increase, increment**.

Incredible, incredulous

Incredible means unbelievable; *incredulous*, unbelieving.

> Frankly, I'm incredulous; the story is incredible.

Infinitives

a. An infinitive is the simple, basic form of a verb, such as *to go, to see, to do*. The *to* is dropped (and understood) after some verbs: *make it (to) work, help them (to) get*, etc.

> Make him rest, if you can.
> We helped him get started on his project.
> They need not come until four.

b. Use an infinitive phrase as follows:
> *Noun, as subject:* To go will be a privilege.
> *Noun, as object:* He wants *to talk* with you.
> *Adjective:* The place *to go* is Spain.
> *Adverb:* He saved his graduation checks *to go* to Italy.
> *Absolute: To exaggerate* a bit, the trip was great!

c. A split infinitive occurs when a word or phrase separates *to* and the verb. Use a split infinitive only when necessary for clarity or emphasis. Notice in the examples below how the emphasis of meaning changes slightly with a shift of the infinitive.

> We want to understand it fully before signing.
> We want to *fully understand* it before signing.

Ingenious, ingenuous

Ingenious means inventive; *ingenuous* means candid or artless.

Inside of a, within

In statements referring to time, the phrase *inside of a* is a colloquial for *within*.

Intransitive verbs

See USAGE; **Transitive verbs.**

Irregardless

Irregardless is a nonstandard word; use *regardless*.

Irony

See PUNCTUATION; **Exclamation point** and **Quotation marks,** *Words different in tone*.

Its, it's

Use *its* as a possessive; *it's*, for *it is*.

> Its concept is new. It's a new concept.

Job, position

Both words mean a post of employment but with this distinction: A laborer who uses physical effort has a *job* and is paid *wages* at an hourly rate. A worker with special training or ability has a *position* and is paid a weekly or monthly *salary*. In personnel terminology, *job* is used for both because it is short; for example, *a clerical job*. (*Job* is also used for a unit of work.)

Junior, Senior, Jr., Sr.

Junior is usually dropped after the death of the father of the same name. *Senior* or *Sr.* is unnecessary and is almost never used unless the two identical names are closely associated (such as business partners) or unless each is so well known that a distinction is needed.

See ABBREVIATIONS; **Jr., Sr.** and PUNCTUATION; **Comma;** *Jr., Sr., II, III*.

Kind, kinds

Use singular verbs and pronouns with *kind*, plural with *kinds*. This guide applies also to *type, types; class, classes*, etc.

That type of machine performs well.
The two types of machines used were . . . .
Avoid: That kind of a machine performs well.

Later, latter

Later means after a time; *latter* means the second of two things.

I shall reply later.   I prefer the latter.

Latest, last

a. While these words can be synonymous, a common distinction is to use *last* to mean at the end in time or place; *latest*, to mean following all others in time only, but not necessarily being the end.

This is the latest edition of the book. It is not the last edition because we have started to work on the next edition.

b. *Last* can also mean the next before the present.

Our latest model is gray; our last model was white.

Lay, lie

a. The transitive verb *to lay* means to put in place. Its principal parts are *lay, laid, laid*.

Lay the mail down.
He laid the mail down.

b. The intransitive verb *to lie* means to recline or rest on. Its principal parts are *lie, lay, lain*.

The mail lies on the table.
It lay there yesterday.

Lead, led

The past tense of *lead* is *led*.

He led the opposition.

Leave, let

Leave means to depart; *let*, to permit or allow.

Lend

See USAGE; **Loan, lend**.

Less, lesser

Less implies that which is smaller in extent but not countable: *less haste, less noise*. *Lesser* implies a difference in extent between two: *the lesser evil, a lesser work*.

Like

a. All reference books agree on these usages:

Adjective: . . . in a like situation.
Pronoun: . . . letters, reports, and the like.
Preposition: . . . type like a professional.

b. Usage of *like* for *as* or *as if* is not accepted in formal writing.

Informal: The report reads like he took pains with it.
Formal: The report reads as if he polished it.

See USAGE; **As, usage of**.

Linking verbs

These verbs *connect* a subject with a predicate noun or adjective. Some examples are:

to be (am, is, was, has been, etc.), act, appear, become, feel, get, grow, look, seem, sound, taste, turn

Loan, lend

Although some writers use *loan* as a noun only, dictionaries show both *loan* and *lend* as verbs. The principal parts are *loan, loaned, loaned,* and *lend, lent, lent.*

Look

When *look* means *appear* (a linking verb), use adjectives with it; when it means to see with the eyes, use adverbs.

    Adjective: Mr. Snyder looked very weary.
    Adverb: He looked wearily at the stack of papers.

Loose, lose

Loose means not tight; *lose,* to suffer a loss.

    It is easy to lose a loose button.

Lot of, lots of

Avoid these phrases in business writing. Use instead: *many, much, a great many, a considerable number,* and the like.

Ltd.

See PUNCTUATION; **Comma;** *Inc., Ltd.*

Mathematics

Use singular forms when you mean the *science* of mathematics.

May, might

Might is the past tense of *may.* Both imply permission, possibility, or opportunity; *can* implies ability.

    The letter says that Mrs. Lee may sell the house.
    She might have sold it, but she reconsidered.
    The realtor says that he can sell it.

See USAGE; **Can, could, would.**

Million

See NUMBERS; **Millions.**

More nearly, most nearly

These phrases are used in formal writing to express comparative and superlative degrees for adjectives that cannot be compared, as *a more nearly perfect circle, the more nearly square design.*

More than one

Although this phrase is plural, the subject that follows it takes a singular verb.

    More than one rule was ignored.

National

See CAPITALIZATION; **Federal.**

Necessary

This word is an adjective. It can be used in business writing to soften a phrase like *you must.* The noun form is *necessity* or *need.*

    It is necessary that you (*or:* You must) . . . .

Necessity, need

Use *necessity of* or *for* or simply *need.*

    There is no necessity for this step.
             or:
    There is no need for this step.

Neither, nor

See USAGE; **Either, neither; Either — or, neither — nor**

News

This word takes singular verbs.

    The latest news is that . . . .

No

See USAGE; **Yes, no.**

Nobody

This word takes singular verbs.

None, no one, not one

None can be either singular or plural; *no one* and *not one* take singular forms.

    None of the students were bored.
    None of the money was spent on improvements.
    Not one of us was able to be there.

See USAGE; **All, any, none, some, more, most.**

Not, and not

When either of these two introduces a phrase in contrast to the subject, the subject determines whether the verb is singular or plural.

    Results, not wishful thinking, count.

Nothing but, nothing else but

Use *nothing but*.

> We can add nothing but our thanks.

Not only, but also

a. In this construction the noun closer to the verb determines whether the forms used are singular or plural.

> Not only the orders but also his report was late.
> Not only the report but also the orders were late.

b. When this construction is used with main clauses, separate by comma.

> Not only was it their first visit here, but it was also their first trip by air.

See PUNCTUATION; **Comma;** *But* and USAGE; **Parallel construction**.

Notorious

This word means *well known for unfavorable reasons*. Used *noted, famed, celebrated*, etc. to imply favorable reasons.

Not so — as

See USAGE; **As — as, not so — as**.

Number

See USAGE; **Amount, number**.

Number, numeral, figure

Use *number* to express the idea of a quantity or sum of something. Numbers can be spelled out in *numerals* or *figures*.

> We spell out small numbers like *two, five, ten*.
> We use figures for large numbers: 1,243, etc.
> There were 15 apples in the basket; *15* is the *number* of apples expressed by the *figures 1* and *5*.

Number of

The meaning intended determines whether this phrase takes singular or plural forms.

> The number of replies that we received is gratifying.
> A number of the replies were critical of our policy.

O, Oh

See PUNCTUATION: **Exclamation point;** *O, Oh*.

Of

See PUNCTUATION; **Comma;** *Of*.

Off, off of

Use *off* alone.

> The part fell off the machine.
> The girl jumped off the wall.

OK, O.K., okay

Use *okay* in formal writing, *OK* or *O.K.* in informal.

Older, oldest

Use *older* in comparing two things, *oldest* in comparing more than two. This guide applies to *elder* and *eldest* also.

> He was the elder of two sons.
> Which of the two books is the older edition?
> They presented an orchid to the oldest mother present.
> *but:*
> My older brother is a doctor; my young brother, a student at Stanford.

One

See USAGE; **We, they, one, you**.

One's, ones

> Saving one's money is a good habit.
> Those forms are not the right ones.

One of the

In formal writing, constructions like *one of the people who* and *one of the things that* take plural forms. In spoken English, the singular forms are often used.

> *Formal:* She is one of the directors who agree that . . . .
> *Informal:* She is one of the people who thinks that . . . .

Oneself

Oneself is preferred to *one's self*.

> Taking oneself too seriously is a foolish practice.

Only

a. Take care to place *only* where it limits according to the meaning of the sentence.

> Only the typists type form letters (not the secretaries).
> The only typist who types form letters is Alan.
> He only types; he does not take dictation.
> He types only form letters requested by the sales department.
> Alan types form letters only when he has spare time.

b. Do not use *only* as a preposition for *except* or *but*.

> *Incorrect:* No one is interested only Mr. Lane.

On, onto, on to

See USAGE ; **In, into, in to**.

Or

When *or* joins two subject words, the verb agrees with the nearer word.

> Only one or two are needed.
> No pencils or paper was furnished.

Oral, verbal

According to the dictionaries, *oral* means spoken; *verbal* refers to words, spoken or written. Although both are commonly used for *spoken*, use the dictionary meaning in formal writing.

> She presented the material verbally and supported it graphically with maps and charts.
> His oral agreement is tantamount to a written contract.
> *Informal:* His verbal contract is . . . .

Out of date, up to date, etc.

Hyphenate these expressions only when used *before* the noun.

> His report is up to date.
> Her up-to-date records saved the day.

See PUNCTUATION ; **Hyphen;** *Compound words as adjectives* .

Owing to

See USAGE ; **Due to**.

Pair, pairs

The plural of *pair* is either *pair* or *pairs*.

> They sent only ten pair(s) of gloves.

See USAGE ; **Two-part objects**.

Parallel construction

If two or more sentence parts are joined by one or more conjunctions, the parts should be of like kinds; that is, all single words of the same part of speech, all phrases, or all clauses.

> The shipment was returned not only because it was late but also because two items were incorrect. *(connecting two clauses)*
> *not:*
> The shipment was returned not only for being late but also because two items were incorrect. *(connecting a phrase and a clause)*
> A good secretary not only is prompt but also shows initiative. *(connecting two verb phrases)*
> *not:*
> A good secretary is both prompt and shows initiative. *(connecting an adjective and a verb phrase)*
> Our plan is to decide on the type of building, to choose an architect, and to let the contracts. *(connecting infinitives)*
> *not:*
> Our plan is to decide on the type of building, choosing an architect, and letting the contracts. *(connecting an infinitive and participles)*

Pardon, excuse

Pardon is used for things of considerable importance; *excuse* for less important ones.

> The company was pardoned for its apparent negligence when the facts were revealed.
> Please excuse the slight delay in answering.

Participles, dangling

A participial construction should modify a related, logical word except when the construction is absolute (modifying nothing).

> *Dangling:* Leaving the office, the letter was dropped.
> *Logical:* Leaving the office, I dropped the letter.
> *Absolute:* The situation having developed, let's accept the changes it necessitates.

Passed, past, pastime

Passed is the past tense and past participle of the verb *to pass*. *Past* is a noun or an adjective meaning previously, a preposition, or an adverb. *Pastime* (often misspelled *passtime* or *pasttime*) is a diversion.

> They passed the time by reading.
> Go two blocks past Elm Street.
> This bill is past due.
> In the past my favorite pastime was reading.

Peeve

The noun *peeve* is not given in all dictionaries. The verb *peeve* is labeled *colloquial*.

Percent, per cent; percentage

While both styles are in common use, the trend is toward *percent*. *Percentage* is always one word and never used with a number. *Proportion* is often better in formal writing.

See NUMBERS; **Percent**.

Person, individual, personage, party, people

A *person* is a human being; an *individual* is one apart from a group; a *personage* is a person of importance; a *party* is a legal term for person (other usage is slang). Use *persons* for small numbers, *people* for large masses.

> The will of the people prevailed.
> The rule affected only thirty persons.

Personal, personnel

Personal means private; *personnel* means a body of persons.

> The letter was personal.
> He drove his personal car, not the company car.
> The office personnel were dismissed at 2:30.

Personally, in person

These terms intensify meaning. Avoid using them in formal writing.

> I personally guarantee each one.
> Mr. Lane made the award in person.

Place compounds

In formal writing, use *anywhere, everywhere, somewhere, nowhere,* and the like. Although some dictionaries recognize *anyplace, everyplace,* and *someplace,* they label them *informal or substandard.*

See USAGE; *Where* **compounds**.

Politics

This word is commonly used with singular verbs.

Position

See USAGE; **Job, position**.

Practical, practicable

Practical means sensible, efficient, or useful. *Practicable* implies something that can be put into practice.

> My practical secretary has suggested a practicable method for handling follow-ups.

Precedence, precedents, precedent

Precedence means priority or preference; *precedents* is the plural of the noun *precedent* and means an earlier occurrence; *precedent* (presEEdent) is an adjective and means earlier in order.

> The guests were seated according to the precedence of their diplomatic positions.
> There are several precedents for that decision.
> The precedent decisions that apply to this case must be considered.

Predominate, predominant

Predominate is a verb meaning to control or surpass; *predominant* is the adjectival form.

> Its good features predominate over its bad ones.
> The predominant features of the plan are good.

Prefixes

See PUNCTUATION; **Hyphen**; *Prefixes, hyphenated* and *joined*.

Prepositions

Prepositions should end a construction only to avoid awkward phrasing or when used in a prepositional idiom.

> A collective noun takes a singular verb when the *group* is thought of.
> He left his car to be worked on.

For prepositional idioms, see USAGE; **Idioms (b)**.

Presume to, presume upon

These are prepositional idioms, each with its own meaning.

> He presumed to offer advice to the company president.
> They presumed upon our generosity.

Prerequisite

As a noun, a *prerequisite for;* as an adjective, to be *prerequisite to.*

Principal, principle

a. *Principal* as an adjective means main; as a noun, it means the main person or a capital sum.

> The principal actor was outstanding in his part.
> The principals in the legal case are present.
> Mrs. Palmer invested the principal of the trust fund and spent the interest therefrom.

b. *Principle* is a noun meaning a rule, guide, truth, etc. It never refers to a person.

> He follows the principle of "least said, soonest mended."

Privileged to, privileged from

These are prepositional idioms.

> They were privileged to hear a great symphony.
> They were privileged from taking the examination.

Proved, proven

Although either word may be used as the past participle of *prove, proved* is preferred.

> You have proved (proven) your point.

Proposition

Correctly used as a noun, *proposition* means an assertion or dignified proposal. Do not use this word as a verb.

Public

As a noun this word is commonly used with singular verbs and pronouns but can take the plural at times.

> The public quickly tires of its favorites.

Quantities

See USAGE; **Amounts, quantities**.

Raise, increase, increment

Business uses all three words for a higher wage or salary. *Raise* is the common word (in Britain, *rise*); *increase* is the more dignified word; *increment* is a personnel word.

Real, really

Use *real* only as an adjective, *really* is an adverb.

> What really worries us is that the real facts are so obscure.

Reason is

The reason is takes a predicate-noun (or noun-clause) construction. *Because* is a conjunction for adverbial clauses; do not use it here.

> The reason we failed is that (*not* because) we were not prepared.

Recipe, receipt

Recipe means a method of procedure (commonly referring to preparing food); common usage for *receipt* is a written statement that something has been received.

> Mrs. Edwards would like to have your recipe for beef Wellington.
> We are enclosing a receipt for your payment.

Redundancy

Redundancy is the needless use of words. The phrases below are redundant. In each one, the italicized word is sufficient for clarity.

both *alike*	*depreciate* in value
close *proximity*	month of *April*
continue on	*repeat* again
customary *practice*	two *twin sisters*

See USAGE; **Consensus of opinion**.

Remainder

See USAGE; **Balance, remainder**.

Requisite

See USAGE; **Prerequisite**.

Resolve

To *resolve* (settle) *something;* to *resolve* (determine) *that;* to *resolve* (separate) *into.*

> We resolved the problem before the deadline.
> We resolve that it won't recur.
> The problem resolved itself into three issues.

Resolved

See CAPITALIZATION; **Whereas, resolved**.

Restrictive clause

See USAGE; **That, which, who** and PUNCTUATION; **Comma;** *Restrictive and nonrestrictive elements.*

Reverend

Use a first name, initials, or title between *Reverend* and the surname.

> Rev. Maxfield Dowell, the Reverend M. A. Dowell, the Reverend Dr. Dowell (in a reference to him)

See ABBREVIATIONS; **Reverend**.

Salary, wages

See USAGE; **Job, position**.

II, 2d, 2nd

See ABBREVIATIONS; **II, 2d, 2nd** and PUNCTUATION; **Comma;** *Jr., Sr., II, III*.

Self (intensive) pronouns

See PUNCTUATION; **Comma;** *Myself, himself, yourself*, etc.

Series lists

See PUNCTUATION; **Special Element, Series**.

Set

See USAGE; **Sit, set**.

Shall, will

Will is commonly used for first, second, and third person, future tense. In formal writing, however, express first person, future, with *shall*, second and third persons, future, with *will*. To express the emphatic future, reverse the usages of *shall* and *will*.

> We shall be happy to accept your offer.
> Nevertheless, I *will* take a stand on this matter.

Should, would

Should is used in uncertainty; *would* is used mainly as a conditional auxiliary verb.

> He should be ready to go soon.
> Do you think we should sign the contract?
> I would have gone except for a previous appointment.
> They would like Italy, I'm sure, once they were there.

Sic

See PUNCTUATION; **Brackets;** *Quoted matter (a)*.

Sit, set

a. *Sit* is intransitive; a person or object sits. The principal parts are *sit, sat, sat*.

> We sat in the lounge and chatted.

b. *Set* is transitive (except when it means to jell or coagulate); a thing is *set* or *placed*. The principal parts are *set, set, set*.

> You *set* something down, and it *sits* there.
> Yesterday you *set* something down, and it *sat* there.

See USAGE; **Transitive verbs**.

Slow, slowly

Both words can be adverbs. Both *drive slow* and *drive slowly* are correct.

So-called

See PUNCTUATION; **Quotation marks;** *Words different in tone (b)*.

Species

This word is both singular and plural.

> That species is extinct.
> These species were grouped for study.

Split infinitives

See USAGE; **Infinitives (c)**.

Sr., senior

See ABBREVIATIONS; **II, 2d, 2nd** and PUNCTUATION; **Comma;** *Jr., Sr., II, III*.

State

See CAPITALIZATION; **Federal**.

Stationary, stationery

Stationary means stable or fixed; *stationery* is writing paper.

Statistics

Use plural forms except when you mean the science of statistics.

Street addresses

See ABBREVIATIONS; **Street addresses**.

Subjunctive mood

In formal writing, the subjunctive mood is commonly used in contrary-to-fact clauses, clauses expressing doubt, clauses expressing wishes, regrets, demands, recommendations, etc.

Subjunctive mood:

If he were here, he would agree with me.
If time were available, I would come.
If that be true, we must act now.
I wish I were confident of the outcome.
We recommend that it be tried.

Conventional (indicative) usage:

I know he was here because he left a note.
If he was (*not* were) here earlier, he didn't leave a note.
If she was planning to go, she didn't tell me.

Professor Porter G. Perrin in his book *Writer's Guide and Index to English* says that, actually, subjunctives are a trait of style rather than a matter of grammar.

Such as

See PUNCTUATION; **Comma;** *Such as*

Suffixes

See PUNCTUATION; **Hyphen;** *Suffixes* and WORDS: COINED; **Suffixes**.

Superior

As an adjective, to be superior *to* a person *in* rank; as a noun, to be the superior *of*.

Sympathetic

To be sympathetic (favorable) *to* or *toward* is colloquial. It is often used in business writing, as *we are sympathetic to the idea*.

Tactics

Use plural verbs and pronouns except when you mean a military science.

Tantamount

To be tantamount (equivalent) *to*.

That, which, who

a. *That* and *which* are not always interchangeable. *That* is preferred for introducing a restrictive clause.

The phrasing that you suggest is good.
The book that you recommend is excellent.

b. *Which* is preferred for introducing a nonrestrictive clause.

The new phrasing, which seems clearer, is better.
Your help, which we need badly, will save the day.

c. *Who* refers to persons, and sometimes to animals. *Who* can introduce either restrictive or nonrestrictive clauses.

The members who favored the amendment voted *Yes*.
Mr. Jones, who was out of town, voted by proxy.
Native Dancer, who won many important races, was a famous racehorse.

d. In formal writing, do not omit *that* as a conjunction.

Formal: We feel that this proposal is fair.
Informal: We feel this idea is a good one.

They

See USAGE; **We, they, one, you**.

Till, until

Until is preferred at the beginning of a sentence.

Titles of books, articles, etc.

a. A title used as a noun takes singular forms.

Executives Report says in its latest issue . . . .

b. For form and style for typewritten titles, see PUNCTUATION; **Special Element, Titles of Published Matter**.

Titles of persons

See ABBREVIATIONS; **Titles** and CAPITALIZATION; **Degrees** and **Titles of persons**.

Together with

See USAGE; **As well as, together with**.

Trademarks

See CAPITALIZATION; **Trademarked names**.

Transitive verbs

Dictionaries label verbs *transitive* or *intransitive*. Transitive verbs take objects. Intransitive verbs do not.

Transitive: Send the letter today.
Intransitive: She arrived this morning.

b. Some verbs are transitive *and* intransitive.

Transitive: I wrote a full report.
She left her luggage at the hotel.
Intransitive: I wrote yesterday.
She left yesterday.

Two-part objects (scissors, gloves, etc.)

Words like scissors, while singular in meaning, take plural verbs and pronouns. Preceded by *pair of*, they take singular forms.

The gloves are new.
This pair of gloves is new.
Two pair (*or* pairs) of gloves were lost.

Type of

Type is a noun or verb; do not use it as an adjective.

This type of process is new.
not:
This type process is new.

Uninterested

See USAGE; **Disinterested, uninterested**

United States

Use *the* before *United States* in formal writing, rephrasing if necessary to avoid an awkward construction. (If necessary, substitute *American*.)

According to laws of the United States . . . .
not:
According to United States laws . . . .

Until

See USAGE; **Till, until**.

Verbal

See USAGE; **Oral, verbal**.

Verbal phrases

See USAGE; **Infinitives** and **Participles**.

Vest

To vest *with* authority; to vest authority *in* a person or agency.

The courts vest a guardian with power to administer an inheritance.
Administration of the estate was vested in the trust department of the bank.

Vice-president

See CAPITALIZATION; **Titles of persons**.

View

As a verb, *to view with;* as a noun, *in view of* or *with a view to*.

We view it with indifference.
In view of the time, we will adjourn.

Void

This word is a noun, a verb, or an adjective.

His resignation left a void in our company.
Please void check No. 435.
She was void of any spark of enthusiasm.

Vulnerable

To be vulnerable (assailable) *to* something *in* some way or place.

He was vulnerable to criticism in his business practices.

Wages, salary

See USAGE; **Salary, wages**.

Weights

See ABBREVIATIONS; **Dimensions and weights** and NUMBERS; **Weights**.

Well

See USAGE; **Good, well**.

We, they, one, you

In business writing, these pronouns are used as indefinite pronouns to refer to the group that the writer represents. Use them consistently within a sentence or a paragraph.

We wired our reply.
If they reject it, we must then . . . .

Whereas

See CAPITALIZATION : **Whereas, resolved**.

Where compounds

Anywhere, everywhere, nowhere, and *somewhere* are adverbs and are written as one word.

See USAGE ; *Place* **compounds**.

Whether, whether — or, whether or not

a. In indirect questions, *whether* is preferred to *if*.

They asked whether he had come.
not:
They asked if he had come.

b. For alternatives, use *whether — or* or *whether or not*. Avoid awkwardness.

State whether you will go or stay.
State whether or not you will go.
not:
State whether you will go or not.

Which, who

See USAGE ; **That, which, who** and **whose**.

While, awhile

a. Use *while* as a connective for time or as a noun. *Awhile*, an adverb, is written as one word.

While Mrs. Lambert was out, her caller arrived.
Once in a while, we find that . . . .
He left awhile ago.

b. *While* can be used for *although*, but it should not be used for *and*.

While we see your point, we do not agree.
not:
We order nails from the H & P Company, while we order hammers from Black and Burns.

Who, whom

Use *who* as the subject of a verb, *whom* as the object of a verb or a preposition, or as the subject of an infinitive.

Send it only to those who asked for it.
Who do you think will be made chairman?
Everyone upon whom I called accepted.
Whom shall I ask first?
Whom did they ask to be chairman?

Whose

Use *whose* as a possessive conjunction if *of which* would be awkward.

The manual for systems and procedures, whose author is unknown, is excellent.
but:
A large box, the contents of which were unknown, stood on the loading dock.

Will

See USAGE ; **Shall, will**.

Within

See USAGE ; **Inside of a, within**.

Yes, no

Type these words in any of these ways (but consistently in a writing).

She will probably say "Yes."   She will probably say Yes.
She will probably say "yes."   She will probably say yes.
She will probably say Yes.

See PUNCTUATION ; **Comma;** *Words that answer*.

Yet

See PUNCTUATION ; **Comma;** *Yet*.

> WORDS:COINED; COMPOUND;
> DIVISION; FOREIGN—Page 733

WORDS : COINED

Coined and picturesque words do not need quotation marks or underlining if they are hyphenated or if they are appropriate to the context; set them off only to avoid misinterpretation.

Her shrug-of-the-shoulders attitude . . . .

Conversions

A *conversion* is the unconventional use of a word. Enclose the word in quotation marks only if the reader may think it is a grammatical error.

a. A noun or noun phrase converted to an adjective:

He is a *meat-and-potatoes* man.
He was in his *comedian* mood.

b. An adjective or adverb converted to a verb:

We *nonstopped* to Dallas.
He *low-keyed* his way into making the sale.

c. A noun converted to a verb:

He *apple-pied* us until we could scarcely move.
They *museumed* their way across Europe.

Hyphens

Use a hyphen to connect compound coinages. See WORDS: COINED; **Conversions** and **Prefixes** and **Suffixes**.

Prefixes

Handle words coined with prefixes according to the following:

ABBREVIATIONS; **Coined verb forms** and PUNCTUATION; **Hyphen**; *Letter prefixes* and *Prefixes, hyphenated*.

Suffixes

a. If a word coined with a suffix would be hard to read, use a hyphen.

He is an uh-er and ah-er (*not* uher and aher).

b. *-able and -ible*. In coinages, use the suffix *-able*, not *-ible*.

electable	put-downable	*yesable*
convinceable	bypassable	

c. *-er and -ee*. Join *-er* to indicate the person acting, *-ee* to indicate the person acted upon. If the verb ends in *e*, drop one *e*.

maintainer, maintainee	berater, beratee
telephoner, telephonee	persuader, persuadee

d. *-ish*. Join to the word unless a hyphen is needed for clarity.

hindsightish	sixty-ish	tycoonish

e. *-ize*. Join to a noun or adjective to form a verb, as *winterize*. If the word ends in a vowel, hyphenate, as *Sohio-ize, bureau-ize*.

f. *-like*. Join the suffix *-like* to the word unless the word ends in *1* or an awkward word would result.

See USAGE; **Suffixes**.

g. *-proof*. To imply imperviousness, add *-proof* to the base word. Use a hyphen only if the word ends in *p* or if an awkward word would result.

See USAGE; **Suffixes**.

h. *Other suffixes*. To coin a word with any other suffix, look up the suffix in the dictionary and follow the examples given.

WORDS: COMPOUND

Compounds are written solid, hyphenated, or open (as separate words). First consult a dictionary for the proper form of a compound. If the word is not given, consult this Reference Guide under one of the following headings:

CAPITALIZATION; **Hyphenated words** and **Titles of persons**

NUMBERS; **Compound numeric adjectives** and **Fractions** and **Hyphenated numbers**

POSSESSIVES; **Compound words**

PUNCTUATION; **Hyphen; Capitalized compound words, Compound words adjectives, Letter prefixes, Prefixes (hyphenated and with mixed usage), Suffixes**

USAGE; *Place* compounds, *Where* compounds

WORDS: COINED

WORD DIVISION

Typewriters without proportional spacing cannot and need not maintain the even right margins of typeset material. But because the reader will be distracted both by an unduly ragged margin and by excessive end-of-line word divisions the best course is to follow (judiciously) these rules:

a. DO NOT DIVIDE:

1. One-syllable words

2. Words of five or fewer letters (preferably *six* or fewer)

into	after	until	proper	notice

3. Abbreviations, numbers, dates, names of persons (Avoid separating titles, initials, and professional and scholastic degrees from a name. If necessary to divide, do so at a logical point: May 14,/1979 or Mr. James A./Hanover.)

4. Two-letter first or last syllables

5. Contractions

6. The last word in over two successive lines of typing

7. The last word in a paragraph or on a page

b. Divide hyphenated words only at the hyphen.

self-criticism   profit-sharing

c. Divide words:

1. After an internal one-letter syllable

criti-cism	tele-vision	sepa-rate

Except: Do not divide *able, ible, icle, ical, cial,* or *sion.*

biolog-ical	change-able	deduct-ible	spe-cial

2. Between two vowels separately pronounced

radi-ator	sci-ence	cli-ents	situ-ation

3. Preferably at a prefix or suffix

mis-spelled	driv-ing	depart-ment	exten-sion

4. Between double consonants unless the base word ends in the double consonant

neces-sary	capil-lary	car-rier	excel-lent
will-ing	tell-ing	careless-ness	staff-ing

but:

discus-sion	impres-sive	impres-sion

5. To improve readability by putting as much of a word on a line as is practical, even though the word has several acceptable points of division

considera-tion (*not* consid-eration)
documenta-tion (*not* docu-mentation)

WORDS: FOREIGN

The English language has evolved from the combination of and additions from various languages, mostly Germanic. The practice of borrowing and adding foreign words is a continuing one; therefore, the secretary often needs to type foreign words.

a. Many "foreign" words have been so accepted into the language that they are considered *Anglicized*. Do not underline Anglicized words. Some common Anglicized words are:

chauffeur	eclair	laissez faire
chic	entree	maitre d' hotel
cliche	ersatz	naive
coiffure	facade	Noel
coup d'etat	faux pas	passe
creche	fete	precis
du jour	hors d' oeuvre	wunderkind

b. Typeset material often uses diacritical marks even with Anglicized words. Some common diacritical marks are:

- ´   Acute accent (French, Spanish)
- `   Grave accent (French, Italian, English)
- ^   Circumflex (French)
- ¨   Dieresis (French, English), crema (Spanish), Umlaut (German)
- ~   Tilde (Spanish)
- ¸   Cedilla (French)

If you find it necessary to use diacritical marks, insert them in ink as shown below.

mañana   tête-à-tête

c. Some foreign terms that are commonly underlined in typewritten material are shown below.

COMMUNICATIONS GUIDE —Page 736

anschluss	manana
cognoscente	noblesse oblige
de trop	nouveau riche
entre nous	rapprochement
et al.	vis-a-vis
joie de vivre	zeitgeist

ARMSTRONG & SONS
Professional Outdoor Advertisers

6858 River Road

Portland, OR 97222

Telephone 503-657-1171

December 10, 19--

Mr. Edward McDaniel
Akron Chamber of Commerce
74 South Main Street
Akron, OH 44308

Dear Mr. McDaniel

This letter is typed in block style with open punctuation.
Every line begins at the left margin. Only essential punctuation marks are used in the opening and closing lines.

The distinctive feature of this letter style is that the
date, the inside address, the salutation, the attention line
(when used), all lines in the body, the complimentary close,
and all signature lines begin at the left margin. No tabulator stops are necessary.

Typing time is accordingly reduced. First, time required
to set tabulator stops and to use the tabulator is saved.
Second, by omitting all except the essential punctuation
marks, the number of typing strokes is decreased.

The use of "open" punctuation is appropriate with this letter
style.

Cordially yours

Janet Harvet

Janet Harvet, Consultant

ao

Fairmeadows East
720 Saint Paul Place   Baltimore, MA 02120   301-631-3363

December 10, 19--

Mrs. Anna James
Caswell-Higgins Associates
Suite 385, Maumee Tower
Toledo, OH 43604

Dear Mrs. James

    SUBJECT: The Modified Block Letter Style

This letter is typed in modified block style with blocked
paragraphs. Open punctuation is used in the opening and
closing lines.

Contrast this style with the block style, and you will notice that the date line has been moved to begin at horizontal
center (although it would be appropriate also to end at the
right margin) and that the closing lines have been blocked
at the horizontal center of the letterhead. All other lines
begin at the left margin. These modifications of the block
style give the style its name -- modified block.

When an attention line is used in this style of letter, it
is begun at the left margin. If a subject line is used, it
is begun at the left margin or centered over the body of the
letter a double space below the salutation.

Although open punctuation is used in this letter, it is
equally appropriate to use mixed punctuation.

    Sincerely yours

    David N. Belz

    David N. Belz, Director

mcn

Commercial Distributors, Inc.
78 UNIVERSITY BOULEVARD • DENVER, CO 80206 • 303-276-4663

    December 10, 19--

Mr. William Summers
The Electromagnetic Corp.
One Erieview Plaza
Cleveland, OH 44114

Dear Mr. Summers:

    This letter is typed in modified block style with in-
dented paragraphs. Mixed punctuation is used in the opening
and closing lines. This punctuation style calls for a colon
after the salutation and a comma after the complimentary
close. All other end-of-line punctuation is omitted in the
opening and closing lines, unless a line ends in an abbreviation that requires the usual abbreviation period.

    Note that the date line is centered (although it could
have been typed to begin at center or to end at the right
margin); the subject line is centered; the first line of
each paragraph is indented 5 spaces (although 10- or 15-space
indentions are also commonly used); the closing lines are
blocked at the horizontal center of the letterhead. All
other lines begin at the left margin.

    Although mixed punctuation is used in this letter, it
would be equally acceptable to use open punctuation.

    Sincerely yours,

    George R. Sanders

    George R. Sanders

ck

ECKERT Equipment Co.

41 Monte Vista Boulevard
Albuquerque, NM 87106
505-575-1685

Dated Today

Office Secretary
Better Business Letters, Inc.
1 Main Street
Clarkstown, NY 10969

SIMPLIFIED LETTER

There's a new movement under way to take some of the monotony out of
letters given you to type. The movement is symbolized by the
Simplified Letter being sponsored by AMS.

What is it? You're reading a sample.

Notice the left block format and the general positioning of the letter.
We didn't write "Dear ----," nor will we write "Yours Truly" or
"Sincerely Yours." Are they really important? We feel just as
friendly toward you without them.

Notice the following points:

1. Date location
2. The address
3. The subject
4. The name of the writer

Now take a look at the Suggestions prepared for you. Talk them over
with your boss. But don't form a final opinion until you've really
tried out The Letter. That's what our secretaries did. As a
matter of fact, they finally wrote most of the Suggestions
themselves.

They say they're sold -- and hope you'll have good luck with
better (Simplified) letters.

Arthur E. Every

ARTHUR E. EVERY - STAFF DIRECTOR, TECHNICAL DIVISION

cc: R. P. Brecht, W. H. Evans, H. F. Grabe

Four Basic Letter Styles. (1) Block style, open punctuation, (2) Modified block style with blocked paragraphs, open punctuation, (3) Modified block style with indented paragraphs, mixed punctuation, (4)
Simplified style

whg 3 villa dr.   blue ash, ohio 45242

December 10, 19--

Dear Henry,

This inside address typed at the end of a letter removes
the business touch and tone from the letter and makes
it more personal.

This letter form is used also for very formal letters,
such as letters to public officials and honored persons.
In addition, letters of appreciation or sympathy or congratulations are typed in this form.

The reference initials are omitted. If the person receiving the letter knows the writer well, it is not necessary that his name be typed as part of the signature.

Cordially,

Bill

Mr. Henry D. Ransom
302 Peachtree Street
Atlanta, GA 30308

PERSONAL AND FORMAL STYLE TYPED ON PERSONAL LETTERHEAD

RMN interoffice memorandum

TO: New Members of the
Stenographic Pool

FROM: Judith L. Reese
Correspondence Supervisor

DATE: December 10, 19--

SUBJECT: Interoffice Correspondence

The interoffice or interdepartment letterhead is used, as the name implies,
for correspondence between offices or departments within the company. One
advantage of this form is that it can be set up quickly. For instance,
this letter requires settings for only the margins and one tabulator stop.
Titles (Mr., Mrs., Dr., etc), the salutation, the complimentary close, and
the formal signature are usually omitted.

Triple-space between the last line of the heading and the first line of the
message. Short messages of no more than five lines may be double-spaced;
longer messages should be single-spaced.

Reference initials should be included. When enclosures are sent, the enclosure notation should appear below the reference initials.

sva

INTEROFFICE MEMORANDUM

J. L. Bell
245 Compton Road
Cincinnati, OH 45215

2″

← 2½″ →

MS ROBERTA SIMPSON
219 KENWAY DRIVE   APT 3
DES MOINES IA 50310

2½″

← 4″ →

CONTINENTAL PRODUCTS
ATTENTION MR ROBERT L OMALLEY
320 EUCLID AVENUE
DES MOINES IA 50313

NOTATIONS TO POST OFFICE

Begin at least three line spaces above the address, below the stamp. Type in all capital
letters. Underline if desired. Such notations
include:

SPECIAL DELIVERY   REGISTERED
HAND STAMP

FORM AND PLACEMENT OF ENVELOPE ADDRESS PARTS FOR OPTICAL CHARACTER READERS

REQUIREMENTS FOR OPTICAL CHARACTER READERS

Post office optical character readers are programmed to scan a specific area on all envelopes; so the address must be completely
within this read-zone, *blocked in style, single-
spaced.* The 2-letter state abbreviations
(typed in upper case) must be used. An apartment or room number should follow the
street address *on the same line.* Acceptable
placements for a No. 10 and a No. 6¾ envelope are specified in the illustration above.
The U.S. Postal Service prefers the use of uppercase letters and no punctuation in envelope addresses.

FOREIGN ADDRESS

The last word in the address
block should be the country
name in all capitals. Where an
address code is used in that
country, it should be placed
on the left side of the last line
or on the next to the last line.

ON-RECEIPT NOTATIONS

Type (in all capitals) a triple space
below the return address and 3
spaces from the left edge of the envelope. Such notations include:

HOLD FOR ARRIVAL
PLEASE FORWARD
CONFIDENTIAL

Type an *attention line* immediately
below the company name.

FORM AND ARRANGEMENT OF BUSINESS LETTER PARTS

Letter Part	Line Position	Horizontal Placement	Points to Be Observed	Acceptable Forms
DATE	If a floating date line is used, the date is typed from 12 to 20 lines from the top of the letterhead or plain sheet, depending upon letter length. A fixed date line is usually typed a double space below the last line of the letterhead.	*Block, Simplified Styles:* Even with left margin. *Modified Block Style:* Begun at center of the sheet; to end flush with right margin; or according to the letterhead.	1. Do not abbreviate names of months. 2. Unusual 2- and 3-line arrangements are not commonly used. 3. Do not use *d, nd, rd, st,* or *th* following the day of the month.	December 14, 19— 2 May 19— (Used primarily in government and military correspondence.)
ADDRESS	*With Floating Date Line:* Typed on 4th line below the date. *With Fixed Date Line:* Typed from 3 to 9 lines below the date, depending on letter length. *Government Letter:* Typed on the 14th line. *Personal Style:* Placed at the left margin 5 or 6 lines below the last closing line.	Single-spaced with all lines even at left margin. Use at least three lines for address. Place business title at end of first line or beginning of second line, whichever gives better balance. For a long company name indent the second line 2 or 3 spaces.	1. Follow addressee's letterhead style. 2. Do not abbreviate *Street* or *Avenue* unless it improves appearance. 3. For the name of a town or city, do not use *City.* 4. Use postal zip codes in addresses. 5. Do not use *%* for *In Care Of.* (This follows the name line.)	Miss Rose Bannaian Manager, Rupp Steel Co. 2913 Drexmore Avenue Dallas, TX 75206 Mr. Russell H. Rupp 68 Devoe Avenue Dallas, Texas 75206 (Refer to the Reference Guide for specific comments.)
ATTENTION LINE	*Preferred:* Typed a double space below address and a double space above salutation.	Typed even with left margin or begun at the paragraph point. Typed even with left margin.	1. Do not abbreviate *Attention.* 2. Unnecessary to use of as in *Attention of Mr. R. H. Rupp.*	Attention Mr. R. H. Rupp Attention Purchasing Agent Attention Mr. L. Cox, Agent
SALUTATION	Typed a double space below last line of address or a double space below attention line. (Note: Omitted in the Simplified style and in interoffice correspondence.)	1. Use *Gentlemen* for a company, a committee, a numbered post-office box, a collective organization made up entirely of men. 2. In addressing women substitute *Ladies* or *Mesdames* for *Gentlemen; Madam* for *Sir; Miss* or *Mrs.* for *Mr.;* use *Ms.* when the marital status of a woman is unknown. 3. Use *Ladies and Gentlemen* for a company, committee, post-office box, or organization made up of men and women.	1. Use *Gentlemen* for a company, a committee, a numbered post-office box, a collective organization made up entirely of men. 2. In addressing women substitute *Ladies* or *Mesdames* for *Gentlemen; Madam* for *Sir; Miss* or *Mrs.* for *Mr.;* use *Ms.* when the marital status of a woman is unknown. 3. Use *Ladies and Gentlemen* for a company, committee, post-office box, or organization made up of men and women.	Dear Mr. Rupp Gentlemen Dear Sir: Dear Russell: Dear Ms. Willis Dear Mrs. Cox Ladies and Gentlemen

SUBJECT (or REFERENCE) LINE	Typed a double space below salutation. Some printed letterheads indicate position for subject or file number (usually at the top of the letterhead).	Typed even with left margin in the block and Simplified styles. (In the Simplified style, the word "Subject" is omitted and the line is typed in all capitals a triple space below last line of address.) *Modified Block Style:* Typed even with left margin, at paragraph point, or centered.	1. *Subject* may be typed in all capitals or with only first letter capitalized. *Subject* may be omitted; if it is used, it should be followed by a colon. 2. Do not abbreviate *Subject;* capitalize important words in the subject line.	Subject: Pension Plan SUBJECT: Pension Plan Pension Plan PENSION PLAN Your File 987 Reference: File #586 Re: File 586
BODY	Typed a double space below salutation or subject (reference) line. *Simplified Style:* Typed a triple space below subject line.	*Block Style:* First line of each paragraph typed even with left margin. *Modified Block Style:* First line of each paragraph typed even with left margin or indented 5 or 10 spaces.	1. Keep right margin as even as possible, avoiding hyphens at ends of lines where possible. 2. For enumerated material, indent 5 spaces from both margins and double-space after each item. (In the Simplified style, indent listed items 5 spaces except when numbered.)	Single-space lines of paragraphs; double-space between paragraphs. A short one-paragraph letter may be double-spaced with indented paragraphs.
SECOND-PAGE HEADING and BODY	*Heading:* Begin approximately 1" (6 blank lines) below the top edge of the sheet. *Body:* Begin on the 3d line from the head, using the same margins as for the preceding page. Do not begin with the last part of a divided word. Include at least two lines of a paragraph.	Mr. Jerry W. Robinson Page 2 (Current Date) ～～～～ Mr. Jerry W. Robinson 2 (Current Date)	Type the second and succeeding pages on plain paper. The heading is typed even with the left margin in block form or in a one-line arrangement (illustrated below). Use the one-line arrangement if a page might be crowded.	
COMPLIMENTARY CLOSE	Typed a double space below the last line of letter body. *Omitted in the Simplified letter style and in interoffice correspondence.*	Begin at the center except in block style where the complimentary close is typed even with the left margin.	1. Do not extend the longest of closing lines noticeably beyond right margin. 2. Capitalize first word only. 3. Avoid contractions.	Very truly yours,* Sincerely yours,* Cordially, or Cordially yours,* Respectfully yours, *Also written with *Yours* as the first word
COMPANY NAME	If used, typed a double space below the complimentary close.	Typed even with the beginning of the complimentary close.	1. Capitalize all letters. 2. Type name exactly as it appears on letterhead.	TRIMOUNT CLOTHING COMPANY JOHNSON & RAND SHOE CO.

FORM AND ARRANGEMENT OF BUSINESS LETTER PARTS (Continued)

Letter Part	Line Position	Horizontal Placement	Points to Be Observed	Acceptable Forms
SIGNATURE (Name and Title of Signer)	Typed 3 blank lines below complimentary close (or company name, if used). *Simplified Style:* All capital letters at least 4 lines below last line of body. NOTE: If both the name and title are used, they may be typed on the same line or the title may be typed on the next line below the typed name. The style giving the best balance should be used.	Typed even with first letter of complimentary close (or company name, if used). *Simplified Style:* Even with left margin.	1. Capitalize important words in title. 2. When dictator's name appears in letterhead, use the title only. 3. Do not use *Mr.* in typing a man's name. (See page 200 for secretarial signatures.)	Harold A. Wenchstern Director of Personnel Brenda Ryan, Manager Purchasing Department *Simplified Style:* LOUIS K. COX – AGENT
IDENTIFICATION NOTATION	Typed a double space below or on the same line with the last of closing lines.	Typed even with the left margin. (For a complete discussion on the use of reference initials, see page 197.)	Omit dictator's initials when his or her name is typed as part of closing lines.	jc JWR/jc jwr/jc JWR:jc JWRobinson/jc
ENCLOSURE	Typed a double space below the identification notation.	Typed even with the left margin.	While *Enc.* and *Encl.* are not preferred forms, they are in common use because they save time.	Enclosure Enc. Encl. Enclosures Enclosures 3 Catalog #23 Encs. 2 Price List #8 Enclosures: Check Contract
POSTSCRIPT	Typed a double space below the identification notation or the last typed line.	Indent or block the postscript according to the style used in other paragraphs of the letter.	Initials of the writer may be typed below the postscript in place of a second signature.	P.S. Or omit the P.S. and write in the same form as a paragraph in the letter.
CARBON-COPY NOTATION	Typed a double space below the identification notation or the last typed line. (If notation not to appear on original; type at top of carbon copies.)	Typed even with the left margin. (When typed at the top of carbon copies, may be centered or placed at the left margin.)	1. *cc* or *Copy to* are generally used to indicate "Carbon Copy to." 2. Use *BC* for "blind copy" if notation is typed on carbon copies only.	cc: BC cc: Mr. H. R. King Miss K. Neilen Copy to Mr. H. R. King, Cashier BC to HRKing
MAILING NOTATION	Typed midway between date and first line of address; may be typed two lines below the last typed line.	Typed even with the left margin.	1. Typed in all capital letters. 2. May be typed on carbon copies only.	SPECIAL DELIVERY REGISTERED MAIL CERTIFIED MAIL
SEPARATE-COVER NOTATION	Typed a double space below last typed line.	Typed even with the left margin.	Indicates method of transportation and number of envelopes or packages.	Separate Cover – Express Separate Cover – Mail 2

PROOFREADER'S MARKS

INSERT MARKS FOR PUNCTUATION

ᵛ Apostrophe

[/] Brackets

: ⊙ Colon

⌃ ʾ/ Comma

ˣˣˣ/ Ellipsis

!/ Exclamation point

-/ Hyphen

⌃ ⌃ Inferior figure

· · ·/ Leaders

(/) Parentheses

⊙ Period

?/ Question mark

ᵛ ᵛ Quotation mark

; ⓢ Semicolon

ᵛ ᵛ Superior figure

OTHER MARKS

|| Align type; set flush

𝑏𝑓 Boldface type

× ⓧ Broken letter

≡ Cₐₚ Capitalize

C+ₛ𝒸 Capitals and small capitals

𝒹 Delete

𝒷 Delete and close up

∧ Insert (caret)

ital Italic, change to

𝐵𝑓 ital Italic boldface

stet Let type stand

lc Lower case type

⊔ Move down; lower

⊓ Move up; raise

⊏ Move to left

⊐ Move to right

ℙ Paragraph

no ℙ ⊏ No new paragraph

out s.c. Out; omit; see copy

⊚ Reverse; upside down

rom Roman, change to

⟲ Run in material

run in Run in material, on same line

Space, add (horizontal)

> Space, add (vertical)

⌣ Space, close up (horizontal)

< Space, close up (vertical)

ⓢₚ Spell out

tr ∩ Transpose

(?) ⓠ Verify or supply information

wf Wrong font

same ℨ/ℯ All marks should be made in the margin on the line in which the error occurs; if more than one correction occurs in one line, they should appear in their order separated by a slanting line.

lc Errors should not be blotted out.

One author →   [1]C. L. Stowell, <u>Contemporary Linguistics</u> (2d ed.; Cincinnati: Mayfair Publishing Co., 1978), p. 99.

Two authors →   [2]G. H. Trice and H. Robert Trice, <u>Basics of Real Estate</u>, edited by
(and editor)   Scott James (Chicago: Business Books, Inc., 1976), p. 86.

Ibid. →   [3]<u>Ibid</u>., pp. 158–160.

Three authors →   [4]B. J. Patterson, Carla Ashcraft–Steffen, and Stanley D. Hardwick, <u>Handbook of Graphic Processes</u> (3d ed.; Sacramento: CP Publications, 1978), pp. 56–59.

Four or more →   [5]Dale Keiger <u>et al</u>., <u>Readings in Management</u> (4th ed.; New York:
authors   MacPherson Book Co., 1977), pp. 115–117.

Unpublished →   [6]Lou Vega, <u>Implementing Affirmative Action Programs</u>, a
material   mimeographed report by the Diaz School of Business, 1978.

Op. cit. →   [7]Patterson, <u>op. cit</u>., p. 125.

Government →   [8]U.S. Treasury Department, Internal Revenue Service, <u>Audit</u>
agency   <u>Guide and Standards for Revenue Sharing Recipients</u>, Publication No. 22P (Washington: U.S. Government Printing Office, 1976), p. 48.

Magazine →   [9]"Mandatory Retirement Under Fire," <u>Executive Update</u>
article   (September 19, 1977), p. 43.

Article from →   [10]E. Martin Ott, "Organizing a Word Processing Center," <u>Ohio</u>
a bound   <u>Business Review</u> (Athens: Graduate School of Business Administration,
volume   Ohio University, 1978), Vol. 25, No. 2 (Summer, 1978), p. 108.

Newspaper →   [11]Susan D. DuChamp, "The New Stereotype––Wonder Women," <u>Atlanta</u>
article   <u>Courier</u> (August 6, 1978), p. 15, col. 1.

Loc. cit. →   [12]Ott, <u>loc. cit</u>.

FOOTNOTE CONSTRUCTION: Indent to paragraph point; single-space; double-space between items. Use quotation marks with titles of publication *parts*; underline titles of *complete* publications. *Ibid*. refers to the immediately preceding source; *loc. cit*. refers to the same location of a previous citation with intervening footnotes; *op. cit*., to a different page of a previous citation.

Newspaper →   DuChamp, Susan D. "The New Stereotype––Wonder Women," <u>Atlanta</u>
article   <u>Courier</u>. (August 6, 1978), p. 15, col. 1.

Four or more →   Keiger, Dale, <u>et al</u>. <u>Readings in Management</u>, 4th ed. New York:
authors   MacPherson Book Co., 1977.

Magazine →   "Mandatory Retirement Under Fire," <u>Executive Update</u> (September 19,
article   1977), p. 43.

Article from →   Ott, E. Martin. "Organizing a Word Processing Center," <u>Ohio Business</u>
a bound   <u>Review</u>. (Athens: Graduate School of Business Administration,
volume   Ohio University, 1978), Vol. 25, No. 2 (Summer, 1978), p. 108.

Three authors →   Patterson, B. J., Carla Ashcraft–Steffen, and Stanley D. Hardwick.
    <u>Handbook of Graphic Processes</u>, 3d ed. Sacramento: CP Publications, 1978.

One author →   Stowell, C. L. <u>Contemporary Linguistics</u>, 2d ed. Cincinnati: Mayfair Publishing Co., 1978.

Two authors →   Trice, G. H., and H. Robert Trice. <u>Basics of Real Estate</u>, edited by
(and editor)   Scott James. Chicago: Business Books, Inc., 1976.

Government →   U.S. Treasury Department, Internal Revenue Service. <u>Audit Guide and</u>
agency   <u>Standards for Revenue Sharing Recipients</u>, Publication No. 22P. Washington: U.S. Government Printing Office, 1976.

Unpublished →   Vega, Lou. <u>Implementing Affirmative Action Programs</u>, a mimeographed
material   report by the Diaz School of Business, 1978.

BIBLIOGRAPHY CONSTRUCTION: Present the items alphabetically by the first word of an item that is not an article. Start each item at the left margin; indent subsequent lines 5 spaces. Invert the order of only the first author's name. Give page references only for citations of *parts* of publications. Omit parentheses around publication facts except for periodicals.

CORRECT FORMS OF ADDRESS AND REFERENCE

Person and Address (Envelope and Letter)	Salutation	Complimentary Close	In Referring to the Person; Informal Introduction	In Speaking to the Person
U.S. PRESIDENT The President The White House Washington, D.C. 20500	Sir Mr. President Dear Mr. President	Respectfully yours Very truly yours	The President Mr. (Name)	Mr. President Sir (in prolonged conversation)
WIFE, U.S. PRESIDENT Mrs. (Last Name Only) The White House Washington, D.C. 20500	Dear Mrs. (Last Name Only)	Respectfully yours	Mrs. (Last Name Only)	Mrs. (Last Name Only)
U.S. VICE PRESIDENT The Vice President United States Senate Washington, D.C. 20510	Sir Dear Mr. Vice President Mr. Vice President	Respectfully yours Very truly yours	The Vice President Mr. (Name)	Mr. Vice President Mr. (Name)
U.S. CHIEF JUSTICE The Chief Justice The Supreme Court Washington, D.C. 20543	Sir Mr. Chief Justice Dear Mr. Chief Justice	Respectfully yours Very truly yours	The Chief Justice	Mr. Chief Justice
U.S. ASSOCIATE JUSTICE Justice (Name) The Supreme Court Washington, D.C. 20543	Sir Madam Mr. Justice Madam Justice Dear Mr. Justice Dear Madam Justice Dear Justice (Name)	Very truly yours Sincerely yours	Mr. Justice (Name) Madam Justice (Name)	Mr. Justice Mr. Justice (Name) Madam Justice Madam Justice (Name)
CABINET OFFICER The Honorable (Name) Secretary of (Office) Washington, D.C. 20520 The Secretary of (Office) Washington, D.C. 20520	Sir Dear Mr. Secretary Madam Dear Madam Secretary	Very truly yours Sincerely yours	The Secretary of ...., Mr. (Name) The Secretary Mr. (Name) The Secretary of ...., Mrs. or Miss (Name) The Secretary Mrs. or Miss (Name)	Mr. Secretary Mr. (Name) Madam Secretary Mrs. or Miss (Name)
SPEAKER OF THE HOUSE OF REPRESENTATIVES The Honorable (Name) Speaker of the House of Representatives Washington, D.C. 20515	Sir Madam Dear Mr. (Name) Mr. Speaker Madam Speaker Dear Madam Speaker	Very truly yours Sincerely yours	The Speaker, Mr. (Name) Mr. (Name) Mrs. or Miss (Name) The Speaker	Mr. Speaker Mr. (Name) Madam Speaker Mrs. or Miss (Name)

CORRECT FORMS OF ADDRESS AND REFERENCE (Continued)

Person and Address (Envelope and Letter)	Salutation	Complimentary Close	In Referring to the Person; Informal Introduction	In Speaking to the Person
U.S. SENATOR, SENATOR-ELECT The Honorable (Name) United States Senate Washington, D.C. 20510 or The Honorable (Name), Senator-Elect	Sir Dear Senator (Name) Madam Dear Senator (Name) Dear Mrs. or Miss (Name)	Very truly yours Sincerely yours	Senator (Name)	Senator (Name) Mr. (Name) Senator (Name) Mrs. or Miss (Name)
U.S. REPRESENTATIVE The Honorable (Name) House of Representatives Washington, D.C. 20515 Representative (Name) House of Representatives Washington, D.C. 20515	Sir Dear Representative (Name) My dear Sir Madam Dear Representative (Name) Dear Mrs. or Miss (Name)	Very truly yours Sincerely yours	Representative (Name) Mr. (Name) Representative (Name) Mrs. or Miss (Name)	Mr. (Name) Mrs. or Miss (Name)
U.S. GOVERNMENT OFFICIAL The Honorable (Name) Director of Bureau of the Budget Washington, D.C. 20503 Librarian of Congress Washington, D.C. 20540	Sir Dear Mr. (Name) Madam Dear Mrs. or Miss (Name)	Very truly yours Sincerely yours	Mr. (Name) Mrs. or Miss (Name)	Mr. (Name) Mrs. or Miss (Name)
AMERICAN AMBASSADOR The Honorable (Name) American Ambassador Paris, France	Sir Dear Mr. Ambassador Madam Dear Madam Ambassador	Very truly yours Sincerely yours	The American Ambassador The Ambassador Mr. (Name) Madam Ambassador Mrs. or Miss (Name)	Mr. Ambassador Mr. (Name) Madam Ambassador Mrs. or Miss (Name)

AMERICAN MINISTER
The Honorable (Name)
American Minister
Ottawa, Canada
	Sir
	Dear Mr. Minister
	
	Madam
	Dear Mrs. or Miss (Name)
	Dear Madam Minister
		Very truly yours
		Sincerely yours
			The American Minister,
			  Mr. (Name)[1]
			The Minister; Mr. (Name)
			The American Minister,
			  Mrs. or Miss (Name)
			The Minister
			Mrs. or Miss (Name)
				Mr. Minister
				Mr. (Name)
				
				Madam Minister
				Mrs. or Miss (Name)

[1] In presenting or referring to American Ambassadors and Ministers in any Latin-American country, say "Ambassador of the United States" or "Minister of the United States."

CORRECT FORMS OF ADDRESS AND REFERENCE (Continued)

Person and Address (Envelope and Letter)	Salutation	Complimentary Close	In Referring to the Person; Informal Introduction	In Speaking to the Person
U.S. REPRESENTATIVE TO THE UNITED NATIONS The Honorable (Name) United States Representa- tive to the United Nations New York, New York 10017	Sir Madam Dear Mr. (Name) Dear Mrs. or Miss (Name) *With Ambassadorial Rank:* Dear Ambassador (Name)	Very truly yours Sincerely yours	Mr. (Name) Mrs. or Miss (Name) Madam Ambassador Mr. Ambassador	Mr. (Name) Mrs. or Miss (Name) Madam Ambassador Mr. Ambassador
FOREIGN AMBASSADOR IN U.S. His/Her Excellency (Name) The Ambassador of France Washington, D.C.	Sir Madam Excellency Dear Mr. Ambassador Dear Madam Ambassador	Respectfully yours Sincerely yours Very truly yours	The Ambassador of..... Mr. (Name) The Ambassador Mr. (Name) Madam Ambassador	Mr. Ambassador Mr. (Name) Madam Ambassador Mrs. or Miss (Name)
FOREIGN MINISTER IN U.S. The Honorable (Name) Minister of Italy Washington, D.C.	Sir Madam Dear Mr. Minister Dear Madam Minister	Respectfully yours Sincerely yours Very truly yours	The Minister of..... Mr. (Name) The Minister Mr. (Name) Madam Minister	Mr. Minister Mr. (Name) Madam Minister Mrs. or Miss (Name)
AMERICAN CONSUL (Name), Esq. The American Consul United States Embassy (Foreign City, Country)	Sir Dear Mr. (Name) Dear Mrs. or Miss (Name)	Very truly yours Sincerely yours	Mr. (Name) Mrs. or Miss (Name)	Mr. (Name) Mrs. or Miss (Name)
FOREIGN CONSUL (Name), Esq. The French Consul (American City, State)	Sir Madam Dear Mr. (Name) Dear Madam (Name)	Very truly yours Sincerely yours	Mr. (Name) Madam (Name)	Mr. (Name) Madam (Name)
GOVERNOR OF A STATE His/Her Excellency the Governor of (State) or The Honorable (Name) Governor of (State) (Capital City, State)	Sir Madam Dear Governor Dear Governor (Name)	Respectfully yours Very truly yours Sincerely yours	Governor (Name) The Governor The Governor of (State)	Governor (Name) Governor
MEMBER, STATE LEGISLATURE The Honorable (Name) The State Senate or The House of Representatives (Capital City, State)	Sir Madam Dear Senator or Representative (Name) Dear Mr. (Name) Dear Mrs. or Miss (Name)	Very truly yours Sincerely yours	Mr. (Name) Senator (Name) Representative (Name) Mrs. or Miss (Name)	Mr. (Name) Senator (Name) Representative (Name) Mrs. or Miss (Name)
MAYOR OF A CITY The Honorable (Name) Mayor of the City of..... (City, State)	Sir Madam Dear Mayor (Name)	Very truly yours Sincerely yours	Mayor (Name) The Mayor	Mayor (Name) Mr. Mayor Madam Mayor

CORRECT FORMS OF ADDRESS AND REFERENCE (Continued)

Person and Address (Envelope and Letter)	Salutation	Complimentary Close	In Referring to the Person: Informal Introduction	In Speaking to the Person
JUDGE OF A COURT The Honorable (Name) Judge of the....Court (Local Address)	Sir Madam Dear Judge (Name)	Very truly yours Sincerely yours	Judge (Name)	Judge (Name)
MILITARY PERSONNEL (Rank) (Name) Post or Name of Ship City, State	Sir Dear (Rank) (Name)	Very truly yours Sincerely yours	(Rank) (Name)	(Rank) (Name)
CLERGY (PROTESTANT) The Reverend (Name), D.D. or The Reverend (Name) Parsonage Address City, State	Reverend Sir Dear Dr. (Name) My dear Sir My dear Madam Dear Reverend (Name)	Respectfully yours Sincerely yours Yours faithfully	The Reverend Doctor (Name) Doctor (Name) The Reverend (Name) Mr. (Name) Mrs. or Miss (Name)	Dr. (Name) Sir Mr. (Name) Mrs. (Name)
RABBI (JEWISH FAITH) Rabbi (Name) Rabbi (Name) D.D. Local Address	Sir My dear Rabbi (Name) My dear Rabbi	Respectfully yours Sincerely yours Yours faithfully	Dr. (Name) Rabbi (Name)	Dr. (Name) Rabbi (Name)
PRIEST (ROMAN CATHOLIC) The Reverend (Name followed by comma and initials of order) Local Address	Reverend Father Dear Father (Name)	Sincerely yours Respectfully yours Yours faithfully	Dr. (Name) Father (Name)	Dr. (Name) Father (Name)
SISTER (ROMAN CATHOLIC) Sister (Name followed by comma and initials of order) Local Address	Dear Sister Dear Sister (Name)	Sincerely yours Respectfully yours Yours faithfully	Sister (Name) Sister	Sister (Name) Sister
PRESIDENT (COLLEGE OR UNIVERSITY) Dr. (Name) or President (Name), (Degree) Name of University City, State	Dear Sir Madam Dear President (Name) Dear Dr. (Name)	Very truly yours Sincerely yours	Dr. (Name)	Dr. (Name)

POSTAL INFORMATION

For rates consult leaflet obtainable at local post office.

FIRST-CLASS MAIL[1]

Kind of Material	Descriptive Information
All first-class mail, except postal and postcards weighing 13 ounces or less (Over 13 ounces air parcel postal rates apply.)	Includes: 1. Matter wholly or partially in writing or typewriting, except authorized additions to second-, third-, and fourth-class mail 2. Matter closed against postal inspection 3. Bills and statements of account
Single postal cards and postcards	Single postal cards — government cards with imprinted stamps. Postcards — private mailing cards; stamps must be affixed.
Double postal cards and postcards	Reply portion of a double postcard does not have to bear postage when originally mailed.
Business reply cards	The senders return these free.
Mail enclosed in business-reply envelopes	A business must first obtain a permit to distribute business reply envelopes from the post office where they are to be returned. The senders return these free.
Priority Mail First-class mail weighing more than 13 ounces	A decreasing rate scale depending on weight. Mail travels by air. No guaranteed delivery time.

[1]First-class mail is discussed on pages 234-235. Weight limit, 70 pounds. Size limit, 100 inches in length and girth.

A reduction in postage rates is given on each piece of presorted mail when 300-500 pieces of mail are presorted according to specifications, which may be obtained from the local post office.

SECOND-CLASS MAIL[2]

Kind of Material	Descriptive Information
Newspapers and periodicals	Must have second-class mail privileges
	Special rates for bulk mailing by authorized nonprofit organizations

THIRD-CLASS MAIL[3]

Kind of Material	Descriptive Information
Circulars, books, catalogs of 24 pages or more and other printed matter, merchandise, seeds, cuttings, bulbs, and plants	Weight less than 16 ounces
	Special rates for bulk mailing by authorized nonprofit organizations
Keys and identification devices (cards, tags, etc.)	

FOURTH-CLASS MAIL[4]

Kind of Material	Descriptive Information
Special fourth-class rate for certain books, films, museum materials, playscripts, and manuscripts, etc.	Package must be marked *Special Fourth-Class Rate* and title of contents shown. See local postmaster.
Library books and educational materials sent between educational, religious, and philanthropic institutions	Package must be marked *Library Rate*. See local postmaster.
	Postage is not differentiated by zone.

[2] Second-class mail is discussed on page 235.
[3] Third-class mail is discussed on page 235.
[4] Special fourth-class mail is discussed on page 237.

TWO-LETTER STATE ABBREVIATIONS*
Approved for Use with ZIP Code *Only*

Alaska	AK	Montana	MT
Alabama	AL	Nebraska	NE
Arizona	AZ	Nevada	NV
Arkansas	AR	New Hampshire	NH
California	CA	New Jersey	NJ
Canal Zone	CZ	New Mexico	NM
Colorado	CO	New York	NY
Connecticut	CT	North Carolina	NC
Delaware	DE	North Dakota	ND
District of Columbia	DC	Ohio	OH
Florida	FL	Oklahoma	OK
Georgia	GA	Oregon	OR
Hawaii	HI	Pennsylvania	PA
Idaho	ID	Puerto Rico	PR
Illinois	IL	Rhode Island	RI
Indiana	IN	South Carolina	SC
Iowa	IA	South Dakota	SD
Kansas	KS	Tennessee	TN
Kentucky	KY	Texas	TX
Louisiana	LA	Utah	UT
Maine	ME	Vermont	VT
Maryland	MD	Virginia	VA
Massachusetts	MA	Virgin Islands	VI
Michigan	MI	Washington	WA
Minnesota	MN	West Virginia	WV
Mississippi	MS	Wisconsin	WI
Missouri	MO	Wyoming	WY

*Canal Zone, District of Columbia, Puerto Rico, and Virgin Islands also included.

WEIGHTS AND MEASURES WITH METRIC EQUIVALENTS

METRIC-ENGLISH EQUIVALENTS
Approximate Values

1 mm	=	0.04 inch
1 cm	=	0.4 inch
1 m	=	39.37 inches
1 km	=	0.6 mile
1 cm²	=	0.16 square inch
1 m²	=	10.8 square feet
1 m²	=	1.2 square yards
1 cm³	=	0.06 cubic inch
1 m³	=	35.3 cubic feet
1 m³	=	1.3 cubic yards
1 ml	=	0.034 ounce
1 cl	=	0.34 ounce
1 l	=	2.1 pints
1 l	=	1.06 quarts
1 l	=	0.26 gallon
1 g	=	0.035 ounce
1 kg	=	2.2 pounds
1 metric t	=	1.1 U.S. ton

ENGLISH-METRIC EQUIVALENTS
Approximate Values

1 inch	=	25.4 mm
1 inch	=	2.54 cm
1 foot	=	0.305 m
1 yard	=	0.91 m
1 mile	=	1.61 km
1 square inch	=	6.5 m²
1 square foot	=	0.09 m²
1 square yard	=	0.8 m²
1 cubic inch	=	16.4 cm³
1 cubic foot	=	0.03 m³
1 cubic yard	=	0.8 m³
1 pint	=	0.47 L
1 quart	=	0.95 L
1 gallon	=	3.79 L
1 ounce	=	28.35 g
1 pound	=	0.45 kg
1 U.S. ton	=	0.9 metric ton

TEMPERATURE CONVERSION

From Celsius to Fahrenheit

$$F = \frac{9}{5} C + 32$$

From Fahrenheit to Celsius

$$C = \frac{5}{9} (F - 32)$$

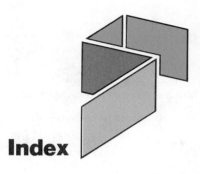

Index